Columbia No

Also by Gene Blottner
and from McFarland

Columbia Pictures Movie Series, 1926–1955: The Harry Cohn Years (2012)

Wild Bill Elliott: A Complete Filmography (2007; softcover 2012)

Universal Sound Westerns, 1929–1946: The Complete Filmography (2003; softcover 2011)

Universal-International Westerns, 1947–1963: The Complete Filmography (2000; softcover 2007)

Columbia Noir

A Complete Filmography, 1940–1962

Gene Blottner

McFarland & Company, Inc., Publishers
Jefferson, North Carolina

Many people assisted me in obtaining information for this book.
The following willingly shared their knowledge or helped me with my research:
Charles Blottner, Gene Carpenter, Larry Floyd, Earl Hagen,
Tony Monczewski, Bill Sasser and Tinsley Yarbrough.

LIBRARY OF CONGRESS CATALOGUING-IN-PUBLICATION DATA

Blottner, Gene, 1938–
Columbia noir : a complete filmography, 1940–1962 / Gene Blottner.
p. cm.
Includes bibliographical references and index.

ISBN 978-0-7864-7014-3 (softcover : acid free paper) ∞
ISBN 978-1-4766-1761-9 (ebook)

1. Columbia Pictures Corporation—Catalogs. 2. Film noir—United States—Catalogs. 3. Motion pictures—United States—Catalogs. I. Title.

PN1999.C57B54 2015 016.79143'75—dc23 2015004487

BRITISH LIBRARY CATALOGUING DATA ARE AVAILABLE

On the cover: Rita Hayworth poster art for *Gilda* (1946) by Columbia Pictures (Photofest)

Printed in the United States of America

McFarland & Company, Inc., Publishers
Box 611, Jefferson, North Carolina 28640
www.mcfarlandpub.com

For Catherine

Table of Contents

Preface

There is no hard, fast definition of film noir. Some just say "I know film noir when I see it" and leave it at that. Merriam-Webster defines film noir as a style of motion picture marked by a mood of pessimism, fatalism and menace. It is further stated that the term was originally applied to American thriller and/or detective films. This is a start but then film critics, historians and fans begin to disagree. There is support for the notion that film noir is a genre, but to the author it seems more fitting to term it a style or mood. A lot of lists seem to support the latter, as evidenced by their inclusion of Western and horror titles.

This book covers all the releases by Columbia Pictures that have been labeled film noir by various sources. There are 169 titles in the crime-gangster, mystery, Western, science fiction, horror and comedy genres. Any title included in any noir festival was an automatic entry, whether it was called a noir or hybrid-noir. For readers who wonder why a particular film was included, I hope I have made it clear why it was. I can only hope that I haven't missed a title.

To give the reader an insight to the entry style and primary sources used for the films covered in this book, the following information may be helpful.

Above the title of each film, there is a tag line used in the advertising copy for that film. Release dates were taken from various sources. If a film is in color and/or a widescreen process, this is noted. If a production company is given screen credit, this is noted.

Alternate Title: If a film used a title other than that given on initial release, it is listed. Working titles will be found in the "Notes and Commentary" section of the entry.

Credits: Each person listed received on-screen billing.

Song(s): All identifiable songs have been named with composers and artists, if known.

Filming Location: This category is included only when the information was available.

Information on songs and location is from IMDb, the Internet Movie Database.

Running Time: In quite a few films, various sources listed different running times. I listed the running time that matched the copy I watched.

Story: This is an encapsulation of the happenings on the screen and not an attempt to describe every scene in detail. The author was able to watch each film, even *Mary Ryan, Detective*, one of the Holy Grail items for which film enthusiasts have been searching. It had been shown only at a couple of noir festivals on the West Coast, but a home video has finally been released.

Notes and Commentary: This covers various facts regarding the film's production as well as comparisons of screenplays to the original source.

Reviews: To give the reader an idea how the film was received by critics on initial release or retrospectively, various reviews are presented.

Summation: My overall appraisal of the film.

Introduction: Film Noir and Columbia Pictures

FILM NOIR: A style of motion picture marked by a mood of pessimism, fatalism and menace. The term was originally applied to American thriller or detective films [Merriam-Webster Dictionary].

The year is 1946. World War II is over. Hollywood has resumed shipping their films to French shores. Among the first group were the following titles: *The Maltese Falcon* (Warner Bros., 1941), *Laura* (20th Century–Fox, 1944), *Murder My Sweet* (RKO, 1944), *Double Indemnity* (Paramount, 1944) and *Woman in the Window* (RKO, 1944). A second group followed that included *This Gun for Hire* (Paramount, 1942), *The Killers* (Universal, 1946), *Lady in the Lake* (Metro-Goldwyn-Mayer, 1946), *The Big Sleep* (Warner Bros., 1946) and *Gilda* (Columbia, 1946). French film critics were amazed at the similarity between the storylines: They were dark, violent and sexually charged. Greed, lust and ambition were at the core of every story. The critics, who were used to seeing American films packed with fully lit, bright scenes, found themselves watching tales shrouded in darkness. The actors and sets were lit equally. The critics, led by Nino Frank, exalted the films and proclaimed them *film noir* or black film. Film historians searched through earlier films and it is generally accepted the first entry of the classic film noir era was *Stranger on the Third Floor*, released by RKO on August 16, 1940.

There are factors that led to the style of film that became known as film noir. Almost everyone is in agreement that German Expressionism, which encompassed many aspects of German culture, especially the cinema, played a role. Early German filmmakers, unable to compete with big-budget, lavish productions from America, decided to emphasize deeper meanings by using symbolism and mise-en-scene, in which set design and lighting play an important part. The way a set was lighted could disguise the lack of production values, with certain areas highlighted and the rest of the set shrouded in darkness. Both the director and cinematographer combine to make the decisions on this aspect. From Europe came noted directors, such as Fritz Lang (*M* [Vereingte Star-Film GmbH, 1931], *Fury* [Metro-Goldwyn-Mayer, 1936] and *You Live Only Once* [United Artists, 1937]), Michael Curtiz (*20,000 Years in Sing Sing* [Warner Bros., 1932] and *Angels with Dirty Faces* [Warner Bros., 1938]), Josef von Sternberg (*Underworld* [Paramount, 1927], *Thunderbolt* [Paramount, 1929] and *Crime and Punishment* [Columbia, 1935]), Rouben Mamoulian (*City Streets* [Paramount, 1931]) and Lewis Milestone (*The Racket* [Paramount, 1938]). Lang and Curtiz brought the Expressionism style to their crime dramas. The films mentioned are now considered to be proto-noir.

Another factor emanated from the change in mystery and crime fiction. Urbane and sophisticated protagonists with chaste relationships with the women they encountered evolved into tough guys and sexy dames. Violence and sex permeated these offerings as in the novels upon which many of them were based: Dashiell Hammett's *The Maltese Falcon* (Knopf, 1930), James M. Cain's *The Postman Always Rings Twice* (Knopf, 1934) and Ernest Hemingway's *To Have and Have Not* (Charles Scribner's Sons, 1937). To further satisfy readers of hard-boiled mystery stories, the monthly pulp magazines *Black Mask* (Popular Publications) with authors Dashiell Hammett, Raymond Chandler and Cornell Woolrich and its close rival *Dime Detective* (Popular Publications) featuring writers John D. MacDonald and Cornell Woolrich could be purchased at newsstands.

A third factor has to be considered. Studios began making films, usually those meant for the lower half of a double bill, with reduced lighting of the sets. Some credit this trend to the popularity of double features. Studios then wanted to make the increased number of films without expenses spiraling out of control. Both money and time were saved, money on less light and both time and money on setting up the scene. It has been said that if there was total darkness in a portion of a set, then no props were needed. Creative directors, producers and cinematographers made good use of the darkness to intensify the tension and suspense.

Most studios, like Columbia, initially considered the film noir style basically for their programmer films. Columbia embraced this style cautiously. *Angels Over Broadway* (1940) was their first noir. The studio released only a handful of noirs until 1944. While the output was strictly "B," Columbia began to receive favorable critical recognition with their Whistler series. Columbia continued to stay low key even though the bigger studios did well with titles like *Laura* (20th Century–Fox), *Ministry of Fear* (Paramount) and *The Woman in the Window* (RKO). The year 1945 saw studios cautiously continuing the production of film noir. With *The House on 92nd Street* (20th Century–Fox), noir began to move out of the studio sound stages to the actual city locations. Columbia stayed basically "in house," although seaside locations were used in the superb *My Name Is Julia Ross*. Nineteen forty-six was the beginning of the boom years for noir. Columbia had two expertly crafted "B" noirs in *Night Editor* and *So Dark the Night* but hit the big time with *Gilda*. With the success of *Gilda*, Columbia began to look to providing more noir productions. In 1947 and '48 there were prestige films: Humphrey Bogart (borrowed from Warners) in *Dead Reckoning*, Glenn Ford in *Framed*, Dick Powell in *Johnny O'Clock* and Orson Welles in *The Lady from Shanghai*. In true noir tradition, each tough guy was pared with a femme fatale: respectively, Lizabeth Scott (from Paramount), the underrated Janis Carter, Evelyn Keyes and Rita Hayworth. Columbia noir began to venture out from the studio with *The Lady from Shanghai* (San Francisco, New York and Mexico) and *Walk a Crooked Mile* (San Francisco). Even so, Columbia tread cautiously, including their western noir, releasing only six or eight pictures annually. In 1950, *All the King's Men* won Academy Awards for Best Picture, Actor (Broderick Crawford) and Supporting Actress (Mercedes McCambridge). Another film released that year that is seen on almost every list of top noirs was *In a Lonely Place*.

In Washington, Tennessee Senator Estes Kefauver headed a special committee to investigate organized crime in interstate commerce. The committee found the FBI was wrong in stating that a nationwide underworld syndicate did not exist. This finding would give new life to noir films, changing the emphasis of corruption of the individual to corruption by an organization or syndicate designed to impact the lives of all citizens. *The Big Heat* (1953) told of corruption in the upper echelons of the police department. *On the Waterfront* (1954) chronicled corruption on the docks of New York and New Jersey, and won many Oscars (see the entry). From 1954 to 1958, Columbia went all-out on noir titles releasing 60 films, exposing corruption in

Rita Hayworth as *Gilda* (1946) and as Elsa Bannister in *The Lady from Shanghai* (1947).

the garment jungle of New York, the boxing rackets and in the cities of Miami, New Orleans, Chicago, Detroit, Houston, Tijuana and Brooklyn. By the late '50s, film noir popularity had greatly diminished thanks to competition first from crime shows on television and secondly from CinemaScope and other widescreen epics that now depicted virtuous heroes. Some film historians believe the classic noir era ended with *Touch of Evil* (Universal-International, 1958).

Other historians disagree, citing such 1959 films as *Anatomy of a Murder* (Columbia) and *Odds Against Tomorrow* (United Artists). From 1960 to 1962, only six Columbia noirs were released. Nineteen sixty-two was an important year for noir entries, with *Cape Fear* (Universal-International) with Gregory Peck and Robert Mitchum, *The Manchurian Candidate* (United Artists) with Frank Sinatra, Laurence Harvey and Angela Lansbury and *Experiment in Terror* (Columbia) with Glenn Ford and Lee Remick. The last Columbia release of the classic noir era was *13 West Street* with Alan Ladd.

The Films

You weren't the first ... and you won't be the last!

Affair in Trinidad

(September 1952)

A Beckworth Corporation Production

Cast: Chris Emery, Rita Hayworth; Steve Emery, Glenn Ford; Max Fabian, Alexander Scourby; Veronica Huebling, Valerie Bettis; Inspector Smythe, Torin Thatcher; Anderson, Howard Wendell; Walters, Karel Stepanek; Dr. Franz Huebling, George Voskovec; Wittol, Steven Geray; Peter Bronec, Walter Kohler; Dominique, Juanita Moore; Uncredited: Olaf, Gregg Martell; Martin, Mort Mills; Coroner, Ralph Moody; Pilot, Robert Boon; Butlers, John Parlow and Albert Szabo; Peters (Reporter), Don Kohler; Airport Clerk, Fred Baker; Stewardess, Kathleen O'Malley; The Bobby, Don Blackman; Jeffrey Mabetes, Joel Fluellen; Fishermen, Roy Glenn and Ivan Browning; Calypso Singer, Charles MacNiles; Neal Emery (corpse), Ross Elliott

Credits: Director and Producer, Vincent Sherman; Assistant Director, Sam Nelson; Story, Virginia Van Lipp and Bernie Giler; Screenwriters, Oscar Saul and James Gunn; Editor, Viola Lawrence; Art Director, Walter Holscher; Set Decorator, William Kiernan; Cinematographer, Joseph Walker; Gowns, Jean Louis; Makeup, Clay Campbell; Hair Stylist, Helen Hunt; Sound, Lodge Cunningham; Musical Directors, Morris Stoloff and George Duning; Choreographer (Hayworth's numbers), Valerie Bettis

Songs: "Trinidad Lady" (Lee and Russell)—danced and sung by Rita Hayworth and Charles MacNiles and "I've Been Kissed Before" (Lee and Russell)—danced and sung by Rita Hayworth (Hayworth's singing was dubbed by Jo Ann Greer)

Production Dates: January 25–March 22, 1952

Running Time: 98 minutes

Story: The death of Rita Hayworth's husband, Ross Elliott, looks to be a suicide. Hayworth is the headliner at Steven Geray's night spot. In his investigation, Inspector Torin Thatcher asks questions about Elliott's involvement with wealthy Alexander Scourby. Thatcher suggests that Hayworth was intimate with Scourby. Later investigation shows Elliott was murdered. Thatcher wants Hayworth to gain Scourby's confidence to get needed evidence. Thatcher believes Scourby was involved in the crime and is engaged in activities threatening world security. Because of a letter he received from Elliott, his brother Glenn Ford comes to Trinidad. Ford is led to believe that Elliott's death was a suicide. Attending a dinner at Scourby's, Ford recognizes the crest on the letter sent to him as Scourby's. Scourby's houseguests are Karel Stepanek, Walter Kohler and George Voskovec and his wife Valerie Bettis. Ford recognizes Voskovec as the author of articles on German V2 rockets. Kohler tells Scourby that his job is finished and that he wants to leave Trinidad. When Kohler attempts to leave, a speeding car runs him down. Scourby is involved in a plot to launch rockets on major United States cities from bases in the Caribbean.

When Hayworth is invited to a party at Scourby's house, Thatcher wants her to try to gain access to his guest house where vital evidence might be found. Ford crashes the party but leaves when Hayworth tells him she has been having an affair with Scourby. Hayworth enters the guest house but as she tries to leave, Scourby, Stepanek and Voskovec enter and she overhears their nefarious plans. She is able to escape undetected but leaves behind a scarf that Scourby gave her. Voskovec finds the scarf and gives it to Bettis, thinking it is hers. Bettis then shows Scourby the scarf. Hayworth is captured by Scourby and his associates. Ford learns that Hayworth has never been involved with Scourby and returns to

Scourby's house. Thatcher proves that Geray and his henchman Mort Mills were in the car that ran down Kohler. At Scourby's house, Ford gets the drop on Scourby and some of his group as they plan to leave with Hayworth. Before Ford can effect a rescue, Voskovec hits him from behind. Ford's pistol discharges, critically wounding Scourby. Knowing his wound is fatal, Scourby tells his associates to dispose of Ford. Scourby plans to kill Hayworth before he dies. Police arrive and a gunfight ensues. Ford is able to gain possession of a pistol and he and Scourby exchange shots. Ford's bullets kill Scourby. Ford and Hayworth leave Trinidad to begin a life together in Chicago.

Notes and Commentary: Though the credits indicate the film was a Beckworth production, this was essentially a ruse to enable Hayworth's salary to be treated as a capital gain and not a salary. Consequently, Hayworth's taxes would be lower.

Hayworth wanted to do her own singing but her voice was just not good enough. Jo Ann Greer was hired to dub Hayworth, as she would do in two subsequent Columbia productions, *Miss Sadie Thompson* (1953) and *Pal Joey* (1957).

Affair in Trinidad was a troubled production. Director Vincent Sherman was hired and then found there was no script, just an initial story treatment. Studio president Harry Cohn was in a position where he had to use Hayworth in a film or she could leave the studio. A script had to be found quickly. The initial script by Virginia Van Upp was never completed. James Gunn was hired to do a complete rewrite. Oscar Saul was brought aboard to add the final polish. Hayworth refused to work until there was a completed script. Cohn applied pressure, giving her the choice of working or going on suspension. Nearly broke, Hayworth gave in. Production finally began in January 1952. Despite generally poor reviews, the film was a major box office hit. The public loved Hayworth.

Reviews: "Rita Hayworth is cast as an entertainer in a Trinidad dive, which affords a promising start but the story meanders into a cliché yarn about a murder and a spy ring." *Variety*, 7/30/52

"An overdone spy melodrama that takes most of its inspiration from *Gilda*." *Motion Picture Guide*, Nash and Ross

Summation: While not wholly an original story idea, it is nonetheless an entertaining international spy noir. Director Sherman did a nifty job of steering the principals through a story that was pasted together. It has been acknowledged that plot elements from *Gilda* (Columbia, 1946) and Alfred Hitchcock's *Notorious* (RKO, 1946) were used. Sherman was able to create some nice suspense in the final reels, which were based on the Hitchcock film. Cinematographer Joseph Walker's shadowy photography adds to the atmosphere of evil.

He Might Have Been a Pretty Good Guy ... If Too Much Power ... and Women ... Hadn't Gone to His Head!

All the King's Men

(January 1950)

A Robert Rossen Production

Cast: Willie Stark, Broderick Crawford; Jack Burden, John Ireland; Anne Stanton, Joanne Dru; Tom Stark, John Derek; Sadie Burke, Mercedes McCambridge; Adam Stanton, Shepperd Strudwick; Tiny Duffy, Ralph Dumke; Lucy Stark, Anne Seymour; Mrs. Burden, Katharine Warren; Judge Stanton, Raymond Greenleaf; Sugar Boy, Walter Burke; Dolph Pillsbury, Will Wright; Floyd McEvoy, Grandon Rhodes; Uncredited: Pa Stark, H.C. Miller; Madison, Houseley Stevenson; Hale, Richard Hale; Helene Hale, Helene Stanley; Puckett, Stephen Chase; Joe Harrison, Earle S. Dewey; Butler, Irving Smith; Football Coach, Phil Tully; File Clerk, Mary Bear; Farmers, Ralph Littlefield and Bill Wolfe; State Troopers, Glen Thompson and Al Wyatt; Sheriff, A.C. Tillman; Speaker of the House, Harold Miller; Drunk at Football Game, John "Skins" Miller; Minister, Louis Mason; Minister at Funeral, Truett Myers; Former Governor Stanton, Wilbur Mack; Doctor, Frank McClure; Receptionist, Reba Waterson; Public Relations Man, Frank Wilcox; Commissioner, William Bruce; Radio Announcer, Edwin Chandler; Bus Man,

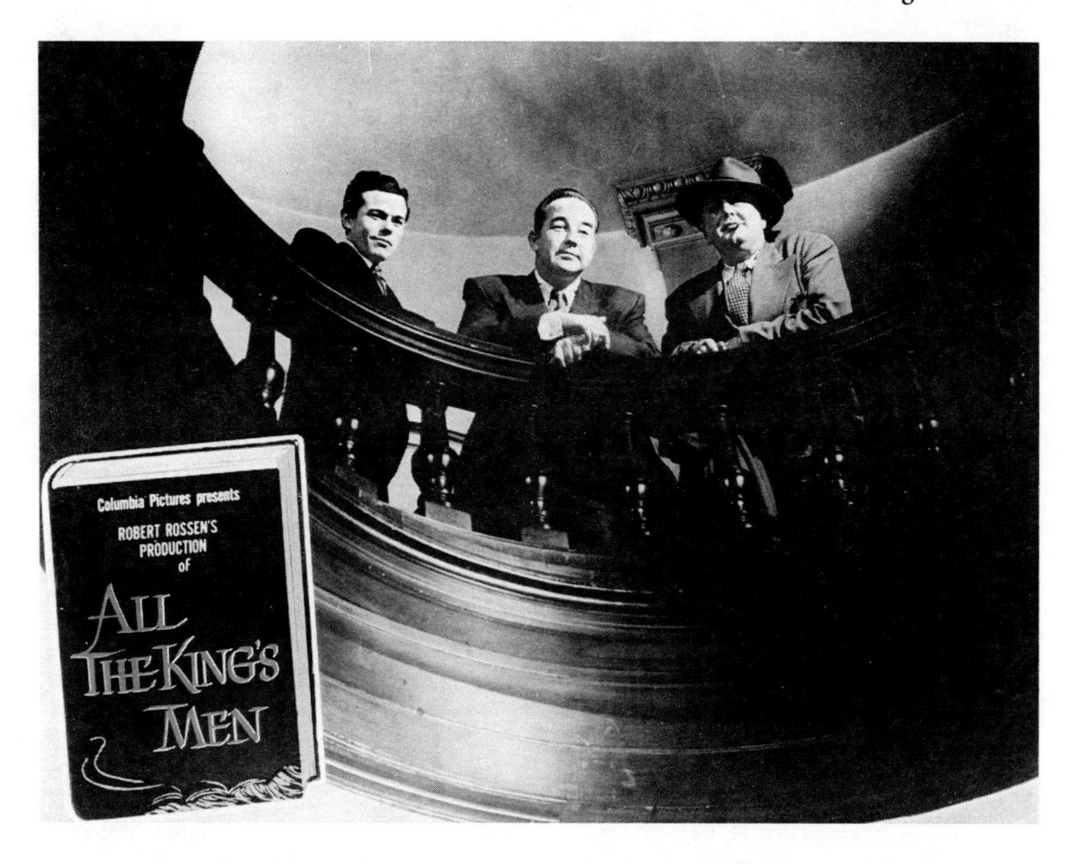

Walter Burke, Broderick Crawford and Ralph Dumke *in All the King's Men* (1950).

George Farmer; Newspaper Office Worker, Charles Ferguson; Dance Caller, Ted French; Young Boy, John Giles; Spokesman for Impeachment, Paul Ford; Senators, Marshall Bradford, Wheaton Chambers, Avery Graves, William E. Green and Nolan Leary; Man Who Tears Down Poster, Tom Coleman; Reporters, William Cottrell and King Donovan; Local Chairman, Paul Maxey; Politicians, Roy Darmour, Tom Ferrandini, Dick Gordon, Sam Harris, Judd Holdren, James Linn, Pat O'Malley, Charles Sherlock and George Taylor; Editors, Robert Filmer and Bert Hanlon; Men in Cheap Bar, Charles Haefeli and Al Thompson; Men in City Bar, Walter Merrill and William Tannen; Stark Strong-arm Man, Frank Hagney

CREDITS: Director and Screenwriter, Robert Rossen; Assistant Director, Sam Nelson; Assistant to the Producer, Shirley Miller; Editor, Al Clark; Art Director, Sturges Carne; Set Decorator, Louis Diage; Cinematographer, Burnett Guffey; Montages, Donald W. Starling; Gowns, Jean Louis; Makeup, Clay Campbell; Hair Stylist, Helen Hunt; Sound, Frank Goodwin; Original Music, Louis Gruenberg; Musical Director, Morris Stoloff; Editorial Advisor, Robert Parrish

FILMING LOCATIONS: Stockton, Fairfield, Suisun and San Joaquin-Sacramento River Delta, California

PRODUCTION DATES: November 29, 1948–January 26, 1949

SOURCE: novel *All the King's Men* by Robert Penn Warren

RUNNING TIME: 110 minutes

STORY: Farmer Broderick Crawford enters politics in a small town, running for city treasurer. He gets a taste of hardnosed politics as everything he tries is rebuffed. Reporter John Ireland interviews Crawford and writes flattering articles about him. Crawford loses the election and studies law and attains his law degree. When tragedy strikes at a local schoolhouse, he decides to re-enter politics. Crawford had warned about an inferior company receiving the bid. Crawford is given encouragement to run for governor, not knowing he is the fall guy primed to split the "hick" vote so the favorite candidate will coast to victory. Campaign advisor Mercedes McCambridge and Ireland let slip that he is being played for a fall guy. After recovering from a drinking binge, Crawford engages in a spirited campaign and barely loses the election. When Crawford runs for the governorship again, McCambridge becomes both his campaign manager and mistress. Ireland also comes on board. Ireland introduces Crawford to his prominent family, which includes the girl he loves, Joanne Dru; an idealistic and excellent physician, Shepperd Strudwick; and an influential judge, Raymond Greenleaf. Waging a vigorous campaign, Crawford wins by a landslide. Greenleaf becomes Crawford's attorney general. Crawford wants Strudwick to head the new medical center he's planning to build. Dru becomes Crawford's mistress to the chagrin of McCambridge. Greenleaf resigns his position when he blocks impeachment of auditor Will Wright. Crawford allows Wright to resign instead. Greenleaf starts a campaign to impeach Crawford. Crawford gets Ireland to dig up dirt about Greenleaf to force him to back off. Ireland finds that Greenleaf was guilty of corruption many years ago when he was desperate for money. Crawford also knows the story and will sully Greenleaf's pristine reputation if he doesn't work with him. Instead Greenleaf commits suicide. Ireland knows the only way Crawford could be aware of Greenleaf's indiscretions is from Dru. Strudwick learns about the relationship between Dru and Crawford and that through Dru's influence, Strudwick was offered the position as head of the medical center. As the impeachment proceedings come to a vote, Crawford has all the "hicks" gather outside the state capitol. A distraught Dru asks Ireland to find Strudwick. The people holler for Crawford. The vote for impeachment fails and Crawford remains governor. As Crawford appears on the capitol steps, Strudwick steps forward and fires shots that mortally wound Crawford. Strudwick is in turn shot down in a hail of bullets. The dazed and crying Dru is told by Ireland, who still loves her, that they have to work together to make the state a better place. Crawford dies not knowing why anyone would end his life.

Notes and Commentary: Warren's Pulitzer Prize–winning novel primarily focused on Jack Burden, his family and his relationships with Anne Stanton and Willie Stark. The screenplay reverses this with the emphasis on Willie. Some major changes from the novel are made. The question of Jack's birth father was omitted, as was Jack's mother's many marriages. Judge Irwin became Judge Stanton in the film. Tiny Duffy is the source that revealed to Adam Stanton that his sister Anne was having an adulterous relationship with Willie. Sadie Burke gave the information to Duffy. In a weak moment, Jack almost tells Sugar Boy, who worshiped Willie, that Duffy was responsible for Willie's death. Jack finally declines knowing that Sugar Boy would gun down Duffy even if it meant his arrest and possible execution. Lucy Stark, to fill the void caused by the deaths of Willie and their son Tom, adopts Tom's illegitimate son.

John Wayne was Robert Rossen's first choice to play Willie Stark. Wayne felt greatly insulted that he was asked to play a part that he felt cast a negative light on the American way of life. He told his agent, Charles K. Feldman, that the script should be shoved up a part of Rossen's anatomy. Eventually Broderick Crawford accepted the part. Wayne was nominated as Best Actor for his performance in *Sands of Iwo Jima* (Republic, 1949) and ironically lost out to Crawford.

In addition to Crawford's win as Best Actor, Mercedes McCambridge won an Oscar for Best Actress in a Supporting Role and the film won Best Picture. Oscar nominees were John Ireland for Best Actor in a Supporting Role, Robert Rossen for Best Director and Screenplay and Robert Parrish and Al Clark for Best Editing.

In 1947, it was reported that Humphrey Bogart was being considered for a lead role.

Although the general release date was January 1950, the film opened in New York on November 8, 1949.

All the King's Men was based on the life of Louisiana Governor Huey Long. Reportedly, Crawford viewed old newsreels of Long. The actor stated that the name Huey Long could not be mentioned on the set.

All the King's Men was adapted for NBC-TV's *The Kraft Theater*. Neville Brand played Willie Stark. The story was broadcast in two parts on May 14 and May 21, 1958.

Columbia remade the movie in 2006 with Sean Penn playing Willie Stark. Even with a stellar cast, this version failed to capture the fancy of either the critics or the moviegoing public.

The novel was adapted by American composer Carlisle Floyd as a full-length grand opera, *Willie Stark*. In 1981, the opera premiered at the Houston Grand Opera.

Reviews: "The rise and fall of a backwoods

political messiah and the mark he left on the American scene is given graphic celluloid treatment. It is a film that vividly impresses with dramatic sureness." *Variety*, 11/9/49

"Robert Rossen has written and directed, as well as personally produced, a rip-roaring film. Consistency of dramatic structure—or of character revelation—is not in it. But it has a superb pictorialism which perpetually crackles and explodes." *The New York Times*, 11/9/49

SUMMATION: This is a truly great film and a wonderful political noir. Broderick Crawford, in his Academy Award–winning role, delivers a great performance as a man who self-destructs on the way to possible greatness. The principal supporting cast comes through with fine performances, especially Mercedes McCambridge, another Academy Award winner, as Crawford's campaign manager and mistress. Robert Rossen directs nicely from his superior script. While making changes from Robert Penn Warren's novel, he maintains its basic essence and thrust. The film justifiably won the Academy Award for Best Picture.

She was a creature of passion who drew around her lovely head a storm of desire and revenge! The best-selling novel becomes the MUST-SEE film of the year!

Anatomy of a Murder

(July 1959)

CAST: Paul Biegler, James Stewart; Laura Manion, Lee Remick; Lt. Frederick Manion, Ben Gazzara; Parnell McCarthy, Arthur O'Connell; Maida Rutledge, Eve Arden; Mary Pilant, Kathryn Grant; Claude Dancer, George C. Scott; Dr. Matthew Smith, Orson Bean; George Lemon, Russ Brown; Alphonse Paquette, Murray Hamilton; Mitch Lodwick, Brooks West; James Durgo, Ken Lynch; Sulo, John Qualen; Dr. Dompierre, Howard McNair; Dr. Harcourt, Alexander Campbell; Dr. Raschid, Ned Weaver; Clarence Madigan, Jimmy Conlin; Sheriff Battisfore, Royal Beal; Lloyd Burke, Joseph Kearns; Duke Miller, Don Ross; Court Clerk, Lloyd Le Vasseur; Army Sergeant 1st Class, James Waters; Judge Weaver, Joseph N. Welch; Uncredited: Pie Eye, Duke Ellington; Muff, "Snuffy," Juror, Mrs. Joseph N. Welch; Jazz Quintet, piano—Duke Ellington, trumpet—Ray Nance, tenor sax—Jimmy Hamilton, bass—Jimmy Woode and drums—Johnny Johnson

CREDITS: Director and Producer, Otto Preminger; Assistant Director, David Silver; Assistant to Producer, Max Slater; Screenwriter, Wendell Mayes; Editor, Louis R. Loeffler; Production Manager, Henry Weinberger; Production Designer, Boris Leven; Cinematographer, Sam Leavitt; Camera Operator, Irving Rosenberg; Lighting Technician, James Almond; Key Grip, Leo McCreary; Wardrobe, Michael Harte and Vou Lee Giokaris; Makeup, Del Armstrong and Harry Ray; Hair Stylist, Myrl Stoltz; Set Dresser, Howard Bristol; Sound, Jack Solomon; Original Music, Duke Ellington; Music Editor, Richard Carruth; Script Supervisor, Kathleen Fagan; Titles Designer, Saul Bass

LOCATION FILMING: Marquette, Ishpeming, Big Bay and Michigamme, Michigan

PRODUCTION DATES: March 23–May 16, 1959

SOURCE: novel *Anatomy of a Murder* by Robert Traver

RUNNING TIME: 160 minutes

STORY: Lee Remick asks lawyer James Stewart to defend her husband Ben Gazzara, accused of murder. Gazzara shot and killed the owner of a local bar and hotel, who raped and beat Remick. Stewart tells Gazzara that he needs a legal excuse for his actions. Gazzara says he must have been crazy. Stewart finally agrees to take the case and persuades Gazzara to write the Army to see if they will provide a psychiatrist to evaluate him. Stewart goes to the bar to question bartender Murray Hamilton. Hamilton refuses to answer questions but tells Stewart that Kathryn Grant is now running both the bar and hotel. Grant is also uncooperative. The trial begins. Stewart enters a plea of not guilty, citing dissociate reaction, an irresistible impulse to shoot. To ensure a conviction, State Attorney General George C. Scott is present to assist local District Attorney Brooks West. Stewart's lawyer friend Arthur O'Connell discovers that Grant was the murdered man's illegitimate daughter. Gazzara's temporary insanity plea is substantiated by psychiatrist Orson Bean. Grant takes the stand and produces the panties that substantiates Remick's rape claim. Scott insinuates that Grant was the murdered man's mistress bur Grant reveals to the court that she was his daughter. Her testimony sways the jury to bring in a verdict of not guilty by reason of temporary insanity. The next day, Stewart and O'Connell seek Gazzara to have him sign a promissory note for the legal fees. They find that Gazzara and Remick had skipped out during the night. Stewart tells O'Connell, now Stewart's partner, that they have a client in Grant: They will administer her estate.

NOTES AND COMMENTARY: Michigan Supreme Court Justice John D. Voelker wrote the source novel using the pseudonym Robert Traver. The story was based on a real-life case in which Voelker was the defense attorney: In Big Bay, a small town in the Upper Peninsula of Michigan, Lt. Coleman Peterson shot and killed bar owner Mike Chenoweth. Peterson believed that Chenoweth had raped his wife Charlotte Peterson. Voelker entered a plea of temporary insanity. Peterson was never institutionalized when a psychiatrist stated that Peterson was now sane. Peterson left the area without paying his legal fee.

Even though the basic thread of Traver's novel was followed, there were some changes. Laura Manion was significantly more promiscuous and sluttish than in the novel. Frederick Manion never had an altercation with fellow prisoner Duke Miller. In the film, this looked to be an opportunity for revenge for Miller. Mary Pilant was not the illegitimate daughter of the murdered man, Barney Quill, in Traver's story. This became the plot line for Mary to produce Laura's panties. In the novel, the panties were never found. Mary's testimony swayed the jury to find Manion not guilty by reason of temporary insanity. In the novel, Paul Biegler's closing argument, which did not find its way to the screen, did the trick. At the novel's end, it looks like a romantic attachment for Biegler and Pilant.

Anatomy of a Murder received six Academy Award nominations: Best Actor: James Stewart; Best Supporting Actors: Arthur O'Connell and George C. Scott; Best Picture; Wendell Mayes for Best Writing, Screenplay; Louis R. Loeffler for Best Editing, and Sam Leavitt for Best Cinematography.

Spencer Tracy and Burl Ives had been offered the role of Judge Weaver. Tracy thought the part was too small. Joseph N. Welch, who really was a judge, accepted the role. In the 1954 televised Un-American Activities hearings, Welch and Senator Joseph McCarthy clashed over communist activity in the United States.

Lana Turner was first considered for the part of Laura Manion. It has been stated that Turner demanded that her gowns be designed by Jean Louis. Producer-director Preminger said that those gowns would not be suitable. Turner later commented that she walked out due to Preminger's unreasonable temperament. Jayne Mansfield also turned down the role. Preminger finally offered the part to Lee Remick, who he really wanted initially. When he thought Turner was set for the part, Remick was offered the smaller part of Mary Pilant. Remick refused that role. Finally, Preminger offered Remick the part she wanted.

The movie became highly controversial because it contained previously forbidden words such as bitch, contraceptive, intercourse, sexual climax, panties, penetration, rape, slut and sperm. The film was subsequently banned in Chicago, Illinois.

REVIEWS: "Not since *Witness for the Prosecution* has there been a courtroom melodrama so beguiling, forceful and enthralling as Otto Preminger's *Anatomy of a Murder*. Its mystery is adult, it is complex and confounding and it is laced with humor and human touches." *Variety*, 7/1/59

"Courtroom histrionics given sizzle and sex by Otto Preminger and Duke Ellington's jazz. Even today, when these issues seem tame, the long drama crackles along." *Motion Picture Guide*, Nash and Ross

"A riveting legal tussle as well as an absorbing psychological drama whose protagonists were far more complex than anything to be found in an ordinary run-of-the-mill courtroom melodrama." *The Columbia Story*, Hirschhorn

SUMMATION: This is a very good courtroom noir, highlighted by some fantastic performances. James Stewart as the crafty defense counselor, Arthur O'Connell as Stewart's associate and George C. Scott as a prosecuting attorney received Academy Award nominations. Eve Arden as Stewart's intelligent, wisecracking secretary, Lee Remick as the rape victim and Ben Gazzara as the man accused of murder contributed greatly to the picture's success. Preminger's direction guided this long motion picture successfully. Cinematographer Sam Leavitt's noirish photography enhanced the final product.

A STRANGE AND WONDERFUL ROMANCE.
BORN BETWEEN HEARTBREAK AND HAPPINESS!

Angels Over Broadway

(October 1940)

CAST: Bill O'Brien, Douglas Fairbanks, Jr.; Nina Barona, Rita Hayworth; Gene Gibbons, Thomas Mitchell; Charles Engle, John Qualen; Hopper, George Watts; Dutch Enright, Ralph Theodore; Louie Artino, Eddie Foster; Eddie Burns, Jack Roper; Sylvia Marbe, Constance Worth; Uncredited: Rennick, Walter Baldwin; Cigarette Girl, Ethelreda Leopold; Vincent (Headwaiter), Edward Earle; Stevie (Sylvia's Escort), Richard Bond; Mr. Hugo, Fred Sweeney; Nightclub Dancer, Carmen D'Antonio; Newsstand Proprietor, Jimmy Conlin; First Cab Driver, John Tyrrell; Second Cab Driver, Billy Wayne; Stage Doorman, William Lally; Court Clerk, Harry Antrim; Police Lieutenant, Lee Phelps; Lunch Room Counterman, Walter Sande; Gamblers, Roger Gray, Jerry Jerome, Al Rhein and Harry Stang

CREDITS: Director, Producer and Story, Ben Hecht; Co-Director, Lee Garmes; Associate Producer, Douglas Fairbanks, Jr.; Editor, Gene Havlick; Art Director, Lionel Banks; Cinematographer, Lee Garmes; Gowns, Kalloch; Music, George Antheil; Musical Director, M.W. Stoloff; Production Assistant, Harold Godsoe

SONG: "Mon Homme" (Yvain)—danced by Carmen D'Antonio

PRODUCTION DATES: June 20–July 16, 1940

RUNNING TIME: 79 minutes

STORY: John Qualen contemplates suicide knowing he will be exposed and arrested as an embezzler. His boss and friend, George Watts, gives Qualen until the next morning to return the money. After a failed suicide attempt, Qualen wanders into a swanky nightclub, where he is thought to be a rich tourist. Grifter Douglas Fairbanks, Jr. wants to steer Qualen into a crooked card game where Fairbanks would receive a cut of the money taken from him. Rita Hayworth thinks Qualen would pay her to be his companion. Former successful playwright Thomas Mitchell has become a celebrity drunk. His career is failing as well as his personal life, having deserted his wife for younger women. Mitchell discovers Qualen's plight and enlists aid from Fairbanks and Hayworth to get the money Qualen needs to salvage his life. Using life as a play, Mitchell concocts a scenario in which Fairbanks would introduce Qualen to the card game run by notorious mobster Ralph Theodore. Mitchell believes that they will let Qualen win one big hand before Qualen has a run of bad cards. After winning, Qualen is to temporally leave the game but actually to leave the hotel. Fairbanks, Hayworth and Mitchell will wait in Fairbanks' hotel room, located on the same floor as the card game. Before Qualen can get to the game, Mitchell passes out in Fairbanks' room. Qualen wins a big hand. Mitchell awakens from his drunken stupor with no recollection of the night's activity. He calls and reconciles with his wife, and leaves to be with her. Qualen leaves the card game but, followed by Theodore's strong-arm man Jack Roper has no choice but to enter Fairbanks' room. Thinking fast, Hayworth suggests Qualen leave by the fire escape outside the window. The window is stuck. Fairbanks steps out to the hall to delay Roper's entry into the room. The door swings open just enough to allow Roper to see what's going on. Fairbanks engages in a fistic encounter with Roper. As the men fight, the window finally opens and Qualen starts down the fire escape. Roper is joined by mob hit man Eddie Foster, and Fairbanks is beaten to the floor. Roper starts down the stairs to head off Qualen. Foster gets to the open window and fires shots at Qualen. Qualen is picked up by police and taken to night court. He explains that money in his possession belongs to Watts. This statement is verified by the police. Through the long night, Fairbanks and Hayworth have become romantically interested in each other. At first resistant, Fairbanks realizes that he and Hayworth are meant for each other.

NOTES AND COMMENTARY: The working title was *Before I Die*.

Ben Hecht received an Academy Award nomination for Best Writing, Original Screenplay. He lost to Preston Sturges and *The Great McGinty*.

REVIEWS: "A synthetic tale of Broadway nightlife. Picture stutters and sputters too often to carefully etch human beings, with result that it develops into an over-dramatic stage play transferred to the screen." *Variety*, 12/31/39

"A melodramatic fantasy that is mordant, tender and quixotic, shot with ironic humor. Beautifully compact. A spare and enormously suspensive story that is as neatly fitted as an O. Henry fable." *New York Times*, 11/18/40

Summation: This fine early noir tells of an individual contemplating suicide after embezzling money for his wife who, in turn, gave it to her lover. John Qualen is perfect in this role, showing loneliness, fear and despair as he's forced to mingle with nefarious underworld figures. He is aided on his journey by some "angels over Broadway," grifter Douglas Fairbanks, Jr., would-be dancer turned prostitute Rita Hayworth and former prize-winning playwright, now a drunk, Thomas Mitchell. Producer-director-writer Ben Hecht gives us a compelling but sometimes verbose narrative. Fortunately the lead actors, especially Fairbanks and Mitchell, are still able to deliver the lines convincingly. Lee Garmes' photography captures the noir atmosphere with dark rainy streets and dark rooms with minimal shards of light that add to Qualen's anguish.

PARIS ... A CITY MADE FOR EXCITEMENT ... EXCITEMENT ON A NIGHT MADE FOR MURDER!

Assignment—Paris

(October 1952)

Cast: Jimmy Race, Dana Andrews; Jeanne Moray, Marta Toren; Nicholas Strang, George Sanders; Sandy Tate, Audrey Totter; Grischa, Sandro Giglio; Anton Borvitch, Donald Randolph; Prime Minister Andreas Ordy, Herbert Berghof; Minister of Justice Vajos, Ben Astar; Biddle, Willis Bouchey; Dad Pelham, Earl Lee; Uncredited: Narrator, William Woodson; Victor, Maurice Doner; Franz, Leon Askin; Kedor, Paul Hoffman; Henry (Bartender), Jay Adler; Jan Czeki, Peter Votrian; Gogo Czeki, Georgiana Wulff; Phone Operators, Don Gibson, Gail Bonney, Mara Marshall, Monique Chantal, Teresa Tudor; Barker, Joseph Forte; Bert, Don Kohler; Miss Oster, Hannelore Axman; Laslo Boros (Tailor), Pal Javor; Larry O'Connell, Victor Sutherland; Waiter, Andre Simeon; American Ambassador, Fay Roope; Gendarme, Maurice Marsac; Maitre d', Marcel De la Brosse; Borvitch's Aide, Gyorgy Naqyajtay; Monitor, Gene Hasler; American Sergeant, Harold Stiller; Colonel Mannix, Paul Birch; Antique Dealer, Charles Radilak; Nurse, Peter Scott; French Reporter, Frank Arnold; Swedish Reporter, Sigfrid Tor; Hungarian Army Officer, Victor Desny; English Reporter, Malcolm Peters; Spanish Reporter, David Morales; Receptionist, Gene Gary; Airport Receptionist, Genevieve Aumont; Radio Budapest Announcer, Paul Frees; Interrogator, Werner Klingler; Doctor, Rolf Lindau; Recorder, Albert Szabo; Military Aide, Ken Terrell; Guard, John Parlow

Credits: Director, Robert Parrish; Assistant Director, Carter DeHaven; Producers, Samuel Marx and Jerry Bresler; Adaptors, Walter Goetz and Jack Palmer White; Screenwriter, William Bowers; Editor, Charles Nelson; Montages, Donald W. Starling; Art Director, John Meehan; Set Decorator, Frank Tuttle; Cinematographers, Burnett Guffey and Ray Cory; Gowns, Jean Louis; Makeup, Clay Campbell; Hair Stylist, Helen Hunt; Sound, Jack Goodrich; Original Music, George Duning; Musical Director, Morris Stoloff

Location Filming: Budapest, Hungary, and Paris, France

Production Dates: Mid–February–early March 1952

Source: story "Trial by Terror" by Paul Gallico

Running Time: 84 minutes

Story: Editor-in-chief of the Paris Office of the *New York Herald-Tribune*, George Sanders brings journalist Marta Toren back from Budapest. An innocent American has been convicted of being a spy and sentenced to 20 years in prison. Toren was working on a story in which Hungarian Prime Minister Herbert Berghof and Yugoslavia President Marshall Tito were plotting against the Russians. Unfortunately, Toren has no proof and so Sanders has no interest. High-ranking Hungarian official Donald Randolph assigns two thugs, Leon Askin and Paul Hoffman, to shadow Toren in hopes she will lead them to an important defector. Toren tells fellow journalist Dana Andrews about her story. When Budapest bureau chief Joseph Forte falls ill, Sanders assigns Andrews to replace him. Because of Andrews' romantic relationship to Toren, he falls under suspicion by the Hungarian government. Andrews finds out that the innocent American is dead and by code sends this information to Sanders in Paris. Andrews receives a photo collaborating Toren's story and is able to hide the photo in Forte's passport. Forte, still seriously ill, is being sent back to Paris. Believing that Andrews is sending sensitive information to Paris, Berghof has him arrested. Andrews' interrogation is tape-recorded and edited so that it sounds as though Andrews admits that he is a spy. Andrews is tortured as he is being prepared for trial. Forte is murdered en route to Paris. In Paris, the incriminating photo is finally found. Sanders attempts to use it as a bargaining chip to effect Andrew's release. Randolph insists that this just a picture of four friendly men and refuses to bargain. In despair, Toren goes back to the newspaper to see if she can find anything that would help Andrews' cause. Sandro Giglio, a filing clerk, is the defector the Hungarians have been looking for. Giglio decides to help Toren and tells her that his daughter has information that will back up her story. Toren retrieves the information only to be captured by Askin and Hoffman and forced to call Giglio and tell him to come home. Giglio arrives and is taken captive by the two thugs. As they try to leave with Giglio, Sanders and the police surround and capture the men and free Giglio. After Sanders promises to relocate Giglio's children to America, Giglio offers himself to be exchanged for Andrews. The exchange is made but Andrews is in a dazed, drugged state. Sanders tells Berghof if any harm befalls Giglio, he will publish the story.

Notes and Commentary: The working title of this film was *European Edition*.

It was based on "Trial by Terror" by Paul Gallico. The story was serialized in seven installments in the weekly *Saturday Evening Post*, beginning with the April 21, 1951, issue. In the story, reporter Jimmy Race is branded a spy by the Hungarian government because he gained entry to the country illegally. Race is broken by torture, confesses to crimes against the state and sentenced to hang. His editor Nick Strang finds Grisha, who has hidden volatile information detrimental to Minister of Justice Ordy's career. Grisha is willing to give Ordy the information that will guarantee Race's freedom. In exchange, Grisha's family is transported to the United States with $100,000 in the bank for them. Race, in a zombie state, is returned. In the book, Grisha is subsequently murdered. Race is in love with Strang's wife. In the film, Race falls for Strang's girlfriend. After all is over, Strang's wife realizes that she is still in love with her husband. Race is weaned off the effects of the drugs but his self-esteem has been shattered. It is uncertain if Race will able to return to his former normal self.

Dana Andrews stated that Paris location shooting was interrupted by possible saboteurs who wanted production stopped.

Reviews: "Hard-hitting espionage thriller. There is an eerie feeling to this film in that much of what is profiled came into very real existence four years later with the abortive Hungarian Revolution." *Motion Picture Guide*, Nash and Ross

"The film emerges as a standard display piece of some palpitating star heroics against a provocative but mildly effective background of totalitarian intrigue." *The New York Times*, 10/25/52

Summation: This is a very effective and well-done Cold War noir. Williams Bowers' screenplay and Robert Parrish's direction produce a suspenseful story of a cocky individual suddenly thrust into a dangerous situation in which he has no control. Dana Andrews plays this part well. An ending leaves the audience uncertain if the individual will recover and if so, at what cost. The photography of cinematographers Burnett Guffey and Ray Cory echoes Andrews and Marta Toren's feelings of despair.

IN THE DARK, WHEN I FEEL HIS HEART POUNDING AGAINST MINE—IS IT LOVE? OR FRENZY? OR TERROR?

Autumn Leaves

(August 1956)
A William Goetz Production

Cast: Milly, Joan Crawford; Burt Hanson, Cliff Robertson; Virginia, Vera Miles; Mr. Hanson, Lorne Greene; Liz, Ruth Donnelly; Dr. Couzzens, Shepperd Strudwick; Mr. Wetherby, Selmer Jackson; Nurse Evans, Maxine Cooper; Waitress, Marjorie Bennett; Mr. Ramsey, Frank Gerstle; Colonel Hillyer, Leonard Mudie; Dr. Masterson, Maurice Manson; Desk Clerk, Bob Hopkins

CREDITS: Director, Robert Aldrich; Assistant Director, Jack Berne; Screenwriters, Jack Jevne, Lewis Meltzer and Robert Blees; Editor, Michael Luciano; Art Director, Bill Glasgow; Set Decorator, Eli Benneche; Cinematographer, Charles Lang; Gowns, Jean Louis; Makeup, Clay Campbell; Hair Stylist, Helen Hunt; Sound, Ferol Redd; Recording Supervisor, John Livadary; Music Composer, Hans Salter; Musical Conductor, Morris Stoloff

LOCATION FILMING: Brentwood, California

SONG: "Autumn Leaves" (Kosma and Prevert) sung by Nat "King" Cole (Note: English lyrics by Johnny Mercer)

PRODUCTION DATES: August 31–October 21, 1955

RUNNING TIME: 107 minutes

STORY: Professional typist Joan Crawford is given symphony tickets. Crawford will go by herself because she has no romantic life. She allowed herself to be tied down by caring for her sick father, Selmer Jackson. After the concert, Crawford stops in a crowded restaurant where Cliff Robertson, a younger man, asks to sit at her table. Reluctantly Crawford allows him to do so. Finally they are enjoying each other's company and Robertson asks Crawford to go to the beach the next day. Crawford accepts. Even though she begins to have romantic feelings for Robertson, she decides to break off the affair because of their age difference. After a month, Robertson comes back into Crawford's life and they get married. Vera Miles comes to their home looking for Robertson. Crawford learns that Miles is Robertson's ex-wife and that Robertson has mental problems. Miles wants Robertson to sign over some property to her. Crawford also learns that Robertson's father, Lorne Greene, who Crawford thought was dead, is very much alive and is in town on business. Crawford visits Greene and hears more disturbing news about Robertson. Crawford, not knowing that Greene and Miles are in a romantic liaison, persuades Robertson to visit his father. Crawford finds out about the relationship but not before Robertson goes to Greene's room. The realization that Greene and Miles are living together leaves Robertson in a state of shock. Robertson tells Crawford that his past life with Miles wasn't important. The marriage broke up when he came home unexpectedly in the middle of the day and went up to their bedroom. Robertson is unable to go further with the story but the event left Robertson traumatized and withdrawn. Greene and Miles want Robertson committed to a sanitarium. Crawford accuses Greene and Miles of being evil. Robertson sees Crawford talking with Greene and Miles but cannot hear the conversation. When Crawford comes back to the house, Robertson accuses her of being in league with Greene and Miles. Robertson suddenly becomes violent and hits Crawford, knocking her to the floor. He then picks up a typewriter and throws it at Crawford, injuring her left hand. As Crawford begins to cry, Robertson is suddenly comes to his senses and has no memory of his violent outburst. Finally Crawford has no choice but have him committed with the hopes he can be cured. Dr. Shepperd Strudwick explains to Crawford that if cured, he might not have the same feelings toward her. After intensive treatment, Robertson is ready for discharge. Robertson has given up his claim to the property to Greene and Miles in exchange for them to stay out of his life. Crawford goes to the sanatorium expecting to be rejected by Robertson but finds that he still loves her.

NOTES AND COMMENTARY: The working title for this film was *The Way We Are*; in order to exploit the Nat "King" Cole song "Autumn Leaves," the film title was changed.

Jack Jevne was the pseudonym for blacklisted writers Jean Rouveral and Hugo Butler. In April 1997, the Writers Guild of America put the proper screenwriting credits in place.

Robert Aldrich originally planned to both produce and direct Rouveral and Butler's screenplay. The completed film was to be released by United Artists. Ultimately William Goetz took over the production end with Aldrich remaining as director.

In one scene, Aldrich wanted Crawford to cry but only slightly. Reportedly Crawford responded, "Which eye?"

REVIEWS: "Joan Crawford has a strong dramatic vehicle. Direction by Robert Aldrich punches every dramatic scene for its full worth." *Variety*, 4/18/56

"*Autumn Leaves* is an intense melodrama about loneliness, despair and mental illness." *Motion Picture Guide*, Nash and Ross

Summation: What a surprise, this film is a noir. Aldrich's direction and the camerawork of Charles Lang elevates what could have been just another woman's picture. Lang, in noir style, keeps normal days on the bright side. As Crawford realizes that she has married a mentally troubled younger man, the scenes darken. In the montage of Robertson's commitment to the sanatorium and Crawford trying to maintain sanity in her work, Lang skews scenes to good effect. *Autumn Leaves* turns out to be a tensely gripping film. Crawford creates a good characterization as an older woman who earlier passed love by only to find possible happiness in the company of a younger man. But it's Robertson who gives the top performance in this film, running the gamut of emotions without a false step. And it's always a delight to see Ruth Donnelly on the screen.

THE UNKNOWN KNIFER ... BEHIND THE SURGEON'S MASK!
THE SHOCKING TRUTH ABOUT "GHOST SURGERY" ...
THE SHAME OF THE MEDICAL PROFESSION!

Bad for Each Other

(January 1954)

Cast: Dr. Tom Owen, Charlton Heston; Helen Curtis, Lizabeth Scott; Joan Lasher, Dianne Foster; Mary Owen, Mildred Dunnock; Dr. Jim Crowley, Arthur Franz; Dan Reasonover, Ray Collins; Mrs. Roger Nelson, Marjorie Rambeau; Dr. Homer Gleeson, Lester Matthews; Dr. Leslie Scobee, Rhys Williams; Rita Thornburg, Lydia Clarke; Uncredited: Pete Olzoneski, Chris Alcaide; Tippy Kashko, Frank Sully; Maid, Louise Franklin; Lucille Grellett, Ann Robinson; Mrs. Cartwright, Katherine Warren; Mrs. Norton, Arlene Harris; Ada Nicoletti, Dorothy Green; Mrs. Olzoneski, Elsie Baker; Dr. Walter Messenger, Grandon Rhodes; Mr. Finer (Jeweler), Reid Kilpatrick; Trooper at Mine Accident, Robert Bray

Credits: Director, Irving Rapper; Assistant Director, James Nicholson; Associate Producer, William Fadiman; Story, Horace McCoy; Screenwriters, Irving Wallace and Horace McCoy; Editor, Al Clark; Art Director, Walter Holscher; Set Decorator, James Crowe; Cinematographer, Frank Planer; Gowns, Jean Louis; Makeup, Clay Campbell; Hair Stylist, Helen Hunt; Sound, Josh Westmoreland; Musical Director, Mischa Bakaleinikoff

Production Dates: April 23–May 21, 1953

Source: novel *Scalpel* by Horace McCoy

Running Time: 83 minutes

Story: Because of his brother's death, doctor Charlton Heston returns to Coalville, Pennsylvania, after ten years of military duty. Coalville residents blame Heston's brother for the mine tragedy that also caused other miners' deaths. Meeting with mine owner Ray Collins, Heston learns his brother was responsible: He used substandard materials, took kickbacks and embezzled money. At a party, Collins' daughter Lizabeth Scott takes an interest in Heston. Coalville physician Rhys Williams wants Heston to leave the Army and join his practice. Scott arranges for Heston to meet Pittsburgh society physician Lester Matthews, who also offers him a job. At Scott's apartment, Scott convinces Heston to accept Matthews' offer. In addition to Scott's charms, Heston takes the position for the money he will receive. Dianne Foster is hired as Heston's nurse. Dr. Arthur Franz, who knew Heston in the service, requests a job with Heston's practice. Due to Foster's urging, Heston gets Franz a job with Williams. Heston proposes marriage to Scott, who accepts. Collins warns Heston that Scott will destroy him and he will truly become a society physician, practicing medicine only for money. At a party, Scott's aunt Marjorie Rambeau becomes ill. Heston recognizes the symptoms of intestinal strangulation. Rambeau is hospitalized for an emergency operation. Matthews is afraid to operate and turns the procedure to Heston. Heston's skill results in a successful operation. Matthews takes credit, making Heston a "ghost surgeon." This situation infuriates Foster, who quits Heston to take a position with Franz. Rambeau learns the truth and renounces Matthews as a fraud. She also believes Heston should open his own practice. A mine explosion brings Heston to the scene to help. Franz is down in the mine trying to care

***Bad for Each Other*, lower left: Lizabeth Scott and Charlton Heston (1954).**

for an injured miner. Heston goes to Franz's side and takes over, stabilizing the miner so he can be moved to the surface. Before Franz can get clear, the mine caves in, killing him. Heston decides to replace Franz in Williams' practice. Scott refuses to leave Pittsburgh for Coalville. Heston goes to Coalville where he will work with Foster.

Notes and Commentary: Some incidents from Horace McCoy's novel *Scalpel* remained in the screenplay; e.g. Owen becomes a society physician due to his social and sexual interaction with Curtis, and his prominence as a physician due to his skill in Mrs. Nelson's operation. The Coalville mine disaster renews his desire to be a healing practitioner. In McCoy's novel, there is no subplot of Owen's possible practice in Coalville or any mention of a "ghost surgeon." Owen is an older man, willing to marry Curtis to ensure a profitable practice in Pittsburgh. Both Dr. Crowley and nurse Lasher, who are engaged to be married, come to work for Owen. Owen and Lasher fall in love and plan to marry. Owen finally realizes that Lasher belongs with Crowley. The mine disaster experience convinces Owen to take a position as associate professor of surgery at Harvard. Curtis realizes her place is with Owen in Cambridge.

In 1950, producer Hal B. Wallis purchased the rights to McCoy's novel for $100,000 and planned to star Burt Lancaster and Patricia Neal in a Paramount production. Lizabeth Scott had also been considered for the picture. Columbia obtained the rights in 1953. The working title for the film was *Scalpel.* Lydia Clarke, who has a small part in *Bad for Each Other,* was Heston's wife. Clarke also appeared with Heston in *The Greatest Show on Earth* (Paramount, 1952) and *Will Penny* (Paramount, 1968).

The ambulance that takes Marjorie Rambeau to the hospital starts the journey as a Cadillac and arrives as a Buick. Heston drives a Kaiser four-door sedan when taking Dianne Foster home but pulls up in a Lincoln two-door hardtop when arriving at the mine.

Reviews: "This is an artificial hodgepodge

of formula drama, cut from the pulp fiction pattern." *Variety*, 12/9/53

Summation: *Bad for Each Other* was released on the *Bad Girls of Film Noir* DVD set. The film is barely noir: The Lizabeth Scott character may be greedy and selfish but certainly not bad as defined in a true noir. The acting by the principals is competent and director Irving Rapper keeps things moving fast enough to make the proceedings qualify as barely acceptable entertainment. The end result is too predictable to make any lasting impact on the audience.

"...THE DOOR'S OPEN ... come on in!" She's the BAIT in a man-trap!

Bait

(February 1954)

Cast: Peggy, Cleo Moore; Marko, Hugo Haas; Ray Brighton, John Agar; Foley, Emmett Lynn; Webb, Bruno VeSota; Waitress, Jan Englund; Chuck, George Keymas; The Devil, Sir Cedric Hardwicke

Credits: Director and Producer, Hugo Haas; Assistant Director, George Loper; Associate Producer, Robert Erlik; Story and Screenwriter, Samuel W. Taylor; Additional Dialogue, Hugo Haas; Dialogue Supervisor, Mark Lowell; Script Supervisor, William Orr; Editor, Robert S. Eisen; Assistant Editor, Harry Eisen; Art Director, William Glasgow; Production Manager, Leon Chooluck; Cinematographer, Edward P. Fitzgerald; Special Effects, Lee Zavitz; Titles and Optical Effects, Jack Rabin and David Commons; Chief Electrician, Don Stott; Makeup, David Newell; Musical Score Composer and Conductor, Vaclav Divina; Orchestrator, Nathan Scott

Filming Location: Bronson Canyon, California

Song: "What Am I Gonna Do?" (Schwab) sung by Edna Neilson and Robert Dale and "No Questions Asked" (Schwab) sung by Edna Neilson and Robert Dale (Songs arranged by Lewis Raymond)

Production Dates: early June–mid–June 1953

Running Time: 79 minutes

Story: John Agar is warned not to enter into an agreement with Hugo Haas to find a lost gold mine, but does so anyway. Agar is ready to abandon the quest when it looks like Haas is mistaken but then, quite by accident, finds the mine. The mine is richer than Haas anticipated and he doesn't want to share with Agar. Agar tells Haas that he is to live up to their equal share bargain. Haas goes to town for supplies and comes back married to Cleo Moore. Moore was looked down upon as an unwed mother. Haas knows that Agar is attracted to Moore and does what he can to kindle a sexual encounter between them. Stating that they're out of salt, Haas tells them he'll go into town to replenish their supply. Haas has hidden the salt to give him this excuse. Agar attempts to ignite a sexual encounter but Moore plans to stay true to her marriage vow. She tells Agar that she was married but paperwork was lost and her husband died before the documents could be replaced. Agar finds the hidden salt and realizes he and Moore have been set up. He knows Haas is outside the cabin, hoping to find the couple in bed; then this "jealous husband" can shoot both and claim all the gold. Agar has Moore pretend to invite him into her bed and turns out all lights. Haas comes through the door only to be overpowered by Agar. Though a major snowstorm is imminent, Agar and Moore plan to take their share of the gold and leave. Haas makes one more attempt on Agar's life. Agar pushes Haas to the cabin floor. Agar and Moore start for town as the winds intensify. In the cabin, Haas realizes his leg was broken in the scuffle and he calls for help. With the high winds, Agar and Moore can't hear him. As Agar and Moore reach the highway and safety, Haas freezes to death with his share of the gold in his grasp.

Notes and Commentary: The working title for this film was *Fever*.

Reviews: "[*Bait*] contains a generous helping of sex and melodrama. While such time-tested ingredients hold audience interest, the story of which they're components is too familiar and evident." *Variety*, 2/17/54

"The short-change begins with the story, which is a pitifully meager affair. It is charitably completed by the comparative brevity of the film, which is the one shining virtue of it." *New York Times*, 2/24/54

"There is something intensely brooding about many of Haas' films, and this one is no exception. Given higher budgets and better scripts, he might have been a second-rate Hitchcock." *Motion Picture Guide*, Nash and Ross

SUMMATION: Although produced on a low budget, this noir of greed and sex turns out to be a pretty good tale. Hugo Haas, who produced, directed and starred, keeps the narrative concise, aided by interjections from Sir Cedric Hardwicke. The other major performers, Cleo Moore and John Agar, perform nicely. Moore plays a sexy young woman, unjustly accused of being an unwed mother and subsequently a slut, but she is actually quite virtuous. Agar is convincing as a young man whose thoughts of riches are somewhat compromised by his raging hormones when he spies Moore. An interesting film.

STICK UP! PICK UP! MURDER! Shot-in-the-streets realism hot from the police files of a great city!

Between Midnight and Dawn

(October 1950)

CAST: Rocky Barnes, Mark Stevens; Dan Purvis, Edmond O'Brien; Kate Mallory, Gale Storm; Ritchie Garris, Donald Buka; Terry Romaine, Gale Robbins; Lt. Masterson, Anthony Ross; Leo Cusick, Roland Winters; Romano, Tito Vuolo; Mrs. Romano, Grazia Narciso; Mrs. Mallory, Madge Blake; Kathy Blake, Lora Lee Michel; Uncredited: Police Dispatchers, Mary Ann Hokanson and Louise Kane; Eddie, Steve Pendleton; Savvy Girl Lookout, Janey Fay; Frightened Girl Lookout, Mary Ellen Kay; Booking Officer, Eric Mack; Policewoman, Ruth Warren; Joe Quist, Philip Van Zandt; Oliver (Attorney), Alex Gerry; Tex, James Brown; Petey Conklin, Billy Gray; Thurlow Conklin, Tony Taylor; Boy, Tommy Mann; Louis Franissi, Jack Del Rio; Yost, Tony Barr; Blake, Wheaton Chambers; Mrs. Blake, Frances Morris; Ziggy, Lee Frederick; Doctor, Gayne Whitman; Judge, William E. Green; Court Clerk, Jack Gargan; Jury Foreman, Nolan Leary; Deputies, Arnold Daly and Tim Daly; Peters, Earl Breitbard; Adams, Peter Mamakos; Waiters, Mike Lally and William H. O'Brien; Detective Captain, Douglas Evans; Reporters, Tom Quinn, Ralph Brooks and Guy Way; Sergeant Bailey, Cliff Bailey; Fred (Jailer), Robert Foulk; Carr, Ted Jordan; Rocco, Marc Krah; Officer Davis, Myron Healey; Officer Nicholls, Richard Karlan; Henpecked Husband, Charles Marsh; Nagging Wife, Maude Prickett; Captain Evans, Sydney Mason; Busboy, Joe Recht; Headwaiter, Ted Stanhope; Detectives, Robert Bice, Chuck Hamilton, Don Kohler, Harry Lauter and Bert Stevens; Policemen, Charles Ferguson and Brick Sullivan; Jurors, Frank O'Connor and Bert Stevens; Driver, Harry Harvey, Jr.

CREDITS: Director, Gordon Douglas; Assistant Director, James Nicholson; Producer, Hunt Stromberg; Story, Gerald Drayson Adams and Leo Katcher; Screenwriter, Eugene Ling; Editor, Gene Havlick; Art Director, George Brooks; Set Decorator, Frank Tuttle; Cinematographer, George E. Diskant; Gowns, Jean Louis; Makeup, Clay Campbell; Hair Stylist, Helen Hunt; Sound, Russell Malmgren; Original Music, George Duning; Musical Director, Morris Stoloff

SONGS: "Please Don't Kiss Me" (Roberts and Fisher)—sung by Gale Robbins, "Either It's Love or It Isn't" (Roberts and Fisher)—sung by Gale Robbins, "I Want to Learn About Love" (Roberts and Lee)—sung by Gale Robbins and "I've Been Working on the Railroad" (traditional)—sung by Mark Stevens and Edmond O'Brien

FILMING LOCATIONS: Los Angeles, California

PRODUCTION DATES: February 14–March 23, 1950

RUNNING TIME: 89 minutes

STORY: Prowl car policemen the Edmond O'Brien and Mark Stevens have been close friends since their stint as Marines in World War II. O'Brien, the older of the two, is hard and cynical about life while Stevens has a kinder outlook. They run afoul of mobster and nightclub owner Donald Buka when they arrest his underling Philip Van Zandt for throwing a stink bomb through shop owner Tito Vuolo's window. Vuolo refuses to identify Van Zandt, and he is released. Before leaving headquarters, O'Brien and Stevens are attracted to Lt. Anthony Ross' assistant, Gale Storm. Storm doesn't want to get involved with either man because her father, a policeman, was killed in the line of duty and she doesn't want to live in fear every time her loved one reports for duty. With Storm's mother Madge Blake's help, O'Brien and Stevens begin taking Storm out. They go to Buka's nightclub where they see notorious gangland boss Roland Winters. Winters wants Buka to join his organization, and Buka refuses. Buka decides to take matters in his own hands and ambushes Winters. The ambush is witnessed and police are notified. The chase is on and O'Brien and Stevens encounter Buka. Gunfire is exchanged. Buka's shot takes out the police radio. Stevens' shots wound Buka and take out driver Van Zandt. Ross and Storm arrive at the scene. Storm is relieved to see O'Brien and Stevens unharmed but throws herself into Stevens' arms. Stevens and Storm plan to marry after Buka's trial. Buka is found guilty but soon engineers a jailbreak. He is able to ambush O'Brien and Stevens' prowl car and his shots mortally wound Stevens. O'Brien vows vengeance. O'Brien and Storm begin hanging out at Buka's nightclub to see if this would unnerve songstress Gale Robbins, Buka's girl. Finally, while overly distraught, O'Brien encounters Robbins at her dressing room and begins hitting her to make her talk. Only Storm's pleas make him stop. When Buka shows up at Robbins' apartment, she wants nothing to do with him. Robbins' apartment is bugged and police surround the building. Buka thinks he's trapped until the building superintendent's daughter, Lora Lee Michel, comes to see Robbins. Buka decides to hold Michel as hostage. O'Brien is able to enter the apartment from the ledge outside a window and gets Michel out of the line of fire but, in doing so, is left open to Buka. As Buka pulls the trigger, Robbins steps in front of O'Brien and takes the fatal bullets. Buka tries to escape but is shot by O'Brien. As O'Brien leaves the crime scene, his demeanor, because of Robbins' sacrifice, is now closer to that of Stevens. Seeing his change, Storm walks arm in arm with him.

Notes and Commentary: The working title for the film was *Prowl Car*. It was first announced that Larry Parks would play one of the lead roles. Both Mark Stevens and Edmond O'Brien demanded top billing. Stevens eventually won out.

Reviews: "There's enough thrill footage to make it an interesting cops-and-robbers melodrama." *Variety*, 9/27/50

"Tough little melodrama" *The Columbia Story*, Hirschhorn

Summation: This is a good, hard-hitting film noir which would have been tougher without the interplay of Edmond O'Brien and Mark Stevens with Gale Storm. Gordon Douglas' direction is brisk and tough with the proper punch to the action scenes. The car chase through the Los Angeles street is first-rate. Cinematographer George E. Diskant's photography is superb, utilizing streaks of light through the darkness and in the exterior scenes using the wet streets to emphasize the terror. The acting of the principals is fine, especially by O'Brien and Stevens. Playing a character who initially has a dark outlook on life, becomes filled with hate but ultimately has a kinder view of the world, O'Brien is believable.

Drama with the shock of a lightning bolt in every scene!

The Big Boss

(April 1941)

Cast: Jim Maloney, Otto Kruger; Sue Peters, Gloria Dickson; Bob Dugan, John Litel; Cliff Randall, Don Beddoe; George Fellows, Robert Fiske; Senator Williams, George Lessey; Tony, Joe Conti; Uncredited: Detective, Ralph Dunn; Jimmie, George Hickman; Blake, George McKay; Radio Announcer, Stanley Brown; Chief Justice, Edmund Elton; Robins, Eddie Laughton; Sheriff Dugan, Ben Taggart; Frank Dugan (boy), Martin Spellman; Bob Dugan (boy), Schuyler Standish; Companions, Roger Gray and Ted Oliver; Prisoner, Ernie Adams; Lynch Mob Leader, Al Bridge

Credits: Director, Charles Barton; Screenwriter, Howard J. Green; Editor, Viola Lawrence; Cinematographer, Benjamin H. Kline

Song: "Pop Goes the Weasel" (traditional)—played on the harmonica first by Martin Spellman and then by Joe Conti

Production Dates: February 19–March 5, 1941

Running Time: 69 minutes

Story: After the death of their father Ben Taggart, two boys (who will grow up to be Otto Kruger and John Litel) go their separate ways. Litel studies law and becomes a state Senator. Kruger embarks on a life of crime before becoming a political boss. This ensures that Kruger's schemes stay just barely legal. Kruger backs Litel to become governor. Reporter Gloria Dickson initially believes that Litel is under Kruger's control but soon finds that he is his own man. Dickson and Litel take a drive and see chain gang convicts working on a private project bossed by Robert Fiske. Litel embarks on a crusade to end this practice, calling it slave labor. Using convicts enables Kruger and his associates to make big profits on their land deals. Fiske, upset about the amount of money he receives, confronts Kruger. The two men fight and in anger Kruger strangles Fiske. Dickson recognizes the picture of the murdered man as the overseer of the chain gang. Fingerprints on Fiske's collar indicate the killer was a deceased escaped convict. Checking Kruger's background indicates that his history only goes back twelve years. Litel believes that Kruger is the supposedly dead convict. Confronted by Litel, Kruger admits that he changed identities with a fellow convict. As Litel takes Kruger to jail, an incident makes him aware that Kruger is his brother. After an agonizing night, Litel plans to resign. Dickson tells Kruger about Litel's decision. Kruger then confesses to Fiske's murder without revealing his real name. Litel remains governor and begins to take a romantic interest in Dickson.

Notes and Commentary: The working title for the film was *Chain Gang*.

Reviews: "Direction paces actors well, involving the audience in the characters' struggles." *Motion Picture Guide*, Nash and Ross

"[M]odest, well-made, competently acted programmer" *The Columbia Story*, Hirschhorn

Summation: This political noir is a formula story. Otto Kruger and John Litel's fine acting carry the story with able assistance from Gloria Dickson and Don Beddoe. A good ending of Kruger going to jail to keep Litel in office gives the story added grit.

A HARD COP AND A SOFT DAME!

The Big Heat

(October 1953)

Cast: Det. Sgt. Dave Bannion, Glenn Ford; Debby Marsh, Gloria Grahame; Katie Bannion, Jocelyn Brando; Mike Lagana, Alexander Scourby; Vince Stone, Lee Marvin; Bertha Duncan, Jeanette Nolan; Tierney, Peter Whitney; Lt. Ted Wilks, Willis Bouchey; Det. Gus Burke, Robert Burton; Larry Gordon, Adam Williams; Police Commissioner Higgins, Howard Wendell; Uncredited: George Rose, Chris Alcaide; Medical Examiner, Joseph Mell; Joyce Bannion, Linda Bennett; Lucy Chapman, Dorothy Green; Retreat Bartender, Sidney Clute; Police Surgeon, Byron Kane; Police Guard Outside Lagana Home, Charles Cane; Lagana's Butler, Ted Stanhope; Lagana's Mother in Portrait, Celia Lovsky; Cab Driver, Donald Kerr; Doris, Carolyn Jones; Mr. Atkins, Dan Seymour; Selma Parker, Edith Evanson; Marge, Kathryn Eames; Al, John Crawford; B-Girl, Laura Mason; George Fuller, Paul Maxey; Councilman Gillen, Douglas Evans; Policeman, John Close; Hettrick, Phil Chambers; Mark Reiner, John Doucette; Harry Shoenstein, Al Eben; Hank O'Connell, Harry Lauter; Intern, Patrick Miller; Bill Rutherford, Robert Stevenson; Hugo, Michael Granger

Credits: Director, Fritz Lang; Assistant Director, Milton Feldman; Producer, Robert Arthur; Screenwriter, Sydney Boehm; Editor, Charles Nelson; Art Director, Robert Peterson; Set Decorator, William Kiernan; Cinematographer, Charles Lang; Gowns, Jean Louis; Makeup, Clay Campbell; Hair Stylist, Helen Hunt; Sound, George Cooper; Musical Director, Mischa Bakaleinikoff

Song: "Put the Blame on Mame" (Fisher and Roberts)—instrumental

Production Dates: March 17–April 18, 1953

Source: *The Saturday Evening Post* serial by William P. McGivern

Running Time: 89½ minutes

Story: Jeanette Nolan's policeman husband commits suicide, leaving a letter incriminating mob boss Alexander Scourby. Seizing the opportunity to live a comfortable life, Nolan contacts and blackmails Scourby. Sgt. Glenn Ford is assigned to the case and is satisfied that there is no foul play. B-girl Dorothy Green gets in touch with Ford and tells him that Nolan's husband was in the process of obtaining a divorce from Nolan. Ford doesn't believe Green's story until her tortured body is found the next day. After Ford questions Nolan again, he is told to stay away from Nolan. Ford refuses to drop the case. After a threatening phone call, Ford goes to Scourby's house to try to get answers. Lt. Willis Bouchey tells Ford to forget Green's murder. A car bomb placed in Ford's car kills Ford's wife, Jocelyn Brando. A meeting with Police Commissioner Howard Wendell makes Ford realize he'll get no official police help in finding Brando's killer. Threatened with suspension, Ford turns in his badge. Ford begins his own investigation and a lead brings him to a bar frequented by the gangster element. In the bar, Ford has a run-in with vicious gangster Lee Marvin. After Marvin abruptly leaves the bar, Marvin's girl, Gloria Grahame, picks up Ford and goes to Ford's hotel room. Mobster Adam Williams sees Ford and Grahame get in a taxi and reports to Marvin.

In the hotel room, Ford turns down Grahame's sexual advances. Grahame returns to Marvin's apartment where the jealous Marvin throws hot coffee in her face. Grahame seeks refuge with Ford and tells him the man who placed the bomb in Ford's car is Williams. Ford confronts Williams and makes him admit that Marvin told him to place the bomb in his car and that he also murdered Green. Ford tells Williams that he plans to spread the word that he squealed. Williams makes an attempt to leave town but is murdered by Marvin. Ford visits Nolan, who admits she's in league with Scourby. Aware that with Nolan's death, Nolan's husband's letter will surface, Grahame goes to Nolan's house and puts three bullets into her. Grahame then goes to Marvin's apartment

The Big Heat (1953).

and throws hot coffee in his face. She tells Marvin that she killed Nolan. Marvin's response is to shoot Grahame. Ford breaks into Marvin's apartment and a gunfight ensues between Marvin and Ford. When Marvin's gun is emptied, Ford captures Marvin. Scourby and Wendell are indicted. Ford is reinstated on the police department.

Notes and Commentary: Changes were made to William P. McGivern's novel as it was adapted for the screen. First were some of the main character names, Mary Ellen Deery to Bertha Duncan, Max Stone to Vince Stone, Brigid Bannion to Joyce Bannion, Lucy Carraway to Lucy Chapman, and Debby Ward to Debby Marsh. There was no Police Commissioner Higgins in the novel. The corrupt official was Lt. Ted Wilks. The honest policeman was Inspector Cranston, whose part was eliminated from the novel. Other prominent characters omitted were newspaper reporter Jerry Furnham and a priest, Father Masterson.

In the novel, the reader did not know Deery was blackmailing Lagana until near the end of the novel. Debby shoots Deery and then mortally wounds herself. After Stone is cornered by Bannion, Stone is shot and killed by a policeman. Lagana is not indicted; a heart attack ended his life. The novel takes place in Philadelphia and the film is situated in the fictional city of Kenport. The intent and basic thrust of McGivern's novel is maintained.

From December 1952 to February 1953, "The Big Heat" was serialized in *The Saturday Evening Post*. Initially William P. McGivern's novel was to be produced by Jerry Wald, who wanted either Paul Muni, George Raft or Edward G. Robinson as Dave Bannion. Columbia paid $40,000 for McGivern's novel.

Columbia wanted Marilyn Monroe for the role of Debby Marsh. 20th Century–Fox wanted too much money so Gloria Grahame got the role. Rex Reason was slated to play either Tierney or Detective Burke. Reason's agent wanted a larger role for Reason. The end result was that Reason did not appear in the film.

In the initial scene with Glenn Ford and Lee Marvin, the musical group at the bar plays "Put the Blame on Mame," a song played in Ford's first Columbia noir, *Gilda*.

Reviews: "Columbia has a taut, exciting crime melodrama in this well-made presentation. It is a cut considerably above the average cops-and-robbers feature in the writing, direction and playing." *Variety*, 9/23/53

"The only concern of the filmmakers is a tense and eventful crime show, and this they deliver in a fashion that keeps you tingling like a frequently struck gong. Mr. Lang can direct a film. He has put his mind to it, in this instance, and he has brought forth a hot one with a sting." *New York Times*, 10/15/53

"A scalding face-full of harsh reality, courtesy Fritz Lang. Starkly photographed and without a continuous score, the absence of which underlines the hard-hitting dialogue and the sound of smacking fists and thudding bullets, this film is a brutal as Lang's *M* was frightening." *Motion Picture Guide*, Nash and Ross

Summation: This is a tough, taut, gritty crime noir. All aspects are first-rate. Ford's portrayal of a cop on the vengeance trail is perfect. Grahame's shading of a gangster's girl who finally realizes the morass of evil she's stepped into is on target. Fritz Lang's directorial skills are very much in evidence as he gets the most of every scene, from the tenderness shown in Ford's home life with Jocelyn Brando to the vicious Lee Marvin throwing hot coffee in Grahame's face. Also to be singled out is the fine cinematography of Charles Lang using shadows and darkness to emphasize the evil that Ford is combating.

Impossible Murder in a Locked Room!

Blind Spot

(February 1947)

Cast: Jeffrey Andrews, Chester Morris; Evelyn Green, Constance Dowling; Lloyd Harrison, Steven Geray; Mike, Sid Tomack; Det. Lt. Fred Applegate, James Bell; Night Watchman, Paul E. Burns; Uncredited: Henry Small, William Forrest; Applegate's Associate, Harry Strang; Officer Harmon, Paul Bryar; Cab Driver, Charles Jordan;

Stakeout Detectives, Steve Benton and Jimmy Gray

Credits: Director, Robert Gordon; Producer, Ted Richmond; Story, Harry Perowne; Screenwriter, Martin Goldsmith; Editor, Henry Batista; Art Director, Cary Odell; Set Decorator, William Kiernan; Cinematographer, George B. Meehan, Jr.; Musical Director, Mischa Bakaleinikoff

Production Dates: September 11–October 2, 1946

Running Time: 73 minutes

Story: Down-on-his-luck author Chester Morris, while in a drunken state, demands an advance from his publisher, William Forrest. Forrest is set to decline. Present at the conversation is mystery writer Steven Geray. Prodded by Geray, Morris comes up with a brilliant locked room mystery. Leaving the office, Morris stops at the bar located on the ground floor of the office building and tells his story to bartender Sid Tomack and then to Forrest's former secretary Constance Dowling. Dowling had just quit her job after having to fend off Forrest's advances. Morris sees that Dowling's dress is ripped. Also, Dowling left the office in a hurry, leaving one ear ring behind. Morris and Dowling form an immediate attachment and Morris tells her about his story. Not remembering whether he told Forrest the complete story, he goes back up to Forrest's office to find out. Forrest's inner office door is locked. Morris, who wants to disassociate himself from Forrest, takes his contract from the files and rips it up. Later, Morris has no memory of his actions until he's confronted by Lt. James Bell. Forrest has been found murdered in his locked office. Bell arrests Morris on the suspicion of murder. Geray intervenes and convinces Bell to release Morris into his custody. Deciding to investigate on his own, Morris goes to Tomack's apartment. He finds Tomack murdered and one of Dowling's earrings on the floor. Retreating to his apartment, Morris finds Dowling waiting for him. Dowling wants to help Morris although she thinks he's a murderer. Morris begins to fall for Dowling, while believing she murdered Forrest. When Morris finds a check for $500 in a coat pocket, he knows he told Forrest the story while Geray was present. Now he thinks Geray is the murderer. Morris and Dowling confront Geray. Under Geray's influence, Morris now remembers how the locked door murder was completed. Geray also convinces Morris that he actually is the murderer. Bell shows up and takes all three to headquarters. The case begins to unravel when Dowling has an earring in her purse. There's an earring in Tomack's apartment and the earring that was found at the Forrest murder scene is missing. Bell knows that only Geray had access to the ring. Geray pulls a gun, so Bell shoots him. Before he dies, Geray confesses: He murdered Forrest over his contract, and the fact Forrest knew that Geray was using a ghost writer for his stories. Tomack was killed because he saw Forrest come back from the staircase after committing the murder. Morris takes Dowling home.

Notes and Commentary: Working titles for *Blind Spot* were *Inside Story* and *Trapped*.

Reviews: "This modest thriller is derivative but clever, and first-time director Robert Gordon keeps the action moving at a brisk pace." *Motion Picture Guide*, Nash and Ross

Summation: Director Robert Gordon efficiently guides this mystery noir to its conclusion with considerable suspense. Chester Morris, taking a break from his Boston Blackie adventures, is quite effective as a man who suddenly becomes a murder suspect. Gordon is able to build and sustain suspense even though most sharp moviegoers guess the identity of the murderer quite early in the proceedings.

ONE OF THE MOST EXCITING CHASE STORIES EVER FILMED!

The Brothers Rico

(September 1957)

A William Goetz Production

Cast: Eddie Rico, Richard Conte; Alice Rico, Dianne Foster; Norah, Kathryn Grant; Sid Kubik, Larry Gates; Johnny Rico, James Darren; Mrs. Rico, Argentina Brunetti; Peter Malaks, Lamont Johnson; Mike Lamotta, Harry Bellaver; Gino Rico, Paul Picerni; Phil, Paul Dubov; Gonzales, Rudy Bond; Vic Tucci, Richard Bakalyan; Joe Wesson, William Phipps; Uncredited: Laundry Truck Driver, James Waters; Miss Van Ness, Patricia Donahue; Estelle (Counter Girl), Estelle Lawrence; Julia Rico, Mimi Aguglia; Jean, Peggy Maley; Nellie, Jane Easton; Ticket Clerk, Marvin Bryan; Pete Selsun, George Cisar; Pedro (Cab Driver), Don Orlando; El Camino Hotel Desk Clerk, George J. Lewis; Second Cab Driver, Sam Finn; Mary Felici, Mimi Gibson; Mrs. Felici, Maggie O'Byrne; Marco Felici, Dean Cromer; El Camino Bellboy, Darren Dublin; Stewardess, Bonnie Bolding; Bank Official, Rankin Mansfield; Bank Officer (Henchman), Pepe Hern; Bank Guard, Robert Malcolm; Pizza Maker, Ernesto Morelli

Credits: Director, Phil Karlson; Assistant Director, Jack Berne; Producer, Lewis J. Rachmil; Story, Georges Simenon; Screenwriters, Lewis Meltzer and Ben Perry; Editor, Charles Nelson; Cinematographer, Burnett Guffey; Art Director, Robert Boyle; Set Decorators, William Kierman and Darrell Silvera; Gowns, Jean Louis; Makeup, Clay Campbell; Hair Stylist, Helen Hunt; Sound, Lambert Day; Recording Supervisor, John Livadary; Musical Composer, George Duning; Music Conductor, Morris Stoloff; Orchestrator, Arthur Morton

Song: "Let's Fall in Love" (Arlen and Koehler)—sung and hummed by Richard Conte

Production Dates: November 23–December 27, 1956

Running Time: 92 minutes

Source: novella *The Brothers Rico* by Georges Simenon

Story: Richard Conte, a former accountant for the Organization, receives a phone call request to meet with mob boss Larry Gates. Gates needs to locate Conte's younger brother, James Darren. Darren and another brother, Paul Picerni, performed a contract hit with Picerni the shooter and Darren the driver. Darren has dropped out of sight with his new bride Kathryn Grant. Grant's brother, Lamont Johnson, is trying to negotiate a deal with the New York D.A. for Darren to testify against the Organization for favorable treatment.

James Darren comforts Kathryn Grant in *The Brothers Rico* (1957).

Gates promises that if Conte finds Darren, he will let Darren leave the States until everything blows over. Conte agrees to look for Darren, not realizing Picerni had been captured by the Organization, tortured and then killed when it was apparent Picerni had no knowledge of Darren's whereabouts. Dianne Foster, who had set up a meeting with an adoption agency, is upset both over missing the meeting and Conte's involvement with the Organization. Conte is able to locate Darren on a farm in a rural California community. Darren tells Conte that he has led the Organization to him and they plan to kill him. Conte still believes Gates will let Darren leave the country until he returns to his hotel room and finds mobster Harry Bellaver waiting for him. Over the phone Conte tries to tell Darren to run but Bellaver gives Darren the choice of surrendering himself to the Organization instead of creating a situation in which Grant and their newborn son may also be killed. Darren has no choice but to acquiesce to save his family's life. Conte is now being transported to Gates. Conte is able to overcome his captor and reaches New York City. He draws money from a bank account to send Foster out of the country and money to be sent to Grant to help her with living expenses. Conte plans to testify against Gates and the Organization. When Gates and his associate Paul Dubov catch up with Conte, there's a gun fight in which Conte is wounded and Gates and Dubov are killed. Conte testifies against the Organization, restoring his good name. He and Foster begin the process of adoption.

Notes and Commentary: The Columbia screenwriters made significant changes in Georges Simenon's short novel. In the book, Eddie Rico is still working for the organization. He is a family man with a wife and three children. In the movie, Eddie is no longer associated with the organization and he and his wife are trying to adopt a child. In both the novel and the film, Eddie tracks down his brother Tony (Johnny in the film) believing he can help his brother and his pregnant wife escape to another country. Only after finding his brother does Eddie realize he was set up and that his brother will be killed. In the book, Eddie was resigned to his fate and returned to his position in the Organization. In the film, Eddie exacts revenge, killing both Sid Kubik and Phil. His testimony to the New York City D.A. helps destroy the Organization. Eddie and his wife now proceed to adopt a child.

When Julia Rico is shown watching television, a clip from *Earth vs. the Flying Saucers* (Columbia, 1956) is shown.

The film was remade as *The Family Rico* (CBS, 1973) with Ben Gazzara.

Reviews: "Okay gangster yarn with good suspense." *Variety*, 8/21/57

"This is a brutal film that offers no hope of ever dismantling an omnipotent crime cartel. Conte's performance is tension-packed and carries an otherwise depressing film, though it is expertly constructed and paced by veteran film noir director Karlson." *The Motion Picture Guide*, Nash and Ross

Summation: This outing is buoyed by a fine performance by Richard Conte. Phil Karlson's sure hand paces the film nicely. Burnett Guffey's cinematography adds to the noirish atmosphere. My only complaint is the script should have followed Simenon's novella more closely. How stunning it would have been to have Conte just realize that he had been used by Larry Gates and his only option would be go back to his life with Foster. This would have made a more memorable film noir.

BIG MAN! BIG GUN! BIG EXCITEMENT!

Buchanan Rides Alone

(August 1958)

Cast: Tom Buchanan, Randolph Scott; Abe Carbo, Craig Stevens; Lew Agry, Barry Kelley; Judge Simon Agry, Tol Avery; Amos Agry, Peter Whitney; Juan de la Vega, Manuel Rojas; Pecos Hill, L.Q. Jones; Waldo Peck, Robert Anderson; Esteban Gomez, Joe DeSantis; Roy Agry, William Leslie; K.T., Jennifer Holden; Nacho, Nacho Galindo; Uncredited: Lafe, Don C. Harvey; Hamp, Roy Jenson; Ivy, Al Wyatt; Nina, Barbara James; Jury Foreman, Terry Frost; Gomez's Friend, James B. Leong; Saloon Gambler, Frank J. Scannell; Saloon Patron, Richard Alexander

Credits: Director, Budd Boetticher; Assistant Director, Jerrold Bernstein; Producer, Harry Joe Brown; Associate Producer, Randolph Scott; Assistant to Producer, David Breen; Screenwriter, Charles Lang; Editor, Al Clark; Art Director, Robert Boyle; Set Decorator, Frank A. Tuttle; Cinematographer, Lucien Ballard; Recording Supervisor, John Livadary; Sound, Jean Valentino; Color Consultant, Henri Jaffe

Location Filming: Sabino Canyon, Tucson, Arizona and Old Tucson, Tucson, Arizona

Production Dates: February 4–27, 1958

Source: novel "The Name's Buchanan" by Jonas Ward

Running Time: 78 minutes

Filmed in Columbia Color

Story: Randolph Scott, on his way from Mexico to west Texas to start a ranch, stops at Agry Town. The border town is run by Judge Tol Avery and his brother Sheriff Barry Kelley. Manuel Rojas comes across the border and guns down Avery's son, William Leslie, for sexually molesting Rojas' sister. Rojas is arrested and is brutally beaten by Kelley's deputy, Robert Anderson. Scott steps in to stop Anderson and lands in jail with Rojas. Kelley plans to hang both men for Leslie's death. Avery's right hand man, Craig Stevens, convinces Avery to stop the hanging. Stevens knows Rojas' wealthy father will pay a considerable sum to have Rojas returned to him. Avery insists both men be given a trial. Scott is found innocent and Rojas is sentenced to hang. Scott is escorted out of town by two of Kelley's deputies, L.Q. Jones and Don C. Harvey. Kelley wants Scott dead because he took $2,000 from Scott. Harvey is shot by Jones, because Jones can't kill a west Texan. Scott promised Jones a full partnership in his ranch. Kelley learns that Rojas' father will send $50,000 with ranch foreman Joe DeSantis. Kelley learns of the transaction and moves Rojas out of the jail so DeSantis will have to deal with him. Anderson takes Rojas to a shack where Scott and Jones are staying. Scott gets the drop on Anderson and his men. Jones is to take Rojas to his ranch while Scott goes to town to retrieve his money. Anderson and his men get free. With fast riding they overtake Jones and Rojas. Jones is shot down and Rojas is taken back to town. They arrive at the jail just as Scott is starting to leave after taking back his money from Kelley. Scott and Rojas are jailed. Stevens, Avery and DeSantis reach the jail looking for Rojas, and Stevens frees the men. Kelley and his deputies return. Guns blaze. Scott and Rojas make a getaway on Avery's wagon, taking Avery along as hostage. DeSantis is wounded after he throws a saddlebag with the money to Rojas. As they cross the short bridge into Mexico, the axle breaks, spilling Scott, Rojas, Avery and the saddlebag onto the ground. In the ensuing gunfight, the deputies are killed and Avery and Kelley shoot each other. Scott sees that Rojas and the money go back to his father. Scott rides to west Texas.

Notes and Commentary: The working title for the film was *The Name's Buchanan*.

Jonas Ward was the pseudonym for prolific western author William R. Cox.

Charles Lang's screenplay was loosely based on Cox's novel. Juan's father, sister and mother play prominent parts in the novel. Buchanan found Juan's sister Maria after she had been raped by Roy Agry. After Juan was sentenced to hang, it is Juan's father's idea to ransom Juan by turning over his vast holdings to Simon Agry. Buchanan effects Juan's release after he brutally beats Waldo Peck. Lew Agry loots the Agry bank of $20,000. Before he can leave town, Buchanan catches up with him. They exchange shots, Lew is killed and Buchanan is wounded. Juan and Gomez take Buchanan to Juan's hacienda. Amos Agry finds the bank money and hides it, planning to go back east in style. Carbo wants the money and figures that Buchanan and Juan took it to the hacienda. Amos decides to warn Buchanan. On the trail, Carbo murders Amos. At the hacienda, Buchanan kills Carbo. In retaliation for Carbo coming to the hacienda, Gomez and his riders burn down Agrytown; the bank money is hidden in the hotel's ruins. For his assistance to Juan and his family, Buchanan is given a gold chain, a belt of silver, a white stallion, a sapphire necklace and a gold ring. Buchanan returns the necklace. Both Maria and servant Lolita have romantic designs on Buchanan. Not wanting to stay in Mexico, Buchanan rides on through the ruins of Agrytown. Buchanan finds a bewildered Simon Agry and gives him a few coins. As Buchanan makes camp for the night, Lolita shows up wanting a sexual relationship with him.

Reviews: "[A] tough, witty western." *Motion Picture Guide*, Nash and Ross

Summation: This is another fine Randolph Scott–Budd Boetticher noir western. In this story, protagonist Scott has to fight against a corrupt judge and a sheriff who have the town under their control. As Scott leaves, the only thing changed is the town is now under the total control of Craig Stevens. Boetticher paces the story nicely, interspersing action logically and ending with a suspenseful shoot-out. The actors acquit themselves well, especially Scott, whose stoic performance holds the proceedings together.

You'll be tense with excitement and limp from excitement!

The Burglar

(June 1957)

CAST: Nat Harbin, Dan Duryea; Gladden, Jayne Mansfield; Della, Martha Vickers; Baylock, Peter Capell; Dohmer, Mickey Shaughnessy; Police Captain, Wendell Phillips; Sister Sara, Phoebe Mackay; Charlie, Stewart Bradley; News Commentator, John Facenda; News Reporter, Frank Hall; Newsreel Narrator, Bob Wilson; State Trooper, Steve Allison; Harbin as a Child, Richard Emery; Gladden as a Child, Andrea McLaughlin; also with Frank Orrison, Sam Elber, Ned Carey, John Boyd, Michael Rich, George Kane, Sam Cresson and Ruth Burnat

CREDITS: Director, Paul Wendkos; Producer, Louis W. Kellman; Screenwriter, David Goodis; Editor, Herta Horn; Art Director, Jim Leonard; Cinematographer, Don Malkames; Makeup, Josephine Ciannella; Hair Stylist, Gary Elliot; Sound Editor Supervisor, Norman Kasow; Sound Engineer, Ed Johnson; Re-Recording Engineer, Albert Gramaglia; Sound Effects, John Peckman; Production Supervisor, Ben Berk; Original Music and Conductor, Sol Kaplan; Solo Bassoonist, S. Schoenbach of the Philadelphia Orchestra; Script Girl, Deedee Schwartz; Technical Advisor, Captain Maurice R. Pliner, Philadelphia Police Department; Re-Recording, Dichter Sound Studios

SONG: "You Are Mine" (Marcucchi and De Angelo)—sung by Vince Carson

FILMING LOCATIONS: Philadelphia, Pennsylvania, Brigantine, New Jersey and Atlantic City, New Jersey

PRODUCTION DATES: late July–late August 1955

SOURCE: novel *The Burglar* by David Goodis

RUNNING TIME: 90 minutes

STORY: Burglar Dan Duryea with his crew Peter Capell, Mickey Shaughnessy and Jayne Mansfield plan to steal a $150,000 necklace from Phoebe Mackay. Duryea breaks into the Mackay residence and begins drilling on the safe when he gets an alert that police are questioning their car outside. Duryea explains to Officer Stewart Bradley and his partner that his car broke down and needs a mechanic. After Bradley and his partner leave, Duryea reenters the house and steals the necklace. As Duryea, Capell and Shaughnessy leave, a car follows them. Capell and Shaughnessy want to fence the necklace immediately but Duryea tells them that it's too hot and they'll have to lay low for awhile. Mansfield is getting unwanted advances from Shaughnessey. Duryea puts Mansfield on a bus to Atlantic City until the necklace can be sold. A young man begins a romantic interlude with Mansfield. In a bar, Martha Vickers entices Duryea to come to her residence where she seduces him. Waking up, Duryea notices that Vickers is not there. He goes outside and finds Vickers talking to someone and realizes they're after the necklace. Duryea persuades Capell and Shaughnessy to go to Atlantic City to get Mansfield. Because of a promise made to Mansfield's father, Duryea feels obligated to take care of her. As they head for Atlantic City, state trooper Steve Allison stops their car, and Shaughnessy and Allison exchange shots. Both men are killed. Duryea and Capell abandon the car and walk through the marsh to Atlantic City where they find a deserted beach house. Duryea goes to Mansfield's hotel and tells her to get rid of any visitors. A visitor leaves and Duryea recognizes the young policeman Bradley and figures out that he followed him from the robbery in his own car. Duryea tries to get Mansfield to come with him. He tells her Bradley is a cop and only wants the necklace. Mansfield refuses because she loves Duryea and he treats her like a daughter. Duryea puts the necklace under one of the pillows and leaves. Bradley follows Duryea back to the shack. Mansfield finds the necklace and puts it in her music box. Bradley calls Vickers and orders her to come to Atlantic City. When Duryea leaves the shack to find a boat to make a getaway, Bradley enters the shack. Bradley and Capell engage in a frantic struggle with Bradley killing Capell. When Duryea returns, he finds himself staring at the gun in Bradley's hands. Duryea tells Bradley he doesn't have the necklace. Bradley is about to shoot Duryea when Vickers enters and convinces Bradley to hold off. Duryea tells Bradley that Mansfield has the necklace. Bradley tells Vickers to keep a gun pointed at Duryea while he retrieves the necklace. Knowing Vickers does care for him, Duryea walks out of the shack to warn Mansfield. Duryea is able to reach Mansfield in time and he tells her to meet him on the pier. Bradley chases after them and finally catches them. Duryea gives Bradley the necklace in exchange for Bradley letting Mansfield go free. As Duryea begins to walk away, Bradley fires a shot into Duryea's back. Bradley continues firing until Duryea collapses to the ground. Police arrive and Bradley is trying to convince them that he killed Duryea in the line of duty. Vickers arrives and states otherwise. Police find the necklace on Bradley and he's taken away in handcuffs.

Notes and Commentary: Although David Goodis adapted the screenplay from his own novel, he makes some significant changes, especially in the story's ending. Policeman Charlie (Stewart Bradley) murders Della (Martha Vickers) for letting Nat (Dan Duryea) go. Charlie catches up to Nat and Gladden (Jayne Mansfield) and forces then to go out on the beach. Charlie begins choking Nat to death. Gladden picks up Charlie's pistol and puts two shots into Charlie's head. With police and spectators coming from all sides, Nat and Gladden retreat into the ocean. Gladden realizes that Nat can't love her like a man and woman but as a father and daughter. She swims furiously away from him. The exertion tires Gladden and she begins to drown. Nat dives to save her. He reaches Gladden but he's too tired to reach the surface and they sink to the ocean floor.

Although the movie was completed in 1955, the release date was held up until 1957 to cash in on Jayne Mansfield's newfound popularity.

The Burglar was remade as *Le Casse* aka *The Burglars* (Columbia, 1972) with Jean-Paul Belmondo, Omar Sharif and Dyan Cannon.

Reviews: "It falls short of being satisfactory entertainment. Poor scripting and direction and overlong footage are strikes against a ready popular acceptance." *Variety*, 5/1/57

"It was a sorry attempt at a film noir which, plot and performance-wise, barely made the grade." *The Columbia Story*, Hirshhorn

Summation: This is an underrated crime caper noir. The direction of Paul Wendkos and the cinematography of Don Malkames enhance David Goodis' story and the resulting tension and suspense. A chase through a funhouse is exciting but doesn't rival Orson Welles' excursion in *The Lady from Shanghai* (Columbia, 1948). The acting is more than adequate. Jayne Mansfield is a pleasant surprise playing a young lady frustrated in her sexual desire for Dan Duryea. Duryea as the burglar carries the film nicely.

WHERE IT'S THE MAN WHO PAYS AND PAYS ... OR ELSE!

Café Hostess

(January 1940)

Cast: Dan Walters, Preston Foster; Jo, Ann Dvorak; Eddie Morgan, Douglas Fowley; Annie, Wynne Gibson; Steve Mason, Arthur Loft; Budge, Bruce Bennett; Scotty, Eddie Acuff; Al, Bradley Page; Tricks, Linda Winters; Daisy, Beatrice Blinn; Willie, Dick Wessel; Nellie, Peggy Shannon; Uncredited: Jones, Walter Baldwin; Policemen, James Blaine and William Lally; Peddler, Frank Austin; Customer Pawing Jo, George Lloyd; Red Connolly, William Pawley; Babe, Veda Ann Borg; Kennedy, George McKay; Café Hostess fighting with Jo, Lorna Gray; Café Hostesses, Betty Compson and Eve Lynne; Kitchen Helper, Mike Lally; Ice Man, Pat McKee; Cab Driver, Ralph Peters; Newsboy, Matty Roubert; Florist, Stephen Soldi; Bartender, John Tyrrell; Waiter, Eddie Laughton; Rocky, James Craig

Credits: Director, Sidney Salkow; Story, Tay Garnett and Howard Higgin; Screenwriter, Harold Shumate; Editor, Al Clark; Art Director, Lionel Banks; Cinematographer, Benjamin Kline; Musical Director, M.W. Stoloff

Production Dates: September 27–October 13, 1939

Running Time: 65 minutes

Story: Sergeant Arthur Loft believes Douglas Fowley, piano player and silent owner of a swank nightclub, is behind a major robbery. The nightclub employs hostesses whose job is to roll customers for their money. Café hostess Ann Dvorak, Fowley's girlfriend, wants out of the racket but Fowley won't let her leave. Dvorak knows if she makes a break, she will end up like Wynne Gibson, former Fowley girlfriend and café hostess. (Gibson tried to break away but Fowley destroyed her chance. Gibson's only choice was to return to the club.) Sailor Preston Foster and his buddies Eddie Acuff and Bruce Bennett enter the club. Foster and Dvorak are immediately attracted to each other, even though Dvorak attempts to steal Foster's wallet. Foster wants Dvorak to leave the club and come to a small town with him. Realizing Fowley has a hold on Dvorak, Foster follows Fowley when he leaves the club. Foster finds where Fowley has stashed the robbery items. Fowley confronts Foster and tells him if he informs Loft, Dvorak will receive a ten-year prison sentence. When Foster tells Dvorak he's sailing in the morning, Fowley decides not to have him killed. When the ship leaves the next morning, Dvorak is at the pier watching it sail away. Leaving, she's pleasantly surprised to find that Foster and his friends remained on shore. Foster and Dvorak resume their romance and Foster convinces her to leave town with him. Returning to her apartment to pack, Dvorak finds Fowley waiting for her. Fowley makes her return to the club. When Foster comes to the club looking for Dvorak, she convinces Foster that she was just playing him for a sap and never planned to go with him. Dvorak does this to prevent Fowley from murdering Foster. As Foster leaves the club, Gibson stops him and tells him Dvorak really loves him. Foster sees Loft and tells him where to find the stolen items. As Loft leaves to retrieve the items, Foster goes to get Dvorak. Fowley gets in Foster's way. The two men begin a fight that results in an all-out brawl in the nightclub. Foster finds Dvorak and she convinces him to leave. Fowley has murder in his heart but the vengeful Gibson plunges a knife into his back. Loft has returned with police officers and order is restored. Loft tells Foster, Dvorak and Foster's friends to get out of town. Just then, Fowley's body is discovered. Loft starts to send an officer after Foster and Dvorak. Gibson speaks up and admits she killed Fowley. Loft reluctantly arrests her.

Notes and Commentary: The working title for the film was *Street of Missing Women*.

The original story had three violations of the Production Code: First, the story had a sordid background and flavor; next, the hero is a thief who goes unpunished, and finally, a murderess is not arrested. The Production Code made the following suggestions: change the background from a dive to a swanky nightclub whose hostesses who would not be B-girls, Jo would not be played as a prostitute but basically a non-criminal in a distasteful situation, and there'd be no suggestion that Jo and Eddie were sexually involved.

Censors in Alberta, Canada and Pennsylvania removed the beginning title card which indicated the story featured B-girls, bar girls and café hostesses.

Reviews: "Sub-par meller about nitery hostessing; for lower-deck dualling" *Variety*, 1/10/40

"Weak melodrama, the varied cast practically overshadows the cumbersome story. Lacking any spark of spontaneity, it simply struggles through the motions, dragging plot development far behind." *Motion Picture Guide*, Nash and Ross

Summation: Performances elevate this crime proto-noir to barely acceptable status. Arthur Loft as the policeman and Douglas Fowley as his antagonist are convincing, showing toughness by their cool demeanor. Preston Foster and Ann Dvorak are acceptable as the romantic leads. Censorship of the time prevented the story from being leaner and tougher. Resorting to a big nightclub brawl to bring matters to a head lessens the noir impact. The screenplay is ordinary. Director Sidney Salkow lacked the skill and expertise to give the story the necessary punch. The photography of Benjamin Kline is quite good. Look at the beginning and ending scenes of the film as the camera follows Loft as he walks through the streets. Also, scenes in the apartment house and in the back alley show Kline's talent.

STORM and TERROR ... LOVE and VIOLENCE!

Cargo to Capetown

(April 1950)

Cast: Johnny Phelan, Broderick Crawford; Kitty Mellar, Ellen Drew; Steve Conway, John Ireland; Sam Bennett, Edgar Buchanan; Rhys, Ted de Corsia; Rik, Robert Espinoza; Singh, Leonard Strong; Uncredited: Captain Richards, Stanley Andrews; Captain Shanahan, Al Hill; Captain Olferi, Trevor Bardette; Sparky Jackson, King Donovan; Judge Van Meeger, Frank Reicher; Charlie (Sailor in Bar), Dick Curtis; Jack (Engineer), Gene Roth; Gomez, Peter Mamakos; Kroll (Second Mate), Gregory Gaye; Cariday, Tom Stevenson; Scar-faced Sailor, Mickey Simpson; Engine Room Oiler, Harry Cording; Captain, Sven Hugo Borg; Engine Room Seaman, George Barrows; Javanese Announcer, Leon Lontoc; Native Loading Boss, Alex Montoya; Engine Room Crewman, Joe Palma; Native Cab Driver, Rodd Redwing; Javanese Jailor, Leo C. Richmond; Tough Sailor, Jack Overman; Helmsman, Charles Sullivan; Brawling Seamen, James Dime, Gil Perkins, David Sharpe and Harry Wilson; Deck Crewmen, Richard Alexander and Blackie Whiteford; Sailors, Ted Jordan, James Logan, Glenn Thompson and Peter Virgo

Credits: Director, Earl McEvoy; Assistant Director, Sam Nelson; Producer and Screenwriter, Lionel Houser; Editor, William Lyon; Art Director, Cary Odell; Set Decorator, Frank Tuttle; Cinematography, Charles Lawton, Jr.; Costumes, Jean Louis; Sound, Frank Goodwin; Original Music, George Duning; Musical Director, Morris Stoloff

Song: "The Girl I Left Behind Me" (traditional)—hummed, whistled and played on concertina by John Ireland

Production Dates: June 27–August 9, 1949

Running Time: 80 minutes

Story: When an oil company is unable to find an experienced captain to transport oil from the Dutch East Indies to Capetown, John Ireland is finally hired. Ireland obtains a crew from the Java jail. Needing an experienced chief engineer, he shanghais Broderick Crawford. Crawford was planning to marry Ellen Drew, an ex-flame of Ireland's. Drew comes aboard the vessel with a gun and demands that Crawford be taken back to port. Ireland disarms Drew and threatens to have her jailed for attempted murder if she tells Crawford that he was shanghaied. When the vessel sails into a raging typhoon, the only casualty is a young native boy, Robert Espinoza, whose leg is crushed by an oil barrel. Faced with delivering the oil on time or saving Espinoza's life, Ireland orders a change of course. Knowing this will mean that Ireland will lose his captain's papers, Espinoza tries to throw himself into the angry sea. He is grabbed by Ireland. Espinoza's effort is too much and he succumbs to his injuries. Through scuttlebutt Crawford learns he was shanghaied. Seaman Ted deCorsia makes an attempt to kill Ireland but fails. Ireland throws deCorsia into the brig. DeCorsia tells Crawford that Drew has been spending time in Ireland's cabin while Crawford has been working below. Crawford's jealousy causes him to slack off on the job. He and Ireland tangle in a brutal fistfight ultimately won by Ireland. To prove that there's nothing between Ireland and Drew, Crawford tells Ireland to perform a marriage ceremony (Crawford and Drew). Drew comes to Ireland to see if Ireland loves her but is rebuffed. After the marriage ceremony, fire breaks out in two of the ship's holds. Only steam can quell the fire. Ireland and Crawford go down into the holds to open the valves. Ireland comes up to the deck only to find Crawford is not with him. Crawford has been overcome by the heat. Ireland goes back into the inferno to save Crawford. The steam finally extinguishes the flames. As Crawford is recovering from his ordeal, he realizes his marriage to Drew was a mistake and will allow her to obtain an annulment. Ireland tells Drew that he always loved her and the two plan to make a life together.

Notes and Commentary: The film was originally to be called *The Tougher They Come*. It was initially released as part of a double feature with *Captive Girl*, a Jungle Jim series entry starring Johnny Weissmuller and Buster Crabbe.

Reviews: "An average shipboard melodrama." *Motion Picture Guide*, Nash and Ross

"The cargo in *Cargo to Capetown* comprised, for the most part, clichés and platitudes. A routine melodrama. Earl McAvoy's direction managed, somehow, to keep it afloat." *The Columbia Story*, Hirschhorn

Summation: Although occasionally exciting, this is a minor, routine adventure noir. Crawford receives top billing but the story's focus is on third-billed Ireland. Lionel Houser's screenplay is episodic and director Earl McAvoy is hard-pressed to sustain the suspense. Acting of the principals is par for the "B" melodrama but such a disappointment after the performances Crawford and Ireland delivered in *All the King's Men* (Columbia, 1949). The fistfight between Crawford and Ireland is outstanding. Too bad the rest of the picture couldn't meet this standard.

IS THIS COP FOR SALE?

The Case Against Brooklyn

(June 1958)

A Morningside Production

CAST: Pete Harris, Darren McGavin; Lil Polombo, Maggie Hayes; Rudi Franklin, Warren Stevens; Jane Harris, Peggy McCay; District Attorney Michael W. Norris/Narrator, Tol Avery; Captain T.W. Wills, Emile Meyer; Finelli, Nestor Paiva; Jess Johnson, Brian Hutton; Sergeant Bonney, Robert Osterloh; Monte, Joseph Turkel; Bobby Helms; Uncredited: George (TV Interviewer), Booth Colman, Ed Reid, Ed Reid; Gus Polumbo, Joe De Santis; Mervin (Bartender), Michael Garth; Sergeant (Steam Room), Herb Vigran; Assistant District Attorney Heller, John Zaremba; Ralph Edmondson, Thomas Browne Henry; Mrs. Carney (Landlady), Cheerio Meredith; Rogers, Dan Riss; Mob Telephone Wiretap Expert in Truck, John Goddard; Laundry Contact Man, Joseph Forte; Rookie Cop, Harry Lauter; Desk Sergeant, Henry Rowland; Thug, Dick Crockett; Policeman, Robert Bice

CREDITS: Director, Paul Wendkos; Assistant Director, Leonard Katzman; Producer, Charles H. Schneer; Story, Daniel B. Ullman; Screenwriter, Raymond T. Marcus; Editor, Edwin Bryant; Art Director, Ross Bellah; Set Decorator, Alfred E. Spencer; Cinematographer, Fred Jackman; Recording Supervisor, John Livadary; Sound, Franklin Hansen, Jr.; Musical Conductor, Mischa Balakeinikoff

SONGS: "Jacqueline" (Garson and Hilliard)—sung by Bobby Helms and "Prize Song" from "Die Meistersinger" (Wagner)

PRODUCTION DATES: December 4—December 17, 1957

SOURCE: story "I Broke the Brooklyn Graft" by Ed Reid in *True Magazine*

RUNNING TIME: 82 minutes

STORY: Organized crime is running rampant in Brooklyn. It is suspected that corrupt police officers are working with the criminal organization. D.A. Tol Avery decides to enlist rookie policemen, working undercover, to break up the mob and arrest its unknown leader. Because of his military background, Darren McGavin is assigned to work on exposing the men behind the illegal gambling. He asks for Brian Hutton to be his partner. Posing as a former Brooklyn resident, McGavin is directed to a horse parlor run by Nestor Paiva. Another lead is Maggie Hayes, widow of garage owner Joe De Santis. De Santis, who was heavily in debt to Paiva, died in a suicide made to look like an accident. Even though McGavin is married to Peggy McKay, he decides to play up to Hayes in hopes of obtaining information. Hutton is able to tap Paiva's phone line but is spotted by Paiva as he leaves the area. Warren Stevens is the mob member responsible for picking up money from the various house parlors and, in a package disguised as laundry, brings payoff money to the police. Stevens tells Sergeant Robert Osterloh that an unknown person was seen in back of Paiva's parlor. Hutton is leery of returning to get the tape but McGavin, who wants to break the case for personal glory, persuades him to get it. As Hutton retrieves the tape, he's confronted by Osterloh. As Hutton attempts to identify himself as a policeman, Osterloh shoots him. McGavin prevents Osterloh's escape. McGavin, trying to bring gang members out in the open, deliberately passes a bad check in Paiva's parlor knowing strong-arm men will be sent to work him over. McGavin's relationship with Hayes has gotten passionate. Only Hayes' hesitation has prevented McGavin from spending the night with her. McGavin is set to take Hayes out again but has a visit from two of Paiva's boys. Initially getting the upper hand, McGavin realizes his best bet is to run. Outside his apartment, McGavin spots Stevens, not knowing he brought the men. Trying to gain entrance to Stevens' car allows the men to work McGavin over, leaving him unconscious on the sidewalk. Police arrive. Stevens tells them that McGavin is just drunk and McGavin is arrested. At the police station, without identifying himself as a policeman, McGavin gets no sympathy from Captain Emile Meyer, who's on the take from the organization. Hayes learns McGavin is married and tells Stevens about McGavin. Stevens has a microphone planted in McCay's apartment and learns that McGavin is a policeman. Stevens tells Meyer to have McGavin released. McGavin goes to McCay. Stevens has an explosive attached to the phone. The phone rings and McCay answers, detonating the bomb. McCay is killed instantly. McGavin is out for vengeance and persuades Hayes to call Stevens up to her apartment.

McGavin's initial instinct to kill Stevens but Hayes tells him that if he does, he's no better that the thugs. Stevens arrives thinking it is a sexual involvement. Hayes gets Stevens to admit his involvement in McCay's death and he warns Hayes to keep her mouth shut. Stevens returns to his laundry truck, unaware that McGavin is hiding in the back. Stevens picks up Meyer who directs Stevens to take him to the boss. The boss is an influential businessman, laundry owner Thomas Browne Henry. Meyer wants out but Henry won't let him. McGavin closes in on Henry and Meyer, not knowing Stevens is behind him. Stevens gets the drop on McGavin and tosses McGavin's pistol down to the laundry factory's floor. Meyer, who is tired of the murders, tries to prevent Stevens from killing McGavin. When Stevens begins firing, his shots kill Meyer and Henry and wound McGavin. After a tense cat-and-mouse chase, McGavin is able to retrieve his pistol and shoot Stevens before passing out. Hayes comes to the hospital to say goodbye to McGavin before leaving Brooklyn.

Notes and Commentary: On-screen, Raymond T. Marcus gets the screenplay credit. The movie was actually written by Bernard Gordon and Julian Zimet. Gordon and Zimet's names were on the Hollywood blacklist and they could not receive screen credit.

Reviews: "Although the ground has been covered before, this is a good melodrama, suspenseful, well plotted and well-acted." *Variety*, 5/14/58

"A tough and gritty melodrama under Paul Wendkos' no-punches-pulled direction." *The Columbia Story*, Hirschhorn

Summation: This is a gem. There is no tacked-on happy ending with Darren McGavin and Maggie Hayes planning a life together. The story is as much the documentation of corruption in the police department as it the dismantling of mob control of illegal gambling. The acting is on target, with McGavin leading the way as a cop determined to make a name for himself regardless of the consequences, almost lowering himself to the level of a thug. Fred Jackman's photography is noteworthy as the shadowy scenes add to the suspense.

THE SHOCK EVENT OF THE MOVIE YEAR!
Actually written in the Death Cell at San Quentin!

Cell 2455 Death Row

(April 1955)

Cast: Whit Whittier, William Campbell; Whit as a Boy, Robert Campbell; Doll, Marian Carr; Jo-Anne, Kathryn Grant; Warden, Harvey Stephens; Hamilton, Vince Edwards; Serl Whittier, Allen Nourse; Hallie Whittier, Diane DeLaire; Whit as a Young Boy, Bart Bradley; Al, Paul Dubov; Nugent, Tyler MacDuff; Monk, Buck Kartalian; Blanche, Eleanor Audley; Hatcheck Charlie, Thom Carney; Lawyer, Joe Forte; Judge, Howard Wright; Uncredited: Opening Narrator, William Woodson; Curley, Joe Turkel; Skipper Adams, Wayne Taylor; Parole Officer, Forrest Lewis; Johnny Albert, Michael Granger; Captain, George Cisar; Guard with Law Books, Robert B. Williams; Reporter, Kerwin Mathews; District Attorney, John Zaremba; Whit's Co-Counsel, Forbes Murray; Guards, Joel Allen, George Berkeley, Ralph Neff and Will J. White; Showgirl, Adelle August; Charley, Joseph Breen; Prisoners, Paul Brinegar and K.L. Smith; Girl, Maureen Cassidy; Plainclothesmen, Alan Dexter and Guy Kingsford; Senior Guard, Glenn Gordon; Officers, John Halloran, John Marshall and James McLaughlin; Wells, Jonathan Haze; Youths, Ivor James and Speer Martin; Slick Mug, Norman Keats; Court Clerk, Kenner G. Kemp; Policemen, Paul Knight, Pat Lawless and Edmund Penney; Prisoner in Car with Whit, Frank Marlowe; Tom, Jerry Mickelsen; Knucklehead, Bruce Morgan; Sonny, Jimmy Murphy; Mug, Ben Pollock; Bud, Bruce Sharpe; Madeline, Marjorie Stapp; Policeman at Whit's Home, Robert Stevenson; Convict, Paul Weber

Credits: Director, Fred F. Sears, Assistant Director, Eddie Saeta; Producer, Wallace MacDonald; Screenwriter, Jack DeWitt; Editor, Henry Batista; Art Director, Robert Peterson; Set Decorator, Frank Tuttle; Cinematographer, Fred Jackman, Jr.; Sound, James Speak; Recording Supervisor, John Livadary; Musical Conductor, Mischa Bakaleinikoff; Technical Advisor, Gino Anselmi

Production Dates: September 28–October 8, 1954

SOURCE: book *Cell 2455 Death Row* by Caryl Chessman

RUNNING TIME: 77 minutes

STORY: As William Campbell waits to be executed at San Quentin, he reflects on his past life. His childhood was happy until an automobile accident crippled his mother, Diane DeLaire. Poverty soon came to the family due to DeLaire's medical bills and the lad drifts into a life of crime to bring food to the household. He also joins a gang but when the members are arrested, he is sent to reform school. Upon release, Campbell begins a crime spree. Arrested again, he is sent to San Quentin. Honor prison Chino is established and Campbell is sent there. With help from gang members Paul Dubov and Buck Kartalian and girlfriend Marion Carr, Campbell escapes from Chino. Freedom is short-lived, and he and Dubov find themselves in Folsom Prison. The authorities believe he is rehabilitated, he is released. Carr wants Campbell to forgo a life of crime but he refuses. With a new gang, he begins preying on the criminal element. Gang leader Michael Granger sends his henchmen after Campbell. In a thrilling car chase, Campbell outmaneuvers his pursuers, causing their car to crash. At this time, a criminal known as the "Red Light Bandit" begins preying on Lover's Lane couples, kidnapping and raping the young women. Police sketches show a likeness to Campbell. Carr believes Campbell is guilty even though he protests his innocence. Police spot Campbell in a stolen car and give chase. Campbell is arrested and charged with kidnapping based on the "Little Lindbergh" law. Campbell's lawyer believes him guilty and refuses to defend him so Campbell decides to defend himself. He is found guilty. For six years, he is able to avoid execution four times. Campbell finally realizes that he only is to blame for being on Death Row. At the last moment, he receives another stay of execution.

NOTES AND COMMENTARY: The basic story of Caryl Chessman's life was pretty closely followed in the screenplay. The main thread eliminated was his marriage. Chessman maintained that he was not the "Red Light Bandit" to the end of his life. He spent 12 years on Death Row. Eight times he received last-minute reprieves. On May 2, 1960, he finally went to the gas chamber. The telephone rang as gas was filling the execution chamber: A judge's secretary was calling to announce another stay of execution. The secretary had initially misdialed, costing Chessman his life.

The working title for this film was *Cell 2455*.

While in prison, Chessman wrote *Cell 2455 Death Row* plus *Trial by Ordeal* (1955), *The Face of Justice* (1957) and *The Kid Was a Killer* (1960).

Alan Alda played Chessman in the television movie *Kill Me If You Can* (Columbia–NBC, 1977).

Alan Ladd's Jaguar Productions had attempted to obtain the rights to Chessman's book but were turned down, so Jaguar fictionalized a story. The released film was called *A Cry in the Night* (Warner Bros., 1956) with Natalie Wood being stalked by Lover's Lane kidnapper Raymond Burr.

REVIEWS: "Good b.o. potential in program and action markets. Direction of Fred F. Sears, although minimizing the psychological aspects, handles the many action sequences with finesse." *Variety*, 4/13/55

"The film tends to fall back on narration instead of portraying motivations through the script and visuals." *Motion Picture Guide*, Nash and Ross

"Motivation wasn't what motivated Wallace MacDonald's production, and the result was a bald narrative depicting a senseless life of crime." *The Columbia Story*, Hirschhorn

SUMMATION: This is a good crime noir by the underrated director Fred F. Sears. Sears adroitly handles the action scenes. The car chase sequences are exciting. Sears keeps the story moving and with a neat performance by William Campbell as an out-of-control criminal. With excellent photography in the noir style by Fred Jackman, Jr., this movie is first-rate. Even on a small budget, the impact of Chessman's story comes through to the audience.

It was legal murder until a reporter and his girl dared to get the inside story!

Chain Gang

(November 1950)

CAST: Cliff Roberts, Douglas Kennedy; Rita McKelvey, Marjorie Lord; Captain Duncan, Emory Parnell; Roy Snead, William "Bill" Phillips; John McKelvey, Thurston Hall; Henry "Pop" O'Donnell, Harry Cheshire; Uncredited:

Convict in Skirmish, Charles Horvath; Senator Harden, Herbert Rawlinson; Joe (Lunch Counterman), John Rogers; O'Donnell's Influential Friend, James Conaty; Langley, Don C. Harvey; Adams, George Eldredge; Zeke, William Fawcett; Yates, Rusty Wescoatt; Reagan, George Robotham; Eddie Jones, Billy Lechner; Dennison, Donald Curtis; Harry Cleaver, William Tannen; Newspaper Office Worker, Bert Stevens; Lloyd Killgallen, Frank Wilcox; Chain Gang Convict, Stanley Blystone; Crane Operator, Eddie Foster; Mrs. Briggs, Dorothy Vaughan; Dr. Evans, Paul E. Burns

CREDITS: Director, Lew Landers; Producer, Sam Katzman; Screenwriter, Howard J. Green; Editor, Aaron Stell; Art Director, Paul Palmentola; Set Decorator, Sidney Clifford; Cinematographer, Ira H. Morgan; Unit Manager, Herbert Leonard; Musical Director, Mischa Bakaleinikoff

PRODUCTION DATES: May 17–May 24, 1950

RUNNING TIME: 70 minutes

STORY: The chain gang system has come under scrutiny but the investigation has been curtailed due to the lack of hard facts. Douglas Kennedy and Marjorie Lord, rival newspaper reporters and romantically involved, are covering the situation. With the help of his boss Harry Cheshire, Kennedy goes undercover as a prison guard at a chain gang camp. Kennedy finds conditions deplorable. The men are no more than slaves, working under the cruel Captain Emory Parnell. The men are forced to work as unpaid labor for William Tannen's construction company. With a camera concealed in a lighter, Kennedy is able to capture incriminating pictures. Lord's stepfather Thurston Hall secretly controls both the newspaper for which she works and Tannen's company. Lord has started writing articles condemning the current chain gang system. Hall wants Lord fired but she instead quits and goes to work for Cheshire. In Hall's study, Tannen sees a picture of Kennedy and Lord and is told that Kennedy is a reporter. This information is relayed to Parnell, who imprisons Kennedy. When one of the prisoners, William "Bill" Phillips, escapes, all available men are sent to bring him back dead or alive. This distraction gives Kennedy a chance to escape. In the woods, Parnell spots Kennedy and fires a shot that hits him. Phillips, who has eluded capture, helps the wounded Kennedy to Dorothy Vaughan's farmhouse. As Phillips leaves the house, he is spotted by the guards and shot and killed. Seeing that Kennedy is wearing a prison guard uniform, she alerts Parnell. Before Parnell and his men can arrive at Vaughan's farm, she tells Kennedy what she has done. Kennedy is on the run before Parnell shows up. Kennedy's searing exposé causes Parnell to be arrested and Hall to be indicted. Kennedy and Lord plan to resume their romance.

REVIEWS: "For supporting booking, *Chain Gang* is an okay melodrama. It doesn't contain many surprises story wise, but manages enough action and pace for the lower case market." *Variety*, 10/4/50

"An uneventful prison melodrama that follows an undercover reporter. The only excitement comes when his cover is blown and he narrowly escapes a shower of bullets and a pack of guard dogs." *Motion Picture Guide*, Nash and Ross

SUMMATION: A somewhat familiar screenplay does not seriously mar the exciting exposé of slavery conditions of chain gangs. Director Lew Landers keeps the story on the move and turns up the suspense when Douglas Kennedy is trying to elude the prison guards. Performances are up to standard, especially Kennedy as the heroic reporter, William "Bill" Phillips as a chain gang convict and Emory Parnell as the ruthless camp boss.

Exposing the inside story!

Chicago Syndicate

(July 1955)

A Clover Production

CAST: Barry Amsterdam, Dennis O'Keefe; Connie Peters, Abbe Lane; Arnie Valent, Paul Stewart; Xavier Cugat and His Orchestra; Joyce Kern, Allison Hayes; David Healey/Narrator, Dick Cutting; Nate, Chris Alcaide; Dolan, William Challee; Detective Lt. Robert Fenton, John Zaremba; Jack Roper, George Brand; Pat Winters, Hugh Sanders; Uncredited: Benny Chico, Xavier Cugat; Al Capone, Al Capone (archive footage); Tony, Gil Frye; Brad Lacy, Mark Hanna; Cleo Allen, Hort-

Chicago Syndicate (1955).

ense Petra; Hugo, Charles Horvath; Mrs. Valent, Carroll McComas; Markey, Joseph Mell

CREDITS: Director, Fred F. Sears; Assistant Director, Leonard Katzman; Story, William Sackheim; Screenwriter, Joseph Hoffman; Editor, Viola Lawrence; Art Director, Paul Palmentola; Set Decorator, Sidney Clifford; Cinematographers, Henry Freulich and Fred Jackman, Jr.; Unit Manager, Leon Chooluck; Sound, Josh Westmoreland; Special Effects, Jack Erickson; Musical Director, Ross DiMaggio

SONGS: "One at a Time" (Raleigh and Wayne)—sung by Abbe Lane with Xavier Cugat and His Orchestra, "Comparsita Mambo" (Rodriguez and DuFault)—played by Xavier Cugat and His Orchestra, "Greek Bolero" (Spartacos)—played by Xavier Cugat and His Orchestra, "Cuban Mambo" (Cugat and Angulo)—played by Xavier Cugat and His Orchestra, "From Here to Eternity" (Karger and Wells)—piano solo and "Let's Fall in Love"(Porter)—piano solo

POEM: "Chicago" from "Chicago Poems" by Carl Sandberg (Holt)

LOCATION FILMING: Chicago, Illinois

PRODUCTION DATES: November 12–24, 1954

STORY: Mob boss Paul Stewart's bookkeeper plans to release information to newspaperman Dick Cutting which would result in Stewart's incarceration. Before Cutting can receive the information, the bookkeeper is murdered. Thinking Stewart would need a new bookkeeper, CPA Dennis O'Keefe is recruited by the police to work his way into Stewart's organization. Letting the word out that he is an eyewitness to the bookkeeper's murder, O'Keefe is brought before Stewart. Impressed by O'Keefe, Stewart gives him a job in one of his legitimate businesses. Believing he can trust O'Keefe, Stewart allows him to audit the mob's books, resulting in O'Keefe recovering sizable amounts of money for Stewart. At a party at Stewart's apartment, Allison Hayes comes on to O'Keefe. Hayes takes O'Keefe to her apartment where O'Keefe learns that Hayes is the murdered bookkeeper's daughter. Hayes is told by the authorities that O'Keefe is trying to bring Stewart down. Finally, Stewart wants O'Keefe to take care of his own personal books using O'Keefe's name. Before O'Keefe can take over, Stewart destroys his personal book. Hayes brings her father's papers to O'Keefe, who finds he had papers microfilmed. They learn that Stewart's mistress, Abbe Lane, picked up the microfilm. O'Keefe believes the only way Stewart can be brought down is to make Lane so jealous that she will reveal pertinent information. Hayes becomes Stewart's new mistress and Lane is discarded. O'Keefe arranges for a phony attempt on Lane's life in order to make her nervous. Lane tells Stewart that he can't get rid of her since she didn't burn the microfilm but hid it. Lane is tortured and her admirer, Xavier Cugat, tells Stewart when the microfilm is hidden. Stewart, O'Keefe and two thugs go to retrieve the microfilm. Hayes calls policeman John Zaremba and tells him where the microfilm is hidden. Directed to burn the microfilm, O'Keefe grabs it and starts running. Stewart and his thugs take chase, shooting at O'Keefe. O'Keefe takes to the tunnels under the Chicago streets. One of the thugs catches up to O'Keefe and a fight ensues, with O'Keefe emerging victorious. O'Keefe takes the thug's gun. O'Keefe returns fire, killing the other thug. A bullet from Stewart wounds O'Keefe. Keefe takes to the streets with Stewart in pursuit. As Keefe is running, Stewart takes careful aim but is cut down by a bullet from Zaremba.

Notes and Commentary: Producer Sam Katzman does not receive billing either on-screen or in the print ads.

King Bros. Productions sued Columbia, Sam Katzman, Clover Productions, and the Katzman Corp. for $1,000,000. King Bros. argued that they had registered the title *The Syndicate* with the MPAA Title Bureau. They charged unfair competition and claimed that the title *Chicago Syndicate* was used "deliberately, willfully and fraudulently."

In one scene, a movie theater marquee advertising *On the Waterfront* (Columbia, 1954) with Marlon Brando can be spotted.

Reviews: "This gang busting melodrama has been put together in suitable style to meet the demands of the general action market." *Variety*, 6/29/55

"This is a standard melodrama in which the bright spot is Allison Hayes, a tall and agreeable young lady who gives considerable aid to the somewhat battered Mr. O'Keefe." *Motion Picture Guide*, Nash and Ross

Summation: This is a good noir docudrama of the breakup of a crime syndicate. Director Fred F. Sears moves the story nicely, even building up some good suspense. Henry Freulich and Fred Jackman, Jr.'s fine camerawork adds to the overall noir effect. The principals acquit themselves nicely.

BEHIND-THE-SCENES STORY ... AS DETECTIVES TRAP KILLER IN SAN FRANCISCO'S CHINATOWN AT MIDNIGHT

Chinatown at Midnight

(November 1949)

Cast: Clifford Ward, Hurd Hatfield; Alice, Jean Willes; Captain Howard Brown, Tom Powers; Sam Costa, Ray Walker; Fred Morgan, Charles Russell; Lisa Marcel, Jacqueline deWit; Hazel Fong, Maylia; Eddie Marsh, Ross Elliott; Uncredited: Joe Wing, Benson Fong; Betty Chang, Barbara Jean Wong; Mrs. Emily Dryden, Josephine Whittell; James Mackintosh (Cleaner), Paul E. Burns; Hotel Proprietor, Victor Sen Yung; Policeman, Steve Pendleton; Pharmacist, Byron Foulger

Credits: Director, Seymour Friedman; Producer, Sam Katzman; Screenwriters, Robert Libott and Frank Burt; Editor, Edwin Bryant; Art Director, Paul Palmentola; Set Decorator, Frank Tuttle; Cinematographer, Henry Freulich; Unit Manager, Herbert Leonard; Musical Director, Mischa Bakaleinikoff

Production Dates: May 19–26, 1949

Running Time: 67 minutes

Story: Master thief Hurd Hatfield brings a gold box to his confederate and lover, Jacqueline deWit. She, in turn, will sell the box to a wealthy customer. DeWit tells Hatfield that she needs a certain white jade vase for another client. To obtain the vase, Hatfield shoots and mortally wounds Benson Fong and his girlfriend Barbara

Jean Wong. To put the police on the wrong track, Hatfield alerts police to the robbery by speaking in Chinese to telephone operator Maylia. Maylia tells police she thinks she would be able to recognize the voice if she heard it again. Looking for a Chinese suspect proves futile, so Police Captain Tom Powers decides to concentrate on locating the vase. The new owner tells deWit that she thinks she has the vase and will notify the police. As Hatfield comes to visit deWit, he finds her getting ready to clear out. Realizing that if caught, deWit will implicate him, Hatfield shoots her as police arrive. Hatfield, after an exchange of shots, is able to leave by the back door. By disposing of his coat and gun in a garbage can, Hatfield eludes his pursuers. The coat is found and, by tracing a laundry tag, police find Hatfield's apartment. Hatfield sees police surrounding the building and walks away. Needing medicine for his malaria condition, Hatfield is able to enter the building disguised as a telegram delivery man. Although he obtains the prescription bottle, he accidentally loses it. Desperate for his medication, Hatfield goes to a pharmacy. Pharmacist Byron Foulger tells Hatfield a prescription is needed. Hatfield tells Foulger his doctor could phone one in. Hatfield picks a physician's name out of the phone book and calls the pharmacy. His call goes through the switchboard and Maylia recognizes Hatfield's voice and notifies police. Powers knows that with Hatfield's medical condition, he is probably staying within blocks of the pharmacy. Policemen and policewomen, pretending to be census takers, comb the area and Hatfield is spotted. When Hatfield sees the police closing in, he takes them on a chase over rooftops, down into alleys and into another apartment house. Hatfield is killed in an exchange of shots.

Notes and Commentary: The film's working title was *Chinatown After Midnight*.

Pharmacist Byron Foulger was correct in not dispensing a prescription drug without a prescription. He was negligent in accepting a prescription over the telephone from an unknown physician without calling the physician back to verify the order.

In the film, Hatfield has a malarial condition caused by the organism plasmodium vivex. It would

Hurd Hatfield as Clifford Ward in *Chinatown at Midnight* (1949).

be reasonable to treat this with the drug Paludrine. The pharmacist's counter offer of treatment with quinine would most likely be ineffective.

Reviews: "This straightforward story of crime and punishment is a neat low-budget film. It has a heightened impact due to a documentary-like format and a sustained pace." *Motion Picture Guide*, Nash and Ross

"The manhunt formula is generally good for some excitement on the screen, so *Chinatown at Midnight* is not without merit." *New York Times*, 11/18/49

Summation: This is a good noir that grips you from the start, pulling you right into the story. Hurd Hatfield is chilling as a cold-blooded and fastidious killer. The supporting cast members acquit themselves well with a special nod to Tom Powers as a low-key but authoritative police captain. Seymour Friedman's direction is on the mark, as is cinematographer Henry Freulich's camerawork.

A City in Terror ... Chills for Millions!

City of Fear

(February 1959)

Cast: Vince Ryker, Vince Edwards; Lt. Mark Richards, John Archer; Dr. John Wallace, Steven Ritch; June Marlowe, Patricia Blair; Sergeant Hank Johnson, Kelly Thordsen; Chief Jensen, Lyle Talbot; Jeanne, Cathy Browne; Pete Hallon, Sherwood Price; Eddie Crown, Joseph Mell; Uncredited: Sailor, Tony Lawrence; Police Sergeant, Larry J. Blake; Landlady, Jean Harvey; Restaurant Proprietor, Michael Mark

Credits: Director, Irving Lerner; Assistant Director, Louis Brandt; Producer, Leon Chooluck; Screenwriters, Steven Ritch and Robert Dillon; Editor, Robert Lawrence; Art Director, Jack Poplin; Set Decorator, Lyle B. Reifsnider; Cinematographer, Lucien Ballard; Wardrobe, Norman Martien; Makeup, Ted Coodley; Sound, Jack Solomon; Original Music and Musical Conductor, Jerry Goldsmith; Property Master, Charles Stokes; Title Designer, Jack Barton; Script Supervisor, Pat Miller; Dialogue Coach, Joe Steinberg; Optical Effects, Westheimer Company

Location Filming: Los Angeles, California

Production Dates: April 7–April 16, 1958

Running Time: 75 minutes

Story: In a daring jailbreak, Vince Edwards steals a container he believes contains pure heroin but it's actually a deadly radioactive substance, Cobalt 60. Edwards eludes capture and makes it to Los Angeles where he is reunited with girlfriend Patricia Blair. Blair touches the container believing it contains only heroin. Police officials John Archer and Lyle Talbot question Blair and two known confederates, Joseph Mell (Edwards' former boss who runs an exclusive shoe store) and small-time crook Sherwood Price. At Mell's store, Mell receives a phone call but is hesitant to talk because Price is standing within earshot. Mell bribes Price to leave the store by giving him a pair of very expensive shoes. That night Edwards meets Mell to discuss a deal to sell the "heroin." Price shows up and demands to be cut in. Archer and Talbot, informed of the container's contents, enlist the aid of Steven Ritch of Air Pollution Control, who states that even touching the container will result in radioactive poisoning. Ritch mobilizes his men to begin searching the area with Geiger counters. One car is found to be radioactive and inside is the body of Price. After days of handling the container, Edwards shows signs of sickness. When Edwards and Mell meet again, they have a falling out and Edwards kills Mell. Police again question Blair, who shows signs of cobalt poisoning. Wanting to save Edwards' life, Blair tells the police where to find him. Alerted by sirens, Edwards goes on the run and holds up in a small restaurant. Over the radio, an announcement is made about the cobalt. The sick Edwards refuses to believe that he doesn't have heroin. He staggers out of the restaurant, collapses to the ground and dies clutching his precious container.

Notes and Commentary: Some sources state that the running time could be 81 minutes but the Sony DVD release is 75 minutes.

Reviews: "A detective story with an atomic twist. Parts of it are good—above its class—and while parts are also not so good, it is never a dull picture and it is occasionally gripping." *Variety*, 1/21/59

"A tense albeit modest melodrama, no world-beater, but above average for its type." *The Columbia Story*, Hirschhorn

Summation: This is a good, grim noir of a man carrying death in his hands. The story benefits from straightforward, tense direction by Irving Lerner, fine photography by Lucien Ballard (making judicious use of darkness and shadows to heighten the suspense) and competent acting by the principals with a special nod to Vince Edwards. Edwards gives a fine portrayal of a man so certain he's on the verge of financial success that he ignores signs of deteriorating health and ultimately, when informed of his folly, still refuses to believe.

SHE WAS WORTH $5,000 ALIVE ... OR DEAD!

Comanche Station

(March 1960)

A Ranown Production

Cast: Jefferson Cody, Randolph Scott; Nancy Lowe, Nancy Gates; Ben Lane, Claude Akins; Frank, Skip Homeier; Dobie, Richard Rust; Station Man, Rand Brooks; John Lowe, Dyke Johnson; Uncredited: Comanche Chief, Joe Molina; Comanche Lance Bearer, Foster Hood; Warrior, Vince St. Cyr; Lowe Boy, John Patrick Holland

Credits: Director and Producer, Budd Boetticher; Assistant Director, Sam Nelson; Executive Producer, Harry Joe Brown; Screenwriter, Burt Kennedy; Editor, Edwin Bryant; Art Director, Carl Anderson; Set Decorator, Frank A. Tuttle; Cinematographer, Charles Lawton, Jr.; Recording Supervisor, John Livadary; Sound, George Cooper; Musical Conductor, Mischa Bakaleinikoff; Color Consultant, Henri Jaffa

Location Filming: Lone Pine, California

Production Dates: June 10–June 26, 1959

Running Times: 74 minutes

Photographed in CinemaScope

Eastman Color by Pathe

Story: Randolph Scott rescues Nancy Gates from the Comanches by trading goods and a rifle for her release. Scott is planning to take Gates to her husband, Dyke Johnson, in Lordsburg. They arrive at a deserted way station. Chased by a Comanche war party, Claude Akins, Skip Homeier and Richard Rust ride hard for shelter at the station. With Scott's help, the Comanches are driven off. Akins and his men have also been looking for Gates: Johnson has offered a $5,000 reward for her return, alive or dead. Gates at first believes Scott rescued her for the reward. She soon finds that for ten years, Scott has been searching for his wife who was taken by the Comanches. Akins plans to kill both Scott and Gates to get the money. Homeier and Rust don't feel good about the plan to kill Gates. Akins doesn't want to force a showdown with Scott until there is no threat of a Comanche attack. During the journey to Lordsburg, Homeier is killed and Akins saves Scott's life. Knowing Akins will make a move, Scott gets the drop on Akins and Rust and takes their weapons. Akins leaves but has a hidden rifle. Akins finds a vantage point where he can ambush Scott and Gates. Rust wants no part in Gates' murder and starts to ride away. Akins shoots Rust in the back, then begins firing at Scott and Gates. Scott is able to get behind Akins. Akins refuses to give up and turns and fires. His shot misses and Scott's shot finishes Akins. Scott delivers Gates to Johnson and finds that Johnson is blind. Not claiming the money, Scott rides away, still alone and still searching for his wife.

Notes and Commentary: This was the last of the collaborations between Randolph Scott and Budd Boetticher. Scott decided to retire but director Sam Peckinpah talked him into co-starring with Joel McCrea in *Ride the High Country* (MGM, 1962). Then Scott retired from the screen after being a star for 30 years.

Reviews: "*Comanche Station* is by any standard a good picture. The screenplay by Burt Kennedy is true to western traditions and at the same time there is romance, although not a conventional love story, and criminal elements for suspense, mystery and excitement. Kennedy does not rely on casting for characterization. The dialog is sparse, but colorful, and humor is not neglected." *Variety*, 12/31/59

"This fine, haunting western was the last of the Randolph Scott–Budd Boetticher collaborations." *Motion Picture Guide*, Nash and Ross

Comanche Station **(1960).**

SUMMATION: In this very good noir western, Randolph Scott rides the dusty trails of greed and deceit. Scott and Claude Akins make worthy antagonists and their acting makes their actions believable. Budd Boetticher keeps Burt Kennedy's fine story taut and tense. Cinematographer Charles Lawton, Jr.'s photography makes the majestic Lone Pine scenery a major contributor to the proceedings.

TWO POWERFUL STARS IN A DRAMA OF
A CONVICT'S LOVE FOR A WARDEN'S DAUGHTER!

Convicted

(August 1950)

CAST: Joe Hufford, Glenn Ford; George Knowland, Broderick Crawford; Malloby, Millard Mitchell; Kay Knowland, Dorothy Malone; Captain Douglas, Carl Benton Reid; Ponti, Frank Faylen; Mapes, Will Geer; Bertie Williams, Martha Stewart; Detective Dorn, Henry O'Neill; Detective Bailey, Douglas Kennedy; Vernon Bradley, Roland Winters; Mackay, Ed Begley; Uncredited: Desk Sergeant, Charles Cane; Freddie, Vincent Renno; Eddie, Frank Cady; Dr. Masterson, William E. Green; Judge, Richard Hale; Mr. Hufford, Griff Barnett; Train Conductor, Tom Kingston; Laundry Room Guards, Fred Graham and Eddie Parker; Yard Guard, Ray Teal; Tex, John Doucette; Grant, Jimmie Dodd; Martha

Lorry, Ilka Gruning; Meireau, Alphonse Martell; Curly, John Butler; Parole Board Members, Marshall Bradford, Harry Harvey and Bradford Hatton; Luigi, Peter Virgo; Whitey, William Vedder; Prison Yard Convict, Harry Cording; Fingerprint Man, Fred F. Sears; Nick (Prison Cook), Jay Barney; Kitchen Guards, James Millican and James Bush; State Attorney Owens, Whit Bissell; Blackie, Benny Burt; Prison Guards, Clancy Cooper, Robert Malcolm and William Tannen; Policemen, Chuck Hamilton and Charles Sherlock

Credits: Director, Henry Levin; Assistant Director, Frederick Briskin; Producer, Jerry Bresler; Screenwriters, William Bowers, Fred Niblo, Jr. and Seton I. Miller; Editor, Al Clark; Art Director, Carl Anderson; Set Decorator, James Crowe; Cinematographer, Burnett Guffey; Sound, Lodge Cunningham; Original Music, George Duning; Musical Director, Morris Stoloff

Production Dates: December 12, 1949–January 19, 1950

Source: play *The Criminal Code* by Martin Flavin

Running Time: 91 minutes

Story: In an argument over a girl, Glenn Ford accidentally kills the son of a prominent citizen. District Attorney Broderick Crawford tells Ford that he'll have to stand trial. Inept legal representation dooms Ford to a prison sentence of one to ten years. As the years pass, Ford becomes hardened and wants to participate in a jailbreak. Cellmate Millard Mitchell advises Ford not to participate because Frank Faylen, a known squealer, is aware of the plan. Ford deals himself in. Ford receives a telegram telling him his father, Griff Barnett, died. An insensitive guard, Fred Graham, prods Ford. Ford retaliates, striking Graham, earning him a week in solitary confinement. The prison break goes on as scheduled. Faylen tips off captain of the guards Carl Benton Reid and so the escaping prisoners are shot and killed. The inmates want to kill Faylen as payback. Crawford becomes the new warden and has Faylen sequestered in a room off of his office until he can transfer him to another facility. Crawford makes Ford a trusty, with the job of chauffeuring him and his daughter Dorothy Malone around town. Ford and Malone soon form a romantic attachment. Events are set in motion to have Mitchell kill Faylen. The inmates start making noise, forcing Crawford to leave his office to make sure there won't be a riot. The noise frightens Faylen and he asks Ford to find out the cause. Ford leaves Crawford's office. Mitchell gains entrance and murders Faylen. Before Mitchell can leave, Ford returns and sees him. Crawford returns, finds the dead man and asks Ford to name the killer. Due to the Criminal Code, Ford remains silent and is sent to solitary. A knife is smuggled into Ford. Mitchell, not wanting Ford to do something rash, obtains a gun and then hits guard James Millican. Mitchell is sent to share Ford's cell. As Mitchell is placed in the cell, he draws his gun and begins firing. Crawford and Reid tell Mitchell to throw the gun out and give himself up. Mitchell gets rid of his gun but takes possession of the knife. Mitchell has a deep hatred for Reid: It was Reid who nailed Mitchell on a minor parole violation that caused him to be sent back to prison. Reid enters the cell. Mitchell grabs him, announces that he killed Faylen and stabs Reid to death. Guard bullets end Mitchell's life. Ford is granted a parole and hopes to make a new start with Malone at his side.

Notes and Commentary: Martin Flavin's play *The Criminal Code* debuted on Broadway on October 2, 1929, at the National Theater with Russell Hardie as the accidental killer, Arthur Byron the warden, Anita Kerry the warden's daughter and Henry Crossen as the prison murderer. The play first reached the screen as *The Criminal Code* (Columbia, 1931) with Phillips Holmes, Walter Huston, Constance Cummings and Boris Karloff. The play was re-made as *Penitentiary* (Columbia, 1938) with John Howard, Walter Connolly, Jean Parker and Marc Lawrence.

The ending of Flavin's play was bleak: Captain Gleason goes to the dungeon to bring Robert Graham to Warden Martin Brady's office. Graham believes Gleason has come to administer another beating to him and, with a knife smuggled in to him, Graham knifes and kills him. Finally Graham enters Brady's office to find a parole was waiting for him. Graham realizes he'll never leave the prison alive.

Review: "Above average prison picture, enough off-beat to hold attention. While plotting is essentially a masculine soap opera, scripting supplies plenty of polish and good dialog to see it through and hold the attention." *Variety*, 7/26/50

"There are some good twists and turns in this well-scripted and tautly directed wrong man story." *Motion Picture Guide*, Nash and Ross

Summation: This is a very good prison noir. Excellent performances are given by Glenn Ford and Broderick Crawford. Ford scores strongly; he has the ability to convey the changes in emotions believably. Crawford matches Ford as a hard but fair district attorney, suddenly thrust into the job as the penitentiary warden. Through his hard-as-nails exterior his character shows genuine compassion at the proper times. Millard Mitchell as a career criminal and Dorothy Malone as the romantic interest add able support. Henry Levin directs with a sure hand and the ever-reliable Burnett Guffey again excels with his photography from a dark solitary cell to the open courtyards.

The brass-knuckled SATURDAY EVENING POST novel of savage vengeance!

Coroner Creek

(July 1948)

A Producers–Actors Production

Cast: Chris Danning, Randolph Scott; Kate Hardison, Marguerite Chapman; Younger Miles, George Macready; Della Harms, Sally Eilers; Sheriff O'Hea, Edgar Buchanan; Abbie Miles, Barbara Reed; Andy West, Wallace Ford; Ernie Combs, Forrest Tucker; Frank Yordy, Joe Sawyer; Leach Conover, William Bishop; Walt Hardison, Russell Simpson; Stew Shallis, Douglas Fowley; Tip Henry, Lee Bennett; Uncredited: McCune, Forrest Taylor; Indian with Withered Arm, Charles Stevens; Charlie Weatherby, Walter Soderling; Bill Arnold, Phil Schumacher; Ray Flanders, Warren Jackson; Jack (Bartender), Joe DeRita; B.J., Dewey Robinson; Townsman in Bar, Paul E. Burns

Credits: Director, Ray Enright; Assistant Director, Aaron Rosenberg; Producer, Harry Joe

Coroner Creek **(1948).**

Brown; Screenwriter, Kenneth Gamet; Editor, Harvey Manger; Art Director, George Van Marter; Set Decorator, George Sawley; Cinematographer, Fred H. Jackman, Jr.; Makeup, Lee Greenway; Sound, William R. Fox; Production Manager, Joe Popkin; Cinecolor Supervisor, Gar Gilbert; Musical Score, Rudy Schrager; Musical Supervisor, David Chudnow

Location Filming: Iverson, California, and Red Rock Crossing, Sedona, Arizona

Production Dates: September 9–October 18, 1947

Source: novel *Coroner Creek* by Luke Short

Running Time: 90 minutes

Color by Cinecolor

Story: Randolph Scott is on the vengeance trail as he looks for the man responsible for his fiancée's death. He is in possession of the man's knife, which she used to commit suicide. Information leads Scott to Coroner Creek and his adversary George Macready. Through hotel owner Marguerite Chapman, Scott learns that Macready's wife, Barbara Reed, is a drunk. When Scott meets Macready he tells all onlookers about Reed's problem. When small ranch owner Sally Eilers sees how Scott stands up to the powerful Macready, she hires him as her foreman. Scott has a run-in with cowhand Joe Sawyer which results in Sawyer being kicked off the ranch. The other ranch hands are Wallace Ford, a man who doesn't look for trouble, and William Bishop, a lazy cowboy; they decide to stay. As Ford shows Scott around the ranch, Macready gunman Douglas Fowley gets the drop on both and Scott's pistol is thrown to the ground. Fowley takes them to a small ranch Macready cowhand Lee Bennett is homesteading. At the homestead is Macready top gun hand Forrest Tucker. Tucker sends Ford away and then gives Scott a savage beating culminating with Tucker stomping Scott's gun hand. Before he can do more with Scott, Ford returns, Scott's pistol in his hand, and gets the drop on Macready's men. Scott regains consciousness and, with Ford keeping his gun on the other men, Scott takes on Tucker in a rugged fight. Scott knocks Tucker out and, in turn, stomps on Tucker's gun hand. Scott tells Bennett that if he remains on the homestead, he will kill him. Frightened, Bennett leaves the area. Sawyer tells Macready that the way to destroy Eilers would be to set a fire to the brush at the entrance to a box canyon; the cattle in the canyon will be destroyed. Macready tells Sawyer to meet him at an out-of-the-way saloon with the intention to kill him. Scott takes Sawyer's place. Macready's shot precipitates an exchange of shots. Chapman is a witness and realizes the type of person Macready is. Enraged, Macready sets fire to the brush, destroying Eilers' cattle. Returning to his ranch, he finds Reed drunk and slaps her. Reed's father, Sheriff Edgar Buchanan, witnesses the scene. Buchanan realizes that Reed has remained married to Macready to keep Buchanan in his job. Both Reed and Buchanan leave the ranch; Buchanan will no longer be Macready's tool. Eilers tells Ford to go take over Bennett's homestead. Tucker and Fowley bring Ford's body into town. Fowley tells Buchanan that he shot Ford in a fair fight. Bishop, who witnessed the incident, says Fowley shot Ford in the back. Buchanan arrests both Fowley and Tucker. Macready breaks the men out of jail, in the process killing Buchanan. In a gunfight, Scott shoots Tucker and captures Fowley. Fowley is forced to tell Scott that Macready is in the town hall. Scott goes after Macready using Fowley as a shield. Macready empties his pistol into Fowley. As Macready tries to retreat up a wooden ladder to the top of the building, Scott throws the knife that ended his fiancée's life. Now Macready understands Scott's hatred. Macready grasps the knife and begins climbing. A rung breaks, sending Macready crashing down with the knife stuck in his chest. Scott believes he can begin a new life with Chapman at his side.

Notes and Commentary: Although screenwriter Kenneth Gamet followed Luke Short's storyline fairly closely, some major changes were made. A major character in the novel, Mac, was deleted, as was a minor character, Della Harms' mother. Chris Danning's fiancée's name, Bess Thornley, was never mentioned in the film. In the book, Apaches murdered Bess while in the film the fiancée took her life using Younger Miles' knife. From the time Danning obtains information on the white man who led the Apache raid on the stagecoach, Gamet follows the book closely. After Miles goes to meet Frank Yordy so he can kill him, the screenplay begins to differ from the book. In the book, Yordy starts the fire that destroys Harms' cattle, while in the film the fire is started by Miles. Only in the film is O'Hea killed. Miles meets his end from bullets from Mac's pistol. Mac reveals himself to be Bess' brother.

This was the first collaboration between Randolph Scott and producer Harry Joe Brown.

Their company Producers–Actors developed with the cooperation of Columbia Pictures.

The working title for the film was *Lawless*. The role of Kate Hardison was first assigned to Ellen Drew. Due to illness, Drew was replaced by Marguerite Chapman. Cinecolor was the color process chosen because of budget limitations.

Reviews: "*Coroner Creek* is a solid western. Enright's direction is tough, emphasizing the violence of the action and the steadfastness of Scott in equal measure. This is a significant western." *The Western*, Pitts

"Columbia has a mighty solid western in *Coroner Creek*. The stress is on deadly gunfighter action and its rough, tough example of straight western fare that pulls no punches. The general worth has been heightened by some knock-down, drag-out fisticuffs that have been rarely matched on the screen." *Variety*, 6/9/48

"An important western that marks the transition from the simple-minded horse operas of the 1930s and 1940s to the later adult themes and sensibilities of the genre." *Motion Picture Guide*, Nash and Ross

Summation: This is a brutal, gripping, exciting top-of-the-line noir western. It's one of the first westerns to have adult overtones in the grim way Randolph Scott exacts his revenge on George Macready, the man responsible for his fiancée's death. The acting is uniformly good. Scott is quite effective as a man hell-bent on revenge. Macready makes a formidable villain. Wallace Ford again shows us why he's one of the best character actors as he changes realistically from a quiet man to a man who can stand up to for what is right. Kudos to cinematographer Fred Jackman, Jr.'s excellent photography from the emphasis on the magnificent Arizona landscapes to the shadowy scenes of sudden violence. Don't miss this important western.

THE LONE WOLF TURNS SPY TO MAKE NAZIS TURN PALE ... and cops turn green with envy!

Counter-Espionage

(September 1942)

Alternate Title: The Lone Wolf in Scotland Yard

Cast: Michael Lanyard, Warren William; Jameson, Eric Blore; Pamela, Hillary Brooke; Inspector Crane, Thurston Hall; Dickens, Fred Kelsey; Anton Schugg, Forrest Tucker; Inspector Stephens, Matthew Boulton; Gustav Soessel, Kurt Katch; Kent Wells, Morton Lowry; Harvey Leeds, Leslie Denison; George Barrow, Billy Bevan; Sir Stafford Hart, Stanley Logan; Police Constable Hopkins, Tom Stevenson; Uncredited: Barrow's Daughter, Heather Wilde; Newspaper Vendor, Robert Hale; Maitre d', Wyndham Standing; Waiter, Lloyd Bridges; Heinrich, Eddie Laughton; Air Warden Williams, Keith Hitchcock; Van Ruhoff, Wilhelm von Brincken; German Telegrapher, William Yetter, Sr.

Credits: Director, Edward Dmytryk; Producer, Wallace MacDonald; Screenwriter, Aubrey Wisberg; Editor, Gene Havlick; Art Directors, Lionel Banks and Robert Peterson; Cinematography, Philip Tannura; Musical Director, M.W. Stoloff

Production Dates: April 10–April 28, 1942

Running Time: 73 minutes

Source: a work by Louis Joseph Vance

Story: In war-torn London, Warren William steals the Beam Detector plan from Stanley Logan's safe. Scotland Yard Inspector Matthew Boulton arrests William but not before William passes the plans to his valet, Eric Blore. William escapes from Scotland Yard only to find German agent Forrest Tucker is waiting for him. Tucker takes William to the head of the spy ring, Kurt Katch. William agrees to sell the plans to Katch. Boulton is killed and his secretary Milton Lowry, a German spy, finds proof that William is working for the British government. William discovers the lair of the German spies and is captured. With timely intervention from Blore and air raid warden Billy Beven, Katch and his spy ring are rounded up.

Notes and Commentary: Eric Blore's character name is listed as Jameson instead of Jamison, as it has been in the earlier series entries. Leonard Carey was Jameson in *The Lone Wolf Spy Hunt* (Columbia, 1939).

In *Counter-Espionage* (1942) Lloyd Brides threatens Warren William and Hillary Brooke.

There has been a discussion of whether Lloyd Bridges appeared in the film or not. It is obviously Bridges, with a mustache, as a German agent in the English pub.

In the film, the street lights were turned off only as the sirens sounded. In reality, a total blackout was imposed. Every day the newspapers listed the time in which all lights were to be extinguished.

Reviews: "Above average series entry." *Motion Picture Guide*, Nash and Ross

"One of the best in the Lone Wolf series" *Variety*, 9/30/42

Summation: This is a first-rate noirish Lone Wolf entry with the accent on adventure and suspense, with comedy almost non-existent this time out. Warren William and Eric Blore are perfect in their roles. The rest of the cast acquit themselves well, especially Hillary Brooke and Billy Bevan. Edward Dmytryk's direction is on target, as he paces the film in fine fashion.

DAVID HARDING EXPOSES INTERNATIONAL INTRIGUE!

Counterspy Meets Scotland Yard

(November 1950)

Cast: David Harding, Howard St. John; Karen Michelle, Amanda Blake; Simon Lang, Ron Randell; Barbara Taylor, June Vincent; Peters, Fred Sears; Bob Reynolds, John Dehner; Hugo Borne (Dr. Victor Gilbert), Lewis Martin; Uncredited: Martin, Harry Lauter; Burton, Jimmy Lloyd; McCullough, Rick Vallin; Hugo Borin (Dr. Ritter), Everett Glass; Martha, Gloria Henry; Professor Schuman, Gregory Gay; Col. Kilgore, Douglas Evans; Fields, Robert Bice; Paul Heisl, Paul Marion; Larry, John Doucette; Jimmy, Don Brodie;

***Counterspy Meets Scotland Yard* (1950).**

Brown, Ted Jordan; Power Company Clerk, Jack Rice; Assistant Lab Technician, George Eldredge; Danning, Taylor Reid; Laundry Man, Al Hill

Credits: Director, Seymour Friedman; Producer, Wallace MacDonald; Screenwriter, Harold Greene; Editor, Aaron Stell; Art Director, Victor Greene; Set Decorator, George Montgomery; Cinematographer, Philip Tannura; Musical Director, Mischa Bakaleinikoff

Production Dates: June 12–June 24, 1950

Source: Based on the radio program *Counterspy* created by Phillip H. Lord

Running Time: 67 minutes

Story: Harry Lauter discovers how top-secret information is getting into the hands of an espionage ring. He is murdered before he can tell his boss, Howard St. John. Scotland Yard is interested in the problem and assigns their top agent, Ron Randell, to help. St. John arranges to have Randell take Lauter's place. Randell's secretary, Amanda Blake, has psychological problems and is a patient of Dr. Lewis Martin. Martin is drugging Blake to learn the secret missile data. The information is taken to the leader, Charles Meredith, in the stopper of an empty water jug. The spies learn Randell is a federal agent and make an attempt to murder him. Randell believes Martin is using a hypnotic drug to obtain information from Blake. St. John places Martin's office under surveillance. Blake goes for her weekly appointment and gives the last of the information. In disguise, Randell visits Martin's office as a patient. Martin's nurse, June Vincent, had met Randell previously and sees through the disguise. Martin attempts to drug Randell and is only partially successful. Randell is able to alert St. John, who then rounds up the espionage ring members. Meanwhile, Randell and Blake have fallen in love and marry.

Notes and Commentary: Ron Randell appears to have had bad luck in Columbia's series efforts. He appeared in the short-lived Bulldog Drummond series, the final Lone Wolf effort and this final Counterspy film.

Reviews: "Cast seems to be having fun, and audiences should too." *Motion Picture Guide*, Nash and Ross

"This modest programmer packs enough excitement to please mystery fans and juvenile audiences." *Variety*, 11/15/50

SUMMATION: This entry was not as good as the initial entry in the Counterspy series, but is still quite entertaining. Director Seymour Friedman paces the story in documentary noir fashion and with the more-than-capable cast, everything works.

A REAL WESTERN! It's really the best ... because it's really the West!

Cowboy

(March 1958)

CAST: Tom Reese, Glenn Ford; Frank Harris, Jack Lemmon; Maria Vidal, Anna Kashfi; Doc Bender, Brian Donlevy; Charlie, Dick York; Paco Mendoza, Victor Manuel Mendoza; Paul Curtis, Richard Jaeckel; Joe Capper, King Donovan; Mr. Fowler, Vaughn Taylor; Senor Vidal, Donald Randolph; Mike Adams, James Westerfield; Don Manuel Arriega, Eugene Iglesias; Alcaide, Frank de Kova; Uncredited: Slim Barrett, Robert "Buzz" Henry; Aunt, Arrapola Del Vando; Charlie's Girl, Bek Nelson; Tucker, William Leslie; Peggy, Guy Wilkerson; Cowhand Bitten by Snake, Strother Martin; Ben (Trail Hand), John L. Cason; Jose, Don Carlos; Rosa, Gloria Rhodes; Bellboy, Don Reardon; Businessman, Paul McGuire; Poker Player, Bill Hale; Cattle Buyers, David McMahon, Russell Thorson and Russ Whiteman; Reese's Gals, Suzanne Ridgeway, Gloria Victor and Juli Reding; Capper's Girl, Joan Bradshaw; Daughter, Pat Kenaston; Peon Boy, John L. Blaustein; Joe, Russ Bender; Trumpeter in Cantina, Rafael Mendez; Older Woman at Hotel Desk, Leoda Richards

CREDITS: Director, Delmer Daves; Assistant Director, Sam Nelson; Producer, Julian Blaustein; Screenwriter, Edmund H. North; Editors, William A. Lyon and Al Clark; Art Director, Cary Odell; Set Decorators, William Kiernan and James Crowe; Cinematographer, Charles Lawton, Jr.; Second Unit Photographer, Ray Cory; Makeup, Clay Campbell; Hair Stylist, Helen Hunt; Recording Supervisor, John Livadary; Sound, Josh Westmoreland; Original Music, George Duning; Musical Conductor, Morris Stoloff; Orchestrator, Arthur Morton; Technicolor Color Consultant, Henry Jaffa; Title Designer, Saul Bass

LOCATION FILMING: Lawton, Oklahoma; El Paso (El Paso Stockyards), Texas; Santa Fe (Bonanza Creek Ranch) and San Ildefonso Pueblo, New Mexico

PRODUCTION DATES: June 14–July 26, 1957

SOURCE: book *On the Trail: My Reminiscences as a Cowboy* by Frank Harris

Color by Technicolor

RUNNING TIME: 92 minutes

STORY: Wealthy Mexican rancher Donald Randolph breaks up a budding romance between his daughter Anna Kashfi and Chicago hotel desk clerk Jack Lemmon. When Lemmon learns that trail boss Glenn Ford plans to drive some of Randolph's cattle to market, Lemmon joins the drive. Lemmon sees that a cowboy's life is tough and has to adapt quickly. At Randolph's ranch, Lemmon meets Kashfi, only to find she's now married to Eugene Iglesias. The trail drive begins. Indians watch closely but decide to attack Lemmon, who is driving a small bunch of strays, instead of hitting the main herd. To save Lemmon, Ford stampedes the main herd into the Indians' path. Lemmon, now hardened, blames Ford for about 200 cattle the cowboys can't recover. The herd reaches the railhead. As the train travels to Chicago, some of the cattle fall in one of the cars. Even though it's dangerous, Lemmon goes into the car to right the cattle. Ford joins Lemmon and together all the cattle regain their footing. In Chicago, Lemmon proves he's now an experienced cowboy by shooting cockroaches that appear on the hotel walls.

NOTES AND COMMENTARY: In the trailer for *Cowboy*, the black and white portion first features veteran western actor Dennis Moore and then in the color portion Jack Lemmon introduces scenes from the film.

Its working titles were *Frontier* and *Reminiscences of a Cowboy*.

ON THE TRAIL: My Reminiscences as a Cowboy reportedly is a semi-autobiographical account of Frank Harris' short life as a cowboy. Other accounts state that Harris obtained accurate accounts of cowboy life from the cowboys he met around the Chicago stockyards.

Many changes were made as Harris' book was adapted for the screen. Tom Reece (note change in spelling) had a partner in Harrel Ford. Reece was an Englishman. Frank Harris had enough money to become a quarter partner. There was never any animosity between Reece and Harris. The lawman who joined the trail drive was Wild Bill Hickok. Hickok left the drive on the return trip at Fort Leavenworth and Harris never heard from Hickok again. Harris wanted to go west on the chance of meeting Senorita Vidal but never saw her again. Other incidents from the novel appeared in the screenplay. There was the horseplay with the rattlesnake that caused a cowboy's death. Cowhand Charlie was knifed in Taos because of his affections for a local senorita. There were multiple incidents in which cattle were down in the cattle cars. Finally Harris learned how to enter the cars and right the cattle. Harris was helped by a cowhand, not Reece. Most of the cattle were destroyed in the Great Chicago Fire. Harris was able to save enough cattle to make a decent profit. With his share of the money, he left cowboy life to attend the University of Kansas and then Heidelberg.

William A. Lyon and Al Clark received Academy Award nominations for Best Editing.

Reviews: "Delightful drama, most realistic and entertaining." *Western Movies*, Pitts

"Although *Cowboy* didn't do well at the box office, it remains a fine film." *Motion Picture Guide*, Nash and Ross

Summation: A very good, tough, noirish western of cowboy life with fine performances by Jack Lemmon and Glenn Ford. Delmer Daves' direction never wavers and keeps the interest on high despite the episodic nature of the story. Charles Lawton, Jr.'s photography captures the beautiful western scenery.

THE FAMOUS TRIALS! ... TRICKS! ... FIXES! ... of the smartest mouthpiece of them all!

Criminal Lawyer

(October 1951)

Cast: Jimmy Regan, Pat O'Brien; Maggie Powell, Jane Wyatt; Tucker Bourne, Carl Benton Reid; Gloria Lydendecker, Mary Castle; Clark Sommers, Robert Shayne; "Moose" Hendricks, Mike Mazurki; Walter Medford, Jerome Cowan; Sam Kutler, Marvin Kaplan; Harry Cheney, Douglas Fowley; Vincent Cheney, Mickey Knox; Frank Burnett, Louis Jean Heydt; Uncredited: Mrs. Johnson, Mary Alan Hokanson; Edward Cranston, Guy Beach; Melville Webber, Wallis Clark; Joey, Jamal Frazier; Captain Loomis, John Hamilton; Bill Webber, Darryl Hickman; Frederick Waterman, Charles Lane; Judge Selders, Lewis Martin; Mike (Bartender), William Newell; Judge Larrabee, Grandon Rhodes; Ed Kelly (City Editor), Arthur Space; Byron Claymore, Harlan Warde; Bailiffs, Kernan Cripps and Pat O'Malley; Receptionist, Amanda Blake; Jury Foreman, Ken Christy; Waiter, Sam Finn; Blonde, Jayne Hazard; Attendant, Joey Ray; Juror, Charles Williams

Credits: Director, Seymour Friedman; Producer, Rudolph C. Flothow; Screenwriter, Harold R. Greene; Editor, Charles Nelson; Art Director, Harold MacArthur; Set Decorator, Frank Tuttle; Cinematographer, Philip Tannura; Musical Director, Mischa Bakaleinikoff

Production Dates: late November–mid–December 1950

Running Time: 74 minutes

Story: Criminal lawyer Pat O'Brien, noted for his use of effective trickery in the courtroom, scores again when murder charges against Mickey Knox, brother of mobster Douglas Fowley, are dismissed. With this victory, O'Brien announces his retirement from the practice of law. He believes he will be appointed a Supreme Court judge and turns over the practice to his partner, Robert Shayne. Shayne enters into a contract to be Fowley's legal counsel for a sizable retainer. Fowley is led to believe that as a judge, O'Brien will rule favorably on any of Shayne's court cases. Later Fowley finds out that O'Brien severed all ties with his former firm. Because of O'Brien's reputation, he is turned down for the judgeship. Carl Benton Reid and Wallis Clark, two men who were against O'Brien as a judge, turn to him when Clark's son, Darryl Hickman, is arrested on a vehicular manslaughter charge. O'Brien's former secretary, Jane Wyatt, convinces him to take the case. Wyatt convinces Reid and Clark to reconsider O'Brien for judge. O'Brien's tricky maneuvers win the case. The verdict distresses Mary Alan Hokanson, widow of the manslaughter victim. Hokanson confronts O'Brien, gun in hand. Unable to pull the trigger, she runs away in tears. O'Brien realizes that in saving Hickman he destroyed Hokanson's life and races after her. Unable to locate O'Brien, his bodyguard Mike Mazurki thinks O'Brien might have gone to see Fowley, because of past arguments. Mazurki goes to Fowley's apartment and finds his body. Mazurki is arrested for murder. Wyatt locates O'Brien, who has taken refuge in alcohol. Sobering up, O'Brien begins working in Mazurki's defense. O'Brien suddenly accuses Shayne of the murder. Shayne confesses and says the murder was committed in self-defense. Shayne and Fowley argued because Fowley was pulling out of their agreement. With Fowley's money gone, the firm would be in financial trouble. O'Brien leaves the courtroom arm in arm with Wyatt, fully expecting to be appointed a Supreme Court judge.

Reviews: "Praiseworthy for its fresh and thoughtful character study." *Motion Picture Guide*, Nash and Ross

"Modest programmer. O'Brien turned in an excellent performance and made the most of Harold R. Greene's efficient screenplay." *The Columbia Story*, Hirschhorn

Summation: This is a good courtroom noir. Director Seymour Friedman briskly directs Harold R. Greene's fine screenplay and gets the most out of a sparkling crew. At the top of his form, O'Brien is believable as a man who temporarily hits the skids when his dream of becoming a judge is shattered. In the fine supporting cast, two performances stand out. Mike Mazurki shows that when a role has depth, he is up to the challenge, from wearing an apron while cooking dinner to emotionally explaining how he came to be O'Brien's man Friday. In a short, telling scene, Mary Alan Hokanson is superb as a distraught widow. Adding to the noir flavor is Philip Tannura's photography, using the darkness to highlight scenes.

YES, this is a beautiful American girl in the arms of a Japanese boy!
A motion picture of startling frankness ... vivid emotions!

The Crimson Kimono

(October 1959)

Cast: Christine Downs, Victoria Shaw; Detective Sgt. Charlie Bancroft, Glenn Corbett; Detective Joe Kojaku, James Shigeta; Mac, Anna Lee; Casale, Paul Dubov; Roma, Jaclynne Greene; Hansel, Neyle Morrow; Sugar Torch, Gloria Pall; Mother, Barbara Hayden; Willy Hidaka, George Yoshinaga; Nun, Kaye Elhardt; Sister Gertrude; Aya Oyama; Charlie (Karate Teacher), George Okamura; Priest, the Reverend Ryosho S. Sogabe; Bob Okazaki, Robert Okazaki; Shuto, Fuji; Uncredited: Ziggy, Walter Burke; Announcer, Robert Kino; Librarian, Stafford Repp; Police Captain, Brian O'Hara; Kendo Referee, Torau Mori; Little Girl, Katie Sweet; Japanese Woman, Chiyo Toto; College Girl, Nina Roman; Waiter, Harrison Lewis; Police Officer, David McMahon; Gardener, Edo Mita

Credits: Director, Producer and Screenwriter, Samuel Fuller; Assistant Director, Floyd Joyer; Editor, Jerome Thoms; Art Directors, William E. Flannery and Robert Boyle; Set Decorator, James M. Crowe; Cinematographer, Sam Leavitt; Costume Designer, Bernice Pontrelli; Makeup, Clay Campbell; Hair Stylist, Helen Hunt; Recording Supervisor, John Livadary; Sound, Josh Westmoreland; Original Music and Musical Conductor, Harry Sukman; Orchestrators, Leo Shuken and Jack Hayes

Location Filming: Los Angeles (Little Tokyo), California

Production Dates: February 16–March 10, 1959

Running Time: 82 minutes

Story: After her performance, burlesque

queen Gloria Pall is chased into the streets and shot down. Detectives Glenn Corbett and James Shigeta are assigned to the case, with Shigeta taking the lead. Pall was working on a new routine to be called the Crimson Kimono. In her dressing room, the detectives find a painting depicting the new act and they begin the search for the artist. Corbett finally locates the artist, Victoria Shaw. Shaw was commissioned to paint the picture by Neyle Morrow. Shaw is able to make a sketch of Morrow. Shigeta finds Fuji, who was to work in Pall's act. Fuji, afraid to talk with the police, makes his escape. At her rooming house, Shaw receives a phone call from Morrow. As she reaches the phone, a shot is fired that misses Shaw. Corbett and Shigeta convince Shaw to move in with them. When Fuji is finally located, it takes both Shigeta and Corbett to subdue him. Fuji is able to lead the detectives to a library where Morrow worked and they find that he had abruptly resigned. Another lead is the wig factory that was consigned to make wigs needed for Pall's routine. Only one employee, Jaclynne Green, recognizes the photo of Morrow but insists that she never met him in person. Shaw is left in Shigeta's care when Corbett meets informant Walter Burke. Burke leads Corbett to Morrow's apartment but Corbett misses Morrow by ten minutes. Shigeta and Shaw begin to have romantic feelings for each other. Shigeta tries to conceal his feelings because Corbett is in love with Shaw and his relationship with Shaw would be interracial. Fighting in their annual Kendo match, Shigeta breaks all rules and gives Corbett a beating. After the match, Shigeta tells Corbett that he and Shaw are in love. Shigeta is unsure to proceed with his relationship with Shaw. He leaves the apartment he shared with Corbett and plans to quit the force. Both Corbett and Shaw track Shigeta in a restaurant and try to convince him to reconsider leaving the force. During the conversation, Shaw spots Morrow. Morrow is captured only to be shot down by Greene. Greene starts running through the streets of Little Tokyo pursued by Shigeta. A bullet from Shigeta brings Greene down. She confesses that she shot Pall because she though Pall was taking Morrow away from her. Greene realized afterwards that Morrow had no romantic interest in Pall. Corbett tells Shigeta that because of Shaw, they no longer can be partners. Shigeta understands and welcomes Shaw in his arms.

Notes and Commentary: The working title for the film was *The White Kimono*. Columbia distributed it on a double bill with *Battle of the Coral Sea* (1959).

The scene in which Gloria Pall was shot was shot on actual Los Angeles streets, at the intersection of 6th and Main. Director Samuel Fuller had three cameras hidden, in a truck, a car and on a rooftop. The traffic was real except Fuller had a father-and-daughter stunt driving team who knew Pall would run in front of them and be shot. Their vehicles would protect her. Pall was quickly taken from the scene. Bystanders, thinking a real murder had been committed, called the police. Fuller needed a close shot but couldn't return until the police had left the scene.

Columbia released the film as just another "B" exploitation film. Another tag line was, "WHY DOES SHE CHOSE A JAPANESE LOVER."

Reviews: "Although Fuller's attempts to probe racial prejudice were undoubtedly motivated by a worthy desire, it doesn't work out very well. The mystery melodrama part of the film gets lost during the complicated romance and the racial intolerance plea is cheapened by its inclusion in a film of otherwise straight action." *Variety*, 9/9/59

"Fuller had an ordinary little murder mystery here that he added an interracial overlay to and attempted to meld the two. It doesn't work, though Fuller's camera is always interesting and his cross-cutting techniques almost bring off the two themes." *Motion Picture Guide*, Nash and Ross

Summation: Director Fuller, working with two main plot themes, almost makes it work in this crime noir. The first, the murder of a burlesque stripper, begins well but gets somewhat lost in the picture's middle and surfaces at the end to bring on a rushed finale. The death of the stripper is satisfactorily explained but not the death of the prime suspect. The resolution of the interracial romance, the second plot theme, seemed forced. After the killer's capture, James Shigeta's decisions to remain on the force and to become romantically involved played like a true throwaway "B" film. To Fuller's credit, his narrative holds the audience's interest, with interesting and intense scenes. The acting of Shaw, Corbett and Shigeta is more than adequate. This was Corbett's acting debut and Shigeta's first American film. Sam Leavitt's fine noir photography helps elevate the film.

WALK INTO HER PARLOR ... and you're caught in a web of intrigue and murder!

The Crooked Web

(December 1955)

A Clover Production

CAST: Stan Fabian, Frank Lovejoy; Joanie Daniel, Mari Blanchard; Frank Daniel, Richard Denning; Herr Koenig, John Mylong; Sgt. Mike Jancoweizc, Harry Lauter; Ray Torres, Steven Ritch; Herr Schmitt, Louis Merrill; Uncredited: Ed, Vince Barnett; Tom Jackson, Van Des Autels; Richard Atherton, Roy Gordon; Don Gillen, George Cisar; Doc Mason, Richard Emory; Charlie Holt, John Hart; German Guard, Harold Dyrenforth; Singer, Judy Clark

CREDITS: Director, Nathan Hertz Juran; Assistant Director, Gene Anderson, Jr.; Story and Screenplay, Lou Breslow; Editor, Edwin Bryant; Art Director, Paul Palmentola; Set Decorator, Sidney Clifford; Cinematographer, Henry Freulich; Sound, Josh Westmoreland; Musical Conductor, Mischa Bakaleinikoff; Unit Manager, Leon Chooluck; Special Effects, Jack Erickson

SONG: "Put the Blame on Mame" (Roberts and Fisher)—played by orchestra in restaurant and "Hold on to Your Heart" (Naylor and Wittkin)—sung by Judy Clark

PRODUCTION DATES: April 4–April 16, 1955

RUNNING TIME: 77 minutes

STORY: Drive-in restaurant owner Frank Lovejoy is enamored of car hop Mari Blanchard. Richard Denning comes on the scene and Blanchard introduces him to Lovejoy as her brother. In reality, Blanchard and Denning are lovers. They

From left to right: Frank Lovejoy, Mari Blanchard, Richard Denning, and Harry Lauter in *The Crooked Web* (1955).

have been hired by Roy Gordon to lure Lovejoy to Germany where he can be tried for the murder of two soldiers, one of them Gordon's son. Denning sets the hook and tells Lovejoy that he needs $3,000 to help finance a trip to Germany to gain possession of a stolen treasure. Blanchard tells Lovejoy that after they've turned the treasure to cash, they can have a honeymoon. The treasure has been buried on a large estate in a graveyard. In the first attempt to take the treasure, German guards interrupt them and Lovejoy, Denning and Blanchard are forced to flee. Believing Denning will double cross him, Lovejoy and Blanchard try their own grab only to find Denning waiting for them. Again German guards arrive and the three flee in a hail of gunfire. Denning and Lovejoy obtain badges and plan to enter the estate as inspectors and take the treasure. Their plan is foiled as the United States Army has take control of the grounds and erected a fence. Denning comes up with a plan to re-enlist in the Army and get assigned to the estate. Once there, he can smuggle the treasure through the gate. Denning's application is turned down because he has a heart murmur. Blanchard begs Lovejoy to re-enlist so the plan can be followed. Lovejoy tells Blanchard if he reenlists, he will be arrested for two murders. His confession is overheard by Denning, German policeman John Mylong and other officers, and Lovejoy is arrested. Denning and Blanchard plan to marry.

NOTES AND COMMENTARY: The working title for the film was *The Big Shock*.

REVIEWS: "Some rather complicated melodramatics are unfurled in this detailing of an elaborate scheme to bring a G.I. killer to justice. It comes off passably well." *Variety*, 11/23/55

"Suffering chiefly from a farfetched plot, a slow mover, this has barely adequate direction." *Motion Picture Guide*, Nash and Ross

"A wildly contrived tale of revenge that stretched the elasticity of belief to snapping point." *The Columbia Story*, Hirshhorn

SUMMATION: This is a bland, below-average crime noir. Nathan Hertz Juran's direction is flat and uninspired and Lou Breslow's screenplay is unbelievable. How could Frank Lovejoy's relationship with Mari Blanchard not become sexual after a year? A director such as Budd Boetticher could have made changes to give the story added punch and "B" director Fred F. Sears could have given the proceedings a brisker and more exciting pace. Henry Freulich's photography adds no suspense. The acting of the principals is adequate at best.

HELL ON EARTH! Skeptical? Don't make up your mind till you see this masterpiece of the macabre!

Curse of the Demon

(July 1958)

CAST: Prof. John Holden, Dana Andrews; Joanna Harrington, Peggy Cummins; Dr. Karswell, Niall MacGinnis; Prof. Harrington, Maurice Denham; Mrs. Karswell, Athene Seyler; Mark O'Brien, Liam Redmond; Mr. Meek, Reginald Beckwith; Lloyd Williamson, Ewan Roberts; Kumar, Peter Elliott; Mrs. Meek, Rosamund Greenwood; Rand Hobart, Brian Wilde; Inspector Mottram, Richard Leech; Detective Simmons, Lloyd Lamble; Superintendent, Peter Hobbes; Chemist, Charles Lloyd-Pack; Librarian, John Salew; Mrs. Hobart, Janet Barrow; Farmer, Percy Herbert; Air Hostess, Lynn Tracy; Uncredited: Narrator, Shay Gorman; Bates (Butler), Walter Horsbrugh; Reporters, Ballard Berkeley and Michael Peake; Children, Anthony John and Anthony Richmond; Girls Playing Snakes and Ladders, the Blake Twins; Ticket Collector, Leonard Sharp; Hobart's Brother, John Harvey (Note: The characters played by Janet Barrow, Percy Herbert and Lynn Tracy were deleted from the United States prints.)

CREDITS: Director, Jacques Tourneur; Assistant Director, Basil Keys; Producer, Hal E. Chester; Screenwriters, Charles Bennett and Hal E. Chester; Editor, Michael Gordon; Assistant Art Director, Peter Glazer; Production Manager, R.L.M. Davidson; Production Designer, Ken Adam; Cinematographer, Ted Scaife; Special Effects, George Blackwell and Wally Veevers; Special Effects Photographer, S.D. Onions; Hair Stylist, Betty Lee; Sound, Arthur Bradburn; Sound Effects Editor, Charles Crafford; Original Music,

Clifton Parker; Musical Conductor, Muir Mathieson; Casting, Robert Lennard; Continuity, Pamela Gayler

Song: "Plain Song" (Sowande) and "Cherry Ripe" (Herrick and Horn)—sung by Athene Seyler, Reginald Beckwith and Rosamund Greenwood

Filming Locations: Elstree, Hertfordshire, Bloomsbury, Wiltshire and London, England

Production Dates: November 9–December 22, 1956

Source: story "Casting the Runes" by Montague R. James

Running Time: 82 minutes

Story: Professor Dana Andrews is summoned to England by colleague Maurice Denham to debunk the witchcraft claims of Niall MacGinnis. Arriving, Andrews is shocked to find Denham is dead, supposedly from accidental electrocution. Actually Denham was killed trying to escape from a monster from Hell. Andrews decides to continue the investigation. Denham's niece, Peggy Cummins, fearing that Andrews will be facing a horrible death, tries to persuade him not to continue. While gathering information in a library, Andrews comes face to face with MacGinnis. In their verbal exchange, it is obvious the two will be enemies. MacGinnis knocks Andrews' papers to the floor, pick's them up and returns them to Andrews. MacGinnis gives Andrews his business card. On the card, it tells Andrews the date of his death. Cummins tells Andrews that Denham found a parchment in his possession with Runic symbols. After Denham read the parchment, the parchment flew from his hands into a nearby fireplace and burned. Visiting MacGinnis, Andrews is told he only has days to live unless he gives up his investigation. At Cummins' house, Andrews discovers he has a parchment with Runic symbols. The parchment attempts to fly into the fireplace but is stopped by a screen. Cummins believes the key to the investigation is a book in MacGinnis' study. Andrews breaks into the house and makes his way to the study when he's suddenly attacked by a cat that has changed into a leopard. The struggle is stopped when MacGinnis enters the study. MacGinnis tells Andrews to leave the grounds by the driveway. Andrews insists that he'll leave by the way he came, through the woods. In the woods, Andrews is chased by a mysterious cloud. As time draws near to the announced time of Andrews' death, a devil worshiper, Brian Wilde, is hypnotized. In this state, he is able to tell Andrews that the only way he can avoid death is to return the parchment to the person who passed it to him. Andrews learns MacGinnis is leaving town on an evening train. Andrews reaches the train as it's pulling out of the station and goes to MacGinnis's compartment. Andrews finds a hypnotized Cummins. MacGinnis brings Cummins out of her trance and attempts to leave the compartment. Andrews blocks his way and tells him if a monster is to appear, MacGinnis will be there to also receive him. Police, who have been following Andrews, arrive and say that MacGinnis is free to leave. Andrews hands MacGinnis his coat. MacGinnis suddenly realizes that Andrews has passed the parchment back to him. The parchment flies from MacGinnis' hands. The train has stopped at a station. MacGinnis gets off and chases the parchment down the railroad tracks. As he tries to pick the parchment up, it bursts into flames. Looking up, he sees the monster from Hell coming toward him. MacGinnis is powerless to escape and is killed. Andrews starts to approach MacGinnis' body but decides to heed Cummins' admonition that it best not to know. Andrews and Cummins leave the station.

Notes and Commentary: This film was released in England as *Night of the Demon*. That version had a running time of 95 minutes. There were some differences in the opening credits from the United States release; both Dana Andrews and Peggy Cummins received above the title credits and Niall MacGinnis appeared alone on the screen after the title. Actors Richard Leech and Reginald Beckwith also received on-screen credit. Opening credits stated this was a Sabre Film Production with Hal E. Chester as executive producer and Frank Bevis as producer. Three scenes were deleted and one scene truncated for the United States version. In the in-flight scene, all footage with the air hostess was deleted. Entire sequences that hit the cutting room floor were one in which MacGinnis tells his mother that he is unable to give up the life of witchcraft, another when Andrews visits Brian Wilde's farm to obtain permission to have him hypnotized, and finally a scene where MacGinnis' mother tells Cummins that Wilde knows the secret of the parchment.

The film was derived from Montague R. James' short story "Casting the Runes." In the story, Karswell seeks witchcraft vengeance on those who cast aspersions on his philosophy of witchcraft. Edward Dunning incurs Karswell's wrath and Karswell slips the parchment to him. Dunning is finally able to pass the parchment back to Karswell. Karswell dies under mysterious circumstances at the time Dunning was supposed to die. No monster appears in the story.

Working titles for the film were *The Bewitched*, *Casting the Runes* and *The Haunted*.

Director Jacques Tourneur, opposed to showing the demon, filmed the scene where Andrews was chased by a "cloud." After Tourneur returned to the United States, either executive producer Hal E. Chester or producer Frank Bevis added scenes with the monster. Other sources state Tourneur was pressed into showing the monster for commercial reasons. Finally Tourneur only wanted to show four frames of the monster picking up Niall MacGinnis and throwing him to the ground. The likeness of the monster was based on 3400-year-old woodcut prints from demonology books.

Curse of the Demon was released as half of a double feature with *The Revenge of Frankenstein* (1958).

Reviews: "Outstanding supernatural horror film with Bennett's literate script and Tourneur's atmospheric visuals." *Motion Picture Guide*, Nash and Ross

"An altogether superior addition, a horror package that somehow never insulted the intelligence." *The Columbia Story*, Hirschhorn

Summation: This is a classic horror noir. Director Jacques Tourneur, like a master chef, combined Charles Bennett and Hal E. Chester's excellent, literate screenplay, Ted Scaife's eerie photography, Clifton Parker's complementary music and fine acting by the principals, especially Niall MacGinnis' riveting performance as a man controlled by witchcraft. The film can stand with such classics as *Cat People*, *Dead of Night* and *The Innocents*. Although both the English and American prints grab the viewer and hold the interest until the final frame, the author prefers the longer version. The author would have preferred that the movie not show (or just barely show) the monster from Hell, but its appearance does the film minimal harm.

GIANT SMUGGLING RING CRACKED BY CUSTOMS AGENT

Customs Agent

(May 1950)

Cast: Bert Stewart, William Eythe; Lucille Gerrard, Marjorie Reynolds; Charles McGraw, Griff Barnett; Charles Johnson, Howard St. John; Thomas Jacoby, Jim Backus; J.G. Goff, Robert Shayne; Uncredited: Al, Denver Pyle; Hank, John Doucette; Perry, Harlan Warde; Pettygill, James Fairfax; Roy Phillips, Clark Howat; Miss Kung, Marya Marco; Watkins, Guy Kingsford; Philip Barton, William "Bill" Phillips; Agents, Robert Bice and George Eldredge; Sergeant, Howard Negley; Policeman, Charles Flynn; Guard, Sam Menacker; Inspector, Kernan Cripps; Head Waiter, Benson Fong; Bartender, Beal Wong

Credits: Director, Seymour Friedman; Producer, Rudolph C. Flothow; Story, Hal Smith; Screenwriters, Russell S. Hughes and Malcolm Stuart Boylan; Editor, Aaron Stell; Art Director, Harold MacArthur; Set Decorator, Sidney Clifford; Cinematographer, Philip Tannura; Technical Advisor, Mel Hanks; Musical Director, Mischa Bakaleinikoff

Production Dates: November 29–December 10, 1949

Running Time: 71 minutes

Story: Following a tip about a Streptomycin smuggling ring, customs agent Clark Howat is shot down in the streets of Shanghai. His partner William Eythe gets some heat because he did not accompany Howat. Tempers flare and chief agent Jim Backus fires Eythe. Eythe goes on a bender. Family friend Griff Barnett attempts to intervene, offering Eythe a job. Eythe refuses and goes on another binge, passing out. Awakening, Eythe finds himself in reputed mobster Howard St. John's house. St. John offers Eythe a lucrative job which Eythe accepts. St. John believes Eythe's knowledge of customs regulations will help him in his smuggling racket. In actuality, Eythe is still a customs agent. Eythe is sent to California. In his luggage, Eythe finds packets of narcotics. Using a smuggler's vest, Eythe brings the drugs into the States. Making it look like he sold the drugs to a buyer, Eythe gets the narcotics into government hands.

St. John's musclemen catch up to Eythe and he is brought to Marjorie Reynolds' house, where Barnett resides. Eythe is told that Barnett is the real leader of the organization. Barnett has a plan to smuggle a large quantity of Streptomycin into China. Eythe is able to alert the West Coast chief agent Robert Shayne that the drug is to be transported to a waiting vessel by a private yacht. The Coast Guard helps bring Barnett, St. John and the rest of the gang to justice.

Reviews: "*Customs Agent* is a good title for the formula action melodramatics that go on for 71 minutes. There's nothing particularly original, plotwise, but the pace and the general action setup slant it as okay." *Variety*, 4/19/50

"Wonderfully shot by craftsman Tannura." *Motion Picture Guide*, Nash and Ross

Summation: This is a good premise for a noir yarn gone astray. Seymour Friedman's direction is both uninspired and uneven. There are a few good moments in the story but for the most part the story lets the viewer down tension- and suspense-wise. The interaction between Eythe and female fatale wannabe Reynolds is never developed to any level past that of teenagers in a '40s family film. The scenes between them are never sensual or passionate. Therefore there is no intensity in the scene where Eythe sees that Barnett is living in the same house with Reynolds. In fact, there is really no sexual tension between Barnett and Reynolds. The ending is wrapped up quickly. There is never any sense that Eythe is in real trouble.

You'll scream with cold CHILLS and ... you'll take this DANGEROUS BLONDE Straight to Your Heart!

Dangerous Blondes

(September 1943)

Cast: Barry Craig, Allyn Joslyn; Jane Craig, Evelyn Keyes; Ralph McCormick, Edmund Lowe; Kirk Fenley, John Hubbard; Julie Taylor, Anita Louise; Inspector Joseph Clinton, Frank Craven; Harry Duerr, Michael Duane; Erika McCormick, Ann Savage; Detective Gatling, William Demarest; "Pop" Philpot, Hobart Cavanaugh; Detective Joe Henderson, Frank Sully; Jim Snyder, Robert Stanford; May Ralston, Lynn Merrick; Uncredited: Office McGuire, Emory Parnell; Announcer Don Wilson, Don Wilson; Scott, Jack Rice; Mrs. Swanson, Minerva Urecal; Lee Kenyon, Stanley Brown; Isabel Fleming, Mary Forbes; Madge Lawrence, Bess Flowers; Roland X. Smith, John Abbott; Detective Temple, Ray Teal; Medical Officer, Emmett Vogan; Detective Matthews, Harry Strang; Bobby Lewis (Reporter), Donald Kerr; Hoodlums, Horace McMahon and Dwight Frye; Pugnacious Man, William Haade; Phillip (Headwaiter), Max Willenz; Night Clerk, Billy Wayne; Mailman, Frank O'Connor

Credits: Director, Leigh Jason; Producer, Samuel Bischoff; Screenwriters, Richard Flournoy and Jack Henley; Editor, Jerome Thoms; Art Director, Lionel Banks; Associate Art Director, Walter Holscher; Set Decorator, Joseph Kish; Cinematographer, Philip Tannura; Original Music, Earl Lawrence; Musical Director, M.W. Stoloff

Production Dates: May 17–June 19, 1943

Source: story by Kelly Roos

Running Time: 81 minutes

Story: Anita Louise comes to the apartment of mystery writer and amateur sleuth Allyn Joslyn and finds Joslyn's wife, Evelyn Keyes. Louise explains there are mysterious happenings on a photo shoot at Edmund Lowe's advertising agency. Lowe runs the agency with two associates, John Hubbard and Michael Duane. While at the apartment, Louise receives a phone call telling her the negatives for the shoot are missing and the shoot will have to be redone that evening. Louise leaves. Keyes decides to go to the agency and leaves a note for Joslyn to follow. At the shoot, a problem arises when wealthy socialite Mary Forbes sees Bess Flowers as one of the models in the scene. Forbes refuses to participate if Flowers is present. Flowers was Forbes' deceased husband's first wife and there is animosity between them. Forbes is the aunt of Lowe's wife Ann Savage. Joslyn arrives and as Keyes is bringing him up to date, the dead body of Forbes is discovered by Louise. Upon Forbes' death, Savage is the sole heir to her fortune. Police Inspector Frank Craven sends detectives to Flowers' apartment. The detectives find Flowers dead from an overdose of sleeping pills with a bloody knife, the murder weapon. Craven declares the case closed. Joslyn thinks the real murderer is still loose and begins his investigation. Shots are fired at Joslyn; hoodlum Horace McMahon beats him up. Joslyn discovers that Savage and Duane were childhood friends. Savage calls Joslyn and starts to tell him the name of the murderer when the connection is broken. Joslyn and Keyes go to Savage's apartment only to find the police already there. Savage is murdered and Lowe is arrested for the crime. Keyes gets a letter from Louise, who has left town, which indicates that Lowe is innocent. Joslyn is able to talk to Lowe at the jail and finds that Louise knows who hired Flowers, and that person is the murderer. Unable to locate Louise, Joslyn has Keyes, posing as Louise, call the agency while Joslyn is there talking with Hubbard and Duane. Hubbard breaks down and pulls a gun with the intention of murdering Joslyn for interfering with his plans. Savage was going to divorce Lowe to marry him but Hubbard didn't want marriage until Savage inherited Forbes' money. When Savage learned the truth, Hubbard had no choice but to murder her also. As Hubbard is about to pull the trigger, a well-placed shot from a police detective kills Hubbard. Joslyn had been followed by the police from the time he left Lowe at the jail.

Notes and Commentary: The film was based on the novel *If the Shroud Fits* by Kelly Roos. This was the second of Roos' Jeff and Haila Troy mystery novels to come to the screen; the first was *A Night to Remember* (Columbia, 1941) with Loretta Young as Nancy Troy and Brian Aherne as Jeff Troy. When Columbia picked up a second Roos novel, a decision was made not to make it as a series and the names of the main characters were changed to Barry and Jane Craig. The basic premise of the novel was kept with Julie Taylor trying to enlist Jeff/Barry in mysterious events at a photo shoot but she was only able to speak with Haila/Jane. In both the novel and the film, the murder victim is Isabel Fleming. There is no attempt in the novel to frame Madge Lawrence. Erika is strangled in both as the motive for the murders remains constant. The murderer in both is Kirk, although exposing him is handled much differently in the screenplay. Haila's life is the one in jeopardy in the novel.

Working titles for this film were *The Case of the Dangerous Blondes* and *Reckless Lady*.

Reviews: "A laugh-packed session here via the antics of Allyn Joslyn and Evelyn Keyes. The film is well paced." *Variety*, 10/13/43

"A low-key thriller which used a come-hither title to conceal a Thin Man–inspired whodunit set against a ritzy, high-society background. A tendency towards over-cuteness, in both the writing and direction, as well in Joslyn's central performance, proved somewhat irksome, though, all things considered, the end result could have been a lot worse." *The Columbia Story*, Hirshhorn

Summation: This is a fairly entertaining but hardly memorable comedy-mystery. A lot of dark scenes have caused the film to be considered recently as noir by some film experts but the plot and execution are not noirish to the author. The denouement is centered on a bluff which is only a mildly satisfactory ending to the proceedings. Performances and direction are nothing special.

WARNING! This man has an irresistible impulse to kill!

The Dark Past

(January 1949)

Cast: Al Walker, William Holden; Betty, Nina Foch; Dr. Andrew Collins, Lee J. Cobb; Laura Stevens, Adele Jergens; Owen Talbot, Stephen Dunne; Ruth Collins, Lois Maxwell; Mike, Berry Kroeger; Prof. Fred Linder, Steven Geray; Frank Stevens, Wilton Graff; Pete, Robert Osterloh; Nora, Kathryn Card; Uncredited: Commentator, Pat McGeehan; Starry-eyed Girl on Bus, Gay Nelson; Old Man on Bus, Sam Harris; McCoy, Edward Earle; Policemen Leaving Headquarters, John McKee and Brick Sullivan; Herb Fuller, Jimmy Lloyd; First Man in Line-up, Lester Dorr; Tough Man in Line-up, Jack Gordon; John Larrapoe, Harry Harvey, Jr.; Young Prisoner, Edwin Mills; Arrested Man Leaving Wagon, Bill Cartledge; Williams, Robert B. Williams; Bobby Collins, Robert Hyatt; Warden

Benson, Selmer Jackson; Agnes, Ellen Corby; Sheriff, Charles Cane; State Policeman at Roadblock, Phil Tully; Mrs. Linder, Hermine Sterler; Al's Father, G. Pat Collins

Credits: Director, Rudolph Mate; Assistant Director, Milton Feldman; Producer, Buddy Adler; Adaptors, Malvin Wald and Oscar Saul; Screenwriters, Philip McDonald, Michael Blankfort and Albert Duffy; Editor, Viola Lawrence; Art Director, Cary Odell; Set Decorator, Frank Tuttle; Cinematographer, Joseph Walker; Gowns, Jean Louis; Makeup, Clay Campbell, Hair Stylist, Helen Hunt; Sound, George Cooper; Original Music, George Duning; Musical Director, M.W. Stoloff

Song: "Air" from Orchestral Suite No. 3 in D Major (Bach)—played by unknown orchestra

Production Dates: May 21–June 21, 1948

Source: play *Blind Alley* by James Warwick

Running Time: 75 minutes

Story: In trying to convince detective Robert B. Williams that prisoner Harry Harvey, Jr., should undergo psychiatric treatment, police psychologist Lee J. Cobb tells him the story of notorious killer William Holden. Holden and his gang (Nina Foch, Berry Kroeger and Robert Osterloh) break into Cobb's lakeside home. In the house are Cobb, his wife Lois Maxwell, his son Robert Hyatt, houseguests Adele Jergens, Stephen Dunne and Wilton Graff, and servants Kathryn Card and Ellen Corby. Card and Corby are tied up in the cellar. Maxwell and Collins are confined to the nursery. The houseguests are taken to an upstairs room under the watchful eye of Osterloh. Holden informs Cobb that they are waiting for a boat to take them across the lake. Cobb begins to psychoanalyze Holden. Steven Geray has repaired Cobb's rifle and brings it to him. Cobb tries to cut the visit short. As Geray starts to leave, he notices a shoe under a curtain and then finds himself face to face with Holden. Holden decides to kill Geray but Cobb deflects Holden's arm and the bullet just wounds Geray. Cobb tells Holden some deep-seated compulsion caused him to shoot Geray and notices that Holden has two paralyzed fingers. Holden gets Foch to watch Cobb while he tries to sleep. Foch tells Cobb that Holden has the same recurrent dream: In the dream, he is surrounded by rain and takes refuge under an umbrella. The umbrella has a hole and Holden is unable to prevent the rain from coming through. The rain hurts Holden and he tries to crawl from beneath the umbrella. Bars surrounding the umbrella prevent him from leaving. Cobb tells Holden if he can discover the meaning of his nightmare, he can stop the dream. As they talk, Cobb realizes Holden hated his father because he came between him and his mother. In the cellar, Card gets free of her bonds and goes to find the police. Through Cobb's help, Holden finds the meaning of the dream: Holden's father G. Pat Collins was wanted by the law and Holden brought the police to arrest him. There was an exchange of shots and Collins was mortally wounded, falling across a table where Holden was hiding. Blood came through a hole in the table. Holden tried to leave but the policemen's legs prevented his escape. The dream is the guilt Holden is suffering for being the instrument of his father's death. Cobb tells Holden every time he killed a man, he was murdering his father, and now he can never kill again. Police arrive at Cobb's house. Using Cobb as a shield, Holden decides to make a break for freedom. He raises his gun to fire at a police officer and now can only see Collins' face. He can't pull the trigger and to his surprise, his fingers are no longer paralyzed. Holden is taken prisoner. Williams decides to let Cobb try psychiatric treatment on Harvey in the hope it will prevent further criminal activity.

Notes and Commentary: The film was based on James Warwick's play and its 1939 adaptation. The story underwent several iterations as it became *The Dark Past*. In the original Broadway play, there are no houseguests. There is a hand-to-hand encounter between Hal Wilson and Fred Landis. When Landis gets the upper hand, he is shot by Wilson's moll, Mazie. Wilson's dream showed that he hated that his mother went with a man she despised and she had a child with him. In a rage, he murdered his half-sister. Wilson kills Mazie before committing suicide. When *Blind Alley* came to the screen, the fight was between Fred and Wilson's henchman Buck. When Fred is the victor, Wilson shoots him. The dream was changed to show he felt guilt for causing his father's death. Every time he murdered someone, Wilson was murdering his father. Finally knowing this, Wilson takes aim at a policeman and sees his father's face. When Wilson is now unable to kill, police bullets finish his life. In *The Dark Past*, Fred Landis becomes Fred Linder, a much older man, Hal Wilson is now Al Walker and Anthony Shelby is Andrew Collins. There is no fight between Fred and Walker, but there is a confrontation in which a shot is fired by Walker but thanks to Collins jarring Walker's arm, Fred is only wounded. As in the movie *Blind Alley*, Walker's dream shows that he been killing his father over and over. When police arrive, Walker takes aim at a policeman and is unable to pull the trigger. Walker is then taken into custody.

The working titles for the film were *Hearsay* and *Blind Alley*. There were three television productions of *Blind Alley: Studio One in Hollywood* (CBS, June 30, 1949) with Jerome Thor, *Broadway Television Theater* (WOR-TV, September 15, 1952) with Ernest Graves and *Kraft Television Theater* (ABC, June 10, 1954) with Darren McGavin.

REVIEWS: "Under Rudolph Mate's skillful direction, the cast builds a firm aura of suspense in the grim period when the thugs hold the upper hand." *Variety*, 12/29/48

"This fast psychological drama is just a little too slick for its own good in that it offers audiences sort of a *Readers Digest* lesson in how the criminal mind functions." *Motion Picture Guide*, Nash and Ross

"A facile psychological thriller. Holden and Cobb worked well together but the sheer predictability of the material robbed the film of any surprises." *The Columbia Story*, Hirschhorn

SUMMATION: This is a very good psychological noir with outstanding performances by William Holden as a psychotic killer and Lee J. Cobb as a psychiatrist. Nina Foch is fine as Holden's moll. Except for the wrap-around story, *The Dark Past* is practically a scene-by-scene remake of *Blind Alley* (Columbia, 1939). The wrap-around story is added to accentuate the need for help for potential young criminals. Excellent photography by Joseph Walker highlights Holden's inner torment. The dream sequence, with minor variations, is the same as in the original film. Director Rudolph Mate's skills keep the tension on high.

SABOTAGE! TREACHERY! INTRIGUE!

David Harding, Counterspy

(July 1950)

CAST: Commander Jerry Baldwin, Willard Parker; Betty Iverson, Audrey Long; Dr. George Vickers, Raymond Greenleaf; Hopkins, Harlan Warde; Charles Kingston, Alex Gerry, and introducing Howard St. John as David Harding; Uncredited: Peters, Fred F. Sears; Frank Reynolds, John Dehner; Barrington, Anthony Jochim; Nurse, Jean Willes; Bartender, Peter Virgo; Newspaper Vendor, Earle Hodgins; Frank Edwards, Steve Darrell; Brown, Jock Mahoney; Burton, Jimmy Lloyd; Baker, Allen Mathews; Man in Theater, Joey Ray; Grady, Charles Quigley; McCullough, John Pickard; Lt. Van Dyke, Grant Calhoun; Sentry, William Henry; Radio Operator, William Tannen; Lt. Iverson, Robert Lowell

CREDITS: Director, Ray Nazarro; Producer, Milton Feldman; Story and Screenwriters, Clint Johnson and Tom Reed; Editor, Henry Batista; Art Director, Harold MacArthur; Set Decorator, Frank Tuttle; Cinematographer, George E. Diskant; Musical Director, Mischa Bakaleinikoff

SONG: "Let's Fall in Love" (Arlen-Koehler)—hummed by Willard Parker

PRODUCTION DATES: January 15–25, 1950

SOURCE: the radio program *Counterspy* created by Phillips H. Lord

RUNNING TIME: 71 minutes

STORY: With the death of Audrey Long's husband Robert Lowell, counterspy Howard St. John suspects that espionage agents are at work at the Molino torpedo plant. He has Commander Willard Parker assigned to take Long's husband's place at the plant. Long was also her husband's secretary. Parker, who is in love with Long, takes the job when he learns that her husband was murdered. In the ensuing investigation, St. John discovers that Harlan Warde is taking pictures of classified information. Parker sees Warde pass something to Long, but Long insists that he was returning a pack of cigarettes. Realizing that Parker is suspicious, Long—a member of the espionage ring—reports to the ringleader, Dr. Raymond Greenleaf. Greenleaf decides that Parker must be killed. Long, who has fallen in love with Parker, alerts authorities who prevent his murder. St. John makes his move and arrests Warde. St. John then spreads rumors that important plans are coming to the facility. The plans are stolen, but St. John has Greenleaf and his men trailed to an out-of-the-way airfield. St. John informs Parker that

David Harding, Counterspy **(1950).**

Long is an enemy agent and the daughter of Greenleaf. St. John allows one agent to escape with the plans, which are phony. In the roundup of the espionage ring, both Long and Greenleaf are killed.

NOTES AND COMMENTARY: When Willard Parker and Audrey Long go to a movie theater, posters of *Sahara* (1943) with Humphrey Bogart can be seen.

Fred F. Sears appeared in 64 films and directed 50 others.

David Harding, Counterspy was a remake of *Walk a Crooked Mile* (Columbia, 1948) with Louis Hayward and Dennis O'Keefe.

REVIEWS: "A fast paced programmer." *Motion Picture Guide*, Nash and Ross

"New series based on the radio program. Good secondary feature." *Variety*, 5/24/50

SUMMATION: This is a decent espionage noir drama and a good start to the series. The treatment remains faithful to the popular radio program. The acting is okay, especially by Willard Parker, Audrey Long, Howard St. John and Raymond Greenleaf. Ray Nazarro paces the film adroitly and has excellent assistance from cinematographer George E. Diskant, who gives the proceedings the desired noir effect.

HUMPHREY BOGART is out with a new woman ... LIZABETH SCOTT

Dead Reckoning

(January 1947)

CAST: Rip Murdock, Humphrey Bogart; Coral Chandler, Lizabeth Scott; Martinelli, Morris Carnovsky; Lt. Kincaid, Charles Cane; Sgt. Johnny Drake, William Prince; Krause, Marvin Miller; McGee, Wallace Ford; Father Logan, James

Dead Reckoning **(1947).**

Bell; Louis Ord, George Chandler; Uncredited: Lt. Colonel Simpson, William Forrest; Mabel, Ruby Dandridge; Pretty Girl at Phone Booth, Lillian Wells; Mike (Bartender), Charles Jordan; Bandleader, Robert Scott; Desk Clerk, Maynard Holmes; Hotel Desk Clerk, Frank Wilcox; Room Service Waiter, Dudley Dickerson; Waiter at the Dixie, Jesse Graves; Morgue Attendant, Syd Saylor; Detective Casey, George Eldredge; Reporter, Garry Owen; Photographer, Alvin Hammer; Bellboy, Stymie Beard; Ed, Matty Fain; Motorcycle Policeman, Ray Teal; Detectives, Chuck Hamilton and Bob Ryan; Priest, Tom Dillon; Nurse, Isabel Withers; Surgeon, Wilton Graff

CREDITS: Director, John Cromwell; Assistant Director, Seymour Friedman; Producer, Sidney Biddell; Story, Gerald Adams and Sidney Biddell; Adaptation, Allen Rivkin; Screenwriters, Oliver H.P. Garrett and Steve Fisher; Editor, Gene Havlick; Art Directors, Stephen Goosson and Rudolph Sternad; Set Decorator, Louis Diage; Cinematographer, Leo Tover; Gowns, Jean Louis; Makeup, Clay Campbell; Hair Stylist, Helen Hunt; Sound, Jack Goodrich; Musical Score, Marlin Skiles; Musical Director, M.W. Stoloff

SONG: "Either It's Love or It Isn't" (Roberts and Fisher)—sung by Lizabeth Scott (Lizabeth Scott was dubbed by Trudy Stevens)

LOCATION FILMING: Philadelphia, Pennsylvania, New York (LaGuardia airport), New York; St. Petersburg, Florida, and Biloxi, Mississippi

PRODUCTION DATES: June 10–September 4, 1946

RUNNING TIME: 100 minutes

STORY: Humphrey Bogart, evading the Gulf City police, takes refuge in a church and wants Father James Bell to hear his story in case he is killed. In flashbacks we see Bogart and fellow paratrooper William Prince brought hurriedly from Paris to receive medals for their wartime service. Prince doesn't want the medal and runs away. Bogart realizes Prince is in trouble and tracks him down. Checking in at the best hotel, Bogart receives a note from Prince. Before they can meet, Prince is murdered. Bogart knows Prince had confessed to murdering Lizabeth Scott's husband prior to entering the service. A witness, George Chandler, works at a local nightclub. Chandler has a letter from Prince to Bogart but cannot hand it to him because tough guy Marvin Miller is watching. At the club Bogart meets Scott. Nightclub owner Morris Carnovsky invites Bogart and Scott to his office for drinks. The drinks are drugged. When Bogart wakes up in his hotel room, he finds a dead Chandler. Bogart hides the body in a laundry cart just before detectives Charles Cane and George Eldredge show up. Bogart believes Carnovsky has Prince's letter and is able to gain entrance to his office. Bogart finds the letter that is in code. Before Bogart can decipher the code, he smells the scent of jasmine and then is struck on the head. When Bogart awakes, he finds himself in the hands of Carnovsky and the sadistic Miller. He refuses to tell them the contents of the letter, and Miller administers a savage beating. Bogart tells Carnovsky that he left an incriminating letter at his hotel. Miller takes Bogart to the hotel when they are met by Cane. A scuffle results and Bogart flees the police. Bogart leaves Bell to see Scott. Scott, who wears jasmine perfume, tells Bogart that he smelled jasmine outside Carnovsky's window. In a tense confrontation, Scott tells Bogart that it was she, not Prince, who in a struggle shot her husband. Scott told all to Carnovsky and gave him the murder weapon. Carnovsky uses the gun to obtain money from Scott. Bogart, who has fallen for Scott, decides to leave town with her after retrieving the murder weapon. Through a friendly underworld contact, Bogart obtains fire grenades. With Scott's help, Bogart enters Carnovsky's office and demands the gun. When Carnovsky initially refuses, Bogart ignites the fire grenades. In fear, Miller jumps through a window and is seriously injured. Carnovsky tells Bogart that Scott is married to him. Her marriage to the murdered man was bigamy. Scott married him because the second husband was in poor health and not expected to live long. As it turned out, he was in good health. Carnovsky insists he was the murderer but Bogart doesn't believe him. Bogart retrieves the gun as the flames begin to completely consume the office. The two men hurry to safety, with Carnovsky in the lead. When Carnovsky opens the door, shots are fired and Carnovsky is killed. As they drive away, Bogart tells Scott that the bullets were meant for him. Scott wants the murder weapon. When Bogart refuses to give it up, Scott shoots him. The wounded Bogart crashes the car into a tree and Scott is badly injured. Bogart now can prove Prince is not a murderer and eligible for military honors. At Scott's bedside, Bogart tells her not to hold on to life and Scott dies.

NOTES AND COMMENTARY: Rita Hayworth was the original choice for the role of Coral Chandler. She was feuding with Harry Cohn and expressed dissatisfaction with the script. Orson Welles, her estranged husband, cast Hayworth as Elsa in the film noir *The Lady from Shanghai* (Columbia, 1948).

Columbia borrowed Humphrey Bogart from Warner Bros. and Lizabeth Scott from Paramount.

There was a reference to the then scandalous photograph taken at the National Press Club in 1945 of Harry Truman playing the piano with leggy blonde Lauren Bacall on top. In an early scene aboard a train, William Prince as Johnny Drake finds he is to receive the Medal of Honor.

Bogart as Murdock remarks that perhaps the president will let Drake "sit on top of his piano."

Dead Reckoning was re-released in 1955 on a double-feature with *I Am the Law* (Columbia, 1938) with Edward G. Robinson.

REVIEWS: "Humphrey Bogart's typically tense performance raises this average whodunit quite a few notches. Film has good suspense and action and some smart direction and photoplay." *Variety*, 1/29/47

"There are a lot of things about the script of *Dead Reckoning* that an attentive spectator might find disconcerting, but the cumulative effect ... is all on the good side of entertainment. For those with a taste for rough stuff *Dead Reckoning* is almost certain to satisfy. All others hereby cautioned to proceed at their own risk." *New York Times*, 1/23/47

"This tricky film noir entry would have been routine had it not been for Bogart's magic. *Dead Reckoning* is a prime example of post–World War I–II film noir, in which the issues are hazy, the hero gropes, and the characters are even more unsavory than the gangsters of the 1930s—as if they were the debris of a war that had claimed the best of humanity." *Motion Picture Guide*, Nash and Ross

SUMMATION: This turns out to be a very satisfactory crime noir, thanks to Bogart's performance. He is able to show both a vulnerable side along with his tough side as he travels through standard noir territory. There are returning war veterans, dark streets and rooms, a sadistic henchman, voiceover narration and of course, a femme fatale. The narrative is a little disjointed and confusing but Bogart's performance smoothes it over. Some of the ending dialogue between Bogart and Lizabeth Scott owes its inspiration to *The Maltese Falcon* (Warner Bros., 1941). Leo Tover's photography aids Bogart in putting the film over.

"My son still loves me! Isn't that a remarkable thing?"

Death of a Salesman

(February 1952)

A Stanley Kramer Company Production

CAST: Willy Loman, Fredric March; Linda Loman, Mildred Dunnock; Biff Loman, Kevin McCarthy; Happy Loman, Cameron Mitchell; Charley, Howard Smith; Ben, Royal Beal; Bernard, Don Keefer; Stanley, Jesse White; Miss Francis, Claire Carleton; Howard Wagner, David Alpert; Uncredited: Subway Guard, Paul Bryar; Miss Forsythe, Elisabeth Fraser; Letta, Patricia Walker; Girls, Beverly Aadland, Wanda Perry and Christa Gail Walker; Boy, Roger Broaddus; Mothers, Jeanne Bates and Gail Bonney

CREDITS: Director, Laslo Benedek; Assistant Director, Frederick Briskin; Associate Producer, George Glass; Screenwriter, Stanley Roberts; Supervising Editor, Harry Gerstad; Editor, William Lyon; Art Director, Cary Odell; Set Decorator, William Kiernan; Cinematographer, Frank Planer; Makeup, Clay Campbell; Hair Stylist, Helen Hunt; Sound, George Cooper; Original Music, Alex North; Musical Director, Morris Stoloff; Production Designer, Rudolph Sternad; Production Manager, Clem Beauchamp

PRODUCTION DATES: August 31–October 1, 1951

SOURCE: play *Death of a Salesman* by Arthur Miller as produced on the stage by Kermit Bloomgarden and Walter Fried

RUNNING TIME: 110 minutes

STORY: Tired and dejected, salesman Fredric March returns home, unable to make his scheduled trip to Boston. His wife, Mildred Dunnock, tells March that their sons are home. The older son, Kevin McCarthy, has been working low-paying jobs in the west. The younger, Cameron Mitchell, is working at a dead-end job, but is able to afford his own apartment and enjoys romancing various women. March is upset at McCarthy's inability to make good. McCarthy tells March that he is going to see a former employer who will give him money to start his own business. Dunnock convinces March to see his boss, David Alpert, and ask for a job in town. Dunnock tells her sons that March is no longer salaried but works strictly on commission. Believing all will be successful, Mitchell arranges to have March and McCarthy meet him at a nice restaurant for dinner. March meets with Alpert, and Alpert fires him. McCarthy's old employer not only does not remember him but has no time to even talk with him. March goes to see his only friend and next door neighbor, Howard Smith. Smith has been lending March money each week to make it look like he's still getting orders.

At the office, March sees Smith's son Don Keefer, a highly successful attorney. Keefer tells March that McCarthy gave up on life a week after he flunked math, making him ineligible to graduate and attend college. Smith gives March enough money to pay his life insurance premium. At dinner, March and McCarthy tell of their uneventful day. March, stunned at McCarthy's failure, remembers that McCarthy came to Boston for his help in convincing the teacher to give him four points to enable him to graduate. McCarthy found March entertaining a young woman, Claire Carleton. Devastated at March's infidelity, McCarthy gave up on life. Later that night, March realizes that McCarthy still loves him. March decides his $20,000 insurance policy will give McCarthy the start he needs. Driving away, March deliberately crashes the car and dies in the impact. At the funeral, Dunnock, unable to cry, laments that the final mortgage payment had been made and now she'll live in the house alone.

NOTES AND COMMENTARY: The film version was faithful to Arthur Miller's stage play. To accommodate the censors, two changes were made. In the Boston hotel scene, a bottle of champagne was added to make it look more like a party than a sexual encounter. In the restaurant scene, Biff and Happy leave with the young ladies and return to the Loman home after spending time with them. In the film, Biff leaves the restaurant by himself and Happy takes both women home.

Death of a Salesman opened on Broadway at the Morosco Theater on February 10, 1949, and ran for 742 performances. Original cast members Mildred Dunnock, Cameron Mitchell, Howard Smith, Don Keefer and Royal Beal reprised their roles in this motion picture adaptation. Kevin McCarthy was in the London production of the play.

In February 1949, the first interest in bringing the play to the motion picture screen was exhibited by the Music Corporation of America with the play's director Elia Kazan and the star Lee J. Cobb. Twentieth Century–Fox would be the potential distributor. Then in September 1949, Miller indicated that he planned to make an independent production with Kazan directing. In August 1950, producers Jerry Wald and Norman Krasna wanted to film the play. In November, it looked as if Paramount would bring the play to the screen with William Wyler as director and producer and Kirk Douglas in the lead. Miller finally sold the rights to Stanley Kramer, who would produce the adaptation for Columbia release. Fredric March, who was Miller's first choice to play Willy Loman, received the lead role.

The Film received five Academy Award nominations: Best Actor, Fredric March; Best Supporting Actress, Mildred Dunnock; Best Supporting Actor, Kevin McCarthy; Best Cinematography, Frank Planer, and Best Musical Score, Alex North. None won the statue.

REVIEWS: "The vise-like grip which held Broadway theatergoers continues undiminished in Stanley Kramer's production of the film version. It's a must see. *Salesman* is a memorable if exhausting film performance." *Variety*, 12/12/51

"[T]his is a very good record of the classic American stage play. Miller's somber stage play retained much of its power in this film version featuring one of March's greatest performances." *Motion Picture Guide*, Nash and Ross

SUMMATION: A powerful noir of a man who is at a dead end in life. Fredric March delivers a sensational performance as a man who sees that the life he reveled in is lost and finally believes that only his death can open doors for a son whom he failed in a crucial time of the son's life. Mildred Dunnock is wonderful as March's long-suffering wife, who in the end cannot cry at her husband's funeral. Kevin McCarthy is truly realistic as the son, who feels his father's infidelities destroyed his life, and ultimately cannot find his way in the world. Laslo Benedek's direction guides the film well, with the excellent support of Frank Planer's photography. Planer's work enhances the dark to ratchet up the drama. The darkness seems to be a part of March's soul.

AT LAST THE SEARCH WAS OVER ...
Now he was face-to-face with the killers who had dishonored his wife!

Decision at Sundown

(November 1957)
A Scott–Brown Production
CAST: Bart Allison, Randolph Scott; Tate Kimbrough, John Carroll; Lucy Summerton, Karen Steele; Ruby James, Valerie French; Sam, Noah Beery; Dr. John Storrow, John Archer;

Sheriff Swede Hansen, Andrew Duggan; Otis (Bartender), James Westerfield; Charles Summerton, John Litel; Morley Chase, Ray Teal; Mr. Baldwin (Barber), Vaughn Taylor; the Reverend Zaron, Richard Deacon; Spanish, H.M. Wynant; Uncredited: Shotgun Guard, Jim Hayward; Abe (Livery Proprietor), Guy Wilkerson; Irv (Deputy Sheriff), Bob Steele; Pete (Deputy Sheriff), Abel Fernandez; Morley's Riders, Frank Chase, Bill Clark, Reed Howes, Pierce Lyden and Frank Scannell; Townsmen, Ethan Laidlaw, Mike Lally, Philo McCullough, Frank Mills, Frank O'Connor, Jack Perrin and Bob Reeves

Credits: Director, Budd Boetticher; Assistant Director, Sam Nelson; Producer, Harry Joe Brown; Associate Producer, Randolph Scott; Assistant to Producer, David Breen; Screenwriter, Charles Lang, Jr.; Editor, Al Clark; Art Director, Robert Peterson; Set Decorator, Frank A. Tuttle; Cinematography, Burnett Guffey; Recording Supervisor, John Livadary; Sound, Jean Valentino; Original Music and Musical Conductor, Heinz Roemheld; Technicolor Color Consultant, Henri Jaffa

Location Filming: Agoura, California

Production Dates: April 1–April 24, 1957

Source: novel *Decision at Sundown* by Vernon L. Fluharty

Running Time: 77 minutes

Color by Technicolor

Story: Randolph Scott and his pal Noah Beery come to the town of Sundown. Scott plans to exact revenge on town boss John Carroll for taking his wife, resulting in his wife committing suicide. Carroll is planning to marry Karen Steele. His mistress, Valerie French, is prepared to give Carroll up. As the wedding begins, Scott breaks it up by telling Steele that soon she'll be married to a dead man. Carroll's paid sheriff Andrew Duggan and his deputies bottle up Scott and Beery in a livery stable. Beery, realizing Scott's vengeance is based on his wife's past, tries to tell him that his wife was a tramp who had many lovers. Scott won't listen. Scott and Beery are told if they give up their quest, they can just ride out of town. Beery decides to leave Scott for awhile, drop his gun and holster in the dirt and get something to eat. Returning to the stable, Beery is gunned down by Duggan's deputy, H.M. Wynant. Scott is able to shoot Wynant in return. The citizens, led by rancher Ray Teal, decide to intervene. They want to see a showdown between first Scott and Duggan and then Scott and Carroll. Carroll, with his high-handed ways, has very few friends in town. Scott and Duggan meet. They draw. Scott is faster and Duggan is killed. In avoiding shots from Duggan, Scott cuts his gun hand on an overturned wagon. Dr. John Archer tends to Scott's hand and reinforces the fact that his wife went off willingly with Carroll. Even though injured, Scott refuses to call off the fight. French tries to persuade Carroll not to face Scott. Even though afraid, Carroll refuses to back down. Scott and Carroll meet. Before either men can draw, a shot rings out. French shoots Carroll in the shoulder, ending the confrontation. Carroll and French leave town. Scott finally realizes his quest for the man who he thought dishonored his wife was an empty one, causing the death of his best friend. In the saloon, Scott gets drunk. Teal wants to thank Scott for ridding the town of Carroll by buying him a drink. Scott violently refuses because if the town had stood up sooner, Beery would still be alive. Scott, who will never find peace within himself, rides out of town.

Notes and Commentary: Charles Lang's screenplay changed the tone of Vernon L. Fluharty's novel into a noir western. Some significant changes were made. The novel has Dr. John Storrow as the father of Lucy Summerville. Storrow's wife Helen left him because of his fondness for alcohol. Charles Summerville, the man Lucy thought was her father, committed suicide. Tate Kimbrough could ruin him because of his involvement in underhanded dealings. Finally Lucy learns that Storrow is her father and persuades him to reunite with her mother. Tate Kimbrough, a coward, does not want to meet Allison and tries to get out of town. His escape is prevented by rancher Morley Chase and his riders. Bart Allison and Kimbrough meet and fight, and Allison shoots him. Lucy tells Allison that she's the woman for him. After getting drunk, Allison plans to leave town when he's shot in the back by Kimbrough's mistress Ruby James. Storrow tells Lucy that after a month, Allison will completely mend. Allison had begun to have strong feelings for Lucy. Lucy feels she and Allison will get together.

Budd Boetticher met Karen Steele as he made preparations to direct *Decision at Sundown*. Enthralled by her beauty, he gave Steele the role of Lucy, a role that previously was going to June Lockhart. Boetticher fell in love with the actress up on the screen and married her. The marriage only lasted three years. Boetticher did use Steele in two more of the Randolph Scott westerns, *Westbound* (Warner Bros., 1959) and *Ride Lonesome* (Columbia, 1959).

The book *Decision at Sundown* was published with Michael Carder name on it as the author. Carder was the pseudonym of Vernon L. Fluharty.

Reviews: "This western stacks up as one of the better new-fangled westerns." *Variety*, 11/6/57

"Highly competent and brooding western; one of Randolph Scott's best." *Western Movies*, Pitts

"*Decision at Sundown* is a superior adult western, thoroughly downbeat, with Scott almost insane in his quest for vengeance." *Motion Picture Guide*, Nash and Ross

Summation: This is a very good western noir with an adult storyline. Boetticher's direction and Scott's performance propel the film to an unexpected conclusion. Boetticher is able to effectively balance violence with mature dialogue. Scott effectively portrays a man who's determined to exact his revenge even though he finally knows he's in the wrong. Valerie French gives a sensitive performance as Carroll's spurned mistress. Boetticher, whose western films usually feature the vistas of the American West, does very well in this town-bound story.

THE NIGHT'S DEADLIEST KILLERS ...
trapped by a waterfront woman's revenge!

The Devil's Henchmen

(September 1949)

Cast: Jess Arno, Warner Baxter; Silky, Mary Beth Hughes; Rhino, Mike Mazurki; Connie, Peggy Converse; Tip Banning, Regis Toomey; Captain, Harry Shannon; Sergeant Briggs, James Flavin; Uncredited: Murray, Julian Rivero; Bill Falls, Paul Marion; May, Ann Lawrence; Baggy, George Lloyd; Dock Police Guard, Lee Phelps; Detective Whalen, Ken Christy; Anderson, William Forrest; Elmer Hood, Al Bridge; Sailor, Ethan Laidlaw

Credits: Director, Seymour Friedman; Producer, Rudolph C. Flothow; Screenwriter, Eric Taylor; Editor, Richard Fantl; Art Director, Harold MacArthur; Set Decorator, James Crowe; Cinematographer, Henry Freulich; Musical Director, Mischa Bakaleinikoff

Production Dates: October 21, 1948–November 3, 1948

Running Time: 68 minutes

Story: Warner Baxter is selling salvage, supposedly plucked out of the harbor, to Regis Toomey. Toomey and Mary Beth Hughes are mixed up in a scheme, selling stolen furs being transported by freighters. The owner of a waterfront café, Peggy Converse, wants to be cut in on the racket. One ship's third mate, Paul Marion, wants a larger cut for his participation. Toomey has Hughes escort Marion to a deserted warehouse where he is murdered. Baxter was following Marion and is accosted by strongman Mike Mazurki. Baxter thinks fast and becomes friends with Mazurki. When Toomey learns that Baxter has a third mate's papers, he wants Baxter to work for him. Baxter is an insurance investigator trying to find out who is stealing cargo from ships. He theorizes that the switch is happening at sea. Baxter's contact person is Julian Rivero, an organ grinder, who is leaving notes in his pet monkey's hat. Captain Harry Shannon, a customer at the café, believes he knows Baxter from the past. With police investigating Marion's murder, Toomey decides they'll make one last haul and leave the area. Investigating, Baxter believes the stolen cargo is being brought into Al Bridge's shop. Baxter is picked to participate in the heist but Mazurki is ordered to stay with Baxter. Needing to get information to the authorities, Baxter purchases Rivero's monkey. Baxter puts a note in the monkey's cap, but Converse intercepts it. Shannon, the brains behind the operation, accompanies Baxter and Mazurki, and the heist goes off without a hitch. Arriving at Bridge's shop, Baxter is surprised that the authorities aren't present. Suddenly the police arrive; there is an exchange of bullets. Mazurki is killed and the rest of the gang is arrested. Converse had taken the note to the police. Her husband had been killed by the gang a few years back, and she was trying to bring the gang to justice. Baxter and Converse plan to see each other socially.

Notes and Commentary: A *Variety* re-

***The Devil's Henchman* (1949).**

viewer incorrectly identified the film as the "latest in the Crime Doctor series."

Reviews: "A decent programmer." *Motion Picture Guide*, Nash and Ross

"The action, and there's plenty of it, is centered on seashore and shipping and gives out with enough suspense and capable acting to rate a good secondary spot on the double bill in first run houses." *Variety*, 7/23/52

Summation: This is a good "B" noir mystery. Warner Baxter, in his first role after the completion of the Crime Doctor series, seems comfortable in the role of Jess Arno. Some familiar faces from low-budget features have prominent parts, and all perform capably. Seymour Friedman's direction provides the necessary pace and suspense. This is a decided improvement on the previous Arno caper, *No Place for a Lady* (Columbia, 1943).

A WEIRD JUNGLE CURSE haunted this beauty! Madden this scientist! Shocked the detective!... The eeriest mystery you'll ever see!

The Devil's Mask

(May 1946)

Cast: Janet Mitchell, Anita Louise; Jack Packard, Jim Bannon; Rex Kennedy, Michael Duane; Louise Mitchell, Mona Barrie; Doc Long, Barton Yarborough; Dr. Karger, Ludwig Donath; Leon Hartman, Paul E. Burns; Prof. Arthur Logan, Frank Wilcox; Uncredited: Narrator, Frank Martin; Willard, Edward Earle; Mendoza, Fred Godoy; Halliday, Richard Hale; Museum Guard, Bud Averill; Frank, Coulter Irwin; Captain Quinn, Thomas E. Jackson; Quentin Mitchell, Frank Mayo; John, John Elliott; Karger's Nurse, Mary Newton; Brophy, Harry Strang

Credits: Director, Henry Levin; Producer,

Wallace MacDonald; Screenwriter, Charles O'Neal; Additional Dialogue, Dwight Babcock; Editor, Jerome Thoms; Art Director, Robert Peterson; Set Decorator, George Montgomery; Cinematographer, Henry Freulich; Musical Director, Mischa Bakaleinikoff

PRODUCTION DATES: February 6–February 23, 1946

RUNNING TIME: 66 minutes

SOURCE: the original radio program "I Love a Mystery" written and directed by Carlton E. Morse

STORY: A plane crashes on takeoff. No lives are lost but all baggage is destroyed except a box containing a shrunken head. The head is taken to the local museum where private detectives Jim Bannon and Barton Yarborough meet Mona Barrie, whose husband owned the museum. Among the exhibits are a case with five Jivaro shrunken heads and a Jivaro blowgun. Barrie is being followed by Michael Duane and thinks she is in danger of being killed. Duane is the boyfriend of Anita Louise, Barrie's stepdaughter. Duane and Barrie visit her uncle. Paul E. Burns, a taxidermist. His shop is decorated like a jungle, with many stuffed animals and one live black leopard, a present from Louise's father, Frank Mayo. Louise tells Burns that she hates Barrie and Prof. Frank Wilcox; she suspects they are lovers based on some love letters from Wilcox to Barrie she found. Louise told Mayo about the letters. Louise also believes that Barrie murdered Mayo when they were on a South America expedition. Barrie has Wilcox show slide photos to Bannon and Yarborough of Mayo on the expedition. While the lights are out, a mysterious figure uses a blowgun to shoot a poison dart into the room, narrowly missing Barrie and Wilcox. As the figure makes his getaway; he is confronted by the butler, John Elliott, who recognizes the intruder. A dart from the blowgun kills Elliott instantly. Louise now believes Mayo is alive and is the murderer. A headless body is found and it is thought that it is Mayo. Bannon and Yarborough go to Burns' shop to verify that the head found in the plane wreckage was that of a Jivaro native. Next the detectives go to the museum to examine the heads on exhibit. One of the heads has red hair, just like Mayo. Bannon examines the cords on the lips of the head and finds a clue that takes him to Burns. Duane is already confronting Burns, telling him that he murdered Mayo. Louise arrives at the taxidermist shop and tells Duane that he must be mistaken. Duane picks up the phone to call the police but Burns had cut the phone cord. Burns then admits that he killed Mayo. Mayo disappeared in South America to come back to San Francisco to see if Barrie and Wilcox were carrying on an affair. When Mayo came to Burns, Burns took this opportunity to kill Mayo because he hated him for killing animals for sport. Bannon arrives at the shop. Burns has already wounded Duane and turns his attention on Bannon. Bannon hides in the jungle so Burns unleashes his leopard to finish him off. Burns dies at the leopard's claws instead. Louise discovers the letters were written prior to Barrie meeting Mayo, and stepmother and stepdaughter are reconciled. In addition, Louise and Duane have fallen in love.

NOTES AND COMMENTARY: The working title for this film was *The Head.*

REVIEWS: "An unassuming whodunit." *The Columbia Story*, Hirshhorn

"Enjoyable programmer from the short-lived 'I Love a Mystery' series." *Motion Picture Guide*, Nash and Ross

SUMMATION: Screenwriters Charles O'Neal and Dwight Babcock fashioned a neat, suspenseful noir murder mystery and Henry Levin directed the tale nicely. Jim Bannon and Barton Yarborough are in fine form as the detectives. Also, a special nod to Anita Louise, who brings off her role convincingly, ranging from anger to hysteria to finally peace within herself. Cinematographer Henry Freulich's camerawork adds to the dark mood of this story, especially in a hypnosis scene with Louise.

"Why would a dame like her go for a guy like me?"

Drive a Crooked Road

(April 1954)

CAST: Eddie Shannon, Mickey Rooney; Barbara Mathews, Dianne Foster; Steve Norris, Kevin McCarthy; Harold Baker, Jack Kelly; Ralph, Harry Landers; Phil, Jerry Paris; Carl, Paul Picerni; Don, Dick Crockett; Uncredited: Garage

Foreman, Mort Mills; Marge, Peggy Maley; James Snyder (Bank Teller), Patrick Miller; Wells, Jeffrey Stone; Pretty Girls, Irene Bolton, Linda Dawson and Diana Dawson; Police Officers, John Close, John Damier, Mike Mahoney and George Paul

Credits: Director, Richard Quine; Assistant Director, Jack Corrick; Producer, Jonie Taps; Story, James Benson Nablo, Adaptor, Richard Quine; Screenplay, Blake Edwards; Editor, Jerome Thoms; Art Director, Walter Holscher; Set Decorator, James Crowe; Cinematographer, Charles Lawton, Jr.; Sound, George Cooper; Musical Director, Ross DiMaggio

Song: "From Here to Eternity" (Karger and Wells)—instrumental

Production Dates: mid–October–early November 1953

Running Time: 83 minutes

Story: Into the life of mechanic and part-time race driver Mickey Rooney comes the beautiful Dianne Foster. Foster is working with her boyfriend Kevin McCarthy and Jack Kelly to persuade Rooney to drive the getaway car in a bank robbery. At first Rooney turns the proposal down. When he believes his acceptance would result into a permanent relationship with Foster, he relents. Feeling sorry for Rooney, Foster wants to tell him that their relationship has no future but McCarthy won't let her. The robbery comes off without a hitch. Afterwards, Rooney finds that Foster is no longer living in her apartment. Rooney goes to McCarthy and Kelly's beach house looking for Foster. McCarthy tells Rooney that he doesn't know where Foster is but Foster comes out of an adjoining room. Foster tells Rooney the truth, that he was used. Believing that Rooney will now go to the police, McCarthy tells Kelly to murder him. Kelly makes Rooney drive. Suddenly Rooney sends the car down an embankment, turning it over. Rooney, though bloodied, survives the crash but Kelly is killed. Rooney takes Kelly's gun and starts walking back to the beach house. Foster's actions have angered McCarthy and he begins slapping her around. Foster runs to the beach but McCarthy catches her. Rooney shows up and tries to get McCarthy to back off. McCarthy kicks Rooney, knocking him down. Simultaneously Rooney fires the gun, killing McCarthy.

***Drive a Crooked Road* (1954).**

The police show up as Rooney is trying to console Foster.

Notes and Commentary: Working titles for this film were *Little Giant, Johnny Big Shot* and *Speedy Shannon.*

Reviews: "An occasionally interesting melodrama proving that crime doesn't pay." *Variety,* 3/17/54

"A crisply done film noir with Rooney taken in by the universal emotional state that was at the root of many noir heroes' problems, loneliness." *Motion Picture Guide,* Nash and Ross

Summation: This is an understated little noir gem. Rooney gives one of his best performances as a lonely little man who is seduced into a criminal act by a beautiful woman. He beautifully understates his role, giving his character added pathos. Kevin McCarthy and Jack Kelly play their parts well, on the surface an open friendly manner but underneath pure ruthlessness and menace. The beautiful Dianne Foster is excellent as the femme fatale who has a change of heart in the treatment of Rooney. Richard Quine directs with a sure hand, moving the story forward to its tragic ending and bringing noir to a high level. Charles Lawton, Jr. camerawork is first-rate, using the shadows to enhance the mood. Don't miss this one.

SAVAGE SUSPENSE SPANS THE GRANITE GORGE!

Edge of Eternity

(December 1959)

Cast: Les Martin, Cornel Wilde; Janice Kendon, Victoria Shaw; Scotty O'Brien, Mickey Shaughnessy; Sheriff Edwards, Edgar Buchanan; Bob Kendon, Rian Garrick; Bill Ward, Jack Elam; Jim Kendon, Alexander Lockwood; Gas Station Attendant, Dabbs Greer; Eli Jones, Tom Fadden; Sam Houghton, Wendell Holmes; Uncredited: Whitmore, John Roy; Dealer, George Cisar; Man at Motel Pool, Don Siegel; Motel Attendant, Hope Summers; Pilot, Buzz Westcott; Suds Reese, Ted Jacques; Deputy Sheriff, George Ross; Coroner, John Ayres; Deputy Radio Operator, William Shaw; Don, Paul Bailey

Credits: Associate Producer and Director, Don Siegel; Assistant Director, Carter DeHaven, Jr.; Producer, Kendrick Sweet; Story, Ben Markson and Knut Swenson; Screenwriters, Knut Swenson and Richard Collins; Editor, Jerome Thoms; Art Director, Robert Peterson; Set Decorator, Frank A. Tuttle; Cinematographer, Burnett Guffey; Makeup, Ben Lane; Hair Stylist, Helen Hunt; Sound, George Cooper; Recording Supervisor, John Livadary; Original Music and Musical Conductor, Daniele Amfitheatrof; Color Consultant, Henri Jaffa; Flying Sequences, Skymasters International

Filming Locations: Kingman, Oatman and Grand Canyon National Park, Arizona

Production Dates: April 27–May 21, 1959

Running Time: 80 minutes

Color by Eastmancolor

Filmed in CinemaScope

Story: An unknown assailant attacks John Roy on a ridge of the Grand Canyon. In the scuffle, the assailant plunges over the cliff to his death. Roy is able to make his way to the shack of Tom Fadden, a caretaker for a mining company. Fadden tries to get Deputy Sheriff Cornel Wilde to come to his shack. Before Wilde can respond, a car recklessly driven by mining operator Alexander Lockwood's daughter Victoria Shaw comes tearing by. Fadden returns to his shack to find Roy dead by hanging. No one can identify the murdered man. Sheriff Edgar Buchanan assigns Wilde to the case. Wilde learns that a worker for a guano company is missing. In addition, Shaw tells Wilde there is still plenty of gold but until the price of gold goes up, it won't be mined. Shaw adds that gold would have to be smuggled into Mexico to be profitable. In a picture in Fadden's shack, Fadden sees the murdered man standing next to Lockwood. An intruder enters the shack and murders Fadden. Through a clue supplied by Shaw, Wilde learns the murdered man's identity and that he was the head of the mining combine. When questioning Lockwood, Wilde sees Lockwood's son Rian Garrick receive a phone call and then rush out of the house followed by Shaw. Wilde follows Shaw. Garrick goes to a small airfield to meet saloon owner Mickey. Shaughnessy, head of a smuggling ring. Shaughnessy admits to Garrick that he murdered Roy and Fadden. Garrick wants no part of murder and tries to back out. The two men fight and Shaughnessy kills Garrick. Shaw drives up and Shaughnessy forces her to accompany him. Wilde arrives and gives chase but a well-aimed shot disables his vehicle. Shaughnessy has a boat waiting for him at Lake Mead. He commandeers a "bucket" to take him and Shaw to safety on the other side of the Grand Canyon. Wilde jumps in, the two men fight and Shaughnessy falls to his death. Wilde and Shaw end in each other's arm.

Notes and Commentary: Working titles for the film were *Rim of the Canyon*, *Dancing Bucket*, *Deadly Is the Canyon* and *Satan's Bucket*.

Initially Felicia Farr was scheduled to play the role of Janice Kendon. When Farr's exclusive contract with Columbia was terminated, she declined the part.

Stunt performers Chuck Couch, Rosemary Johnson and Guy Way, who doubled for the stars in the Grand Canyon sequence, were professional aerialists.

Reviews: "Well-made meller set in the beauty of the Grand Canyon. A tightly made melodrama, for mood and excitement, taken sparkling advantage of Arizona's Grand Canyon. A moderately budgeted film that is entertaining, slickly produced and to the point." *Variety*, 11/4/59

"Exciting modern-day western actioner. Superb location photography by Burnett Guffey and exciting direction by Siegel help gloss over the rather weak script and make this film well worth watching." *Motion Picture Guide*, Nash and Ross

Summation: This is a routine noir murder mystery set in the vistas of the Grand Canyon and surrounding vicinity. Siegel keeps the story moving fast enough to possibly whisk plot contrivances by most moviegoers. It stretches credulity to believe the murderer knows exactly when to strike at Fadden's shack. There is no groundwork laid to direct or misdirect the audience to the killer. Siegel does move into high gear when the chase begins and keeps the tension building until the exciting conclusion.

THE INSIDE STORY BEHIND THE MOST AMAZING CRASH-OUT IN CRIME ANNALS!

Escape from San Quentin

(September 1957)

A Clover Production

Cast: Mike Gilbert, Johnny Desmond; Robbie, Merry Anders; Roy Gruber, Richard Devon; Hap Graham, Roy Engel; Richie, William Bryant; Curley Gruber, Ken Christy; Mack, Larry Blake; Uncredited: Lang, Paul Bryar; Piggy, Don Devlin; Mendez, Victor Millan; Sampson, John Frederick; Jerry, Dean Fredericks; Georgie, Barry Brooks; Bud, Lennie Smith; Georgia Gilbert, Peggy Maley; Police Lieutenant, Tristram Coffin; Policemen, Dennis Moore and Terry Frost; Border Guard, Dan White

Credits: Director, Fred F. Sears; Assistant Director, Leonard Katzman; Producer, Sam Katzman; Screenwriter, Raymond T. Marcus; Editor, Saul A. Goodkind; Art Director, Paul Palmentola; Set Decorator, Sidney Clifford; Cinematographer, Benjamin H. Kline; Sound, Josh Westmoreland; Original Music and Musician, Laurindo Almeida; Technical Advisors, Hank Coffin and the Cessna Aircraft Co.

Location Filming: Lake Enchanto, Malibu, California

Song: "Lonely Lament" (Desmond)—sung by Johnny Desmond

Production Dates: June 4–June 14, 1957

Running Time: 81 minutes

Story: Convict Richard Devon wants fellow inmate Johnny Desmond to join him in breaking out of their prison camp. Desmond initially refuses, but changes his mind after receiving a letter advising him that his wife, Peggy Maley, wants a divorce. Complicating the escape plans is inmate Roy Engel, who wants to participate. Desmond, who is a pilot, and Devon plan to hijack one of the small planes and fly to Oregon. The addition of Engel might make a risky takeoff. As Desmond tries to get the plane in the air, Devon gets on board and clubs Engel until he drops to the runway. Desmond has to land the low-on-fuel plane on a lonely highway. Desmond and Devon steal a car and head for Los Angeles where Devon's father

Ken Christy has Devon's stolen money. Though badly hurt, Engel is also able to escape. Engel rounds up his old gang and plans to take Devon's money. The gang keeps a close watch on Christy. By hiding in William Bryant's truck, Devon is able to contact Christy. Engel grabs Bryant and forces him to take him to Devon. Meanwhile, Desmond contacts Marley's sister, Merry Anders, and asks her to get a message to Marley. Marley wants nothing to do with Desmond. Anders goes back to Desmond with the news. Anders has a crush on Desmond. At the motel, using Bryant as a shield, Engel busts into Devon's room. Christy has brought some of the money. Engel grabs it and shoots Bryant in the leg. Leaving the motel, Engel is recognized by two policemen. There's an exchange of gunfire, and one of the policemen's shots ruptures the gas tank of Engel's car, engulfing the car in a ball of flame. Knowing Desmond is soft on Anders, Devon treats Desmond and Anders as prisoners and drives to Tijuana. Christy is supposed to bring the rest of the stolen money to Tijuana but sends a note to meet on the California side. Devon decides to go back across the border. Seeing the wounded Bryant as a liability, Devon throws him down an elevator shaft. Devon owes lawyer Victor Millan money so he takes him along. At the motel where Devon is to meet Christy, Anders tells Millan about Devon. Devon locks Millan and Anders in the bathroom, planning to kill them before he leaves. Desmond convinces Devon that he can rent a plane from a nearby airfield and he can fly Devon and himself to safety. Instead Desmond goes to the motel office to call the police only to find police already there. The police thought Devon was a drug smuggler, especially since they caught Christy with a suitcase full of money. Desmond tells the police that the motel room is a hostage situation and suggests that he and a plainclothes policeman enter the room and capture Devon. Devon is suspicious of the situation. When Millan breaks a window, Devon panics and fires a shot at the policeman. Desmond pushes the policeman to safety while taking a bullet in the shoulder. In the melee, the room is thrown into darkness. Desmond and Devon engage in a savage struggle until Desmond gains the upper hand. Although Desmond has to return to prison, it may not be for long because of his part in Devon's capture. It looks like Anders will wait for him.

Notes and Commentary: Blacklisted screenwriter Bernard Gordon used the pseudonym Raymond T. Marcus.

Review: "A prison melodrama of no distinction whatsoever." *The Columbia Story*, Hirschhorn

Summation: Exciting and brutal noir of escaped criminals on the run. Underrated director Fred F. Sears keeps the story moving at a fast clip utilizing unique camera angles and close-ups to good advantage. Sears, when on his game as he is here, could direct these "B" crime noirs as well as anyone. Richard Devon is quite good as the violent Roy Gruber with the aura of menace. Top-billed Johnny Desmond turns in an okay performance except when he tries a little too hard to act tough. Benjamin H. Kline's camerawork compliments Sears' direction.

Slipping Silently Out of the Fog ... Came MURDER!

Escape in the Fog

(April 1945)

Cast: Paul Devon, Otto Kruger; Eileen Carr, Nina Foch; Barry Malcolm, William Wright; Schiller, Konstantin Shayne; Hausmer, Ivan Triesault; George Smith, Ernie Adams; Uncredited: Policeman on Bridge, Robert B. Williams; Mr. Boggs, Harrison Greene; Thomas (Butler), John Elliott; Hilary Gale, Leslie Denison; Chang Yong, Wing Foo; Kolb, Noel Cravat; Hotel Doorman, Chuck Hamilton; Mrs. Devon, Mary Newton; Taxi Driver, Shelley Winters; Lieutenant Commander, Tom Dillon; Harbor Patrol Navy Officer, Frank O'Connor; Port Director, Emmett Vogan; Bartender, Frank Mayo; Police Desk Sergeant, Ralph Dunn; Officer Sullivan, Eddie Parker; Gil Brice, John Tyrrell; Simmons, Charles Jordan; Screaming Woman, Jessie Arnold; Chinese Boy, Chin Kuang Chow; Chinese Man, William Yip; Detective, Edmund Cobb; Policemen, Dick Jensen, Elmo Lincoln and Joe Palma; Plainclothesman, LeRoy Taylor; Accident Witness, Heinie Conklin

CREDITS: Director, Oscar Boetticher, Jr.; Producer, Wallace MacDonald; Screenwriter, Aubrey Wisberg; Editor, Jerome Thoms; Art Director, Jerome Pycha, Jr.; Cinematographer, George Meehan

PRODUCTION DATES: December 6–December 22, 1944

RUNNING TIME: 63 minutes

STORY: On a foggy night, Nina Foch is walking across a bridge over the San Francisco Bay when a cab pulls up. Men come out of the cab, fighting. Konstantin Shayne, Ivan Triesault and Noel Cravat force William Wright to the ground. One man is prepared to plunge a knife into Wright when Foch screams. Foch has had a bad dream but her screams bring hotel guests William Wright and Harrison Greene to investigate. Foch recognizes Wright as the victim in the dream and tells him about it. They become romantically interested in each other. Army officer Wright is a psychological warfare expert. At the hotel, he receives a new assignment and is told to report to Otto Kruger in San Francisco. Hotel employee Ernie Adams, a German spy, alerts chief spy Shayne that Wright is returning. Wright convinces Foch to come to San Francisco with him. Wright receives a dangerous assignment and is handed a packet that must not land in enemy hands. Shayne, a clock maker taking care of Kruger's prize grandfather clock, has installed a recording device and learns of Wright's assignment. The spies kidnap Wright and obtain the packet. After Wright leaves Foch, she has a premonition that Wright is in danger and goes to Kruger. Kruger dismisses Foch. After Foch leaves, Kruger receives a phone call substantiating Foch's fears. Foch goes to the bridge and her dream becomes reality. In the struggle, Wright tosses the packet into the bay. Foch's screams alert policeman Robert B. Williams, who fires at the spies, driving them off. Wright tells Foch the packet will float and he starts a search. The packet landed on a Navy vessel and was returned to police in Half Moon Bay. Shayne has placed an ad in the paper stating he found the packet. Foch answers the ad and is captured. Triesault's attempt to obtain the packet fails and he is arrested. The arrest is seen by Adams, who informs Shayne. Shayne sends Wright a note to bring the packet or Foch will die. Wright alerts the police and walks into the trap. At Kruger's home, he notices that his clock has stopped and, investigating, finds the recording device. Kruger and his men head for Shayne's watch repair shop. Meanwhile, Adams brings Wright to the back of Shayne's shop. Wright's leg is shackled to an iron bar. As Shayne and Adams prepare to leave the shop, Shayne turns on the gas, giving Wright and Foch ten minutes to live. Wright is able to send a signal. Passersby smash the shop's window. Kruger and his men arrive and release the captives. Kruger has the area surrounded. Shayne and Adams go to the rooftops. Shayne decides they should split up. Adams is to provide a diversion so Shayne can escape through the dragnet. Wright sees movement on the roof and is able to get behind Shayne. Adams positions himself behind Wright. Shayne and Adams fire at Wright at the same moment. Wright ducks in time so that Shayne and Adams kill each other. Wright and Foch plan to marry.

NOTES AND COMMENTARY: The working title of this film was *Out of the Fog*. According to *The Hollywood Reporter*, initially the film was to be directed by William Castle. The female lead was to have been Lynn Merrick.

The film opens with a shot of the San Francisco Bridge. The camera closes in to show Nina Foch on the bridge walkway where she is asked by a policeman if she's there to kill herself. Unfortunately the real San Francisco Bridge does not have such a walkway. Screenwriter Aubrey Wisberg may have confused that bridge with the Golden Gate Bridge.

REVIEWS: "A nifty spy thriller with sturdy production values. [Boetticher] has given plot fast, suspenseful direction to mark it as first-class supporting feature." *Variety*, 5/18/45

"A far-fetched, undistinguished programmer..." *The Columbia Story*, Hirschhorn

"A forgettable programmer which would have been forgotten by now had director Boetticher not gone to direct a number of good westerns in the 1950s starring Randolph Scott. This minor entry offers no clue to his talent." *Motion Picture Review*, Nash and Ross

SUMMATION: A brisk pace is the salvation of this spy noir. Director Boetticher (billed as Oscar Boetticher, Jr.) guides the story with a sure hand, glossing quickly over the contrived plot elements. The aspect of lovely Nina Foch having a dream forewarning danger to William Wright, a man she has never met, and then losing this gift, is hard to believe. George Meehan's photography adds tension and suspense as he clothes the proceedings in darkness or fog. Foch as the damsel drawn into danger takes the acting honors with the rest of the cast more than adequate.

TERROR ... TENSION ... ALMOST MORE THAN THE HEART CAN BEAR!

Experiment in Terror

(June 1962)

A Blake Edwards Production

A Geoffrey–Kate Production Picture

ALTERNATE TITLE: The Grip of Fear

CAST: John Ripley, Glenn Ford; Kelly Sherwood, Lee Remick; Toby Sherwood, Stefanie Powers; Brad, Roy Poole; Popcorn, Ned Glass; Lisa, Anita Loo; Nancy Ashton, Patricia Huston; Special Agent, Gilbert Green; Captain Moreno, Clifton James; Masher, Al Avalon; Chuck, William Bryant; FBI Agent #1, Dick Crockett; Landlord, James Lamphier; and Ross Martin as Red Lynch; Uncredited: Janie (FBI Switchboard Operator), Barbara Collentine; FBI Office Secretary, Mary Ellen Popel; Louella Hendricks, Judee Morton; Welk, Frederic Downs; Penny (Bank Teller), Mari Lynn; Raymond Burkhardt (Bank Manager), William Sharon; Dave (Toby's Boyfriend), Harvey Evans; Coroner, William Remick; Radio Man, George Moorman; Truck Driver, Harold Goodwin; Chinese Waiter, Tommy H. Lee; Pastor, Beal Wong; Hospital Superintendent, Fay McKenzie; Yung (Attorney), Clarence Lung; Joey Soong, Warren Hsieh; Drunk, Sidney Miller; Nurse, Audrey Swanson; Dick, Edward Mallory; Taxi Driver, Gil Perkins; Saleswoman, Karen Norris; Hangout Waitress, Helen Jay; Hangout Cook, Mario Cimino; Helicopter Pilot, Bob Dempsey; TV Director, Russ Whiteman; Man at Ballpark, Ray Kellogg; Stadium Announcer, Robert Coffey; Edna, Sherry O'Neal; FBI Agents, James T. Callahan, Fred Coby, Kenny Johnson, Kelly McCormick, Bill Neff, Richard Norris, David Tomack and Ken Wales; Baseball Players, Harvey Kuenn, Don Drysdale, Wally Moon and John Roseboro; Dodgers Game Announcer, Vin Scully

CREDITS: Director and Producer, Blake Edwards; Assistant Director, Sam Nelson; Associate Producer, Don Peters; Screenwriters, the Gordons; Editor, Patrick McCormack; Art Director, Robert Peterson; Set Decorator, James M. Crowe; Cinematographer, Philip Lathrop; Makeup, Ben Lane; Sound, Lambert Day; Sound Supervisor, Charles J. Rice; Original Music, Henry Mancini; Orchestrators, Leo Shuken and Jack Hayes; Script Supervisor, Betty Abbott

SONGS: "Nancy" (Mancini)—played by Jimmy Rowles, "Gwine to Rune All Night (De Camptown Races)" (Foster), "When the Saints Go Marching In" (traditional), "Bill Bailey, Will You Please Come Home" (Cannon), "Wiegenlied, Op. 49, No. 4 (Lullaby)" (Brahms) and "Listen to the Mockingbird" (Milburn)—played by unknown organist

LOCATION FILMING: San Francisco and Fairfax, Marin County, California

SOURCE: novel *Operation Terror* by the Gordons

RUNNING TIME: 123 minutes

STORY: Returning home from a party, Lee Remick enters her garage and is accosted by a shadowy figure, Ross Martin. Martin tells her that she must steal money from her bank or either she or her younger sister Stefanie Powers will be killed. After Martin leaves, Remick calls FBI Agent Glenn Ford. Before Remick can tell of her plight, Martin enters the house and breaks the connection. Knowing Remick's name, Ford starts a search and finally is connected with Remick. Afraid to have the FBI come to her house, Remick arranges to have Ford meet her at the bank in the morning. Remick never saw her assailant's face but knows he has an asthmatic condition because of his strange way of breathing. Ford requests Remick to play along with the caper until he can identify the mystery man. Remick tells Powers never to be alone to minimize the chance that Martin will strike at her. From FBI files, Martin is the only one identified with an asthmatic condition. Good police work finally identifies Anita Loo as a possible girlfriend. Loo provides minimal assistance since Martin has given financial assistance to her son Warren Hsieh's medical condition. Finally, Martin is ready to strike. Remick is told to steal $100,000 and then follow his directions. To ensure Remick's cooperation, Martin kidnaps Powers and locks her in a fur storage room. Martin's instructions take Remick to a baseball game at Candlestick Park. No one approaches Remick during the game.

Meanwhile, FBI agents follow clues that lead them to the fur storage room and Powers is rescued. As Remick leaves the game, Martin makes his move. Ford and the other agents have been watching Remick. Ford grabs Martin as other agents hustle Remick to safety. Martin breaks away and fires a shot into the crowd. The crowd parts and Martin runs to the baseball field. Standing on the pitcher's mound, Martin prepares to fire again. Ford fires two bullets, killing Martin. Powers is brought to the ball park and she and Remick are reunited.

Notes and Commentary: The basic plot of the Gordons' novel *Operation Terror* was followed very closely. Some minor changes were made. The story was moved from Los Angeles to San Francisco. Ross Martin's character name was changed to Lynch from Dillon and Anita Loo's character became Lisa instead of Shiri. The names of other minor characters were also changed. A hint of romance between Ripley and a FBI secretary was eliminated. In the book the finale took place at the Los Angeles Rams–Baltimore Colts football game at the Coliseum instead of a baseball game at Candlestick as depicted in the film.

Experiment in Terror was John Ripley's second appearance on the motion picture screen. Broderick Crawford played FBI Agent Ripley in *Down Three Dark Streets* (United Artists, 1954). The Gordons wrote screenplays for both films that were adapted from their novels.

The ticket to the baseball game shows the date as August 18, 1961.

Reviews: "The film treatment embraces a number of unnecessary character bits that merely extend the plot and despite their striking individual reaction, deter from the suspense buildup." *Variety*, 12/31/61

"Not satisfied with a fairly straightforward 'war of attrition' plot, director Blake Edwards gussied up *Experiment in Terror* with far too many arty, self-conscious, cutely angled shots for his picture's good. The end result was less an experiment in terror than an experiment in lily-gilding." *The Columbia Story*, Hirschhorn

Summation: This is a quite good caper noir. Philip Lathrop's photography complements the mood of the film brilliantly. Glenn Ford is fine and Stefanie Powers also does well, especially in the scene where, partially undressed, she fears rape from Ross Martin. But the acting honors go first to Remick who plays a woman terrified for her life but able to overcome these fears. Martin can be singled out for a beautifully restrained performance that conveys fear to Remick without unnecessary histrionics. The Gordons' screenplay could have been shortened to intensify the suspense; the scenes with informant Ned Glass and murder victim Patricia Huston, although in the novel, only served to lengthen the proceedings.

IS THIS THE FACE THAT LAUNCHED A THOUSAND CRIMES?

The Face Behind the Mask

(January 1941)

Alternate Title: Behind the Mask

Cast: Janos Szabo, Peter Lorre; Helen Williams, Evelyn Keyes; Jim O'Hara, Don Beddoe; Dinky, George E. Stone; Watts, John Tyrrell; Benson, Al Seymour; Harry, Stanley Brown; Jeff, James Seay; Johnson, Warren Ashe; Chief O'Brien, Charles C. Wilson; Terry Finnegan, George McKay; Uncredited: Ship's Stewart, David Oliver; Pedestrian Lighting Cigarette, Eddie Foster; Police Officer 643, Lee Shumway; Hotel Cook, Ralph Peters; Tenant Who Cooks in Room, Al Hill; Man Who Calls Fire Department, Jack Gardner; Burn Treatment Nurse, Mary Currier; Burn Treatment Physician, Ben Taggart; Shocked Nurse, Claire Rochelle; Jonathan Harris (Watchmaker), Walter Soderling; Stimson (Clerk), Harry Strang; Man on Dock Who Loses Wallet, John Dilson; Flophouse Manager, Al Bridge; Dr. Beckett, Edwin Stanley; Dr. Cheever, Frank Reicher; Gas Station Attendant, Chuck Hamilton; Mrs. Perkins, Sarah Edwards; Mr. Perkins, Joel Friedkin; Mike Cary (Pilot), Sam Ash, Detective, Lee Phelps

Credits: Director, Robert Florey; Producer, Wallace MacDonald; Story, Arthur Levinson; Screenwriters, Allen Vincent and Paul Jarrico; Editor, Charles Nelson; Art Director, Lionel Banks; Cinematographer, Franz Planer; Musical Director, Morris Stoloff

***The Face Behind the Mask* (1941).**

LOCATION FILMING: Oxnard Sand Dunes, Oxnard, California

PRODUCTION DATES: November 6–26, 1940

RUNNING TIME: 69 minutes

SOURCE: the radio play "Interim" by Thomas Edward O'Connell

STORY: Immigrant Peter Lorre is befriended by Police Lieutenant Don Beddoe who directs him to a hotel run by George McKay. Another tenant, Al Hill, accidentally starts a fire and Lorre's face is horribly burned. Because of his facial scars, Lorre is unable to find work. He is contemplating suicide when he meets small time thief George E. Stone. Lorre and Stone become friends. When they're broke and Stone is ill, Lorre turns to crime to obtain money. Lorre decides to become a gang leader in order to obtain money to restore his face. Before Lorre can see the primary plastic surgeon Frank Reicher, his assistant Edwin Stanley constructs a facial mask. Former gang leader James Seay, released from prison, makes an unsuccessful attempt to take back leadership. Reicher tells Lorre that he waited too late, that surgery cannot help him. Despondent as he leaves the physician's office, he bumps into the blind Evelyn Keyes. Although Lorre continues his life of crime, he begins spending time with Keyes. Keyes gets Lorre to tell his story since coming to America. Because of his love for Keyes, Lorre turns over gang leadership to Seay. Lorre tells Stone that he and Keyes are getting married and moving to a small town to live. Seay thinks Lorre is working with Beddoe and wants to get even. Seay tortures Stone until he tells where Lorre is living. Seay goes to Lorre's house and distracts Lorre while his men attach an explosive to Lorre's car radio. Stone is shot and thrown from a speeding car. The wounded Stone is able to get the word to Lorre about the bomb. Knowing Keyes is getting into the car, Lorre races to warn her. He is too late: The explosion mortally wounds Keyes. Lorre plans revenge. Stone tells Lorre that Seay and his gang plan to leave the area by plane. Lorre sends Beddoe a note to meet him in a western desert. Lorre takes pilot Sam Ash's place and with the plane now out of fuel, lands the plane in the desert where there's no chance for any of them. After a week, Beddoe shows up at the rendezvous point to find everyone dead.

Notes and Commentary: The Face Behind the Mask was one of twelve Columbia feature films added to the "Son of Shock" package released to television in 1958. The other sixty-one features in the package were Universal releases.

It has been reported that Peter Lorre's "mask" was created with white powder and two pieces of adhesive tape to immobilize the sides of his face. Lorre's facial expressions then gave the illusion of a mask.

Peter Lorre was difficult to work with during the filming of this production. He started by drinking his breakfast and reinforcing himself through the morning. By the afternoon, Lorre became indifferent to Robert Florey's direction. Florey consequently tried to direct Lorre's most important scenes during the morning hours.

Reviews: "This is not so much to scare audiences as make them a little sick. Production, acting and story, paradoxically, are all of a fairly high order, but it's all too unpleasant." *Variety*, 12/31/40

"Despite a certain pretentiousness toward things psychological, [this] may safely be set down as another bald melodramatic exercise in which the talents of Peter Lorre are stymied by hackneyed dialogue and conventional plot manipulations." *New York Times*, 2/7/41

"Intriguing and well-acted with strong direction." *Blockbuster Video Guide to Movies and Videos 1995*

"A stylish film about human suffering." *Motion Picture Guide*, Nash and Ross

Summation: What a fine example of "B" moviemaking. This is not a horror film but an excellent study of a man's descent into a life of crime through unforeseen circumstances and his subsequent inability to revert to a normal life. In depicting this individual, Peter Lorre gives one of the best performances of his career. Evelyn Keyes, as the blind girl with whom Lorre hopes to find happiness, delivers a sensitive performance. George E. Stone is fine as Lorre's best friend who is not horrified by his facial disfigurement. The film is directed with a sure hand by Robert Flory, who makes every scene count. Excellent photography by Franz Planer in both the dark scenes and the final desert scenes intensifies the dramatics.

JUST TIME ENOUGH ... to change his clothes ... his girl and his name!

Face of a Fugitive

(May 1959)

A Morningside Production

Cast: Jim Larsen aka Ray Kincaid, Fred MacMurray; Sheriff Mark Riley, Lin McCarthy; Ellen Bailey, Dorothy Green; Reed Williams, Alan Baxter; Janet Hawthorne, Myrna Fahey; Purdy, James Coburn; Deputy George Allison, Frances deSales; Alice Bailey, Gina Gillespie; Danny Larsen, Ron Hayes; Jake (Barber), Paul Burns; Uncredited: Deputy, Bill Clark; Stableman, Hal K. Dawson; Eakins, Stanley Farrar; Stockton, James Gavin; Burton, Robert "Buzz" Henry; Charlie (Bartender), Harrison Lewis; Minister, Rankin Mansfield; Haley, John Milford

Credits: Director, Paul Wendkos; Assistant Director, Leonard Katzman; Executive Producer, Charles H. Schneer; Producer, David Heilwell; Story, Peter Dawson; Screenwriters, David T. Chandler and Daniel B. Ullman; Editor, Jerome Thoms; Art Director, Robert Peterson; Set Decorators, Louis Diage and Bill Calvert; Cinematographer, Wilfrid M. Cline; Recording Supervisor, John Livadary; Sound, Harry Mills; Original Music and Musical Conductor, Jerrald Goldsmith; Color Consultant, Henri Jaffa

Location Filming: Bell Ranch, Santa Susana; Corriganville, Simi Valley and Jamestown, California

Production Dates: October 8–October 28, 1958

Running Time: 81 minutes

Eastman color by Pathe

Story: Bank robber Fred MacMurray is being escorted to jail by Deputy Bill Clark. At a train stop, MacMurray gets the upper hand and forces Clark to release him. At the same time MacMurray's younger brother, Ron Hayes, shows up, to MacMurray's displeasure. Since Hayes has two waiting horses, MacMurray decides to ride off with him. In the escape, Hayes and Clark exchange shots. Both hit their target; Clark is killed and Hayes is seriously wounded. Hayes brought

MacMurray a change of clothes and some money. Hayes succumbs to the wound and MacMurray throws him in a river. MacMurray seeks refuge on a train as a passenger. When the train is stopped by Sheriff Lin McCarthy, MacMurray is able to pass himself off as a mine inspector. At the end of the line, MacMurray gets off the train and becomes acquainted with McCarthy's sister, Dorothy Green. MacMurray finds he cannot ride out of town because deputies have been posted by the only trail leaving the town. Non-residents cannot leave the area until reward posters arrive. McCarthy has a more pressing problem. Big ranch owner Alan Baxter has fenced in public grazing land and refuses to allow others to use it. McCarthy cuts the barbed wire fence. Irate, Baxter wants to settle the dispute with guns. McCarthy tries to walk away but Baxter continues to push the issue until MacMurray steps in. Baxter promises to repair the fence in the morning. Green and McCarthy's girlfriend Myrna Fahey are grateful. McCarthy gives MacMurray a job as deputy, and MacMurray escorts Green home. On the way to Green's home, they see townspeople by the river where the body of Hayes has washed ashore. At Green's home, MacMurray and Green discover they are romantically attracted to each other. Back in town, MacMurray sees Hayes' body and realizes McCarthy and Hayes would be about the same age. Believing Baxter might gun him down, McCarthy is hesitant to marry Fahey. MacMurray convinces McCarthy to marry Fahey immediately. Next morning, McCarthy and MacMurray ride out to the cut fence. McCarthy decides to ride back to town to see the reward poster. On the way, McCarthy rides to the fence that has now been repaired by Baxter's ranch hand James Coburn. As McCarthy approaches the fence with wire cutters, Coburn draws his gun. Before Coburn can fire, MacMurray shoots the gun out of Coburn's hand. MacMurray follows with shots that cut the fence with the wire wrapping around Coburn. McCarthy rides on to town. MacMurray starts to help free Coburn from the wire until he sees Baxter and other ranch hands riding toward him. MacMurray rides away to take refuge in a ghost town. Baxter and his men follow. A gunfight ensues. Finally the only combatants are Baxter and an injured and wounded MacMurray. Baxter is stalking MacMurray in an old dark building. McCarthy and Green show up at the ghost town. McCarthy opens a door, with sunlight shining on Baxter. A bullet from MacMurray ends Baxter's life. MacMurray is brought out of the building and placed in a wagon with Green tending to him. First McCarthy tells Green that MacMurray might not be the man pictured on the poster. Then McCarthy, who is also a lawyer, tells Green he'll defend MacMurray making certain a jury will know what he did to help the town.

Notes and Commentary: The working title of this film was *Justice Ends with a Gun*.

Reviews: "A fair program western which attempts to be offbeat and succeeds in being downbeat. Acceptable entertainment." *Variety*, 4/29/59

"Fairly entertaining oater with Fred MacMurray good as the fugitive." *Western Movies*, Pitts

Summation: This is a good western noir with a fine performance by Fred MacMurray. He plays a bank robber who slowly turns from a life of crime. First MacMurray defends novice Sheriff Lin McCarthy because he doesn't want McCarthy to meet an early death like his younger brother. Also, MacMurray finally finds a woman he could love. MacMurray's transformation is realistic with MacMurray showing his difficulty in making the change. James Coburn effectively shows his nasty and tough side as he does rancher Alan Baxter's bidding. Screenwriter Daniel B. Ullman's touch elevated a number of '50s western programmers.

A DATE WITH DESTINY! ... in a city of sudden death!

Fire Over Africa

(November 1954)

A Frankovich–Sale Production

Alternate Title: Malaga

Cast: Joanna Dana, Maureen O'Hara; Van Logan, Macdonald Carey; Frisco, Binnie Barnes; Augie, Harry Lane; Dupont, Leonard Sachs; Danny Boy, Jim Lilburn; Farrell, Hugh McDermott; Soames Howard, Guy Middleton; Mustapha, Ferdy Mayne; Pebbles, Eric Corrie; Potts, Bruce Beeby; Signor Amato, Derek Sydney; Mons.

Ducloir, Jacques Cey; Tiger, Mike Brendall; Aziz, Antonio Casas; Hotel Clerk, Dino Galvani; Uncredited: Jakie, Meinhart Maur; Captain Civil, Rafael Giron

Credits: Director, Richard Sale; Assistant Director, Basil Keys; Second Unit Director, David Eady; Producer, M.J. Frankovich; Screenwriter, Robert Westerby; Editor, A.S. Bates; Assistant Editor, A.H. Rule; Art Directors, Vincent Korda and Wilfred Shingleton; Cinematographer, Christopher Challis; Camera Operator, A. Ibbetson; Wardrobe, Bridget Sellers; Makeup, Tony Sforzini; Hair Stylist, Gladys Atkinson; Production Manager, Fred Gunn; Original Music and Musical Director, Benjamin Frankel; Continuity, Olga Brook; Technicolor Color Consultant, Joan Bridge

Song: "Malaga" (Frankel)

Location Filming: Malaga, Andalucia, Spain and Shepperton, Surrey, England

Production Dates: Early November–mid–December 1953

Running Time: 84 minutes

Color by Technicolor

Story: Tangier is a smugglers' paradise. Tangier produces sudden riches and sudden death. Former OSS agent Maureen O'Hara is assigned to find the leader of the ring. Arriving in Tangier, she draws interest from boat owner Macdonald Carey, minor smuggler Leonard Sachs and syndicate henchman Harry Lane. At the hotel, O'Hara meets with her boss Hugh McDermott, who alerts her to two possible hangouts, Binnie Barnes' bar and Ferdy Mayne's shop. After O'Hara leaves the meeting, McDermott is murdered. Mayne runs the smuggling operation out of a back room of his shop. Sachs has hijacked some of Mayne's cargo and makes arrangements with Carey to transport the cargo to Malaga. Mayne sends Lane to retrieve the cargo but his attempt to murder Carey and Sachs fails. O'Hara threatens to leave Sachs until he produces a key that will blow the lid off the smuggling operation. Sachs tells O'Hara that eight countries will pay a lot for this information. Sachs gives O'Hara the key before he is murdered by Lane. O'Hara is able to escape the same fate. Carey catches up with O'Hara and takes the key. In turn O'Hara fires two shots into Carey's chest and takes back the key. Fortunately, Carey had an armored vest under his shirt and the impact only rendered him unconscious. At the hotel Dino Galvani looks at the key and is able to tell O'Hara how to find the information. Realizing that Lane has spotted her, O'Hara decides to take refuge at Barnes' bar after passing the key to a confederate. Lane catches up with O'Hara and instead of receiving help from Barnes, Barnes reveals that she is the secret head of the smuggling operation. Barnes tells Lane to kill O'Hara. Lane refuses, believing O'Hara will make a good hostage. Barnes and Lane argue. Lane kills Barnes and takes O'Hara with him. Carey has gone to the authorities. Carey has been working undercover. Sachs' information has been recovered and they have enough proof to arrest Barnes and Mayne. Carey goes to Barnes' bar. With her dying breath, Barnes tells Carey where Lane has taken O'Hara. Lane has gone to a beach where men are trying to transport all the smuggling operation information to a new location. As Carey and soldiers arrive, Lane finally realizes he has to kill O'Hara. In a struggle, O'Hara wounds Lane. Lane advances toward O'Hara but Carey arrives in time to shoot Lane. O'Hara not only finds that Carey was working undercover but with McDermott's death, Carey is now her boss. As the two are now interested in each other romantically, Carey tells O'Hara that he'll make the relationship permanent. O'Hara has no objection.

Notes and Commentary: The working titles for the film were *Port of Spain* and *Malaga*. *Malaga* was the title of the United Kingdom release.

The producers considered Errol Flynn and Indian actress Nimmi for starring roles. Originally the film was to be shot in Morocco and Kenya.

Reviews: "A ludicrous North African adventure. The highly predictable script detracts from any possible enjoyment of the action." *Motion Picture Guide*, Nash and Ross

"There were some pretty Technicolor shots of the exotic locale, though the ear was less well served by Robert Westerby's screenplay." *The Columbia Story*, Hirschhorn

Summation: This attempt at an international crime noir is pretty far-fetched. Robert Westerly's screenplay is filled with too many holes and Richard Sale's fast-paced direction isn't good enough to cover them up. Maureen O'Hara is miscast as the formed OSS agent turned undercover agent. Even though she is quite attractive, she doesn't exude the raw sex appeal that's needed to deal with the lowlife element. Macdonald Carey is adequate as the undercover hero. This was O'Hara and Carey's second teaming after the lackluster western *Comanche Territory* (Universal-International, 1950). The author noted the lack of chemistry between the stars in that opus and it's also quite noticeable in this one. Even as an action film, this one doesn't make the grade.

THEY HIT THE JACKPOT in the world's richest gambling house!

5 *Against the House*

(June 1955)

A Dayle Production

Cast: Al Mercer, Guy Madison; Kay Greylek, Kim Novak; Brick, Brian Keith; Roy, Alvy Moore; Ronnie, Kerwin Mathews; Eric Berg, William Conrad; Francis Spiegelbauer, Jack Dimond; Virginia, Jean Willes; Uncredited: Jean, Kathryn Grant; Blonde Student, Adelle August; Brunette Student, Jana Mason; Holdup Man, Frank Gerstle; Police Detective, John Larch; Young Man, Don Oreck; Cashier, Geraldine Hall; Lt. Anderson, Tom Greenway; Lift Operator, Pete Kellett; Casino Guard, George Cisar; Older Guard, Robert F. Simon; Younger Guard, Thom Carney

Credits: Director, Phil Karlson; Assistant Director, Milton Feldman; Producers, Stirling Silliphant and John Barnwell; Associate Producer, Helen Ainsworth; Screenwriters, Stirling Silliphant, William Bowers and John Barnwell; Editor, Jerome Thoms; Art Director, Robert Peterson; Set Decorator, Frank Tuttle; Cinematographer, Lester White; Gowns, Jean Louis; Recording Supervisor, John Livadary; Sound, Harry Smith; Original Music, George Duning; Musical Conductor, Morris Stoloff

5 *Against the House* (1955).

Songs: "The Life of the Party" (Hackady and Mure)—sung by Kim Novak and "I Went Out of My Way" (Bliss)—sung by Kim Novak (Novak's singing was dubbed by Jo Ann Greer)

Location Filming: Reno and Las Vegas, Nevada, Mill Valley and Lake Tahoe, California

Production Dates: November 11–December 1, 1954

Source: novel *5 Against the House* by Jack Finney, serialized in *Good Housekeeping* magazine (July–September 1951)

Running Time: 83 minutes

Story: When returning from summer jobs, law students Guy Madison, Brian Keith, Alvy Moore and Kerwin Mathews stop for an hour's fun at Harold's Club in Reno. While there, there is a holdup attempt by Frank Gerstle. Policeman John Larch states it is impossible to rob the club. Madison and Keith are older students. Both are Korean War veterans. Because of a head injury, Keith sometime exhibits violent tendencies. Back at college, Madison resumes his romance with Kim Novak, now a featured singer at a local nightclub. Madison wants to marry Novak but she is hesitant. Mathews works out a plan to rob Harold's but doesn't plan to keep the money if successful. Keith and Moore join in but a fourth man is needed. They want Madison to participate but know he won't. Madison is asked to join them on a school break to Reno. Madison agrees to go when Novak thinks Reno would be a nice place to get married. Before leaving, unbeknownst to the others, Keith purchases a pistol. Madison finally finds out about the heist and tries to talk them out of it. Keith produces his pistol, says the heist is on and they will keep the money. Believing Keith will kill innocent people, Madison agrees to participate. Threatening to kill Madison, Keith forces Novak be a part of the robbery. The plan works and Keith takes the money out of Harold's. Mathews tries to stop Keith but Keith knocks him to the ground. Keith begins running away and Madison gives chase. Novak has alerted the police. Madison asks Novak to ask police to stand back while he talks with Keith. Madison breaks Keith down and places him in police hands. Madison asks that Keith be given psychiatric help. Madison and Novak still plan to get married.

Notes and Commentary: Even though Jack Finney's novel and the screenplay center on the robbery of Harold's Club, the thrust of the novel is drastically changed. Of course names are changed: Tina Greyleg became Kay Grelek, Guy became Roy and Jerry became Ronnie. Only Al and Brick retained their names in the transition to the screen, but neither are war veterans. All four students are in favor of holding up Harold's Club. Tina becomes the fifth when she helps plan the heist. On the way to Reno, Al and Tina get cold feet. Brick tells Al that if he backs out, he'll give Tina such a beating that it will leave a psychological scar. The robbery goes off perfectly until Al leaves Harold's with the money bag and there is no getaway car. Al hides on the roof of the club where he stashes the bag. The five decide to hide out in Reno until the heat's off. On the trip to Reno, at a traffic stop a young boy saw Brick at the wheel and wrote his name on the dusty trailer. The young boy is brought to Reno where he recognizes Brick. Brick gives up the names of his accomplices and all are arrested. Al finally reveals the location of the bag. The bag turns out to be of value only to Harold's: All that's in it are checks made out to the club. The five are released because Harold's decides not to prefer charges because there was no armed robbery, the bag never left the premises and Harold's does not want the unwelcome publicity. Al, Tina, Guy and Jerry go back to the college town. Brick decides to go his own way.

Guy Madison's popularity as TV's Wild Bill Hickok probably made producers believe that audiences would not buy into Madison as a potential thief. Therefore the screenplay had Madison enter the heist reluctantly with the thought of stopping Brian Keith when others were out of harm's way.

Initially Stirling Silliphant obtained an option on Finney's story. United Artists would distribute the film, Frank Tashlin would direct and Tashlin's wife, Mary Costa, would have the female lead. Tashlin dropped out of the project. Peter Godfrey would now direct and Milly Vitale would replace Costa. Columbia became interested in the project. Phil Karlson would direct with Kim Novak in the female lead. The four students would be Guy Madison, Alvy Moore, Robert Horton and Roddy McDowall. In the final cut, Brian Keith would replace Horton and Kerwin Mathews replaced McDowall.

Kim Novak trained to do her own singing but ultimately Jo Ann Greer did the vocalizing.

Reviews: "Suspenseful melodramatics. The direction by Phil Karlson is a large factor in making the characterizations well valued and the suspense tight." *Variety*, 5/18/55

"A gripping little thriller. The nifty direction

was by Phil Karlson, who, when it came to laying on the suspense, didn't miss a trick." *The Columbia Story*, Hirschhorn

SUMMATION: An okay crime noir that passes muster thanks to Brian Keith's fine performance. He is totally believable as a man who passes himself off as a light-hearted individual but, because of mental illness from a war injury to his brain, has underlying violence waiting to be unleashed. Director Karlson is able to generate suspense during the heist and its aftermath. Acting of the other principals is on target and Kim Novak, on the verge of stardom, is very attractive.

NEVER FORGET ... when a man is close enough to KISS YOU ... he is close enough to KILL YOU!

Footsteps in the Fog

(June 1955)

An M.J. Frankovich Production

CAST: Stephen Lowry, Stewart Granger; Lily Watkins, Jean Simmons; David Macdonald, Bill Travers; Elizabeth Travers, Belinda Lee; Alfred Travers, Ronald Squire; Inspector Peters, Finlay Currie; Herbert Moresby, William Hartnell; Dr. Simpson, Frederick Leister; Magistrate, Percy Marmont; Mrs. Park, Margery Rhodes; Brasher, Peter Bull; Constable Burke, Barry Keegan; Rose Moresby, Sheila Manahan; Grimes, Norman Macowan; Corcoran, Cameron Hall; Jones, Victor Maddern; Constable Farrow, Peter Williams; Vicar, Arthur Howard; George Bishop; Mark Daly; W. Thorp Devereaux; Hedges, Eric Chitty; Philip Holles

CREDITS: Director, Arthur Lubin; Assistant Director, Ronald Spencer; Producer, Maxwell Seaton and M.J. Frankovich; Adaptor, Arthur Pierson; Screenwriters, Dorothy Reid and Lenore Coffee; Editor, Alan Osbiston; Art Director, Wilfred Shingleton; Cinematographer, Christopher Challis; Camera Operator, A. Dempster; Costume Designer, Beatrice Dawson; Costumes for Stewart Granger, Elizabeth Haffenden; Makeup, N. Smallwood; Hair Stylist, Bette Lee; Sound Supervisor, John Cox; Sound Recordists, A. Ambler and Red Law; Original Music and Musical Conductor, Benjamin Frankel; Production Manager, Fred Gunn; Continuity, Betty Forster; Technicolor Color Consultant, Joan Bridge

SONG: main theme "The 'Lily Watkins' Tune" (Frankel)—played by an orchestra conducted by Benjamin Frankel

PRODUCTION DATES: mid–November 1954–mid–January 1955

SOURCE: short story "The Interruption" by W.W. Jacobs

RUNNING TIME: 90 minutes

Color by Technicolor

Filmed in CinemaScope

STORY: After the death of his wife, Stewart Granger was inwardly pleased: Her fortune now belonged to him. When he looks for his wife's jewelry, housemaid Jean Simmons tells Granger his wife gave it to her. Simmons then tells Granger that she knows he murdered his wife. She also wants to become the housekeeper. Granger wants to form a partnership with Ronald Squire and also marry his daughter Belinda Lee. Simmons informs Granger that she will be the only woman in the house. On a foggy night, Simmons leaves the house to post a letter. Granger decides that he can kill Simmons and escape in the fog. Granger murders the wrong woman. In his escape, Granger drops the walking stick he used in the crime. Granger is arrested and put on trial. Simmons' perjured testimony sets Granger free. In order for Simmons to live in the house without fearing Granger, she tells him she has send her sister, Sheila Manahan, a sealed letter to be opened upon her death. Granger, who wants to marry Lee, devises a plan to get rid of Simmons. He professes his love and says that they will marry when they begin life in America. Simmons believes him and writes Manahan to destroy the letter. Manahan sets fire to the letter but her husband, William Hartnell, retrieves it before the fire can consume it. Hartnell wants to blackmail Granger but shows it to barrister Bill Travers, whom he mistakes for Granger. Travers takes the letter to the police. Granger puts his plan into action to be rid of Simmons: Feigning illness, he sends Simmons to bring Dr. Frederick Leisler. Simmons says she'll be back with the doctor in five minutes. Granger works fast, consumes poison and places the incriminating bottle in Simmons' room. Leaving the house, Simmons is approached by police and taken to the police station. At the station, Simmons swears she didn't write the letter and demonstrates her handwriting which is quite different from the letter. On leaving the station, Simmons signs out in her normal handwriting. Now the police know Simmons did write the note. Simmons returns to the house where she sees a dying Granger. The police arrive. Granger accuses Simmons of poisoning him and also of murdering his wife. As Simmons is being led away, Granger expires.

Notes and Commentary: Working titles for the film were *Interruption*, *Rebound* and *Deadlock*. Patricia Medina had been considered for the part of Lily Watkins. Robert Goldstein was to produce the film.

Stewart Granger was borrowed from MGM to co-star with his wife Jean Simmons. They had last worked together in *Young Bess* (MGM, 1953). Granger and Simmons wanted to make a film in England and agreed to star in the film if the script was rewritten. They almost turned the film down when they learned the director was Arthur Lubin, noted for comedies with Abbott and Costello and Francis the Talking Mule. On daily trips to Shepperton Studios, Granger and screenwriter Lenore Coffee rewrote the script.

W.W. Jacobs' short story contained only three characters, Spencer Goddard, housekeeper Hannah and the doctor. Goddard poisons his wife. Hannah takes the wife's jewelry and implies she knows Goddard is a murderer. Hannah has left a letter with her sister. Goddard decides to set up Hannah as a murderess by sending Hannah for the doctor. He takes poison. Hannah is unable to locate the doctor. She returns too late and Goddard dies.

Reviews: "Well-acted but slow moving movie." *Motion Picture Guide*, Nash and Ross

"CinemaScope and Technicolor did nothing to alleviate the tedium engendered by *Footsteps in the Fog*." *The Columbia Story*, Hirschhorn

Summation: This is a good Gothic noir featuring fine performances by Granger and Simmons. Both believably play vile characters that either murder or blackmail to gain their goal in life. Dorothy Reid and Lenore Coffee's screenplay moves steadily forward to its ironic conclusion. Cinematographer Christopher Challis uses fog and darkness to the desired effect of creating tension and suspense.

ENEMY A-BOMB SMUGGLED INTO U.S.

The 49th Man

(May 1953)

Cast: John Williams, John Ireland; Paul Reagan, Richard Denning; Margo Wayne, Suzanne Dalbert; Commander Jackson, Robert C. Foulk; Lt. Magrew, Touch Connors; Buzz Olin, Richard Avonde; FBI Agent in Montage, William R. Klein; Blonde Woman, Cicely Brown; Agent Reynolds, Tommy Farrell; Box of Taffy Man at Penn Station, Joseph Mell; Andy, Robert Hunter; Leo Wayne, Peter Marshall; Uncredited: Mack, Lee Morgan; Sheriff Ramirez, Nesdon Booth; Narrator, Gerald Mohr; Agent Gray, Michael Colgan; Technician, Steve Pendleton; Pilot, Tom McKee; Lifeguard, Sandy Sanders; Agent who Received Lifeguard Report, Barney Phillips; Penn Station Counterman, Morgan Brown; Lindsley (Lab Technician), Lester Dorr; Sands, Clark Howat; Go-Between with Satchel, Heinie Conklin; Courier who Got Bag at Bar, Bud Osborne; Agent Maurice Leroux, Jean Del Val; Agent Manning, Chris Alcaide; Bass Player in Quartet, Bert Dodson; Dave Norton, George Milan; Pierre Neff, George Dee; Cabaret Singer, Genevieve Aumont; Corrigan, Boyd "Red" Morgan; Submarine Chief, Robert B. Williams

Credits: Director, Fred F. Sears; Assistant Director, Milton Feldman; Producer, Sam Katzman; Associate Producer, Charles H. Schneer; Story, Ivan Tors; Screenwriter, Harry Essex; Editor, William A. Lyon; Art Director, Paul Palmentola; Set Decorator, Louis Diage; Cinematographer, Lester White; Sound, George Cooper; Musical Director, Mischa Bakaleinikoff

Location Filming: Iverson, California

Production Dates: December 11–22, 1952

Running Time: 73 minutes

Story: After a car crash, a box with mysterious contents was taken to scientists at Los Alamos. It was confirmed that the box contained part of an atomic bomb. Chief Investigator Richard Denning assigns John Ireland to the case. Although other atom bomb parts are recovered, a mass of uranium attached to a submarine slips through. All clues point to Marseilles, France. Undercover, Ireland gets assigned to the sub as it returns to Marseilles. In Marseilles, Ireland learns that the Café Henri might offer a clue. At the club, Ireland meets clarinet player Richard Avonde, Peter Marshall and his wife Suzanne Dalbert. Marshall and Dalbert have suspicious backgrounds. After the meeting, Avonde drops out of sight. Ireland finds the source of the metal cases used to transport the atomic material. Forty-eight cases comprised the initial shipment and Avonde ordered four additional cases. Ireland tells Marshall and Dalbert the sub has been recalled to the States. Ireland and agent Robert Hunter watch Dalbert pass a package containing microfilm to an unknown sailor stationed on the sub. Before they can react, both men are struck from behind. Hunter is able to tear the assailant's coat prior to blacking out. Hunter learns that Lt. Touch Connors' uniform was torn and follows Connors to the Café Henri. Connors meets the sub commander Robert C. Foulk. Foulk is identified as the man who ordered the 48 metal cases. Ireland and Hunter board the sub to arrest Foulk and Connors, but Hunter turns on Ireland. Ireland is taken captive and drugged. When Ireland regains consciousness, he finds himself in Washington D.C. as Boyd "Red" Morgan's captive. Ireland is able to escape and call Denning. Denning then calls Morgan to tell him where Ireland is waiting. Ireland sees Morgan first and makes his escape. Ireland makes his way to Denning's office where he not only finds Denning but also Foulk and Connors. It turns out the 48 cases were part of a war game to test defenses against the possible smuggling of atomic bombs into the United States. As Denning, Foulk and Connors begin to congratulate Ireland on his good work, Ireland tells them there are four additional boxes to be found. Ireland begins to look for Avonde, Marshall and Dalbert. Dalbert is found murdered in Marseilles. Ireland tracks Avonde to a rest home. Avonde tells Ireland that Marshall is on the way to a small airport and that he plans to drop an atomic bomb on San Francisco. Ireland and other agents get to the airport in time to keep the plane from taking off. Marshall is killed in a gunfight. Foulk is present to try to defuse the bomb but is unable to do so. Ireland flies to an atom bomb test site where the bomb is exploded harmlessly with less than a minute to spare.

Notes and Commentary: The working title for this film was *49 Men*.

In the opening, Lordsburg, New Mexico is misspelled Lordsburgh.

Talent agent Abner J. Greshler purchased the rights to Ivan Tors' story in 1951. Subsequently Greshler sold the rights to Columbia who turned the story over to Sam Katzman's Esskay Picture Corporation. Screenwriter Harry Essex reworked the story for the big screen.

Reviews: "Fast-paced and entertaining." *Motion Picture Guide*, Nash and Ross

"The use of library wartime footage gave *The 49th Man* a documentary-like feel to it, but it was still just a low-budget programmer." *The Columbia Story*, Hirshhorn

Summation: This is a good docu-noir filmed realistically and smartly acted. Fred F. Sears' direction generates some nice suspense. The photography by Lester White firmly complements Sears' direction. The story moves forward in a logical manner with a couple of nice plot twists thrown in to intensify audience interest.

"I don't care what any other man meant to you!"

Framed

(May 1947)

Cast: Mike Lambert, Glenn Ford; Paula Craig, Janis Carter; Steve Price, Barry Sullivan; Jeff Cunningham, Edgar Buchanan; Beth, Karen Morley; Jack Woodworth, Jim Bannon; Uncredited: Jane Woodworth, Barbara Woodell; Trucking Manager, Charles Cane; Trucking Assistant Manager, Walter Baldwin; Bartender, Sid Tomack;

Framed (1947).

Dishwasher, Snub Pollard; Policemen, Kenneth MacDonald and Crane Whitley; Judge, Al Bridge; Julio, Eugene Borden; Sandy (Assayer), Paul E. Burns; Café Janitor, Martin Garralaga; Desk Clerk, Art Smith; Houseman, William Stubbs; Crap Shooters, Nacho Galindo and Cy Malis; Paperboy, David Fresco; Man in Coffee Shop, Robert Kellard; Woman in Coffee Shop, Lillian Wells; Jail Guard, Harry Strang; Bank Clerk, Fred Graff; Policemen, Stanley Andrews and Gene Roth; Bank Guard, Jack Baxley

Credits: Director, Richard Wallace; Assistant Director, Herman Webber; Producer, Jules Schermer; Story, John Patrick; Screenwriter, Ben Maddow; Editor, Richard Fantl; Art Directors, Stephen Goosson and Carl Anderson; Set Decorators, Wilbur Menefee, Sidney Clifford and Fay Babcock; Cinematography, Burnett Guffey; Gowns, Jean Louis; Sound, George Cooper; Original Music, Marlin Skiles; Musical Director, M.W. Stoloff

Location Filming: Lake Arrowhead, California

Production Dates: September 6–October 30, 1946

Running Time: 82 minutes

Story: Mining engineer Glenn Ford comes to a small town looking for a job. He is arrested for reckless driving and sentenced to ten days in jail because he can't pay the fine. Janis Carter, a café waitress, pays the fine, pays for a room for Ford and leaves him money. Carter tells Barry Sullivan, vice-president of a local bank, that Ford is the man they're looking for. Carter and Sullivan plan to steal $250,000 from the bank and place it in Carter's safe deposit box. They also plan to murder Ford, making it look like an auto accident, and pass the corpse off as Sullivan. Carter and Sullivan will leave town to start a new life. Ford finds a job working with miner Edgar Buchanan. Buchanan has discovered a rich vein of silver and goes to Sullivan for a loan. Carter, learning of Ford and Buchanan's relationship, manages to have Sullivan turn down Buchanan's loan request. An angry Buchanan leaves the bank. With bank examiners arriving in a few days, Ford needs to be murdered quickly. Ford is told that Sullivan might reconsider Buchanan's request. Sullivan, Carter and Ford go to Buchanan's mine and Sullivan tells Ford the loan will be approved. On the return to town, Sullivan suggests they stop at his mountain cabin for drinks. When Ford realizes that Carter and Sullivan have been having an affair, he begins drinking until he passes out. Ford is placed in Sullivan's car. When they reach the murder spot, Carter strikes Sullivan instead of Ford. Sullivan and his car are sent over a cliff. The next day Carter tells Ford that Sullivan died in the cabin during an altercation between Ford and Sullivan. Ford can't go to the police because Carter will be implicated as an accessory. Evidence then points to Buchanan as Sullivan's murderer. Ford visits Buchanan in jail and from their conversation he now believes Carter is the murderer. Carter tells Ford that she's going to pick up her final check as a waitress but in reality she is going to empty out her safe deposit box. Ford confronts Carter at the bank because he knows Carter killed Sullivan. Carter starts to leave the bank but sees two police officers waiting for her (Ford called the police). As Carter is being taken to the police station, she looks back at Ford. Ford walks away, knowing the woman he loved is a murderess.

Notes and Commentary: The working title for this film was *They Walk Alone.*

It was noted in *The Hollywood Reporter* that Charles Lawton was the cinematographer from September 6 through October 4. On October 5, Burnett Guffey took over this responsibility.

In initial bookings, *Framed* played on a double bill with *King of the Wild Horses* (Columbia, 1947) with Preston Foster.

Reviews: "Taut melodrama, another in the unscrupulous women cycle." *Variety*, 3/5/47

"Apparently convinced that the wages of sin are always the same and that crime has never paid off, Columbia has fashioned a workmanlike and fairly taut illustration of these axioms. An unpretentious effort which manages to be realistic and absorbing, despite a set of sordid circumstances and characters." *New York Times*, 5/26/47

Summation: This is a wow of a crime noir. Glenn Ford is perfect as a man trying to get a break being sidetracked by a woman who knows how to use sex to get what she wants out of life. Janis Carter shows again she can portray the perfect femme fatale. Her expression of sexual satisfaction as she watches the car with Sullivan go over the cliff rivals her expression in *Night Editor* (Columbia, 1946) as she watches a woman being murdered. Richard Wallace provides firm direction assisted by noir master cinematographer Burnett Guffey.

THE WHOLE NAKED TRUTH about the rackets in New York's Garment Center!

The Garment Jungle

(April 1957)

Cast: Walter Mitchell, Lee J. Cobb; Alan Mitchell, Kerwin Mathews; Theresa Renata, Gia Scala; Artie Ravidge, Richard Boone; Lee Hackett, Valerie French; Tulio Renata, Robert Loggia; George Kovan, Joseph Wiseman; Tony, Harold J. Stone; Ox, Adam Williams; Mr. Paul, Wesley Addy; Dave Bronson, Willis Bouchey; Fred Kenner, Robert Ellenstein; Tulio's Mother, Celia Lovsky; Uncredited: Alfredi, Jon Shepodd; Latzo, Jud Taylor; Miller, Dick Crockett; Joanne, Suzanne Alexander; Stephanie, Ellie Kent; Fitting Model, Gloria Pall; Receptionist, Eve Brent; Announcers, Shirley Buchanan, Millicent Deming and William Woodson; Young Operator, Joan Granville; Elderly Operator, Irene Seidner; Truck Driver's Helper, Dale Van Sickel; Truck Driver, George Robotham; Salesmen, Hal Taggart and Paul Knight; Buyer, Lillian Culver; Garment Worker, Sid Melton; Bartender, Bob Hopkins; Elevator Operator, Archie Savage; Models, Anna Lee Carroll, Laurie Mitchell, Kathy Marlowe, Peggy O'Connor, Bonnie Bolding, Joanna Barnes, Marilyn Hanold, June Tolley and Dorothy Kellogg; On-Line Models, Jann Darlyn, Madelyn Darrow and June Kirby

Credits: Director, Vincent Sherman; Assistant Director, Irving Moore; Producer, Story and Screenplay, Harry Kleiner; Editor, William Lyon; Art Director, Robert E. Peterson; Set Decorators, William Kiernan and Frank A. Tuttle; Cinematographer, Joseph Biroc; Gowns, Jean Louis; Makeup, Clay Campbell; Hair Stylist, Helen Hunt; Recording Supervisor, John Livadary; Original Music, Leith Stevens; Orchestrator, Arthur Morton

Location Filming: New York City and the garment districts of both New York City and Los Angeles

Production Dates: October 13–December 7, 1956; retakes mid–December 1956

Source: article "Gangsters in the Dress Business" by Lester Velie (*Reader's Digest*, July 1955)

Running Time: 88 minutes

Story: Kerwin Mathews wants to work with his father Lee J. Cobb in the garment business. Cobb, still upset over the death of his partner Robert Ellenstein, is reluctant to bring Mathews into the firm because of the friction with the unions. Cobb has worked with mobster Richard Boone to use strong-arm tactics to keep unions out of his business. Cobb is unaware that Ellenstein's death was actually murder, committed by Boone's chief henchman Wesley Addy. Valerie French, Cobb's girlfriend, convinces him to put Mathews to work. Robert Loggia is trying to unionize Cobb's business and intimates that Ellenstein's death was not an accident. Mathews seeks addition information and goes to see Loggia. Mathews also meets Loggia's wife Gia Scala, who is afraid for Loggia's life because of retaliation by Boone's henchmen. Addy and his men break up a union meeting and beat up Loggia and union president Willis Bouchey. When Loggia confronts Cobb and Boone in Cobb's office, Boone threatens Loggia. To force Cobb to allow his workers to join the union, the union forms a picket line outside Cobb's shop and no trucker is to be allowed in or out. Addy and his men plus union traitors jump Loggia and murder him. Mathews wants Cobb to go to the D.A. Boone tries to put the union traitors to work in Cobb's shop, but Cobb has had enough and breaks with Boone. Cobb tells Mathews that he has books detailing his relationship with Boone. Cobb promises Mathews that the shop will be unionized. Boone has Cobb murdered. French has the books and gets them to Mathews and Scala. As Mathews

Kerwin Matthews and Gia Scala in *The Garment Jungle* (1957).

goes to contact the police, he is grabbed and taken to Boone in Cobb's office. Boone tells Mathews that he'll run the business under his direction. Mathews then tells Boone that he has Cobb's books that will topple Boone's crime empire. Boone begins giving Mathews a beating to find the books' location. Scala brings the police and Boone is arrested. Mathews takes over the business, improves working conditions and plans to make a life with Scala.

NOTES AND COMMENTARY: The working title of the film was *Garment Center*. Glenn Ford and Henry Fonda were contenders for the role of Alan and Elaine Stritch was considered for the role of Lee Hackett.

Robert Aldrich directed until he came down with the flu. Vincent Sherman replaced Aldrich. Sherman thought he was only a temporary director until studio boss Harry Cohn asked Sherman not only to complete the picture but to reshoot almost 70 percent of Aldrich's work. Cohn wanted more of the Kerwin Mathews–Gia Scala romance. Sherman was surprised that he received sole directorial credit. Aldrich insists that he never watched the film.

In Lester Velie's *Reader's Digest* article, the inspiration for the film, Velie mentions there were shops that remained non-union and that a union organizer was knifed to death. In addition, countless workers were beaten to persuade them not to go union. Velie adds that a high-ranking mobster was arrested but he is concerned that there still could be a higher-up.

REVIEWS: "Realistic and intense..." *Variety*, 4/25/57

"Realism was the key-note in *The Garment Jungle*, a tough hard-hitting drama." *The Columbia Story*, Hirschhorn

SUMMATION: While a good exposé crime noir, this should have been much better. Almost offsetting the realistic, taut, gritty story is an unnecessary subplot of Kerwin Mathews' romance with Gia Scala and the routine crime story ending. From the first time the camera lingers on the lovely Scala, only the uninitiated would not realize that she would end up with Mathews. In one of the final scenes, it is too implausible that Scala knows to bring the police to Cobb's office for a simple, quick wind-up. The murder of Loggia is riveting, a great scene. The film has some fine acting, from veterans Lee J. Cobb and Richard Boone to newcomers Robert Loggia and Scala. Mathews tries hard but he's simply not in their league. Joseph Biroc's photography is outstanding, especially in Loggia's death scene. Sherman's direction emphasized the Mathews–Scala relationship which pleased studio boss Harry Cohn.

SEEKING VENGEANCE ... WOULD HE FIND LOVE ... or MURDER?

The Gentleman from Nowhere

(September 1948)

CAST: Earl Donovan/Robert Ashton, Warner Baxter; Catherine Ashton, Fay Baker; F.B. Barton, Luis Van Rooten; Fenmore, Charles Lane; Larry Hendricks, Wilton Graff; Edward Dixon, Grandon Rhodes; Vincent Sawyer, Noel Madison; Uncredited: Detectives, Harry Strang and Kernan Cripps; Bill Cook, Don Haggerty; Miss Kearns, Victoria Horne; Marshal, Robert Emmett Keane; Henry Thompson, William Forrest; Salesman, Charles La Torre; Barber, George Humbert; District Attorney, Selmer Jackson; Judge, John Hamilton; Bailiff, Stanley Blystone; Bondsman, Charles Jordan; Maid, Netta Packer; Henchman, Ethan Laidlaw

CAST: Director, William Castle; Producer, Rudolph C. Flothow; Screenwriter, Edward Anhalt; Editor, Henry Batista; Art Director, George Brooks; Set Decorator, Frank Kramer; Cinematography, Vincent Farrar; Musical Director, Mischa Bakaleinikoff

PRODUCTION DATES: May 3–May 15, 1948

RUNNING TIME: 65 minutes

STORY: During a fur robbery at a storage company, watchman Warner Baxter is wounded. While he is recovering, insurance investigator Luis Van Rooten notices Baxter's strong resemblance to a missing chemist wanted for stealing $200,000 from the Wilshire Chemical Company. Van Rooten tells the company president Grandon Rhodes and the board chairmen that he's located the chemist. A background check on Baxter proves that he was just a watchman. Company attorney Charles Lane tries to buy off Van Rooten, stating an investigation will damage company holdings. Van Rooten persuades Baxter to impersonate the chemist and Fay Baker, the chemist's wife, agrees to go along with the deception. Baker believes her husband was framed and ran because he could not prove his innocence. Baker suspects that chairman Noel Madison is the guilty party. Madison and Baker's husband disagreed on allowing the company to distribute his brand of whiskey. Another chairman, Wilton Graff, is in love with Baker and wants Baxter to give her up. Thinking Baxter is the chemist, the board wants him to produce a formula for synthetic foods that will save the company from ruin. Baker has the notes and shows them to Baxter. Baxter is offered his old job if he reveals the formula. Madison wants to break with the company and start a new venture with Baxter. Baxter will agree if Madison helps him find the man who framed the chemist. Madison and Baxter sneak into the company to search for evidence. A mystery man attacks them, throwing Madison over a railing to his death. Baxter sees a mystery woman at the scene and believes it to be Baker. Fearing Baxter will be the next victim, Lane wants Van Rooten to send Baxter to New York. Van Rooten agrees and offers to drive Baxter to the airport. Lane tampers with a headlight and then makes a mysterious phone call. En route, Baxter realizes that Baker still loves her husband and that Van Rooten is an honest investigator. Baxter then reveals that he really is the missing chemist. Baxter has a plan to reveal the murderer. A truck rams the car, killing Van Rooten and injuring Baxter. At the chemical firm meeting the next morning, Lane is surprised to see Baxter walk through the doorway. Rhodes believes Baxter is not the chemist. This fact reveals him as the man who framed Baxter. Baxter names Rhodes' secretary, Victoria Horne, as his accomplice. Baxter and Baker are reunited.

Summation: This is a somewhat interesting but confusing noir with a hurried ending. Without police presence, the murderer is revealed, another is accused of being an accomplice, and a third who earlier was shown assisting in a murder plot was never mentioned as being involved in the plot. All this happens in a matter of minutes. The acting is average in this "B" mystery. Director William Castle keeps things moving and, as mentioned, too fast at the finale. The real culprit is screenwriter Edward Anhalt.

There NEVER was a woman like Gilda!

Gilda

(March 1946)

Cast: Gilda, Rita Hayworth; Johnny Farrell/Narrator, Glenn Ford; Ballin Mundson, George Macready; Detective Obregon, Joseph Calleia; Uncle Pio, Steven Geray; Casey, Joe Sawyer; Capt. Delgado, Gerald Mohr; Gabe Evans, Robert Scott; German Cartel Member, Ludwig Donath; Thomas Langford, Don Douglas; Uncredited: Cartel Members, Robert Board, Eduardo Ciannelli, Jean De Briac, Jean Del Val, Herbert Evans, Sam Flint, Ernest Hilliard, George Humbert, Frank Leyva, Oscar Loraine, Forbes Murray and Philip Van Zandt; Huerta, George J. Lewis; Newsman, Julio Abadia; Blackjack Dealers, Sam Appel, Eugene Borden and Erno Verebes; Girl at Carnival, Nina Bara; Gamblers at Roulette Table, Symona Boniface and Bess Flowers; Assistant Croupiers, Jack Chefe, Lou Palfy, Albert Pollet and George Sorel; Doorman, Jerry De Castro; Servant, Leander De Cordova; Cashier, Jack Del Rio; Bendolin's Wife, Fernanda Eliscu; Banco Dealer, Nobel G. Evey; Bartender, Fred Goday; Policemen, Lew Harvey and John Merton; Holdup Man, Ted Hecht; Gambler at Banco Table, Stuart Holmes; Waiters, Herman Marks, Joe Palma and Ralph Navarro; Roulette Croupier, Alphonse Martell; Little Man, Saul Martell; Judge, Ramon Munox; Harpy, Soretta Raye; Maria, Rosa Ray; German, Lionel Royce; Clerk, Robert Tafur; Escort, Russ Vincent; Crap Game Spectator, Blackie Whiteford

Credits: Director, Charles Vidor; Assistant Director, Arthur S. Black; Producer, Virginia Van Upp; Assistant to the Producer, Norman Deming; Story, E.A. Ellington; Adaptation, Jo Eisinger; Screenwriter, Marion Parsonnet; Editor, Charles Nelson; Art Directors, Stephen Goosson and Van Nest Polglase; Set Decorator, Robert Priestley;

Cinematographer, Rudolph Mate; Gowns, Jean Louis; Makeup, Clay Campbell; Hair Stylist, Helen Hunt; Sound, Lambert Day; Music Directors, M.W. Stoloff and Marlin Skiles

Songs: "Amado Mio" (Roberts and Fisher)—sung by Rita Hayworth and "Put the Blame on Mame" (Roberts and Fisher)—sung by Hayworth (Note: Rita Hayworth's voice was dubbed by Anita Ellis)

Production Dates: September 4–December 10, 1945

Running Time: 110 minutes

Story: After winning money in a crap game with loaded dice, Glenn Ford almost loses his money to hold-up man Ted Hecht. The robbery is prevented by George Macready. Macready gives Ford a card allowing him to enter a local casino. Ford finds that Macready runs the casino and ultimately Macready offers Ford a job. Soon Ford is the casino's manager. Macready takes a trip, leaving Ford in complete charge. When Macready returns, he has a wife, Rita Hayworth. Hayworth and Ford were lovers in the past and had a bitter break-up. There is an attempt on Macready's life. Macready is in control of a tungsten cartel. Led by Ludwig Donath, German agents want Macready to relinquish control to them. In a meeting with the Germans, one is killed, forcing Macready to leave the country. Macready is followed by both Ford and police officer Joseph Calleia. As Macready makes his escape over the ocean, the plane explodes. Macready parachutes out unseen and is picked up by a waiting boat. While married to Macready, Hayworth had been seen in the company of many men. To punish Hayworth for hurting him in their relationship, Ford pretends that he loves her and, believing Macready dead, they marry. Ford then makes certain Hayworth lives a solitary life. She is frustrated in her attempts to obtain either a divorce or annulment. Meanwhile, Ford takes control of the cartel. Calleia begins pressuring Ford to give him the names of the cartel members so they can be prosecuted. In defiance of Ford, Hayworth comes to the casino and begins to perform a striptease. Ford has the routine stopped before Hayworth can remove her dress. Calleia tells Ford that he and Hayworth are really in love. He puts Ford under arrest and Ford is not allowed to leave the casino. Ford finally gives Calleia the information that he wants. Calleia brings Hayworth to the casino. Ford finds that Hayworth's supposed infidelities (while wed to Macready) were only an act. They plan to leave the country. Macready, who was deeply in love with Hayworth, shows up and plans to murder them both. A casino employee, Steven Geray, kills Macready. Calleia declares Macready's death a justifiable homicide. Hayworth and Ford leave the casino together.

Notes and Commentary: Glenn Ford had two of his teeth broken in this film. After Rita Hayworth had been brought back to Argentina by Don Douglas, Hayworth slapped Ford across both sides of his face. The blows were hard enough to do damage but Ford stood his ground until the take was completed.

The photograph of Glenn Ford as a baby is of Ford's real-life son, Peter Ford.

While filming the legendary "Put the Blame on Mame" number, Hayworth wore a corset. A few months earlier, she had given birth to her first daughter, Rebecca.

It was reported in the *Los Angeles Examiner* that Edmund Goulding would direct *Gilda*. Ultimately, the job went to Charles Vidor. This was Ford's first picture after four years in the service.

Reviews: "Practically all the s.a. [sex appeal] habiliments of the femme fatale have been mustered for *Gilda* and when things get trite and frequently farfetched, somehow, at the drop of a shoulder strap, there is always Rita Hayworth to excite the filmgoer." *Variety*, 3/20/46

"Despite close and earnest attention to this nigh-onto-two-hour film, this reviewer was utterly baffled by what happened on the screen. It simply did not make sense. A slow, opaque, unexciting film." *New York Times*, 3/15/46

"Hayworth at her peak. Rita is the main reason to see *Gilda*. The torrid, turgid plot of this myth of misogyny needn't be dwelled on in depth. *Gilda* is an erotic landmark to be especially considered today, when erotic thrillers dominate the box office and television screens." *Motion Picture Guide*, Nash and Ross

Summation: This is a good noir thanks to the sexual charge Hayworth gives to the story whenever it starts to slow down. The story is basically a boy meets girl, boy loses girl and boy finally gets girl story with dark noir trappings. The movie is all Hayworth, who dominates every scene she's in. Ford, as her lost lover and Macready as a ruthless crime boss turn in good performances. Rudolph Mate's excellent photography truly stands out as the darkness emphasizes the evil that surrounds the principals. This is one of the memorable film noir efforts of the '40s.

THE 10-HOUR MANHUNT ... that tore New York apart!

The Glass Wall

(Columbia, April 1953)

CAST: Peter, Vittorio Gassman; Maggie, Gloria Grahame; Nancy, Ann Robinson; Inspector Bailey, Douglas Spencer; Tanya, Robin Raymond; Tom, Jerry Paris; Mrs. Hinckley, Elizabeth Slifer; Eddie, Richard Reeves; Freddie, Joe Turkel; Mrs. Zakoyla, Else Neft; Toomey, Michael Fox; Monroe, Nesdon Booth; Fat Woman, Kathleen Freeman; Girl Friend, Juney Ellis; Jack Teagarden; Shorty Rogers and his Band; Uncredited: Narrator, Michael Fox; Club Manager, Lou Krugman; Fat Woman's Friend, Dorothy Neumann; Police News Broadcaster, Roy Engel; Musician in Men's Room, Joseph Mell; Louis (Street Dancer), Dick Monda; Street Dancer, Alvin Freeman; Lieutenant Reeves, Barney Phillips; Giggling Man in Arcade, Richard Collier; Man in Alley with Showgirl, Snub Pollard; Taxi Driver's Friend, Frank Mills

CREDITS: Director, Maxwell Shane; Assistant Director, Richard Dixon; Assistant Director (New York), Ben Berk; Producer, Ivan Tors; Associate Producer, Ben Colman; Screenwriters, Ivan Tors and Maxwell Shane; Supervising Editor, Stanley Frazen; Editor, Herbert L. Strock; Cinematographer, Joseph F. Biroc; Art Director, Serge Krizman; Production Designer, George Van Marter; Production Manager, C.M. Florance; Sound, William A. Wilmarth; Lighting Effects, Robert Jones; Special Effects, Jack Rabin and David Commons

LOCATION FILMING: New York City (United Nations Building, Times Square)

PRODUCTION DATES: Early May–mid–June 1952

RUNNING TIME: 82 minutes

STORY: Vittorio Gassman is a stowaway on a ship bringing immigrants to New York City. Since he was on board illegally, Inspector Douglas Spencer denies him entry. Gassman claims he can be allowed to come to America because he saved an American pilot's life during World War II. All he knows about the man he saved is that he is a clarinet player who worked in the Times Square area. Since Gassman is not allowed to leave the ship, he decides to escape and find the man he saved. Jumping from the ship to the pier below, he injures some ribs. Gassman finds his way to Times Square where, hungry, he stops in a restaurant. In the restaurant, a down-on-her-luck Gloria Grahame swipes Kathleen Freeman's coat. Chased by Freeman and others, Grahame drops the coat. Police join the hunt and Gassman helps Grahame elude the authorities. Gassman coerces Grahame to take him to her rooming house. Grahame and Gassman begin to have strong feelings for each other. Meanwhile the former pilot, Jerry Paris, sees Gassman's picture in the newspaper. Paris' fiancée Ann Robinson has arranged an audition for a spot with Jack Teagarden's band. Paris goes to the club to play with Teagarden, who tells Robinson that he has the job. After one set, Paris realizes he has to go to the immigration authorities to help Gassman. After an altercation with the landlady's son, Gassman and Grahame leave the rooming house and take refuge in the subway. Spotted by police, Grahame is apprehended but Gassman makes his escape with a daring leap in front of an oncoming subway train. Paris and Grahame convince Spencer that Gassman should be able to stay in America legally. Since the ship is scheduled to depart at 7 a.m., Gassman must be found before then or be branded a fugitive from justice and deported. Gassman believes his only chance to be heard is to gain access to the United Nations building. As he reaches the building, he's spotted by Grahame, Paris and Spencer. With two policemen, they call to Gassman. Unaware that they want to help him, Gassman flees into the building, finally ending up on the roof. Gassman prepares to jump when Paris calls out to him. Paris tells Gassman that he will sponsor him. Gassman leaves the building with Paris and Grahame.

NOTES AND COMMENTARY: There were a couple of firsts for this film: It was the first American film of Vittorio Gassman and the first to be made in the newly constructed United Nations building. United Artists was going to release this film before the producers settled on Columbia Pictures. Movie titles seen on various theater marquees are *My Six Convicts* (Columbia, 1952), *Red Mountain* (Paramount, 1951) and *Tomorrow Is Too Late* (RKO, 1952).

REVIEWS: "It lives up to its entertainment intentions sufficiently to rate as regulation heavy-drama screenfare." *Variety*, 3/4/53

"Documentary style photography and atmospheric lighting work very nicely. A brief appearance by Teagarden and Rogers and his band, along with a hard jazzy score, gives the story an even more kinetic feel." *Motion Picture Guide*, Nash and Ross

SUMMATION: The Glass Wall is included in the *Bad Girls of Film Noir* DVD set. There's nary a bad girl to be seen but top-billed Gloria Grahame does a fine job as a woman down on her luck. Jerry Paris registers well as the musician for whom Gassman is searching. But it's Gassman who steals the movie with a fine performance as an immigrant wanting to live in a free country. He captures each mood properly and makes the audience feels his anguish without engaging in unnecessary histrionics. Maxwell Shane directs in such a manner that the audience is kept in suspense. An added bit of enjoyment are the scenes in which Jack Teagarden shows why he was a premier jazz trombonist.

LISTEN TO THOSE CHIMES! LISTEN TO THOSE ROARS! LISTEN TO THOSE CHEERS!

The Good Humor Man

(June 1950)

A S. Sylvan Simon Production

CAST: Biff Jones, Jack Carson; Margie Bellew, Lola Albright; Bonnie Conroy, Jean Wallace; Stuart Nagle, George Reeves; Johnny Bellew, Peter Miles; Inspector Quint, Frank Ferguson; Uncredited: Fat Customer, Maxine Glass; Willie, Jimmy Lagano; Street Cleaner, Emil Sitka; Man in Elevator, Ferris Taylor; Elevator Starter, Garry Owen; Meek Man, Chester Clute; Ambrose, Leslie Bennett; Junior, Billy Gray; Bobby, Timmy Hawkins; Eddie, Gilbert Barnett; Stoker, Jack Overman; Slick, David Sharpe; Fats, Chick Collins; John, Eddie Parker; Officer Daley, Richard Egan; Officer Rhodes, Pat Flaherty; Desk Sergeant, Edgar Dearing; Detectives, George Magrill and Brick Sullivan; Lavery, Robert Emmett Keane; Gardener, Chester Conklin; Fat Inmate, Babe London; Streetwalkers, June Smaney and Lenore Lombard; Big Woman, Ann Kunde; Small Woman, Rose Plumer; Elmer Darby, Lorin Raker; Bride, Victoria Horne; Roger (Bridegroom), Jack Rice; Mr. Watkins, Paul E. Burns; Mr. Lankford, William Forrest; Typist, Mary Bear; Doctor, Edward Keane; Factory Guard, Robert B. Williams; Laundryman, Harry Tyler; Steven, Arthur Space; Fat Man in Park, Vernon Dent; Susan, Susan Simon; Policemen, Robert Malcolm and Frank Sully; Football Player, Teddy Infuhr; Claude, Jackie Jackson; Rollie, Bill McKenzie; Fat Boy, George McDonald

CREDITS: Director, Lloyd Bacon; Assistant Director, Paul Donnelly; Screenwriter, Frank Tashlin; Editor, Jerome Thoms; Art Director, Walter Holscher; Set Decorator, James Crowe; Cinematographer, Lester White; Gowns, Jean Louis; Makeup, Clay Campbell; Hair Stylist, Helen Hunt; Sound, George Cooper; Musical Score, Heinz Roemheld; Musical Conductor, Morris Stoloff

SONGS: "Margie" (Conrad, Robinson and Davis)—played over title credits and throughout the film and "The Wedding March" (Mendelssohn)—played in the final scene

PRODUCTION DATES: May 23–July 13, 1949

SOURCE: story "Appointment with Fear" by Roy Huggins in *The Saturday Evening Post* (September 28, 1946)

RUNNING TIME: 80 minutes

STORY: Good Humor man Jack Carson wants to marry Lola Albright, secretary for private investigator George Reeves. Reeves wants to date Albright. Reeves gets fresh with Albright, which leads to Carson smearing Reeves' face with ice cream. Albright loves Carson but she won't get married because she's the sole support for her younger brother, Peter Miles. Carson and Miles are both members of the local Captain Marvel fan club. When driving home, Carson prevents thugs David Sharpe, Chick Collins and Eddie Parker from kidnapping Jean Wallace. The next night Wallace hails Carson and persuades him to stand guard over her until morning. In return Wallace will buy all the ice cream in Carson's truck. Carson makes it impossible for anyone to enter the house. The next morning Carson finds a lifeless Wallace on the floor with bruise marks on her throat. Even though he knows he'll be the prime suspect, he reports the murder to police Inspector Frank Ferguson. When the police arrive, the corpse is gone. Carson's ice cream truck was used in a murder and robbery and Carson is suspected of being involved in that crime. Carson convinces Albright to help him clear himself. Carson and Albright are able to find Wallace's apartment. Entering, they find Wallace's body on a bed. The three thugs come to the apartment. Carson and Albright are able to hide and hear them talk about the exact amount of money taken in the robbery. Carson starts to call Ferguson when Wallace puts a gun in his back and makes him drop the phone. Wallace was never dead but has a symptomatic epileptic condition that puts her in a temporary deathlike coma. Arthur Space, an accomplice of Wallace, arrives and they plan to murder Carson and Albright. Carson and Albright turn the tables and capture the criminals. Learning that Ferguson is going to Reeves' office, Albright calls Reeves, not knowing Reeves is the gang leader. Albright tells Reeves that until he can get in touch with Ferguson, she and Carson will take refuge in the Captain Marvel clubhouse. Reeves send the thugs to take care of Carson and Albright. A slapstick chase ensues. Miles sees the thugs chasing Albright and Carson and rounds up Captain Marvel Fan Club members. Reeves joins the thugs. Things look grim for Carson and Albright until Miles and his pals spring into action. By the time Ferguson and the other policemen arrive, the crooks are begging to go to jail. Albright finally agrees to marry Carson.

Notes and Commentary: The source for this film was a mystery story starring P.I. Stuart Bailey from the *Saturday Evening Post* magazine. None of the characters from the source material appear in this film. Screenwriter Frank Tashlin lifted the neat locked room murder idea along with having the corpse disappear before the police arrive on the scene. In the story the "corpse" is being victimized by her scheming sister. In the film the "corpse" is part of a crime ring. In both, the young woman had systematic epilepsy which made her appear to be dead.

When Jack Carson and Lola Albright pass a movie theater, a poster for the noir *The Undercover Man* (Columbia, 1949) with Glenn Ford can be seen.

Reviews: "Eighty minutes of fun and frolic... Nifty slapstick fun." *Variety*, 05/31/50

"A surprisingly successful resurrection of Mack Sennett–style slapstick." Genuinely funny." *Motion Picture Guide*, Nash and Ross

Summation: This film provides a good combination of slapstick comedy and noir. Carson is perfect as the naïve but good-hearted lug who gets involved with murder and mayhem. Giving it her best and almost matching Carson's antics is the lovely Lola Albright. Director Lloyd Bacon takes Frank Tashlin's energetic script and really runs with it, culminating in one of the most boisterous and fun-filled slapstick chases to hit the screen.

Don't Condemn Janet Ames until you've Seen the Picture!

The Guilt of Janet Ames

(April 1947)

Cast: Janet Ames, Rosalind Russell; "Smitty" Cobb, Melvyn Douglas; Sammy Weaver, Sid Caesar; Katie, Betsy Blair; Susie Pearson, Nina Foch; Walker, Charles Cane; Carter, Harry von Zell, Junior, Bruce Harper; Nelson, Arthur Space; Joe Burton, Richard Benedict; Danny, Frank Orth; Uncredited: Frank Merino, Hugh Beaumont; Police Sergeant Vicks, Thomas E. Jackson; Surgeon, Edwin Cooper; Susie's Father, Emory Parnell; Nurses, Victoria Horne, Wanda Perry, Kathleen O'Malley and Eve March; Doctors, Pat Lane and Fred Howard; Ambulance Attendant, Steve Benton; Student Nurse, Doris Houck; Headwaiter, William Trenk; Policeman, George Riley; Hospital Janitor, John Farrell; Orderly, Bill Wallace; Drunk Customer, John Berkes; Ambulance Surgeon, William Challee; Chauffeur, Michael Towne; Dr. Morton, William Forrest; Marian (Nurse Receptionist), Isabel Withers; Masher, Denver Pyle; Emmy Merino, Doreen McCann; Sidney, Ray Walker

Credits: Director, Henry Levin; Assistant Director, Milton Feldman; Story, Lenore Coffee; Screenwriters, Louella MacFarlane, Allen Rivkin and Devery Freeman; Editor, Charles Nelson; Art Directors, Stephen Goosson and Walter Holscher; Set Decorators, George Montgomery and Frank Tuttle; Cinematographer, Joseph Walker; Gowns,

Jean Louis and Travis Banton; Makeup, Clay Campbell; Hair Stylist, Helen Hunt; Sound, Frank Goodwin; Music, George Duning; Musical Director, M.W. Stoloff

Location Filming: Mojave Desert, California

Production Dates: July 12–August 13, 1946; September 5–September 19, 1946

Running Time: 83 minutes

Story: Rosalind Russell, walking trancelike, is hit by a car as she crosses the street to enter a seedy bar. She is taken to a hospital. In her purse is the Medal of Honor and a piece of paper with five names. Reporter Harry Von Zell, covering the hospital beat, recognizes Melvyn Douglas' name. Douglas, once a top-flight reporter, is now out of a job. After returning from serving in World War II, he has taken solace in alcohol. Douglas is located and persuaded to come to the hospital. Douglas is shown the list and recognizes all the names. Russell tells the doctors that she's unable to walk even though there is no medical reason for her condition. Douglas tells Russell that he knows all the men on her list. In the war, Russell's husband threw himself on a live grenade, saving the lives of the five men. Russell, bitter because of her husband's death, wants to meet the men to see if they were worth saving. Douglas tells Russell that he's a student of the novel *Peter Ibbetson*, in which Ibbetson, while in prison, could transport himself in his mind to places outside. Douglas tells Russell that he can paint word pictures in which she can meet the five men. Through Douglas, she is transported and finds that one man, Richard Benedict, wants a house with his girl Betsy Blair, a second has forsaken a lucrative life to follow his dreams, a third, Hugh Beaumont, has a daughter, and the fourth, Sid Caesar, aspires to a career in show business. Russell now realizes the fifth man is Douglas, who tells her that he's a successful reporter. Russell never really loved her husband and fears that he sacrificed his life because he had nothing for which to live. Russell and Douglas begin to become romantically attached. Douglas runs away to his favorite bar where he admits that as Russell's husband's commanding officer, he ordered the man to fall on the grenade. This memory drove him to take refuge in alcohol. Douglas tells this to Russell, who tells him that her husband acted instinctively and never heard Douglas' command. The two decide to face life together.

Notes and Commentary: The working title for the film was *My Empty Heart*.

This was a troubled production. Charles Vidor was assigned to direct and Virginia Van Upp would produce. They had worked together on *Gilda* (Columbia, 1946). The two had disagreements about the script. Van Upp collapsed from the stress and Vidor sued Columbia in order to terminate his contract. Production closed down. Script changes were made. Helen Deutsch was Van Upp's replacement. Vidor refused to work with Deutsch. Deutsch wanted out but Columbia president Harry Cohn refused to allow her to quit. Henry Levin took over the directorial reins and received solo screen credit. Neither Van Upp nor Deutsch received on-screen credit. Vidor lost his suit with Columbia who, in return, sued him. Vidor finally bought out his contract.

Reviews: "The people who thought up the story hit upon a good idea. What this picture lacks in large doses is dramatic interest, and there isn't much the principals ... can do about that." *The New York Times*, 5/23/47

"It was either a ludicrous con or a fascinating exercise in psychology, enjoyment of it depending on the viewer's own state of mind. A tighter, more convincing screenplay would have helped matters considerably." *The Columbia Story*, Hirschhorn

Summation: This noirish melodrama has, on the surface, much to offer. There are dark sets, rainswept streets, Daliesque dream sequences and sincere acting. But alas, the screenplay fails to convince. It is too much to believe that two people can rid themselves of their guilt feelings and find true romance in a little over two hours. Too much hokum no matter how cleverly it's served.

SUDDEN DEATH ON GUNMAN'S WALK!

Gunman's Walk

(July 1958)

Cast: Lee Hackett, Van Heflin; Ed Hackett, Tab Hunter; Cecily "Clee" Chouard, Kathryn Grant; Davy Hackett, James Darren; Deputy Sheriff

Gunman's Walk **(1958).**

Will Motely, Mickey Shaughnessy; Sheriff Harry Brill, Robert F. Simon; Purcell Avery, Edward Platt; Jensen Sieverts, Ray Teal; Bob Selkirk, Paul Birch; Curly, Michael Granger; Judge, Will Wright; Uncredited: Paul Chouard, Bert Convy; Black Horse, Chief Blue Eagle; Cook, Paul E. Burns; Bartender, Paul Bryar; Mr. Johnson, Ewing Mitchell; Mrs. Stotheby, Dorothy Adams; the Reverend Arthur Stotheby, Everett Glass; Girl, Gloria Victor; Doctor, Harry Antrim; Storekeeper, Joseph Hamilton; Wranglers, Jack Barry, Wayne Burson, John L. Cason, Brett Halsey, Walt La Rue, and Allen Pinson; Cattlemen, George J. Lewis, Robert Malcolm, David McMahon, Irving Mitchell and Russell Thorson; Dance Hall Girls, Judy Cannon, Shirley Haven, Bek Nelson and Peggy Whitney; Townsmen, Wheaton Chambers, Watson Downs, Sam Flint, Charles Heard, Pierce Lyden, Frank Mills, Alan Reynolds and Hal Taggart; Townswomen, Constance Cameron and Lucille Vance

CREDITS: Director, Phil Karlson; Assistant Director, Sam Nelson; Producer, Fred Kohlmar; Story, Ric Hardman; Screenwriter, Frank Nugent; Editor, Jerome Thoms; Art Director, Robert Peterson; Set Decorator, Frank A. Tuttle; Cinematography, Charles Lawton, Jr.; Makeup, Clay Campbell; Hair Stylist, Helen Hunt; Sound, Lambert Day; Recording Supervisor, John Livadary; Original Music, George Duning; Musical Conductor, Morris Stoloff; Orchestrator, Arthur Morton; Technicolor Color Consultant, Henri Jaffe

SONG: "I'm a Runaway" (Karger and Quine)—sung by Tab Hunter

LOCATION FILMING: Sonoita, Rain Valley, Patagonia, Elgin and San Rafael Valley, Arizona

PRODUCTION DATES: December 10–23, 1957

Color by Technicolor

Filmed in CinemaScope

RUNNING TIME: 95 minutes

STORY: Van Heflin sends his sons Tab Hunter and James Darren to the Indian trading post to find wranglers to help round up horses and drive them to Jackson City, Wyoming. At the post, they find Kathryn Grant, an attractive half-breed, working for Indian agent Edward Platt. Hunter's intentions toward Grant are less than honorable. While trying to apologize for Hunter, Darren begins to fall for Grant. Three men are available for the drive, and one is Grant's brother Bert Convy. Hunter is upset to learn that Convy is considered perhaps the best wrangler in the area. Hunter and Convy ride hell bent for leather to rope an elusive white mare. As they ride on the edge of a steep precipice, neither rider will give way. Hunter deliberately shoves Convy over the edge to his death. Witnesses report to Platt, who has Hunter brought before Judge Will Wright. Wright is about to hold Hunter for trial when horse trader Ray Teal comes forward and lies that the incident was an accident. Hunter is released. Teal, counting on Heflin's generosity, tells him that he's missing ten horses. Heflin tells Teal to look over his stock and if he can spot his horses, he can take them. The tenth horse Teal picks is the white mare. As Teal drives the horses through town, Hunter spots the white mare. Hunter tells Teal he can't have the mare but Teal pulls a gun. As Hunter walks away, he draws his pistol, turns and fires. His bullet creases Teal's gun hand and Teal's gun falls to the ground. Hunter then fires another bullet into Teal's body. In grave condition, Teal is taken to Dr. Harry Antrim's office. Sheriff Robert F. Simon attempts to arrest Hunter, but Hunter refuses to surrender his pistol. To prevent bloodshed, Heflin takes Hunter's gun, and Hunter is jailed. Heflin makes a deal with Teal to say that the incident was a misunderstanding and to stick to the false story about Convy's death. Incensed about being jailed, Hunter makes his escape while gunning down Deputy Mickey Shaughnessey. Heflin hopes to reach Hunter before the sheriff's posse does, and asks Darren to accompany him. Sick of guns and killing, Darren refuses. Heflin tells Darren to stay with Grant and never step foot on his range again. When Heflin reaches Hunter, he realizes that Hunter has turned into a ruthless killer. The two face off in a gunfight. Heflin's bullet finds its mark, ending Hunter's life. Heflin throws away his gun. Returning to town, Heflin finds Darren and Grant waiting. Heflin asks them to ride with him and Hunter's body to the ranch. Breaking down in tears, Heflin is comforted by Darren and Grant.

NOTES AND COMMENTARY: The working title for the film was *The Slicks*. Rudolph Maté was initially assigned as director. When a rough cut of *Gunman's Walk* was screened for Columbia president Harry Cohn, Cohn reportedly cried at the ending. He declared Karlson a great director and promised him top projects. Before this could come about, Cohn died.

REVIEWS: "One of the most interesting of the Westerns of the fifties that center on the conflict between a father and a son. Nugent's screenplay is a little facile, making Heflin and Hunter ciphers rather than characters but Karlson, remorselessly pushing the film to its inevitable conclusion, directs impressively." *The Western*, Hardy

"Okay psychological oater with Van Heflin excelling as the patriarch." *Western Movies*, Pitts

"Complex and interesting film. The film is direct, moving intensely towards its inevitable climax." *Motion Picture Guide*, Nash and Ross

"Director Phil Karlson skillfully juggled the tensions inherent in the behavior of his central trio and drew from his three stars well-rounded, and clearly differentiated performances." *The Columbia Story*, Hirschhorn

SUMMATION: This is a very good western noir that tells the story of one man's spiral into his own destruction. Tab Hunter, cast against type, perfectly essays this young man as he attempts to emulate and surpass the deeds of his father. Van Heflin gives a fine, measured performance as the father, who only realizes too late the monster his son has become. James Darren is very believable as the son who realizes that settling matters with guns has become a thing of the past and is comfortable being his own person. Kathryn Grant plays the part of the Indian maiden who inspires lust in Hunter and love and caring in Darren.

BOGART PULLS NO PUNCHES ... If You Thought On the Waterfront Hit Hard ... Wait Till You See This One!

The Harder They Fall

(April 1956)

CAST: Eddie Willis, Humphrey Bogart; Nick Benko, Rod Steiger; Beth Willis, Jan Sterling; Toro Moreno, Mike Lane; Buddy Brannen, Max Baer; George, Jersey Joe Walcott; Jim Weyerhause, Edward Andrews; Art Leavitt, Harold J.

Stone; Luis Agrandi, Carlos Montalban; Leo, Nehemiah Persoff; Vince Fawcett, Felice Olandi; Max, Herbie Faye; Danny McKeogh, Rusty Lane; Pop, Jack Albertson; Uncredited: Frank, Val Avery; Oklahoma City Ring Announcer, Bill Baldwin; Fight Fan, Emily Belser; Bakersville Boxer, Phil Berger; Mrs. Benko, Tina Carver; Benko's Son, Tony Blankley; Benko's Daughter, Penny Carpenter; Alice, Marian Carr; Chicago Television Announcer, Edwin Chandler; Gus Dundee, Pat Comiskey; Mrs. Harding, Lillian Culver; Shirley, Patricia Dane; Joey, Vinnie De Carlo; Chief Firebird, Abel Fernandez; Priest, Paul Frees; Minister, Everett Glass; San Diego Referee, Benny Goldberg; Gus Dundee's Doctor, Michael Granger; Joey, Joe Greb; Locker Room Guard, William Henry; Tommy, Tommy Herman; San Diego Ring Announcer, Bob Hopkins; Chicago Ring Announcer, Peter Leeds; New York Ring Announcer, Harry Lewis; Reporter in Hospital, Mort Mills; Dundee Referee, Frank Mitchell; New York House Doctor, Irving Mitchell; Sailor Rigazzo, Matt Murphy; Milk Fund Referee, Jimmy O'Gatty; Mrs. Harding's Lawyer, William Roerick; Salinas Referee, Wally Rose; Brannen's Manager, J. Lewis Smith; Chicago House Doctor, Ferris Taylor; Milk Fund Fighter, Pat Valentino; Salinas Boxer, Ulysses Williams; Oklahoma Referee, James Wilson; Fighters, Al Baffert, Tommy Garland, Charles Horvath, Roy Jensen, Tony Pavelec, Jack Roper and Fred Scheiwiller; Statuesque Blonde, Julie Benedic; Fight Managers, George Cisar and Matty Fain; Reporters, Jack Daly, Robert Gamble, Don Kohler, Dennis Moore, Richard Norris, Alan Reynolds, Sandy Sanders and Mark Scott; Las Vegas Showgirls, Dorothy Gordon and Joanne Rio; Referees, Frank Hagney, Joe Herrera and Abe Roth; Fight Fan, Vic Holbrook; Vince's Girlfriends, Elaine Edwards, Pat Lawler and Diana Mumby; Ring Announcer, Joseph Mell; Girls, Jean Smith and Angela Stevens; Pretty Girl, Gloria Victor

Credits: Director, Mark Robson; Assistant Director, Milton Feldman; Producer and Screenwriter, Philip Yordan; Editor, Jerome Thoms; Art Director, William Flannery; Set Decorators, William Kieman and Alfred E. Spencer; Cinematographer, Burnett Guffey; Makeup, Clay Campbell; Hair Stylist, Helen Hunt; Sound, Lambert Day; Recording Supervisor, John Livadary; Original Music, Hugo Friedhofer; Orchestrator, Arthur Morton; Music Conductor, Lionel Newman; Technical Advisor, John Indrisano

Location Filming: Beverly Hills and Los Angeles, California, Chicago, Illinois and New York, New York

Production Dates: October 31–December 29, 1955

Source: novel *The Harder They Fall* by Budd Schulberg

Running Time: 109 minutes

Story: Mob connected fight promoter Rod Steiger brings his new fight discovery, Mike Lane, from Argentina to New York City. Although gigantic in size, Lane is muscle-bound with a powder-puff punch and a glass jaw. Steiger hires down-on-his-luck former sportscaster Humphrey Bogart as publicity agent. Bogart suggests that California would be the best place to begin Lane's professional career. Bogart's articles and connection with other sports writers get Lane tremendous publicity. After a string of fixed fights, Lane believes he has a powerful punch. Bogart's wife Jan Sterling wants him to sever his relationship with Steiger but Bogart, looking for a big payoff after a heavyweight championship fight, refuses. The two become estranged. Lane is scheduled to fight the winner of the Max Baer–Pat Comiskey fight. Baer gives Comiskey a severe beating. Comiskey, through not fully recovered, signs not only to fight Lane but to throw the fight. In the fight, a blow from Lane causes a brain hemorrhage. Comiskey later dies on the operating table and Lane mistakenly thinks his blow was the cause. Bogart convinces Lane that the fights were fixed and that he did not kill Comiskey. Baer, angry that Lane receives credit for Comiskey's death, vows to destroy him in the ring. Lane takes a severe beating although he scores one knockdown. Knowing Lane's boxing career is now at an end, Bogart goes to Steiger to pick up both his and Lane's prize money. Bogart receives $26,000 and finds Lane's contract has been sold to a sleazy fight promoter who plans to schedule fights until Lane can no longer fight. Lane's purse after expenses only comes to $49.07. Bogart is now thoroughly disgusted with the fight racket. Bogart checks Lane out of the hospital and places him on a plane to Argentina after giving him $26,000. Bogart and Sterling reconcile after he tells her he's left Steiger's employ. Bogart tells Steiger he doesn't frighten him and then starts writing a series of articles on Steiger and the crooked fight game.

Notes and Commentary: The major characters' last names were changed as Budd Schulberg's

The Harder They Fall (1956).

novel reached the screen. In addition, Eddie and Beth were lovers in the book and not a married couple. Major characters in the novel either made an abbreviated appearance in the film or were totally eliminated. Nick's wife had adulterous affairs with all the leading boxers in Nick's stable, especially Toro. Shirley, a popular madam in the boxing circles, is not seen in the film. The novel is followed closely until the end. The novel was more noir than the film. In the novel, Toro does not return to Argentina. His contract was sold to a sleazier fight promoter who plans to barnstorm Toro against local fighters until he's too broken-down and punch drunk to go on. Eddie, because of his support of Toro, is now dismissed by the fight boys. Beth, seeing that Eddie will never amount to much, leaves him. Eddie, washed-up, ends up in bed with Shirley, who only takes to bed beaten fighters.

Schulberg's novel was first purchased by Dore Schary at RKO, with hopes of having Robert Mitchum and Joseph Cotten as the leads. When Howard Hughes gained control of RKO, he tried to exchange the rights to the story to Warner Bros. for Errol Flynn's services. Warners wanted the story as a vehicle for Humphrey Bogart and Edward G. Robinson. The deal fell through. Finally, Columbia's Jerry Wald bought the rights from Hughes.

Many thought the novel (and therefore also the movie) was a thinly disguised story of the boxing career of Primo Carnera. Carnera thought so too and sued Columbia for $1.5 million, claiming invasion of privacy. The suit was dismissed, the judge declaring that Carnera was a public figure and that his rights to privacy had been waived. (Max Baer, who played Buddy Brannen, the boxer who ends Toro's bid for a heavyweight championship, also ended Primo Carnera's bid years before.)

The film received an Academy Award nomination for Best Black and White Cinematography. One of the screen's premier cinematographers, Burnett Guffey won Academy Awards for his work on *From Here to Eternity* (Columbia, 1953) and *Bonnie and Clyde* (Warner Bros., 1967) and received nominations for *Birdman of Alcatraz* (United Artists, 1963) and *King Rat* (Columbia, 1966).

The film was released in two different versions. In one, Eddie demands that boxing be abolished. In the DVD version viewed by the author, Eddie wants a federal investigation into the crooked actions behind the boxing scene.

Reviews: "*Fall* is sufficiently well done, is such rousing fare, that it still rates as a strong drawing despite the sanguine sightseeing." *Variety*, 3/28/56

"With all the arcane of the fight game that Mr. Yordan and Mr. Robson have put into it—along with their bruising, brutish fight scenes—it makes for a lively, stinging film." *The New York Times*, 5/10/56

"Nothing about it is pretty, with director Mark Robson moving the story along at a frenetic pace and Burnett Guffey's stark black-and-white photography lending a grim feel to the movie. All the performers are excellent, especially Bogart, in what would be his final screen appearance." *Motion Picture Guide*, Nash and Ross

Summation: Although this is a superior sports noir thanks to fine performances by Bogart as the sports writer and Rod Steiger as the fight promoter, tight direction by Mark Robson and brilliant photography by cinematographer Burnett Guffey, adherence to author Schulberg's novel would have made it more memorable. To Bogart's credit, his acting skill makes his break from Steiger seem realistic.

From dark to dawn... From dives to dames... From cops to killers...

Hell Is a City

(November 1960)

A Hammer Film Production

Cast: Inspector Martineau, Stanley Baker; Don Starling, John Crawford; Gus Hawkins, Donald Pleasence; Julia Martineau, Maxine Audley; Chloe Hawkins, Billie Whitelaw; Furnisher Steele, Joseph Tomelty; Doug Savage, George A. Cooper; Devery, Geoffrey Frederick; Lucky Lusk, Vanda Godsell; Clogger Roach, Charles Houston; Tawney Jakes, Joby Blanshard; Laurie Lovett, Charles Morgan; Bert Darwin, Peter Madden; Bragg, Dickie Owen; Cecily, Lois Daine; Commercial Traveler, Warren Mitchell; Silver Steele, Sarah Branch; Sam, Alastair Williamson; Superintendent, Russell Napier; Uncredited: Headquarters PC, Philip Bond; Fingerprint Officer, John Harvey; Older Sister in the Hospital, Doris Speed; Plainclothes Police Driver, John Comer; Prostitute, Marianne Stone; Pub Customer, Val Guest

Credits: Director and Screenwriter, Val Guest; Assistant Director, Philip Shipway; Producer, Michael Carreras; Editor, John Dunsford; Supervising Editor, James Needs; Art Director, Robert Jones; Cinematographer, Arthur Grant; Makeup, Colin Garde; Hair Stylist, Pauline Trent; Sound, Leslie Hammond and Len Shilton; Original Music–Conductor, Stanley Black; Music Recording Director, A.W. Lumkin; Music Recorded, The Associated British Studios Orchestra; Camera Operator, Moray Grant; Casting Director, Robert Lennard; Assistant Casting Director, David Booth; Wardrobe Mistress, "Jacky" Jackson; Production Manager, Don Weeks; Continuity, Doreen Dearnaley

Filming Location: Manchester, England

Source: novel *Hell Is a City* by Maurice Proctor

Running Time: 95 minutes

Story: John Crawford, a man whom Inspector Stanley Baker has known since childhood, is serving a 14-year prison sentence for jewelry theft. The jewelry was never recovered. Crawford breaks out of prison and gets in contact with the other three members of his gang, Charles Houston, Joby Blanshard and Laurie Lovett. Crawford, needing some ready cash, comes up with a plan to rob bookmaker Donald Pleasence's courier Lois Daine as she goes to the bank with a bag with money chained to her wrist. To save time, Crawford throws Daine in a waiting car. In the car Daine continues to struggle. Crawford strikes Daine with a club, killing her. Daine is thrown in a ditch on the side of the road. A passing motorist, Warren Mitchell, sees the incident and notifies the police. Baker and Detective Geoffrey Frederick respond to the call and notice malachite green dye on her fingertips. Crawford now needs a place to stay while he retrieves the jewels. Furniture dealer Joseph Tomelty, who lives with his deaf-mute daughter Sarah Branch, turns him down, as does old girlfriend Vanda Godsell. Crawford takes refuge in Pleasence's house where he plans to have sex with Pleasence's wife, Billie Whitelaw. Whitelaw had affairs with almost everybody before marrying Pleasence. Unexpectedly Pleasence comes home and Crawford hides in the attic. Next morning, Pleasence hears movement in the attic and investigates. Before he can enter the attic, Crawford strikes him on his head and renders him unconscious. Before leaving, Crawford takes Whitelaw into her bedroom. Baker believes Whitelaw has important information and she tells him that Crawford was in the house. Baker now realizes that Crawford was involved in the robbery and murder of Daine. To get a lead on his confederates who now have money to spend, police raid gambling dens. Pub owner George A. Cooper, detained because traces of the dye are found on his fingers, points out Morgan and Houston as two men with a lot of money. Morgan and Houston are arrested and name Blanshard as the third member of Crawford's crew. Blanshard is arrested before he can leave town. Crawford breaks into Tomelty's place to retrieve the jewels that he had hidden there. Crawford retrieves the jewels but is unable to leave before Branch come up to clean the furniture stored in the attic. Unable to scream, Branch begins throwing furniture through windows, attracting the attention of the police. In a rage, Crawford fires a shot into Branch, seriously wounding her. Crawford takes to the roof with Baker in pursuit. Baker and Crawford have a shootout in which both men are hit. Baker continues the chase and finally catches Crawford. The men fight with Baker pushing Crawford off the roof but still holding on to him. Other police officers arrive and take Crawford into custody. Crawford will now hang for his crimes. As Baker recuperates, he becomes restless staying at home in the company of his wife Maxine Audley, with whom he no longer feels comfortable (he wants children and she doesn't). Baker chooses to walk the dark streets of Manchester alone.

Notes and Commentary: The main thrust of Maurice Proctor's novel was faithfully translated to the screen. There were some changes, modifications and deletions in order not to have an overlong feature. Most of the major changes occurred in the latter stages of the film. In the novel, the bullet fired by Don Starling kills Silver. The film's ending differs from the novel: When approached by the prostitute, Martineau, upset with an unhappy marriage, decides to go with her. The moment ends when she recognizes Martineau. Martineau is then tempted to leave his wife for Lucky Lusk until she reveals she can't stand children. He then walks the streets alone. The alternate ending of the film is like the book's ending as Martineau and his wife decide that children would revitalize their marriage.

The original British release ran 98 minutes. Some salty dialogue was deleted for American audiences.

An alternate ending was filmed. Stanley Baker comes home to his wife Maxine Audley after he had been walking the streets of Manchester. Baker repeats his desire for them to have children. Audley recognizes Baker's need and decides to overcome her fear of having children.

Columbia Pictures acquired the distribution rights for the United States in September 1959 as part of a deal with Hammer Productions. Warner Bros. received the global distribution rights to an Associated British Picture Corporation production.

The novel was published in the United States as *Murder Somewhere in the City*.

Reviews: "Great police yarn with authentic backgrounds, taut screenplay and first class performances, especially by Stanley Baker. A very satisfying film." *Variety*, 5/18/60

"A mild but workmanlike little suspense melodrama. The import is engrossing, making crisp, restrained use of a cops-and-robbers chase yarn to line up a persuasive gallery of characters while shaping a lifelike, if reminiscent movie mosaic." *The New York Times*, 1/19/61

"Satisfying British crime drama, which features a realistic performance from Baker and a script that keeps the action building." *Motion Picture Guide*, Nash and Ross

Summation: This is a taut, well-done cops-and-robbers noir. Stanley Baker gives a superior performance as a detective who feels more at home in dealing with crime than at home dealing with an unhappy marital situation. The rest of the performances are more than satisfactory. Val Guest's direction and screenplay keeps the viewer's attention glued to the screen. Arthur Grant's cinematography captures each scene perfectly and adds to the mounting tension.

TERROR OVER TEXAS as organized crime moves in!
The Screen Hits a Gusher of Excitement!

The Houston Story

(February 1956)

A Clover Production

Cast: Frank Duncan, Gene Barry; Zoe Crane, Barbara Hale; Paul Atlas, Edward Arnold; Gordon Shay, Paul Richards; Madge, Jeanne Cooper; Louie Phelan, Frank Jenks; Emile Constant, John Zaremba; Chris Barker, Chris Alcaide; Willie Lucas, Jack V. Littlefield; Duke, Paul Levitt; Marsh, Fred Krone; Kalo, Pete Kellett; Uncredited: Clara Phelan, Claudia Bryar; Spiro, Mickey Simpson; Taxicab Driver, Frank Sully; Inspector Gregg, Roy Engel; Detective Talbot, Clark Howat; Don Stokes, Charles H. Gray; Café Customer, Jack Stoney; Arresting Policeman at Café, Brick Sullivan

Credits: Director, William Castle; Assistant Director, Gene Anderson, Jr.; Producer, Sam Katzman; Screenwriter, James B. Gordon; Editor, Edwin Bryant; Art Director, Paul Palmentola; Set Decorator, Sidney Clifford; Cinematographer, Henry Freulich; Sound, Josh Westmoreland; Musical Conductor, Mischa Bakaleinikoff; Special Effects, Jack Erickson; Unit Manager, Leon Chooluck

Song: "Put the Blame on Mame" (Roberts and Fisher)—sung by Barbara Hale

Filming Locations: Houston, Texas

Production Dates: early May; July 8–20, 1955

Running Time: 79 minutes

Story: Through nightclub singer Barbara Hale, oil driller Gene Barry meets territorial mob boss Edward Arnold. Barry has a plan to divert oil from existing wells and sell the oil on the black market. The expected take: five million dollars. Arnold has to take the idea to his boss, John Zaremba. Barry has a girlfriend, Jeanne Cooper, who runs a diner that caters to oil workers, but he has more than a passing interest in Hale. Hale is Arnold's second-in-command Paul Richards' girl. Hale could be interested in Barry if his scheme pans out and gives him the key to her house. Zaremba okays the idea. Arnold suggests that when the plan starts rolling, Barry could be eliminated. Zaremba wants no violence, especially since Barry seems to be smart and could have more good ideas. A dummy corporation is formed with Barry's friend Frank Jenks as the president. Jenks would be the fall guy if things went wrong, leaving Barry and Arnold in the clear. Barry tells Arnold that costs could be cut if a pipeline could be established to a small refinery. To hijack the pipes, Barry has to work with Richards. There is no love lost between the two. Barry tapes a conversation with Richards in which he emphasizes there is to be no violence in the hijacking. Richards orders his men to shoot the truckers if necessary. Henchman Chris Alcaide kills one of the men. Zaremba is furious. When Barry plays back the conversation, Zaremba replaces Richards in the organization with Barry. Barry tells Jenks to buy out a small refinery but the owner refuses. Barry knows that the refinery gets its oil from two wells and if the wells are blown up, the refinery would have to be sold. Barry tells Richards he has a chance to partially redeem himself by blowing up the wells. Barry arranges to have police in the vicinity and when they hear the explosions, they pursue and arrest Richards. Since he believes Arnold informed the police, Richards gives up Arnold as the local head of the rackets. A confused Arnold, hearing that he's a wanted man, tries to run but is shot down in an exchange of bullets with the police. Hale tries to tell Barry that now is the time to cut and run before the syndicate decides to replace him. Barry believes that he's too valuable to the organization and decides to stay. Zaremba is upset with all the violence and decides to send two henchmen, Pete Kellett and Charles H. Gray, to kill Barry. Kellett and Gray go to Barry's office, where they find and pistol-whip Jenks. The incident is overheard by Barry and he decides to go on the run. Jenks calls the police and tells them that gangsters are after Barry. Barry tells Hale to meet him at Cooper's diner. Hale, when contacted by the killers, tells them she has no idea where to find Barry. Barry asks Cooper to go to his apartment to retrieve clothes and $100,000 from his wall safe. Cooper arrives at the apartment to find Hale cleaning out the safe. Hale tells Cooper that Barry wants her to go on the run with him but she's taking the money and going on her own. Leaving the apartment, Hale is grabbed by Kellett and Gray. The killers promise Hale that if she gives up Barry, she can go on her way. Believing them, Hale tells them Barry is at the diner. She is then shot and dumped out of the moving car. Cooper calls the police and tells them where Barry can be found. The killers arrive first. There is a gunfight in which Barry is wounded and the killers are killed. The police surround the diner. Jenks and Cooper arrive. Jenks asks Barry to give himself up. Realizing there is no other option, Barry surrenders to the police as Cooper and Jenks watch him being taken away.

NOTES AND COMMENTARY: Lee J. Cobb was signed to play the part of Frank Duncan. While filming scenes in Houston, Cobb collapsed from exhaustion and was hospitalized. With three more days of location filming left, director William Castle, who resembled Cobb, filled in for him in long shots. The film was put on hold. Upon learning that Cobb would not be available for several months, Castle recast the part with Gene Barry.

SUMMATION: This is a very good, hard-hitting crime noir. Castle's direction is on target, highlighting good action sequences throughout. The photography of Henry Freulich is superb, effectively using the dark to highlight tension and suspense. The screenplay by James B. Gordon (pseudonym for Robert E. Kent) plays up violence and sex. The ending with Barry being led away, under arrest, watched by the only two people who care for him, is a neat touch. Barbara Hale is excellent as a hard-as-nails femme fatale who knows the score and almost makes it to safety. Edward Arnold, in one of his last roles, shows his acting skills, primarily in the scene when he realizes his empire has crashed around him and for the first time has to think of flight. Barry is fine as a smart guy who turns out to be too smart for his own good.

SHE WAS BORN TO BE BAD ... TO BE KISSED ... TO MAKE TROUBLE!

Human Desire

(September 1954)

CAST: Jeff Warren, Glenn Ford; Vicki Buckley, Gloria Grahame; Carl Buckley, Broderick Crawford; Alec Simmons, Edgar Buchanan; Ellen Simmons, Kathleen Case; Jean, Peggy Maley; Vera Simmons, Diane DeLaire; John Owens, Grandon Rhodes; Uncredited: Yard Dispatcher, Don C. Harvey; John Thurston, Carl Lee; Train Conductor, John Zaremba; Prosecutor Gruber, Dan Riss; Gruber's Assistant, Hal Taggart; Brakeman, Paul Brinegar; Police Chief, John Maxwell; Lewis, Olan Soule; Duggan, Dan Seymour; Man who Asks Vicki to Dance, John Pickard

CREDITS: Director, Fritz Lang; Assistant Director, Milton Feldman; Producer, Lewis J. Rachmil; Screenplay, Alfred Hayes; Editor, Aaron Stell; Art Director, Robert Peterson; Set Decorator, William Kiernan; Cinematographer, Burnett Guffey; Gowns, Jean Louis; Makeup, Clay Campbell; Hair Stylist, Helen Hunt; Recording Supervisor, John Livadary; Original Music, Daniele Amfitheatrof; Music Conductor, Morris Stoloff

LOCATION FILMING: Reno, Oklahoma (the Santa Fe railroad junction)

PRODUCTION DATES: December 14, 1953–January 25, 1954

SOURCE: novel *La Bête Humaine* by Emile Zola

RUNNING TIME: 90 minutes

STORY: Assistant railroad yard master Broderick Crawford is blamed for an incident that costs the company significant money. He argues with his boss Carl Lee and is fired. Crawford believes that his wife, Gloria Grahame, can get his job back by appealing to Grandon Rhodes, who has significant influence with the railroad. Grahame is hesitant because her previous relationship with Rhodes was sexual. They travel to Chicago where Grahame has sex with Rhodes to get Crawford his job back. When Crawford finds how Grahame influenced Rhodes, he's consumed with jealousy. Realizing that Rhodes will be traveling on the same train that evening, Crawford forces Grahame to send him a note telling him she wants to meet him in his compartment. At the appointed time, Rhodes is surprised to see the angry Crawford, who murders Rhodes and pockets Grahame's note. In trying to return to their compartment, they see Glenn Ford, an engineer who works for the railroad. Crawford tells Grahame to lure Ford away. They go to an empty compartment where Ford kisses Grahame before Grahame leaves to return to Crawford. The next morning, Ford finds out that Grahame is Crawford's wife. Rhodes' body is found and an inquest is held. Grahame tells Ford that she entered Rhodes' compartment and found him dead. Infatuated with Grahame, he lies at the inquest, saying he saw no one leave Rhodes' car at the time of the murder. After the inquest, the relationship between Crawford and Grahame is strained. Grahame can't leave Crawford because he holds the note over her. Crawford begins drinking and gambling. Grahame begins an adulterous affair with Ford. When Crawford's actions get him fired again, he decides that he and Grahame will leave town. Grahame entices Ford to murder Crawford so they can have an open relationship. Ford encounters a drunken Crawford but is unable to murder him although he does retrieve Grahame's note. Having the note, Grahame leaves Crawford on the morning train. Crawford forces his way into Grahame's compartment. Grahame tells Crawford that she had a willing sexual relationship with Rhodes, hoping to entice him to divorce his wife and marry her. Enraged, Crawford strangles Grahame. Ford decides to begin a relationship with fireman Edgar Buchanan's daughter, Kathleen Case, who has always loved him.

Notes and Commentary: Emile Zola's 1890 novel *La Bête Humaine* was set in France in the 1880s and the screenplay was updated to 1950s America with all character names changed. The screenplay followed the basic premise of the novel with some major exceptions. The engineer in the novel had a mental problem, a "blood lust" to murder any woman he might sexually desire. In both, the engineer has knowledge that a railroad employee has murdered a man of prominence. The motive for the murder stemmed from the man of prominence having had sex with the employee's wife, even though in both the novel and screenplay, this man's influence saved the railroad employee from being fired. In both, the wife uses her sexual charms to keep the engineer from stating what he knows to the authorities. The engineer and the wife fall in love. The railroad employee begins to drink and gamble. The wife wants the engineer to murder her husband so they can be together openly. The engineer agrees but is unable to follow through. At this point the novel and the screenplay differ greatly. In the novel the lovers plan to murder the husband but in a sexual moment before the husband arrives, the "blood lust" strikes the engineer and he murders the wife. An innocent man, who is silently in love with the wife, is charged with the murder and circumstances tie the husband to the earlier murder. No suspicion is cast on the engineer, who now begins an affair with his fireman's mistress. The fireman attempts to throw the engineer off a speeding train. The two men begin a furious struggle with both falling under the wheels of the train and being decapitated. As the story ends, the runaway train is speeding across France.

Zola's novel was first filmed as *La Bête Humaine* (Paris Film, 1938), directed by Jean Renoir. Jean Gabin and Simone Simon played the engineer and the railroad employee's wife.

The rights to Zola's novel were purchased by producers Jerry Wald and Norman Krasna in September 1950. Fritz Lang would direct with Barbara Stanwyck, Robert Ryan and Paul Douglas in the lead roles. (The four worked together in 1952's *Clash by Night.*) Columbia obtained the rights in December 1952. Originally Peter Lorre was sought to play Jeff Warren. Lorre disliked Lang from their association in the filming of *M* (Nero-Film AG, 1931). Rita Hayworth was the first choice for the role of Vicki. After her marriage to Dick Haymes, Hayworth withdrew from the film. Then Olivia de Havilland and subsequently Jennifer Jones were considered to replace Hayworth. With the success of *The Big Heat* (Columbia, 1953), it was finally decided to cast Glenn Ford and Gloria Grahame. Unfortunately, Harry Cohn disliked the downbeat tone of Zola's novel. The sexual tones inherent in the novel and the earlier film were decidedly toned down to the disappointment, especially, of Lang. He directed in a tyrannical manner. The third major cast member Broderick Crawford lifted Lang off the floor by his lapels after he unnecessarily yelled at Grahame. Lang finished directing the film, satisfying his commitment to Columbia, and left by mutual consent for Metro-Goldwyn-Mayer.

Reviews: "The development is contrived and the characters shallow. The scenario lacks any genuine suspense or excitement and the players down the line impart slight conviction to their parts." *Variety*, 8/11/54

"Among the assorted troubles with Columbia's *Human Desire* is there isn't a single character in it for whom it builds up the slightest sympathy—and there isn't a great deal else in it for which you're likely to have the least regard. This film has been directed in a flat, lethargic fashion by the usually creative Fritz Lang." *New York Times*, 8/7/54

"This sordid little tale is not nearly as sensuous or sexual as the French version, nor is it very suspenseful. The only person we can root for is Ford, and even he sleeps with a married woman. Guffey's moody photography serves to make this movie look better than it actually is." *Motion Picture Guide*, Nash and Ross

SUMMATION: Although the film is not truly faithful to Zola's novel, it is nevertheless satisfactory entertainment. Thanks to the acting of the principals and the cinematography of Burnett Guffey, the result is a successful film noir. Grahame sizzles as the femme fatale and Crawford is first-rate as the brutish husband prone to unthinkable violence. Kathleen Case registers strongly as the woman who knows she's the right woman for Glenn Ford. Though he disliked the final screenplay, Fritz Lang's directorial skill still surfaces.

A weird death sentence from the mystic east!

I Love a Mystery

(January 1945)

CAST: Jack Packard, Jim Bannon; Ellen Monk, Nina Foch; Jefferson Monk, George Macready; Doc Long, Barton Yarborough; Jean Anderson, Carole Mathews; Justin Reeves, Lester Matthews; Uncredited: Gimpy, Ernie Adams; Vovaritch, Leo Mostovoy; Miss Osgood, Isabel Withers; Street Musician, Pietro Sosso; Mr. G's Doorkeeper, Harry Semels; Dr. Han, Gregory Gay; Capt. Quinn, Joseph Crehan; "Pegleg" James Anderson, Frank O'Connor

CREDITS: Director, Henry Levin; Producer, Wallace MacDonald; Screenwriter, Charles O'Neal; Editor, Aaron Stell; Art Director, George Brooks; Set Decorator, Joseph Kish; Cinematography, Burnett Guffey; Sound, Edward Bernds

George Macready, Jim Bannon and Barton Yarbrough in *I Love A Mystery* (1945).

Production Dates: October 23–November 9, 1944

Running Time: 70 minutes

Source: the original radio program "I Love a Mystery" written and directed by Carlton E. Morse

Story: A car crashes and the dead body of George Macready is brought to the morgue. At the Silver Samovar nightclub, detectives Jim Bannon and Barton Yarborough rehash the events of the past three days. In flashbacks we see that at the nightclub they met Macready and his companion Carole Mathews. Macready tells them that he's scheduled to die in three days and that a peglegged man with a satchel large enough to hold his head is following him. Bannon and Yarborough agree to help Macready. Leaving the nightclub with Mathews, Macready is followed. The detectives confront the peglegged man, Frank O'Connor, but he is able to get away. Macready tells the detectives that problems began when he and his wife Nina Foch were on a trip to the Orient. They were followed by a mysterious street musician, Pietro Sosso, even to the streets of San Francisco. Sosso confronts Macready and leads him to a meeting with Lester Matthews, who states that he is the leader of the Barokan, a secret society. Matthews offers to pay Macready $10,000 for his head, which is needed to replace that of the deceased sacred one. Foch receives a letter prophesying that she would be an invalid in three days. Dr. Gregory Gay, who is working with Foch, verifies that she is indeed paralyzed. Bannon figures out that Foch is faking. Bannon finds that in the event of a divorce, the wealth of the couple will go to charity. Only by death can the survivor inherit the money. In his investigation, Bannon encounters an Oriental seller who knows Foch. Bannon guesses that Matthews is the so-called leader of the Barokan. Bannon has a plan to draw out O'Connor but Mathews interferes. O'Connor retreats to his rooming house not realizing he's being followed, and he is brutally murdered. Next Mathews meets the same fate. With the cooperation of the police, Bannon has telegrams sent to Foch, Matthews and Gay, telling them he knows who the murderer is, and asks the murderer to meet him at one of Macready's warehouses. The three meet secretly in Foch's bedroom, knowing that not one of them is the murderer, and refuse to rise to the bait. Matthews is ready to back out of the scheme but Foch wants to carry it through. As Matthews leaves Macready's house, he's murdered. Macready confronts Foch and tells her that he is the murderer and that she will one day be killed by him. Afraid that Bannon will figure out his scheme, Macready goes to the warehouse to kill Bannon. Bannon and Macready scuffle but Macready is able to get away. In his haste to escape, his car crashes and Macready is killed. Yarborough thinks everything is neatly wrapped up. Bannon states there's still one loose end: No one knows what happened to Macready's head.

Notes and Commentary: The initial entry of the series was based on the radio program episode "The Head of Jonathan Monk." The character was changed to Jefferson Monk in the film. *Variety* indicated that Columbia intended to produce two films annually for five years. The series was terminated after three episodes.

Jim Bannon had his own series again in 1949 when he played Red Ryder in four films for Eagle-Lion.

The notes played by the street musician were lifted from Tchaikovsky's *Fifth Symphony*.

Reviews: "A preposterous, thoroughly tasteless and rather nasty little thriller." *The Columbia Story*, Hirshhorn

"Shaky direction and script, but good performances from Bannon and Foch." *Motion Picture Guide*, Nash and Ross

"Fairly suspenseful low-budget chiller." *Variety*, 2/28/45

Summation: This is a good, film noirish murder mystery with supernatural overtones in the tradition of the popular radio show. Bannon and Yarborough stand out as the detectives, but it's George Macready's show as the beleaguered man marked for death. Director Henry Levin paces the story to its wow finish.

Scandalous secrets only murder can silence!

I Love Trouble

A S. Sylvan Simon Production
A Cornell Production

(January 1948)

Cast: Stuart Bailey, Franchot Tone; Norma

Shannon, Janet Blair; Mrs. Caprillo aka Jane Breeger and Janie Joy, Janis Carter; Boots Nestor, Adele Jergens; Hazel Bixby, Glenda Farrell; Keller, Steven Geray; Ralph Johnson, Tom Powers; Mrs. Johnson, Lynn Merrick; Reno, John Ireland; Martin, Donald Curtis; John Vega Caprillo, Eduardo Ciannelli; Lt. Quint, Robert H. Barrat; Herb, Raymond Burr; Uncredited: High School Girl, Nan Holliday; Gus, Garry Owen; Warehouse Foreman, Harry Tyler; Angel, Martha Montgomery; Blonde at Club Zoro, Claire Carleton; Butler, Vesey O'Davoren; Recording Detective, Lane Chandler; Gracie, Isabel Withers; Janitor, Paul E. Burns; Miss Phipps, Roseanne Murray; Betty, Karen X. Gaylord; Eunice (Maid), Louise Franklin; Lab Man, Douglas D. Coppin; Plainclothesman, Gene Roth; Policeman at Crime Scene, John Hart

Credits: Director-Producer, S. Sylvan Simon; Assistant to Producer, Earl McEvoy; Screenwriter, Roy Huggins; Editor, Al Clark; Art Directors, Stephen Goosson and Carl Anderson; Set Decorators, Wilbur Menefee and Louis Diage; Cinematographer, Charles Lawton, Jr.; Gowns, Jean Louis; Sound, Frank Goodwin; Original Music, George Duning; Musical Director, M.W. Stoloff

Location Filming: Westwood Village, Westwood, Los Angeles, California

Production Dates: May 14–June 19, 1947

Source: novel *The Double Take* by Roy Huggins

Story: Private investigator Franchot Tone is hired by Tom Powers to investigate the background of his wife, Lynn Merrick. The trail leads to a Portland gambling club run by Steven Geray. Geray allows Tone to rummage through old posters of performers that worked in a now-defunct nightclub. Tone spots and takes a photograph of Merrick. Tone is told that Merrick left the city with comic Sid Tomack, who now runs a restaurant. Tomack tells Tone that she started using a stage name with her new act. Tone makes the rounds of the booking agencies without success. Janet Blair comes to Tone's office telling him that she's the sister of the woman for whom he's looking. Tone has his doubts when Blair makes no comments after looking at Merrick's picture. Donald Curtis, chauffeur for Janis Carter, offers Tone money to drop the case. Tomack calls Tone and tells him that he has important, expensive information. Arriving at Tomack's restaurant, Tone hears three shots and finds the murdered Tomack. Geray's henchmen John Ireland, Raymond Burr and Eddie Marr kidnap Tone. A drug is injected into Tone to render him unconscious. Before the drug fully takes effect, Tone makes it look like he climbed out of a window when, in fact, he hid under the bed. Returning to his office, Tone learns that Merrick and Tomack met in the coffee shop the day Tone first talked to Tomack. Tone believes Merrick shot Tomack and tells Powers he'll have to report this to Lt. Robert H. Barrat. Powers tells Tone that Merrick left town. Merrick is found dead and Tone is framed for the crime. Barrat puts Tone under arrest but Tone's secretary, Glenda Farrell, helps him escape. He returns to his apartment where Carter is waiting for him. Powers calls and Tone tells him he has an unopened letter from Merrick that he's planning to turn over to the police. Tone figures out that Merrick, hiding from Geray, assumed Carter's identity. Geray comes to the apartment and verifies this and states that Merrick disappeared after stealing a large amount of money from him. Arriving, Blair confirms that Carter is her sister. Carter mentions that Merrick was Geray's wife. Powers turns up and accuses Tone of murder. Tone deduces that Merrick murdered Tomack and then Powers killed Merrick. Tone tells Powers that Merrick was using him as a hideout from Geray. As Powers prepares to kill Tone, a shot rings out. Barrat, who had earlier been called by Tone, wounds Powers and then takes him into custody. Tone and Blair decide a romance is in order.

Notes and Commentary: The working title for this film was *The Double Take*. It was based on Roy Huggins' novel *The Double Take*. The novel was followed fairly faithfully until the discovery of the murder of Mrs. Johnson. In the novel, the plot went through a gambling casino boss to work up to the conclusion. The film deviated by having Stuart Bailey framed for both murders. The denouncement in both occurs in Bailey's apartment. Only in the film are any of the women present. Before Ralph Johnson can murder Bailey, Lt. Quint shoots Johnson. In the film, Johnson is wounded and arrested. In the novel, the bullet kills Johnson. In the novel, Norma ends up with Bailey the next day. This was the first screen appearance of private eye Stuart Bailey. Ten years later Bailey showed up in *Girl on the Run* (Warner Bros., 1958) with Efrem Zimbalist, Jr. in the role. This led to Zimbalist playing the character on the hit Warner Bros. series *77 Sunset Strip* (1958–1964).

Reviews: I Love Trouble spins its involved melodramatics at a good pace. Production polish is excellent. Lensing by Charles Lawton, Jr. is top-notch. Neatly paced whodunit." *Variety*, 12/24/47

"The mystery has plenty of unexpected sidelights to hold audience interest through the shallow story." *Motion Picture Guide*, Nash and Ross

Summation: This is a good detective noir with Franchot Tone playing to perfection a wisecracking sleuth. John Ireland and Raymond Burr play truly sinister henchmen. Glenda Farrell is outstanding as Tone's secretary-assistant. Roy Huggins does a good adaptation of his novel, elevating the story with some snappy dialogue. S. Sylvan Simon brings a good, well-paced, hard-hitting story to the screen. Charles Lawton, Jr.'s camerawork is first-rate, especially in the scenes in and around Geray's gambling club and the scenes where Tone is captured and beaten by Geray's henchmen.

THE BOGART SUSPENSE PICTURE WITH THE SURPRISE FINISH

In a Lonely Place

(May 1950)

A Santana Production

Cast: Dixon Steele, Humphrey Bogart; Laurel Gray, Gloria Grahame; Detective Sergeant Brub Nicolai; Frank Lovejoy; Captain Lochner, Carl Benton Reid; Agent Mel Lippman, Art Smith; Sylvia Nicolai, Jeff Donnell; Mildred Anderson, Martha Stewart; Charlie Waterman, Robert Warwick; Lloyd Barnes, Morris Ankrum; Ted Barton, William Ching; Paul, Steven Geray; Singer, Hadda Brooks; Uncredited: Fran Randolph, Alix Talton; Henry Kesler, Jack Reynolds; Effie, Ruth Warren; Martha, Ruth Gillette; Mr. Swan, Guy Beach; Junior, Lewis Howard; Joe,

Frank Lovejoy, Carl Benton Reid, Gloria Grahame and Humphrey Bogart are *In a Lonely Place* (1950).

Arno Frey; Hatcheck Girl, Pat Barton; Airline Clerk, Robert Lowell; John Mason, Don Hamin; Waiter, George Davis; Tough Girl, Melinda Erickson; Officer, John Jahries; Dr. Richards, David Bond; Post Office Clerk, Myron Healey; Actress in Convertible, June Vincent; Bartender, Cosmo Sardo; Angry Husband in Convertible, Charles Cane; Young Boy Seeking Autographs, Billy Gray; Flower Shop Employee, Davis Roberts; Dave (Parking Lot Attendant), Frank Marlowe

Credits: Director, Nicholas Ray; Assistant Director, Earl Bellamy; Producer, Robert Lord; Associate Producer, Henry S. Kesler; Adaptation, Edmund H. North; Screenwriter, Andrew Solt; Editor, Viola Lawrence; Art Director, Robert Peterson; Set Decorator, William Kiernan; Cinematographer, Burnett Guffey; Gowns, Jean Louis; Makeup, Clay Campbell; Hair Stylist, Helen Hunt; Sound, Howard Fogetti; Original Music, George Antheil; Musical Director, Morris Stoloff; Technical Advisor, Rodney Amateau

Song: "I Hadn't Anyone Till You" (Noble)—sung by Hadda Brooks

Location Filming: Beverly Hills and West Hollywood, California

Production Dates: October 25–December 1, 1949

Source: novel *In a Lonely Place* by Dorothy B. Hughes

Running Time: 94 minutes

Story: Humphrey Bogart, a screenwriter with no recent hit movies, is offered the job of adapting a bestselling novel. Bogart has no desire to read the novel. He asks Martha Stewart, who thought the novel was great, to come to his apartment and tell him the story. Enthralled at being in the presence of a celebrity, Stewart breaks her date with her boyfriend Jack Reynolds. After a half-hour, Bogart has heard enough. He gives Stewart $20 and directs her to a taxi stand. A few hours later, Bogart is awakened by Army buddy Frank Lovejoy, now a police sergeant, who tells him that he's wanted at police headquarters. Captain Carl Benton Reid informs Bogart that Stewart was murdered. Bogart is the prime suspect until Bogart's neighbor, Gloria Grahame, tells police that she saw Stewart leave Bogart's apartment alone. Bogart tells Lovejoy and his wife Jeff Donnell that he believes Reynolds is the murderer and describes how the murder was carried out. Bogart and Grahame become romantically attached. Bogart, now happy and contented, begins work on the screenplay. Grahame is questioned again by Reid because he believes Bogart, who has a violent past, is the murderer. When Bogart finds out by chance that Grahame had again been questioned, he becomes angry and gets behind the wheel of his car. Grahame gets in the car and tries to calm down Bogart. Bogart's wild driving gets him into a minor accident with Don Hamin. When Hamin calls Bogart names, Bogart begins hammering Hamin with his fists. As Hamin lies on the ground beaten, Bogart picks up a large rock. Only Grahame's calling out to him stops him from striking Hamin. The incident frightens Grahame and although she loves Bogart, she's afraid of him. Grahame plans to leave for New York. Bogart, now wanting to marry Grahame quickly, forces her to accept an engagement ring. At an engagement party, Bogart finds that Grahame gave the finished script to his agent Art Smith. This upsets Bogart and he strikes Smith. As Bogart apologizes to Smith, Grahame returns to her apartment. Thoroughly afraid of Bogart, she plans to leave for New York on the first flight she can get. Bogart confronts Grahame and finds that she's leaving him. Again in anger, Bogart begins choking her. The phone rings. Bogart takes his hands off Grahame and, in a daze, answers the phone. Lovejoy has been trying to reach Bogart to tell him Reynolds committed the murder just as Bogart indicated. Reid gets on the line to apologize to Grahame. Grahame tells Reid the news is too late. Bogart knows his actions doomed their relationship and he walks out of Grahame's life.

Notes and Commentary: Dorothy B. Hughes' novel was completely reworked. In the novel, Dixon Steele was not only much younger, but a serial rapist and killer. Steele meets Laurel Gray and falls in love with her. Steele believes Gray will marry him. Her sudden disappearance begins to unnerve Steele. Steele plans to murder Gray when she returns to her apartment. Steele sees a woman dressed like Gray returning to her apartment. He is shocked when he discovers the woman is Sylvia Nicolai, wife of detective Brub Nicolai. Gray, fearing Steele, had taken refuge with the Nicolais. Steele, under arrest, finally admits his guilt.

Humphrey Bogart's Santana Productions purchased the rights to Hughes' novel. Bogart wanted his wife Lauren Bacall for the role of Laurel Gray. Warner Bros., who had Bacall under contract, refused to loan her out. Next Ginger Rogers was considered for the role. Director Nicholas Ray made a successful case to have his wife, Gloria Grahame, play the part.

A problem arose, with Ray and Grahame's marriage coming to an end. This fact was kept secret, for fear that disclosure of their marital status would mean the removal of Ray as director. It was written into Grahame's contract that she would have to obey any request from Ray during the hours of filming. Also, Grahame was forbidden to say or do anything that would delay production. Ray, not being able to return home at night, slept at the studio, using the excuse he had to work late into the night in preparation for the next day's shooting.

Andrew Solt's screenplay had murder suspect Bogart, a man with violent tendencies, become so enraged at the thought of Grahame leaving him that he strangles her. After the scene was filmed, Ray had second thoughts about the ending. He cleared the set of all but essential personnel and a new ending was filmed. Now Bogart almost commits the crime, but stops. Bogart is cleared of the suspicion of murder but his actions doom the romance between him and Grahame.

The original adaptation by Edmund H. North adhered closely to Hughes' novel. John Derek was considered for the role of Dixon Steele. Even though North received screen credit, his version was not used. Bogart was extremely pleased with Solt's screenplay. The working title for the film was *Behind the Mask*.

REVIEWS: "Humphrey Bogart as a temperamental, fistic-loving screenwriter, generates *In a Lonely Place* into a box office winner. Andrew Solt's screenplay makes for a forceful drama." *Variety*, 5/17/50

"Humphrey Bogart is in top form in his latest independently made production ... and the picture is a superior cut of melodrama." *New York Times*, 5/18/50

"Superior film noir, brilliantly directed by the gifted Ray..." *Motion Picture Guide*, Nash and Ross

SUMMATION: This more than a great film noir, this is a great picture. This is a film in which everything fits together perfectly. Bogart, in one of the finest roles in his storied career, is perfect as the on-the-edge, individual who finally finds love but loses it because of his violent tendencies. Grahame is on the mark with her portrayal of a woman who finally finds a man she could love but is unable to overcome her fear of him. Ray directs with a sure hand, slowly bringing the suspense to a boiling point. Ray improves on Andrew Solt's otherwise fine screenplay with his imaginative and just-right ending to the story. Burnett Guffey's photography is top-notch, especially in the scene in which Bogart describes how the murder was committed. Don't miss this one.

"I'm takin' over this town ... again! I'm gonna throw Detroit wide open! Dice, dames, the horses, the numbers—the works! And no one better get in my way!"

Inside Detroit

(January 1956)

A Clover Production

CAST: Blair Vickers, Dennis O'Keefe; Gus Linden, Pat O'Brien; Joni Calvin, Tina Carver; Barbara Linden, Margaret Field; Gregg Linden, Mark Damon; Max Harkness, Larry Blake; Ben Macauley, Ken Christy; Pete Link, Joseph Turkel; Sam Foran, Paul Bryar; Hoagy Mitchell, Robert Griffin; Jenkins, Guy Kingsford; Toby Gordon, Dick Rich; Preacher Bronislav, Norman Leavitt; Ethel Linden, Katherine Warren; Uncredited: On-Screen Commentator, John Cameron Swayze; Narrator, William Woodson; Tom Vickers, William Bryant; Blair's U.A.W. Friends, William Boyett, John Pickard and Paul Sorenson; Recreation Hall Manager, Wally Campo; Reporter at Hospital, Cosmo Sardo; Doctor, George Eldredge; Earl Heaton, President of United Auto Workers, Earl Heaton; Harry, Stanley Adams; Reller, James Anderson; Mrs. Jenkins, Helen Brown; Irate Plant Worker, Paul Brinegar; Pharmacist, George Cisar; Witness at Car Accident, Eddie Parker

CREDITS: Director, Fred F. Sears; Assistant Director, Gene Anderson, Jr.; Screenwriters, Robert E. Kent and James B. Gordon; Editor, Gene Havlick; Art Director, Paul Palmentola; Set Decorator, Sidney Clifford; Cinematographer, Henry Freulich; Unit Manager, Leon Chooluck; Sound, Harry Smith; Special Effects, Jack Erickson; Musical Conductor, Mischa Bakaleinikoff; Technical Advisor, William Martin

SONGS: "Silent Night" (Mohr and Gruber, tr. Young)—sung by male chorus and "St. James Infirmary Blues (anonymous)—played by jazz combo

Production Dates: June 20–July 2, 1955

Location Filming: Detroit, Michigan

Story: At the Union Hall, Joseph Turkel plants a bomb that explodes, killing Dennis O'Keefe's brother William Bryant and three other union members. O'Keefe blames his nemesis Pat O'Brien, although O'Brien has five days left on his prison term. O'Brien's daughter Margaret Field tells O'Keefe her father is innocent. O'Brien is upset that the explosion did not kill O'Keefe. Upon his release from prison, O'Brien plans to take over the country's unions plus control the rackets in Detroit. Although married with a daughter (Field) and a son, Mark Damon, O'Brien resumes his affair with Tina Carver. Carver, who waited five years for O'Brien's release, wants him to divorce his wife and marry her. O'Brien refuses. Damon believes O'Keefe framed O'Brien and goes to O'Keefe's apartment, gun in hand. Damon is subdued by O'Keefe and police detective Larry Blake. O'Keefe gets Damon placed in his care. O'Keefe and Blake take Damon to a party where he sees his father's unsavory companions. Upset, Damon leaves the apartment but is joined by Carver, who seduces him. O'Brien wants his men hired to work in a plant controlled by O'Keefe's union. To achieve this, gang members Turkel and James Anderson work over plant hiring boss Guy Kingsford and threaten his family. Worker preacher Norman Leavitt is protesting the hiring of O'Brien's men when steel beams are dropped on him. The murder is witnessed by O'Keefe and Field, who obtained a job at the plant to see if O'Keefe's suspicions were justified. O'Brien's men begin to take over the plant. Damon falls in love with Carver, who offers him a partnership in her modeling firm, not knowing this is a front for illegal activities. Kingsford finally decides to talk about O'Brien's activities but is murdered by Turkel before he can meet O'Keefe at the police station. At a roadhouse, O'Keefe shows Field that there is a romantic attachment between Damon and Carver. Upset, Field leaves the road house, driving recklessly and smashing into a tree. O'Keefe puts pressure on Damon, who leads O'Keefe and Blake to information that would convict Carver. Pressure is then put on Carver to cooperate with the authorities with the choice of jail or deportation. Carver agrees to work with O'Keefe and Blake. Damon tells O'Brien that he plans to marry Carver. O'Brien goes to Carver's apartment for a showdown, planning to have Turkel kill Carver. Waiting outside the apartment, O'Keefe and Blake watch the scene unfold. When Turkel tries to shoot Carver, Blake shoots Turkel. Blake is hit by a bullet from O'Brien's gun. O'Keefe dives into the apartment and picks up Turkel's gun. O'Keefe and O'Brien exchange shots, with O'Keefe wounding and capturing O'Brien. O'Brien's crime scheme is ended.

Notes and Commentary: Producer Sam Katzman is credited in the print ads but does not receive on-screen credit. *Inside Detroit* was actor Mark Damon's big screen debut.

From various sources, it is suggested that this film was based incidents in the life of United Auto Workers president Walter Reuther and his brother.

Reviews: "Fair melodrama. A familiar good-verses-racketeer type of actioner." *Variety*, 12/14/55

"Though strictly a formula piece and woefully naïve about the realities of crooked unions, it's a competently produced and acted piece. The pseudodocumentary style fits the film's mood." *Motion Picture Guide*, Nash and Ross

Summation: This is a good gritty "B" yarn of one man's crusade against mob rule in Detroit. Fred F. Sears' direction keeps the story continuously moving and holds the audience's interest. The acting is average for this sort of film with special mention to Margaret Field's fine performance as O'Brien's daughter who finally realizes her father is a mob boss. Kudos to screenwriters Robert E. Kent and James B. Gordon for not having the film end with Field in O'Keefe's arms. Henry Freulich's cinematography is on target.

SHE PULLED THE STRINGS ... HE PULLED THE TRIGGER... together, they ruled the mob!

Joe Macbeth

(February 1956)

Cast: Joe MacBeth, Paul Douglas; Lily MacBeth, Ruth Roman; Lennie, Bonar Colleano; Mr. del Luca, Gregoire Aslan; Banky, Sidney James;

Big Dutch, Harry Green; Angus, Walter Crisham; Ruth, Kay Callard; Ross, Robert Arden; Second Assassin, George Margo; Rosie, Minerva Pious; Tommy, Philip Vickers; Benny, Mark Baker; Marty, Bill Nagy; Al (First Assassin), Alfred Mulock; Uncredited: Duffy, Nicolas Stuart; Patsy, Shirley Douglas; Mae, Louise Grant; Johnny, Robert O'Neill; Mugsy, Johnny Ross; Ruth, Teresa Thorne; Joan, Sheila Woods; Chef, Victor Baring; Sandwich-board Man, Beresford Egan; Physician, Launce Maraschal

Credits: Director, Ken Hughes; Assistant Director, Phil Shipway; Producer, M.J. Frankovich; Associate Producer, George Maynard; Screenwriter, Philip Yordan; Editor, Peter Rolfe Johnson; Assistant Editor, John Jympson; Cinematographer, Basil Emmott; Camera Operator, Bernard Lewis; Wardrobe, Jean Fairlie; Makeup, R. Bonnor-Morris and Terry Terrington; Hair Stylist, Nina Broe; Sound Editor, Alfred Cox; Sound Recordists, W.H. Lindop and Ken Cameron; Original Music, Trevor Duncan; Music Supervisor, Richard Taylor; Production Designer, Alan Harris; Production Manager, "Freddie" Pearson; Continuity, Splinters Deason

Production Dates: early May–early July 1955

Running Time: 90 minutes

Story: Under orders from mob kingpin Gregoire Aslan, Paul Douglas murders Aslan's number 1 man Philip Vickers. Douglas next marries Ruth Roman and Aslan takes over Vickers' night club. Flower vendor Minerva Pious, who now tells fortunes, predicts that Douglas will live in Vickers' mansion and will become the mob boss. Aslan gives Douglas the key to the mansion and orders him to murder rival mob boss Harry Green. Douglas has Green poisoned. Pious again reads the future and predicts someone will die in the mansion. Aslan is invited to spend the night and Roman tells Douglas this is his chance to murder Aslan and become kingpin. Extremely reluctant but prodded by Roman, Douglas fatally stabs Aslan. Douglas becomes the mob boss and makes his friend, Sidney James, his number one man. Douglas' rough and ruthless ways upset the men, especially James' son Bonar Colleano. Pious tells Douglas to watch out for Colleano. Douglas brings in two assassins, Alfred Mulock and George Margo, to murder Colleano. In the murder attempt, the assassins kill James but Colleano escapes. At a dinner party for his men, Douglas explains that James and Colleano will not be present. Unexpectedly, Colleano does arrive. Douglas is so unnerved that in a hallucination, he sees James in the empty chair. Roman calms down Douglas and tells all the men to leave the house. As the mob leaves, they agree that Colleano should be the new mob boss. To control Colleano, Douglas sends the assassins to kidnap Colleano's wife Kay Callard and their infant son. Unaware of Douglas' plan, Roman arrives at Colleano's apartment to convince Callard to have Colleano work with Douglas. As she enters the apartment building, the assassins are leaving. In the apartment, Roman finds the dead bodies of Callard and her son. Upon receiving word of his family's demise, Colleano vows vengeance on Douglas and sends word to Douglas that he's coming for him. Roman now believes that she sees blood on her hands. Roman keeps leaving her bed only to be told to return by Douglas. Douglas makes ready for Colleano, believing that he and the assassins can repel any attack. The assassins believe that they weren't paid for an all-out battle and decide to leave. When they walk out of the mansion, they are gunned down. Douglas is now frightened to the point that he begins to shoot at shadows. When the library door opens, Douglas fires and then realizes he just killed Roman. Before Douglas can fully reflect on his actions, bullets to his back end his life. With Douglas and Roman dead, Colleano plans to dissolve the mob. As he leaves the mansion, police sirens and the sound of gunfire are heard.

Notes and Commentary: Joe MacBeth is a modernized telling of William Shakespeare's tragedy *Macbeth*. The fortune teller replaces the three witches. Some of the character names have been modernized, e.g. Banquo becomes Banky, Duncan becomes del Duca and Lady Macbeth is now Lily Macbeth. As in the play, the predictions come true. In the play, Macbeth sees the ghost of Banquo and in the film, Banky is a hallucination of Joe's. Lady Macbeth descends into madness after the deaths of Banquo's son's wife and child. Lily Macbeth begins to go mad after seeing Lennie's dead family. As in the play, Banquo (Banky)'s son ends Joe Macbeth's reign as mob kingpin.

It took about nine years to bring Philip Yordan's screenplay to the screen. In 1947, the screenplay was going to be filmed in Chicago with Robert Cummings as star. In 1949, Lew Ayres and Shelley Winters were in the running to star in the film. In 1954, Mike Frankovich was now the producer and he wanted John Ireland and Joanne Dru in the leads. Finally in March 1955, Frankovich made a deal to produce the film in London for release through Columbia Pictures.

Review: "A dreadful underworld melodrama." *The Columbia Story*, Hirschhorn

SUMMATION: This is a grim, gripping, violent and intense crime noir. Even though director Ken Hughes is somewhat hamstrung by having to follow the basic plot of Shakespeare's tragic play, he draws nice performances from the leads and consequently keeps the audience involved. Anyone familiar with the play knows basically how the story will end. Douglas is fine as a man who uses bluff and swagger to hide his inadequacies and his inability to lead. He shows us that he's a soldier, not a leader, and does best when following orders. Roman is a vicious, conniving femme fatale. Murder means nothing to her in elevating Douglas to kingpin of the mob. Only when she sees the dead bodies of innocents does the horror of her deeds begin to bring her to the brink of insanity. British noir master cinematographer Basil Emmott drapes the scenes in darkness with shards of light enveloping Douglas and Roman in a path leading to their demise. Hughes' brisk direction helps the audience to somewhat overlook the fact that with all the deaths, there is no police investigation. Since no police appear in the screenplay, I would have liked it better not to have heard police sirens and gunfire at the end. This probably was added to appease the censors to signify that all corruption was wiped out.

Johnny was a guy with a record ... with the cops ... or with a doll!

Johnny Allegro

(June 1949)

CAST: Johnny Allegro, George Raft; Glenda, Nina Foch; Vallin, George Macready; Schultzy, Will Geer; Addie, Gloria Henry; Pelham Vetch, Ivan Triesault; Pudgy, Harry Antrim; Roy, William "Bill" Phillips; Uncredited: Desk Clerk, Fred F. Sears; Waiter, Cosmo Sardo; Elevator Boy, George Offerman, Jr.; Maintenance Man, Eddie Acuff; Jeffrey, Sol Gorss; Servant, Matilda Caldwell; Grote, Walter Rode; Gray, Paul E. Burns; Nurse, Mary Baer; Dr. Jaynes, Frank Dae; Frank, Thomas Browne Henry; Treasury Agent, Steve Pendleton; Operator, Larry Thompson; Coast Guard Officer, Harlan Warde; Guards, Chuck Hamilton, Joe Palma and Brick Sullivan

CREDITS: Director, Ted Tetzlaff; Assistant Director, Earl Bellamy; Producer, Irving Starr; Story, James Edward Grant; Screenwriters, Karen DeWolf and Guy Endore; Editor, Jerome Thoms; Art Director, Perry Smith; Set Decorator, Frank Tuttle; Cinematographer, Joseph Biroc; Gowns, Jean Louis; Sound, Jack Goodrich; Original Music, George Duning; Musical Director, M.W. Stoloff

LOCATION FILMING: Los Angeles County Arboretum and Botanic Garden, Arcadia, California

PRODUCTION DATES: December 15, 1948–January 25, 1949

RUNNING TIME: 81 minutes

STORY: Florist George Raft, after escaping from Sing Sing years previously, is going straight. Because of a chance encounter with Nina Foch, who has ties to the underworld, Raft is asked by Treasury Agent Will Geer to help break up a counterfeiting scheme. If Raft survives the mission, Geer will put in a good word on his behalf. Foch receives a message to leave town on a private plane and asks Raft to help her avoid police scrutiny. To get away, Raft has to shoot police officer Harry Antrim. The bullets fired were blanks. Telling Foch that he's now on the run from the police, Raft convinces her to take him to her final destination, an island owned by George Macready, who Raft learns is Foch's husband. To stay on the island, Raft has to surrender his gun. Macready professes that he prefers the bow and arrow to a gun. Raft learns that a foreign power is paying Macready to flood the United States with counterfeit money, thus damaging the economy. Macready finally has a falling-out with Ivan Triesault and Walter Rode, the foreign country's agents. He dispatches both men with a silver-tipped arrow. Macready decides to move the coun-

Johnny Allegro **(1949) with (left to right) Ivan Triesault, George Raft, Walter Rode and George Macready.**

terfeit money off the island. Raft is able to send information to Geer, who has a boat offshore. In trying to remove papers from a desk drawer, Macready uses Raft's gun to blast the lock only to discover that the gun is loaded with blanks. Foch, who is in love with Raft, tells him where to find the counterfeit money. After Raft stops underling William "Bill" Phillips from removing the money, he finds himself hunted by Macready. With Foch watching, Macready finally has a clear shot at Raft. As Macready prepares to shoot the arrow, Foch hits his arm and the arrow misses. Angered, Macready begins to beat Foch. Raft intervenes. The two men fight and Raft delivers a blow that sends Macready off a cliff to his death. As Raft and Foch are being taken back to the mainland, Geer promises to put in good words on their behalf.

Notes and Commentary: The working titles for this film were *The Big Jump* and *Hounded*.

Reviews: "*Johnny Allegro* is a typical George Raft melodrama. It has been given good production presentation, excellent direction and photography." *Variety*, 6/1/49

"Despite being little more than a potboiler, *Johnny Allegro* had enough originality in the plot to keep it moving, and one can recognize many of its twists and turns in subsequent spy films." *Motion Picture Guide*, Nash and Ross

"A diverting crime melodrama. It was all too far-fetched for words but it was fun while it lasted." *The Columbia Story*, Hirschhorn

Summation: This is an entertaining minor crime noir. The story, which borrows from "The Most Dangerous Game," is briskly directed by Ted Tetzlaff with nice photography by Joseph Biroc. The acting meets the demands of the story. George Macready again is the consummate villain, a classical music devotee whose method of dispatching his adversaries is with bow and silver-tipped arrow. Nina Foch is properly alluring. Raft's understated acting fits the mood of the script perfectly.

JOHNNY WAS SMART... TOO SMART TO TANGLE WITH WOMEN!

Johnny O'Clock

A J.E.M. Production
(January 1947)

Cast: Johnny O'Clock, Dick Powell; Nancy Hobson, Evelyn Keyes; Inspector Koch, Lee J. Cobb; Nelle Marchettis, Ellen Drew; Harriet Hobson, Nina Foch; Guido Marchettis, Thomas Gomez; Charlie, John Kellogg; Chuck Blayden, Jim Bannon; Slatternly Woman Tenant, Mabel Paige; Phil, Phil Brown; Uncredited: Turk, Jeff Chandler; Mrs. Wilson, Virginia Farmer; Punchy, Kit Guard; Fishermen, George Lloyd and Al Hill; Policeman at Waterfront, Kenneth MacDonald; Hatcheck Girl, Robin Raymond; Practical Dealers, George Alesko, Fred Beecher, Ralph Freeman, Joe Helper, Edward Margolis, Thomas H. O'Neil, Jack C. Smith and Bill Stubbs; Waiter, John Berkes; Fleming, Matty Fain; Marion, Victoria Faust; Redcap, Jesse Graves; Dry Cleaner, Shimen Ruskin; Floorman, John P. Barrett; Card Players, Brooks Benedict, Jeffrey Sayre and Bill Wallace; Dealers, Gene Delmont, Cy Malis, Bob Perry, Charles Perry, Cy Schindell, Sammy Shack, Charles St. George and Ralph Volkie; Detectives, Raoul Freeman and Carl Saxe; Bodyguards, Allen Mathews and Charles Mueller; Policeman, Robert Ryan; Businessman, Charles Marsh

Credits: Director, Robert Rossen; Assistant Director, Carl Hiecke; Producer, Edward G. Nealis; Associate Producer, Milton Holmes; Story, Milton Holmes; Screenplay, Robert Rossen; Editors, Warren Low and Al Clark; Art Directors, Stephen Goosson and Cary Odell; Set Decorator, James Crowe; Cinematographer, Burnett Guffey; Gowns, Jean Louis; Sound, Jack Haynes; Production Associate, Lehman Katz; Technical Advisor, John P. Barrett; Musical Score, George Duning; Musical Director, M.W. Stoloff

Song: "What'll I Do" (Berlin)—played by various orchestras throughout the film

Production Dates: July 10–September 6, 1946

Running Time: 95 minutes

Story: Getting ready to go to work, junior partner and casino overseer Dick Powell finds his former girlfriend (now the wife of senior partner Thomas Gomez) Ellen Drew has left an unusual and expensive watch for him. Police Inspector Lee J. Cobb wants to ask questions about the shooting of a rival casino owner by crooked cop Jim Bannon. Hatcheck girl Nina Foch is distraught because Bannon wants to end their romantic relationship. Powell plans to return the watch, dodges questions from Cobb and tells Foch to forget about Bannon. At the casino, Powell and Bannon have a conversation in which each warns the other to stay out of his way. In addition Bannon plans to talk with Gomez, just back from a Mexican vacation, to discuss plans to become his new partner. Powell sees Drew in the casino and asks Foch to return the watch. Later a bloody coat jacket is fished out of the river. Cobb investigates and finds Foch took the coat to a dry cleaner and the coat belonged to Bannon. Going to Foch's room, Cobb smells gas and finds her dead, an apparent suicide victim. Cobb also finds the watch that Powell gave to Foch. Cobb notifies Evelyn Keyes, Foch's sister. Powell meets with Drew and learns that Foch never returned the watch and goes to Foch's room to search for it. In the room he finds Keyes and a Mexican coin on the floor. An autopsy shows Foch was poisoned. Powell and Keyes become romantically involved. Bannon's body is found in the river. Cobb has Powell and Gomez brought to police headquarters and tells them they both have motives to have murdered Bannon. Cobb believes Bannon murdered the casino owner. Then, Cobb shows Gomez the watch he found in Foch's room. Gomez sees the watch is identical to one Drew gave him. Leaving the police station, Powell tells Keyes he's taking her to the airport. Powell's man, John Kellogg, who has switched allegiance to Gomez, tells Gomez where to find Powell. Gomez tells Drew that their marriage is over and that Powell will be killed. After Powell drops Keyes off at the airport, there is an attempt on his life. Keyes now realizes that Powell was trying to send her away to protect her, and decides to stay. Powell makes Kellogg confess he saw Foch's murder. Powell and Keyes start running. Powell plans to pay Gomez off in his own time. Powell goes to Gomez to dissolve their partnership and take money owed him. After Powell gets the money, Gomez pulls a gun. Powell tells Gomez that he knows he killed Foch and Bannon. Powell also pulls a gun. Shots

Johnny O'Clock (1947).

are exchanged. Gomez is killed and Powell is wounded. Drew tells Powell that if he stays with her, she'll back his claim of self-defense. Hearing the gunshots, the police enter the building. Cobb finds the body. A spurned Drew tells Cobb that Powell tried to hold up Gomez and then shot him in cold blood. Powell is hiding in the house. In the confusion, Keyes comes in the house and finds Powell. Keyes refuses to leave him. Cobb wants Powell to give himself up. Because of Keyes' love, Powell decides to do so. As Powell, Keyes and Cobb start for the police station, Cobb tells Powell things will work out.

Notes and Commentary: This was the initial film from producer Edward G. Nealis and celebrity lawyer Jerry Giesler. It was the first film directed by Robert Rossen, and Jeff Chandler's screen debut.

Columbia borrowed film editor Warren Low from Paramount, Lee J. Cobb from 20th Century–Fox and Thomas Gomez from Universal.

When this film was made, the casino set was the most expensive set constructed in Hollywood after the lifting of wartime regulations. On the set were fourteen gambling rooms. Fifty thousand dollars worth of gambling equipment was shipped from Las Vegas for the set.

Lux Radio Theater presented *Johnny O'Clock* on its May 12, 1947, broadcast with Powell, Cobb and Marguerite Chapman.

The director first named to helm *Johnny O'Clock* was Charles Vidor but he refused to work for Harry Cohn. Cohn then gave Rossen the opportunity to direct. Charles Enfield with Enterprise Pictures heard *Johnny O'Clock* was a good film and asked to see it prior to its release. Cohn refused and told Enfield that he took a chance and he should too. Enfield then signed Rossen to direct *Body and Soul* (United Artists, 1947), a wonderful film noir boxing film.

REVIEWS: "This is a smart whodunit, with attention to scripting, casting and camerawork lifting it above the average. Pic has action and suspense, and certain quick touches of humor to add flavor." *Variety*, 2/5/47

"The slowness and general confusion of the plot for two-thirds of the film does not make for notable excitement, and the shallowness of the mystery as to who's doing all the killing relieves it of any great suspense." *New York Times*, 3/27/47

"This was Rossen's first directorial assignment and it's a good mixture of crime melodrama and black humor, personified in the tough-guy personality of Powell. Rossen's direction is slick and Powell and supporting cast do much to keep interest high." *Motion Picture Guide*, Nash and Ross

SUMMATION: This is a good noir mystery. Robert Rossen's screenplay has sharp, biting dialogue and his strong direction moves the story to a satisfactory conclusion. Powell is believably tough and Cobb is outstanding as the cop trying to nab a murderer. Thomas Gomez is fine as the killer who finds his wife loves Powell. The women in the film are terrific: Evelyn Keyes, drawn into the mystery because of the death of Foch; Ellen Drew, the two-timing broad married to the wealthy Gomez but prefers Powell, and Nina Foch, a naïve young girl who falls in love with a killer cop. Burnett Guffey's photography has great inventive camera angles and dark scenes that signify evil.

"I'M GONNA KILL YOU, JUBAL ...
FOR WHAT YOU DID TO MY WIFE!"

Jubal

(April 1956)

CAST: Jubal Troop, Glenn Ford; Shep Horgan, Ernest Borgnine; "Pinky" Pinkham, Rod Steiger; Mae Horgan, Valerie French; Naomi Hoktor, Felicia Farr; Shem Hoktor, Basil Ruysdael; Sam, Noah Beery, Jr.; Reb Haislipp, Charles Bronson; Carson, John Dierkes; McCoy, Jack Elam; Dr. Grant, Robert Burton; Uncredited: Jake Slavin, Robert Knapp; Charity Hoktor, Juney Ellis; Jim Tolliver, Don C. Harvey; Cookie, Guy Wilkerson; Bayne, Larry Hudson; Tolliver Boys, Mike Lawrence and Robert "Buzz" Henry; Matt, William Rhinehart

CREDITS: Director, Delmer Daves; Assistant Director, Eddie Saeta; Producer, William Fadiman; Screenwriters, Russell S. Hughes and Delmer Daves; Editor, Al Clark; Art Director, Carl Anderson; Set Decorator, Louis Diage; Cinematographer, Charles Lawton, Jr.; Second Unit Photographer, Ray Cory; Gowns, Jean Louis; Makeup, Clay Campbell; Hair Stylist, Helen Hunt; Recording Supervisor, John Livadary; Sound, Harry Smith; Original Music, David Raksin; Orchestrator, Arthur Morton; Musical Conductor, Morris Stoloff; Technicolor Color Consultant, Henri Jaffa

LOCATION FILMING: Jackson Hole, Wyoming (Grand Teton Range and Lake Jackson)

Song: "Beautiful Dreamer" (Foster)—played by Ernest Borgnine on the player piano

Production Dates: July 28–September 13, 1955

Source: novel *Jubal Troop* by Paul I. Wellman

Color by Technicolor

Filmed in CinemaScope

Running Time: 100 minutes

Story: Drifter Glenn Ford is given a job on Ernest Borgnine's ranch. From the beginning Ford faces enmity from top hand Rod Steiger. Borgnine's wife Valerie French wants to replace Steiger as her lover with Ford but he rebuffs her advances. Ford's hard work earns Borgnine's admiration and Ford is made foreman. Ford further earns Steiger's hatred when he stops Steiger from moving Basil Ruysdael and his family and followers off Borgnine's range. Ford is kidded that he allowed them to stay because he was attracted to Ruysdael's daughter, Felicia Farr. The attraction between Ford and Farr causes Farr's fiancé Robert Knapp to become jealous. Charles Bronson, who had been traveling with Ruysdael, is hired to work through the roundup season. Ford and Bronson become fast friends. At the roundup camp, French brings Borgnine a letter from the Cattleman's Association. Because of a mountain lion threat, Borgnine asks Ford to see French back to the ranch. French thinks she will be able to seduce Ford since no man has resisted her charms. As French begins to prepare herself in her bedroom, Ford rides away. Back at the roundup camp, Steiger plants the seeds of jealousy in Borgnine's mind. Borgnine rides to his ranch to see if Ford is with French. He finds French asleep and alone in their bed and kisses her and starts to walk away. Awakening, French calls out Ford's name. Confronted by Borgnine, French declares she and Ford are lovers. Borgnine finds Ford drinking at a saloon and starts shooting. One shot wounds Ford, who fires back in self-defense, killing Borgnine. Bronson, who had left the camp to find Ford, takes him to Ruysdael's camp. Ruysdael agrees to shelter Ford and have Farr look after him. Steiger goes to Borgnine's ranch to take Borgnine's place running the ranch and sleeping with French. French wants no part of Steiger so Steiger savagely beats her. Steiger incites the cowboys in the area to hunt down Ford. The jealous Knapp tells Steiger where Ford is hidden. Bronson stalls Steiger and the cowboys to give Ford time to reach Borgnine's ranch. Ruysdael tells Knapp that he is no longer wanted in his group. At Borgnine's ranch, Ford finds the battered French, who says that Steiger hurt her. Steiger and the men arrive. Farr has followed them. Men rush in the barn to assist French. Steiger makes an unsuccessful attempt to kill Ford, and then tries to ride away. Ford stops Steiger. The men state that French told them about Steiger before she died. The cowboys circle Steiger. Ford leaves Steiger to western justice and rides away with Farr and Bronson.

Notes and Commentary: The working title for the film was *Jubal Troop*.

Less than 100 pages of Paul I. Wellman's novel were used as the basis for the screenplay. The novel was episodic in nature with the sprawling story telling of Jubal's adventures as a small-time rancher, a big-time cattle baron and an oil well entrepreneur. Troup met Naoma (Naomi in the film) after he left Seth Horgan's ranch and spent the novel falling in love with her, losing her, finding her again, finally marrying and divorcing before the two reconciled in the final pages. In the segment devoted to Jubal's time on the Horgan ranch, only three characters were directly involved: Seth Horgan, his wife Mae and Jubal. The segment reminded me of a Hugo Haas screenplay with the older rancher, the sexy and provocative wife and the young, virile ranch hand. When Seth has to spend the night away from the ranch, the wife seduces Jubal. Jubal ignores the wife's continuing advances, so she tells her husband of the affair. The rancher tries to shoot Jubal but Jubal returns fire, killing the rancher. When Jubal decides to leave and won't take the now widow, she tells the townspeople she was raped. A posse catches up to Jubal and plans to string him up. The widow has a change of heart and implores the posse not to hang Jubal. Jubal is able to make his escape.

Initially producer-director Sam Wood obtained the rights to Wellman's novel. Gary Cooper and Irene Dunne would be the stars. Wood's death shelved the project. In 1953, Alan Ladd was slated to take the lead with Raoul Walsh as director.

Although it is indicated that this is Felicia Farr's first motion picture, she had previously appeared in *Timetable* (United Artists, 1956). *Jubal* was Valerie French's first American production.

There was thought of filming another part of Wellman's novel with Glenn Ford in the lead. The project was eventually abandoned.

Reviews: "The strong point of this gripping dramatic story ... is a constantly mounting suspense." *Variety*, 12/31/55

"Sagebrush Shakespeare—a pistol-packin' Othello, deftly done. An unusually good story that could fit in almost any milieu." *Motion Picture Guide*, Nash and Ross

Summation: This is a tough, taut adult noir western. Delmer Daves' direction paces the story in a leisurely fashion that accentuates the suspense until violence suddenly erupts. The acting is excellent. Ford exhibits a quiet strength that hides his inner insecurity while Borgnine's boisterous manner fits his character perfectly. Steiger builds his villainous character carefully. Valerie French is sultry, exuding raw sex, where Felicia Farr is pretty as the nice girl men hope to meet.

RUNNING FROM THE ARMS OF LOVE INTO THE EMBRACE OF MURDER!

Key Witness

(October 1947)

Cast: Milton Higby, John Beal; Marge Andrews, Trudy Marshall; Larry Summers, Jimmy Lloyd; Sally Guthrie, Helen Mowery; Albert Loring, Wilton Graff; Martha Higby, Barbara Reed; John Ballin, Charles Trowbridge; Custer Bidwell, Harry Hayden; Uncredited: Beat Policeman, Stanley Blystone; Driver, Ray Harper; Officer Johnson, Robert B. Williams; Nurse Sibley, Victoria Horne; Johnny, Buddy Gorman; Messenger, Joe Recht; Smiley, William Newell; Racetrack Policeman, Earle Hodgins; Jim Guthrie, Douglas Fowley; Dr. Jergins, Arthur Space; Receptionist, Claire Carleton; Coroner, John Hamilton; Policeman, Kernan Cripps; Norris, Pat O'Malley; Dillon, Eddie Dunn; Crandall, Edward Keane; Edward Clemmons, Selmer Jackson; Chaplin, Emmett Vogan; Warden, Charles C. Wilson

Credits: Director, D. Ross Lederman; Producer, Rudolph C. Flothow; Story, J. Donald Wilson; Adaptation, Edward Bock and Raymond L. Schrock; Screenwriter, Edward Bock; Editor, Dwight Caldwell; Art Director, Harold MacArthur; Set Decorator, Albert Rickerd; Cinematographer, Philip Tannura; Musical Director, Mischa Bakaleinikoff

Production Dates: April 7–17, 1947

Running Time: 67 minutes

Story: In trying to elude police in a small Arizona town, John Beal is hit by a car and hospitalized. Beal reflects on his recent past. After his wife Barbara Reed goes to visit her aunt, fellow worker Jimmy Lloyd convinces Beal to go with him to the race track. Beal hits a daily double which is very lucrative. He is supposed to go to dinner with Lloyd and two lady friends, Trudy Marshall and Helen Mowery. An intoxicated Beal arrives at Mowery's apartment and passes out. Beal is placed on a bed. Mowery tells Lloyd and Marshall to go on to dinner and she and Beal will join them later. Mowery's ex, Douglas Fowley, shows up and sees a man's hat. When Fowley tries to enter the bedroom, Mowery produces a gun. There is a struggle and a shot is fired. Beal investigates and finds Mowery's dead body. Thinking he'll be arrested, Beal leaves the apartment through a window. Before Beal hits the road, he leaves a note and money for Reed. Beal becomes a hobo and teams up with William Newell. The men find a dead body beside a railroad track. Beal takes the dead man's identification and places his watch on the dead man's wrist. With Beal's name as the dead man in the paper, wealthy Charles Trowbridge believes Beal is his long-lost son. Against his better judgment, Beal moves in with Trowbridge. Feeling useless and bored, Beal convinces Trowbridge to allow him to mass produce his novelty inventions. One such invention comes into Lloyd and Marshall's hands. They believe someone stole Beal's inventions and that money is owed Reed. Lloyd and Marshall investigate and talk to Trowbridge's lawyer, Wilton Graff, who denies any wrongdoing. Believing the inventor murdered Beal, Lloyd calls the police. Lloyd is told that Fowley has confessed to Mowery's murder. Reed, Lloyd and Marshall confront the inventor and discover Beal is alive. The joy of reunion is short-lived when Graff accuses Beal of murdering Trowbridge's son and has him arrested. Beal is convicted of murder and is sentenced to be executed. At the last minute, Beal receives a reprieve. Newell shows up at the prison to substantiate Beal's story. Finally there is a happy reunion as Trowbridge accepts Beal and Reed as his family.

Notes and Commentary: The working title for the film was *Destiny*.

Reviews: "Very insubstantial B film. The continuity is incomprehensible and the acting is unbelievable. This is an excellent lesson in how not to make a movie." *Motion Picture Guide*, Nash and Ross

"A tacky little quickie which was ill-served by both the actors and the screenplay." *The Columbia Story*, Hirschhorn

Summation: This is a slack little "B" noir that is lacking in suspense. Uninspired direction, indifferent acting and an improbable storyline doom this film. On the plus side, Philip Tannura's dark photography ably hides the lack of good production values. In the 67-minute running time the audience suffers more anguish than star John Beal. It's a relief to finally see THE END show up on the screen.

The Suspense is Killing!

Kill Her Gently

(October 1958)

A Fortress Film Production

Alternate Title: Convicts for Hire

Cast: Jeff Martin, Griffith Jones; Kay Martin, Maureen Connell; William Connors, Marc Lawrence; Lars Svenson, George Mikell; Dr. Jimmy Landers, Shay Gorman; Raina, Marianne Brauns; Inspector Raglan, Frank Hawkins; Uncredited: Constable Brown, Roger Avon; Truck Driver, John Gayford; Detective Sgt. Thompson, Patrick Connor; Bank Clerk, Jonathan Meddings; Bank Manager, Peter Stephens; Barmaid, Susan Neill; Slade, David Lawton; Mrs. Douglas, Elaine Wells

Credits: Director, Charles Saunders; Assistant Director, Douglas Hermes; Producer, Guido Coen; Screenwriter, Paul Erickson; Editor, Margery Saunders; Art Director, Harry White; Cinematographer, Walter J. Harvey; Makeup, Jill Carpenter; Hair Stylist, Helen Penfold; Sound Supervisor, Fred Turtle; Sound Mixer, Baron Mason; Original Music and Music Conductor, Edwin Astley; Production Manager, John "Pinky" Green; Camera Operator, Gus Drisse; Continuity, Pamela Carlton

Running Time: 75 minutes

Story: Returning home from London, Griffith Jones picks up two hitchhikers, Marc Lawrence and George Mikell, whom he knows to be escaped convicts. Jones makes a deal with Lawrence and Mikell to take over his home and murder his wife, Maureen Connell. In exchange, Jones will give them £1000 and arrange safe passage to Lisbon. Jones is surprised to learn Marianne Brauns, a maid he fired, is still on the premises, living in a room over the garage. Jones goes to the bank but necessary funds to cover the check have not been deposited. Jones makes arrangements to sell his car for £800. Connell tells Mikell that Jones is a mental patient. A friend of the family, Dr. Shay Gorman, calls to arrange an appointment for followup care on Jones. Brauns, who needs help in packing, enlists Lawrence's help. Brauns recognizes Lawrence as an escaped convict and grabs his pistol. A struggle follows, a shot is fired and Brauns is killed. Because of this incident, Lawrence and Mikell fight. Connell is able to gain possession of the pistol. Jones comes home and takes charge. Connell finds that Jones is working with the convicts. Jones wants Connell dead because she had him admitted to a mental institution. Jones also believes Connell and Gorman are having an affair. When Mikell tries to stop Lawrence from harming Connell, Jones shoots him. Lawrence has had enough and wants to help Connell get away. Jones starts looking for Connell, who now has help from Gorman. Gorman shows up because he couldn't reach Connell by phone. Hearing sirens, Jones decide to make a getaway after running down Lawrence. The dying Lawrence fires a shot that mortally wounds Jones. His vehicle crashes and he is pronounced dead.

Notes and Commentary: The film was released in Great Britain in December 1957.

Reviews: "The plot is over-familiar and the treatment is not suspenseful enough to give it fresh value." *Variety*, 9/7/58

"The story is old hat with no freshness in the telling." *Motion Picture Guide*, Nash and Ross

Summation: Even with a ludicrous title, the

film turns out to be a fairly suspenseful British noir thanks primarily to Maureen Connell's performance as the woman in jeopardy. Director Charles Saunders keeps the tight story moving with no dull patches in the 75-minute running time. Walter J. Harvey's camerawork aids in the tension. The final shot of Connell and Shay Gorman standing silently on opposite sides of the living room speaks volumes.

ONE WOMAN BRINGS TERROR TO 8,000,000 PEOPLE!

The Killer That Stalked New York

(December 1950)

Alternate Title: Frightened City

Cast: Sheila Bennet, Evelyn Keyes; Matt Krane, Charles Korvin; Dr. Ben Wood, William Bishop; Alice Lorie, Dorothy Malone; Francie Bennet, Lola Albright; Treasury Agent Johnson, Barry Kelley; Health Commissioner Ellis, Carl Benton Reid; Dr. Cooper, Ludwig Donath; Anthony Moss, Art Smith; Sid Bennet, Whit Bissell; Mayor of New York, Roy Roberts; Belle, Connie Gilchrist; Skrip, Dan Riss, Officer Houlihan, Harry Shannon; Uncredited: Narrator, Reed Hadley; Danny, Walter Burke; Willie Dennis, Jim Backus; Walda Kowalski, Beverly Washburn; Mrs. Kowalski, Celia Lovsky; Treasury Agent Owney, Richard Egan; Joe Dominic, Peter Virgo; Charlie, Charles Watts; Nurses, Edythe Elliott and Mary Alan Hokanson; Elderly Doctor, Everett Glass; General, Charles Evans; Colonel, Roy Engel; Dr. Penner, Arthur Space; Mr. Kowalski, Lester

Charles Korvin and Evelyn Keyes embrace as Lola Albright looks on in *The Killer That Stalked New York* (1950).

Sharpe; Police Commissioner, James Pierce; Health Department Investigator, Paul Picerni; Walda's Uncle, John Bleifer; Jerry, Tommy Ivo; Mrs. Dominic, Angela Clarke; Pinkie, Billy Gray; Photographer, Norman Leavitt; Boy Outside Willie's Place, Teddy Infuhr; Tom the Wino, Peter Brocco; Wise Guy, Ray Walker; Drug Company Executives, George Baxter, Alex Gerry and Paul Keast; Policeman, Robert Foulk

Credits: Director, Earl McEvoy; Assistant Director, James Nicholson; Producer, Robert Cohn; Adaptation and Screenplay, Harry Essex; Art Director, Walter Holscher; Set Decorator, Louis Diage; Editor, Jerome Thoms; Cinematographer, Joseph Biroc; Costumes, Jean Louis; Sound, Russell Malmgren; Musical Score, Hans J. Salter; Musical Director, Morris Stoloff

Location Filming: New York (Brooklyn, Manhattan and Port of New York) and Los Angeles (300 block of South Broadway)

Production Dates: November 29–December 24, 1949

Running Time: 76 minutes

Source: Based on the article "Smallpox, the Killer That Stalks New York" by Milton Lehman in *Cosmopolitan* magazine (April 1948)

Story: Diamond smuggler Evelyn Keyes returns from Cuba followed by Treasury agent Barry Kelley. Keyes had mailed diamonds to her husband Charles Korvin. The only thing Keyes smuggles in from Cuba is the smallpox virus. At the train station, Keyes phones Korvin and tells him she is being followed. Korvin tells Keyes to check in at a hotel. Korvin is in no hurry to see Keyes since he's having an affair with Keyes' younger sister Lola Albright. Although Keyes is feeling ill, she manages to shake Kelley. Keyes seeks aid at a local clinic and Dr. William Bishop gives her medicine. Unwittingly Keyes infects a young girl, Beverly Washburn. Keyes goes to Korvin and tells him the diamonds are in the mail. Washburn's illness is diagnosed as smallpox. A campaign is begun to prevent an epidemic and to find the carrier. Korvin receives the diamonds but does not tell Keyes. He takes all the money from Keyes' purse and leaves. In time, Keyes not only finds what Korvin did but about the affair with Albright. Keyes approaches Albright and finds Korvin has ditched her also. Korvin tries to sell the diamonds to fence Art Smith. Smith tells Korvin the diamonds are hot and it will be ten days before he can handle them. Keyes finds out from Smith when Korvin will return. In despair, Albright commits suicide. It finally becomes evident to the authorities that Keyes is the diamond smuggler and smallpox carrier. Korvin returns to Smith, who doesn't want to deal with him. Korvin steals the money and kills Smith. As Korvin leaves Smith's office, he finds Keyes with a gun in her hand. Keyes, who was planning to kill Korvin, changes her mind when she sees Smith's dead body. Keyes calls the police. As the police arrive, Korvin tries to escape. His only chance is to leap to an adjacent building. Korvin's jump is short and he falls to his death. Keyes climbs out on the ledge with thoughts of suicide. Bishop is able to talk her into coming back in Smith's office. Before Keyes succumbs to the smallpox, she gives the necessary information to quell the epidemic.

Notes and Commentary: The film was based on Milton Lehman's *Cosmopolitan* story "Smallpox, the Killer That Stalked New York." The screenplay was made more dramatic by making the smallpox carrier an attractive diamond smuggler. The actual carrier was Eugene LaBar, an American exporter of leather goods from Mexico. Although LaBar spread the virus through an area of New York City and into the village of Millbrook, LaBar and a young pregnant woman, Carmen Acosta, were the only casualties. New York City vaccinated 5,265,000 persons. Some actual touches were repeated in the screenplay. Mayor William O'Dwyer was umpiring the neighborhood boys in a baseball game when commissioners came to discuss the smallpox issue. Pharmaceutical companies ran out of single dose vials of vaccine. Permission was given to provide the vaccine in multi-dose vials. When needles ran short, six sewing machine companies came through. An Army Medical Center laboratory in Washington D.C. provided the smallpox diagnosis. The city was alerted with the phrase, "Be safe, be sure, be vaccinated," which was used in the screenplay.

Lehman's story was first purchased by producer Allen Miner, who intended to produce a movie with Lew Ayres starring as the doctor. Miner finally sold the rights to Columbia for $40,000.

The Killer That Stalked New York was completed and trade shown more than six months before it was finally released. Before Columbia could release *Killer*, 20th Century–Fox brought out *Panic in the Streets* with a similar theme. *Killer* was put on the shelf until *Panic* had run its course.

There was a lapse in continuity as Sheila's

height is listed as 5'4" but on the bulletin sent out by teletype, Sheila is 5'2".

Reviews: "A melodramatic yarn that is nothing more than a cops-'n'-robbers' story with a twist." *Variety*, 12/6/50

"The script of Harry Essex ... has a bad tendency to ramble and confuse two separate hunts [smallpox carrier, diamond smuggler]. The performances of the principal characters, while adequate, have little punch. A potentially but not sufficiently intriguing film." *New York Times*, 1/5/51

"Melodrama ran haywire in which Evelyn Keyes had a full-throttle dramatic role that allowed her to run the gamut of emotions from the coolly confident to the desperate." *The Columbia Story*, Hirshhorn

Summation: Evelyn Keyes' dynamic performance propels the film into a taut, suspenseful noir. Keyes is riveting as a woman with a deadly disease whose thirst for vengeance keeps her going. Earl McEvoy's direction is sure-handed and tough.

Written in brutal honesty and profound compassion!

Knock on Any Door

(April 1949)

A Santana Production

Cast: Andrew Morton, Humphrey Bogart; District Attorney Kerman, George Macready; Emma, Allene Roberts; Adele Morton, Susan Perry; Vito, Mickey Knox; Judge Drake, Barry Kelley; introducing John Derek as Nick Romano; Uncredited: Carl Swanson (Bartender), Vince Barnett; Officer Dan Hawkins, Thomas Sully; Detective Interrogating Romano, Al Hill; Junior, Houseley Stevenson; Kid Fingers Carnahan, Jimmy Conlin; Butch, Dewey Martin; Squint Zinsky, Sid Melton; Sunshine, Davis Roberts; Purcell, Pierre Watkin; Corey, Gordon Nelson; Assistant District Attorney, Myron Healey; Miss Holiday, Helen Mowery; Elkins, Curt Conway; Ma Romano, Argentina Brunetti; Maria Romano, Joan Baxter; Angie Romano, Carol Coombs; Julian Romano, Dick Sinatra; Jimmy, Sumner Williams; Duke (Fence), Sid Tomack; Gussie, Jody Gilbert; Reformatory Guards, Eddie Parker and Al Ferguson; Larry (Barber), Garry Owen; Nelly Watkins, Cara Williams; Aunt Lena, Florence Auer; Waiter, Charles Camp; Piano Player, Dooley Wilson; Cashier, George Chandler; Juan Rodriguez, Pepe Hern; Teenage Girls in Courtroom, Lorraine Comerford and Ann Duncan; Courtroom Spectator, Franklyn Farnum; Prison Warden, Sam Flint; Jury Members, Homer Dickenson, Stanley Dubin, Mary Emery, Betty Hall, Joy Hallward, Jack Jahries, John Mitchum, Netta Packer, Rose Plumer, Franz Roehn, Mabel Smaney, Evelyn Underwood

Credits: Director, Nicholas Ray; Assistant Director, Arthur S. Black; Producer, Robert Lord; Associate Producer, Henry S. Kesler; Screenwriters, Daniel Taradash and John Monks, Jr.; Editor, Viola Lawrence; Art Director, Robert Peterson; Set Decorator, William Kiernan; Cinematographer, Burnett Guffey; Gowns, Jean Louis; Makeup, Clay Campbell; Hair Stylist, Helen Hunt; Sound, Frank Goodwin; Musical Score, George Antheil; Musical Director, M.W. Stoloff; Technical Advisors, National Probation and Parole Association

Location Filming: Lake Arrowhead, San Bernardino National Forest, California

Production Dates: August 2–September 17, 1948

Source: novel *Knock on Any Door* by Willard Motley

Running Time: 100 minutes

Story: An unidentified holdup man runs out of a bar followed by police officer Thomas Sully. An exchange of shots follows, with Sully falling to the ground. The holdup man approaches, fires three more shots into the fallen policeman and then plunges the gun into a nearby rain barrel. All possible suspects are picked up and one of them, John Derek, is finally charged with the murder. Derek, proclaiming his innocence, asks attorney Humphrey Bogart to defend him. As the trial begins, Bogart, himself a product of the slums, tells the story of how Derek chose a life of crime. Derek becomes soured on life when his father, an innocent man, dies in prison. Derek begins stealing, first watches, then cars, before being arrested and sent to a harsh reformatory. Upon release, Derek meets a nice girl,

Susan Perry, but stops seeing her because he can't give up his life of crime. Arrested again, Derek goes to prison. Bogart decides to become Derek's mentor. Derek again meets Perry and they fall in love. They decide to marry when Perry tells Derek she'll help him go straight. Derek is unable to hold any job for any length of time and feels the only way he can obtain money is to steal it. Even learning that Perry is pregnant can't deter Derek from committing crimes. Distraught, Perry commits suicide. The trial begins with Bogart doing a good job of discrediting District Attorney George Macready's witnesses. Bogart knows the outcome of the trial rests on how Derek handles himself with Macready's cross-examination. Macready is ruthless in his questions but strikes a nerve when he brings up Perry's suicide. Knowing he's to blame for Perry's final actions, Derek breaks down and admits his guilt. Derek then changes his not guilty plea to guilty. Bogart makes an impassioned plea to save Derek from a death sentence, stating that society's failures are equally at fault. Derek is sentenced to die in the electric chair. Bogart tells Derek that he'll devote his life to trying to help other young men escape the slums and lives of crime.

Notes and Commentary: Willard Motley's book was sanitized by the Production Code as the screenplay was written. The police cruelty, as depicted in the novel, was largely eliminated, as was Nick Romano's bisexuality. Motley told the story in chronological order so the reader knew that Nick was guilty of murder. The screenplay told of Nick's background in flashbacks. Nick's interaction with his family life was almost entirely deleted. The Andrew Morton character in the film was a combination of the Andrew Morton and Grant Hollowell characters in the book. The interaction of Nick and Nelly Watkins was downplayed; the screenplay eliminated the one night stand they had after his marriage to Emma. This resulted in an out-of-wedlock child as chronicled in Motley's sequel, *Let No Man Write My Epitaph*.

Motley's book was also serialized in William Randolph Hearst newspapers and was printed in abridged form in *Look* magazine and *Omnibook*.

Producer Mark Hellinger obtained the rights to Motley's novel but he died before a film could be produced. Bogart, a partner in Hellinger's company, purchased the rights for his Santana production company. *Knock on Any Door* would be the first of six Santana films to be released through Columbia. Three others would star Bogart: *Tokyo Joe* (1949), *In a Lonely Place* (1950) and *Sirocco* (1951). The other two were *And Baby Makes Three* (1949) with Robert Young and *The Family Secret* (1951) with John Derek and Lee J. Cobb.

Reviews: "Strong melodrama dealing with juvenile delinquency. It's a hard-hitting, tight melodrama. Nicholas Ray's direction gives the film a hard, taut pace that compels complete attention." *Variety*, 2/23/49

"A pretentiously 'social' melodrama. The whole thing appears to be fashioned for sheer romantic effect." *New York Times*, 2/23/49

Summation: The story is somewhat watered down from the original source. Police brutality and corruption is for the most part absent from the screenplay. Thanks to Bogart's performance, Ray's direction and Burnett Guffey's cinematography, the film is an effective noir courtroom drama. Bogart is highly effective as the lawyer who defends and then makes an impassioned speech about society and juvenile delinquency. John Derek brings life to his part as a troubled youth with the motto, "Live fast, die young and leave behind a good-looking corpse." Other performers of note are Allene Roberts as the nice girl who falls in love with Derek and George Macready as the ruthless prosecuting attorney. Columbia's favorite noir cinematographer Guffey captures the proper atmosphere.

THE STAGE SENSATION THAT MADE BROADWAY CHEER BECOMES A MIGHTY SCREEN TRIUMPH!

Ladies in Retirement

(September 1941)

A Lester Cowan Production in association with Gilbert Miller

Cast: Ellen Creed, Ida Lupino; Albert Feather, Louis Hayward; Lucy, Evelyn Keyes; Emily Creed, Elsa Lanchester; Louisa Creed, Edith Barrett; Lenora Fiske, Isobel Elsom; Sister Theresa, Emma Dunn; Sister Agatha, Queenie Leonard; Bates, Clyde Cook

Credits: Director, Charles Vidor; Screenwriters, Reginald Denham and Garrett Fort; Editor, Al Clark; Production Designer, David Hall; Cinematographer, George Barnes; Costumes, Walter Plunkett; Original Music, Ernst Toch; Music Director, M.W. Stoloff; Art Director, Lionel Banks

Song: "Tit Willow" from the operetta *The Mikado* (Gilbert and Sullivan) sung by Isobel Elsom and Louis Hayward

Production Dates: May 15–June 26, 1941

Running Time: 91 minutes

Source: the play by Reginald Denham and Edward Percy

Story: To prevent her sisters Elsa Lanchester and Edith Barrett from being placed in a London asylum, housekeeper-companion Ida Lupino persuades her employer, Isobel Elsom, to allow them to come to Elsom's cottage. Elsom believes that the stay will be short but Lupino hopes a permanent arrangement can be made. After Lupino has left for London, Louis Hayward, her nephew, arrives at the cottage needing money to replace the sum he's embezzled at his bank job. Elsom feels sorry for him, goes to an old bake oven which now doubles as a safe, and gives him the sum he needs. While at the cottage, Hayward meets Evelyn Keyes, the maid, and begins to make romantic overtures. As he leaves, Hayward requests that Lupino not be told of his visit. The sisters arrive and after six weeks, Elsom has had enough. She tells Lupino the sisters have to go. When Lupino balks, Elsom fires her. Lupino arranges for her sisters to explore an old castle, gets Keyes out of the house and then strangles Elsom. Lupino tells her sisters that she bought the cottage but tells everyone else that Elsom is on a long journey, with no clear plans when she will return. Hayward returns to the cottage, now wanted by the police for embezzlement of more funds. Hayward eventually puts the pieces together and figures out that Lupino murdered Elsom and is using her funds. Hayward has Keyes impersonate Elsom. Lupino thinks she's seeing a ghost and faints. Hayward forces Lupino to admit her crime and wants to make the cottage his permanent home. Lupino gets word that police are in the area looking for Hayward. Hayward attempts to get away but is caught. Keyes overhears Hayward's escape plans and, coming face to face with Lupino, screams and races from the cottage. Lupino realizes the only way to protect her sisters is to surrender to the authorities.

Notes and Commentary: The film garnered two Academy Award nominations. One went to Lionel Banks and George Montgomery for Best Art Direction–Interior Decoration, black and white. The second went to Morris Stoloff and Ernst Toch for Best Scoring of a Dramatic Picture. (Montgomery did not receive on-screen credit.)

The play was based on a true incident: Euphrasie Mercier murdered her companion Elodie Menetret and later assumed her identity in order to maintain a home for herself and her two insane sisters. The play debuted on Broadway at the Henry Miller Theater on March 26, 1940. The cast consisted of Flora Robson (Ellen Creed), Patrick O'Moore (Albert Feather), Evelyn Ankers (Lucy), Jessamine Newcombe (Emily Creed), Estelle Winwood (Louisa Creed), Isobel Elsom (Lenora Fiske) and Florence Edney (Sister Theresa). The play ran for 151 performances, closing on August 3. Elsom reprised her stage role in the motion picture.

The film follows the play quite closely. Some scenes are somewhat rearranged for increased dramatic effect. The character of Bates, completely off-stage in the play, is seen consistently throughout the film. This allows the film to get out of the confines of the cottage. Also added was a second nun, Sister Agatha. In the play there is no mention of Albert being captured by the police.

Rosalind Russell was originally announced to star as Ellen Creed. Some of the actresses considered for the roles of the Creed sisters were Lillian Gish, Pauline Lord, Laurette Taylor, Judith Anderson and Helen Chandler.

Ida Lupino, who was borrowed from Warner Bros., was married to co-star Louis Hayward.

A radio adaptation was presented by *Lux Radio Theater* on September 27, 1943, with Ida Lupino as Ellen Creed.

There have been two television presentations, the first on *Robert Montgomery Presents* (NBC, 1951) with Lillian Gish, Una O'Connor and Betty Sinclair and then on *Lux Video Theater* (NBC, 1954) with Claire Trevor, Elsa Lanchester and Edith Barrett.

The 1941 film interesting opening credits. Ida Lupino and Louis Hayward's names appeared to be floating on the waters of a swamp. The remaining credits had the names appearing on tombstones and signs.

Ladies in Retirement was remade as *The Mad Room* (Columbia, 1969) with Shelley Winters and Stella Stevens. This time out, the character names were changed.

Reviews: "An exercise in slowly accumulating terror with all the psychological trappings of a Victorian thriller. Painstakingly done, beautifully photographed and tautly played." *New York Times*, 11/7/41

"The film version of *Ladies in Retirement* has been produced with general excellence of script, direction, acting and mounting. Somber tale, for critical attention but dubious b.o. [box office]." Variety, 9/10/41

SUMMATION: This is an excellent tale that grips the audience with mounting suspense, thanks to fine acting, especially that of Ida Lupino, direction by Charles Vidor and exceptional camerawork by George Barnes. Barnes creates a film noir atmosphere, using darkness with streaks of light to intensify the suspense. The scene in which Lupino thinks she sees the ghost of Isobel Elsom is especially well photographed for maximum effect. Lupino excellently conveys the torment of someone driven to murder in order to provide a haven for her two insane sisters. Louis Hayward almost matches Lupino as Elsom's nephew, a petty thief who sees an opportunity to benefit from Lupino's duplicity, which ultimately dooms the two.

"I told you ... you know nothing about wickedness."

The Lady from Shanghai

(June 1948)

CAST: Elsa Bannister, Rita Hayworth; Michael O'Hara, Orson Welles; Arthur Bannister, Everett Sloane; George Grisby, Glenn Anders; Sidney Broome, Ted De Corsia; Judge, Erskine Sanford; Goldie, Gus Schilling; District Attorney Galloway, Carl Frank; Jake, Louis Merrill; Bessie, Evelyn Ellis; Cab Driver, Harry Shannon; Uncredited: Cab Driver, Joe Palma; Garage Attendant, Joe Recht; Yacht Captain, Sam Nelson; Bartender, Peter Cusanelli; Port Steward/Peters, Philip Morris; Schoolteacher at Aquarium, Jessie Arnold; Truck Driver, Maynard Holmes; Assistant District Attorney, Richard Wilson; Court Clerk, John Elliott; Jury Foreman, Charles Meakin; Li, Wong Chung; Ticket Seller, Jean Wong; Ticket Taker, Wong Artarne; Old Lady, Edythe Elliott; Old Woman, Dorothy Vaughan; Policemen, Steve Benton, Eddie Coke, Al Eben, Milton Kibbee, Harry Strang, Norman Thomson and Philip Van Zandt; Reporters, William Allard, Robert Gray, Alvin Hammer, Byron Kane and Mary Newton; Police Lieutenant, Joseph Granby; Guards, Herman Elliott and Edward Piel, Sr.; Chinese Girls, Doris Chan and Billy Louie; Man Outside Cantina, Errol Flynn

CREDITS: Screenwriter and Producer, Orson Welles; Assistant Director, Sam Nelson; Associate Producers, Richard Wilson and William Castle; Editor, Viola Lawrence; Art Directors, Stephen Goosson and Sturges Carne; Set Decorators, Wilbur Menefee and Herman Schoenbrun; Cinematography, Charles Lawton, Jr.; Gowns, Jean Louis; Sound, Lodge Cunningham; Original Music, Heinz Roemheld; Musical Director, M.W. Stoloff

LOCATION FILMING: Acapulco, Guerrero, Mexico; New York City (Central Park); San Francisco and Sausalito, California

SONGS: "Please Don't Kiss Me" (Roberts and Fisher)—sung by Rita Hayworth (dubbed by Anita Ellis), Na Baixa do Sapateiro (Bahia) (Barroso) and Amado Mio (Roberts and Fisher)

PRODUCTION DATES: October 2, 1946–February 27, 1947

SOURCE: novel *If I Die Before I Wake* by Sherwood King

RUNNING TIME: 87 minutes

STORY: After rescuing Rita Hayworth from a group of thugs in New York's Central Park, seaman Orson Welles is offered a job on her husband Everett Sloane's yacht. During the voyage to the West Coast, Hayworth indicates that she wants to begin an affair with Welles. Sloane's law partner Glenn Anders offers Welles $5,000 to confess that he killed him (Anders). Anders would not be murdered but plans to disappear to a tropical island to live a peaceful life. Welles won't be convicted because a body would never be found. Hayworth decides to leave Sloane and go away with Welles. Welles tells Hayworth of the plot but she tells him that it's a scheme concocted by Sloane. Sloane's employee, Ted De Corsia, confronts Anders and tells him that he knows he plans to frame Welles for a crime of which he's innocent. Anders then shoots De Corsia. Welles and Anders drive away to perpetrate the supposed murder. Still alive, De Corsia tells Hayworth that Anders plans to murder Sloane. The plan to "murder" Anders is put in motion. Welles fires his pistol as Anders escapes in a speed-

Rita Hayworth entrances Orson Welles in *The Lady from Shanghai* (1948).

boat. Welles calls Sloane's home, and De Corsia tells Welles he's the fall guy before dying. Welles hurries to Sloane's office where he's detained by policemen and he sees the body of Anders. Welles is arrested. Sloane, who has never lost a case, defends Welles. District Attorney Carl Frank makes the case that Welles murdered in order to be with Hayworth. As Welles and Sloane wait for the jury's verdict, Sloane tells Welles he lost the case on purpose so Welles would finally be executed. As the jury returns to the courtroom, Welles swallows medication. As order is being restored to the courtroom, Welles, who has not completely succumbed to the medication, overpowers his guards and makes his escape. From a courtroom window, Hayworth sees the fleeing Welles and follows him to a Chinese theater. There Welles tells her that if he can find the gun that shot Anders, he can prove his innocence. As Hayworth and Welles embrace, Welles finds the murder weapon on Hayworth. Welles figures that Anders was supposed to murder Sloane but when Anders shot De Corsia, Hayworth had to kill Anders. The drug finally takes effect and Welles blacks out. Hayworth has Welles taken to a deserted amusement park. Welles comes to and makes it to the hall of mirrors where he meets Hayworth. Sloane arrives and tells Hayworth that he left a letter with Frank explaining the plot and clearing Welles. Sloane and Hayworth begin shooting at each other. As bullets smash the mirrors, bullets finally find their mark and Sloane is killed. Hayworth is mortally wounded. Hayworth begs Welles to stay with her. Welles leaves knowing Hayworth will be dead before he can return with the police. Welles figures he'll die trying to forget Hayworth.

Notes and Commentary: Except for changing the story's locale from New York to San Francisco and the protagonist's name from Laurence Planter to Michael O'Hara, Welles pretty well follows the storyline of Sherwood King's novel *If I Die Before I Wake* until Planter takes the stand and accuses his lawyer, Bannister, of the crimes. Planter is found guilty and imprisoned in Sing Sing. A policeman finally believes Planter is innocent. To become independently wealthy, Elsa Bannister murders her husband, attempting to make the death look like suicide. The detective finds Elsa's fingerprints both on the gun and the bullets which proves her guilty of all murders. Planter is declared innocent just hours before his intended execution. Planter takes up residence in Tahiti.

Working titles for this film were *Black Irish*, *If I Die Before I Wake* and *Take This Woman*.

Welles' first choice for the role of Elsa was French actress Barbara Laage. Next it was announced that Ida Lupino had the role before Rita Hayworth was finally cast. It has been reported that Columbia studio boss Harry Cohn was more than displeased when Welles had Hayworth's auburn tresses cut and dyed blonde. Elsa in King's novel had long red hair.

Welles was in Boston for the premiere of a musical version of Jules Verne's "Around the World in 80 Days." To open, he needed $50,000 for the costumes. Welles called Cohn and asked if he would wire the sum. In exchange Welles told Cohn that he would produce, direct and star in a motion picture for Columbia. Cohn asked the name of the project. Welles was standing in a phone booth with a rack of paperback novels nearby. Welles spotted the title *If I Die Before I Wake* and gave that as the title of his proposed project. As it turned out, director William Castle had the rights to the story. The rights were assigned to Welles, and Castle worked on the production as an associate producer. Reportedly Welles took an immediate dislike to the novel and rewrote the story in three days.

The yacht used in the film belonged to Errol Flynn. His stipulation was that it only could be used when he was on board.

There were numerous production delays, some attributed to Welles' script and location changes. Other delays were due to Hayworth's illness, the heart failure of assistant cameraman Donald Ray Cory while filming in Acapulco and the illness of cinematographer Charles Lawton, Jr. During Lawton's absence, Rudolph Maté filled in.

Reviews: "Entertainment value suffered from the striving for effect that features Orson Welles' production, direction and scripting. Script is wordy and full of holes which need the plug of taut storytelling and more forthright action." *Variety*, 4/14/48

"For a fellow who has as much talent with a camera as Orson Welles and whose powers of pictorial invention are as fluid and as forcible as his, the gentleman certainly has a strange way of marring his films with sloppiness which he seems to assume that his dazzling exhibitions of skill will camouflage." *The New York Times*, 6/10/48

"This remarkably inventive if decidedly confusing film noir stars Welles as a wandering Irishman. Replete with humorous self-deprecating narration, marvelous performances, and typically Wellesian visuals, *The Lady from Shanghai* dazzles as much as it obfuscates. An uneven film, perhaps, but one which only seems to improve with age." *Motion Picture Guide*, Nash and Ross

Summation: This is another Welles classic. He brings his tremendous abilities to this film and elevates what could be a routine murder mystery into a work of classic proportions. The acting is excellent, Hayworth, Sloane and of course Welles are perfect in their roles. Hayworth, with her hair cut and dyed blonde, is still seductive and alluring. The camerawork of Charles Lawton, Jr. successfully captures Welles' vision of the story. The final scenes at the hall of mirrors must be seen to be believed. This is a major moment in motion picture history.

WHEN SIX GUNS SPOKE THE LAW ... a sheriff had no friends!!

The Last Posse

(July 1953)

Cast: Sheriff John Frazier, Broderick Crawford; Jed Clayton, John Derek; Sampson Drune, Charles Bickford; Deborah, Wanda Hendrix; Robert Emerson, Warner Anderson; Ollie Stokely, Henry Hull; Todd Mitchell, Will Wright; Frank White, Tom Powers; Arthur Hagan, Raymond Greenleaf; Judge Parker, James Kirkwood; Dr. Pryor, Eddy Waller; Art Romer, Skip Homeier; Will Romer, James Bell; George Romer, Guy Wilkerson; Uncredited: Mrs. Mitchell, Mira McKinney; Mrs. White, Helen Wallace; Heckler, Frank J. Scannell; Indian, Billy Wilkerson; Mr. Farley, Paul Maxey; Bartender, Brick Sullivan; Uncle Will, Monte Blue; Davis, Harry Hayden; Mexican Girl, Rita Conde; Posse Riders, Frank Ellis, Frank Hagney and Reed Howes; Townsmen, Stanley Blystone, Bob Burns and Franklyn Farnum

CREDITS: Director, Alfred Werker; Assistant Director, Jack Corrick; Producer, Harry Joe Brown; Story, Seymour and Connie Lee Bennett; Screenwriters, Seymour and Connie Lee Bennett and Kenneth Gamet; Editor, Gene Havlick; Art Director, George Brooks; Set Decorator, Frank Tuttle; Cinematographer, Burnett Guffey; Sound, Lambert Day; Musical Director, Ross DiMaggio

LOCATION FILMING: Alabama Hills, Lone Pine, California

PRODUCTION DATES: mid–October–late October 1952

RUNNING TIME: 73 minutes

STORY: Ruined by big rancher Charles Bickford, small rancher James Bell asks Bickford for a loan to start over. When Bickford refuses, Bell, his son Skip Homeier and brother Guy Wilkerson take money Bickford just received in selling Bell's cattle. With John Derek, his ward and foreman, Bickford organizes a posse. Realizing Bickford is planning to gun down the robbers rather than bring them to justice, the Citizens Committee made up of Warner Anderson, Will Wright, Tom Powers and Raymond Greenleaf join the posse. Drunken sheriff Broderick Crawford, an adversary of Bickford, catches up to the posse and takes charge. The robbers are chased into a blind canyon. Bell, Homeier and Wilkerson attempt to climb over the rocks. Wilkerson falls to his death. After the men have surrendered, Bickford guns them down. Crawford tells Derek that he knows Bickford killed his father but Bell, the only witness, was afraid to testify. Bickford then fires two shots into Crawford. As Bickford prepares to fire another shot into Crawford, Derek shoots Bickford. The Citizens Committee sees their chance. They propose to split the stolen money between them and Derek would gain possession of Bickford's ranch. They believe Crawford will die before he can testify otherwise. They return to town and an inquest is held. Derek is in a quandary about whether to lie or not. Crawford gets out of bed, gets dressed and takes a seat to listen to the testimony. When Derek tells the truth, the Citizens Committee surrenders the money. Although they will not be prosecuted, their reputations are tarnished. As Derek goes over to thank Crawford, he finds that Crawford died the moment he sat down.

NOTES AND COMMENTARY: The working title was *Posse*.

Raymond Greenleaf's character is introduced at the Founders Day Meeting as Arthur but his first name on the bank window is Albert.

REVIEWS: "The entertainment is just fair, mostly because the story loses impact under a choppy flashback treatment. The action stuff is good, however, as are the character performances, and the outdoor lensing of rugged scenery and plot types is excellent." *Variety*, 6/10/53

"A confusing but compelling western complicated by flashbacks and flash forwards." *Motion Picture Guide*, Nash and Ross

"An interesting film courtesy of Werker's forceful direction and Guffey's superb cinematography." *The Western*, Hardy

SUMMATION: This is a taut, suspenseful noir western with some good acting especially by Broderick Crawford as a once-tough lawman, now a drunk holding onto his job in a now peaceful town. Charles Bickford scores as a hard, ruthless rancher who will not let murder stand in his way in getting what he wants. Director Alfred Werker intersperses some good action with tension-packed scenes. The use of flashbacks and the dark theme of greed and murder qualify this as noir. Cinematographer Burnett Guffey captures the grandeur of the Alabama Hills of Lone Pine, California, as well as the darkness of the small western town. A well-done film.

ONLY THE BRAVE OR CRAZY CROSS THE LAWLESS STREET...

...or the Marshal of Medicine Bend!

A Lawless Street

(December 1955)
A Scott–Brown Production

CAST: Marshal Calem Ware, Randolph Scott; Tally Dickenson, Angela Lansbury; Harner Thorne,

Warner Anderson; Cora Dean, Jean Parker; Dr. Amos Wynn, Wallace Ford; Cody Clark, John Emery; Asaph Dean, James Bell; Molly Higgins, Ruth Donnelly; Harley Baskam, Michael Pate; Dooley Brion; Don Megowan; Mrs. Dingo Brion, Jeanette Nolan; Uncredited: Dingo Brion, Frank Hagney; Tony Cabillo (Barber), Harry Tyler; Juan Tobrez, Don Carlos; Abe Deland, Frank Ferguson; Hiram Hayes, Peter Ortiz; Mayor Kent, Harry Antrim; Willis, Charles Williams; Hotel Clerk, Hal K. Dawson; Saloon Waiter, Victor Adamson; Bartender, Frank J. Scannell; Saloon Patron, Ethan Laidlaw; Townsmen, Kermit Maynard and Reed Howes; Dean Ranch Hand, John L. Cason

CREDITS: Director, Joseph H. Lewis; Assistant Director, Abner E. Singer; Producer, Harry Joe Brown; Associate Producer, Randolph Scott; Assistant to Producer, David Breen; Screenwriter, Kenneth Gamet; Editor, Gene Havlick; Art Director, George Brooks; Set Decorator, Frank Tuttle; Cinematographer, Ray Rennahan; Recording Supervisor, John Livadary; Sound, Frank Goodwin; Original Music and Musical Conductor, Paul Sawtell; Choreographer, Jerry Antes; Technicolor Color Consultant, Henri Jaffe

SONG: "Mother Says I Mustn't" (Hunt)—sung by Angela Lansbury and female quartet

LOCATION FILMING: French Ranch, Thousand Oaks, California

PRODUCTION DATES: May 5–25, 1955

SOURCE: novel *Marshal of Medicine Bend* by Brad Ward

RUNNING TIME: 77 minutes

STORY: Marshal Randolph Scott pictures the town of Medicine Bend as an unchained beast ready to strike. Rancher Frank Hagney attempts to murder Scott but is shot and killed in return. The attempt was thought to be from an old grudge until $100 in gold pieces is found in his pocket. Complicating matters for Scott is the arrival of noted entertainer Angela Lansbury, Scott's wife. She left him years ago, unable to withstand Scott's dangerous profession. Unknown to Scott, prominent businessman Warner Anderson and saloon owner John Emery are plotting to take control of the town and make it a wide-open mining town. Scott is the only obstacle. With Scott out of the way, wealthy cattleman James Bell would be forced to not only relinquish control of Medicine Bend but would have to stay out. Anderson is carrying on an adulterous relationship with Bell's wife, Jean Parker. Lansbury realizes she's still in love with Scott despite his violent past. Hagney's son Don Megowan begins busting up Emery's saloon. Emery brought money collected to help out Hagney's widow to the ranch. Scott, not wanting to shoot Megowan, engages him in a tough fistic encounter and wins but injures his gun hand. Anderson brings in noted gunman Michael Pate to face Scott. The men meet and Pate's shot hits Scott. Dr. Wallace Ford declares Scott dead and has him taken to the jail. Pate's shot actually creased Scott's skull, rendering him unconscious. With Scott out of the way, Medicine Bend becomes a lawless town. Anderson rides to Bell's ranch to tell him of Scott's death and to stay out of town. He also tells Bell that he no longer has any interest in Parker. Parker goes to town and tells Ford she would testify against Anderson and Emery. Scott recovers and again enforces the law in Medicine Bend, starting by closing up every saloon, saving Emery's for last. Scott and Pate face each other again, and this time Scott guns down Pate. Anderson and Emery decide to clear out. In the confusion, Anderson shoots Emery, thinking it's Scott. When Anderson tries to escape, Bell and his cowhands capture him. Scott realizes that his kind of law is no longer needed. He turns in his badge so he can go to a ranch he owns. As he leaves, Ford tells Scott that he has the perfect medicine for him, his wife Lansbury. When the town went wild, she saw how much a lawman like Scott was needed. Scott and Lansbury head for the ranch.

NOTES AND COMMENTARY: The working titles for the film were *The Street Without Law*, *The Marshal of Medicine Bend* and *My Gun Commands*.

Although Kenneth Gamet's screenplay holds true to the basic plot of Brad Ward's novel, changes were made. Dorry Dean, Asaph Dean's brother, became Harner Thorne in the film. Instead of being captured by Asaph and his cowhands, Dean is shot and killed by Calem Ware. Saloon owner Cody Clark has the affair with Cora Dean. Cora comes to Cody as he is trying to leave town. Cody tells Cora that they're through. Asaph enters the room and, instead of putting a bullet into Cody, allows him to leave town. He then tells Cora to come back to the ranch with him.

REVIEWS: "Good Randolph Scott action feature for the western fan." *Variety*, 11/23/55

"A well-written western, in which Scott's character is more complex than the usual western hero." *Motion Picture Guide*, Nash and Ross

Summation: This is a superior western noir in the capable hands of noir director Joseph H. Lewis. Lewis, known for his edgy direction, starts matter off in fine style in his tracking shots and finally close-up shots of gunman Frank Hagney's face and gun. Lewis uses striking camera angles. Scenes of Scott and Wallace Ford in the darkened jail cell with shards of light barely penetrating the darkness, and then with Scott alone in the cell, equal anything noir has to offer. The audience can sense Scott's despair in losing Lansbury and perhaps his life as he has to face the wide-open town. Scott is outstanding as a mortal man who has to put on an invincible front to keep law and order. Chipping in with telling performances are the only two people who know the truth behind the façade, Ruth Donnelly as Scott's cheerful but fearful landlady and Ford, the town doctor who also knows Scott's secret. This is a good tale of a man standing up to corruption in a small western town.

Ripped Raw and Roaring from Real Life!

Let No Man Write My Epitaph

A Boris D. Kaplan production (October 1960)

Cast: Judge Bruce Mallory Sullivan, Burl Ives; Nellie Romano, Shelley Winters; Nick Romano, James Darren; Barbara Holloway, Jean Seberg; Louie Ramponi, Ricardo Montalban; Flora, Ella Fitzgerald; Max, Rudolph Acosta; Grant Holloway, Philip Ober; Fran, Jeanne Cooper; Goodbye George, Bernie Hamilton; Wart, Walter Burke; Night Court Magistrate, Francis De Sales; Nick Romano as a Child, Michael Davis; Uncredited: Mike (Saloon Owner), Nesdon Booth;

Let No Man Write My Epitaph **(1960) starring Shelly Winters, James Darren and Burl Ives.**

Eddie, Don Easton; Bum at Bar, Tom London; Barney, David McMahon; Exotic Dancer, Carmen D'Antonio; Ruthie, Marjorie Stapp; Startled Motorist, Dale Van Sickel; Night Court Bailiff, Guy Way; Florist Shop Manager, Peter Brocco

CREDITS: Director, Philip Leacock; Assistant Director, Sam Nelson; Producer, Boris D. Kaplan; Screenwriter, Robert Presnell, Jr.; Editor, Chester W. Schaeffer; Art Director, Robert Peterson; Set Decorator, Armor Goetten; Cinematographer, Burnett Guffey; Makeup, Ben Lane; Hair Stylist, Helen Hunt; Sound, Josh Westmoreland; Orchestrator, Arthur Morton

SONGS: "I Can't Give You Anything but Love" (McHugh and Fields)—sung by Ella Fitzgerald, "Angel Eyes" (Dennis and Brent)—sung by Ella Fitzgerald and "Reach for Tomorrow" (McHugh and Washington)—sung by Ella Fitzgerald

PRODUCTION DATES: November 30, 1959–January 15, 1960

RUNNING TIME: 106 minutes

SOURCE: novel *Let No Man Write My Epitaph* by Willard Motley

STORY: Shelley Winters works as a B-girl in the Chicago slums to provide for her son James Darren, an aspiring concert pianist. Supporting Winters in her goal are a number of denizens of the area: former judge Burl Ives, cab driver Rudolph Acosta, singer Ella Fitzgerald and others. Winters forms a sexual attachment to Ricardo Montalban, a major narcotics dealer. When Winters threatens to end the affair, Montalban introduces her to narcotics in order to prolong their relationship. When Darren realizes the depth of Winters' addiction, he goes to Montalban's office planning to kill him. Fitzgerald is in the office, trying to obtain narcotics when Darren enters. Montalban overpowers Darren and plans to turn him into a junkie. When Fitzgerald tells Ives that Darren is Montalban's captive, Ives breaks into Montalban's office. Even though Montalban shoots him three times, Ives is able to strangle Montalban before succumbing to his wounds. Winters plans to wean her way off narcotics while Darren continues to pursue a career as a concert pianist.

NOTES AND COMMENTARY: Willard Motley's novel was distilled down to one theme, that of a junkie mother trying to protect her son from a life in the Chicago slums. There is nothing of Nellie continuously prostituting herself to obtain drugs to support her habit and at the novel's end, she is still a junkie for life, depending on a daily fix from her son Nick. Nick was changed from an artist to a promising concert piano player. Also, the fact that Nick is eventually hooked on narcotics and does successfully take the cure is eliminated. Narcotic czar Frankie (Louie in the film) Ramponi is killed by a fellow mobster who he tried to cheat out of money. Judge Sullivan dies in his bed. The Romano family is nowhere to be found in the film. Also missing is a doomed romance between Nick's uncle Louie and his black lover Judy. The novel has a downbeat ending; the only ray of hope is the possibility that Nick can stay away from narcotics and find happiness with Barbara (Bonny) Holloway, the daughter of wealthy freelance writer Grant Holloway. Nick is told that Holloway was his father's attorney, with screenwriter Robert Presnell, Jr. ignoring the fact that Andrew Morton was the lawyer in *Knock on Any Door* in both the novel and 1949 Columbia release. The working title for the film was *Reach for Tomorrow*.

A March 1958 edition of the *Los Angeles Times* reported that Harry Cohn purchased the rights to Motley's novel. Cohn must have seen an advance copy since he died on February 27, 1958, and the novel was published in June. The novel was a sequel to Motley's earlier work *Knock on Any Door*, filmed by Columbia in 1949. Initially Lana Turner was considered for the role of Nellie Romano. The role finally went to Shelley Winters on the heels of her performance in *The Diary of Anne Frank* (20th Century–Fox, 1959) for which she would win the Best Supporting Actress Academy Award. Henry Silva was first mentioned for the role of Louie Ramponi. Winters wanted George C. Scott but the part finally went to Ricardo Montalban. Michael Callan was first announced to play Nick Romano. Winters wanted James Darren and he ended up with the part.

Columbia intended to film the production in Chicago but the winter weather would prevent this. Art director Robert Peterson went to Chicago and sketched the skid row area, which was then reproduced on the Columbia Ranch in Burbank, California.

When you see scenes with Winters keeping her left hand hidden in her pocket, it was because she injured it in a scene with Burl Ives. Winters accidentally slammed her hand in a car door, crushing cartilage and ligaments.

The novel's title came from Irish Nationalist rebel leader Robert Emmet's speech in 1803 after he had been sentenced to be beheaded. Emmet stated, "Let no man write my epitaph. Let my character and motives repose in obscurity and peace, till other times and other men can do them justice."

Reviews: "An occasionally moving but rather mild film... This is not a bad picture, nor an especially good one—just pretty good, everything considered." *The New York Times*, 11/11/60

"This is a heavy-handed drama further dragged down by weak performances. Director Leacock did manage to create a properly gritty mood for the film." *Motion Picture Guide*, Nash and Ross

Summation: The film is punctuated with only three gripping scenes, two near the conclusion of the story only to be followed by a most absurd ending. Slack direction by Philip Leacock and a primarily toothless script waste some good acting by Ricardo Montalban as a ruthless drug dealer and a surprisingly nice performance by premier jazz songstress Ella Fitzgerald as a junkie singer–piano player. Scenes with Fitzgerald begging money for drugs, James Darren battling his mother Winters over her drug use and massive Burl Ives breaking through Montalban's office door, taking three bullets in his body before strangling Montalban cry for much more in this picture. The ending, which must be seen to be believed, shows a radiant Winters, who was begging for drugs, telling one and all that she will take the cure. Fitzgerald, who also needed drugs badly, is happily performing at the local bar while Darren is walking off into the distance with socialite Jean Seberg. That ending is pure hokum and further dilutes what emotional power the film might have had.

TOO HOT... TOO BIG... FOR TV! The manhunt they had to put on the giant-sized movie theater screen!

The Lineup

(June 1958)

A Frank Cooper Production

Cast: Dancer, Eli Wallach; Julian, Robert Keith; Sandy McLain, Richard Jaeckel; Dorothy Bradshaw, Mary LaRoche; Larry Warner, William Leslie; Inspector Al Quine, Emile Meyer; Inspector Fred Asher, Marshall Reed; Philip Dressler, Raymond Bailey; The Man, Vaughn Taylor; Cindy Bradshaw, Cheryl Callaway; Staples, Robert Bailey, and co-starring Warner Anderson as Lt. Guthrie; Uncredited: Porter, Bert Holland; Dr. Turkel, George Eldredge; Lab Technicians, Charles Stewart and Jack Carol; Boys, Chuck Courtney and Dee Pollock; Manager, William Marsh; House Boy, Frank Tang; Communications Sergeant, Clayton Post; Chester McPhee, Francis DeSales; Supervisor, Kay English; Porter Foreman, Al Merin; Salisbury, Billy Snyder; Stewardess, Kathleen O'Malley; Attendant, Jack Moyles; Lefty Jenkins (Cab Driver), Guy Way; Truck Driver, Dick Crockett; Norm Thompson, John Maxwell; Jeffers, Junius Matthews; Men at Lineup Viewing, Paul Kruger, Mike Lally, Charles Morton, Forbes Murray and Cap Somers

Credits: Director, Don Siegel; Assistant Director, Irving Moore; Second Unit Director, Lawrence Butler; Producer, Jaime del Valle; Assistant to Producer, William Beaudine, Jr.; Screenwriter, Stirling Silliphant; Film Editor, Al Clark; Art Director, Ross Bellah; Set Decorator, Louis Diage; Cinematographer, Hal Mohr; Recording Supervisor, John Livadary; Sound, Stanford Haughton; Musical Conductor, Mischa Bakaleinikoff; Story Editor, Fred Eggers; Technical Advisor, Inspector John Kane S.F.P.D.

Location Filming: San Francisco, California (Nob Hill, Golden Gate Bridge, Bay Bridge, Russian Hill, Fort Scott Road, U.S. Custom House, 11 Kent Street, 2011 Bayshore Boulevard at Hester Avenue, 2090 Jackson Street, Mark Hopkins Hotel, Pier 41, Steinhart Aquarium (Golden Gate Park), Sutro Baths and the Embarcadero)

Song: "Polly Wolly Doodle" (traditional) played on a calliope

Production Dates: September 30–October 29, 1957

Source: the CBS-TV series *The Lineup* created by Lawrence L. Klee

Running Time: 86 minutes

Story: When an attempt to steal luggage from Raymond Bailey goes awry, Police Lt. Warner

Anderson and his partner Inspector Emile Meyer become aware of a new wrinkle in the smuggling of heroin into San Francisco. Unsuspecting travelers come into possession of packets containing the drug; then they are taken from the traveler. Cold-blooded killer Eli Wallach and his partner Robert Keith are brought to San Francisco to collect drugs from three individuals. The first, seaman William Leslie, tries to hold up Wallach for additional money. Wallach then shoots Leslie. In the second collection, Wallach has to shoot house boy Frank Tang to take the heroin. Wallach and Keith run into problems trying to take the third packet: Mary LaRoche's little daughter Cheryl Callaway found the packet secreted in her doll and thought it was face powder for the doll. Wallach and Keith are convinced the Man, Vaughn Taylor, will think they're holding out on him and will send hit men to kill them. Wallach decides to take LaRoche to tell Vaughn the story. Wallach meets Taylor, who tells Wallach that he's dead for discovering his identity. Enraged, Wallach murders Taylor. Good police work locates Wallach's car. With LaRoche and Callaway as captives, Wallach and Keith try to escape capture. The chase is on and Wallach's car ends up on an unfinished portion of the freeway. Wallach goes out of control and shoots down Keith. Wallach tries to escape on foot, holding Callaway as hostage. Wallach puts Callaway down and attempts to jump to safety on another part of the freeway. In midair Wallach is shot, his body falling to the road below.

Notes and Commentary: This was Eli Wallach's first movie role after his debut in *Baby Doll* (Warner Bros., 1956), directed by Elia Kazan. Wallace believed he was working in a routine thriller but soon saw that he'd been handed a very demanding role in a well-directed film by Don Siegel. At the film's premiere, Wallach's wife began to get upset when she thought Wallach's character might shoot hostage Mary LaRoche.

The climactic chase took place on the Embarcadero (I-480) Freeway that was currently under construction. Stuntman Guy Way was driving the car that had to come to a sudden stop at the edge of the unfinished freeway. No trickery was used in filming this shot. Way doubled driver Richard Jaeckel. Way's girlfriend doubled Mary LaRoche. Professional stuntmen also stood in for Eli Wallach and Robert Keith. Way pulled the stunt off, stopping beautifully at the freeway's edge, a five-story sheer drop. The event was so harrowing that Way's girlfriend was hysterical for several days. If a tire blew or if Way slid too fast, the car would have gone over the edge. The scene was filmed from a fifth floor window of the city's YMCA.

Siegel was opposed to the film's title, wanting to distance it from the popular TV show. Siegel wanted to call the film *The Chase*. Siegel may have been correct as the grosses for the film were disappointing. Most film critics dismissed it as an ordinary crime drama.

Reviews: "A moderately exciting melodrama ... short on action until the final, well-plotted and photographed climax." *Variety*, 5/7/58

"A brutal but absorbing crime tale, it probes the evil character of a contract killer who murders without mercy until he is faced with a dilemma which causes his downfall." *Motion Picture Guide*, Nash and Ross

Summation: This is a taut, suspenseful and well-acted crime noir, highlighted by Eli Wallach's brilliant portrayal of a stone cold killer and Don Siegel's fast, realistic and on-the-target direction. The film would be too tough and brutal for '50s TV. With a spectacularly conceived chase at the end, audiences were left limp.

MOBSTERS INVADE TEAMSTERS! Drivers Fight Crime and Corruption in Battle for Control of Truck Industry!

The Long Haul

A Maxwell Setton Production
(December 1957)

Cast: Harry Miller, Victor Mature; Lynn, Diana Dors; Joe Easy, Patrick Allen; Connie Miller, Gene Anderson; Frank, Peter Reynolds; Casey, Liam Redmond; Doctor, John Welsh; Nat Fine, Meier Tzelniker; Butch Miller, Michael Wade; Mutt, Dervis Ward; Jeff, Murray Kash; Ship Captain, Ewen Solon; Sam MacNaughton, Jameson Clark; George Miller, Wensley Pithey;

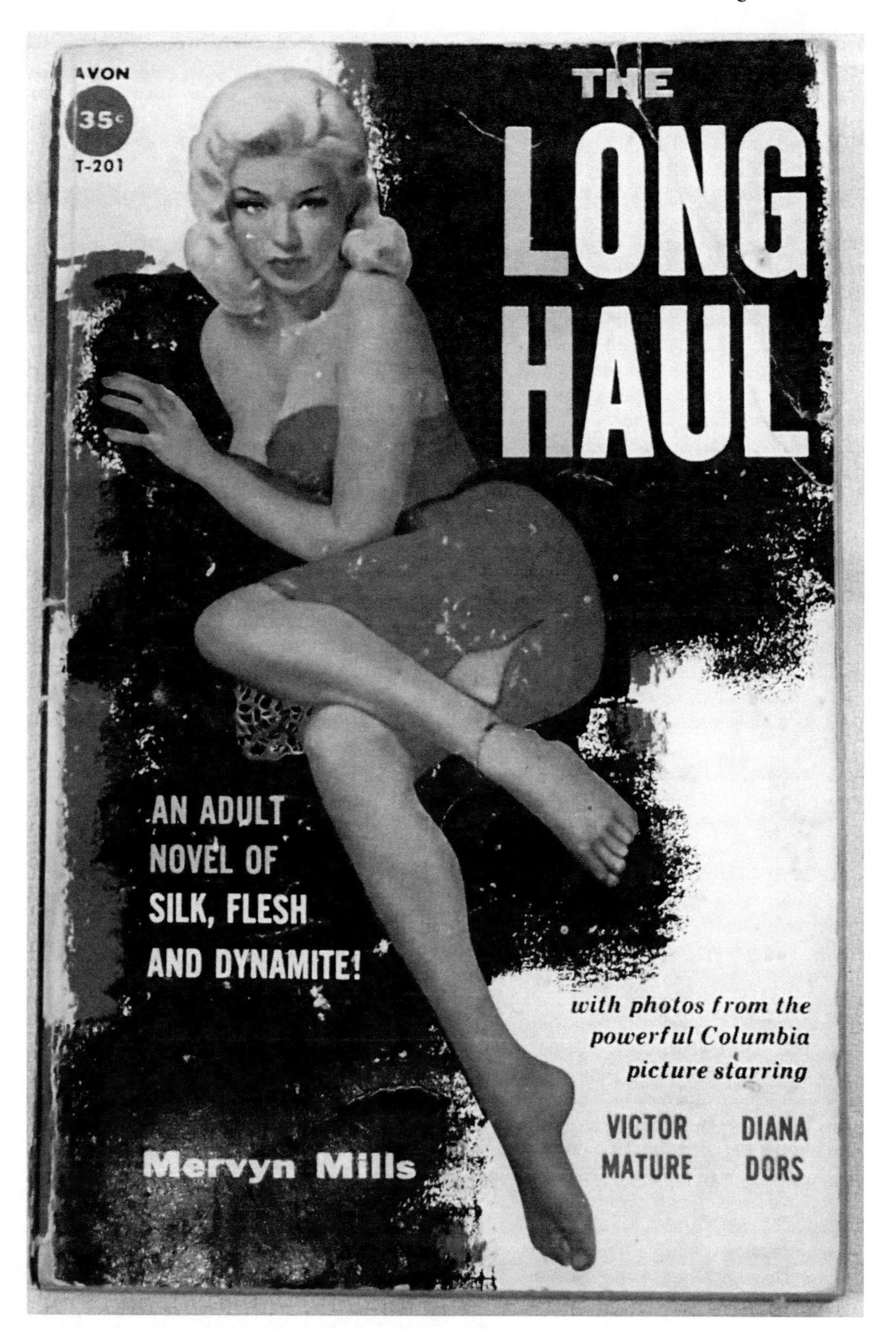

Avon's paperback cover to the book based on *The Long Haul* (1957).

Uncredited: Superintendent Macrea, John Harvey; Army Sergeant, Roland Brand; Young Liverpool Driver, Norman Rossington; Hotel Manager, Madge Brindley; Foreman, Stanley Rose; Depot Manager, Barry Raymond

Credits: Director and Screenwriter, Ken Hughes; Assistant Director, Ronnie Spencer; Producer, Maxwell Setton; Associate Producer and Production Designer, Tom Morahan; Editor, Raymond Poulton; Art Director, John Hoesli; Cinematographer, Basil Emmott; Camera Operator, Jack Mills; Makeup, Eric Carder; Hair Stylist: "Bobbie" Smith; Sound, Peter Thornton; Sound Recorders, A. Ambler and Bob Jones; Production Manager, Fred Gunn; Assembly Cutter, John Jympson; Continuity, Yvonne Richards; Music Supervisor, Richard Taylor; Music Composer, Trevor Duncan; Music Conductor, Reynell Wreford

Scottish Location: Second Unit Director, Tom Morahan; Unit Manager, R.L.M. Davidson; Lighting Cameraman, Hylton Craig; Assistant Director, Fred Slark; Operator, Harold Haysom; "Leyland" Technical Assistant, Dick Rayner

The producer gratefully acknowledges the assistance and facilities made available to the production by Leyland Motors Limited.

Location Filming: London, England, and Scotland

Production Dates: February 18–April 24, 1957

Source: novel *The Long Haul* by Mervyn Mills

Running Time: 88 minutes

Story: Victor Mature, an American stationed in England, is discharged from the Army. His English wife, Gene Anderson, does not want to go to the United States even though Mature's good friend has a job opening for him. Anderson talks Mature into staying in Liverpool for a few months before going. Mature gets a truck driving job with Anderson's uncle, Wensley Pithey. Mature has a run to Glasgow with fellow trucker Liam Redmond. Mature doesn't know Redmond is in on a plan to have two of Patrick Allen's hoods, Dervis Ward and Murray Kash, hijack some of the freight when they stop for food. Mature's quick fists break up the robbery attempt. In Glasgow, Mature is unable to get a load to take back to Liverpool. When Mature confronts Allen about this, Mature is roughed up by Ward and Kash and thrown into a back alley. Allen's girlfriend, Diana Dors, finds Mature and helps him. Because of his honesty, Mature, not Redmond, gets the job of transporting Scotch to Glasgow. Redmond notifies Allen. Allen finds Mature at a truck stop and unsuccessfully tries to make a deal with him. Dors, who had accompanied Allen, comes in the restaurant and they have an argument. When Mature gets back in his truck, he finds Dors in the passenger seat; she wants to get away from Allen. The relationship gets steamy, Mature stops at a hotel on the road and they take a room for a few hours. As Mature starts back to his truck, he sees it being hijacked and immediately blames Dors for setting him up. Mature, who now wants to go back to the States, tells Anderson about his affair with Dors. Mature also loses his job. Anderson still refuses to go with Mature. Allen tells Peter Reynolds, Dors' brother, to find Dors. Needing money, Mature decides to help Redmond in a hijacking scheme. Part of the scheme is to destroy Redmond's truck to make it look like all the cargo was lost in an accident. Things go awry and Redmond is killed. Mature goes to Allen for his money. When Mature leaves, Reynolds tells him where Dors is and that she's waiting for him. The affair is rekindled. Allen wants Mature to transport furs to a freighter heading for America. Mature will remain on the ship. Allen sees Dors with Reynolds. She pleads with Mature to meet her. He relents, but has to bring along his son Michael Wade. Mature tells Dors they will have to break up because he can't leave Anderson and Wade. Returning home, Anderson and Mature argue over his meeting with Dors. In the heat of the argument, Mature finds out that his good friend is really Wade's father. With his back to the wall, Mature consents to drive a truckload of stolen furs. Allen, who has located Dors, plans to clear out with her after receiving money for the stolen goods. Allen murders Reynolds and plans to do the same to Mature after the furs are delivered. Because of police roadblocks, Mature is forced to drive the truck through rough terrain. When the truck gets bogged down in a creek, Allen tries to kill Mature. Boxes of furs fall on Allen, pushing him underwater to his death. Mature and Dors plan to leave on a freighter to America when Mature realizes that Anderson is penniless. Taking money to Anderson, Mature learns that Wade has a brain injury and needs hospitalization. Even though Mature loves Dors, he knows his loyalty is with Anderson and Wade. The police take him into custody. A tearful Dors knows her only choice is to go back to her roots.

Notes and Commentary: On the original release in England, sources listed the running time as 100 minutes.

The Long Haul was first slated for production in 1956 by Todon Productions and Warwick Film Productions. Marlon Brando and Robert Mitchum were considered for the leads. Maxwell Setton Productions gained control of the project. Initially, Setton negotiated with Allied Artists before signing a contract for Columbia distribution.

Mervyn Mills' novel is yet to be made into a film. The screenwriters took only the initial outline of a truck driver who has an affair with a mobster's beautiful girl and loses his job. The truck driver then drifts into criminal activities. Only two character names are used from the novel, the mobster's girl Lynn and the truck driver's wife Con, lengthened to Connie in the film. In the novel, the truck driver joins a mob and pulls off a caper. Jealous of the mistress, the wife goes to the police. The police close in on the truck driver and he escapes capture by committing suicide.

The film was released as half of a double feature with *The Hard Man* (Columbia, 1957) with Guy Madison.

Reviews: "A domestic triangle thriller, interwoven with hijackers and graft that makes good entertainment for the general run of patrons." *Variety*, 9/4/57

Summation: This is a gritty, gripping British film noir with good performances from Victor Mature, Diana Dors, Patrick Allen and Gene Anderson. The very adult and yet action-packed screenplay was well-written and directed by Ken Hughes. The cinematography by Basil Emmott adds to the tension and realism. This story of a man sinking into a life of crime as his marriage disintegrates is definitely noir.

THE SECRET OF TREASURE MOUNTAIN! A true story of love, jealousy and murder ... of $20,000,000 in buried gold!

Lust for Gold

(June 1949)

Cast: Julia Thomas, Ida Lupino; Jacob Walz, Glenn Ford; Pete Thomas, Gig Young; Barry Storm, William Prince; Wiser, Edgar Buchanan; Deputy Ray Covin, Will Geer; Sheriff Lynn Early, Paul Ford; Uncredited: Floyd Buckley, Hayden Rorke; Cowboy in Lobby, Kermit Maynard; Coroner, Eddy Waller; County Clerk, Virginia Farmer; Walter, Jay Silverheels; Matron at Pioneer Home, Virginia Mullen; Martha Bannister, Elspeth Dudgeon; Bill Bates, Paul E. Burns; Young Martha Bannister, Karolyn Grimes; Ramon Peralta, Antonio Moreno; Ludi, Arthur Hunnicutt; Parsons (Assayer), Will Wright; Eager Onlooker at Assayer's Office, William Tannen; Oldtimer in Assayer's Office, Si Jenks; Luke (Saloon Owner), Tom Tyler; Lucille (Saloon Girl), Myrna Dell; Saloon Girl, Suzanne Ridgeway; Luke's Bartender, Robert Malcolm; Boy, Billy Gray; Man in Saloon hit by Pete Thomas, Trevor Bardette; Joe (Town Butcher), Harry Cording; Barber, Percy Helton; Man in Barber Shop, John Doucette; Husband, Alvin Hammer; Wife, Maudie Prickett; Mrs. Butler, Anne O'Neal; Townsmen, Richard Alexander, Hank Bell, George Chesebro, Edmund Cobb, Tex Cooper, Eddie Fetherston and Bill Wolfe; Townswoman, Dorothy Vernon

Credits: Director and Producer, S. Sylvan Simon; Assistant Director, James Nicholson; Associate Producer, Earl McEvoy; Screenwriters, Ted Sherdeman and Richard English; Editor, Gene Havlick; Art Director, Carl Anderson; Set Decorator, Sidney Clifford; Cinematography, Archie Stout; Makeup, Clay Campbell; Hair Stylist, Helen Hunt; Wardrobe (Miss Lupino), Jean Louis; Sound, Lodge Cunningham; Original Music, George Duning; Musical Director, M.W. Stoloff

Location Filming: Superstition Mountains, Arizona

Production Dates: October 25–December 13, 1948

Source: book *Thunder Gods Gold* by Barry Storm

Running Time: 90 minutes

Released in Sepiatone

Story: William Prince is searching for his grandfather Glenn Ford's lost gold mine. Four men have been murdered in that area over the past two years. A sheriff and his deputies Will Geer and Jay Silverheels warn Prince about looking for the mine. At the Pioneer Home, old-timer Paul E. Burns tells Prince the story of Ford and his gold strike. Ford and his partner Edgar Buchanan followed two men, Antonio Moreno and Arthur Hunnicutt, into the Superstition Mountains. Moreno and Hunnicutt locate treasure hidden years before by Moreno's brother. Ford and Buchanan murder the two men. In turn, Ford kills Buchanan. Ford goes on a spree in Tom Tyler's Phoenix saloon. Bakery shop owner Ida Lupino tells her husband Gig Young that she wants to meet Ford but he's not to tell him that they are married. Tired of Ford and his antics, Tyler tells bartender Robert Malcolm to drug Ford's next drink. Ford leaves the saloon before the drug fully takes effect. He is shooting into the saloon when the drug renders him unconscious. Lupino take this opportunity to take Ford into her store. The next morning Lupino pretends not be interested in Ford's wealth. Consequently Ford begins to become romantically interested in her. Ford gives Lupino a map to the mine and tells her to meet him there. When the relationship becomes intense, Young wants Lupino to stop seeing Ford. Lupino tells Young that she really loves him and is only trying to get Ford's gold. Ford overhears this conversation. Young sees the map and forces Lupino to go with him to the mine. After they reach the mine, they realize Ford has them stranded with no food or water. In desperation to prove her love for Ford, Lupino kills Young. There's an earthquake that causes an avalanche that causes Lupino to be buried under rocks and seals the entrance to the mine. With this information, Prince is further encouraged to find the mine, not realizing he is being stalked by an unknown man with a high-powered rifle. Prince finds markers that might lead to the mine entrance and he's accosted by Geer. Geer has been looking for the mine for twenty years. Knowing he's about to be murdered, Prince begins a desperate struggle with Geer. As Geer has gained the upper hand and is about to finish Prince, a rattlesnake bites Geer, causing Geer to lose his footing and go over a cliff. Prince wants to stay and see if he can find the entrance to the mine, which will be revealed when the moon shines down though an opening in the rocks. The moon shines through but the patch of moonlight keeps moving, giving different possible entrances. Prince realizes that he will never be able to locate the entrance and leaves it to others to search.

Notes and Commentary: Lust for Gold was based on Barry Storm's *Thunder Gods Gold.* In the modern part of the film, a murderous deputy sheriff tries to do Storm in. In real life, there were attempts on Storm's life but no one was brought to justice. In the film Storm was Jacob Walz's grandson but in reality there was no family tie. In the flashback, the story is faithful up until Walz meets Julia Thomas. Thomas and her husband never traveled to Walz's mine and there was no confrontation in which Julia kills Pete with an earthquake then burying Julia and covering the mine entrance. In real life, Walz met Julia when he was 69. Julia was a German-speaking quadroon who ran an ice cream parlor. A friendship developed and when Julia needed money to be sent to her wandering husband to keep him from coming home, Walz gave it to her. Finally, in his 80s and near death, Walz made a rough map showing the location of the mine. Even with the map, Julia forgot other directions and admonitions and was never able to locate the mine.

The film's working titles were *Superstition Mountain*, *Greed* and *Bonanza*. The film was reviewed as *For Those Who Dare* by *The Hollywood Reporter*.

Originally, Glenn Ford was scheduled to play both Jacob Walz and his descendant Barry Storm. Ford declined, believing it was just a gimmick. William Prince got the part of Storm.

Barry Storm, the pseudonym of John Griffith Climenson, took exception to being portrayed as the grandson of Jacob Walz. Reportedly the suit he brought was settled out of court.

George Marshall was originally signed to direct but was replaced by producer S. Sylvan Simon before cameras rolled.

Ace stuntman Davy Sharpe doubled Prince in his fight with Will Geer.

Reviews: "A tense, intelligent and often thrilling adventure. The saga makes a neat addition to the roster of good Western dramas which have come our way." *The New York Times*, 7/4/49

Summation: This is a fine western noir with some good action and suspense. Acting honors go to Ida Lupino as a devious femme fatale and Glenn Ford as a man whose second nature is murder. Will Geer plays his part a little too slimy to be fully believable. Of special note is the fine job by screenwriters Ted Sherdeman and Richard English in writing the dialogue for William Prince's narration.

THE MOST GRIPPING MOTION PICTURE YOU'VE EVER SEEN!

M

(March 1951)

Cast: Martin Harrow, David Wayne; Inspector Carney, Howard Da Silva; Dan Langley, Luther Adler; Charlie Marshall, Martin Gabel; Lt. Becker, Steve Brodie; Pottsy, Raymond Burr; Riggert, Glenn Anders; Mrs. Coster, Karen Morley; Sutro, Norman Lloyd; Blind Balloon Vendor, John Miljan; MacMahan, Walter Burke; Chief Regan, Roy Engel; Jansen, Benny Burt; Lemke, Lennie Bremen; Mayor, Jim Backus; Last Little Girl, Janine Perreau; Little Girl at Model Train Window, Frances Karath; Elsie Coster, Robin Fletcher; Watchman, Bernard Szold; Mrs. Stewart, Jorja Curtright; Uncredited: Harry Dennis, Peter Virgo; Policeman Giving Ticket for Jaywalking, Dick Wessel; Second Rorschach Test Subject, William Schallert; Detective Questioning Blonde, William Newell; Harry Greer, Norman Leavitt; Harrow's Landlady, Virginia Farmer; Little Girl, Sherry Jackson; Father, Alvin Hammer; Detectives, Brick Sullivan and Ray Walker; Hood, Tom Kennedy; Men in Mob, Frank O'Connor and Jack Roper; Woman in Mob, Tiny Jones

Credits: Director, Joseph Losey; Assistant Director, Robert Aldrich; Producer, Seymour Nebenzal; Associate Producer, Harold Nebenzal; Screenwriters, Norman Reilly Raine and Leo Katcher; Additional Dialogue, Waldo Salt; Editor, Edward Mann; Art Director, Martin Obzina; Set Decorator, Ray Robinson; Cinematographer, Ernest Laszio; Makeup, Ted Larsen; Sound, Leon Becker; Sound Re-recordist, Mac Dalgleish; Original Music, Michel Michelet; Musical Conductor, Bert Shefter; Production Supervisor, Ben Hersh; Production Layout, John Hubley; Script Supervisor, Don Weis

Location Filming: Alta Vista Apartments, Bradbury Building and Bunker Hill in downtown Los Angeles, California

Production Dates: June 5–July 7, 1950

Running Time: 88 minutes

Story: The city is terrorized by the serial murders of young girls. The shoes of the children are taken. The murderer, David Wayne, lures the little girls to a deserted area and kills them. Inspector Howard Da Silva raids all mob-controlled businesses in hopes of uncovering the murderer. Luther Adler, once a respected lawyer, reports to mob boss Martin Gabel of Da Silva's latest raid. Gabel remarks that mob profits are drastically down because of Da Silva's actions. Gabel decides his men must find the murderer. Da Silva receives a list of persons recently released from mental institutions and entrusts Lt. Steve Brodie to check them out. In the course of his investigation, Brodie goes to Wayne's rooming house. As he searches Wayne's room, the only unusual thing he finds is a shoestring attached to a lamp switch. Gabel's men locate Wayne with a young girl, Janine Perreau. To help identify Wayne, one man writes an M on the back of Wayne's coat. As the men close in on Wayne and Perreau, they are able to slip into an office building at closing time. Brodie and Da Silva go to Wayne's room, a more thorough search turning up the children's shoes. Gabel knows Wayne is hiding in the office building. Wayne has been locked inside and is struggling frantically to get out. His actions are heard, and Gabel and his men break into the room. Perreau is safe. The men capture Wayne. Suddenly an alarm is sounded. Gabel and his men make their escape. Perreau is returned to her home. Wayne is taken to a mob garage. Two of Gabel's men, Lennie Breman and Benny Burt, are apprehended. In order to force the men to give valuable information, Da Silva tells them they will be indicted for murder. Burt breaks down and tells Da Silva where to find Wayne. Gabel wants to turn Wayne over to the police through a news reporter. Gabel's gang wants to kill Wayne. Wayne breaks for safety but is quickly surrounded and given a severe beating. Gabel stops the mob. In order to buy time, Gabel orders Adler to plead Wayne's case. Wayne wants to talk for himself. Wayne tells the crowd that his mother told him all men are evil. He has to do horrible things so he can be punished. Wayne killed the children to save them from evil men. Adler tells the crowd that Wayne belongs in a mental institution. Adler then blames Gabel for his downfall and denounces Gabel's criminality. In a rage, Gabel shoots Adler. The police show up, arrest Gabel and take Wayne into custody.

Notes and Commentary: This film was a remake of the German film *M* (Verinigte Star–Film GmbH, 1931) with Peter Lorre. Fritz Lang directed and Seymour Nebenzel was the producer. Nebenzel also produced the remake, which adheres closely to Lang's original except the mob boss does not shoot the child murderer's defense attorney.

Initially United Artists was set to distribute the 1951 film.

It has been reported that the state of Ohio would not allow the film to be shown. The producing company, Superior Films, took the matter to the U.S. Supreme Court. Ohio finally allowed the film to be shown uncut in 1954.

Reviews: "Strictly adult fare. *M* is the psychological study of a killer's twisted mind. Whether it is entertainment depends on the individual viewer. Although loaded with suspense, pic is at times morbid and gruesome, reaching a dynamic climax that is tops for high tension." *Variety*, 3/7/51

"The film is a surprisingly good remake of Fritz Lang's German masterpiece of 1931." *Motion Picture Guide*, Nash and Ross

Summation: This is a grim, unrelenting study of a man whose mental illness forces him to murder little girls. Wayne gives a fine portrayal of this man who commits gruesome crimes in order to be finally punished. Joseph Losey's direction highlights tension and suspense as both the law and the underworld try to capture Wayne. Cinematographer Ernest Lazio's use of darkness duplicates the darkness of the child killer's mind. This is a story definitely not for the squeamish.

RAGING WITH THE VIOLENT PASSIONS OF
A WILD FRONTIER ... A LAWLESS ERA!

The Man from Colorado

(December 1948)

Cast: Colonel Owen Devereaux, Glenn Ford; Captain Del Stewart, William Holden; Caroline Emmet, Ellen Drew; Big Ed Carter, Ray Collins; Doc Merriam, Edgar Buchanan; Johnny Howard, Jerome Courtland; Sergeant Jericho Howard, James Millican; Nagel. Jim Bannon; York, Wm. "Bill" Phillips; Uncredited: Easy Jarrett, Denver Pyle; Corporal Dixon, James Bush; Morris, Mikel Conrad; Mutton McGuire, David Clarke; Jack Rawson, Ian MacDonald; Charlie Turnbull, Clarence Chase; Roger MacDonald, Stanley Andrews; Powers, Myron Healey; Rebel Major, David York; Tom Barton, Walter Baldwin; Bartender, Ray Teal; Parry, Craig Reynolds; Parks, Fred Graham; Jones, Eddie Fetherston; Sanders, Phil Holder; Deputies, Ben Corbett and Herman Hack; Glory Hill Townsmen, Emile Avery, Tex Cooper, Kansas Moehring and Blackie Whiteford; Miner, Fred F. Sears; Veteran, Fred Coby, Matron, Symona Boniface

Credits: Director, Henry Levin; Assistant Director, Wilbur McGaugh; Second Unit Director, Arthur Rosson; Producer, Jules Schermer; Story, Borden Chase; Screenwriters, Robert D. Andrews and Ben Maddow; Editor, Charles Nelson; Art Directors, Stephen Goosson and A. Leslie Thomas; Set Decorators, Wilbur Menefee and Sidney Clifford; Cinematographer, William Snyder; Gowns, Jean Louis; Sound, George Cooper; Original Music, George Duning; Musical Director, M.W. Stoloff; Technicolor Color Director, Natalie Kalmus; Associate Technicolor Color Director, Francis Cugat

Location Filming: Corriganville and Iverson, California

Songs: "When Johnny Comes Marching Home" (Lambert)";Beautiful Dreamer" (Foster)

Production Dates: February 24–May 26, 1948

Running Time: 98 minutes

Filmed in Technicolor

Story: At the close of the Civil War, in a skirmish out west, Union troops have a Confederate troop trapped. Confederate Major David York raises a white flag but Colonel Glenn Ford chooses to ignore it. Only York escapes death. Returning to camp, Ford hears the news that the war is over. Ford insists that the camp remain on full alert. Sergeant James Millican, happy the war is over, gets drunk on duty and Ford plans to have him court-martialed. Millican is able to escape. Ford is appointed federal judge and asks his best friend William Holden to be federal marshal. Holden accepts because he feels Ford is mentally unstable and Holden wants to try to help Ford keep an even balance. Both Ford and Holden are in love with Ellen Drew but she accepts Ford's proposal of marriage. Ray Collins' mining company takes over the small miners' gold claims because they had not been worked for three years. In a court trial, Ford upholds the mining company even though the reason the claims had not been worked was because the men were serving in the Union Army. Collins first gives the miners work but then fires all of them. The miners join Millican to form an outlaw band. Millican and his men rob Collins' office safe. In the robbery, Millican kills one of Collins' workers. Holden arrests Millican's brother, Jerome Courtland, along with other gang members. Ford wants to hang Courtland. Holden asks Ford to delay Courtland's trial to give him time to bring in Millican. Holden locates Millican and tells him if he doesn't come in, Courtland will hang. Millican allows Holden to bring him in. Before they can reach town, the men see Courtland hanging from a tree. Holden resigns as federal marshal. Ford plans to hang the men captured with Courtland. Holden and Millican effect a rescue. Drew begins to fear Ford. Holden receives notice that Drew needs to see him. Thinking this might be a trap, Holden goes anyway. Ford captures Holden and prepares to hang him. Drew obtains Ford's diary in which Ford has detailed his mental problems. With Dr. Edgar Buchanan's help, Drew helps Holden escape from jail. In the escape, Ford shows up and fires a shot, hitting Holden. Holden is taken to the former miner's town. When the townspeople refuse to surrender Holden, Ford sets fire to the town. All the townspeople are allowed to leave. Only Holden, Drew, Buchanan and Millican are left. Ford, in a rage, goes into the blazing inferno to get Holden. Before he can shoot Holden, Millican jumps him. Ford and Millican struggle. Part of a burning structure falls on both and kills them. Holden, reinstated as federal marshal, will go to Washington to have the small miners' claims returned to them.

NOTES AND COMMENTARY: Edmund Goulding was first hired to direct the film but creative differences with producer Jules Schermer caused his dismissal. Charles Vidor was then chosen to direct. Problems began almost immediately. Vidor and Glenn Ford disliked each other. A few years earlier Ford had testified against Vidor in a court case. Vidor wanted to get out of his Columbia contract to begin work at Warner Brothers. Vidor claimed Columbia president Harry Cohn's profane verbal abuse was grounds to void the contract. Ford testified that Cohn's language was natural for him and not to be taken seriously. Additionally, Vidor's own verbal rants came back to haunt him. On the *Man from Colorado* set, Vidor refused to talk directly to Ford and began to work slowly in order to throw the picture over budget. Ford complained to Cohn and with costs rising, Cohn replaced Vidor with Henry Levin, who received sole directorial credit.

The film acted like conventional film noir, having a man returning from a war with mental disorders. He then has a problem adjusting to his past life.

A deep gorge is called for in the script. To create this, a 1500-foot mountain in the San Fernando Valley in California was dynamited.

The western town inhabited by the miners was constructed in Corriganville, California. When the climactic fire scene got out of control, Ford and Holden participated in fighting the fire until firemen arrived. Footage of the town's destruction would be used in *Gene Autry and the Mounties* (Columbia 1950) and *Brave Warrior* (Columbia 1952).

Melvyn Douglas was first announced as Ford's co-star. Eventually Ford's old friend Holden was borrowed from Paramount.

The brooch worn by Ellen Drew in the ballroom scene was once worn by Julia Dickerson Gilpin, wife of William Gilpin, Colorado's first governor. It was first worn in June 1861 at Gilpin's inaugural ball.

REVIEWS: "While the action values of *The Man from Colorado* have been dissipated to some extent by the introduction of psychiatric motives, there's enough color and excitement to ensure healthy returns for this post–Civil War western." *Variety*, 1/24/49

"*The Man from Colorado* kicks up quite a bit of dust and literally ends in a blaze of destruction as a town and Mr. Ford are reduced to ashes, but somehow very little excitement is generated on the screen" *The New York Times*, 1/21/49

SUMMARY: This is a good western noir with some fine action sequences interspersed with the story of a man's descent into madness. Glenn Ford's performance carries the picture. He effectively shows his inner torment as he realizes that something is wrong with him but is unable to control his brutal actions. The only major misstep is Ford's makeup. From the beginning the makeup is excessively dark, making it look like this could turn into a monster melodrama. Even so, the film is worth viewing.

He came a thousand miles—to kill a man he'd never seen!

The Man from Laramie

(August 1955)

A William Goetz Production

CAST: Will Lockhart, James Stewart; Vic Hansbro, Arthur Kennedy; Alec Waggoman, Donald Crisp; Barbara Waggoman, Cathy O'Donnell; Dave Waggoman, Alex Nicol; Kate Canady, Aline MacMahon; Charley O'Leary, Wallace Ford; Chris Bolt, Jack Elam; Frank Darrah, John War Eagle; Tom Quigby, James Millican; Fritz, Gregg Barton; Spud Oxton, Boyd Stockman; Padre, Frank DeKova; Uncredited: Dr. Selden, Eddy Waller; Mule Drivers, Jack Carry, Bill Catching, Frank Cordell and Frosty Royce

CREDITS: Director, Anthony Mann; Assistant Director, William Holland; Screenwriters, Philip Yordan and Frank Burt; Editor, William Lyon; Art Director, Cary Odell; Set Decorator, James Crowe; Cinematographer, Charles Lang; Makeup, Clay Campbell; Hair Stylist, Helen Hunt; Recording Supervisor, John Livadary; Sound, George Cooper; Original Music, George Duning; Orchestrator, Arthur Morton; Musical Conductor, Morris Stoloff; Technicolor Color Consultant, Henri Jaffe

SONG: "The Man from Laramie" (Lee and Washington) by a chorus

LOCATION FILMING: Bonanza Creek Ranch, Taos Pueblo, Taos, and Tesuque Pueblo, New Mexico

PRODUCTION DATES: September 29–November 26, 1954

SOURCE: novel *The Man from Laramie* by Thomas T. Flynn in *The Saturday Evening Post*

Color by Technicolor

Photographed in CinemaScope

RUNNING TIME: 104 minutes

STORY: Posing as a freighter, James Stewart arrives in the small town of Coronado, controlled by rancher Donald Crisp. He delivers supplies to Crisp's niece Cathy O'Donnell, who runs the mercantile store. Stewart's mission is to find the person who sold repeating rifles to the Apaches that resulted in the massacre of cavalry troops. A victim of the tragedy was Stewart's younger brother. Stewart has a run-in with Crisp's son, arrogant Alex Nicol, and Crisp's foreman Arthur Kennedy. Small rancher Aline MacMahon wants Stewart as her foreman because he stands up to Crisp's men. Stewart turns her down. When Stewart returns to the area, he is framed for the murder of the town drunk, Jack Elam. MacMahon bails Stewart out of jail. As MacMahon's foreman, Stewart goes looking for stray cattle on Crisp's land. Nicol sees Stewart and begins throwing lead. In the gunfight, a bullet from Stewart's pistol wounds Nicol's gun hand. Crisp's men then surround Stewart. Nicol orders his men to hold Stewart and he shoots Stewart's gun hand. Nicol then rides away. Crisp's cowhands help Stewart mount his horse. Stewart rides toward MacMahon's ranch. Nicol rides up into the mountains where rifles and ammunition intended for the Apaches is hidden. He starts to signal the Apaches when his partner in the venture, Kennedy, arrives to stop him. The men argue, draw their guns and Kennedy kills Nicol. In reviewing invoices, Crisp discovers that Nicol ordered fence wire that the ranch does not use. Crisp thinks Nicol actually ordered guns for the Apaches and wants to begin searching to see if Nicol was a gunrunner. Kennedy tries to dissuade Crisp from making a thorough search. When Crisp begins taking the trail that will lead to the guns, Kennedy pushes him over a cliff. Stewart finds Crisp, unconscious but still alive, and takes him to MacMahon's ranch. Kennedy arrives at MacMahon's ranch, expecting to hear of Crisp's death. When Crisp regains consciousness and asks to talk with Stewart, Kennedy goes on the run. Crisp tells Stewart that Kennedy killed Nicol and tried to kill him. Stewart trails after Kennedy and only catches up after he has signaled the Apaches. As the Apaches draw closer, Stewart makes Kennedy help him propel the wagon load of guns and ammunition over a cliff. The guns and ammunition are destroyed as the wagon hits the side of the mountain, explodes and burns. Stewart is unable to gun down an unarmed man and lets Kennedy ride away. Apaches quickly surround Kennedy and kill him. Stewart is now ready to return to Laramie. Crisp and MacMahon plan to get married. O'Donnell plans to go east and Stewart invites her to stop off in Laramie and ask for him.

NOTES AND COMMENTARY: Thomas T. Flynn's western novel was pared down as it reached the screen. The novel had three subplots and the man behind the gunrunning plot was Frank Darrah, a handsome businessman who planned to marry Alec Waggoman's niece Barbara. The first plot was Will Lockhart's quest to find the man who sold guns to the Apaches, resulting in his brother's death. The second plot dealt with Waggoman's son Dave and his foreman Vic Hasbro's rustling stock from Alec's stock. The third plot had Darrah and Hasbro planning the deaths of Alec and Dave Waggoman. Barbara would then inherit the ranch. With Darrah's marriage to Barbara, he and Hasbro would then control the ranch. In the novel, Darrah kills Chris Bolt and Dave Waggoman and almost kills Lockhart. Hasbro attempts to murder Alec and is killed in a gunfight with Lockhart. There is no doubt that Lockhart and Barbara will marry as she tends to Lockhart's wounds.

Reviews: "Rugged western film fare using good characterizations to make dramatic points as story of vengeance is unfolded with explosive violence." *Variety*, 6/29/55

"Exciting revenge melodrama with fine production values." *Western Movies*, Pitts

Summation: This is an excellent, gripping, brutal and violent noir western. Everything works in this film: acting, direction, screenplay and cinematography. James Stewart plays a man consumed by revenge who endures personal hardships to uncover the gunrunner. Stewart, a consummate actor, makes his role become real as he displays a wide range of emotions, especially rage and fear. Both emotions are handled superbly in the extremely violent scene when Alex Nicol puts a bullet through his gun hand. Arthur Kennedy nearly matches Stewart's performance as he allows greed and a lust for power to rule his otherwise calm, reasonable persona. Alex Nicol is the psychotic son of wealthy rancher Donald Crisp. His futile attempt to match the toughness of his father would signal his downfall. Noir director Anthony Mann guides the excellent screenplay of Philip Yordan and Frank Burt by interspersing gritty violent scenes with fine characterizations of the actors. Cinematographer Charles Lang's photography brings a sense of dread in both the vast western landscapes and the dark streets of the small western town. A film not to be missed.

DEATH RIDES THE ROLLER COASTER!! ... with a killer at the controls!

Man in the Dark

(April 1953)

Cast: Steve Rawley, Edmond O'Brien; Peg Benedict, Audrey Totter; Lefty, Ted de Corsia; Arnie, Horace McMahon; Cookie, Nick Dennis; Dr. Marston, Dayton Lummis; Jawald, Dan Riss; Uncredited: First Policeman, Robert B. Williams; Nurse Receptionist, Maudie Prickett; Clinic Guard, Leonard Bremen; Interne, Shepard Menken; Flannigan, Mickey Simpson; Assistant Surgeon, Carleton Young; Nurse, Mary Alan Hokanson; Wheelchair Patient, Sayre Dearing; Detective, Howard Negley; Detective Driver, Frank Fenton; Gate Guard, Frank O'Connor; Armored Car Guard, Guy Way; Pursuing Detective, Chris Alcaide; Policeman, Fred Aldrich; Freddie (Bartender), Paul Bryar; Slavin, William Tannen; Post Office Clerk, Ted Stanhope; Yellow Cab Driver, Frank Sully; Herman, John Harmon; Mayme, Ruth Warren

Credits: Director, Lew Landers; Assistant Director, Irving Moore; Producer, Wallace MacDonald; Story, Tom Van Dycke and Henry Altimus; Adaptor, William Sackheim; Screenwriters, George Bricker and Jack Leonard; Editor, Viola Lawrence; Art Director, John Meehan; Set Decorator, Robert Priestley; Cinematographer, Floyd Crosby; Sound, Lodge Cunningham; Musical Director, Ross DiMaggio

Location Filming: Pacific Ocean Amusement Park, Los Angeles, California

Production Dates: February 27–March 17, 1953

Running Time: 70 minutes

Filmed in 3-D and in Sepia tone

Story: At a prominent clinic, Edmond O'Brien undergoes an operation to remove not only criminal tendencies but all recollection of his former life. He had engineered an armored car robbery, netting $130,000. Insurance investigator Dan Riss is still on O'Brien's trail, believing he still knows where the money was stashed. Robbery confederates Ted de Corsia, Horace McMahon and Nick Dennis kidnap O'Brien from the clinic.

Man in the Dark **(1953).**

O'Brien is taken to de Corsia's apartment. Waiting for O'Brien is his former girlfriend Audrey Totter. Totter wants O'Brien to tell her where he hid the money. They then would escape from his confederates. Believing O'Brien could have hidden the money at the house where he lived before his arrest, de Corsia takes O'Brien there. A clue is found that could lead them to the money but O'Brien still can't remember where he left the money. As a last resort, de Corsia gives O'Brien one hour to come up with the answer. In reality, O'Brien is given the opportunity to escape. He and Totter go on the run, followed by de Corsia and his confederates. From dreams, O'Brien believes the answer lies at a nearby amusement park. His memory proves correct and he collects the money. Totter wants O'Brien to return the money and give up his life of crime. O'Brien plans to keep the money. McMahon grabs Totter while de Corsia and Dennis close in on O'Brien. O'Brien takes refuge on a roller coaster ride. Seeing de Corsia and Dennis waiting, O'Brien leaves the car at the top of the structure. De Corsia and Dennis begin climbing to get O'Brien. O'Brien is grabbed by de Corsia and the two men fight. A roller coaster car comes speeding toward the men. O'Brien gets out of the way but de Corsia is hit by the car and knocked off the structure to his death. Dennis begins firing shots at O'Brien. Dan Riss and the police arrive and an officer shoots Dennis. O'Brien is able to reach the ground and gets out of view of Riss. Totter sees O'Brien but decides not to call out. O'Brien realizes that he loves Totter and a crime-free life and decides to return the money.

Notes and Commentary: The working title of the film was *The Man Who Lived Twice*. Supposedly this is a remake of *The Man Who Lived Twice* (Columbia, 1936) with Ralph Bellamy. Only the character names Slick Rawley aka James Blake and the premise of a brain operation to remove memory and criminal tendencies are used. In the original screenplay, Blake becomes a noted physician. When his former identity is revealed to the police by his gangster girlfriend, Blake is arrested, tried and found guilty. There is an outpouring of requests to pardon Blake. He is now free to resume his medical practice and get married.

Man in the Dark was Columbia's first 3-D

release. The film beat Warner Bros.' *House of Wax* to the theaters by two days to be the first major studio 3-D release. *Bwana Devil* was the first 3-D film of the 1950s but it was an independent production released through United Artists.

REVIEWS: "Story, scripting and performances are all mediocre, which puts the whole level on the attraction of the stereoscopic effects. Landers' direction relies on climaxes in 3-D and consequently falls short in building up tension." *Variety*, 4/8/53

"The story is a drably written thing, unimaginative, unintelligent and undistinguished by visual stunts. There is one salvation: the picture is in sepia, anyhow, so when looked at through the dark glasses, it can barely be seen." *New York Times*, 4/9/53

SUMMATION: First you have to suspend belief that a brain operation will remove all memory of a former life. This plot is reminiscent of a Boris Karloff horror effort of the early '40s. Once you can get by that, the picture is a smooth crime noir in which a man learning of his unsavory past must decide on the path his life must take. Edmond O'Brien takes on this role to good effect. Other performances are adequate. Well-staged dream sequences help O'Brien regain important aspects of his former life. A neat nighttime climax on a roller coaster after a harrowing chase through a crowded amusement park brings the film home to a satisfying climax.

"Townsmen, I've been pushed as far as I'm gonna go... NOW I'M COMING BACK!"

Man in the Saddle

(December 1951)

A Scott–Brown Production

ALTERNATE TITLE: The Outcast

CAST: Owen Merritt, Randolph Scott; Laurie Bidwell, Joan Leslie; Nan Melotte, Ellen Drew; Will Isham, Alexander Knox; Fay Dutcher, Richard Rober; Hugh Clagg, John Russell; Cultus Charley, Alfonso Bedoya; Bourke Prine, Guinn "Big Boy" Williams; Pay Lankershim, Clem Bevens; George Vird, Cameron Mitchell; Juke Vird, Richard Crane; Lee Repp, Frank Sully; Uncredited: Tom Croker (Bartender), George Lloyd; Ned Bale, Frank Hagney; Love Bidwell, Don Beddoe; Wrangler, Tennessee Ernie Ford; Sheriff Medary, James Kirkwood; Isham Riders, John Crawford, Herman Hack, Jim Mason and George Wallace; Mexican Informant, Peter Virgo; Townsmen at Stable, Frank Ellis and Reed Howes; Indian Servant, Rosa Turich; Townsmen, Bob Burns, Curley Gibson, David O. McCall, G. Raymond Nye, Frank O'Connor and Charles Rivero; Townswomen, Ada Adams and Dorothy Phillips

CREDITS: Director, Andre De Toth; Assistant Director, Willard Reineck; Producer, Harry Joe Brown; Associate Producer, Randolph Scott; Assistant to Producer, Herbert Stewart; Screenwriter, Kenneth Gamet; Editor, Charles Nelson; Art Director, George Brooks; Set Decorator, Frank Tuttle; Cinematographer, Charles Lawton, Jr.; Sound, Frank Goodwin; Original Music, George Duning; Musical Director, Morris Stoloff; Technicolor Color Consultant, Francis Cugat

FILMING LOCATIONS: Alabama Hills, Lone Pine, California; French Ranch, California, and Iverson, California

SONG: "Man in the Saddle" (Lewis and Murphy)—sung by Tennessee Ernie Ford

PRODUCTION DATES: April 17–May 15, 1951

SOURCE: novel *Man in the Saddle* by Ernest Haycox

RUNNING TIME: 87 minutes

Filmed in Technicolor

STORY: Joan Leslie decides to marry wealthy rancher Alexander Knox instead of the man she loves, Randolph Scott, a small rancher in the valley. Leslie wants the position, wealth and respectability that Knox can give her. Little does Leslie know that Knox has hired gunman Richard Rober to kill or drive Scott out of the valley. After Rober has caused the death of two of Scott's ranch hands, Scott decides to strike back. Leslie wants to avoid further bloodshed by leaving Knox and beginning anew with Scott elsewhere. After Scott shoots up one of Knox's line camps, Rober brings his men to Scott's ranch. Scott, engaging the men in a gunfight, is wounded in the leg. Neighboring rancher Ellen Drew's arrival causes Rober and his men to ride off. Drew takes Scott to an out-of-the-way cabin. Knox ranch hand John Russell, who is love with Drew, finds out that Drew is sheltering Scott. Fiercely jealous, he decides to track down and kill both of them. Before Russell can carry out his threat, Scott engages Russell in a vicious hand-to-hand struggle. The fight ends when Scott's head strikes a large rock. Drew shows up, rifle in hand, and Russell rides off. Leslie has left the ranch and Knox thinks she's with Scott. Russell comes back to the ranch and starts talking about Scott and a woman. Knox thinks Russell's remarks are about Leslie and fires three fatal shots into him. Scott is planning to continue his campaign against Knox. His only help comes from his cook Alfonso Bedoya and neighboring ranch owner Guinn "Big Boy" Williams. Williams captures Knox ranch hand Frank Sully and Bedoya's skill with knives convinces Sully to talk. He tells Scott that Rober murdered his two ranch hands and Knox killed Russell. Disguised as Mexicans, Scott and his companions take Sully to Sheriff James Kirkwood. Knox is tipped off and is waiting in town. Scott reaches Knox at the hotel and offers to dismiss the murder claim if he will sell out and leave the valley. Knox agrees when he finds Leslie will leave with him. An angry Rober comes to the hotel and begins firing. Bullets hit Knox and as he dies, he leaves the ranch to Leslie, asking her never to sell. Scott and Rober enter into a gunfight through the dusty, windy streets of the town. Finally at close range, the men exchange shots. Rober is killed and Scott is wounded. Drew again is there to tend to Scott's wound and they go off together.

NOTES AND COMMENTARY: This western noir was the first collaboration between director Andre De Toth and star Randolph Scott. Four Warner Bros. westerns followed, *Carson City* (1952), *Thunder Over the Plains* (1953), *Riding Shotgun* (1954), *The Bounty Hunter* (1954), plus *The Stranger Wore a Gun* (Columbia, 1953). De Toth is known for his noirs, having directed *Dark Waters* (United Artists, 1944), *Pitfall* (United Artists, 1948), *Slattery's Hurricane* (20th Century–Fox, 1949), *Crime Wave* (Warner Bros., 1954) and *Hidden Fear* (United Artists, 1957) and the western noirs *Ramrod* (United Artists, 1947) and *Day of the Outlaw* (United Artists, 1959).

The basic story outline of Ernest Haycox's novel is followed by screenwriter Kenneth Gamet. Some changes were made to tighten the narrative. Nan Malotte was a combination of two characters, Helen Tague and Nan Malotte. Sally Bidwell became Laurie Bidwell. Her brother, Starr Bidwell, was omitted because he really did nothing to further the story. George Vird did not have a brother. Juke Slover was just a close friend. Pay Lankershim joined with Bourke Prine and Cultus Charley in Owen Merritt's fight against Will Isham. Merritt kills both Isham and Isham's foreman Fay Dutcher. Both incidents happened near or at Merritt's ranch. With the fight over, Merritt knows there is no future with Sally Bidwell because the shadow of Isham will always be between them. Also, Merritt, in his struggle against Isham, has fallen in love with Nan Malotte.

REVIEWS: "Bang-up Randolph Scott western, strong on action for outdoor fans. Picture makes excellent use of Technicolor, High Sierra scenery, a top-notch plot and plenty of rugged action." *Variety*, 11/14/51

"Some excellent photography during the nighttime raids and De Toth's skillful direction make for one heck of a western." *Motion Picture Guide*, Nash and Ross

SUMMATION: This is a very good western noir. Scott is fine as a rancher who loses the woman he loves and then has to go on the run to defend himself against the machinations of a man who thoroughly hates him. The supporting cast backs Scott nicely. Alexander Knox is excellent as Will Isham, whose hate for Scott and love for Joan Leslie leads him to a path of destruction. Leslie does a fine turn as the woman both men love who finally realizes she will honor her marriage vows. De Toth, is an adept noir director, guides this film to a satisfactory conclusion. Charles Lawton, Jr.'s photography is exemplary with fantastic nighttime scenes of violence as well as daytime scenes that showcase beautiful scenic vistas.

SHE SENT HIM TO THE GALLOWS ... then risked her life to save him!

The Man Who Dared

(May 1946)

CAST: Lorna Claibourne, Leslie Brooks; Donald Wayne, George Macready; Larry James, Forrest Tucker; District Attorney Tyson, Charles

D. Brown; Felix, Warren Mills; Reginald Fogg, Richard Hale; Judge, Charles Evans; Sergeant Arthur Landis, Trevor Bardette; Sergeant Clay, William Newell; Uncredited: Bones, Brooks Benedict; Shargis, Tom Kingston; Andy White, Franklin Parker; Marty Martin, Arthur Space; Sibyl Wilson, Doris Houck; Ferris (Policeman), Ralph Dunn; Bailiffs, George Lloyd and Harry Tyler; Court Clerk, Pat O'Malley; Jury Foreman, William E. Lawrence; Bob (Tyson's Secretary), Robert Kellard; Mrs. Cheever, Margaret McWade; Police Sergeant, Joe Palma; Police Radio Announcer, Art Gilmore; Turnkey, Phil Arnold; Nurse, Jessie Arnold; Policemen, Harry Anderson and Jack Perrin; Passenger, Wally Rose

Credits: Director, John Sturges; Producer, Leonard S. Picker; Story, Maxwell Shane and Alex Gottlieb; Screenwriter, Edward Bock; Additional Dialogue, Malcolm Stuart Boylan; Editor, Charles Nelson; Art Director, George Brooks; Set Decorator, James Crowe; Cinematographer, Philip Tannura; Musical Director, Mischa Bakaleinikoff

Production Dates: February 13–February 26, 1946

Running Time: 66 minutes

Story: Newspaperman George Macready uses his column to call for the elimination of circumstantial evidence in murder trials. Macready, on trial for the murder of Franklin Parker, does not allow his lawyer Richard Hale to mount an effective defense. Finally, Macready's fiancée Leslie Brooks' testimony is enough to insure a guilty verdict. The verdict is just what Macready wanted. He tells Brooks and Hale that he hired Parker to get evidence that would prove that an innocent man was being convicted of murder. Parker calls Macready to tell him he has the proof. Macready arrives at Parker's house to find Parker mortally wounded. Macready finds a handwritten note indicating gangster Arthur Space shot him and Parker has a piece of cloth torn from Space's clothes. Brooks has followed Macready. Macready realizes that this is the perfect opportunity to show how harmful circumstantial evidence can be. He fires a shot out a window and allows

Leslie Brooks is interrogated in *The Man Who Dared* (1946).

Brooks to see him race to his car and drive off. Before he's arrested, Macready gives the evidence to fellow newspaperman Forrest Tucker to keep until he's convicted. Tucker would them present the evidence and Macready would go free. After Macready's conviction, Tucker leaves to get the evidence. After retrieving the items, Space's men, Brooks Benedict and Tom Kingston, kidnap Tucker. Space destroys the evidence and has his men drive a car over Tucker. Tucker survives but lapses into a coma. In Tucker's possession is Macready's gun. Ballistics expert Trevor Bardette proves this is the gun that killed Parker. Macready is transported to prison by Sergeant William Newell. Proud of his gun, Newell shows how the barrel can be removed and replaced. Macready is able to overcome Newell and make a getaway. Macready goes to Tucker's hospital room. Tucker regains consciousness long enough to state that Space had kidnapped him. Eluding police, Macready calls copy boy Warren Mills to meet him at the murder house. Macready wants to retrieve the bullet that he fired out of the murder house window. Using physics principles Mills directs the police to the bullet. Macready goes to Space's apartment to get possession of Space's gun. The two men fight. Macready is able to take Space to Bardette's office. Macready gets Bardette to pull photos of murder bullets of Parker and another recent murder. The bullets match. Macready has an iron-clad alibi for the other murder. Macready gives Space's gun to Bardette and tells him a bullet from Space's weapon will match the bullet he fired out the murder house window. Space had exchanged gun barrels. Space is arrested and Macready is cleared.

Notes and Commentary: The working title for the film was *One Life Too Many*.

William Castle was originally assigned to direct but was given *The Return of Rusty* (Columbia, 1946) instead. John Sturges was then given the directorial reins. This was Sturges first time as director of a feature film. His directorial career lasted thirty years. He specialized in westerns, including *Bad Day at Black Rock* (MGM, 1955) and *The Magnificent Seven*] (United Artists, 1960).

Reviews: "An entertaining thriller, it was well assembled by John Sturges and well played." *The Columbia Story*, Hirschhorn

Summation: This is an exciting, gripping and suspenseful crime noir. First-time feature film director John Sturges directs with a steady hand and holds audience interest. Usually cast as a villain, George Macready excels as a man willing to put his life on the line to show the perils of circumstantial evidence in murder trials. Cinematographer Philip Tannura's understanding of the use of darkness to heighten suspense adds to the story's effectiveness.

"$30,000 AND AN ALIAS WILL BE THIS MAN'S PASSPORT TO DEATH"

The Mark of the Whistler

(October 1944)

Cast: Lee Selfridge Nugent, Richard Dix; Pat Henley, Janis Carter; Joe Sorsby, Porter Hall; "Limpy" Smith; Paul Guilfoyle; Eddie Donnelly, John Calvert; Uncredited: Voice of the Whistler, Otto Forrest; Landlady, Minerva Urecal; Fireman, Walter Baldwin; Children's Aid Society Woman, Edna Holland; Mailman, Jack Rice; Bank Guard, Edgar Dearing; M.K. Simmons, Howard Freeman; Newspaper Photographer, Donald Kerr; Haberdasher, Eddie Kane; Perry Donnelly, Matt Willis; Sellers, Arthur Space; Tom, Matt McHugh; Men's Room Attendant, Willie Best; Truck Driver, Bill Raisch

Credits: Director, William Castle; Producer, Rudolph Flothow; Story, Cornell Woolrich; Screenwriter, George Bricker; Editor, Reg Browne; Art Director, John Datu; Set Decorator, Sidney Clifford; Cinematographer, George Meehan; "Whistler" Theme Music, Wilbur Hatch

Production Dates: July 31–August 14, 1944

Running Time: 61 minutes

Source: Suggested by the Columbia Broadcasting System program "The Whistler."

Story: Richard Dix, down on his luck, decides to claim the dormant bank account of a man with the same name. After careful preparation and giving the right answers, Dix receives over $29,000. Leaving the bank in a hurry and not

***The Mark of the Whistler* (1944) with John Calvert and Richard Dix.**

wanting to be photographed for the newspapers, Dix accidentally knocks over a crippled street beggar, Paul Guilfoyle. After seeing Dix's picture in the paper, John Calvert and his brother Matt Willis plan to murder Dix. Calvert finds Dix in a nightclub with newspaper reporter Janis Carter. Sensing trouble, Dix is able to leave the club by a hidden back window. Before he can reach his hotel, Dix is joined in his cab by Guilfoyle, who tells him that men are waiting for him. Dix asks Guilfoyle to go to his hotel room and retrieve a small box for him. When Guilfoyle takes the box, the top opens and Guilfoyle sees the money. Leaving the hotel, Guilfoyle is trailed by Calvert. Guilfoyle gives the box to Dix and tells him if he's in trouble to come to his apartment. When Guilfoyle leaves, Calvert introduces himself to Dix as a policeman and tells him he's under arrest. Dix is taken to Calvert's home. Calvert believes Dix is the true owner of the dormant account; Calvert's father was falsely imprisoned and consequently lost his mind as a result of the account owner's duplicity. Calvert plans to exact his revenge on Dix. Dix tries to tell Calvert he's not the person he's looking for, to no avail. Transporting Dix to a secluded area to kill him, Calvert's vehicle is involved in a traffic accident, giving Dix a chance to escape. As fate would have it, Dix is on the street where Guilfoyle resides. Dix goes to Guilfoyle's apartment where he finds that Guilfoyle is the real owner of the account. As Calvert tries to break into the apartment, the police arrive. In a gunfight, Calvert is killed. Dix will have to serve prison time for fraud even though Guilfoyle tried to have charges dropped. Guilfoyle had removed the money from the box before giving it to him. Guilfoyle tells Dix they will go into business together when he is released from prison. Also, Carter wants to renew a budding romance with Dix.

Notes and Commentary: The film is based on the short story "Dormant Account" by Cornell Woolrich which appeared in the May 1942 issue of *Black Mask* magazine. Screenwriter George Bricker followed Woolrich's story closely, with only a few changes. Bricker named his protagonist Lee Selfridge Nugent instead of George

Palmer. A female reporter is added as a possible romantic interest for Nugent. At the end of the screenplay, the bank insists Nugent must serve prison time for fraud even though "Limpy" wanted charges dropped, whereas in Woolrich's story "Limpy's" pleas are successful and no jail time is imposed.

Dormant Account was also the working title for this film.

REVIEW: "Direction is evenly paced and performances are up to par." *Motion Picture Guide*, Nash and Ross

"Moderately entertaining." *Variety*, 11/1/44

SUMMATION: Another good noir Whistler film in which director William Castle builds the suspense nicely. Richard Dix is fine in the lead and John Calvert is properly sinister. George Meehan chips in with some great camerawork, especially in the scene in the dark with Dix and Paul Guilfoyle.

LIPS vs. GUNS! CURVES vs. FISTS!
Undercover girl smashes giant shoplifting ring!

Mary Ryan, Detective

(January 1950)

CAST: Mary Ryan, Marsha Hunt; Captain Billings, John Litel; Estelle Byron, June Vincent; Sawyer, Harry Shannon; Joey Gunney, William "Bill" Phillips; Mrs. Sawyer, Katharine Warren; Wilma Hall, Victoria Horne; Uncredited: Belden,

Mary Ryan, Detective (1950).

John Dehner; Mike Faber, Arthur Space; Riley, Kernan Cripps; Chester Wiggin, Chester Clute; McBride, Clancy Cooper; Tom Cooper, Robert B. Williams; Patsy Hall, Doreen McCann; Sammy, Ben Welden; Chuck, Paul Bryar; Johnson, Jim Nolan; Baker, Charles Russell; Mrs. Simpson, Isabel Randolph; Munsell, Robert Emmett Keane; Gordon, Jimmy Lloyd; Parker, Eddie Dunn; Commissioner Ward, Pierre Watkin; Evans, Stanley Blystone; Watchman, Paul E. Burns; Mrs. Morse, Bess Flowers; Jones, I. Stanford Jolley; Matron, Ruth Warren; Policeman, Ralph Dunn; Party Guests, Gertrude Astor, Paul Bradley, Alyn Lockwood and Larry Steers

CREDITS: Director, Abby Berlin; Producer, Rudolph C. Flothow; Story, Harry Fried; Screenwriter, George Bricker; Editor, James Sweeney; Art Director, George Brooks; Set Decorator, William Kiernan; Cinematographer, Vincent Farrar; Musical Director, Mischa Bakaleinikoff

LOCATION FILMING: Huntsinger Turkey Farms, San Fernando Valley, California

PRODUCTION DATES: June 16–28, 1949

RUNNING TIME: 68 minutes

STORY: June Vincent, Victoria Horne and her little daughter Doreen McCann are shoplifters. With Detective Marsha Hunt's assistance, Vincent and Horne are arrested. Both refuse to reveal the identity of the fence who buys their stolen merchandise. Captain John Litel assigns Hunt to go undercover and she becomes well-versed in shoplifting techniques. Next, under an assumed name, Hunt is placed in Horne's cell. Winning Horne's confidence, Hunt is told to contact Arthur Space. Space puts her to work as a maid at a society party. Hunt steals a valuable necklace from a policewoman posing as a society woman. William "Bill" Phillips helps Hunt elude capture and takes her to a turkey ranch owned by Harry Shannon and his wife, Katherine Warren. Shannon is the fence and he ships the stolen merchandise inside smoked turkeys. Inside a turkey, Hunt places a message to be given to Litel. Hunt is forced to participate in a robbery of a fur warehouse. The robbers meet resistance and Phillips is shot. Hunt is able to remove the bullet and save his life. Finally, Litel receives Hunt's note. Vincent escapes from jail and goes to the farm. She tells Shannon that Hunt is a policewoman. Shannon is about to kill Hunt when Phillips starts a gunfight. Phillips, Shannon and Warren are killed. Litel and other police arrive to arrest the rest of the gang. Litel sends Hunt on a well-deserved vacation.

NOTES AND COMMENTARY: According to *Noir City, Mary Ryan, Detective* was slated to be the first of a series. Marsha Hunt had been brought before the House on Un-American Activities Committee as a result of liberal articles she had written and had appeared in Communist literature. She was asked to renounce these articles but she refused and was subsequently blacklisted. The plans for a series were then dropped.

The Huntsinger Turkey Farm, an actual turkey farm, had served as a front for criminal charges until closed down by Federal authorities.

REVIEWS: "It has too uniform pacing, a negligible romantic interest and a fairly thin story that doesn't provide the opportunity for a constant degree of excitement." *Variety*, 11/9/49

"A tepid and decidedly minor addition to Hollywood's annals of crime. Most of the action occurs on a turkey farm, which is poetic justice." *The New York Times*, 11/4/49

"The plot is strictly formula with standard acting and production values. Hunt is a little too perky for her role and it's difficult to swallow her as a hard-boiled detective." *Motion Picture Guide*, Nash and Ross

SUMMATION: This is a fairly entertaining "B" crime noir thanks to Marsha Hunt.

EXPOSED! The big mob's attempt to take over the billion-dollar vacation-land bankroll!

Miami Expose

(September 1956)
A Clover Production

CAST: Lt. Bart Scott, Lee J. Cobb; Lila Hodges, Patricia Medina; Oliver Tubbs, Edward

Arnold; Louis Ascot, Michael Granger; Anne Easton, Eleanore Tanin; Ray Sheridan, Alan Napier; Tim Grogan, Harry Lauter; Morrie Pell, Chris Alcaide; Chief Charles Landon, Hugh Sanders; Stevie Easton, Barry L. Connors; Uncredited: Mayor of Miami, Randy Christmas; Harry Tremont, Lauren Gilbert

Credits: Director, Fred F. Sears; Assistant Director, Gene Anderson, Jr.; Producer, Sam Katzman; Story and Screenwriter, James B. Gordon; Editor, Al Clark; Art Director, Paul Palmentola; Set Decorator, Sidney Clifford; Cinematography, Ben H. Kline; Sound, Josh Westmoreland; Musical Conductor, Mischa Bakaleinikoff

Location Filming: Miami and the Everglades, Florida, and Havana, Cuba

Production Dates: mid–March–April 9, 1956

Running Time: 75 minutes

Story: Rival mobs want to legalize gambling in Florida and make Miami the Las Vegas of the East. To discourage the Cuban mob, the United States mob resorts to eliminating the competition. When her husband is murdered by Alan Napier's hired killer Chris Alcaide, Patricia Medina flees to Cuba to stay with Cuban gang boss Michael Granger. Miami police lieutenant Lee J, Cobb follows, as does Alcaide. After attempts on her life, Medina agrees to return to Miami with Cobb. On leaving the plane, Medina collapses. She has been poisoned, but quick medical attention saves her life. To draw Napier out into the open, newspapers report that Medina died. Napier has hired shady lobbyist Edward Arnold to form a committee of prominent citizens to back support for legalized gambling in Florida with Napier the gambling commissioner. Napier furnishes Arnold with facts he can use to blackmail those who won't cooperate. To protect Medina, she is taken to Cobb's cabin deep in the Everglades. To safeguard her and keep her company are Cobb's girlfriend Eleanore Tanin, Tanin's young son Barry L. Connors and police detective Harry Lauter. Granger, who is in love with Medina, finds out that she is alive. Granger and his men search the Everglades and find Cobb's cabin. When prominent businessman Lauren Gilbert is murdered, Arnold is brought in for questioning. In the police station, Cobb lets Arnold overhear a conversation that tells him Medina is alive. Napier tells Arnold that, if he wants to live, he must leave Miami for South America. Alcaide tells Napier that Granger has been taking trips into the Everglades and that is where Medina must be. Alcaide hires the same boat owner that Granger hired. Before leaving, the owner contacts Cobb. The boat owner takes as much time as he can until he's threatened with death by Alcaide. Cobb, machine gun in hand, leads police officers to try to head off Alcaide. Lauter has been alerted and when Alcaide and his men arrive, Lauter, Tanin and Medina open fire. In the heat of the battle, Cobb and his men arrive. With a few bursts of his machine gun, the fight is over. Alcaide demands that Cobb shoot him but Cobb belts him instead. Medina identifies Alcaide as her husband's murderer. This connects the crimes to Napier. Arriving at Napier's resident, Cobb finds Napier dead, shot by Arnold. Mob takeover in Florida has been thwarted.

Notes and Commentary: The working titles for this film were *Shakedown on Biscayne Bay*, *Shakedown on Biscayne Drive*, *Biscayne Bay* and *Miami Shakedown*. Dennis O'Keefe was originally set to star in the film.

Story and screenwriter Robert E. Kent used the pseudonym James B. Gordon.

Producer Sam Katzman had additional funds to apply to his feature films when Columbia discontinued the cliffhanger serials he had been producing. This allowed location filming in Cuba and the Everglades.

This was Edward Arnold's final film. It was reported that he was fatally stricken on the set.

Reviews: "It's in the same familiar 'mob' pattern as [Katzman's] recent *The Houston Story* and the earlier *The Miami Story*. Format is observed too religiously and dialogue and situations resultantly are often trite and telegraphed." *Variety*, 7/25/56

"[A] fair low-budget crime picture helped tremendously by the presence of Cobb." *Motion Picture Guide*, Nash and Ross

Summation: This is an interesting low-budget crime noir thanks to firm, speedy direction by Fred F. Sears. Cobb humanizes his role with his interplay with policeman's widow Eleanore Tanin and his obvious affection for Tanin's son Barry L. Connors. Sears takes another story of how mob corruption was defeated in a large city and paces the film to hold the audience interest. A great scene: Cobb coming off the police boat with his machine gun blazing.

HOW MIAMI PUT THE HEAT ON THE MOB

The Miami Story

(May 1954)

Cast: Mick Flagg, Barry Sullivan; Tony Brill, Luther Adler; Ted Delacorte, John Baer; Gwen Abbott, Adele Jergens; Holly Abbott, Beverly Garland; Frank Alton, Dan Riss; Police Chief Martin Belman, Damian O'Flynn; Robert Bishop, Chris Alcaide; Johnny Loker, Gene Darcy; Louie Mott, George E. Stone; Uncredited: Senator, George A. Smathers; Detective Simmons, Al Hill; Charles Earnshaw, Tom Greenway; Clifton Staley, John Hamilton; Gil Flagg, David Kasday; Harry Dobey, Wheaton Chambers; Police Lieutenant, Ray Kellogg; Henchman, Peter Mamakos

Credits: Director, Fred F. Sears; Assistant Director, Charles S. Gould; Producer, Sam Katzman; Story and Screenwriter, Robert E. Kent; Editor, Viola Lawrence; Art Director, Paul Palmentola; Set Decorator, Sidney Clifford; Cinematography, Henry Freulich; Special Effects, Jack Erickson; Sound, Josh Westmoreland; Unit Manager, Herbert Leonard; Musical Director, Mischa Bakaleinikoff

Production Dates: November 12–19, 1953

Running Time: 75 minutes

Story: After two Cuban gangsters are murdered by mob kingpin Luther Adler's right hand man John Baer. Beverly Garland, who was traveling with them, goes into hiding. A citizens committee, led by Tom Greenway, decides to fight fire with fire to destroy Adler's crime empire. One of the members, Dan Riss, believes an ex-criminal, Barry Sullivan, is the answer. Sullivan, under an alias, is living on an Indiana farm with his son David Kasday. After placing Kasday in good hands in Orlando, Sullivan continues on to Miami where he finally agrees to help the committee. Sullivan poses as the leader of a Cuban gang that plans to close Adler down and take over crime in Miami. Believing Sullivan's cover story, Garland goes to Sullivan's hotel room. Garland tells Sullivan that she's trying to locate her sister Adele Jergens, who is Adler's mistress. Sullivan and Garland go to Adler's nightclub. Sullivan tells Adler that he has the ability to have his club shut down. Trying to obtain information about Sullivan's plans, Garland is badly beaten. In retaliation, Sullivan has the club immediately shut down. Baer removes $300,000 in checks just prior to the raid. Adler directs Baer to take the checks out of town to be cashed. Baer is intercepted by Sullivan. Sullivan suggests that if Baer guns down Adler, Sullivan will let him take over the Miami operation. Sullivan has the upper hand until he finds that Adler has kidnapped Kasday. Adler forces Sullivan to allow him to reopen his club. After a television camera is installed in an air vent in Adler's office, the club reopens. Adler plans to make Kasday an orphan. In Adler's office, Baer makes his move, planning to shoot Adler. In desperation, Adler promises Baer greater power while admitting he is the ultimate crime boss. Baer fires and finds that Sullivan loaded the gun with blanks. Police raid the club. Sullivan convinces the police to allow Adler to escape, figuring Adler will lead him to Kasday. Adler and Baer escape in a small craft followed by Sullivan in a police launch. Adler is able to elude the police. Sullivan decides to head for Adler's launch. When Adler and Baer arrive, they're greeted by Sullivan and the police. Adler is easily arrested. Baer tries to get away in the small craft. Sullivan follows. The two men fight with Sullivan finally victorious. Sullivan is reunited with Kasday. They return to Sullivan's Indiana farm. Garland comes to visit and never leaves.

Notes and Commentary: George Raft was considered for the role of Mick Flagg.

Reviews: "A suspenseful melodrama. The script is a swiftly paced chronicle of how a gambling and white slave syndicate was supposedly smashed in Miami." *Variety*, 3/3/54

"*The Miami Story* is an old one essentially but is divertingly told." *The New York Times*, 5/15/54

"The plot was basic, but tautly scripted by Robert E. Kent and tightly directed by Fred F. Sears. The result was a fast-paced crime melodrama." *The Columbia Story*, Hirschhorn

Summation: Director Fred F. Sears' no-nonsense direction of Robert E. Kent's taut screenplay delivers a fast-moving, exciting crime noir. Acting of the principals is above par with Barry Sullivan scoring as a tough ex-criminal bent on bringing down Luther Adler's crime syndicate. Adler almost matches Sullivan's performance as a mob boss who will stop at nothing to prevent his downfall. On the distaff side, Adele Jergens (bad sister) and Beverly Garland (good sister) are not only attractive but deliver performances that enhance the story. Henry Freulich's excellent photography adds to the story's enjoyment.

ONLY A GHOST KNEW THE SECRET BEHIND SIX MURDERS ... and he wasn't talking to the cops!

The Missing Juror

(November 1944)

Cast: Joe Keats, Jim Bannon; Alice Hill, Janis Carter; Henry Wharton/Jerome Bentley, George Macready; Tex Tuttle, Jean Stevens; Willard Apple, Joseph Crehan; Uncredited: Marcy, Carole Mathews; Inspector Davis, Cliff Clark; Detective Cahan, Edmund Cobb; Cullie, Mike Mazurki; George Szabo, George Lloyd; Ben (Deputy Sheriff), Al Bridge; Clem Poskins, Victor Travers; Sergeant Regan, John Tyrrell; Officer Garrett, William Hall; Newsboy, Danny Desmond; Sergeant Murphy, Harry Strang; Mac, Charles C. Wilson; Ellen Jackson, Cecil Weston; Nurse, Nancy Brickman; Sugar Chappel, Shelby Payne; Town Sheriff, Walter Baldwin; Priest, Pat O'Malley; Judge, Sam Flint; Train Conductors, Dell Henderson and Frank O'Connor; Tom Pierson, Trevor Bardette; Doctor, Ernest Hilliard; Wally, William Newell; Chief of Detectives at Lineup, Ray Teal; District Attorney, Forbes Murray; Wharton's Attorney, George Anderson; Albert Leonard, Jack Perry; Warden, Edwin Stanley; Porter, Jesse Graves; Joe (Train Engineer), Milton Kibbee; Court Clerk, Pat Lane; Bailiff, Chuck Hamilton; Reporter, Jack Gardner

Credits: Director, Oscar Boetticher, Jr.; Producer, Wallace MacDonald; Story, Leon Abrams and Richard Hill Wilkinson; Screenwriter, Charles O'Neal; Editor, Paul Borofsky; Art Director, George Brooks; Set Decorator, George Montgomery; Cinematographer, L.W. O'Connell; Musical Director, Mischa Bakaleinikoff

Production Dates: July 10–25, 1944

Running Time: 66 minutes

Story: After the fourth member of George Macready's murder trial jury dies in a mysterious accident, reporter Jim Bannon believes someone is actually committing murder. Macready was convicted on George Lloyd's perjured testimony. Just prior to Macready's execution, Lloyd is gunned down. Before Lloyd dies, he exonerates Macready. The man behind Macready's girlfriend's murder was a jealous rival. The strain of waiting in death row has destroyed Macready's mind and he is transferred to a mental hospital. When a fire consumes Macready's room, the body is presumed to be his. Bannon begins interviewing the remaining members of the jury and become enamored with antique dealer Janis Carter. Through Carter, he meets Macready, now disguised as the jury foreman. Macready tells Bannon he will reveal the killer's identity at dawn. Macready makes an unsuccessful attempt on Bannon's life. Trevor Bardette confesses to the crimes but Bannon proves he's not the murderer. Macready murders another juror. He then abducts Carter and takes her to his house, planning to hang her from a rafter. Bannon races with the local police to Macready's house. As the rope tightens around Carter's neck, Deputy Sheriff Al Bridge fires three shots into Macready. The threat to the jurors over, Bannon and Carter now have time for romance.

Notes and Commentary: The working title was *Tomorrow We Die.*

The music heard over the opening credits would be reworked for the theme music for the Durango Kid series at Columbia.

Reviews: "Well-balanced direction keeps the suspense going up to the very end." *Motion Picture Guide*, Nash and Ross

Summation: This is an interesting but only mildly suspenseful revenge noir. Oscar Boetticher, Jr.'s direction keeps the story on the move, cinematographer L.W. O'Connell's photography is sometimes inventive, and George Macready gives a fine performance as a man driven to insanity. But the end result is a just barely above-average motion picture.

HUNTED MEN AND THEIR WOMEN—one step ahead of the relentless pursuit of the law

Mr. District Attorney

(February 1947)

ALTERNATE TITLE: District Attorney

CAST: Steve Bennett, Dennis O'Keefe; Craig Warren, Adolphe Menjou; Marcia Manning, Marguerite Chapman; Harrington, Michael O'Shea; James Randolph, George Coulouris; Miss Miller, Jeff Donnell; Berotti, Steven Geray; Ed Jamison, Ralph Morgan; Franzen, John Kellogg; Uncredited: Marsden, Ralf Harolde; Mrs. Marsden, Joan Blair; Longfield, Charles Trowbridge; Gang Leader, Robert Barron; Defense Attorney, Frank Wilcox; Gallentyne, Holmes Herbert; Captain Lambert, Cliff Clark; Party Guest, Arthur Space; Peter Lantz, Frank Reicher; Judge, Forbes Murray; Newsboy, Johnny Duncan; Doorman, Gene Roth

CREDITS: Director, Robert B. Sinclair; Assistant Director, James Nicholson; Producer, Samuel Bischoff; Story, Sidney Marshall; Adaptation, Ben Markson; Screenwriter, Ian McLellan Hunter; Editor, William Lyon; Art Directors, Stephen Goosson and George Brooks; Set Decorator, Earl Teass; Cinematographer, Bert Glennon; Gowns, Jean Louis; Sound, Jack Goodrich; Musical Director, M.W. Stoloff

SOURCE: the radio program "Mr. District Attorney" created by Phillips H. Lord

PRODUCTION DATES: July 29, 1946–September 5, 1946

RUNNING TIME: 81 minutes

STORY: Marguerite Chapman, a suspected murderess, has a key position with racketeer George Coulouris. Coulouris wants to begin an

The mob is under the gun in *Mr. District Attorney* (1947).

affair with Chapman. She wants marriage and wealth before love. District Attorney Adolphe Menjou's assistant Dennis O'Keefe is prosecuting one of Coulouris' associates. Chapman begins an affair with O'Keefe and obtains information that destroys O'Keefe's case. O'Keefe proposes to Chapman, who puts him off. Menjou interferes and forces Chapman to give up O'Keefe. Chapman marries Coulouris. O'Keefe learns what Menjou did and resigns. Chapman murders another of Coulouris' associates who had decided to give information to Menjou. Chapman arranges for O'Keefe to work for Coulouris. She also verifies that O'Keefe still loves her. Coulouris is murdered and O'Keefe is thought to be the murderer. Nightclub owner Steven Geray observed the murder and goes to Chapman's apartment, accusing Chapman of the crime. Menjou arrives and Geray gets the drop on him. Chapman shoots Geray, telling Menjou she did it to save his life. Menjou believes O'Keefe to be innocent. Wearing a wire, O'Keefe goes to Chapman's apartment, where she confesses. She wants to marry O'Keefe and take over Coulouris' rackets. O'Keefe plans to turn Chapman in. Chapman tries to push O'Keefe off the balcony to the pavement eight stories below. O'Keefe moves aside and Chapman plunges to her death. Menjou welcomes O'Keefe back as his assistant.

Notes and Commentary: The film begins with the same statement as the radio program.

Mr. District Attorney is given a name in this film; on the radio program he was called either Mr. D.A. or boss.

The producers wanted Tallulah Bankhead and Edward G. Robinson for roles in this film.

This was director Robert B. Sinclair's first post-war film assignment.

Reviews: "[A] lukewarm thriller." *The Columbia Story*, Hirschhorn

"It is a rather haphazard version of the ether whodunit with cloudy storyline that will not always be clear to ticket buyers." *Variety*, 12/25/46

Summation: This good crime melodrama is faithful to the radio program. The taut screenplay emphasizes the film noir genre highlighted by Sinclair's direction and Bert Glennon's cinematography. The acting is first-rate. Marguerite Chapman scores strongly as a female fatale who will stop at nothing to get what she wants. Dennis O'Keefe matches Chapman as an aspiring assistant district attorney who is out of his depth in his dealings with Chapman. Adolphe Menjou sparkles as Mr. District Attorney.

YOU CAN'T KEEP RUNNING FOREVER ... BECAUSE A BULLET CAN TRAVEL FASTER THAN YOU CAN...

Mr. Soft Touch

(August 1949)

Cast: Joe Miracle, Glenn Ford; Jenny Jones, Evelyn Keyes; Early Byrd, John Ireland; Mrs. Hangale, Beulah Bondi; Rickle, Percy Kilbride; Susan Balmuss, Clara Blandick; Rainey, Ted de Corsia; Yonki, Stanley Clements; Barney Teener, Roman Bohnen; Sergeant Garrett, Harry Shannon; Uncredited: Muggles, Gordon Jones; Fanner, Jack Gordon; Victor Christopher, Ray Mayer; Clara Christopher, Angela Clarke; Officer Miller, Mikel Conrad; Judge Fuller, Charles Trowbridge; Sonya, Lora Lee Michel; Al, William Rhinehart; Percentage, Leon Tyler; Alex, William Edmunds; Piano Mover, Ralph Volkie; Yonzi's Cohorts, Gene Collins and Myron Welton; Gardner, William Vedder; Donna, Helene Stanley; Receptionist, Gay Nelson; Tenant, Mary Field; Overweight Man, Peter Cusanelli; Slatternly Woman Tenant, Mary Gordon; Massive Woman, Edith Leslie; Tomboy, Peggy Miller; Ugly Old Maid Tenant, Maudie Prickett; Jackie, Teddy Infuhr; Old Woman, Ilka Gruning; Fat Santa Claus, Paul Maxey; Skinny Santa Claus, Olin Howland; Santa Claus, Ralph Littlefield; Squad Car Policemen, Tom Coffey and Ray Teal; Tollgate Policeman, Ralph Dunn; Gus, Shimen Ruskin; Doctor, Myron Healey; Buddy, Wally Rose; Policeman, Brian O'Hara; Old Man, William A. Cokos; Driver, Al Murphy; Fire Chief, Al Hill; Used Car Salesman, Frank O'Connor; Little Boy, Tony Taylor; Henchman, Mike Lally

Credits: Directors, Henry Levin and Gordon Douglas; Assistant Director, Milton Feldman; Producer and Story, Milton Holmes; Screenwriter, Orin Jannings; Editor, Richard

Fantl; Art Director, George Brooks; Set Decorator, Frank Tuttle; Cinematographers, Joseph Walker and Charles Lawton, Jr.; Gowns for Miss Keyes, Jean Louis; Makeup, Clay Campbell; Hair Stylist, Helen Hunt; Sound, George Cooper; Original Music, Heinz Roemheld; Musical Director, M.W. Stoloff

Location Filming: San Francisco, California

Production Dates: August 9–September 23, 1948

Running Time: 93 minutes

Story: Glenn Ford, a returning veteran, is chased by mobsters led by Ted de Corsia. Ford arrives in San Francisco to find that the nightclub of which he is part-owner is under mob control and his partner dead. Ford takes $100,000 from the mob as payment for his interest. He has a ticket on a ship to Japan but the ship doesn't depart for 36 hours. Circumstances place Ford in the custody of social worker Evelyn Keyes at the Settlement House. Ford thinks that this would be a good place to hide and also to hide his money until he can leave the country. Ford and Keyes become attracted to each other. Columnist John Ireland, who believes Ford is in the right, comes to the Settlement House on a hunch that Ford is there. Ford sees the Settlement House is in need and arranges to have new towels, blankets and bathtubs delivered. Ireland finally sees Ford, who refuses to help him in his crusade against the mob. Ford plans to leave the country and wants Keyes to come with him. In retaliation, Ireland tips off de Corsia as to Ford's whereabouts. Ford sees de Corsia and his men and slips the money to Keyes. De Corsia and his cohorts grab Ford. Believing the money is in the Settlement House, de Corsia sends Ford to bring the money to him. In the Settlement House, Keyes returns the money to Ford. De Corsia sets the Settlement House on fire. Ford is able to get the money out only to have it grabbed by the mob. Ford goes to the nightclub and, using a secret entrance, enters the office of mob boss Roman Bohnen. Using strong-arm tactics, Ford gets his money back. Making his escape, Ford is chased by de Corsia and his men. To elude capture, he enters the Settlement House, disguised as a Santa Claus. Thinking Ford will return to the Settlement House, de Corsia and his men cover all entrances. Ford gives his money to help rebuild the Settlement House. As he leaves, Keyes chases after him. When Keyes calls Ford's name, de Corsia realizes who he is and fires three shots into Ford's body. Keyes cradles Ford as he lies in the street.

Reviews: "Moderately entertaining..." *Variety*, 7/27/49

"The use of two directors, Levin and Douglas, shows in the uneven pace and the stereotyped performances." *Motion Picture Guide*, Nash and Ross

Summation: This is an unusual hybrid of comedy and noir which comes off as a slightly above-average motion picture. The first two-thirds is basically comedy that is predictable but does generate a few chuckles. The final third is a suspenseful, nicely filmed noir. Ford and Keyes are fine as the leads and the chemistry sparkles between them. The big surprise is the abrupt and ambiguous ending. Ford is critically wounded and lying in the gutter, with three bullets in his back. Paper promoting the film shows Ford and Keyes surrounded by a medic and a cluster of onlookers. The film has a tight close-up of the two principals, with the movie audience assuming they are all by themselves. Interestingly, de Corsia is not shot or captured and the mob stays in place with only the loss of money to bother them. Also, the audience is left to wonder about the fate of Ford and Keyes. The film is worth watching just for the noir portion.

CRUEL ... CUNNING ... COLD AS ICE ... nothing like it since The Killers

The Mob

(October 1951)

Cast: Johnny Damico, Broderick Crawford; Mary Kiernan, Betty Buehler; Thomas Clancy, Richard Kiley; Police Lt. Banks, Otto Hulett; Smoothie aka Blackie Clegg, Matt Crowley; Gunner, Neville Brand; Joe Castro, Ernest Borgnine; Police Sgt. Bennion, Walter Klavun; Peggy Clancy, Lynne Baggett; Doris Clancy, Jean Alexander; Police Commissioner, Ralph Dumke; Tony, John Marley; Uncredited: Fred (Pawnbroker), Peter Prouse; Officer Bill Gerrity, Art Millan; Cigar Store Proprietor, Don De Leo; District Attorney,

Carleton Young; Man Leaving Phone Booth, Ethan Laidlaw; Ship's Mate, Robert Anderson; Crewman, Ernie Venneri; Bruiser (Big Longshoreman), Don Megowan; Jack (Longshoreman), Charles Bronson; Russell (Hotel Clerk), Jay Adler; Culio, Frank DeKova; Plainclothesman, Fred Coby; Detective Mason, Jess Kirkpatrick; Waiter, Charles Marsh; Dock Worker in Bar, Fred Aldrich; Gas Station Attendant, Emile Meyer; Johnson (Mobile Unit #3 Officer), Paul Dubov; Daniels (Mobile Unit #2 Officer), Harry Lauter; Prowl Car #2 Officer, David McMahon; Thug Beating Mary, Robert Foulk; Nurse at Reception Desk, Virginia Chapman; Clegg's Doctor, Lawrence Dobkin; Policewoman Nurse, Mary Alan Hokanson; Policeman Cullen, Paul Bryar; Paul, Ken Harvey; Prowl Car Driver, Richard Irving; Talbert, Michael McHale; Joe, Al Mellon; Plotter, William Pullen; Radford, Duke Watson; Policemen, Sydney Mason and Ric Roman; Heathcliff Damico (in picture), Fred F. Sears

Credits: Director, Robert Parrish; Assistant Director, James Nicholson; Producer, Jerry Bresler; Screenwriter, William Bowers; Editor, Charles Nelson; Art Director, Cary Odell; Set Decorator, Frank Tuttle; Cinematographer, Joseph Walker; Makeup, Clay Campbell; Hair Stylist, Helen Hunt; Sound, Lodge Cunningham; Original Music, George Duning; Musical Director, Morris Stoloff

Production Dates: January 11–February 8, 1951

Source: novel *Waterfront* by Ferguson Findley

Running Time: 87 minutes

Story: After purchasing an expensive ring for his fiancée Betty Buehler, police officer Broderick Crawford sees a man gunned down in the dark, wet streets. The shooter identifies himself as a police lieutenant and says he just ended the life of a cop-killer. Crawford allows the man to walk away before he realizes something is wrong with his story. The murdered man turns out to be a man out to bust up the mob's hold on the longshoreman unions. Even though Crawford only got a partial view of the murderer's head, he is assigned to go undercover and work his way into the mob and ferret out the murderer. Crawford's only contact will be Lieutenant Otto Hulett. Crawford gets work on the docks and, dropping the name of mobster Ernest Borgnine, whom he has never met, he replaces Frank DeKova in an easy job. Crawford and DeKova engage in a fight with Crawford emerging victorious. The only dockworker to befriend Crawford is Richard Kiley. Gunman Neville Brand takes Crawford to a meeting with Borgnine. Brand takes Crawford's pistol and fires a shot into a wall. When Borgnine allows Crawford to leave, he knows he's being set up. DeKova is murdered and Crawford is arrested. Crawford undergoes intensive questioning by Sergeant Walter Klavun. Ballistics proves his gun did not fire the fatal shot. Hulett is able to intercede and get Crawford released. Crawford believes Klavun is under mob influence. Bartender Matt Crowley tells Crawford where he can find Brand. Crawford and Brand engage in a brutal fight with Crawford victorious. Crawford has Brand quietly arrested. Borgnine decides to find out what Crawford knows about Brand's disappearance. Kiley knocks out Borgnine and reveals to Crawford that he's an undercover agent trying to arrest Borgnine. Kiley had found out that Crawford is a police officer. Crawford convinces Kiley to keep the arrest quiet. Crowley believes Crawford killed Brand and tells him the big boss has a job for him. Crowley tells Crawford that he is to kill someone. Crawford won't agree until he talks to the head man. The boss turns out to be Crowley, who with a wig turns out to be the murderer Crawford is looking for. The man Crowley wants him to kill is a policeman. Crowley is unaware that policeman is Crawford. Buehler has been led to Crowley's headquarters by Klavun. Before Beuhler's torture can be resumed, Crawford begins a gunfight. The police who have been trailing Crawford arrive. All are captured or killed except Crowley who, though wounded, escapes. Buehler is taken to a local hospital. Through the efforts of mob doctor Lawrence Dobkin, Crowley is a patient on the same floor. After Crawford comes to visit Buehler, Crowley enters the room with the intention to murder both. Crowley closes the blinds for privacy. Before Crowley can act, nurse Mary Alan Hokanson enters to check on Buehler and opens the blinds. Before Crowley can pull the trigger, he is shot by a police marksman. Hokanson is a police officer.

Notes and Commentary: William Bowers' screenplay followed Ferguson Findley's storyline closely. There were changes in character names. Johnny Malone became Johnny Damico and Joe Cigar became Joe Castro.

Prior to publication as a novel by Duell, Sloan and Pearce, the Findley yarn was serialized in *Collier's* (July 22–August 19, 1950).

The working titles for this film were *Waterfront* and *Remember That Face*. *The Mob* was re-released in 1957.

Reviews: "*The Mob* is solid corner-of-the-month stuff for the leather-jacket and blue-jean trade. Fist fights, gunfire and some salty dialog and sexy interludes involving Crawford with Lynne Baggett enliven the proceedings considerably. Tensely paced entrée." *Variety*, 9/5/51

"While not at all a pleasant film, *The Mob* is a gripping, violent drama that will satisfy fans of the crime genre." *Motion Picture Guide*, Nash and Ross

"*The Mob* was a thoroughly professional cops-and-robbers melodrama that benefited from a taut and exciting screenplay and from the central performance by Broderick Crawford. One of the better crime pictures of the year." *The Columbia Story*, Hirschhorn

Summation: This is a gritty, gripping and exciting crime noir with fine acting by Broderick Crawford as an undercover cop assisted by tough guys Neville Brand and Ernest Borgnine. The intense direction of Robert Parrish from a well-done William Bowers screenplay provides excellent entertainment. Both police and the mob do not hesitate to use violence to gain their particular advantage. Joseph Walker's camerawork takes advantage of the dark to intensify the proceedings and further brand the film as noir.

DOUBLE RATES FOR WOMEN ... because a woman is always double-trouble!

Murder by Contract

(December 1958)

Cast: Claude, Vince Edwards; Marc, Phillip Pine; George, Herschel Bernardi; Billie Williams, Caprice Toriel; Mr. Moon, Michael Granger; Mary, Cathy Browne; Harry (Hotel Room Waiter), Joseph Mell; Miss Wiley, Frances Osborne; Detective Shooting Tear Gas, Steven Ritch; Janet Brandt; Hall of Records Clerk, Davis Roberts; James William Mayflower, Don Garrett; Miss Wexley, Gloria Victor; Uncredited: Hotel Take-Out Delivery Man, William H. O'Brien

Credits: Director, Irving Lerner; Assistant Director, Louis Brandt; Producer, Leon Chooluck; Screenwriter, Ben Simcoe; Editor, Carlo Lodato; Set Director, Jack Poplin; Property Master, Jack Gorton; Set Dresser, Lyle B. Reifsnider; Cinematographer, Lucien Ballard; Special Effects, Jack Erickson; Photographic Effects, Jack Rabin and Louis DeWitt; Makeup, Ted Larsen; Wardrobe, Norman Martien; Sound, Jack Solomon; Musical Composer and Player, Perry Botkin; Script Supervisor, Elinore Donahoe; Dialogue Coach, Joe Steinberg

Location Filming: Glendale (train station), California; Los Angeles (Hall of Records, Ventura Freeway and Hollywood Freeway), California; Pacific Coast Highway (Thelma Todd House), California; San Fernando Valley (Ventura Freeway), California and Studio City (golf driving range), California

Production Dates: completed early February 1958

Running Time: 81 minutes

Story: In order to obtain an expensive house that he desires, Vince Edwards becomes a contract killer. A mob boss convinces underling Michael Granger to hire him. After two successful kills, the mob boss directs Edwards to kill Granger. Next, Edwards receives a contract to travel to Los Angeles to kill Caprice Toriel. Edwards is surprised to find his next victim is a woman. She is scheduled to testify against the mob boss. Edwards is escorted around the Los Angeles area by two local hoods, Phillip Pine and Herschel Bernardi. Edwards is hesitant to attempt the job until he is certain Pine and Bernardi aren't being followed. Finally Edwards is ready to carry out his assignment. Edwards cannot directly access the house because of the police presence. Edwards diverts electricity from high voltage wires to the line connected to Toriel's television so that there will be an explosion when Toriel turns it on. When Toriel uses a remote to turn on the television, the set explodes but she is unharmed. Alarmed, Toriel insists that her companion in the house be a woman. Gloria Victor is assigned. Edwards purchases an archery set and turns Bernardi into a proficient bowman. Bernardi will shoot blunted arrows into Toriel's front door. When the curious Toriel opens the door, Edwards, using a high-powered rifle, will shoot. The plan goes forth, the door opens and Edwards fires. A body falls to the ground. Instead of Toriel, the victim was Victor, who was garbed in Toriel's negligee. Edwards decides to abort the job and return home. Pine and Bernardi are assigned to kill Edwards if he doesn't go through with the job. Edwards is taken to an abandoned movie studio. Edwards overpowers Pine and kills him and then overtakes the fleeing Bernardi and dispatches him also. Edwards then decides to carry out the job if his fee is doubled. From the Hall of Records, Edwards learns that a large drainage pipe leads into Toriel's house. He gains entrance to the house. At first Toriel thinks Edwards is a policeman but quickly learns that he is there to kill her. Edwards plans to strangle Toriel with his necktie as she plays the piano. Because he really doesn't wants to murder a woman, Edwards hesitates long enough to be spotted by the police. He attempts to escape through the drainage pipe. Shots are exchanged and he is killed.

Notes and Commentary: *Murder by Contract* influenced Martin Scorsese in his direction of *Mean Streets* (Warner Bros., 1973) and *Taxi Driver* (Columbia, 1976).

The former Charlie Chaplin Studio was the location used for the abandoned movie studio.

Reviews: "Suspenseful story of a paid killer's last assignment. The production has the benefit of mounting suspense, after a haphazard opening, and the story is sufficiently interesting." *Variety*, 12/10/58

"Ben Simcoe's screenplay piled on the suspense." *The Columbia Story*, Hirschhorn

Summation: In this neat "B" crime noir, the suspense builds slowly but finally settles in for the final twenty minutes. Vince Edwards carries the story as a man who chooses this dangerous life in order to achieve some lifetime ambitions. His performance is realistic throughout. On the negative side, Phillip Pine and Herschel Bernardi are given meaningless and uninteresting dialogue that hampers the production. Perry Bodkin's music and guitar-playing is only an asset during the suspenseful moments of the film, distracting in the others.

Just as he killed his wife ... just as he'd kill his bride...
This man will kill anyone who stands in his way!

My Name Is Julia Ross

(November 1945)

Cast: Julia Ross, Nina Foch; Mrs. Hughes, Dame May Whitty; Ralph Hughes, George Macready; Dennis Bruce, Roland Varno; Sparkes, Anita Bolster; Mrs. Mackie, Doris Lloyd; Uncredited: Bertha, Joy Harington; Peters, Leonard Mudie; Alice, Queenie Leonard; Uniformed Policeman, Leyland Hodgson; McQuarrie, Reginald Sheffield; Gatekeeper, Charles McNaughton; the Reverend Lewis, Olaf Hytten; Mrs. Robinson, Ottola Nesmith; Mr. Robinson, Harry Hays Morgan; Dr. Keller, Evan Thomas; Nurse, Marilyn Johnson; Plainclothes Policeman, Milton Owen

Credits: Director, Joseph H. Lewis; Producer, Wallace MacDonald; Screenwriter, Muriel Roy Bolton; Editor, Henry Batista; Art Director, Jerome Pycha, Jr.; Set Decorator, Milton Stumph; Cinematographer, Burnett Guffey; Sound, Lambert Day; Musical Director, Mischa Bakaleinikoff

Production Dates: July 19–August 4, 1945

Running Time: 64 minutes

Source: the novel *The Woman in Red* by Anthony Gilbert

Story: In London, Nina Foch is desperately looking for a job as a secretary. Dame Mae Whitty is looking for someone with no family ties or any close friends. Finding that Foch has none, Whitty and her son George Macready decide to hire her if she can start immediately. Foch didn't mention that she was friendly with Roland Varno because Varno was engaged to be married. Returning to her boarding house, Foch learns that Varno's engagement fell through because Varno is really in love with Foch. Foch tells Varno about her new job and plans to meet him the next night after her duties are completed. Foch goes to Whitty's residence that night as instructed. She is drugged and, while asleep, all of her identification and clothes are destroyed by Whitty and her confederate Anita Bolster. When Foch awakens, she is told that she is the wife of Macready and that they're at their mansion in Cornwall, miles from London. Foch protests but is told by Whitty that she has a mental problem. Meanwhile, Varno starts an unsuccessful search. Foch's attempts to escape are thwarted. Whitty and Macready are trying to drive Foch crazy in the hopes that she will commit suicide. When Foch finds a secret panel in her bedroom, she enters and overhears Whitty and Macready planning her death. Macready is mentally unbalanced and in a homicidal rage he murdered his well-to-do wife. Foch's death by suicide or accident is needed in order for Macready to claim his wife's estate. By trickery, Foch is able to mail a letter to Varno. Whitty sends another confederate, Leonard Mudie, to intercept the letter at Varno's boarding house. Rooming house owner Doris Lloyd notices the theft and races after Mudie. Whitty and Macready make another unsuccessful attempt to murder Foch and she races back into her bedroom. When Whitty and Macready hear Foch's scream, they run to Foch's bedroom window and see what looks like her body on the rocks below. Whitty encourages Macready to quickly get to the body to make sure Foch is dead. Finding Foch alive, Macready picks up a rock to crush her head. Macready's attempt is stopped by Varno and policeman Milton Owen. Foch had actually thrown her gown out of the window and then escaped through the secret passage. Leaving the mansion, she was met by Varno and Owen. Quickly they devised the ploy to prove Macready's intention to murder Foch. As Macready attempts to escape, Owen hollers for him to stop. When Macready doesn't, Owen fires a bullet that ends Macready's life. Peters was arrested in London. Owen now arrests Whitty and Bolster. Varno and Foch return to London together. En route, Varno asks Foch to marry him and she accepts.

NOTES AND COMMENTARY: The working title for this movie was *The Woman in Red*.

Anthony Gilbert was the pseudonym for Lucy Beatrice Malleson. She wrote over 50 detective novels featuring Arthur Crook, an eccentric but brilliant lawyer who used his detective skills to prove his clients innocent. *The Woman in Red* featured Crook but Columbia screenwriters deleted his role in their adaptation. Although the

Joy Harington and Nina Foch in *My Name Is Julia Ross* (1945).

initial premise is the same in both the novel and the film, the screenplay changes the focus from a routine spy novel to a Victorian film noir. In the novel, it is necessary for Julia Ross to die by suicide or accident to cover up the death of a government agent. With Crook's help, Ross escapes the clutches of Mrs. Ponsonby (Hughes in the film) and Sparks. Ponsonby has no son so Macready's part was created by the screenwriters. Ross is persuaded to be recaptured so the elusive Peters can also be apprehended. Ross has a boyfriend in the novel, Colin (Dennis in the film) Bruce, and they also plan to marry.

This film was remade as *Dead of Winter* (MGM, 1987) with Mary Steenburgen and Roddy McDowall. The 1955 television adaptation "My Name Is Julia Ross" ran on *Lux Video Theater* with Fay Bainter and Beverly Garland.

Reviews: "Mystery melodrama with a psychological twist runs only 64 minutes but it's fast and packed with tense action throughout. Acting and production are excellent." *Variety*, 11/14/45

"While Joseph Lewis, the director, succeeds in creating an effectively ominous atmosphere, he has not been as adept in handling the players, and that, we suspect, is why *My Name Is Julia Ross* misses the mark." *New York Times*, 11/9/45

"An excellent example of *film noir*, with a lean plot and atmospheric camera work. *My Name Is Julia Ross* is harrowing and suspenseful." *Motion Picture Review*, Nash and Ross

Summation: The film is a definite improvement over the book, which was a fairly routine spy novel. Director Lewis, known for his edgy direction in "B" western films, adapts well to film noir. His direction of Muriel Roy Bolton's screenplay combined with Burnett Guffey's camerawork result in a highly suspenseful outing. Nina Foch's performance is the final ingredient to make the film work. She registers the proper realistic emotions to meet the demands of the script. Acting honors also go to George Macready whose subtle interpretation of a homicidal maniac adds to the suspense. This is a fine example of how an intelligent film can be made on a limited budget.

A WOMAN SCREAMS! A KILLER STRIKES! AND "THE WHISTLER" STALKS HIS PREY!

Mysterious Intruder

(April 1946)

Cast: Don Gale, Richard Dix; Detective Taggart, Barton MacLane; Joan Hill, Nina Vale; James Summers, Regis Toomey; Freda Hanson, Helen Mowery; Harry Pontos, Mike Mazurki; Elora Lund, Pamela Blake; Detective Burns, Charles Lane; Uncredited: Voice of the Whistler, Otto Forrest; Edward Stillwell, Paul E. Burns; Reporters, Donald Kerr and Dan Stowell; Desk Clerk, Charles Jordan; Woman in Window, Jessie Arnold; Dr. Connell, Selmer Jackson; Rose Denning, Kathleen Howard; Mr. Brown, Harlan Briggs; Kelly, Kernan Cripps; Henry, Stanley Blystone; Police Desk Sergeant, Harry Strang; Miss Gordon, Isabel Withers; Jimmy, Jack Carrington; Policeman Outside Stillwell's Store, Joe Palma; Davis, Arthur Space

Credits: Director, William Castle; Producer, Rudolph C. Flothow; Story and Screenwriter, Eric Taylor; Editor, Dwight Caldwell; Art Director, Hans Radon; Set Decorator, Robert Priestley; Cinematographer, Philip Tannura; Sound, Jack Haynes; Musical Director, Mischa Bakaleinikoff; "Whistler" theme music, Wilbur Hatch

Production Dates: December 6–20, 1945

Running Time: 61 minutes

Source: the Columbia Broadcasting System Program "The Whistler"

Story: Seedy private investigator Richard Dix is hired by Paul E. Burns to find Pamela Blake. Burns has some of Blake's mother's heirlooms that might be worth a fortune. Dix decides to pass Helen Mowery off as the heir. After Mowery meets Burns, tough guy Mike Mazurki shows up and murders Burns and takes Mowery. Mowery returns to Dix when he tells reporters Mowery was only pretending to be the heir. Mowery leads Dix to Mazurki's house. Dix breaks in and finds Mazurki passed out. Police detectives Barton MacLane and Charles Lane arrive and shots are fired. Mazurki is killed. Seen leaving the house, Dix is arrested. Blake sees the newspaper article about Burns' death and calls the police. Dix is released. Blake is instructed to meet with Dix to find the valuable heirlooms. Dix tells Blake he will find them. Dix confronts Mowery and makes her confess that she was working with Mazurki and she had a boyfriend call the police. Mowery hoped the police would shoot Dix. Mowery also shows Dix a newspaper clipping about some rare Jenny Lind recordings worth $200,000. Someone comes to Mowery's door and Dix leaves through the back entrance. Harlan Briggs, who owns the shop next to Burns' place, shows Dix a secret passage into Burns' store. Dix learns that Mowery was murdered. Apartment manager Regis Toomey found her body. Dix decides to enter the store and finds Briggs' dead body. In Burns' store, Toomey and a confederate, Arthur Space, are looking for the Jenny Lind recordings. Toomey and Space locate the recordings and start to leave only to be confronted by Dix. Toomey was working with Mowery and wants to make a deal with Dix. Dix takes the box with the recordings. Shots are exchanged and it looks like Toomey and Space are hit. From a tip, MacLane and Lane enter the store from the front door. Dix leaves by the secret passage and calls the police. Dix hears someone coming through the passage and, thinking it's the killers, fires a shot. Shots are returned. One bullet goes through the box (smashing the recordings) and into Dix's body, killing him. MacLane and Lane fired the shots.

Notes and Commentary: The working title for this film was *Murder Is Unpredictable*.

Reviews: "Though routine in plot, this is a well-paced film with some good moments of suspense. Though classically hard-boiled, Dix's characterization has a soft spot, as well as providing some humor within the mystery. Some interesting camerawork and a tightly plotted script make this a nifty programmer." *Motion Picture Guide*, Nash and Ross

"Nicely paced whodunit with Richard Dix, [it] provides a consistently entertaining hour's entertainment." *Variety*, 3/27/46

Summation: This is a fine mystery film noir. Dix's portrayal of a private investigator working on the edge of the law is excellent. The fine supporting cast includes such worthies as Barton MacLane, Regis Toomey, Mike Mazurki, Pamela Blake and Charles Lane. William Castle's direction and Philip Tannura's cinematography complement Eric Taylor's first-rate story.

EVERY DAY WAS MARDI GRAS FOR THE MOBSTERS AND THEIR DOLLS!

New Orleans Uncensored

(March 1955)

Cast: Dan Corbett, Arthur Franz; Marie Reilly, Beverly Garland; Alma Mae, Helene Stanton; Zero Saxon, Michael Ansara; Scrappy Durant, Stacy Harris; Big Mike, Mike Mazurki; Joe Reilly, William Henry; Jack Petty, Michael Granger; Charlie, Edward Stafford Nelson; Themselves, Al Chittenden, President, General Longshore Workers, Local 1418 (ILA); Joseph L. Scheuering, Superintendent of Police, City of New Orleans; Victor Schiro, Senior Councilman, City of New Orleans; Howard L. Dey, Fire Chief, City of New Orleans; Pete Herman; Ralph Dupas and Judge Walter B. Hamlin as Wayne Brandon

Credits: Director, William Castle; Assistant Director, Leonard Katzman; Producer, Sam Katzman; Story, Orville H. Hampton; Screenwriters, Orville H. Hampton and Lewis Meltzer; Editors, Gene Havlick and Al Clark; Art Director, Paul Palmentola; Set Decorator, Sidney Clifford; Cinematographer, Henry Freulich; Special Effects, Jack Erickson; Sound, Josh Westmoreland; Musical Director, Mischa Bakaleinikoff; Unit Manager, Leon Chooluck

Location Filming: New Orleans, Louisiana

Production Dates: August 17–27, 1954

Running Time: 75 minutes

Story: Arthur Franz arrives in New Orleans to purchase a Landing Ship Medium to use in starting his own shipping business. Needing money to finish payment, Franz gets a job as a dock worker, working with dock manager William Henry. Franz finds that cargo leaves the docks without being checked. Mob boss Michael Ansara is attempting to gain control of the docks, getting rich by pilfering and smuggling. Henry finally has had enough and asks to quit Ansara. Ansara agrees but sends henchmen Frankie Ray and Mike Mazurki to silence Henry. With investigators starting to get too close to the truth, Ansara has the honest Franz made dock manager. Franz has become close with Henry's widow Beverly Garland and her brother Stacy Harris. Harris tries to warn Franz about the dangers of working with Ansara and is told that Franz told everything Harris told *him* to Ansara. In a rage, Harris starts hitting Franz. In self defense, Franz throws a mild punch resulting in Harris's immediate death. Garland tells Franz that Harris had a bad heart. Franz goes to the authorities to offer his help in stopping mob rule on the docks. Franz begins placing transmitters in valuable cargoes so police can trace their movement through the city. A transmitter is discovered and Ansara figures that Franz was responsible. After Franz is beaten into unconsciousness, Ansara puts Franz's fingerprints on the gun that killed Henry and keeps the gun. Ansara goes to the docks to help get stolen merchandise back to the dock before the authorities seize it. With mob moll Helene Stanton's help, Franz gets free and goes after Ansara. At the docks the men exchange shots. Both men are wounded. Ansara shot Franz with the gun that killed Henry. This puts the finishing touches in toppling Ansara's plan of ruling the docks. Franz and Garland plan to start a shipping business.

Notes and Commentary: The working title for the film was *Riot on Pier 6*.

Pete Herman was a bantamweight world champion from 1917 to 1921. He lost the championship and then regained it in July 1921. He lost the championship for good two months later. Herman operated a club in the New Orleans French Quarter. He was inducted into the National Boxing Hall of Fame and the Louisiana Sport Hall of Fame.

When this film was shot, Ralph Dupas was a ranked contender as a lightweight fighter. He fought in the welterweight division but lost a title bout with Emile Griffith. In 1963, Dupas became the light middleweight champion. His reign was short: He lost in September, kayoed by Sandro Mazzinghi. Dupas was later inducted into the World Boxing Hall of Fame and the Louisiana Sport Hall of Fame.

Reviews: "The entertainment that results is only fair at best." *Variety*, 2/16/55

"Liberal use of the New Orleans docks and other city sites as film settings lends some authenticity to the movie..." *Motion Picture Guide*, Nash and Ross

Summation: At time the looks like it could have been a respectable "B" crime noir but a rushed and improbably happy ending ruined all chances. Inexplicably, Michael Ansara keeps in his possession a murder weapon he will use to frame Arthur Franz. Franz then convinces mob moll Helene Stanton to help him get free to chase down Ansara. By screenwriters' luck, Ansara wounds Franz in a gunfight, with the bullet conveniently remaining in his body to be compared with bullets that killed William Henry. Director William Castle doesn't pace the script fast enough so the audience has time to think about holes in the script. Stacy Harris is killed when Franz hits him with a pulled punch (Harris has a bum heart). It would have made more sense for Harris to have succumbed from the exertion he placed on his heart from the blows he landed on Franz. The talented Beverly Garland gives a good performance as the unhappy widow of William Henry, showing both disappointment in her life and later grief over Henry's death. The beautiful Helene Stanton pulls out all the stops as a femme fatale gangster moll who knows how to use her body to get what she wants. This one of the few Sam Katzman crime exposés that fails to rate as good entertainment.

THE SHOCK STORY OF A DOUBLE-CROSS
that started with a kiss ... and ended in murder!

Night Editor

(March 1946)
Alternate Title: The Trespasser
Cast: Police Lt. Tony Cochrane, William Gargan; Jill Merrill, Janis Carter; Martha Cochrane, Jeff Donnell; Johnny, Coulter Irwin; Crane Stewart, Charles D. Brown; Police Lt. Ole Strom, Paul

E. Burns; Police Capt. Lawrence, Harry Shannon; Douglas Loring, Frank Wilcox; Doc Cochrane, Robert Kellard; Uncredited: Street Sweeper Driver, John Tyrrell; Max, Robert Emmett Keane; Swanson, Charles Marsh; Necktie, Lou Lubin; Doc Cochrane as a boy, Michael Chapin; Tusco, Anthony Caruso; Coroner, Emmett Vogan; Dickstein, Ed Chandler; Butler, Frank Dae; Benjamin Merrill, Roy Gordon; Bank Manager, Douglas Wood; Phillips, Charles Wagenheim; Fat Man in Library, Vernon Dent; Clerk, Jimmy Lloyd; Luke, Murray Leonard; Bartender, Harry Tyler; District Attorney Bill Halloran, Jack Davis

CREDITS: Director, Henry Levin; Producer, Ted Richmond; Story, Scott Littleton; Screenwriter, Hal Smith; Editor, Richard Fantl; Art Director, Robert Peterson; Set Decorator, James Crowe; Cinematographers, Burnett Guffey and Philip Tannura; Sound, Lambert Day; Musical Director, Mischa Bakaleinikoff

PRODUCTION DATES: December 26, 1945–January 12, 1946

RUNNING TIME: 68 minutes

SOURCE: Based on the radio program "Night Editor" by Hal Burdick

STORY: Newspaper reporter Coulter Irwin has not been home for a week and now is afraid to go. The paper's night editor Charles D. Brown tells him the story of policeman William Gargan's affair with socialite Janis Carter. Gargan and Carter are both married. In his car, Gargan takes Carter to a secluded spot to break off the affair. Carter is able to seduce Gargan. In the throes of their lovemaking, another car pulls up and its driver kills the woman passenger. Gargan lets the murderer escape to avoid a personal scandal. Gargan is assigned to the case and learns that Carter knew the murdered woman and also the murderer. The murderer is banker Frank Wilcox, whom Gargan also recognizes. Gargan wants Carter to go with him to police headquarters and tell the truth. Carter refuses. When an innocent man is accused of the crime, Gargan looks for other evidence to convict Wilcox. Carter is now having an affair with Wilcox and provides an alibi for him. Gargan goes to arrest Wilcox and finds him

Janis Carter and William Gargan conspire in *Night Editor* (1946).

in a passionate embrace with Carter. Carter stabs Gargan in the back with an ice pick. Gargan hands over his prisoners and surrenders his badge before collapsing. As the story ends, Irwin leaves the news room. In the lobby, Irwin realizes the cigar stand owner is Gargan and that Gargan's family stood by him. Irwin now knows the importance of family and decides to go home.

NOTES AND COMMENTARY: The working title for *Night Editor* was *Inside Story*.

Night Editor was released on DVD as part of the *Columbia Bad Girls of Film Noir Collection* in 2010.

REVIEWS: "[A]n inept cop drama." *The Columbia Story*, Hirshhorn

"This is a classic example of film noir with its analogies between sex and violence, women who use sex to get what they want, and the basic negativity toward people in general. Gargan is dull and ineffectual in his role ... but this may have been the intention." *Motion Picture Guide*, Nash and Ross

"Cockeyed police-sleuth meller. It's an instance of a good idea gone haywire via slipshod production and faulty direction." *Variety*, 4/3/46

SUMMATION: This is a good film noir that was supposed to be the first in an anthology series similar to that of the Whistler. Henry Levin nicely directs the story with flawless performances by Gargan and Janis Carter. The cinematography by Burnett Guffey and Philip Tannura is first-rate. The delicate shadings of black and white add immensely to the film noir tale. It would have been a stronger film noir if Gargan had succumbed to Carter's murder attempt and the wrap-around story had been eliminated.

WITH A GASP IN YOUR THROAT ... AND A GUN IN YOUR BACK! YOU WILL LIVE ALL THE SUSPENSE AND REALISM!

The Night Holds Terror

(July 1955)

CAST: Gene Courtier, Jack Kelly; Doris Courtier, Hildy Parks; Victor Gosset, Vince Edwards; Robert Batsford, John Cassavetes; Luther Logan, David Cross; Captain Cole, Edward Marr; Detective Pope, Jack Kruschen; Phyllis Harrison, Joyce McClusky; Bob Henderson, Jonathan Hale; Stranske, Barney Phillips; TV News Broadcaster, Roy Neal; Reporter, Joel Marston; Police Technician, Guy Kingsford; Uncredited: Narrator, William Woodson; Mr. Courtier, Stanley Andrews; Steven Courtier, Charles Herbert; Deborah Courtier, Nancy Zane; Mrs. Osmond, Barbara Woodell; Reporter, John Phillips

CREDITS: Director, Producer and Screenwriter, Andrew Stone; Assistant Director, Melville Shyer; Editor, Virginia Stone; Cinematographer, Fred Jackman, Jr.; Sound, Theron Triplett; Original Music, Lucien Cailliet

SONG: "Every Now and Then" (V. Stone)

PRODUCTION DATES: November 30–December 20, 1954

RUNNING TIME: 86 minutes

STORY: Jack Kelly, on his way home from work, picks up hitchhiker Vince Edwards. Edwards produces a gun and forces Kelly to drive to a secluded area. They are followed by another car with gang boss John Cassavetes and gang member David Cross. The crooks need money and to save his life, Kelly agrees to sell his car and give Cassavetes the money. Car dealer Barney Phillips can't give Kelly cash until the next day. Cassavetes, Edwards and Cross take over Kelly's house, intimidating Kelly's wife Hildy Parks. Kelly gets the money but Cassavetes takes Kelly with him as a hostage. Parks tells Cassavetes that if she doesn't hear from Kelly in 30 minutes, she will notify the police. Parks confides in her neighbor Joyce McCluskey, who convinces her to call the police. Parks finally calls the police and an all points bulletin is put out. Cassavetes finally lets Kelly call home. Kelly is able to tell Parks that Cassavetes has a police radio in his car and Parks is able to alert the police before the APB goes out on the air. Cross tells Cassavetes that Kelly's father, Stanley Andrews, owns a large supermarket chain and they should hold Kelly for ransom. Cassavetes tells Parks the ransom is $200,000. While Cassavetes is away, Kelly convinces Cross to help him overcome Edwards. By helping Kelly escape, Cross will avoid a kidnapping charge. As Kelly and Cross attempt to get away, Cassavetes returns. Cassavetes kills Cross and keeps Kelly as hostage. They reach another phone to finalize the ransom details. The call is traced. Police arrive and shots are fired. Edwards is hit and Cassavetes is taken into custody. Kelly is safe.

Notes and Commentary: The working title for the film was *Terror in the Night*. It was based on a real-life incident: In February 1953, Eugene Courtier and his family were held hostage by Leonard D. Mahan, Jr. and two other individuals. In the film, Mahan was identified as Robert Batsford.

Two lawsuits resulted. In August 1955 Mahan's family sued Columbia Pictures, Ben Cohen and Andrew Stone for $750,000 citing invasion of privacy. They stated that the family was ostracized and Mahan, Sr., lost his job. They requested that the picture not be shown. This request was dismissed by a Superior Court judge. A second suit was filed in November 1955, again for $750,000 and a share in the film's profits against Columbia Pictures, Andrew Stone and Eugene Courtier. They stated the film was made without Mahan, Jr.'s, permission and did not mention his insistence of innocence which might adversely impact any chance for an early parole. The author could not determine the outcome of the latter lawsuit.

Reviews: "Taut, well-played melodramatics. Stone's writing and direction keep the theatrics subdued, letting the situation itself and how the hoods and victims react build the tight mounting expectancy that earmark this one as a believable suspense feature." *Variety*, 7/13/55

"A tense film noir based on a true story. A well-constructed, powerful film." *Motion Picture Guide*, Nash and Ross

Summation: This fine, gritty kidnap caper noir features good performances by Jack Kelly and Hildy Parks as the terrorized couple and John Cassavetes, Vince Edwards and David Cross as the terrorizers. Director Stone keeps the suspense on high, alternating between police and telephone company procedure and the actions of the kidnappers. Great photography by Fred Jackman, Jr. enhances this taut story.

SHEER TERROR ... and RAPTURE
THE BLACK BAG ... with $350,000 in loot
THE BLACK DRESS ... with a beautiful pickup girl inside!
THE BLACK NIGHT ... made for lovers ... and killers!

Nightfall

(February 1957)

A Copa Production

Alternate Title: Night Fall

Cast: James Vanning, Aldo Ray; John, Brian Keith; Marie Gardner, Anne Bancroft; Laura Fraser, Jocelyn Brando; Ben Fraser, James Gregory; Dr. Edward Gurston, Frank Albertson; Red, Rudy Bond; Uncredited: Bartender, Gene Roth; Hostess, Arline Anderson; Spanish Woman, Maria Belmer; Spanish Man, Orlando Beltran; Cashier, Art Bucaro; Shoeshine Boy, Walter Smith; Fashion Commentator, Winifred Waring; Models, Joan Fotre, Annabelle George, Pat Jones, Lillian Kassan, Betty Koch, Jane Lynn; Taxi Driver, Eddie McLean; Man on Bus with Radio, Robert Cherry; Bus Driver, George Cisar

Credits: Director, Jacques Tourneur; Assistant Director, Irving Moore; Producer, Ted Richmond; Screenwriter, Stirling Silliphant; Editor, William A. Lyon; Art Director, Ross Bellah; Set Decorators, William Kiernan and Louis Diage; Cinematographer, Burnett Guffey; Gowns, Jean Louis; Makeup, Clay Campbell; Hair Stylist, Helen Hunt; Recording Supervisor, John Livadary; Sound, Ferol Redd; Original Music, George Duning; Musical Conductor, Morris Stoloff; Orchestrator, Arthur Morton; Fashion Show, J.W. Robinson Company of California

Songs: "Nightfall" (Lewis, DeRose and Harold)—sung by Al Hibbler; "Nocturne Op. 9 No. 2" (Chopin)—piano solo and "Red River Valley" (traditional)—played by a western band

Filming Locations: Beverly Hills, California, Hollywood Blvd., Los Angeles, California

Production Dates: March 20–April 9, 1956

Source: novel *Nightfall* by David Goodis

Running Time: 78 minutes

Story: In a Los Angeles bar, Anne Bancroft makes the acquaintance of Aldo Ray. Ray is a man on the run from both the police and murderous bank robbers. Leaving the bar with Bancroft, Ray's past catches up with him when Brian Keith and Rudy Bond accost him. They take Ray to a deserted oil rig and promise to let him go if he will give them the $350,000 that he took from them. Ray tells them that he doesn't remember what happened to the money. Ray remembers that Keith and Bond had an automobile accident and that he and Dr. Frank Albertson tried to help them. Keith suffered a fractured left arm that Albertson bandaged. Keith forces Ray to give them his driver's license and registration. Ray now focuses his thoughts on his present situation. Seizing an opportunity, Ray engages in a violent struggle with Keith and Bond. Ray is victorious and is able to escape. Believing Bancroft was in league with the men, Ray goes to her apartment. Bancroft tells Ray she thought the men were police and Ray was being arrested. Now Ray believes Bancroft is in danger from Keith and Bond and tells her she'll have to leave with him. While waiting for Bancroft to pack, he tells of the meeting with Keith and Bond. Ray and Albertson are taken to their campsite. Bond decides he will shoot Albertson with Ray's rifle and then force Ray to commit suicide. Bond shoots Albertson. Ray fires his one bullet at Bond. The shot goes wild. As Ray tries to flee, he falls. Bond fires. The shot misses but clips a piece of rock that strikes Ray in the head, rendering him unconscious. Bond thinks the shot killed him. Keith and Bond leave. Before Ray can continue the story, Keith and Bond show up at Bancroft's apartment. Ray and Bancroft escape through the back door. Ray and Bancroft go to Ray's apartment. They are seen by James Gregory, an insurance investigator who has Ray under surveillance. Ray continues his story. When coming to, Ray reached for Albertson's medical bag. When he opened the bag, he saw the bank money. Ray heard a car returning. Knowing it was the robbers, Ray started running over the snow-covered countryside. After crossing a stream, Ray eluded his pursuers. Traveling through the heavy snow, Ray finally realized he'd lost the money bag. Ray tells Bancroft that he wants to go back to Wyoming, find the money and return it to the authorities. Snow has abated in Wyoming and the roads are now clear. Ray buys two bus tickets. Gregory follows him. Bancroft goes to work as a fashion model and sees Keith and Bond in the audience. When Ray shows up, Bancroft warns him and they leave quickly. Bancroft tells Ray she's going to Wyoming with him. The two have fallen in love. Reaching Wyoming, Gregory tells Ray he believes he's innocent of any crime. Ray tells Gregory the whole story. Ray, Bancroft and Gregory retrace the route he took as he fled from the bank robbers. They reach a shack where Ray thinks he dropped the money bag only to find Keith and Bond are already there. The robbers found the money bag. Keith convinces Bond to tie up Bancroft and Gregory. Bond wants to murder Ray. Keith disagrees. The two robbers hold a gun on each other. Bond fires three quick shots, killing Keith. Ray takes advantage of the situation and retrieves Keith's rifle. Bond gains shelter in a snow plow and heads toward the shack where Bancroft and Gregory are being held. Ray gains access to the cab. The two men fight. Ray turns the plow from the shack. Both men fall out of the plow and roll in front of the oncoming plow. Ray is able to dive out of the way. Bond is killed by the plow. Gregory retrieves the money. Ray and Bancroft have each other.

Notes and Commentary: The main theme of David Goodis' novel reached the screen but major changes were made in the execution of the screenplay. Vanning was traveling alone in Colorado when he came upon a car wreck with three men, one injured. The men had stolen from a Seattle bank $300,000 ($350,000 was stolen in the film). When Vanning stops, he is taken captive at gunpoint. Vanning is taken to a Denver hotel but is allowed to escape with a pistol and the money. A confederate, Harrison (a character not in the film), plans to murder Vanning after he has left the hotel. By circumstance, Vanning shows Harrison the pistol before shooting him. Vanning escapes through snow country, losing the bag with the money. Vanning ends up in New York City rather than Los Angeles, where the story is concluded. Vanning finally regains his memory, having been a victim of regressive amnesia, and plans to take Fraser to Colorado to retrieve the money.

Winifred Waring, who plays the fashion commentator in the film, was fashion director for the J.W. Robinson Company in Beverly Hills.

Reviews: "Although there's a generous slice of mystery, action and suspense in *Nightfall*, this modest budgeter adds up to only fair entertainment." *Variety*, 12/5/56

"Terrific film noir, expertly directed..." *Motion Picture Guide*, Nash and Ross

Summation: Nightfall is a minor but entertaining crime noir. Performances are satisfactory with a special nod to Rudy Bond as a psychotic killer. His performance brings true terror and menace to the story, elevating it to a higher level. Stirling Silliphant's to-the-point noir screenplay of a man sought by both police and crooks checks in at a crisp 78 minutes. An added pleasure is the fine camerawork of Burnett Guffey, who handles both the dark, mean streets of Los Angeles and the snow-covered Wyoming countryside with authority.

MEN BEWARE! These girls have LOVE in their hearts! ... and MURDER on their minds!

Nine Girls

Columbia
(February 1944)

Cast: Grace Thornton, Ann Harding; Mary O'Ryan, Evelyn Keyes; Jane Peters, Jinx Falkenburg; Paula Canfield, Anita Louise; Roberta Halloway, Leslie Brooks; Eve Sharon, Lynn Merrick; "Butch" Hendricks, Jeff Donnell; Alice Blake, Nina Foch; "Tennessee" Collingwood, Shirley Mills; Shirley Berke, Marcia Mae Jones; Capt. Brooks, Willard Robertson; Walter Cummings, William Demarest; Horace Canfield, Lester Matthews; Uncredited: Photographer, Grady Sutton

Credits: Director, Leigh Jason; Producer, Burt Kelly; Screenwriters, Karen DeWolf and Connie Lee; Adaptor, Al Martin; Editor, Otto Meyer; Art Directors, Lionel Banks and Ross Bellah; Set Decorator, Fay Babcock; Cinematographer, James Van Trees; Original Music, John Leipold; Musical Director, M.W. Stoloff

Production Dates: October 26–December 9, 1943

Source: play *Nine Girls* by Wilfred H. Pettitt

Running Time: 78 minutes

Story: Prior to a sorority initiation of two pledges, Shirley Mills and Marcia Mae Jones, tension begins to run high. The rich but unpopular Anita Louise has three other sorority sisters who have reason to hate her. Louise is trying to break up Jinx Falkenberg's romance. She plans to blackmail Nina Foch for not writing a thesis for her. Because Evelyn Keyes told Falkenberg of Louise's attempt to derail her romance, Louise plans to spread information about Keyes' brother that will prevent her from obtaining a desired teaching position. The initiation is to take place at chaperone Ann Harding's mountain cabin. All arrive except Louise. A news broadcast informs them that Louise's dead body was found in an arroyo. They plan to leave but Police Captain Willard Robertson and his associate William Demarest arrive to question Harding and the girls. Robertson asks them not to leave so everyone would be easily accessible. The girls begin to suspect each other of murder. Robertson returns with a plaster cast of a shoe found at the murder site. Before all the shoes can be examined, the lights go out. Under the cover of darkness, Harding places a pair of shoes in the furnace. The smell of burning leather alerts Robertson and all he's able to salvage is enough of the shoe to let him know that it was the one that he sought. A nervous Keyes begins to think she's the prime suspect. Keyes tells Harding that it was she who called Louise the night of the murder. Harding suggests that Louise write a note to Louise's father, Lester Matthews, telling him of the phone call and offering her condolences. Harding dictates the letter, which is a disguised suicide note. Harding offers Keyes a sedative. As Keyes starts to drink, a scream causes the liquid to be spilled. The next morning, Robertson plans to take Harding and the girls to police headquarters. One of the sorority sisters, Jeff Donnell, notices that her target pistol is missing. As everyone leaves, someone makes certain the cabin door is unlocked. Keyes is the last to leave. She finds that someone had tampered with her car. All the others cars have driven off before she can signal for help. Keyes goes back to the cabin. The front door opens, Harding enters with the target pistol in hand. She tells Keyes that Louise stood in her way to marry Matthews. In an argument, she killed Louise. Harding tells Keyes that she plans to kill her, making it look like a suicide. Harding pulls the trigger but the hammer falls on an empty chamber. Robertson enters, arrests Harding and tells her that he unloaded the pistol.

Notes and Commentary: Wilfred H. Pettitt's Broadway play was completely reworked as the story reached the screen. There were nine girls but the Paula Canfield character never appeared in the play. There was no chaperone in the play so the murderer was one of the nine girls. In Act One, we learn that Mary killed Paula and then gets Alice to begin writing a letter to her mother expressing her sorrow over Paula's death. Alice has a letter from Paula hinting that someone was making her highly nervous. Mary burns the letter. She then gives Alice a drug-laced liquid that kills her and uses the letter to her mother as a suicide note. Another student, Eve, believes Alice was murdered and begins her investigation. Before submitting to arrest, Mary makes an unsuccessful attempt on Eve's life. Mary killed Paula because she believed Paula took from her the man she wanted to marry. That marriage would have made a comfortable life for Paula and her impoverished parents.

Nine Girls opened on Broadway on January 13, 1943, at the Longacre Theater. It closed January 16. Pettitt copyrighted the play under the title *This Little Hand.*

Shelley Winters was initially scheduled to make her motion picture debut in this film.

Reviews: "*Nine Girls* is a really entertaining piece with a nice mix between the comedy and suspense. The direction is well handled. The photography is a cut above most other films of this level. There is a lush quality that is rarely found in B movies." *Motion Picture Guide*, Nash and Ross

Summation: This is a very good suspenseful mystery noir. Director Leigh Jason adroitly balances the suspense with some not-too-intrusive comedy scenes. The breakfast scene with William Demarest and Jeff Donnell is a delight. Acting is good with Evelyn Keyes delivering a standout performance as the co-ed in peril.

WILL ECSTASY BE A CRIME ... in the terrifying world of the future?

1984

(September 1956)

A Holiday Production

Cast: Winston Smith of the Outer Party, Edmond O'Brien; O'Connor of the Inner Party, Michael Redgrave; Julia of the Outer Party, Jan Sterling; Charrington (Junk Shop Owner), David Kossoff; Jones, Mervyn Johns; R. Parsons, Donald Pleasence; Selina Parsons, Carol Wolveridge; Outer Party Announcer, Ernest Clark; Inner Party Official, Patrick Allen; Rutherford, Ronan O'Casey; Outer Party Orators, Michael Ripper and Ewen Solon; Prisoner, Kenneth Griffiths; Uncredited: Kalador, Bernard Rebel; Telescreen (Voice), Anthony Jacobs; Woman (Voice), Barbara Cavan; Special Woman, Barbara Keogh; Big Brother, John Vernon

Credits: Director, Michael Anderson; Assistant Director, F. Slark; Producer, N. Peter Rathvon; Assistant Producer, Ralph Bettinson; Screenwriters, William P. Templeton and Ralph Bettinson; Editor, Bill Lewthwaite; Art Director, Terence Verity; Assistant Art Directors, Peter Glazier and Len Townsend; Cinematographer, C. Pennington Richards; Camera Operator, R. Day; Wardrobe, Barbara Gray; Makeup, L.V. Clark; Hair Stylist, H. Montsash; Sound Recordist, A. Bradburn; Recording Director, Harold King; Dubbing Editor, A. Southgate; Original Music, Malcolm Arnold; Musical Conductor, Louis Levy; Music Played by the London Symphony Orchestra; Production Supervisor, John Croydon; Production Manager, G.R. Mitchell; Special Effects, B. Langley, G. Blackwell and N. Warwick; Casting: R. Lennard; Continuity, Gladys Goldsmith

Production Dates: early June–August 8, 1955

Source: novel *1984* by George Orwell

Running Time: 90 minutes

Story: After major nuclear war, the Earth is divided up into three countries. London is the capital of Oceania. To keep citizens in line, there are continuous wars and constant observation of all members of the outer and inner parties. Fed up with the system and "Big Brother," Edmond O'Brien is attracted to Jan Sterling but the Anti-Sex League forbids unauthorized contact between men and women. Finally the two meet clandestinely. O'Brien makes arrangements with junk shop owner David Kossoff to use rooms on his second floor. O'Brien believes Inner Party member Michael Redgrave has similar feelings toward "Big Brother." O'Brien and Sterling meet with Redgrave and begin to make plans to overthrow "Big Brother." After O'Brien receives a forbidden book, O'Brien and Sterling are arrested. They find that Kossoff had surveillance installed to watch every move they made in the rented room. Redgrave's true colors are shown as he plans to brainwash both and have them renounce each other. O'Brien holds out until he's faced with his greatest fear, rats. Finally O'Brien and Sterling are allowed to meet once more and they admit that they renounced each other. Shouts from a rally divert O'Brien. When O'Brien looks back, Sterling is gone. Enthusiastically, O'Brien joins in the shouts of praise for "Big Brother."

Notes and Commentary: Reportedly two endings were filmed. In the version released in the United Kingdom, Winston Smith and Julia are executed. For the United States version, which is more faithful to Orwell's novel, Smith and Julia are brainwashed and profess loyalty to "Big Brother."

The opening credits indicate that the screenplay was freely adapted from George Orwell's novel. The screenplay focuses primarily on the relationship between Smith and Julia. The other part of Orwell's novel that dealt with Oceania and its philosophies was greatly truncated. Only enough was brought to the screen to allow the audience to see the hold that "Big Brother" and the Inner Party had on the rest of the population. Changes were made in two character names: O'Brien became O'Connor and Goldstein was renamed Kalador.

From the publication of Orwell's novel, there was interest in bringing it to the screen. Charles K. Feldman obtained rights in 1949. Then Robert Maxwell and Bernard Luber announced they would produce the novel in 1951. Frank McCarthy in 1954 wanted to produce the film with Anthony Mann as director. Finally N. Peter Rathvon co-produced with Associated British Picture Corp. Initially it was intended to be an all–British production. Rathvon decided to cast Edmond O'Brien in the title role to insure better bookings in the United States.

Reviews: "A sinister glimpse of the future, *1984* is a grim, depressing picture." *Variety*, 12/31/55

Summation: In this well-done sci-fi noir, Edmond O'Brien is excellent as Smith, who doesn't believe in the "Big Brother" philosophy but is eventually brainwashed. Michael Redgrave does a fine job as a man who leads O'Brien into making the decision to oppose "Big Brother" only to betray him. Jan Sterling makes a fine love interest for O'Brien. Director Michael Anderson paces the story to completely absorb the audience to the dark ending. C. Pennington Richards' noir photography adds substance, interest and involvement to the story.

A story as warm and moving as Going My Way ... but with brass knuckles!

On the Waterfront

An Elia Kazan Production
A Horizon Picture
(October 1954)

Cast: Terry Malloy, Marlon Brando; Father Barry, Karl Malden; Johnny Friendly, Lee J. Cobb; Charley Malloy, Rod Steiger; Kayo Dugan, Pat Henning; Glover, Leif Erickson; Big Mac, James Westerfield; Truck, Tony Galento; Tillio, Tami Mauriello; "Pop" Doyle, John Hamilton; Mott, John Heldabrand; Moose, Rudy Bond; Luke, Don Blackman; Jimmy, Arthur Keegan; Barney, Abe Simon, and introducing Eva Marie Saint as Edie Doyle; Uncredited: Longshoreman's Mother, Scottie MacGregor; J.P. (Johnny's Banker), Barry Macollum; Slim, Fred Gwynne; Dues Collector, Zachary Charles; Gillette, Martin Balsam; Cab Driver, Nehemiah Persoff; Tommy Collins, Thomas Handley; Mrs. Collins, Anne Hegira; Sidney, Dan Bergin; Specs, Mike O'Dowd

Credits: Director, Elia Kazan; Assistant Director, Charles H. Maguire; Producer, Sam Spiegel; Assistant to Producer, Sam Rheiner; Screenwriter, Budd Schulberg; Editor, Gene Milford; Art Director, Richard Day; Cinematography, Boris Kaufman; Production Manager, George Justin; Makeup, Fred Ryle; Hair Stylist,

Mary Roche; Sound, James Shields; Original Music, Leonard Bernstein; Wardrobe Supervisor, Anna Hill Johnstone; Wardrobe Mistress, Flo Transfield; Script Supervisor, Roberta Hodes; Dialogue Supervisor, Guy Thomajan

Location Filming: Hoboken, New Jersey

Production Dates: November 17, 1953–January 26, 1954

Source: an original story by Budd Schulberg suggested by articles by Malcolm Johnson

Running Time: 108 minutes

Story: Lee J. Cobb has Marlon Brando entice Eva Marie Saint's brother to the roof of his apartment. Then, Cobb's men hurl him to the pavement below so he won't testify to the Waterfront Crime Commission. Brando just thought Cobb's men would lean on him so he would remain quiet. Saint wants to find the murderer and enlists Father Karl Malden's aid. Malden wants the support of the longshoremen but only Pat Henning will stand up against Cobb and his corrupt union. Saint believes Brando has information she needs. The two begin to associate and to fall in love. Fearing Henning will talk, cargo is dropped on him, killing him instantly. Brando starts to weaken and tells both Malden and Saint that he lured Saint's brother to the roof under Cobb's direction. Seeing Brando might cooperate with the crime commission, Cobb has Brando's brother, Rod Steiger, talk to him. In a taxicab, Steiger is unable to deter Brando from testifying and is unable to kill him. After Brando gets out of the cab, driver Nehemiah Persoff delivers Steiger into Cobb's hands. Steiger is murdered and an unsuccessful attempt is made on Brando's life. Brando testifies before the crime commission. Cobb retaliates, telling Brando he'll never work on any dock again. The next morning Brando goes down to the docks looking for work. Every man is picked except Brando. Brando challenges Cobb and they engage in a brutal fight. When Brando gains the upper hand, Cobb has his men give Brando a brutal beating. A ship needs to have cargo unloaded but the longshoremen refuse to work. Malden tells the injured Brando if he leads the men to the job, Cobb's hold on the union will be broken. As Brando leads the men to work, Cobb, knowing he will be indicted, vows he will return and exact revenge.

Notes and Commentary: Reporter Malcolm Johnson received an assignment to cover a waterfront murder. In his investigation, he found the waterfront piers from Brooklyn to Hoboken were a territory akin to the Wild West where violence ruled and murders were almost never solved. Johnson published a series of articles in the *New York Sun* under the title "Crime on the Waterfront." They would win Johnson a Pulitzer Prize. Johnson wrote about the crime and corruption that abounded, from cargo shipments mysteriously vanishing, arbitrary charges to shippers to load and unload cargo and the ease with which narcotics and other illegal goods could pass through the ports. Almost all the important positions in the ILA were filled by men with long criminal records.

Most of all, he wrote about man's inhumanity to man, the deplorable conditions in which the longshoremen had to work. First was the shape-up to select men for work instead the use of hiring halls that were present in all other ports in the United States and foreign countries. The shape-up required men to gather around and see who would be chosen to work. Since there was more longshoreman than were needed, a lot of men were without work. Shape-ups were held twice a day to choose men for four hours of work. Favoritism abounded. To get work, in many instances, the workers had to kick back part of their pay or they continuously stayed in debt. A longshoreman would borrow from a loan shark, get a job that would just cover the loan and then the cycle would start again. Those who complained would either be beaten or murdered.

Budd Schulberg acquired the rights to the story and began writing a screenplay. Visiting the docks himself, he verified the accuracy of Johnson's articles. Some of the real-life persons found themselves as closely drawn characters in the film, Father Barry was modeled on the "waterfront priest," Father John "Pete" Corridan; Johnny Friendly was a composite of International Longshoreman's Association leader Michael Clemente and former Murder Inc. boss Albert Anastasia; and longshoreman Brownie became Kayo Dugan. The project was turned down by Darryl F. Zanuck at 20th Century–Fox and initially by Harry Cohn at Columbia. Schulberg resisted pressure to make Communists the bad guys instead of the union officials. The part of Terry Malloy was originally written for John Garfield. With his death, Marlon Brando was the top choice. When Brando kept returning the script unread, Frank Sinatra and Montgomery Clift were considered, with Sinatra finally winning out. Producer Sam Spiegel, using the ploy of having Brando watch someone test for the part, hooked Brando into signing for the role. An irate Sinatra sued Columbia for breach of contract. I don't know the details of the suit disposition but Sinatra later worked at Columbia in *Pal Joey* (1957). With Brando in the lead and the low budget, Harry Cohn then agreed to distribute the picture.

On the Waterfront was honored with eight Academy Awards, Best Picture (Sam Spiegel), Best Director (Elia Kazan), Best Actor in a Leading Role (Marlon Brando), Best Actress in a Supporting Role (Eva Marie Saint), Best Film Editing (Gene Milford), Best Art Direction–Set Decoration (Richard Day), Best Cinematography, Black and White (Boris Kaufman) and Best Writing, Story and Screenplay (Schulberg). Lee J. Cobb, Karl Malden and Rod Steiger all received nominations for Best Actor in a Supporting Role. Leonard Bernstein received a nomination for Best Music, Scoring of a Dramatic or Comedy Picture.

Working titles for this film were *Crime on the Waterfront*, *Bottom of the River* and *Waterfront*. The title *Waterfront* was rejected since this was the title of a current syndicated television series starring Preston Foster.

Reviews: "*On the Waterfront* is packed with strongarm dramatics. Hard hitting entertainment." *Variety*, 7/14/54

"A small but obviously dedicated group of realists has forged artistry, anger and some horrible truths into *On the Waterfront*, as violent and indelible a film record of man's inhumanity to man as come to light this year. It is an uncommonly powerful, exciting and imaginative use of the screen by gifted professionals. *On the Waterfront* is moviemaking of a rare and high order." *New York Times*, 7/29/54

Summation: This is a great film, very deserving of the Academy Awards it received. The film was gripping, honest, brutal and emotional. Acting was superb, especially that of Brando, Saint, Malden and Cobb. Director Kazan is able to bring the proper emotions to every scene which keeps the audience riveted throughout. Cinematographer Boris Kaufman is able to emphasize the despair and poverty level of the longshoremen and their families. Schulberg is to be commended for bringing a totally honest and realistic story to the screen.

"I CONFESS I'm the kind of girl every man wants—but shouldn't marry!"

One Girl's Confession

(April 1953)

A Hugo Haas Production

Cast: Mary Adams, Cleo Moore; Dragomie Damitrof, Hugo Haas; Johnny, Glenn Langan; Smooch, Ellen Stansbury; Father Benedict, Anthony Jochim; Gardener, Burt Mustin; Gregory Stark, Leonid Snegoff; Warden, Jim Nusser; Police Officer, Russ Conway; Girl, Mara Lea; District Attorney, Gayne Whitman; Gambler, Leo Mostovoy; Old Lady, Martha Wentworth; Uncredited: Kibitzer, Frank Mills; Bar Manager, Roy Engel; Dock Worker, Joseph Mell

Credits: Director, Producer and Screenwriter, Hugo Haas; Assistant Director, Leon Chooluck; Associate Producer, Robert Erlik; Editor, Merrill G. White; Associate Editor, Robert Eisen; Art Director, Rudi Feld; Cinematographer, Paul Ivano; Camera Operator, Eddie Fitzgerald; Makeup, Gustaf Norin; Sound, Ben Winkler; Original Music, Vaclav Divina; Musical Conductor, Adolph Heller; Chief Electrician, Dan Stott; Script Supervisor, Joe Franklin; Dialogue Supervisor, Mark Lowell

Production Dates: August 18–August 30, 1952

Running Time: 73 minutes

Story: Cleo Moore is a waitress working for Leonid Snegoff, who financially ruined her father. When Moore observes Snegoff engaging in an illegal transaction, she decides to steal the money. Snegoff has Moore arrested. Moore admits that she stole the money but refuses to disclose where it's hidden. Moore is sentenced to one to ten years in jail. Because of her exemplary attitude and good behavior, Moore is pardoned after three years. The prison priest Anthony Jochim drives Moore to town and tells her the money she stole is cursed. Moore finds that Snegoff, because of problems with the law, is now living in South America. She gets a job as waitress in Hugo Haas' bar. Moore rebuffs Haas' sexual advances and also gets romantic interest from fisherman Glenn Langan. Langan needs money to purchase a new boat and new equipment. Moore plans to lend Langan the money and to go into partnership with him. Before Moore can give Langan any money, she finds that Haas, a compulsive gambler, has lost his business and has written a bad check. Feeling sorry for him, Moore tells him where to find the money. After a long length of time, Haas returns empty-handed and Moore is devastated. Later, hearing this bar is reopening, Moore finds that Haas still is the owner. Also, she has moved to a swanky apartment. Haas has a big party at his apartment. Haas' girlfriend, Ellen Stansbury, takes the drunken Haas to his bed where he passes out. After Stansbury and the other guests leave, Moore gains entrance and begins screaming at Haas, wanting her money. Moore gets too close and Haas, still drunk, grabs her in a crushing grip. There is an empty bottle on the bed, Moore grabs it and hits Haas on the head. Moore is able to break Haas' grasp as he fall out of bed. Stansbury come back and tells Moore that Haas is dead. She also reveals to Moore that Haas' newfound wealth was the result of Haas gambling with a Turkish sailor and winning $48,000. Moore goes to the spot where she buried the money and finally locates it. Moore leaves the money at an orphanage before turning herself into the police for killing Haas. Officer Russ Conway calls Haas' apartment and finds that Haas is alive. Moore goes back to the orphanage to retrieve the money but she is too late; the nuns now have it. Moore, going to the waterfront, is approached by Haas, who offers her a job as hostess at his bar. Fisherman Langan wants Moore to join him on his boat. Haas indicates life with Langan will bring her the happiness she's seeking.

Notes and Commentary: The working titles for the film were *Story of a Bad Girl* and *Tough Girl.*

Reviews: "It is a plodding programmer, using up 73 minutes of film to no avail. Hackneyed, uninspired plot." *Variety*, 3/11/53

"Mundane plot is performed and directed in an equally mundane manner." *Motion Picture Guide*, Nash and Ross

Summation: This is a tawdry noir with an ironic ending. Director Hugo Haas does manage to generate moments of suspense as "bad girl" Cleo Moore attempts to start a new life with stolen money. Moore exudes sex but manages to remain chaste as she is pursued by both Haas and Glenn Langan. Visually Moore fits the bill but in the acting area she's barely adequate. Director Haas directs star Haas capably. He has an especially good scene as he realizes that he gambled away his business and has written a bad check. Langan is basically decoration and someone for Moore to be with at the film's end. Screenwriter Haas has fashioned a story that will hold interest but more forceful direction and acting would have been welcome.

A murderously funny story, magnificently cast ... marvelously made!

Our Man in Havana

Columbia (1960)

Cast: Jim Wormold, Alec Guinness; Dr. Hasselbacher, Burl Ives; Beatrice Severn, Maureen O'Hara; Capt. Segura, Ernie Kovacs; Hawthorne, Noel Coward; 'C,' Ralph Richardson; Milly Wormold, Jo Morrow; Cifuentes, Gregoire Aslan; Hubert Carter, Paul Rogers; General, Raymond Huntley; Professor Sanchez, Ferdy Mayne; Admiral, Maurice Denham; Lopez, Jose Prieto; MacDougal, Duncan Macrae; Svenson, Gerik Schjelderup; Officer, Hugh Manning; Dr. Braun, Karel Stepanek; Teresa, Maxine Audley; Beautiful Woman, Elisabeth Welch; Striptease Girl, Yvonne Buckingham; Uncredited: Man at the Film Introduction, Enrique Almirante; Rudy, Timothy Bateson; Man beaten by Police, Rene de la Cruz; Black-haired Girl, Madeleine Kasket; Canadian Girl, Shan Lawrence; Louis (waiter), John Le Mesurier; Dark-haired Woman, Anne Padwick; Prostitute, Rachel Roberts

Credits: Director and Producer, Carol Reed; Assistant Director, Gerry O'Hara; Associate Producer, Raymond Anzarut; Screenwriter, Graham Greene; Editor, Bert Bates; Art Director, John Box; Assistant Art Director, Syd Cain; Cinematographer, Oswald Morris; Camera Operator, Denys N. Coop; Costume Designer, Phyllis Dalton; Costumes and Wardrobe, Arthur Newman and Betty Adamson; Hairdresser, Gordon Bond; Makeup, Harry Frampton; Sound Supervisor, John Cox; Sound Recordists, John W. Mitchell and Red Law; Sound Editor, Ted Mason; Music Played by Frank and Lawrence Deniz; Music Unit Manager, James H. Ware; Continuity, Margaret Shipway

Songs: "La Bella Cubana" (Jose White Lafitte, composer); "Domitila, donde vas?" (Diaz)—sung by three street musicians

Filming Location: Havana, Cuba

Production Dates: April 13–May 13, 1959 (Havana, Cuba); May 18–August 7, 1959 (London, England)

Source: Our Man in Havana by Graham Greene

Running Time: 111 min.

Filmed in CinemaScope

Story: British secret agent Noel Coward wants to recruit fellow Englishman Alec Guinness, an owner of a vacuum cleaner shop in Cuba, as "our man in Havana." Guinness is hesitant but relents because the additional money would enable him to purchase a coveted horse and accompanying country club membership for teenage daughter, Jo Morrow. Coward, through orders from his superior Ralph Richardson, tells Guinness to begin recruiting agents, but Guinness' efforts prove futile. He confides in his close friend Burl Ives, who tells Guinness to invent secret agents as well as classified information. Using names from the list of members of the club country Guinness fabricates his list of agents. Later, Ives summons Guinness to his apartment, which is in shambles. Ives explains that someone tried to recruit him as an agent but he refused.

One night, entering his shop, Guinness notices that shadow cast by the vacuum display looks like a weapon. Using the display as a model, Guinness makes drawings of the weapon system, which he locates in the mountains of Cuba, and reports to headquarters that one of his "agents," a commercial airline pilot, discovered the threat. In sharing this news Guinness gains credibility and a secretary, Maureen O'Hara and a radio operator, Timothy Bateson are sent to join his staff. O'Hara tells Guinness that London wants photographs of the weapon system. Inspired by a comic strip in which a pilot is killed when his plane crashes into a mountain, Guinness decides that's how his "agent" will die. A message Guinness sends informing headquarters that his agent will obtain photographs is intercepted and Ives receives a phone call reporting that the agent died in an automobile accident.

As Guinness and O'Hara start to warn the other faux agents, Chief of Police Ernie Kovacs detains the two and threatening Guinness with deportation, insists that Guinness must report to him. Guinness confronts Ives who now believes that the fake reports are factual. Guinness reports to Coward in Jamaica, who informs him of plans to poison Guinness at an upcoming trade luncheon.

On the return flight, Guinness meets a rival vacuum cleaner promoter, Paul Rogers, who will also attend the luncheon. At the event, Ives intercepts Guinness and tells him to leave. Guinness refuses a plate of food that is quickly grabbed by a waiter before anyone else can taste it. Rogers, who is seated across from Guinness, offers him a drink which Guinness deliberately spills. A dog, who had snuck into the room, laps up the liquor, and in a few minutes, dies.

Kovacs comes to Guinness's shop and takes him to a bar to identify the now murdered Ives. Guinness confesses to O'Hara that he invented everything and he has deceived the secret service. Guinness invites Kovacs to his shop to play a game of checkers with miniature bottles of scotch and bourbon being used as game pieces. As a piece is taken, the contents of the bottle will be consumed. Soon, Kovacs has passed out. Guinness takes Kovacs' pistol and goes looking for Rogers. Finding Rogers, Guinness take him first to a bar then to a brothel where the two exchange fire and Rogers receives a fatal bullet. Guinness returns to his shop and Kovacs awakes, not realizing Guinness had ever left.

Kovacs serves Guinness with deportation papers and he is ordered to report to Secret Service Headquarters in London. As he prepares to face Richardson and the top brass, Guinness prepares for the worst. To save face and avoid admitting that the Secret Service had been duped, Richardson tells Guinness that his post was shut down, the construction of the weapon system had proved a failure and had been dismantled. For his fine work Guinness is promoted to a member of their training staff and decorated as an Officer of the Most Excellent Order of the British Empire.

As Guinness and O'Hara leave headquarters, they see a street vendor, who shows them a toy weapon made in Japan in the shape of vacuum cleaner parts.

Notes and Commentary: The script by Graham Greene follows his novel closely. Some scenes in the novel, which do not further the plot, have been deleted. A few scenes have been presented in a different order. The ironic ending of the film is not in the book.

Greene based the story on German spies who during World War II submitted false reports to continue getting paid. Grahame planned to have an Englishman do the same to satisfy the material demands of his wife. The British film censors were not in favor of a subject unfavorable to the secret service. Greene finally updated the story to '50s Havana and replaced the wife with a daughter.

Alfred Hitchcock was interested in filming Greene's novel. Greene was not really interested in Hitchcock making the film so he asked 50,000 pounds. As Hitchcock backed off, Greene offered the project to his friend Carol Reed for less money.

Columbia wanted Lauren Bacall for the role of Beatrice. Bacall wasn't available so the studio gave the part to Maureen O'Hara, who was under contract. Jean Seberg was the first choice as Milly, but Seberg decided to make *Breathless* (UGC, 1960) instead. Jo Morrow, who was also under contract, then received the role.

The comic strip "Rock Cain" that would be Guinness's inspiration for his aviator "agent's" death is credited to Syd Cain. An inside joke, Cain was the assistant art director.

Reviews: "The hot-house world of international espionage was the target which Graham Greene so successfully and humorously demolished in his novel. In its film incarnation, under the meticulous aim of director Carol Reed, a bullseye was struck once again." *The Columbia Story*, Hirschhorn

"Based on the Graham Greene novel, this turns out to be polished, diverting entertainment, brilliant in its comedy but falling apart towards the end when undertones of drama, tragedy and message crop up" *Variety,* 12/31/59

"The nub of the farce is in the spoofing of the elaborate techniques of spies, and in this area this picture is grand." *New York Times*, 1/28/60

Summation: What a brilliant satirical espionage noir. Perfectly cast, with Alec Guinness as the hapless individual picked to become a secret agent, Burl Ives, as Guinness' best friend, who is unwittingly drawn into the intrigue, Ernie Kovacs, forgoing his flair for comedy, to portray a ruthless chief of police, and Noel Coward as the agent who recruits "our man in Havana. Maureen O'Hara is just fine as a novice agent who falls for Guinness and vice versa. But Guinness is the key and he carries the part well, using both his comedic and dramatic skills in this story of a spy who invents his reports that suddenly develop into actual espionage and murder. Graham Greene's story is compellingly brought to the screen by director Carol Reed. Reed exacts excellent performances from the cast as he adroitly paces the story to its conclusion, with no false notes. Cinematographer Oswald Morris' photography is superb, capturing the bright sunlight of Havana as well as the world of noir, with shades of darkness and unusual camera angles. A cinema treat not to be missed.

EXPOSE! CONFIDENTIAL STORY BEHIND THE BLACKMAIL PHOTO RACKET!

Over-exposed

(April 1956)

Cast: Lily Krenshka aka Lila Crane, Cleo Moore; Russell Bassett, Richard Crenna; Mrs. Payton Grange, Isobel Elsom; Max West, Raymond Greenleaf; Shirley Thomas; Roy Carver, James O'Rear; Coco Fields, Donald Randolph; Horace Sutherland, Dayton Lummis; Uncredited: Les Bauer, Jack Albertson; Doris, Norma Brooks; Club Customer Photographed by Lila, George Cisar; Renee, Jeanne Cooper; Jerry, Dick Crockett; Mrs. Grannigan, Helen Eby-Rock; Martha, Geraldine Hall; Mrs. Gulick, Edna Holland; Freddy (Bellboy), Bill McLean; Fran, Joan Miller; Steve (Bartender), Frank Mitchell; Mario, Leo Mostovoy; Matt (Thug), Eddie Parker; Judge Evans, Voltaire Perkins; Policemen, Robert Bice, Charles J. Conrad and William H. O'Brien; Taxi Driver, Chuck Carson; Studio Thug, John L.

***Over-Exposed* (1956) starring Cleo Moore.**

Cason; Operator, Bob Hopkins; Police Sergeant, Robert B. Williams; Hysterical Woman, Diane DeLaire; Reporter, Roger Smith

CREDITS: Director, Lewis Seiler; Assistant Director, Abner E. Singer; Producer, Lewis J. Rachmil; Story, Richard Sale and Mary Loos; Screenwriters, James Gunn and Gil Orlovitz; Editor, Edwin Bryant; Art Director, Carl Anderson; Set Decorator, Robert Priestley; Cinematographer, Henry Freulich; Gowns, Jean Louis; Makeup, Clay Campbell, Hair Stylist, Helen Hunt; Sound, Josh Westmoreland; Musical Conductor, Mischa Bakaleinikoff

PRODUCTION DATES: October 11–24, 1955

RUNNING TIME: 80 minutes

STORY: Cleo Moore, caught in a raid in a clip joint, is ordered out of town. Instead she meets freelance photographer Raymond Greenleaf, who becomes her mentor and teaches her the photography business. Moore strikes out on her own and travels to New York, where it's difficult to find a job. When a building fire breaks out, Moore takes exclusive photos. Thanks to reporter Richard Crenna, Moore obtains her first professional credit. Crenna also gets Moore a job at Jack Albertson's nightclub. Moore takes a picture of mob lawyer Dayton Lummis with a woman. To keep the picture from being published, Lummis persuades nightclub owner Donald Randolph to hire her. At the club, socialite Isobel Elsom allows Moore to take her picture because they both know Greenleaf. Moore does such a great job that Elsom allows the picture to be published. Moore's photographic talents are soon in great demand. At the club, Moore accidentally takes a picture of a mobster and another individual. Soon the mobster is suspected of murder, and the picture would ruin his alibi. Moore puts the photo in a file. Feeling a need to get away, Moore goes to Maine where Crenna is vacationing. Crenna wants to marry Moore but she is unwilling to give up her career. Moore returns to New York. Elsom is celebrating her birthday and insists Moore take pictures. In the midst of dancing, Elsom collapses and dies. Moore takes a picture of Elsom's collapse. Columnist James O'Rear offers to buy the picture from Moore, who refuses.

O'Rear is able to steal the negative and the picture is published. Everyone thinks Moore sold the photo and her career is ruined. To re-establish herself, Moore plans to blackmail the mobster in order to have O'Rear admit that the picture was published without her permission. Moore tells Lummis that the mobster can have every copy except one. On the way to meet with the mobster, Moore is kidnapped. Crenna calls Moore's studio. Thug John L. Cason, who's there searching it for the photo, just takes the receiver off the hook. Crenna goes to investigate and overcomes Cason. Crenna forces Cason to tell that Moore was taken to a mob warehouse. Crenna arrives to see Moore being beaten. Crenna is able to rescue Moore. Moore decides to take the picture to the police. Moore accepts Crenna's proposal to marry him and work with him on news assignments.

Notes and Commentary: After completion of the film, Columbia sent Cleo Moore on an extensive promotional tour. The tour caused Moore to miss out on two loanouts. Moore demanded and received her contract release.

Reviews: "A mild meller for the program market. Lewis Seiler's direction tosses in a melodramatic punch here and there but the overall result fails to excite." *Variety*, 2/29/56

Summation: This is a good little noir about a woman's lust for money and fame that puts her on noir city's mean streets. Cleo Moore is effective and Raymond Greenleaf, as Moore's mentor, gives good support. Other acting credits are average for a "B" feature. The story holds audience interest. Both Lewis Seiler's direction and Henry Freulich's photography are effective.

THEY GAVE HER A BAD NAME and she lived up to it!

Pickup

(July 1951)

A Forum production

Cast: Jan Horak, Hugo Haas; Betty, Beverly Michaels; Steve, Allan Nixon; Professor, Howland Chamberlain; Irma, Jo-Carroll Dennison; Waiter, Mark Lowell; Secretary, Marjorie Beckett; Driver, Art Lewis; Doctor, Jack Daley; Joe, Bernard Gorcey

Credits: Director-Producer, Hugo Haas; Assistant Director, Louis Brandt; Producer-in-Charge, Leon Chooluck; Co-Producer, Edgar E. Walden; Screenwriters, Hugo Haas and Arnold Phillips; Editor, Douglas W. Bagler; Art Director, Rudi Feld; Cinematographer, Paul Ivano; Camera Operator, Ed Fitzgerald; Wardrobe Supervisor, Izzy Berne; Makeup, Dave Grayson; Sound Recordist, John R. Carter; Original Music, Harold Byrns; Musical Conductor, Harold Byrns with the Los Angeles Chamber Symphony Orchestra; Property Master, William Veady; Technician Supervisor, Walter Thompson; Master Electrician, Joseph Edesa

Production Dates: early March 1950

Source: novel *Hlidac cislo 47* (*Watchman 47*) by Joseph Kopta

Running Time: 78 minutes

Story: Despondent over the death of his dog, railroad dispatcher Hugo Haas goes into town to purchase a puppy. Unable to strike a deal with the owner, Haas wanders through the town. Down-on-her-luck Beverly Michaels, who has been displaying her legs to the male population, spies Haas and decides to let him pick her up. Haas and Michaels do the town until a mysterious dizziness overcome Haas and he hurries home. The next week, Haas drives her to his home. The only thing Michaels finds attractive about Haas is his bank book which shows he has $7,300. Haas' relief dispatcher Allan Nixon knows of Michaels' unsavory reputation and makes a play for her. Michaels responds until she finds that Nixon has no money. When Michaels is evicted from her room, she convinces Haas to marry her. Too late she finds she'll have to wait until Haas' retirement in six years to spend his money. While inspecting the tracks, Haas again falls prey to the dizziness which results in his hearing loss. Michaels is overjoyed: Now Haas can retire and she can get her hands on his money. Haas goes into town to talk with his boss. Crossing a street, he does not hear an approaching car. The impact knocks him to the road—and he regains his hearing. To make Michaels happy, Haas now plans to pretend his hearing is lost and still retire with his pension.

Haas returns home to tell Michaels the good news. Before he can, Nixon enters the house and Haas has to continue the pretense. Haas now hears that Michaels never cared for him and would like to have an affair with Nixon. The next time the tracks have to be inspected, Michaels wants Nixon to push Haas over a cliff to his death, making it look like an accident. Haas decides to write a letter to his boss telling of his duplicity. Haas gives the letter to his good friend Howland Chamberlain to take to his boss. Hass and Nixon inspect the tracks and reach the place where Nixon can kill Haas. Michaels waits anxiously. When Nixon enters the house, she thinks all has gone her way until Haas comes in. Michaels is disgusted and goes out with some friends. Haas gets Nixon drunk so he can't perform his duties and Haas has to take over. Michaels returns and states she doesn't need either Haas or Nixon. Enraged, Nixon begins to strangle Michaels but Haas stops him. They learn Haas can hear. Michaels leaves. Haas send Nixon home. Chamberlain brings Haas news that he can keep his job. In addition, Chamberlain brings Haas a puppy to replace the dog he lost.

Notes and Commentary: It has been stated that Edgar E. Walden received screen credit a month after the film had been released. I attempted to obtain a copy of Kopta's novel but no copy in English was available.

Reviews: "Fairly satisfactory drama of middle-aged man tricked by young floozy." *Variety*, 7/18/51

"An inept but oddly fascinating noir with a plot mirrored in nearly every one of Haas' films to follow." *Motion Picture Guide*, Nash and Ross

Summation: This is easily one of Haas' best noirs. As his leading lady, and I use the word loosely, Beverly Michaels is quite good as a slutty femme fatale. Usually Haas' leading ladies are sexy but ultimately chaste. Michaels is willing to use her body in any way to get what she wants. She has to marry Haas to have a chance to spend his money and she uses her feminine wiles to entice the younger Allan Nixon to possible commit murder for her. Haas' direction and screenplay (co-written with Arnold Phillips) build nicely until the soft ending. The strangulation of Michaels by Nixon is stopped by Haas and she is allowed to go her way, making faces at Haas' best friend. Haas sends Nixon home to his old girlfriend and Haas ends up with a puppy licking his face. A stark ending would have elevated this film.

EXPOSED! The international narcotics kings ... and their women! THIS IS A PICTURE ABOUT DOPE!

Pickup Alley

(August 1957)

A Warwick Film Production

Alternate Title: Interpol

Cast: Charles Sturgis, Victor Mature; Gina Broger, Anita Ekberg; Frank McNally, Trevor Howard; Amalio, Bonar Colleano; Breckner, Andre Morell; Varolli, Martin Benson; Helen, Dorothy Alison; Captain Baris, Peter Illing; Fayala, Eric Pohlmann; Curtis, Sydney Tafler; Salko, Alec Mango; Murphy, Lionel Murton; Bartender, Danny Green; Singer, Yana; Joe, Sidney James; Guido, Marne Maitland; Kalish, Harold Kasket; Luggage Clerk, Van Boolen; Allison, Brian Nissen; Badek, Peter Elliott; English Tourist, Charles Lloyd Pack; Interrogator, Al Mulock; Vincent Cashling, Alfred Burke; Man with Tick, Maurice Browning; Warden, Cyril Shaps; Customs Inspector, Paul Stassino; Amalio's Brother, Gaylord Cavallaro; The Monk, Brian Wilde; Company Man, Russell Waters; Borgese, Richard Molinas; Morgue Attendant, Wolfe Morris; Uncredited: Monello, Umberto Fiz; Child, Anthony John; Drug Addict, Betty McDowell; Abbata, Alfredo Rizzo; Policeman, Kevin Stoney

Credits: Director, John Gilling; Assistant Directors, Bluey Hill and Alec Gibb; Second Unit Director, Max Varnel; Producers, Irving Allen and Albert R. Broccoli; Associate Producer, Phil C. Samuel; Screenwriter, John Paxton; Editor, Richard Best; Art Director, Paul Sheriff; Assistant Art Directors, Maurice Fowler and Syd Cain; Cinematographer, Ted Moore; Second Unit Cinematographer, Stan Pavey; Camera Operators, Skeets Kelly and Harold Haysom; Wardrobe Supervisor, Elsa Fennell; Makeup, Roy Ashton; Hair Stylist, Bill Griffiths; Sound Editor, Don Saunders; Sound Recordists, Norman Coggs and Len Shilton; Original Music, Richard Bennett; Musical Conductor, Muir Mathieson; Orchestra, Sinfonia of London; Production Manager, Cecil R. Foster Kemp; Casting, Nora Roberts; Location Manager, John Cabrera; Continuity, Olga Brook and Kay Rawlings

Song: "Anyone for Love" (Lee and Washington)—sung by Yana

Location Filming: Athens, Greece; Genoa, Rome, Lazio and Liguria, Italy; Lisbon, Portugal; London, England; Paris, France; New York City, New York

Production Dates: August 15–November 13, 1956

Source: book *Interpol* by A.J. Forrest

Running Time: 92 minutes

Filmed in CinemaScope

Story: Dorothy Alison desperately tries to reach her brother, narcotics agent Victor Mature, to tell him that she has found the leader of a major narcotics ring, Trevor Howard. Howard murders Alison before she can relay this information. Howard's name is known but the authorities have no photograph of him. Howard uses Anita Ekberg to bring money to his accomplice Alec Mango. After taking the money, Mango attempts to force himself on Ekberg. When a furious struggle ensues, Ekberg produces a pistol and shoots Mango. Terrified, she rushes to Howard, who tells her that he will protect her only if she continues to act as his courier. Howard has a plan to bring a large amount of heroin into the United States. At Mango's apartment, Mature and other Interpol agents only find blood but no body. Fingerprints identify Ekberg and when she travels to Lisbon, Mature follows. The trail finally leads to Rome. Howard believes Mature is getting too close and there is an unsuccessful attempt to murder him. In Athens, another Howard accomplice, Eric Pohlmann, has been arrested. Mature and other agents finally force Pohlmann to lead them to Howard. Mango, who was only wounded by Ekberg, is being held by Howard. When the authorities arrive, Howard murders Mango and escapes over the rooftops. Howard has arranged for the narcotics to be shipped by freighter to New York, hidden in the back of a refrigerator. Howard plans to fly to New York and tells Ekberg that she must accompany him. Before she can leave, Mature arrests her and shows her that she didn't kill Mango. Mature learns which ship is transporting the narcotics and flies to New York, unaware that Howard is on the same plane. When the ship docks, it is thoroughly searched but the narcotics are not found. All the agents leave the dock except Mature. The narcotics are removed from the back of the refrigerator and placed in two bags which are then placed in a waiting truck. Mature sees Howard remove the bags and gives chase. Mature and Howard exchange shots, and one of Mature's bullets ends Howard's criminal career. Ekberg identifies the body as Howard and the case is closed.

Notes and Commentary: The working titles for the film were *Interpol*, *Half Past Hell* and *The Most Wanted Woman*. The film was released as *Interpol* in the United Kingdom.

A.J. Forrest's non-fiction work *Interpol* was the source of some of the story ideas of the motion picture. Forrest told of the United States sending special agents across the Atlantic to work with Interpol and of hiding narcotics in secret compartments on vessels coming into New York.

The Production Code Administration, a division of the Motion Picture Association of America, requested that the word "dope" be removed from ads. In the latest DVD release, that word is back in the tagline.

In September 1957, *Pickup Alley* was double-billed with *The Brothers Rico* (Columbia, 1957).

Reviews: "A fast-moving action melodrama..." *The Columbia Story*, Hirschhorn

"Howard's the only bright spot in this dark alley." *Motion Picture Guide*, Nash and Ross

Summation: This is a well-done international crime noir. Between John Paxton's taut, plausible script, John Gilling's sure-handed direction and nice acting from the principals, the story never wavers. The action sequences are nicely handled, interwoven into the plot adroitly. A special mention has to be mentioned of Ted Moore's outstanding cinematography. His striking camera angles and masterful use of darkness to light intensifies the tension and suspense. Although Victor Mature handles the lead well, it is the acting of Anita Ekberg and Trevor Howard that really stand out. Ekberg is truly believable as one who has gotten in over her head in a criminal enterprise and can't see any way out. Howard brilliantly underplays the maniacal aspect of his character. He is always forceful. Talking low and distinctly, Howard is quite a man of menace.

MURDER BY A MAD MAN WHO LOVED ... TO KILL!

The Power of the Whistler

(April 1945)

Cast: William Everest, Richard Dix; Jean Lang, Janis Carter; "Francie" Lang, Jeff Donnell; Charlie Kent, Loren Tindall; Constantina Ivaneska, Tara Birell; Kaspar Andropolous, John Abbott; Uncredited: Voice of the Whistler. Otto Forrest; Motorist, I. Stanford Jolley; Stage Door Guard, Forrest Taylor; Flotilda, Nina Mae McKinney; Locksmith, Jack George; Richards, Stanley Price; Pharmacist, Cy Kendall; Joe Blainey, Murray Alper; Cake Delivery Man, Frank Hagney; Police Captain, Crane Whitney; Western Union Agent, Walter Baldwin; John Crawford, Kenneth MacDonald; Highway Patrolman, Robert Williams; Motorcycle Patrolmen, Eddie Parker and Frank J. Scannell

Credits: Director, Lew Landers; Producer, Leonard S. Picker; Screenwriter, Aubrey Wisberg; Editor, Reg Browne; Art Director, John Tatu; Set Decorator, Sidney Clifford; Cinematographer, L.W. O'Connell; "Whistler" theme music, Wilbur Hatch

Production Dates: December 6–20, 1944

Running Time: 66 minutes

Source: the Columbia Broadcasting System Program "The Whistler."

Story: While crossing a street, Richard Dix is struck by a car and hits his head on a lamppost, causing amnesia. In a Greenwich Village café, Janis Carter sees Dix and reads his fortune with a deck of cards. The forecast is death within twenty-four hours and Carter warns him. Finding Dix has amnesia, Carter decides to help him and enlists her sister, Jeff Donnell, to help. During the search for Dix's identity, small animals are found dead. Don-

A police officer observes the anxious Janis Carter and Richard Dix in *Power of the Whistler* (1945).

nell discovers that Dix had a prescription filled for a deadly poison and then had a birthday cake sent to Dr. Kenneth MacDonald at the Hudson Mental Institute in Woodville. Unbeknownst to Carter, Dix regains his memory, including the fact that he wants to murder the judge who had him committed to the mental institution. Dix convinces Carter to travel with him. Donnell goes to the police with information that proves Dix is a homicidal maniac. On the way to the judge's house, Carter becomes suspicious and breaks away. Dix stalks Carter as the police close in. Dix traps Carter in a barn. Carter seizes a pitchfork and drives it into Dix's body, killing him.

Notes and Commentary: As a pharmacist, I couldn't help noticing that Cy Kendall filled a prescription for a deadly poison, without knowing the patient's name and that the physician was deceased. In this case the physician had been dead for about fifty years.

Reviews: "Chilling suspense story. Dix is cast in a tough part which he is unable to pull off." *Motion Picture Guide*, Nash and Ross

"Fair mystery chiller for the duals." *Variety*, 3/28/45

Summation: The story builds well to a harrowing suspenseful conclusion! Lew Landers does a fine job of directing with excellent cinematography by L.W. O'Connell.

What did Prisoner 17242 have on the warden's wife?

Prison Warden

(December 1949)

Cast: Warden Victor Burnell, Warner Baxter; Elisa Burnell, Anna Lee; Capt. Peter Butler, James Flavin; Albert Gardner, Harlan Warde; Captain Bill Radford, Charles Cane; English Charlie/Watkins, Reginald Sheffield; Dr. Ray Stark, Harry Antrim; Uncredited: Postman, Frank Jenks; Ethel, Margaret Wells; Guard, George Eldredge; Mr. Greene, Harry Hayden; Governor, Charles Evans; McCall (Gate Guard), Clancy Cooper; Stone, Peter Virgo; Convict with Cards, Ben Welden; Lanning, William "Bill" Phillips; Ludy (Convict Refusing Quarry Work), George J. Lewis; Toulouse, Heinie Conklin; Mr. Webb, John Hamilton; County Deputy Stewart, Lee Phelps; Second County Deputy, Kernan Cripps; Lt. Davis, Edgar Dearing; Women's Committee Members, Lois Austin, Gail Bonney, Marcella Cisney, Dorothy Conlon and Sarah Selby; Seeley, Mike Mahoney; Henley, Jack Overman; Cory, Frank Richards; Maloff, Nick Volpe; Prison Guard, Frank O'Connor; Convicts, Michael Browne, Paul Bryar and Robert Malcolm

Credits: Director, Seymour Friedman; Producer, Rudolph C. Flothow; Screenwriter, Eric Taylor; Editor, James Sweeney; Art Director, Carl Anderson; Set Decorator, James Crowe; Cinematographer, Henry Freulich; Musical Director, Mischa Bakaleinikoff

Production Dates: April 25–May 5, 1949

Running Time: 62 minutes

Story: Warner Baxter's wife, Anna Lee, goes to the state prison to meet with her lover Harlan Warde. She tells Warde their plans to effect his escape have been altered. Warde maintains he's innocent of his embezzlement charge. Lee contrived to marry Baxter because he had planned to become warden of the prison. Baxter had second thoughts and turned down the position. Governor Charles Evans asks Baxter to review prison conditions and persuade Dr. Harry Antrim not to resign his position. Baxter sees evidence of possible prison brutality and favoritism. Antrim tells Baxter he'll stay if Baxter becomes warden. Baxter is finally persuaded to take the position and begins cleaning up the deplorable conditions. Entitled to have a chauffeur, Lee asks for Warde. Her request is turned down until Warde saves Baxter's life when two convicts attempt to kill him. In trip to town while Lee is shopping, Warde gets possession of a pistol. Lee tells Warde that she will help him get paroled. Warde guesses correctly that Lee now loves Baxter. On a trip to Lee's hairdresser, Warde pulls a gun and tells her that he actually stole the money. Warde kidnaps Lee and forces her to accompany him to Mexico. When Lee does not show up for her hair appointment, Baxter is alerted. Alerted, the police begin to close in. In the car, Lee begins to struggle with Warde for possession of the ignition key. She is pushed from the speeding car down an embankment. With Lee out of the car, police open fire, bullets ending Warde's life as the car crashes through a guardrail. After an extended hospital stay, Lee is finally ready to be discharged. Lee is about to tell Baxter of her involvement with Warde but Antrim advises her to keep the story to herself.

REVIEW: "An undistinguished effort. Scenes of prison brutality spiced up Eric Taylor's platitudinous screenplay but not enough to keep audiences involved." *The Columbia Story*, Hirshhorn

SUMMATION: This is an interesting prison noir. Convict Harlan Warde is a homme fatale who draws Anna Lee into his plan to break out of prison. Because of her relationship with Warde, Lee almost loses her life and her chance of happiness. Seymour Friedman directs briskly and Eric Taylor's screenplay holds the interest. Acting is average for a "B" programmer.

THE SUSPENSE DRAMA OF THE YEAR!
"Just squeeze the trigger," she whispered. "Then take the money—and me!"

Pushover

(August 1954)

CAST: Paul Sheridan, Fred MacMurray; Rick McAllister, Phil Carey, and introducing Kim Novak as Lona McLane; Ann Stewart, Dorothy Malone; Lt. Carl Eckstrom, E.G. Marshall; Paddy Dolan, Allen Nourse; Uncredited: Bank Guard, Kenneth A. Smith; Harry Wheeler, Paul Richards; Bank Teller, Ann Loos; Assistant Bank Manager, John De Simone; Bank Executive, Hal Taggart; Beery (Mechanic), James Anderson; Detective Briggs, Phil Chambers; Detective Schaeffer, Walter Beaver; Detective Harris, Richard Bryan; Detective Fine, Alan Dexter; Detective Peters, Don C. Harvey; Man Who Annoys Ann, Paul Picerni; Bartenders, Robert Carson and Mort Mills; Bar Patron Who Tries to Pick Up Lona, Tony Barrett; Hobbs, Joe Bailey; Billings, Robert Forrest; Molly Burnett, Ann Morriss; Young Man, Dick Crockett; Young Woman, Marion Ross; Boy, John Tarangelo; Detectives, Mel Welles and Jack Wilson

CREDITS: Director, Richard Quine; Assistant Director, Jack Corrick; Producer, Jules Schermer; Associate Producer, Philip A. Waxman; Screenwriter, Roy Huggins; Editor, Jerome Thoms; Art Director, Walter Holscher; Set Decorator, James Crowe; Cinematographer, Lester H. White; Gowns, Jean Louis; Makeup, Clay Campbell; Hair Stylist, Helen Hunt; Sound, John Livadary; Original Music, Arthur Morton; Musical Conductor, Morris Stoloff

PRODUCTION DATES: January 16–February 13, 1954

SOURCE: novel *The Night Watch* by Thomas Walsh and the novel *Rafferty* by William S. Ballinger

RUNNING TIME: 88 minutes

STORY: Paul Richards and a confederate hold up a bank and steal $210,000. In the process bank guard Kenneth A. Smith is killed. The police locate Richards' girl, Kim Novak, and assign Detective Fred MacMurray, under the guise of an ordinary citizen, to talk with her. The relationship quickly becomes sexual. Lt. E.G. Marshall assigns MacMurray, Philip Carey and Allen Nourse to stake out Novak's apartment; he wants Richards taken alive. One night, Novak leaves and MacMurray follows her to his place. Novak deduces correctly that MacMurray is a policeman who is trying to locate Richards and the money. Novak uses her sexual charms to convince MacMurray to kill Richards and the two of them would take the money. MacMurray finally agrees to the plan. Novak tells MacMurray that Richards is coming to her apartment the next night. Novak receives Richards' call and, as planned by MacMurray, leaves the apartment. Carey tails her. MacMurray tries to get in touch with Nourse, whose stakeout position is in a car in front of the apartment. Nourse, thinking that all is quiet, goes across the street to a bar for a drink. When MacMurray finally locates Nourse, they see Richards enter the apartment building. When Richards comes out, MacMurray and Nouse grab Richards and take him to his car. The money is in a satchel in the trunk. MacMurray pushes Richards into Nourse and then shoots Richards. MacMurray tells Nourse that Richards jumped him and he had to shoot; he then suggests that they put Richards in the trunk and drive the car to another destination. This way Marshall will think the confederate killed Richards and MacMurray won't have to report that Nourse was drinking on duty. Nourse agrees only if the money stays with the body. MacMurray reluctantly agrees. MacMurray has to go to Novak's apartment to receive a phone call that it's all clear for her to return. As MacMurray leaves, he finds Novak's next door neighbor, Dorothy Malone, asking for ice. He quickly closes the door but not before Malone has gotten a good look at his face. Finally Nourse realizes MacMurray is after the money and pulls a gun. The two men struggle and the gun goes off, killing Nourse. MacMurray searches for the car but Nourse had moved it. From the roof of the apartment building, Novak spots the car. Malone tells Carey that she saw a man in Novak's apartment. While Novak decoys Carey, MacMurray moves Richards' body. After Richard's body is found, Marshall decides to question Novak in her apartment. MacMurray is summoned to the apartment to bring the stakeout log. Leaving the apartment, MacMurray is seen by Malone. Malone calls police headquarters. Headquarters calls MacMurray to tell him that Malone saw the man who was in Novak's apartment. Knowing Malone can identify him, MacMurray goes to Malone's apartment and takes her captive. MacMurray and Novak attempt to leave the building, taking Malone with them. Carey finds that Malone called the police and rushes to her apartment only to find it empty. MacMurray tells Malone to get the money from Richards' car. Carey intervenes, telling Malone to take shelter and begins firing at MacMurray. MacMurray tells Novak to run as he makes a break for the car only to be shot by police. As MacMurray lies dying in the wet street, Novak comes back. He asks Novak if she would have gone with him without the money. As she is being placed in a police car, Novak has no comment.

Notes and Commentary: *Pushover* is based on two novels, the characters and main storyline based on Thomas Walsh's *The Night Watch*. In the film the protagonist is shot and killed. In the novel, he is captured and begs to be killed. The first names of some characters were changed, Jane Stewart becoming Ann, Frank Eckstrom becoming Carl, Molly Burnett becoming Ellen and Walter Sheridan becoming Paul. On the last change, possibly the producer noted that MacMurray played Walter Neff in *Double Indemnity* (Paramount, 1944) and the similarity in plot. From William S. Ballinger's *Rafferty* came the idea of a detective on stakeout becoming enthralled with the woman he's watching and subsequently committing murder while attempting to acquire the spoils of a bank robbery.

The working titles for this film were *The Killer Wore a Badge*, *322 French Street* and *The Night Watch*.

When Kim Novak comes out of the movie theater, the titles of the double feature are shown: *It Should Happen to You* (Columbia, 1954) with Judy Holliday and *The Nebraskan* (Columbia, 1953) with Philip Carey. It's interesting that detective Paul Sheridan didn't comment to fellow detective Rick McAllister how much he resembled actor Philip Carey. Maybe Paul just kept his eyes on Lona McLane.

Reviews: "*Pushover* is a cops-n-robbers meller whose suspense holds up despite its mite too long 88 minutes running time." *Variety*, 7/28/54

"This modest Columbia melodrama is a creditable job for about half the time. Quietly performed by the star and his supporting cast, under Richard Quine's intelligent direction, the story opens with deceptive slowness, mounting in suspense." *The New York Times*, 7/31/54

"Sharply directed by Quine, with an interesting reprise by MacMurray of his *Double Indemnity* role, *Pushover* is a compelling story of a man whose morals become twisted by a dangerous and somewhat naïve femme fatale. In fact, what makes *Pushover* a success, is the image that newcomer Kim Novak brings to the screen." *Motion Picture Guide*, Nash and Ross

Summation: Director Richard Quine guides the audience through a highly suspenseful crime noir aided by the stark photography of Lester H. White. White shows us Los Angeles through darkness and wet streets. Reminiscent of his role in *Double Indemnity*, MacMurray is still highly effective as his sexual desire for femme fatale Novak leads to disaster and his death. In her first starring role, Novak's sexuality explodes from the screen and she is quite good as the seductress.

ALL HONEY ON THE OUTSIDE ... ALL FURY ON THE INSIDE!
She knows how to bring out the worst ... in the best men in town!

Queen Bee

(November 1955)

A Jerry Wald Production

CAST: Eva Phillips, Joan Crawford; Avery "Beauty" Phillips, Barry Sullivan; Carol Lee Phillips, Betsy Palmer; Judson Prentiss, John Ireland; Jennifer Stewart, Lucy Marlow; Ty McKinnon, William Leslie; Sue McKinnon, Fay Wray; Miss Breen, Katherine Anderson; Ted Phillips, Tim Hovey; Trissa Phillips, Linda Bennett; Uncredited: Miss George, Willa Pearl Curtis; Sam, Bill Walker; Dr. Pearson, Olan Soule, Maid, Juanita Moore; Man Who Brings Eva Home, Robert McCord

CREDITS: Director and Screenwriter, Ranald MacDougall; Assistant Director, Irving Moore; Editor, Viola Lawrence; Art Director, Ross Bellah; Set Decorator, Louis Diage; Cinematographer, Charles Lang; Camera Operator, Emil Oster; Gowns, Jean Louis; Makeup, Clay Campbell; Hair Stylist, Helen Hunt; Sound, Lambert Day; Recording Supervisor, John Livadary; Original Music, George Duning; Musical Director, Morris Stoloff; Orchestrator, Arthur Morton; Miss Crawford's Jewelry by Ruser of Beverly Hills

PRODUCTION DATES: March 22–May 5, 1955

SOURCE: novel *Queen Bee* by Edna Lee

RUNNING TIME: 95 minutes

STORY: Lucy Marlowe comes to live in the southern mansion of Joan Crawford and Barry Sullivan. Other family members are Sullivan's sister Betsy Palmer and his two children, Tim Hovey and Linda Bennett. Marlowe overhears Palmer tell John Ireland that she wants their engagement to remain a secret. Crawford and Sullivan have an unhappy marriage to the point that Sullivan takes refuge in alcohol. Palmer tells Marlowe that she hates Crawford. Ireland announces his engagement to Crawford. Crawford, who was in love with Ireland before she married Sullivan, wants to rekindle their affair but Ireland says their relationship is over. Crawford promises Ireland that she will have her revenge. Sullivan tells Marlowe that Crawford tricked him into marriage by claiming he got her pregnant. Sullivan and Marlowe become romantically interested in each other. Sullivan insists Palmer and Ireland get married immediately. Crawford tells Palmer that she and Ireland once had an affair. Finding this to be true, Palmer is devastated and commits suicide. Upon hearing the news, Crawford become ill and hires Nurse Katherine Anderson to take care of her. When Anderson starts mistreating his children, Sullivan fires her. Crawford tells Sullivan if Anderson leaves, she will spread the word that he and Marlowe are carrying on an adulterous affair. Mistakenly Ireland believes that Sullivan had told Palmer about his affair with Crawford. Marlowe sets him straight that it was Crawford. Crawford tells Sullivan to stay away from Marlowe. Sullivan becomes the loving and attentive husband to Crawford, even buying her an expensive bracelet that she had always wanted. Ireland deduces correctly that Sullivan plans to engineer an automobile crash that will kill Crawford and Sullivan himself as they drive to a party. Ireland arranges to drive Crawford to the party. Sullivan knows that Ireland intends to carry out his (Sullivan's) own plan to crash the car, and drives quickly to prevent the "accident." Sullivan is too late. Ireland drives the car through a guard rail and it crashes and burns, killing Crawford and Ireland. The next morning as Sullivan goes to the police station, Marlowe accompanies him.

NOTES AND COMMENTARY: Edna Lee's novel was told through the eyes of Jennifer Stewart. Changes were made as her novel came to the screen. Avery Phillips' sister's name was changed from Purl to Carol Lee. Eva is not an "outsider" but the center of Atlanta society. The intense infatuation that Ty McKinnon has for Jennifer is virtually eliminated. The sexual affair between Eva and Jud is an ongoing affair, even after the announced engagement between Jud and Carol Lee. Avery is the driver in the car crash that kills Eva and him. Jen, still not interested in a marriage with Ty, is content to care for Avery's children and bask in the memory of Avery.

The film received Academy Award nominations for Charles Lang's cinematography and Jean Louis' costume design.

REVIEWS: "It is a rather anguished soap opera, plus the brittle polish expected of a Crawford vehicle." *Variety*, 10/19/55

Summation: This is a gripping, somewhat gothic noir set up nicely by Charles Lang's photography. Lang sets the stage, with the opening exterior shot giving a 3-D illusion to the dark shadows of evil that permeate the Southern mansion. The performances are good, especially by Joan Crawford and Barry Sullivan. The screenplay was too pat to have Ireland the instrument of Crawford's destruction. It would have been more noirish if the novel's ending had been filmed.

A WILD WEB OF VIOLENCE DREW THEM IRRESISTIBLY TOWARD ONE ANOTHER!

The Reckless Moment

(November 1949)

Cast: Martin Donnelly, James Mason; Lucia Harper, Joan Bennett; Bea Harper, Geraldine Brooks; Tom Harper, Henry O'Neill; Ted Darby, Shepperd Strudwick; David Harper, David Bair; Nagel, Roy Roberts; Uncredited: Sybil, Frances E. Williams; Desk Clerk, Paul E. Burns; Drummer, Danny Jackson; Blond, Claire Carleton; Gambler, Billy Snyder; Pete (Bartender), Peter Brocco; Wrestler, Karl "Killer" Davis; Card Player, Joe Palma; Liza, Penny O'Connor; Dennie, Bruce Gilbert Norman; Bridget, Sharon Monaghan; Bob (Newspaper Vendor), Charles Marsh; Post Office Clerks, Harry Harvey and Norman Leavitt; Tall Man in Post Office, Boyd Davis; Catherine Feller, Ann Shoemaker; Drug Clerk, Everett Glass; Magazine Clerk, Buddy Gorman; Mike, Louis Mason; Receptionist, Pat Barton; Pawnbroker, John Butler; Mrs. Loring, Kathryn Card; Bank Guard, Pat O'Malley; Bank Official, Charles Evans; Old Lady, Jessie Arnold; Waitress, Celeste Savoi; Newsboy, Joe Recht; Policemen, Mike Mahoney and Glenn Thompson; Police Lieutenant, William Schallert

Credits: Director, Max Ophuls; Assistant Director, Earl Bellamy; Producer, Walter Wanger; Adaptors, Mel Dinelli and Robert E. Kent; Screenwriters, Henry Garson and Robert Soderberg; Editor, Gene Havlick; Art Director, Cary Odell; Set Decorator, Frank Tuttle; Cinematographer, Burnett Guffey; Gowns, Jean Louis; Sound, Russell Malmgren; Original Music, Hans J. Salter; Musical Director, Morris Stoloff

Location Filming: Balboa and Los Angeles, California

Production Dates: March 17–April 15, 1949

Source: story "The Blank Wall" by Elisabeth Sanxay Holding in *The Ladies' Home Journal*

Running Time: 81 minutes

Story: Joan Bennett travels from Balboa to a seedy Los Angeles hotel to confront Shepperd Strudwick and tell him to stay away from her 17-year-old daughter, Geraldine Brooks. Strudwick says that, for a financial consideration, he will. Strudwick arranges to meet Brooks at her Balboa boat house. The meeting turns sour when Brooks realizes Strudwick only wants money from her, and she angrily strikes him with a heavy flashlight. The next morning Bennett finds Strudwick's body: He had fallen on an anchor that was lying on the beach. Bennett gets Strudwick's body and the anchor into the family speedboat, dropping the anchor in the middle of the bay and depositing the body in an out-of-the way swamp. James Mason shows up with a packet of love letters sent by Brooks to Strudwick and says he will give them to Bennett for $5,000. The alternative is that he will turn them over to the police. Bennett tries futilely to come up with the money. Mason begins to have strong feelings for Bennett but can't just drop the request because he's working with mobster Roy Roberts. All Bennett can raise is $800. Mason tells Bennett her worries are over because the police have arrested a minor thug for the murder. But the thug is released and Roberts wants the $5,000. Roberts believes Mason has gone soft and approaches Bennett in the boat house. Mason shows up and the two men fight. Although Mason is severely injured in the fight, he is able to overpower and strangle Roberts. Bennett goes to the house to obtain bandages. Upon returning, she sees Mason driving away with the dead Roberts in the passenger seat. Accompanied by maid Frances E. Williams, Bennett follows. Mason deliberately crashes through a guard rail into a large tree. Bennett rushes to the dying Mason, who gives her the packet of letters and tells her to quickly leave the scene of the accident. Later Bennett learns that before he died, Mason confessed to the murder of Strudwick.

The Reckless Moment (1949).

Notes and Commentary: The working title for the film was *The Blank Wall.*

The basic theme of Elisabeth Sanxay Holding's story was followed, with some changes. The family name was Holley. Bea's grandfather caused the death of Ted Darby. In the climax of the story, after Donnelly strangles his crime boss Nagle, he carries the body away in a chest (with Lucia's help) and burns it. Donnelly, a known crook, is wanted by the police for questioning. When apprehended, Donnelly confesses to both the murders of Darby and Nagle, allowing Lucia's family to escape scandal.

Director Max Ophuls requested that Columbia allow him to have two adjoining sets lighted at the same time because he wanted to film a continuous tracking shot from one set to the other. Columbia turned down his request. This was his last American film.

Reviews: "A tense melodrama, projecting good mood and suspense." *Variety*, 10/19/49

Summation: This is a very good noir with an excellent performance by Joan Bennett as a mother trying to prevent scandal. James Mason does a nice turn as a small-time grifter who wants to help Bennett primarily because she reminds him of his mother. Ophuls' direction effectively paints the picture of a middle-class family and the underworld encroachment. Visual effects are superb as Ophuls' vision is vividly brought to the screen by the master cinematographer Burnett Guffey. The long tracking shots are outstanding.

THE BRIDE DISAPPEARS INTO A MAZE OF MYSTERY!

The Return of the Whistler

(March 1948)

Cast: Ted Nichols, Michael Duane; Alice Dupres Barkley, Lenore Aubert; Gaylord Traynor, Richard Lane; Charlie Barkley, James Cardwell; Mrs. Barkley, Ann Shoemaker; Mrs. Hulskamp, Sarah Padden; Uncredited: Voice of the Whistler, Otto Forrest; Jeff Anderson, Olin Howland; Hotel Painter, William Newell; Crandall, Fred F. Sears; Hart, Robert Emmett Keane; Captain Griggs, Edgar Dearing; George Sawyer; Jack Rice; Sam, Eddy Waller; Sybil, Ann Doran; Arnold, Trevor Bardette; Traynor's Secretary, Abigail Adams; Older Nurse, Isabel Winters; Dr. Grantland, Wilton Graff; Male Nurses, Steve Benton

***The Return of the Whistler* (1948).**

and Kenner G. Kemp; Nurse, Dolores Castle; Police Sergeant, Harry Strang

Credits: Director, D. Ross Lederman; Producer, Rudolph C. Flothow; Story, Cornell Woolrich; Screenwriters, Edward Bock and Maurice Tombragel; Editor, Dwight Caldwell; Art Director, George Brooks; Set Decorator, James Crowe; Cinematographer, Philip Tannura; Musical Director, Mischa Bakaleinikoff; "Whistler" theme music, Wilbur Hatch

Production Dates: October 13–23, 1947

Running Time: 63 minutes

Source: the Columbia Broadcasting System Program "The Whistler"

Story: Michael Duane and Lenore Aubert stop at a justice of the peace to get married but the justice had just been called away. While they are in the house, two mysterious men disable their car. Duane and Aubert barely make it to "The Inn" where only Aubert is able to get a room. The next morning, Aubert is missing. Duane tells private investigator Richard Lane that Aubert was married to an American soldier who had been killed on their wedding day. Aubert recently came to the United States to be with her husband's relatives. At his apartment, Duane finds Aubert's marriage certificate. Lane hits Duane and takes the certificate. Duane finds a lead and eventually meets James Cardwell, who tells Duane that he is Aubert's husband. Duane is allowed to see Aubert, who verifies this fact. After Duane leaves, it becomes evident that Aubert was forced to lie at the point of a gun. Cardwell and his mother, Ann Shoemaker, are behind a scheme to steal a fortune that belongs to Aubert. Cardwell then meets Lane, who hands him the marriage certificate. Duane discovers that Cardwell had lied to him and plans to talk to Aubert. Meanwhile, Lane finds that Cardwell is not Aubert's husband and begins his investigation. Aubert has been taken to a sanitarium. Duane is able to rescue Aubert before Cardwell confronts him. Duane defeats Cardwell in a short fistfight. As male nurses begin to subdue Duane, Lane shows up with the police. Cardwell, Shoemaker and other family members are arrested. Duane and Aubert finally marry.

Notes and Commentary: The screenplay was adapted from Cornell Woolrich's story "All at Once, No Alice," first published in the March 2, 1940, issue of *Argosy* magazine. Significant changes were made in bring Woolrich's story to the screen, but the basic premise is maintained. The couple in the short story are James Cannon and Alice Brown. In the story, they are married by the justice of the peace but then unable to find a suitable room for the night's lodging. Alice is able to spend the night in a small closet in a local hotel and James finds a room at the YMCA. The next morning the hotel employees and the justice of the peace insist they have never heard of her. The police become involved. Finally Detective Ainslie sees proof that Alice exists. James remembers that Alice told him she worked as a maid for a Beresford family. Following up, James and Ainslie discover that Alice's real name is Alma Beresford. Alma was rich but told James she was a maid so as not to frighten him away because of their difference in social standing. Alma had loved James and wanted to marry him. Alma's guardian, Hastings, planned to murder Alma to inherit her fortune. Hastings had bribed the hotel employees and the justice of the peace to deny any knowledge of Alma. Hastings's plans are thwarted by Ainslie and James. James plans to legally marry Alma, with Ainslie as best man.

Reviews: "Shoddy script has a hard time holding any level of suspense." *Motion Picture Guide*, Nash and Ross

"Fairish whodunit. With some judicious editing the film could have been a superior suspense thriller." *Variety*, 3/3/48

Summation: This engrossing Whistler noir episode isn't as suspenseful as some previous entries but the story unfolds at a nice pace and holds the viewer's interest. Acting is up to par but Richard Dix is sorely missed.

HOT ON TAX-DODGERS TRAIL!

Revenue Agent

(February 1951)

Cast: Steve Daniels, Douglas Kennedy; Marge King, Jean Willes; Sam Bellows, Onslow Stevens; Harry Reardon, William "Bill" Phillips; Lt. Bob Ullman, Ray Walker; Cliff Gage, David Bruce; Ernie Medford, Archie Twitchell; Uncredited: Narrator, James Seay; Chief Agent Hunter, Eddie Kane; Augustus King, Lyle Talbot; Mexican Bank Official, Paul Bradley; Al Chaloopka, Rick Vallin; Policeman at Roadblock, Terry Frost; Mine Caretaker, Frank Ellis; Fireman, Frank O'Connor; Officer in Squad Car, Judd Holdren; Sergeant Wallace, Fred Kelsey; Uster, William Fawcett; U.S. Border Patrolman, John Hart; Mexican Officer, Alex Montoya

Credits: Director, Lew Landers; Producer, Sam Katzman; Screenwriters, William Sackheim and Arthur A. Ross; Editor, Edwin Bryant; Art Director, Paul Palmentola; Set Decorator, Sidney Clifford; Cinematographer, Ira H. Morgan; Unit Manager, Herbert Leonard; Musical Director, Mischa Bakaleinikoff

Production Dates: July 11–19, 1950

Running Time: 72 minutes

Story: When Lyle Talbot learns that his wife Jean Willes is having an affair with his boss Onslow Stevens, he decides to tell Internal Revenue about Stevens' tax evasion. Before Talbot can meet with agent Douglas Kennedy, he's murdered by William "Bill" Phillips, an associate of Stevens. A clue alerts Kennedy to questionable bank accounts in Mexico. Using an alias, he tries to join the gang. An attempt to put Kennedy out of the picture fails. Kennedy tells Stevens, Phillips and another associate, Archie Twitchell, that he's a Revenue Agent but he would rather have the money promised him than turn them in. A trial run is scheduled with fake gold bars hidden in a sedan. Kennedy is able to alert officers at a road block in time and Stevens begins to have greater confidence in Kennedy. Stevens decides to make one last shipment of gold to Mexico and then close down operations. With the help of agent David Bruce, pictures of Stevens' sedan are taken so an exact duplicate can be assembled. On the drive to the Mexican border, the party is detained long enough to switch cars. Stevens' sedan is torn apart but there is no trace of gold. A few miles from the border, a stop is made at William Fawcett's shop. The gold has been sent to Fawcett to hide in the sedan just before it crosses the border. One look under the car tells Fawcett that the cars have been switched. Kennedy is captured and forced to make certain that the border crossing can be made without incident. After crossing, Stevens is to draw all the money out of the bank while Phillips and Twitchell kill Kennedy at an abandoned quarry. Suddenly, Kennedy whirls, kayoes Twitchell with a well-delivered punch and pushes Phillips off balance enough so he can make a break for freedom. Phillips chases and corners Kennedy, then he finds his gun is empty. The two men fight and Phillips falls from a high platform to his death. Overhearing that Stevens has gone to the airport to fly to Mazatlan, Kennedy arrives in time to pull him from the plane and arrest him. Stevens had to pay the income tax and penalty on the money he had deposited in the Mexican banks. In addition, he was sent to Federal Prison for conspiracy and tax evasion. The gold that was smuggled into Mexico was not recovered. Twitchell was still at large in Mexico.

Reviews: "Good program melodrama built around work of income tax agents. Actionful." *Variety*, 12/6/50

"Fast-paced and hard-hitting yarn that centers on the work of the Internal Revenue Service in uncovering a plot to sneak $1 million in gold dust out of the country. Told in a documentary style, the tension is maintained throughout." *Motion Picture Guide*, Nash and Ross

Summation: A minor gem that needs to be re-discovered, this is a gritty, hard-hitting and realistic melodrama. The acting is uniformly good with a special nod to Douglas Kennedy as the Revenue agent who finally cracks the case. Veteran director Lew Landers' quick pacing allows no lull in the story. Ira H. Morgan's camerawork compliments the story. There are no romantic interludes to dilute the impact of the William Sackheim–Arthur A. Ross story.

This is the man called "Brigade" ... hot as the revenge that drove him ... hated by the woman he saved!

Ride Lonesome

(February 1959)
A Ranown Production

Cast: Ben Brigade, Randolph Scott; Carrie Lane, Karen Steele; Sam Boone, Pernell Roberts;

Billy John, James Best; Frank John, Lee Van Cleef; Whit, James Coburn; Uncredited: Charlie, Dyke Johnson; Indian Chief, Boyd Stockman; Outlaws, Boyd "Red" Morgan, Roy Jenson and Bennie Dobbins

CREDITS: Director and Producer, Budd Boetticher; Assistant Director, Jerrold Bernstein; Executive Producer, Harry Joe Brown; Screenwriter, Burt Kennedy; Editor, Jerome Thoms; Art Director, Robert Peterson; Set Decorator, Frank A. Tuttle; Cinematographer, Charles Lawton, Jr.; Recording Supervisor, John Livadary; Sound, Harry Mills; Original Music and Musical Director, Heinz Roemheld; Color Consultant, Henri Jaffa

LOCATION FILMING: Alabama Hills, Lone Pine, California, and Olancha Dunes, Olancha, California

PRODUCTION DATES: August 14–28, 1958

RUNNING TIME: 74 minutes

Filmed in CinemaScope and Eastman Color by Pathe

STORY: Bounty hunter Randolph Scott takes outlaw James Best into custody. As Best is captured, he yells to his cohorts to find his brother Lee Van Cleef. Scott plans to take Best to Santa Cruz to face a charge of murder. At a swing stage station, Scott finds old adversary Pernell Roberts, Roberts' pal James Coburn and the station man's wife Karen Steele. With Indians on the warpath, they band together on the trek to Santa Cruz. Indians killed Steele's husband. Roberts tells Scott that he and Coburn need to take Best to Santa Cruz so that they will be granted amnesty. Scott refuses to relinquish Best. Roberts realizes that Scott has been traveling slowly and in the open and wants Van Cleef to catch up. The meeting place is a clearing outside Santa Cruz with a hanging tree. Many years before, as sheriff of Santa Cruz, Scott was responsible for sending Van Cleef to prison. Van Cleef got revenge by kidnapping and hanging Scott's wife from the hanging tree. As Van Cleef confronts Scott, he sees Best seated on a horse with a rope around his neck. Scott goads Van Cleef into charging at him by making Best's horse bolt. There is an exchange of shots and Scott's finds the mark, killing Van Cleef. Scott then fires a shot that severs the rope strangling Best, who drops to the ground unharmed. Roberts then confronts Scott about taking Best. To Robert's surprise, Scott turns Best over to Roberts, stating he no longer has any use for him. Roberts, Coburn and Steele take Best on to Santa Cruz. Looking back, Roberts sees black smoke rising from the clearing. Scott burns the hanging tree, exorcising the demons that have haunted him over the years.

NOTES AND COMMENTARY: To get the ending he wanted for the characters played by Pernell Roberts and James Coburn, director Budd Boetticher had to battle with the Columbia executives. He finally won. Positive audience reaction proved Boetticher was right.

After *Buchanan Rides Alone*, the Columbia brass made an attempt to fire producer Harry Joe Brown. Randolph Scott and Boetticher stated that they would make no westerns at Columbia without Brown. With the success of the previous collaborations, the studio gave in. Ranown (from Randolph and Brown) Productions was formed and this film and *Comanche Station* (Columbia, 1960) were filmed.

Scott was impressed with James Coburn, making his first feature film, and requested additional scenes be written for him. The result was the impressive scene in which Roberts asks Coburn to be his business partner. Coburn's reaction always delights movie audiences.

Roberts is given the line, "There are some things a man just can't ride around." Randolph Scott used an almost identical line in "The Tall T" (Columbia 1957).

REVIEWS: "High grade oater. [Boetticher] had a tough, honest screenplay by Burt Kennedy and he has given it perception and tension." *Variety*, 2/18/59

"Using all the elements of B westerns (as well as Eastmancolor and CinemaScope) *Ride Lonesome* is an intelligent western making good use of old formulas." *Motion Picture Guide*, Nash and Ross

SUMMATION: The collaboration of star Scott, director Boetticher, screenwriter Kennedy and cinematographer Charles Lawton, Jr. resulted in a taut, superior western noir. Boetticher perfectly balances action, characterizations, humor and tension. Lawton captures the bleakness of the trek through the beautiful Lone Pine scenery. It is to Kennedy's credit that there is no fistfight between the stars over Steele, nor is it confirmed that Steele will end up with Roberts, even though he's willing. This very adult western shows that talent can make a gem on a low budget.

LAW AND ORDER VS. THE UNDERWORLD ...
for control of the teen-gangs!

Rumble on the Docks

(December 1956)

A Clover Production

Cast: Jimmy Smigelski, James Darren; Della, Laurie Carroll; Joe Brindo, Michael Granger; Rocky, Jerry Janger; Chuck, Robert Blake; Pete Smigelski, Edgar Barrier; Anna Smigelski, Celia Lovsky; Dan Kevlin, David Bond; Frank Mangus, Timothy Carey; "Stomper" Tony Lightning, Dan Terranova; Poochie, Barry Froner; Wimpy, Don Devlin; Cliffie, Stephen H. Sears; Ferdinand Marchesi, Joseph Vitale; Gotham, David Orrick; Officer Fitz, Larry Blake; Gil Danco, Robert C. Ross; Sully, Steve Warren; Bo-Bo, Don Garrett; District Attorney Fuller, Joel Ashley; Kid with Wallet, Salvatore Anthony; Freddie Bell and the Bellboys (Jack Kane on saxophone, Frankie Brent on bass-guitar, Russ Conti on piano, Chick Keeney on drums and Jerry Mayo on trumpet); Uncredited: Tops, Terry Frost; Dormeyer, Michael Mark, Police Captain Callahan, Paul Bryar; Lou "Peanuts" Bassett, Benny Burt; Judge, Robert Shayne

Credits: Director, Fred F. Sears; Assistant Director, Willard Sheldon; Producer, Sam Katzman; Screenwriters, Lou Morheim and Jack DeWitt; Editor, Jerome Thoms; Art Director, Paul Palmentola; Set Decorator, Sidney Clifford; Cinematographer, Benjamin H. Kline; Sound, Josh Westmoreland; Musical Conductor, Mischa Bakaleinikoff

Song: "Get the First Train out of Town" (Bell and Latanzi)—performed by Freddie Bell and the Bellboys

Location Filming: San Pedro, California

Production Dates: July 10–21, 1956

Source: novel *Rumble on the Docks* by Frank Paley

Running Time: 82 minutes

Story: James Darren and Robert Blake, members of the Diggers gang, prevent two members of the rival Stompers gang from raping Laurie Carroll. Carroll invites Darren to take her to the Settlement House dance. Mob boss Michael Granger and his henchman Timothy Carey use intimidation to try to stop Darren's father Edgar Barrier from printing inflammatory statements against Granger in his weekly newspaper. Barrier hates Granger for engineering an "accident" that broke Barrier's back, leaving him crippled. Barrier wants to break the mob stronghold on the Brooklyn docks. At the dance, the Stompers break in, and a rumble ensues until police sirens are heard. Running away, Darren is stopped by Granger, who takes Darren to his apartment. One of the piers has been abandoned and a new longshoreman's local is formed with Joseph Vitale in charge. All the participants of the dance rumble are arrested. Granger's lawyer David Orrick gets Darren released. Leaving the courthouse, Darren meets Carroll and they begin walking home. They hear an ambulance siren and they discover that Vitale was the victim of a hit and run murder. Youthful eyewitnesses identify Benny Burt as the driver. Granger convinces Darren to perjure himself and testify that Burt was not the driver. Granger holds a victory party in his apartment. Barrier and Darren's mother, Celia Lovsky, arrive and Barrier disowns Darren as his son. Darren retreats to his room where Carroll's little brother, Barry Froner, tells him that Carroll needs him. The Diggers grab Darren and take him to the garage where Darren works. Carroll tells Darren that she can prove he lied and will take the stand if he doesn't change his testimony. Granger discovers that Darren is missing and decides to have him murdered so he can't be cross-examined. Granger gets a phone call telling him where to find Darren. Blake sees Granger and Carey enter the garage and goes to Barrier for help. Barrier goes to Darren's aid while Blake calls the police. Granger and Carey have Darren cornered when Barrier breaks in and disrupts the planned murder. Barrier is shot and wounded. Police sirens are heard and Granger and Carey are apprehended. The mob's hold on the longshoremen is broken. Darren has a steady girlfriend in Carroll and now plans to go to a local college.

Notes and Commentary: Frank Paley's *Rumble on the Docks* was slightly re-worked to resemble the superior *On the Waterfront* (Columbia, 1954) but the screenwriters kept the gist of the story intact. Della's part was reworked to remind viewers of Eva Marie Saint's Edie Doyle and there was a courtroom scene that would signal the end of mob control of the Brooklyn Docks. So viewers wouldn't think this was a complete copy, Paley's Father Kevlin ran the Settlement House. In the novel, Della had heart trouble and would spend most of the story confined to bed. Jimmy's father was primarily wheelchair-bound. There were modifications in the ending. In the novel, Jimmy finds a gun and, in a shootout, fires two shots into Brindo's face, killing him. To escape from the garage, Jimmy fires a shot into the henchman's leg. Jimmy is afraid of being arrested for murder and also fears mob retribution and plans to leave Brooklyn on a freighter. Only when Jimmy believes that two friends have been arrested does he surrender to police. The novel ends abruptly as Jimmy is now going to testify in court for the prosecution, the mob making plans and Jimmy reading a note from Della and realizing that she cares for him.

It was announced that Robert Kent would produce the film but Sam Katzman is the only producer named on the on-screen credits. James Darren was billed as "introducing."

Rumble on the Docks was released on a double feature with *Don't Knock the Rock* (Columbia, 1956) with Bill Haley and the Comets. In some print advertisement, there was an asterisk on RUMBLE to tell theatergoers it meant "teen-age gang war."

Summation: This pocket version of *On the Waterfront* (Columbia, 1954) is nevertheless entertaining. James Darren renders a dynamic performance in his film debut. Timothy Carey provides good menace as mob boss Michael Granger's right hand man. Director Fred F. Sears does a fine job keeping the interest on high as he moves the storyline briskly to its conclusion.

THE MAN FROM "THE MOB" IS MAKING ANOTHER KILLING!

Scandal Sheet

(January 1952)

A Motion Picture Investors Production

Cast: Mark Chapman aka George Grant, Broderick Crawford; Julie Allison, Donna Reed; Steve McCleary, John Derek; Charlotte Grant, Rosemary DeCamp; Charlie Barnes, Henry O'Neill; Biddle, Harry Morgan; Lt. Davis, James Millican; Judge Elroy Hacker, Griff Barnett; Frank Madison, Jonathan Hale; Uncredited: Bailey, Jay Adler; Pete, Don Beddoe; Heeney, Charles Cane; Mrs. Rawley, Kathryn Card; Doc O'Hanlon, Cliff Clark; Mary, Victoria Horne; Joe, Matt Willis; Needle Nellie, Ida Moore; Mrs. Allison, Katherine Warren; Baxter, Pierre Watkin; Edwards, Eugene Baxter; Jordon, Luther Crockett; Conklin, Raymond Largay; Joey (Office Boy), Ralph Reed; Elkins, Ric Roman; Toothless Bum, Harry Hines; Mrs. Penwick, Edna Holland; Drunk in Heeney's Bar, John "Skins" Miller; Addled Bum, Garry Owen; Janitor, Guy Wilkerson; Telephone Operator, Pat Williams; Telephone Operator, Shirley Ballard; *New York Express* Board Member, Jack Perrin; Reporters, Chuck Colean, Tom Kingston, Mike Mahoney and Peter Virgo; Newspapermen, Kenner G. Kemp, Frank O'Connor and Jeffrey Sayre; Bums in Heeney's Bar, Blackie Whiteford and Harry Wilson; Policeman, Duke Watson

Credits: Director, Phil Karlson; Assistant Director, Frederick Briskin; Producer, Edward Small; Screenwriters, Ted Sherdeman, Eugene Ling and James Poe; Editor, Jerome Thoms; Art Director, Robert Peterson; Set Decorator, William Kiernan; Cinematographer, Burnett Guffey; Gowns, Jean Louis; Makeup, Clay Campbell, Hair Stylist, Helen Hunt; Sound, Jack Goodrich; Original Music, George Duning; Musical Director, Morris Stoloff

Production Dates: late April–mid–May 1951

Source: novel *The Dark Page* by Samuel Fuller

Running Time: 82 minutes

Story: Hard-driving executive editor Broderick Crawford's newspaper is promoting a Lonely Hearts dance. At the dance, Crawford is reunited with Rosemary DeCamp. Crawford, who has since changed his name, walked out on his marriage to DeCamp over twenty years previously. Crawford goes with DeCamp to her nearby apartment. Crawford wants to give DeCamp money to leave town, get a divorce and stay out of his life. DeCamp wants to resume their marriage. When she sees this is not possible, DeCamp plans to ruin Crawford's life. Their argument turns physical, Crawford pushing DeCamp. Her head hits an iron pole, killing her instantly. Crawford removes all traces of DeCamp's identity, even tearing off her badge of admission to the Lonely Hearts Dance. Crawford also takes a pawn ticket. Crawford's best reporter John Derek goes to the scene to cover the story. DeCamp is found in her bathtub. Police Lieutenant James Millican is ready to write off the death as an accident. Looking around, Derek notices the Lonely Hearts tag was torn off, leaving the pin, rather than just removed. Derek suspects murder and tells Crawford he's planning to pursue the investigation. Crawford tries to deter Derek but can't without looking suspicious. Crawford decides to pick up the item at the pawn shop. Before he's able to do so, he is approached by former newspaperman Henry O'Neill, now a drunk. Crawford brushes off O'Neill and gives him money—and, accidentally, the pawn ticket. Redeeming the pawn ticket, O'Neill is given a suitcase. In the suitcase are two pictures, one taken on DeCamp's wedding day, but the groom is turned so the face is unrecognizable. The second shows a youthful Crawford and DeCamp on a beach. O'Neill immediately knows Crawford murdered DeCamp and contacts reporter Donna Reed. Reed turns the telephone over to Derek, who doesn't believe the ramblings of O'Neill. O'Neill then plans to take his story to a rival newspaper. Crawford, who has been informed of O'Neill's call, intercepts him and brutally murders him. Derek feels he's at a dead end in the city and believes his only chance is to find the person who performed the marriage ceremony. Crawford makes an inquiry to see if Judge Griff Barnett can be reached but is told Barnett no longer lives in the area. Crawford begins to feel safe. As it looks like their investigation is stalled, Derek receives a phone call from Barnett. Derek telegraphs Crawford that he's bringing evidence to break the case. Crawford meets Barnett but after all the years, Barnett doesn't recognize him. Barnett tells Derek that he could recognize Crawford's angry voice. Crawford gets perturbed and suddenly Barnett knows Crawford is the man. Crawford pulls a gun. Reed brings Millican to interview Barnett. Crawford decides to shoot his way to freedom but Millican returns fire, killing Crawford. Derek writes the biggest story of his career.

Notes and Commentary: The working title of the film was *The Dark Page*. The thrust of Samuel Fuller's novel *The Dark Page* was followed to a point. Character names were slightly altered and in some instances changed. One major change is newspaperwoman Julie Allison chases newspaperman Lance McCleary instead of the other way around in the film. The screenplay began to deviate from the novel after the justice of the peace sent word he could give vital information in the Lonely Hearts murder. Chapman goes to the justice's residence and strangles him. McCleary approaches an old newspaperman and is able to find that John Grant (now Chapman) married Charlotte Faith. Chapman believes his only recourse is to murder McCleary. McCleary tells Chapman that, if he murders him, he'll go on killing, and possibly even his current wife Rose will be a victim. Chapman, instead of shooting McCleary, commits suicide. McCleary brings Chapman's body to the newspaper office and lays him across his desk. Then Julie and McCleary leave the office to get drunk.

Initially John Payne was penciled in to star in a Sidney Buchman production of Fuller's novel. Then William Holden was slated to co-star with Broderick Crawford in a Jules Schermer production. Fuller finally sold his novel to H-F Productions for $15,000. Director Howard Hawks began working on pre-production. Then the property was sold to Monterey Productions who then sold it to Motion Picture Investors. Columbia purchased the rights for $10,000 from Motion Picture Investors.

Reviews: "Story is full of twists and generates fair suspense..." *Variety*, 1/9/52

"*Scandal Sheet* is an intense, gripping crime drama that hurtles along like an express train." *Motion Picture Guide*, Nash and Ross

Summation: This is a superior crime noir. Director Phil Karlson takes Fuller's excellent novel and delivers a solid suspense story *and* gives moviegoers a look behind the scenes at the tabloid newspaper business. Crawford delivers another of his fine performances. Burnett Guffey's photography is first-rate. Note the final scenes as Crawford's face goes in and out of the shadows.

Tension that's too much to bare!

Screaming Mimi

(April 1958)

A Sage Production

Cast: Virginia Wilson/Yolanda Lange, Anita Ekberg; Bill Sweeney, Philip Carey; Joann "Gypsy" Masters, Gypsy Rose Lee; Dr. Greenwood/Bill Green, Harry Townes; Ketti, Linda Cherney; Charlie Weston, Romney Brent; Red Norvo Trio (Red Norvo on xylophone, Jimmy Wyble on guitar, Red Wooten on bass, unknown drummer); Uncredited: Homicidal Maniac with Knife, Sol Gorss; Dr. Robinson, Stephen Ellsworth; Nurse, Dick Ryan; Paul (Bartender), Frank J. Scannell; Nightclub Patron, Franklyn Farnum; Waiter, Hank Mann; Lola Lake in Photo, Jeanne Cooper; Mac, Paul E. Burns; Captain Bline, Alan Gifford; Dr. Mapes, Thomas Browne Henry; Walter Krieg, Oliver McGowan; Raoul Reynarde, Vaughn Taylor; Jan, Betsy Jones-Moreland; Ben (Cab Driver), Frank Marlowe; Mrs. Myers, Ruth Warren; Detective Roberts, Tom McKee; News Vendor, Heinie Conklin; Thelma, Sarah Padden; Detectives, Pat Collins, David McMahon and Phil Tully

Credits: Director, Gerd Oswald; Assistant Director, Jerrold Bernstein; Producers, Harry Joe Brown and Robert Fellows; Assistant to Producers, Harry Joe Brown, Jr.; Screenwriter, Robert Blees; Editors, Gene Havlick and Jerome Thoms; Art Director, Cary Odell; Set Decorator, Frank A. Tuttle; Cinematographer, Burnett Guffey; Sound, Josh Westmoreland; Recording Supervisor, John Livadary; Choreographer, Lee Scott

Songs: "Put the Blame on Mame" (Fisher and Roberts) sung by Gypsy Rose Lee with the Red Norvo Trio; "Sweet Genevieve" (Tucker and Cooper) sung by unknown male singers; "Let's Fall in Love" (Porter) played by Red Norvo Trio

Location Filming: Carrillo Beach, California

Production Dates: September 16–October 9, 1957

Source: novel *Screaming Mimi* by Fredric Brown

Running Time: 79 minutes

Story: While showering after an ocean swim, Anita Ekberg is attached by a knife-wielding homicidal maniac, Sol Gorss. Ekberg's life is saved when her half-brother Romney Brent shoots and kills Gorss. The incident causes Ekberg to go into traumatic shock and she is hospitalized in a sanitarium. The incident also affects Brent, who fashions a sculpture showing a frightened Ekberg. In the sanitarium, Dr. Harry Townes takes a personal interest in Ekberg's case and begins to treat her at no charge. Finally, Townes arranges for Ekberg's release. Ekberg gets a job as an exotic dancer in Gypsy Rose Lee's nightclub. Townes is now her manager. Walking home, Ekberg is attacked and receives a knife wound. Further damage is prevented by the intervention of her Great Dane, Devil. Reporter Philip Carey takes an interest primarily because of the physical attributes of Ekberg. Carey decides to research recent slasher crimes. One victim is murdered with a figurine of a frightened woman at the scene. While interviewing Ekberg, Carey sees an identical figurine in her dressing room. Late one night, Carey finds Ekberg walking at the scene of her attack. Carey and Ekberg become romantically involved, Carey taking her back to her apartment where he spends the night. Carey thinks he might have broken Townes' control over Ekberg. Townes now wants to quickly take Ekberg out of the country. In his investigation, Carey finds that Brent is the sculptor. Brent tells Carey the story behind the figurine but has been told her half-sister died in the sanitarium. Carey believes the figurine is key to the solution of the crime and plays it up with a front page story. Townes knows Ekberg still has a figurine and demands that Ekberg give to him. Ekberg refuses and has Devil push Townes through a window. Mortally injured, Townes confesses that is the killer. Ekberg and Devil leave before they can be questioned by the police. Carey tracks Ekberg down. He realizes that Ekberg slashed the victim when she saw the figurine in her hands. Fearing arrest, Ekberg turns Devil on Carey. Carey tries to calm the animal. Suddenly the police arrive and take things in hand. Ekberg is sent back to the sanitarium. Carey can only stand and watch as the woman he loves is taken away.

Notes and Commentary: The basic storyline of Fredric Brown's novel is followed in the screenplay.

The major difference is the screenplay's emphasis on Yolanda Lange/Virginia Wilson (Bessie Wilson in the novel) rather the novel's emphasis on Sweeney. The novel is told in the first person by Sweeney so any knowledge of Yolanda is either seen directly by Sweeney or told to him. In the film, Sweeney and Yolanda have a sexual encounter, which never happened in the novel. The nightclub proprietor in the film is lesbian Gypsy Rose Lee and in the novel the club is owned by mobster Harry Yahn and run by his manager Nick. The screenplay depicts the events in straightforward fashion while in the novel the events unfold as Sweeney discovers them. In the novel, there were three murders; this is reduced to one in the film.

For most of the film, the Red Norvo Trio is a quartet. The drummer is absent in the final number played. Most of the musical score, especially the main title theme, is taken from Leonard Bernstein's score from *On the Waterfront* (Columbia, 1954).

Screaming Mimi was released on the lower half of a double bill with *This Angry Age* (Columbia, 1958).

Reviews: "This psychological meller fails to rise above the calibre of a typical 'B' programmer." *Variety*, 3/19/58

Summation: This is a gripping, suspenseful noir directed with a sure hand by Gerd Oswald, who builds the tension nicely. Burnett Guffey's camerawork aids Oswald and the actors in keeping the audience engrossed until the final scene. Even though most of the audience will be focused on Anita Ekberg's physical charms, her acting meets the demands of the part. Philip Carey, usually more at home in western ventures, does a nice job as the reporter who comes under the spell of Ekberg. An added treat for jazz fans is the fine music supplied by Red Norvo and his sidemen in the nightclub sequences.

THE WHISTLER'S GREATEST LOVE MURDER!

The Secret of the Whistler

(November 1946)

Cast: Ralph Harrison, Richard Dix; Kay Morrell, Leslie Brooks; Jim Calhoun, Michael Duane; Edith Harrison, Mary Currier; Linda Vail, Mona Barrie; Joe Conroy, Ray Walker; Laura, Claire Du Brey; Uncredited: Voice of the Whistler, Otto Forrest; Jorgenson, Byron Foulger; Girls at Party, Doris Houck and Nancy Saunders; Dr. Winthrop, Charles Trowbridge; Fred, Fred "Snowflake" Toones; McLaren, John Hamilton; Messenger Boy, Fred Amsel; Dr. Gunther, Arthur Space; Miss Bailey, Barbara Woodell; George, Ernie Adams; Henry Loring, Jack Davis; Butler, Ernest Hilliard; Detective Lieutenant, Pat Lane; Detective, Tony Shaw

Credits: Director, George Sherman; Producer, Rudolph Flothow; Story, Richard H. Landau; Screenwriter, Raymond L. Schrock; Editor, Dwight Caldwell; Art Director, Hans Radon; Set Decorator, Robert Bradfield; Cinematographer, Allen Siegler; Musical Director, Mischa Balaleinikoff; "Whistler" theme music, Wilbur Hatch

Production Dates: July 15–August 1, 1946

Running Time: 65 minutes

Source: the Columbia Broadcasting System program "The Whistler"

Story: Mary Currier, who has a heart problem, purchases a tombstone for herself. Her husband Richard Dix, an untalented artist, lives on Currier's money. Once Dix learns Currier has a short time to live, he begins an affair with gold digger Leslie Brooks and wants to marry her. Under the care of a new physician, Currier returns to good health. She also discovers Dix's affair with Brooks and plans to divorce him. Dix decides to murder Currier before she can begin divorce proceedings by adding poison to one of her medications. Housekeeper Claire Du Brey finds Currier's dead body. The death is attributed to Currier's heart condition. In her diary, Currier stated she is going to divorce Dix and that Dix put something in her medication. Brooks finds the prescription bottle and verifies that poison was added. Dix overhears the conversation and goes into a rage and strangles Brooks. Brooks had called the police. The police arrive and shoot Dix as he tries to escape. The page in the diary would have exonerated Dix in his wife's death.

Reviews: "One of the best in the series." *The Columbia Story*, Hirshhorn

"Engrossing as usual and well acted." *Motion Picture Guide*, Nash and Ross

"Excellent suspense enhanced to the mood of lurking danger." *Blockbuster Video Guide to Movies and Videos, 1995*

Summation: This was another fine noir entry in the Whistler series. Buoyed by George Sherman's direction, telling performances by Dix, Leslie Brooks, Mary Currier and Clair Du Brey, the film generates genuine suspense. Raymond L. Schrock's screenplay adaptation of Richard H. Landau's story keeps you guessing to the end how fate will trip up Dix.

EXPOSE OF THE $8,000,000,000
GAMBLING SYNDICATE AND ITS HOODLUM EMPIRE!

711 Ocean Drive

(July 1950)

Cast: Mal Granger, Edmond O'Brien; Gail Mason, Joanne Dru; Carl Stephans, Otto Kruger; Vince Walters, Barry Kelley; Trudy Maxwell, Dorothy Patrick; Larry Mason, Donald Porter; Lt. Pete Wright, Howard St. John; Gizzi, Robert Osterloh, and introducing Sammy White as Chippie Evans; Uncredited: Steve Marshak, Bert Freed; Joe Gish, Carl Milletaire; Rocco, Charles La Torre; Peterson (Chauffeur), Fred Aldrich; Tim, Charles Jordan; Mendel Weiss, Sidney Dubin; Detective Carter, Jay Barney; Mal's Date, Cleo Moore; Chippie's Date, Gail Bonney; Sonny, Ralph Montgomery; Flirty Man at Bar, Harry Lauter; Boxer, Joe Gray; Auto Repair Mechanic, Walter Sande; Al (Las Vegas Bookmaker), Al Hill; Kelly (Boulder Dam Policeman), Chuck Hamilton; Boulder Dam Guide, William Getts; Boulder Dam Tourist, George Magrill

Credits: Director, Joseph M. Newman; Assistant Director, Charles L. Smith; Producer, Frank N. Seltzer; Screenwriters, Richard English and Francis Swann; Editor, Bert Jordan; Set Decorator, Howard Bristol; Cinematographer, Frank N. Planer; Camera Operator, Edward Fitzgerald; Production Designer, Perry Ferguson; Production Manager, Orville Fouse; Property Master, Arnold Goode; Gown Designer, Odette Myrtil; Gown Executor, Athena; Women's Wardrobe, Greta Isgrigg; Furrier, A. Teitelbaum; Makeup, Jack Byron; Hair Stylist, Ann Locker; Sound Mixer, James Gaither; Original Music, Sol Kaplan; Musical Director, Emil Newman; Dialogue Director, Jack Herzberg; Technical Advisors, Lt. William Burns, L.A.P.D., and Edward Block

Location Filming: Gilmore Stadium, Hollywood, Los Angeles, and Palm Springs, California and Boulder Dam, Arizona–Nevada Border

Running Time: 102 minutes

Story: Telephone repairman Edmond O'Brien is introduced to bookmaker Barry Kelley by his local bookie Sammy White. Interested in making more money, O'Brien begins working for Kelly and quickly updates Kelley's communication system of reporting race results. O'Brien pressures Kelley to make him a partner. When Kelley is killed by a small time bookie, O'Brien takes charge. The operation now becomes so profitable that it is noticed by the Eastern Syndicate headed by Otto Kruger. Kruger thinks it's time to expand to the West Coast and sends his right hand man Don Porter to talk with O'Brien. O'Brien becomes interested in the arrangement when he meets Porter's wife, Joanne Dru. O'Brien is to have a 50–50 split. Dru, who is not in love with Porter, gets romantically attached to O'Brien. Things are fine with O'Brien until he discovers the split is 70–30 and he's on the short end. Porter begins to take exception to O'Brien's interest in Dru and pushes her downstairs with her injuries requiring a hospital stay. Through an exclusive clothier, Robert Osterloh, O'Brien arranges a hit on Porter and then steps into Porter's place in the organization. Kruger vows to find the man behind Porter's death. Osterloh gets greedy and blackmails O'Brien. O'Brien pays off but when he realizes this is only the first payment, murders Osterloh. Now O'Brien knows it's time to drop out of sight but wants to collect money he believes the organization owes him. With White and Dru, O'Brien sets up a sting in which he knows the winner of a race before the results are revealed to the Las Vegas bookies. Dru and White clean up. Dru is able to get all her winnings in cash while White is forced to take a check. The police find evidence to arrest O'Brien for murder and Lt. Howard St. John goes after him. Kruger gets a tip that O'Brien engineered the sting and that White has been seen in town. O'Brien sends White to cash the check but White is picked up by Kruger's strong arm boys. Before White meets his fate, he tells Kruger where to find O'Brien. Kruger decides to pass this information on to St. John. When White fails to return, O'Brien and Dru start into town to look for him. On the way, they pass St. John and other policeman going the opposite direction. The chase is on. O'Brien's hopes of getting into Arizona are dashed when a road block is set up at Boulder Dam. O'Brien and Dru join the tourists at the dam in hopes of entering Arizona on foot. St. John spots the two and the chase continues inside the dam. The pace is too great for Dru and police take her into custody. Emerging into the sunlight, O'Brien sees Dru in custody and begins exchanging shots with the police. Finally police bullets end O'Brien's life.

Notes and Commentary: The film's working title was *Blood Money*. Producer Frank Seltzer testified before the Senate Crime Investigating Committee that he was pressured by Las Vegas gamblers to stop filming at Boulder Dam, Lake Mead, Palm Springs, Las Vegas and at a prominent Los Angeles restaurant. The gamblers did not like the film's presentation of crooked racing wire operations that included "past posting" to cheat bookies. "Past posting" means to place a wager on a race in which the outcome is known. Seltzer said $77,000 was spent to create stage reproductions of actual filming locations. To get the film completed, Seltzer had five members of the Los Angeles police gangster squad assigned as protection. The Las Vegas Chamber of Commerce said the charges were false and wanted revisions in the script to eliminate "falsehoods and fantasy." Seltzer was only concerned that measures would be taken to destroy the film.

Congress authorized the Boulder Dam project. The dam was then named the Hoover Dam after the sitting president, Herbert Hoover. When Franklin D. Roosevelt became president, he found that he could not change the name. His Interior Secretary Harold Ickes proclaimed that the dam would be known as Boulder Dam in any and all references. In 1947, Congress passed a resolution restoring the name Hoover Dam. The motion picture's script and highway signage indicated Boulder Dam.

Barry Kelley's name was spelled correctly in the print ads but misspelled Kelly in the opening credits.

Reviews: "Fast moving melodrama about gambling." *Variety*, 7/19/50

"Joseph H. Newman's direction kept the proceedings fast and snappy." *The Columbia Story*, Hirschhorn

Summation: This is a very good crime noir. O'Brien's well-done and believable performance propelling the story to the tragic conclusion. There is a fine supporting cast headed by Otto Kruger as the suave syndicate head, Sammy White as O'Brien's close friend and the beautiful Joanne Dru as the woman O'Brien must possess. Joseph M. Newman's direction never wavers and moves the story briskly.

FIRST THE SHADOW ON THE WINDOW... THEN THE TERROR THROUGH THE DOOR!

The Shadow on the Window

(March 1957)

Cast: Tony Atlas, Phil Carey; Linda Atlas, Betty Garrett; Jess Reber, John Barrymore, Jr.; Gil Ramsey, Corey Allen; Joey Gomez, Gerald Sarracini; Petey Atlas, Jerry Mathers; Sgt. Paul Denke, Sam Gilman; Captain McQuade, Rusty Lane; Dr. Hodges, Ainslie Pryor; Bigelow, Paul Picerni; Stuart, William Leslie; Molly, Doreen Woodbury; Girl, Ellie Kent; Uncredited: Ben Canfield, Watson Downs; Conway (Truck Driver), Nesdon Booth; Jim Warren, Jack Lomas; Felipe, Don Carlos; Dr. Turnesa, Michael Garrett; Postman, Norman Leavitt; Bus Driver, Ralph Montgomery; Dispatcher, Jim Hayward; Bessie Warren, Eve McVeagh; Bartender, Paul Bryar; Mrs. Bergen, Nora Marlowe; Myra, Angela Stevens; Myra's

Husband, Mort Mills; Lounger, Joe Turkel; Polikoff, Mel Welles; Gil's Father, Henry Corden; Policemen, Bill Erwin and Joe Quinn; Desk Sergeants, Curtis Cooksey and Russ Whiteman; Miller, Dave Barry; Proprietor, George Cisar; Sgt. Nordli, Carl Milletaire; Bergen, Julian Upton; Unshaven Man, Billy Nelson

CREDITS: Director, William Asher; Assistant Director; Irving Moore; Producer, Jonie Taps; Screenwriters, Leo Townsend and David P. Harmon; Editor, William A. Lyon; Art Director, Robert Peterson; Set Decorators, William Kiernan and Robert Priestley; Cinematographer, Kit Carson; Sound, Lambert Day; Original Music, George Duning; Musical Conductor, Morris Stoloff; Orchestrator, Arthur Morton

FILMING LOCATIONS: Downtown Los Angeles and Puente, California

PRODUCTION DATES: July 9–August 1, 1956

SOURCE: story "Missing Witness" by John and Ward Hawkins (*Cosmopolitan*, June 1954)

RUNNING TIME: 73 minutes

STORY: Child Jerry Mathers sees hoodlums John Barrymore, Jr., Corey Allen and Gerald Sarracini attack his mother Betty Garrett and farmer Watson Downs in a robbery attempt. Garrett is rendered unconscious and Downs is murdered. Mathers goes into shock and wanders aimlessly away, unseen by the attackers. Mathers is finally taken to a police precinct where he's recognized as Detective Sergeant Phil Carey's son by Sergeant Sam Gilman. Carey and Garrett have separated. Mathers is unable to comprehend or answer questions. At the crime scene, Barrymore and Allen want to kill Garrett but Sarracini refuses to allow it. Carey and Gilman attempt to retrace Mathers' path in order to find Garrett. Allen suggests that he borrow his father's car and they can all drive to the border. In taking the car keys, Allen also finds a gun. Police work leads Carey and Gilman to Allen's address. A running gunfight ensues and Allen is killed. Carey is able to pinpoint the area where the crime was committed. Carey takes Mathers to the area and there is a flicker of recognition. Barrymore is jumpy because Allen hasn't returned. He finds a gun and takes charge. Barrymore is about to shoot Garrett when Sarracini jumps him. In the struggle, the gun goes off and Sarracini is killed. Police surround the house but are noticed by Barrymore. Carey and Gilman break into the house. Barrymore tells them to back off or he will shoot Garrett. A shot by a policeman spooks Barrymore and he tries to escape. Finally cornered, he gives up. Garrett learns that Mathers is outside and runs to him. Seeing his mother, Mathers is finally able to speak. Carey joins them and it looks like the family will be reunited.

NOTES AND COMMENTARY: The working title was *The Missing Witness*. In John and Ward Hawkins' story, Tony and Linda are not married but they are in the screenplay. Also, the screenplay had Petey help locate the farmhouse. In the story, Tony gets the vital lead to find Linda from a local banker. Blake Edwards was originally slated to direct the film.

REVIEWS: "A manhunt cued by a small, shock-muted boy gives a good thriller pace to this melodrama." *Variety*, 2/27/57

SUMMATION: A taut little crime noir directed briskly by William Asher. Betty Garrett displays excellent acting range as she worries about her missing child as she tries to keep from being killed. Jerry Mathers, wordless, is able to display proper emotion in his state of shock.

HE KNEW TOO MUCH TO TALK!

Shadowed

(September 1946)

CAST: Carol Johnson, Anita Louise; Fred Johnson, Lloyd Corrigan; Detective Lt. Braden, Michael Duane; Mark Bellaman, Robert Scott; Edna Montague, Doris Houck; Ginny Johnson, Helen Koford [Terry Moore]; Tony Montague, Wilton Graff; Lester Binkey, Eric Roberts; Lefty, Paul E. Burns; Uncredited: Eddie, Jack Overman; Waitress, Wanda Perry; Tillie, Sarah Edwards; Policeman at Golf Course, Pat Flaherty; Caretaker at Golf Course, Ernie Adams; Ed (Patrolman), Ralph Dunn; Inspector Monck, Jack Lee; Bunker (Henchman), Fred Graff; Sellers, Jack Davis; Billie Benson, Virginia Cruzon (newspaper photo only)

Shadowed **(1946).**

CREDITS: Director, John Sturges; Producer, John Haggott; Story, Julian Harmon; Screenwriter, Brenda Weisberg; Editor, James Sweeney; Art Director, Hans Radon; Set Decorator, Bill Calvert; Cinematographer, Henry Freulich; Musical Director, Mischa Bakaleinikoff

PRODUCTION DATES: June 18–July 3, 1946

RUNNING TIME: 64 minutes

STORY: Small businessman Lloyd Corrigan's motto is "Good Fences Make Good Neighbors." An avid golfer, he decides to play a round by himself. He makes a hole-in-one and memorializes the ball with his initials and date. Believing this is his lucky ball, Corrigan uses it on the next hole and drives it into the woods. In searching for the ball, he discovers the body of a murdered woman and finds a packet containing counterfeiting plates. Hearing the murderers Wilton Graff and Doris Houck, Corrigan hides. Graff finds Corrigan's golf ball and, believing the owner to be hiding nearby, tells him that he will find him. Corrigan is afraid to go to the police, fearing harm will come to his daughters Anita Louise and Helen Kofort. At the golf course, Moore finds an elk's tooth that belongs to Corrigan and begins to think her father might be a murderer. The killers begin a campaign of terror and intimidation to prevent Corrigan from going to the police. Gang member Paul E. Burns sees Corrigan attempt to mail the packet to the police but is able to stop him. Louise finds the packet in Corrigan's desk and puts the plates in a city trash container. Police believe Corrigan has important information. Corrigan, not knowing what he should do, hides in his office. Graff kidnaps Kofort. Burns and Graff locate Corrigan and demand the plates. When Corrigan tells them he doesn't have them, they begin to beat him. Finally they offer to exchange Kofort for the plates and Corrigan agrees. Burns and Houck bring Kofort to the office. Corrigan wants Kofort to be taken to a place of safety before turning over the plates. Graff has had enough and plans to shoot Corrigan. Houck, who doesn't want to be further involved in murder, starts for the window to yell for help. Graff guns Houck down. Seeing his opportunity, Corrigan hits Graff with a heavy garden tool. Burns quickly surrenders.

Corrigan is now a local hero with a new motto, "No man liveth to himself alone."

NOTES AND COMMENTARY: The working title for the film was *The Gloved Hand*. Initially Leslie Brooks was slated to play the part of Carol Johnson.

Columbia received special permission from the Treasury Department to photograph both genuine and counterfeit currency to publicize and exploit this film. The practice was usually prohibited. In conjunction with the screening of *Shadowed*, the Secret Service demonstrated in theater lobbies how counterfeit money could be detected.

REVIEWS: "An uninspired programmer." *Motion Picture Guide*, Nash and Ross

"A listless murder melodrama. Producer John Haggott's programmer had little going for it and audiences left the cinema under-nourished." *The Columbia Story*, Hirschhorn

SUMMATION: This is a superior little "B" crime noir. Lloyd Corrigan, in a rare lead role, gives an excellent performance, displaying a range of emotions from showing a gentle side to showing fright from intimidation to heroics in protecting his daughter Kofort. Kofort also registers strongly. John Sturges' fine direction moves the story briskly. Cinematographer Henry Freulich innovative use of shadows and darkness intensify Corrigan's feeling of terror and helplessness.

SOMETIMES SHE GETS BURNED
MOSTLY SHE GETS WHAT SHE WANTS!

She Played with Fire

(September 1958)

A Frank Launder–Sidney Gilliat Production

ALTERNATE TITLE: Fortune Is a Woman

CAST: Oliver Branwell, Jack Hawkins; Sarah Moreton, Arlene Dahl; Tracey Moreton, Dennis Price; Mrs. Moreton, Violet Farebrother; Clive Fisher, Ian Hunter; Old Abercrombie, Malcolm Keen; Michael Abercrombie, Geoffrey Keen; Fred Conner, Patrick Holt; Berkeley Reckitt, John Robinson; Sgt. Barnes, Michael Goodliffe; Detective Constable Watson, Martin Lane; Mr. Jerome, Bernard Miles; Charles Highbury, Christopher Lee; Vere Litchen, Greta Gynt; Willis Croft, John Phillips; Ambrosine, Patricia Marmont

CREDITS: Director, Sidney Gilliat; Assistant Director, Douglas Hermes; Associate Producer, Leslie Gilliat; Adaptor, Val Valentine; Screenwriters, Sidney Gilliat and Frank Launder; Editor, Geoffrey Foot; Art Director, Wilfred Shingleton; Assistant Art Director, Frank Willson; Cinematographer, Gerald Gibbs; Camera Operator, Alan Hume; Dress Designer, Anthony Mendleson; Makeup, Colin Garde; Hair Dresser, Betty Sheriff; Sound, John Aldred and Red Law; Sound Supervisor, John Cox; Original Music, William Alwyn; Musical Director, Muir Mathieson; Orchestra, The Royal Philharmonic; Production Manager, Roy Parkinson; Dubbing Editor, Chris Greenham; Casting, Paul Sheridan; Continuity, Phyllis Crocker; Special Effects, Wally Veevers and George Samuels

LOCATION FILMING: Shepperton Studios, Surry, England, and London, England

PRODUCTION DATES: September 6–November 20, 1956

SOURCE: novel *Fortune Is a Woman* by Winston Grahame

RUNNING TIME: 95 minutes

STORY: Insurance investigator Jack Hawkins is assigned to assess damages from a fire at Lowis Manor. Living at the manor are Dennis Price, his mother Violet Farebrother and his wife Arlene Dahl. Hawkins and Dahl had been romantically involved five years previously. The damage turns out to be minor except to one valuable painting. When Price has an asthma attack, Hawkins is asked to take Dahl to a play. Their romance is rekindled. When investigating another claim, Hawkins sees a painting that was supposed to be destroyed in the Lowis Manor fire. Hawkins believes Price is involved in insurance fraud and that the paintings hanging in Lowis Hall are fakes. Knowing the manor is supposed to be deserted while undergoing renovations, Hawkins enters through an unlocked window and finds Price's dead body. Suddenly he hears breathing but cannot see anyone. Upon further investigation,

Hawkins finds a fire in the basement. Unable to put out the fire, he calls for help, using Price's name. Hawkins leaves before help arrives. In the insurance settlement, Dahl receives £30,000. Hawkins, who withheld evidence because of his love for Dahl, believes she was Price's accomplice. Hawkins finds evidence that Dahl is innocent and tells her of Price's plot. Dahl plans to return her inheritance to the insurance company. Hawkins and Dahl marry and are unable to return the money before they embark on their honeymoon to France. After they return to England, blackmailer Bernard Miles demands £15,000 for his unnamed client. Dahl and Hawkins are unable to return the money because they are under suspicion of insurance fraud. Hawkins and Dahl follow Miles in order to find the person behind the blackmail plot. The blackmailer is Ian Hunter, an old family friend. Hawkins tells Hunter that they plan to talk to authorities. Hawkins tells all to his employers. Dahl goes back to Lowis Manor and Hawkins follows. He finds Dahl with Farebrother. Farebrother confesses that she was in the Manor on the night of Price's death. She knew Price planned to set fire to the manor and tried to stop him. The fire had already started. Price and Farebrother struggled. Price crashed through a second floor railing to his death. Dahl convinces Farebrother to tell the story to the authorities. Hawkins thinks he should resign but is persuaded to stay on.

Notes and Commentary: The basic plot of Winston Grahame's novel *Fortune Is a Woman* is followed. Some characters are consolidated to move the story quicker. A major difference is there was no previous romance between Oliver Branwell and Sarah Moreton. They had met briefly years earlier when he changed a flat tire for her and she, in turn, gave him a ride to his destination. The ending was altered. Mrs. Moreton is being driven to confess to the authorities when she suddenly leaps from the speeding car to her death. Branwell then tells the whole story, including his failure to report the fraud. Because of a compassionate plea from Dent, a character only mentioned briefly in the film, Branwell is allowed to keep his job.

The working title for this film was *Fortune Is a Woman*. This title was used in the Great Britain release.

Reviews: "The suspense is occasionally bogged down by intricate plot development." *Variety*, 3/20/57 (Note: This film was reviewed by *Variety* as *Fortune Is a Woman*.)

Summation: Director Sidney Gilliat is able to develop some suspenseful moments aided by the fine camerawork of Gerald Gibbs. Some very good dream sequences enhance the production. There is some good acting by Jack Hawkins and Arlene Dahl, the latter playing a character who is thought to be a femme fatale but turns out to be a good woman.

THEIR MARRIAGE MADE THEM FUGITIVES...

Shockproof

(January 1949)

Cast: Griff Marat, Cornel Wilde; Jenny Marsh, Patricia Knight; Harry Wesson, John Baragrey; Mrs. Marat, Esther Minciotti; Sam Brooks, Howard St. John; Frederick Bauer, Russell Collins; Tommy Marat, Charles Bates; Uncredited: Barry, Gilbert Barnett; Monte, Frank Jaquet; Logan, Frank Ferguson; Dr. Daniels, Ann Shoemaker; Joe Wilson, King Donovan; Florrie Kobiski, Claire Carleton; Joe Kobiski, Al Eben; Clerks, Fred F. Sears and Jimmy Lloyd; Switchboard Operator, Isabel Withers; Policemen, Chuck Hamilton and Brian O'Hara; Policeman in Park, James Flavin; Mrs. Terrence, Virginia Farmer; Race Caller, Earle Hodgins; Proprietor, Lester Sharpe; Manager, Charles Marsh; Border Patrolman, George J. Lewis; Man in Car, Paul Bryar; Emmy, Shirley Adams; Girl, Yolanda Lacca; Stella, Argentina Brunetti; Hamburger Man, Charles Jordan; Teenage Boy, Buddy Swan; Boy at Wedding, Norman Oldstead; Sam Green (Pawnbroker), John Butler; Foreman, Crane Whitley; Drunk, Robert R. Stephenson; "Kid" (Knife Wielder), Richard Benedict; Police Inspector, Arthur Space; Police Lieutenant, Cliff Clark; Nurse, Nita Mathews; Newspaper Buyer, Eddie Foster

Credits: Director, Douglas Sirk; Assistant Director, Earl Bellamy; Associate Producer, Earl McEvoy; Screenwriters, Helen Deutsch and Samuel Fuller; Editor, Gene Havlick; Art Director,

Carl Anderson; Set Decorator, Louis Diage; Cinematographer, Charles Lawton, Jr.; Gowns, Jean Louis; Makeup, Clay Campbell; Hair Stylist, Helen Hunt; Sound, Lodge Cunningham; Musical Score, George Duning; Musical Director, M.W. Stoloff

LOCATION FILMING: Los Angeles, California (Bradbury Building, 304 South Broadway and Bunker Hill)

PRODUCTION DATES: June 28–August 9, 1948

RUNNING TIME: 79 minutes

STORY: After spending five years in jail for murder, Patricia Knight is paroled. She had gone to prison so her lover John Baragrey could go free. Knight reports to parole officer Cornel Wilde, who almost immediately begins to fall under her spell. Wilde admonishes Knight and tells her that she cannot be in the company of Baragrey. Baragrey has plans for Knight and is delighted to find that Wilde has fallen for her. He wants Knight to entice Wilde into a marriage that they will have to keep secret for at least two years. Baragrey will then have the hold on Wilde that he needs. As Wilde falls for Knight, she also falls for him. The two marry but Knight does not tell Baragrey. Baragrey finds that the couple got married in Las Vegas and threatens to destroy Wilde's career. As Baragrey begins to read an old love letter from Knight to Wilde, Knight shoots and seriously wounds him. Wilde is first on the scene and reads the note, thinking the worst. Wilde takes Knight into custody. When Knight persuades Wilde that she shot Baragrey to save his career, Wilde decides to take her to Mexico where they can start a new life together. Fate takes a hand and they are unable to leave the country. Wilde gets a job at an oil well. When their pictures appear in an article in the local paper, they realize they are living on borrowed time and decide to give themselves up. The police bring Knight and Wilde to Baragrey's hospital bed. Baragrey admits to the police that the shooting was accidental. Wilde tells police that Knight did not violate her parole since she was continuously in his custody. The two are free to go.

NOTES AND COMMENTARY: The working title for the film was *The Lovers*.

The original screenplay ended with Wilde shooting it out with police to prevent Knight's arrest. Screenwriter Helen Deutsch then re-wrote the ending to have Wilde and Knight decide to surrender themselves to the police. Another director replaced Douglas Sirk to film the unbelievable ending. The movie that Knight, Wilde and Charles Bates go to see is *Last Days of Boot Hill* (Columbia, 1947), a Durango Kid western.

REVIEWS: "While never credible, story does point up the standard melodramatics and good playing to keep it all interesting." *Variety*, 1/26/49

"Up until the contrived ending forced on the director, this is a taut, well-made example of film noir." *Motion Picture Guide*, Nash and Ross

SUMMATION: For the first 78 minutes, this is a good film noir. Unfortunately a totally unbelievable ending was tacked on to this production. Perhaps Wilde falls for femme fatale Knight a little too easily but the mood of the story more than made up for it. This is Knight's film and she plays it to the hilt, first using her charms to bait Wilde before actually falling in love with him. Her performance is flawless every step of the way. John Baragrey offers good support. Douglas Sirk's direction captures the futility of lovers Knight and Wilde trying to escape their true destiny. It is reported that Sirk had no part in the so-called happy ending and has vilified it. To think the totally despicable Baragrey would have a change of heart and swear that the nearly mortal gunshot wound was an accident is beyond belief. Then for the police to allow Knight and Wilde to waltz off arm in arm without charging them for car theft and resisting arrest (for starters) additionally tests the audience's credulity. Wilde tells the police that Knight did not violate parole by leaving the area since she was with him. This new ending derailed a perfectly good noir.

SHOCKING ... what this woman dared for love!

The Sign of the Ram

(March 1948)

An Irving Cummings Production

CAST: Leah St. Aubyn, Miss Susan Peters; Mallory St. Aubyn, Alexander Knox; Sherida Binyon, Phyllis Thaxter; Christine St. Aubyn, Peggy Ann Garner; Dr. Simon Crowdy, Ron Randell; Clara Brastock, Dame May Whitty; Jane St. Aubyn, Allene Roberts; Logan St. Aubyn, Ross

Ford; Catherine Woolton, Diana Douglas; Uncredited: Station Master, Gerald Rogers; Perowen, Paul Scardon; Emily, Margaret Tracy; Vicar Woolton, Gerald Hamer; Mrs. Woolton, Doris Lloyd

Credits: Director, John Sturges; Assistant Director, James Nicholson; Producer, Irving Cummings, Jr.; Screenwriter, Charles Bennett; Editor, Aaron Stell; Art Directors, Stephen Goosson and Sturges Carne; Set Decorators, Wilbur Menefee and Frank Tuttle; Cinematographer, Burnett Guffey; Gowns, Jean Louis; Makeup, Clay Campbell; Makeup, Helen Hunt; Sound, Jack Goodrich; Original Music, Hans J. Salter; Musical Director, M.W. Stoloff

Song: "I'll Never Say I Love You"—sung by Susan Peters (dubbed by Dorothy Ellers)

Production Dates: July 14–August 23, 1947

Source: novel *The Sign of the Ram* by Margaret Ferguson

Running Time: 84 minutes

Story: Phyllis Thaxter arrives in Cornwall to fill the position of secretary-companion to wheelchair-bound Susan Peters. Other members of the household are Peters' husband, Alexander Knox, and her three children, Allene Roberts, Ross Ford and Peggy Ann Garner. Peters' doctor, Ron Randell, announces his intention to marry Roberts. Sensing Peters' displeasure, Randell calls her family "a little band of slaves." Peters will approve the marriage if Randell will live in her mansion, which Randell refuses to do. Peters then poisons Roberts' mind against Randell and that breaks up the relationship. Ford's sweetheart Diana Douglas, an aspiring artist, returns to Cornwall and the two plan to marry. Douglas, a foundling, is told by Peters that her birth father was insane and she could only enter into a childless marriage. The distraught Douglas attempts suicide only to be saved by Knox. Ford traveled to London to investigate Douglas' background and finds that Peters' claim was false. Ford tells Knox that he will never go back to Peters' house. Roberts now knows Peters' lies broke up her relationship with Randell and they plan to marry. Garner believes that Thaxter's coming to work for Peters caused the family to break up and she poisons Thaxter. The housekeeper, Margaret Tracy, discovers Thaxter in time to prevent her death. Knox confronts Peters and in the exchange Peters accuses the loyal Knox of being in love with Thaxter. This is hurtful to Knox since his only love is Peters. Peters, now believing that she will be left in the house without any family, decides her only way out is suicide and she hurls herself over a cliff to the water and rocks below. This fulfills the prophecy of the sign of the ram to die a violent death.

Notes and Commentary: Screenwriter Charles Bennett followed the basic thrust of Margaret Ferguson's novel but made changes that moved the story into the gothic noir realm. After Bennett initially shows the St. Aubyn home as a place of happiness and contentment, it becomes apparent this is true only if Leah St. Aubyn controls her husband and children. Bennett wisely eliminates some of Ferguson's characters. In the novel, there is a fourth child, Andrew, who is only present in a few pages and does nothing to further the narrative. Busybody Mabel (Clara in the film) Brastock has a constant companion, Cicely Burnham, who also adds nothing to the story. In the novel, Mallory St. Aubyn and Sherida Binyon fall in love but only after Leah's death is there hope a romance can be kindled. The screenplay has Leah accuse Mallory of being in love with Sherida, which angers him to the point of not wanting to be near her because there is no truth to the accusation. Leah does interfere with proposed nuptials between her stepson Logan and Catherine Maitland (Woolton in the film) and with her physician Simon Crowdy and stepdaughter Jane. In both, Logan leaves the family home to marry Catherine, after Catherine's suicide attempt. In the novel, the romance between Crowdy and Jane is broken up by Leah because Crowdy instilled a will to live in Leah after being crippled with a romantic relationship between them. Leah reminds Crowdy of that when he tells her that he plans to marry Jane. After Leah's death, Crowdy grips Jane's hand, suggesting the possibility of their renewing their romance. The film ends on a tragic noir note with an empty wheelchair at the cliff's edge and the fact that Leah had now hurled herself into the rocks and water below. The author softens the ending by having the reader possibly think that with Leah's death, the people involved can now live a normal life. The character name Perowen is given to the station master in the book and the butler in the film.

Susan Peters was a brilliant actress who received a 1942 Academy Award nomination for Best Actress in a Supporting Role for her performance in MGM's *Random Harvest*. In January 1945 she was on a duck-hunting trip in the Cuyamaca Mountains near San Diego. When she reached down for her rifle, it accidentally discharged, sending a bullet into her spine. The incident left Peters paralyzed from the waist down. Peters had no interest in returning to the screen until Charles Bickford brought Margaret Ferguson's *The Sign of the Ram* to her attention. Unfortunately, the film was not successful with either the critics or the moviegoing public, and it would be her farewell screen appearance. Peters played a wheelchair-bound detective in the NBC television series *Miss Susan* aka *Martinsville U.S.A.* (1951) and toured in two plays, *The Glass Menagerie* and *The Barretts of Wimpole Street*, before her untimely death on October 23, 1952.

Reviews: "[A] flat and fatuous fable about the mischievous deeds of a selfish dame. Plainly the story is claptrap. The direction of John Sturges is such that the illogic and the pomposity are only magnified." *The New York Times*, 3/4/48

"Despite some good performances, *The Sign of the Ram* suffers from weak scripting and lackluster direction and never really gets off the ground." *Motion Picture Guide*, Nash and Ross

Summation: This is an engrossing, absorbing, very good gothic noir highlighted with fine acting, especially by Susan Peters as a woman who feels she has to have complete control over her family. Director John Sturges builds the tempo of the story to a thundering crescendo.

BEYOND CASABLANCA—in Damascus ... Destiny in a low-cut gown lies in wait for BOGART!

Sirocco

(June 1951)

A Santana Production

Cast: Harry Smith, Humphrey Bogart; Violette, Marta Toren; Colonel Feroud, Lee J. Cobb; General LaSalle, Everett Sloane; Major Jean Leon, Gerald Mohr; Balukjiaan, Zero Mostel; Nasir Aboud, Nick Dennis; Emir Hassan, Onslow Stevens; Flophouse Proprietor, Ludwig Donath; Achmed, David Bond; Uncredited: Arthur, Vincent Renno; Omar, Martin Wilkins; Major Robbinet, Peter Ortiz; Colonel Corville, Edward Colmans; Sergeants, Al Eben and Sam Scar; Barber, Peter Brocco; Hamal, Jay Norvello; Rifat, Leonard Penn; Dancer, Carmen D'Antonio; Bartender, Sammy Slack; Hungarian, John Bleifer; Greek, Peter Mamakos; Egyptian, Louis Merrill; Lieutenant Collet, Harry Guardino; Master Sergeant, Harry Cording; Flower Vendor, Julian Rivero; Hysterical Woman, Marta Mitrovich; Arab Singer, Abdullah Abbas; Cart Drivers, George Khoury and Joe Sawaya; Feisal, Jeff Corey; Bus Driver, Myron Marks; Wealthy Syrian, Dan Seymour; Syrian, Eddie Le Baron; Orderly, Ric Roman; Lieutenant, Paul Fierro; Officer, Paul Marion; Syrian Boy, Neyle Morrow; Guard, Tristram Coffin; Soldier, Felipe Turich

Credits: Director, Curtis Bernhardt; Assistant Director, Earl Bellamy; Producer, Robert Lord; Associate Producer, Henry S. Kesler; Screenwriters, A.I. Bezzerides and Hans Jacoby; Editor, Viola Lawrence; Art Director, Robert Peterson; Set Decorator, Robert Priestley; Cinematography, Burnett Guffey; Makeup, Clay Campbell; Hair Stylist, Helen Hunt; Sound, Lodge Cunningham; Original Music, George Antheil; Musical Director, Morris Stoloff

Production Dates: early November–late December 1950

Source: novel *Coup de Grace* by Joseph Kessel

Running Time: 96 minutes

Story: In 1925, France undertakes to rule Syria. To stop Arab resistance, General Everett Sloane orders five Syrian hostages to be executed for every French soldier killed. Colonel Lee J. Cobb wants to make a truce with emir Onslow Stevens. Sloane finally agrees with Cobb. Lieutenant Harry Guardino is sent to meet with the Arabs. In the guise of being a merchant of food goods, Humphrey Bogart is also running munitions to the Arabs. Bogart sees Marta Toren, Cobb's mistress, and decides to win her favor. Of all the merchants, Cobb accuses Zero Mostel of supplying arms to the Syrians. Seeing that Bogart is interested in Toren, Cobb forbids her to talk to him. Incensed, Toren tells Cobb she wants to leave him. Cobb threatens to kill her. Mostel is able to finger Bogart as the gun runner. When Bogart plans to go to Cairo, Toren begs him to take her with him. Before they can leave Damascus, French soldiers arrive. Bogart escapes but Toren is captured. The Syrians want no part of fugitive Bogart. Cobb takes charge of Toren and sends her back to her quarters. Guardino is found dead and Sloane wants to carry the fight to the Syrians. An informer tells Cobb where Bogart can be captured. Cobb wants Bogart to arrange a meeting between himself and Stevens. In return, Bogart will receive a pass to leave Damascus. Cobb also arranges a pass for Toren. Bogart and Toren plan to travel to Cairo together. Bogart takes Cobb to meet Stevens. Bogart is told never to come to the Syrian hideout again. Before Bogart is handed his pass, Sloane wants to know Cobb's whereabouts. At first, Bogart refuses to help but then agrees to take Major Gerald Mohr to ransom Cobb. Bogart believes £10,000 will deliver Cobb. Cobb tells Stevens he wants a 24-hour ceasefire so both sides can confer. Bogart delivers the money. Cobb and Mohr are allowed to leave. Bogart is detained and is accused of being in the employ of the French. He is finally allowed to leave, only to be killed. With Bogart's death, Cobb and Mohr notice the absence of gunfire signaling the possibility of a truce.

Notes and Commentary: Joseph Kessel's 1931 novel *Coup de Grace* was translated into English by Katherine Woods. It was subsequently published by Random House as *Sirocco*.

Alas, Kessel's novel never actually made it to the screen. Kessel told of a love triangle: an Arab, Hippolyte, who is a master sergeant in the French Army; French Colonel Feroud, secretly the brilliant Arab fighter Mehemet Pasha; and Violette, a 15-year-old who dances naked at a local restaurant. Feroud is dangerously infatuated with Violette, who becomes Hippolyte's mistress. Hippolyte is unable to accept the idea of Violette with Feroud and murders her. Feroud is grateful the spell Violette held over him is broken. Feroud decides to take Hippolyte with him to the mountain country and continue the fight. For the screen, Violette was transformed into a woman of the world (obviously the screen wasn't ready for a love affair between a mature man and a 15-year-old girl). Restaurant owner Arthur is the only other character with a role in both the novel and the film. The character Harry Smith and the gunrunning plot was an invention of the screenwriters.

At one point during shooting, producer Robert Lord thought about replacing director Curtis Bernhardt. Perhaps Lord thought Bernhardt's forte was not as an action director. Another possible reason for Lord's displeasure was Bernhardt's annoyance that the film was shot on the Columbia back lot and not on location in Damascus. Screenwriter A.I. Bezzerides intervened and Bernhardt finished the picture.

A story surfaced that may have caused the producers some consternation. At an early screening, Arab-American audience members began to go into hysterics in a scene in which Bogart is walking through a crowded bazaar and a voice shouts, "Ya hallah deen bayak!" American audiences joined in the laughter when the line was translated as "Goddamn your father."

Reviews: "Near East atmosphere is excellently created but yarn plays off too evenly, and cryptically, to excite more than fair entertainment." *Variety*, 6/6/51

"There is so little substance in this morally unrelenting tale of the career of a munitions smuggler that one looks for some marginal compensation in the way of color and atmosphere, at least. And even in those departments, the film is disappointingly short." *New York Times*, 6/14/51

"Even though many of the same elements as seen in *Casablanca* are here, it just doesn't jell, mainly because the ending is so hopeless and the love story between Bogart and Toren seems contrived." *Motion Picture Guide*, Nash and Ross

Summation: This noir offers pretty good entertainment but it's certainly not up to the entertainment standard set by *Casablanca* (Warner Bros., 1942). Bogart gives his usual good performance; there's also good acting by Lee J. Cobb as an idealistic soldier, Marta Toren as the deceptive mistress and Everett Sloane as a no-nonsense officer. Director Bernhardt keeps the story on the move and cinematographer Burnett Guffey's camerawork aids in the suspense department.

...They were all brunettes ... all under 30 ... and they all crossed the path of "THE SNIPER"

The Sniper

(May 1952)
A Stanley Kramer Company Production

Cast: Lt. Frank Kafka, Adolphe Menjou; Eddie Miller, Arthur Franz; Sgt. Joe Ferris, Gerald

Mohr; Jean Darr, Marie Windsor; Insp. Anderson, Frank Faylen; Dr. James G. Kent, Richard Kiley; Landlady, Mabel Paige; May Nelson, Marlo Dwyer; Checker, Geraldine Carr; Uncredited: Pete, Jay Novello; Police Interlocutor, Ralph Peters; Chadwick, Max Palmer; Intern, Sidney Miller; Sam, Herb Latimer; Sandy, Danni Sue Nolan; Mayor, Harry Cheshire; Chief of Police, Cliff Clark; Officer Rivers, Robert Foulk; Policemen, Fred Hartman, Don Michaelian, David McMahon, Verne Martell and Renaldo Viri; Police Lineup Organizer, Rory Mallinson; Policeman at Darr Murder Scene, J. Anthony Hughes; Policeman with Teletypes, Kernan Cripps; Boy, Danny Mummert; Mapes, George Dockstader; Flaherty, Leslie Sketchley; Mr. Liddell, Carl Benton Reid; Peter Eureka, Byron Foulger; TV Announcer, Roy Maypole; Al, Paul Marion; Bartender, Al Hill; Warren Fitzpatrick, Grandon Rhodes; Millie, Karen Sharpe; Mr. Harper, Harlan Warde; Police Photographers, Robert B. Williams and Clark Howat; Nurse, Elizabeth Whitney; Wise, John Brown; Mr. Stonecroft, John Eldredge; Women Talking to Policeman, Betty Shute and Patricia Toun; Desk Nurse, Isabel Withers; Woman Dunked at Concession, Robin Raymond; Detective, Howard Negley; Detective at Lineup, Steve Darrell; Old Man, Willis West; Spectator, Norman Nazarr; Rookie Cop, John Bradley; Bumped Woman's Husband, Nolan Leary; Tony Debiaci, Ralph Smiley; George Tinman, John Pickard; Joey, Joseph Mell; Jailer, Frank Kreig; Suspect, Ralph Volkie; Tom, Victor Sen Yung; Mr. Alpine, Charles Wagenheim; Woman at Darr Murder Scene, Gail Bonney; Man in Pajamas at Darr Murder Scene, Harry Harvey; Ambulance Man, Steve Pendleton; Cleaner, Dudley Dickerson; Man on Cable Car, John Butler; Concessionaire, Mike Lally; Attendant, Barry Brooks; Motorcycle Policeman, Bruce Cameron; Outfielder, Tommy Hawkins; Child, Lucas Farara; Manager, Charles Marsh; Woman on Street, Jean Willes; Mrs. Fitzpatrick, Lilian Bond; Shooting Gallery Concessionaire, George Chesebro; Drunk in Bar, Charles Lane; Man at Carnival Dunking Concessionaire, Frank Sully; Smokestack Painter, Ralph O. Clark; Man Pressing Clothes, Wally Cox; Cop in Darr's Apartment, Chuck Hamilton; Guy with Glasses Pressing Clothes, Ken Terrell

Credits: Director, Edward Dmytryk; Assistant Director, Milton Feldman; Associate Producers and Story, Edna and Edward Anhalt; Screenwriter, Harry Brown; Editor, Aaron Stell; Art Director, Walter Holscher; Set Decorator, James Crowe; Cinematographer, Burnett Guffey; Production Designer, Rudolph Sternad; Production Manager, Clem Beauchamp; Sound, Frank Goodwin; Music Score, George Antheil; Musical Director, Morris Stoloff; Editorial Supervisor, Harry Gerstad

Location Filming: San Francisco, California (Telegraph Hill and Francisco Street) and Long Beach, California

Songs: "Pennies from Heaven" (Johnston and Burke)—played by Marie Windsor and Plaisir D'Amour (Martini)—played by Marie Windsor

Production Dates: September 24–October 20, 1951

Running Time: 88 minutes

Story: After deciding not to shoot a woman coming home from a date, mentally disturbed Arthur Franz, recently released from prison, takes a walk through the city. Franz makes a futile attempt to contact the prison psychiatrist. Realizing he needs help badly, Franz deliberately burns his right hand and then goes to an emergency room. Interne Sidney Miller, knowing the wound is self-inflicted, is about to send Franz for psychiatric help when serious accident victims arrive. Franz is then sent home. Franz, a driver for a dry cleaner, feels mistreated by entertainer Marie Windsor. Franz stalks and shoots Windsor, beginning a series of killings. Franz sends a note to the police asking them to stop him before he kills more. Lt. Adolphe Menjou and Sgt. Gerald Mohr are assigned to the case. From a tip from police psychiatrist Richard Kiley, they begin to look for men who have a history of assaulting women. Franz is on the list. Franz is told by his supervisor Geraldine Carr that he needs to have a clean bandage on his hand when he returns to work. Enraged, Franz kills another woman, leaving his bandage on a tree. Carr, reading about the incident, notifies Menjou. Instead of reporting to work, Franz is planning to shoot another woman when he's spotted by smokestack painter Ralph O. Clark. When Clark shouts a warning, Franz shoots him and retreats to his rooming house. Police arrive and surround the house. Menjou, Mohr and uniformed policemen enter Franz's room. They find Franz sitting on his bed, cradling his rifle, tears streaming down his face.

Notes and Commentary: Producer Stanley Kramer hired Edward Dmytryk a member of the Hollywood Ten, as director. This was Dmytryk's first American assignment after being blacklisted. In the late forties Dmytryk had been persuaded to include communist sentiments in some of his films. He appeared before the House Un-American Activities Committee but refused to cooperate and name names. Dmytryk was cited for contempt of Congress. He fled to England and directed two films before returning to the United States. After serving several months in jail on the contempt charges, Dmytryk finally testified before HUAC and named names and was able to resume his Hollywood career. *The Sniper* brought him in contact with actor Adolphe Menjou. It was feared that the two would not be able to work together because of their political differences. No problems developed. Menjou received criticism for working with Dmytryk. Asked by his fellow reactionaries why he accepted the role, he stated, "Because I'm a whore."

The Production Code tried to shut production down by saying the film violated section 27 paragraph 4 of the code, which said that perversion cannot be the subject of a motion picture. Screenwriter Edward Anhalt faced the board and denied that there was any perversion. The board insisted that the film implied the sniper got an orgasm every time he shot a woman. Anhalt countered that it would only be perversion if he got an orgasm from shooting men. The Production Code office backed down and the film was made.

In interviewing for the role of Eddie Miller, Arthur Franz made such a positive impression on producer Stanley Kramer that he immediately called in Dmytryk. Both agreed that Franz was right for the role.

Dmytryk wanted a different look to the rooftop chase and he wanted clotheslines filled with laundry. He challenged a sketch artist to come up with a novel idea. The artist came up with the conception of the chase through flapping sheets.

Studio president Harry Cohn saw the film in a screening room and said it stank and would never make a nickel. Cohn's prediction proved to be accurate. In later years, the film would become popular as a tautly directed film noir as well as a comment on society's failure to address social concerns.

Reviews: "Extremely well-done suspense melodrama on sex criminals." *Variety*, 3/19/52

"A taut psychological police drama." *Motion Picture Guide*, Nash and Ross

Summation: This noir is a compelling look at a mentally disturbed individual branded a sex criminal because of his assaults against women. This is a terrific movie thanks to Franz's brilliant performance. He displays his mental anguish by facial expressions better than a sea of dialogue. Top-billed Adolphe Menjou, with a neat job of acting, only offers support to Franz. A first-rate noir is delivered thanks to the talents of Franz, cinematographer Burnett Guffey and director Dmytryk, no stranger to the noir world. It took many years for this fine film to receive the appreciation it deserves.

TEEN AGE GIRL ... VS. KILLER-WITH-A-GIMMICK!

The Snorkel

(July 1958)

A Hammer Production

Cast: Paul Decker, Peter Van Eyck; Jean Edwards, Betta St. John; Candy Brown, Mandy Miller; Inspector, Gregoire Aslan; Wilson, William Franklyn; Maria (Maid), Marie Burke; Julio (Gardener), Henri Vidon; John Holmes' dog Flush as Toto; Uncredited: Hotel Clerk, David Ritch; Waiter, Armand Guinie; Station Sergeant, Robert Rietty; Hotel Proprietor, Irene Prador

Credits: Director, Guy Green; Assistant Director, Tom Walls; Producer, Michael Carreras; Associate Producer, Anthony Nelson-Keys; Screenwriters, Peter Myers and Jimmy Sangster; Editor, James Needs; Art Director, John Stoll; Cinematographer, Jack Asher; Camera Operator, Len Harris; Wardrobe, Molly Arbuthnot; Makeup, Phil Leakey; Hair Stylist, Henry Montsash; Sound, Jock May; Re-recorder, Ken Cameron; Original Music, Francis Chagrin; Music Conductor, John Hollingsworth; Production Manager, Don Weeks; Location Manager, Renzo Lucidi; Continuity, Doreen Dearnaley

Location Filming: San Remo, Italy

Production Dates: early September–late October 1957

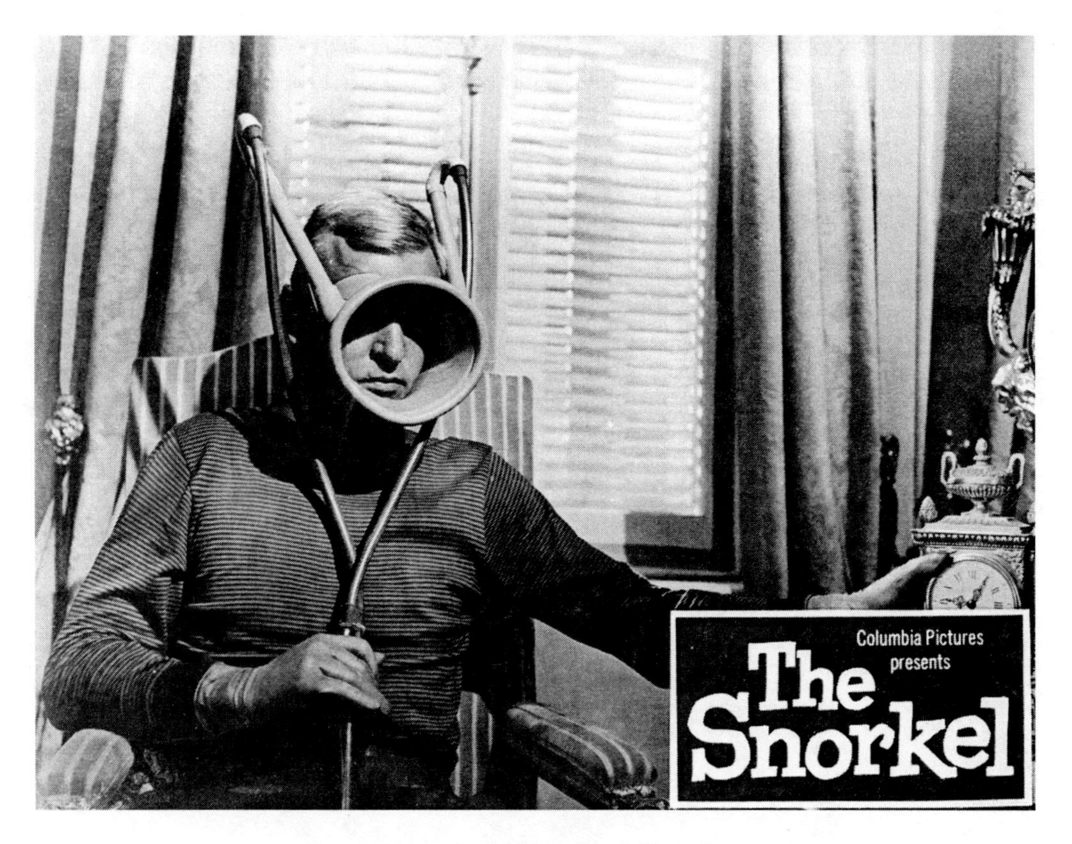

Peter Van Eyck in *The Snorkel* (1958).

Source: story "The Snorkel" by Anthony Dawson

Running Time: 90 minutes

Story: In an Italian villa, Peter Van Eyck murders his wife by asphyxiation in a room locked from the inside. He avoids the effects of the gas by using a snorkel piped to outside air. To avoid detection, Van Eyck can hide in a space under the floor boards. Inspector Gregoire Aslan declares the death to be a suicide but the murdered woman's teenage daughter Mandy Miller believes that somehow Van Eyck murdered her. Miller also believes that Van Eyck murdered her father. Miller, home for holidays, is accompanied by her companion, Betta St. John. Because of the tragedy, Miller, St. John and Van Eyck take rooms at a hotel in town. Miller sees a billboard advertising a man using a snorkel and thinks that's how Van Eyck could have survived in the room. Miller enters Van Eyck's room and finds his passport, which shows he was in a neighboring French village at the time of the death. Miller's dog Flush finds a snorkel in Van Eyck's wardrobe. Van Eyck thinks the dog is too inquisitive and poisons him. Afraid of Miller's tenacity in trying to prove him a murderer, he next attempts to drown her during a beach picnic. Only the timely intervention of St. John stops Van Eyck. Van Eyck tells St. John that it is best that he and Miller stay away from each other and goes to a small hotel just across the Italian-French border. Using his snorkel, Van Eyck swims back to the villa. Pretending that he's a member of Aslan's police department, Van Eyck requests that Miller come to the villa. Miller arrives to find Van Eyck, who tells her he found her mother's suicide note. Miller accepts a glass of milk, unaware that it is drugged. Van Eyck plans to murder her in the same manner as he did her mother. Before the gas can kill her, St. John and British consul William Franklyn arrive, break down the door and rescue Miller. Meanwhile, Van Eyck has retreated to his hiding place under the floor boards. Miller insists Van Eyck tried to murder her and is hiding in the room. Miller swears that if St. John and Franklyn can prove Van Eyck is not in the room, she'll never say anything about him again. The search of the room proves futile. Miller notes they haven't looked for a possible passage behind a heavy cabinet. The cabinet is moved over the trap door to Van Eyck's hiding place. Miller, St. John and Franklyn leave. Van Eyck quickly realizes his plight. Miller comes back to the room for one more glance and hears Van Eyck's pleas to be rescued. Miller ignores Van Eyck and leaves the villa. As Miller is leaving the town, she has a change of heart and tells Aslan to look under the floor in the sitting room.

Notes and Commentary: It's only a movie: Knowledgeable sources state that it would be impossible for Van Eyck's character to receive fresh air from the outside using a snorkel with such long hoses. *The Snorkel* was released on the bottom half of a double feature with *The Camp on Blood Island* (Columbia, 1958).

Reviews: "Not greatly distinguished but nonetheless manages to be more absorbing that the usual low-budget program film. For those who are looking to kill time." *The New York Times*, 9/18/58

"[An] ingenious murder mystery. A clever film that works." *Motion Picture Guide*, Nash and Ross

Summation: This is a quite-good suspense noir featuring fine performances by Peter Van Eyck and Mandy Miller. Van Eyck is the handsome, personable, cold-blooded murderer and Miller is the teenage girl who knows his true nature. The story revolves in an exciting, suspenseful cat-and-mouse game between the two. Miller's dog Flush, is engaging and talented and adds to the story. The ever-lovely Betta St. John is mainly window dressing in this one. Anthony Dawson's story and the screenplay collaboration of Peter Myers and Jimmy Sangster is a winner. Guy Green's direction is on target, focusing on the talents of Van Eyck and Miller.

Most Baffling of Mysteries!

So Dark the Night

(October 1946)

Cast: Henri Cassin, Steven Geray; Nanette Michaud, Micheline Cheirel; Pierre Michaud, Eugene Borden; Mama Michaud, Ann Codee; Dr. Boncourt, Egon Brecher; Widow Bridelle, Helen Freeman; Uncredited: Commissioner Grande, Gregory Gaye; Dr. Manet, Jean Del Val; Peasant Woman, Esther Zeitlin; Bootblack, Cynthia Caylor; Flower Girl, Nanette Bordeaux; Philippe (Chauffeur), Billy Snyder; Leon Achard, Paul Marion; Pere Cortot, Emil Rameau; Georges (Hunchback), Brother Theodore; Jean Duval, Louis Mercier; Newspaper Woman; Adrienne D'Ambricourt; Bank President, Alphonse Martell; Antoine, Frank Arnold; Proprietor, Marcelle Corday; Postmaster, Andre Marsaudon

Credits: Director, Joseph H. Lewis; Producer, Ted Richmond; Story, Aubrey Wisberg; Screenwriters, Martin Berkeley and Dwight Babcock; Editor, Jerome Thoms; Art Director, Carl Anderson; Set Decorator, William Kiernan; Cinematographer, Burnett Guffey; Sound, Frank Goodwin; Musical Score, Hugo Friedhofer; Musical Director, M.W. Stoloff

Location Filming: Rowland V. Lee Ranch, Canoga Park, Los Angeles, California

Production Dates: December 8–20, 1945

Running Time: 71 minutes

Story: Paris' number one detective Steven Geray takes his first vacation in eleven years at the inn of Eugene Borden and Ann Codee in the small village of St. Margo. On meeting Borden and Codee's daughter Micheline Cheirel, Geray falls in love. Cheirel's fiancée, Paul Marion, becomes jealous. Cheirel plays up to both men but decides to marry Geray. Marion breaks into the engagement party and tells Cheirel that he will win her back. When Marion leaves, Cheirel follows him. Both Marion and Cheirel disappear. Cheirel's body is found in the river with evidence that she had been strangled. At Marion's farm, he is found strangled. The only clue is a footprint under Marion's body. Geray takes on the case but is unable to identify the murderer. Geray receives a note that another will die. Codee is found dead, strangled like the others. Geray begins to brood over his inability to solve the case. Widow Helen Freeman takes a shoe from Geray's room and later accuses him of being the killer. Freeman wants Geray to take her to Paris. Believing himself incompetent, Geray returns alone to Paris headquarters where, from the footprint, he describes the possible murderer to

Commissioner Gregory Gaye and police sketch artist Frank Arnold. From the sketch, Geray deduces that he is the murderer. Geray insists on an investigation. Police physician Egon Brechel concludes that Geray might be schizophrenic. Geray overpowers a police guard and returns by train to St. Margo, where his mission is to murder Borden. Codee wanted Cheirel to marry Geray, accumulate money and possessions and then divorce Geray and marry Marion. Borden was opposed to a marriage between Geray and Cheirel. Geray and Borden engage in a violent struggle. Geray gains the upper hand and is about to strike Borden with a fireplace poker when a shot rings out. Gaye's bullet mortally wounds Geray. In Geray's last moments, he breaks the glass windows of the inn before confessing his guilt to Gaye.

Notes and Commentary: There are conflicting stories of the origin of *So Dark the Night*. One source mentions that the film was suggested by a story from the "Whistler" radio program. Another states the source was a *Reader's Digest* story by Aubrey Wisberg. The author reviewed all *Reader's Digest* magazines from January 1939 through June 1946 with no success. The author contacted the Index Department of *Reader's Digest* and the result that they had no record of any stories published by Wisberg.

The scenes at the bridge and the river were filmed at the Rowland V. Lee ranch. The house was built by Republic for *I've Always Loved You* (1946). The rest of the exteriors were filmed on the Columbia backlot.

As director Joseph H. Lewis was prepared to begin production on *So Dark the Night*, Columbia president Harry Cohn called Lewis into his office and offered him the chance to direct a big budget production, *The Jolson Story* (1946). Lewis told Cohn that he preferred to finish *So Dark the Night*. Lewis always wanted to see his productions to completion.

Reviews: "Above-par whodunit marred by weak screenplay. A 'B' that has 'A' quality." *Variety*, 9/18/46

"An outstanding film noir programmer. *So Dark the Night* is an engrossing crime drama that succeeds on many levels. As a character study it is amazingly complex and draws a detailed portrait of the tortured detective played by Geray. On a visual level the film is extremely effective, making brilliant use of light, shadow, rain and a motif of frames within frames that trap the characters in their environment. *So Dark the Night* is a bit obscure but well worth uncovering." *Motion Picture Guide*, Nash and Ross

Summation: Lewis' direction and Burnett Guffey's cinematography combine to produce a quite good and totally engrossing noir. Lewis is known for his unusual camera angles and edgy direction. Guffey is able to make maximum use of the dark and the scene in which Steven Geray encounters an angular town set predestines his mental status. Geray, in a rare starring role, is perfect in his role, and Micheline Cheirel is fine as a femme fatale. A "B" noir well worth viewing.

SHE KISSED HIS LIPS ... they were COLD!
SHE TOUCHED HIS WRIST ... there was NO PULSE!
SHE SCRATCHED HIS ARM ... there was NO BLOOD!
SHE WAS MARRIED TO A WALKING DEAD MAN!

The Soul of a Monster

(August 1944)

Cast: Lilyan Gregg, Rose Hobart; Dr. George Winson, George Macready; Dr. Roger Vance, Jim Bannon; Ann Winson, Jeanne Bates; Fred Stevens, Erik Rolf; Uncredited: Police Driver, Brian O'Hara; Police Sergeant, John Tyrrell; Disabled Warehouseman, Al Thompson; First Newsboy, Norman Salling; Man in Bar, Charles Sullivan; Woman in Bar, Grace Leonard; Sedan Driver, Milton Kibbee; Woman in Sedan, Ruth Lee; Workmen, Cy Malis and Charles Perry; Mrs. Kirby, Ida Moore; Ervin, Ervin Nyiregyhazi; Wayne, Ernest Hilliard; Talkative Policeman, Harry Strang; Second Newsboy, Buddy Swan; Truck Driver, Ray Teal; Piano Player, Clarence Muse; Waiter, Al Hill; Nurse, Ann Loos; Mrs. Jameson (Housekeeper), Edith Evanson

Credits: Director, Will Jason; Producer,

Ted Richmond; Screenwriter, Edward Dein; Editor, Paul Borofsky; Art Directors, Lionel Banks and George Brooks; Set Decorator, Fay Babcock; Cinematographer, Burnett Guffey; Musical Director, Mischa Bakaleinikoff

SONGS: "Spanish Rhapsody" (Liszt)—played by Ervin Nyiregyhazi, "Mephisto Waltz" (Liszt)—played by Ervin Nyiregyhazi, "Boogie Woogie Special"—played by Clarence Muse, "Ain't That Just Like a Man"—played by Clarence Muse, and "Ava Maria" (Schubert)—sung by a boys' quintet

PRODUCTION DATES: May 25–June 13, 1944

RUNNING TIME: 61 minutes

STORY: Noted physician George Macready is near death. Neither the medical skills of Dr. Jim Bannon nor the prayers of pastor Erik Rolf can improve his condition. Frustrated, Macready's wife Jeanne Bates prays to any source that can help. Mysteriously a strange but beautiful woman, Rose Hobart, arrives and takes over caring for Macready. Miraculously, Macready recovers but is now a cold, cruel and callous individual. Hobart's power over Macready estranges him from Bates. The only person Hobart fears is Rolf and she compels Macready to try to murder him. Macready stalks Rolf through the city streets and is about to strike when Rolf turns with a cross in his hands. Macready turns and flees. Bannon notices a change in Macready. In the throes of an argument, Bannon grabs Macready's wrists and cannot feel a pulse. After an operation, Bannon accidentally cuts Macready with a sharp scalpel but there is no blood. Bannon confides in Rolf, who tells Bannon to stay away from Macready. Bannon confronts Macready anyway and Hobart helps Macready rebuff him. Seeing that Bannon is a danger to her, she makes an emergency call for medical assistance. Bannon walks out of his house only to be run down by Hobart. In critical condition, Bannon summons Macready to his side. Hobart advises Macready to let Bannon die. Macready is arrested for murder but is released on bail. Rolf tells Macready to break the hold Hobart has on him. Bates goes to church to pray for Macready. Macready confronts Hobart, who tells him that she murdered Bannon. Realizing he is now just an instrument for Hobart's evil, Macready begins to break the spell she holds over him. Hobart decides to murder Macready, making it look like suicide. Hobart shoots Macready but he keeps advancing toward her. Hobart empties her gun into Macready just as he pushes her through a window to her death. All this has been a dream and we're back at the beginning of the story. As Bates prays for Macready, he opens his eyes to begin his recovery.

NOTES AND COMMENTARY: The working title for this film was *Death Walks Alone*.

Columbia had used up their pre-war supply of blank cartridges. Rose Hobart was the first to use the new ammunition when she fired six bullets into George Macready.

The Soul of a Monster was released to television as part of the *Son of Shock* package of 21 films.

REVIEWS: "This one's an entry for the all-time looney prize! A preposterously foolish film." *The New York Times*, 09/09/44

"Time, thought and money were three ingredients absent from *Soul of a Monster*, a horror entry which on a scale of one to ten did well to register a two." *The Columbia Story*, Hirschhorn

SUMMATION: The copout ending reduces a fairly entertaining horror-noir to a bunch of hooey. Despite Burnett Guffey's brilliant photography, Edward Dein's screenplay causes the film to come up empty. Perhaps if you can skip the ludicrous final minutes, the horror-noir fan could derive some enjoyment from the film. The acting is acceptable and Will Jason's direction is competent but only Guffey's contribution is truly worthy of note.

WITH A WARM EMBRACE ... A COLD COMMAND TO KILL!

Spin a Dark Web

(October 1956)

ALTERNATE TITLE: Soho Incident

CAST: Bella Francesi, Faith Domergue; Jim Bankley, Lee Patterson; Betty Walker, Rona Anderson; Rico Francesi, Martin Benson; Buddy, Robert Arden; Tom Walker, Joss Ambler; Bill Walker, Peter Hammond; Inspector Collis, Peter Burton; Sam, Sam Kydd; Mick, Russell West-

***Spin a Dark Web* (1956).**

wood; Audrey, Patricia Ryan; McLeod, Bernard Fox

Credits: Director, Vernon Sewell; Assistant Director, Douglas Hermes; Producer, George Maynard; Screenwriter, Ian Stuart Black; Editor, Peter Rolfe Johnson; Assistant Editor, John Jympson; Cinematographer, Basil Emmott; Wardrobe, Jean Fairlie; Makeup, R. Bonnor-Moris; Hair Stylist, Joyce James; Sound, W.H. Lindop; Production Manager, "Freddie" Pearson; Production Designer, Ken Adam; Original Music, Robert Sharples; Musical Supervisor, Richard Taylor; Continuity, Splinters Deason; Camera Operator, Bernard Lewis

Song: "Love Me, Love Me Now" (Paul and Roberts)—sung by Julie Dawn

Location Filming: Walton-on-Thames, Surry, England

Production Dates: early June–August 12, 1955

Source: novel *Wide Boys Never Work* by Robert Westerby

Running Time: 76 minutes

Story: Lee Patterson wants to get money without working and looks up a Canadian Army friend, Robert Arden, who now works for gambling crime boss Martin Benson. Benson has no interest in hiring Patterson but his (Benson's) sister Faith Domergue intercedes and Patterson gets a job. Boxer Peter Hammond wins a fight instead of taking a dive. Benson sends henchman Bernard Fox to impress on Hammond's father, Joss Ambler, the importance of following his orders. Ambler refuses. Fox gets angry and Hammond hits him. When Hammond turns his back, Fox strikes Hammond on the head with a club, killing him. Fox, on the run, demands money from Benson. Domergue wants him killed. Patterson delivers money to Fox after stopping at Ambler's house to offer condolences to Hammond's sister, Rona Anderson. Anderson is in love with Patterson. Domergue takes Patterson to her apartment where she seduces him. Benson has a horse that is a cinch to win an important race and he wants to bet large sums at sensational odds. To insure there is no conversation from the race track and the bookies, Benson has Patterson build an apparatus to accomplish this. That night, after a victory party, Fox sneaks into Benson's apartment and takes more money. While getting away, he is seen by Patterson, who follows Fox and sees him hole up in a nearby warehouse. Benson, Domergue, Patterson and Benson's cronies enter the warehouse and finally flush out Fox. Domergue implores Benson to kill Fox, which he does. Patterson doesn't mind breaking the law but he draws the line at murder. As Patterson tries to leave, Domergue offers her body to make him stay. Patterson pushes Domergue away; Benson and his gang arrive and Patterson fights his way free. He plans to ship out to Canada and begin a new life. Benson and Domergue agree that Patterson must be killed so he can't testify against them. Benson, Domergue, Arden and another tough, Russell Westwood, break into Ambler's residence. When Patterson calls to say goodbye to Anderson, Domergue answers the phone. Domergue tells Patterson that he has 20 minutes to come to Anderson's aid or she will be killed. Patterson calls Inspector Peter Burton and fills him in on the situation. Patterson arrives at Ambler's residence but the police are spotted. Domergue tells Burton that unless he lets them through the police blockade, Anderson will be killed. In the getaway car, Arden is driving and Patterson is forced to accompany Domergue and Benson. The car leaves with Westwood left behind. Patterson tells Arden that Benson and Domergue will leave him behind also. The car is stopped in a wooded area so Benson can march Patterson and Anderson into the woods to be murdered. Arden checks the boot and realizes Patterson is correct. At that point, Domergue murders Arden. The shots distract Benson, and Patterson grabs him. Domergue fires two shots that hit and kill Benson. Facing Patterson, Domergue fires a shot into his body. As she attempts to drive off, the police arrive and arrest her. Patterson spends one month in a prison hospital recuperating. This is the sentence imposed on him. Also, Patterson is released on two years' probation under Ambler's supervision.

Notes and Commentary: Robert Westerby's novel has yet to be filmed. In this movie, only the name Jim Bankley is used. There is no femme fatale in the story. The novel tells of a young man who wants the easy life rather than work for a living. His life spirals downward until his only choice is to return home. The author then tells that it would only be a matter of time before he would become a wide boy again. (A wide boy, also known as a spiv, is a petty crook who will turn his hand to anything as long as it doesn't involve honest work.)

The working title for this film was *44 Soho Square.*

Reviews: "Melodrama of fairly entertaining quality. As a gangster pic, it stirs up sufficient thrills entertainment for lowercase dates on the dual market." *Variety*, 9/26/56

Summation: The web wasn't spun dark enough. The film is mediocre at best, with uninspired direction and barely competent acting. Director Vernon Sewell is unable to put the needed punch in the film to make it memorable. The tension is missing and there is only a modicum of suspense as Lee Patterson races to get to Rona Anderson's house in the required 20 minutes. The acting is flat; Patterson's acting is primarily put on monotone through all his trials and tribulations. Faith Domergue, though sultry, is unable to put the spin on her femme fatale role to be completely alluring. Except for a few brief scenes, Basil Emmett's camerawork is just routine. Kudos to screenwriter Ian Stuart Black for only scripting a 76-minute feature!

The off-guard surprise ... the mounting suspense ... the unconventional twist ... that place it in the top company of great action dramas!

State Secret

(October 1950)
Alternate Title: The Great Manhunt
A Frank Launder–Sidney Gilliat Production

Cast: Dr. John Marlowe, Douglas Fairbanks, Jr.; Lisa, Glynis Johns; Baba, Olga Lowe; Teresa, Theresa Van Kye; Colonel Galcon, Jack

Hawkins; General Niva, Walter Rilla; Dr. Revo, Karel Stepanek; Dr. Poldoi, Leonard Sachs; Theodor, Herbert Lom; Buckman, Robert Ayres; Clubmen, Howard Douglas, Martin Boddey, Russell Waters and Arthur Howard; Prada, Carl Jaffe; Bendel, Gerard Heinz; Andre, Leslie Linder; Man at Telephone Box, Leo Bieber; Shop Woman, Nelly Arno; Barber, Paul Demel; Taxi Driver, Danny Green; State Policeman, Anton Diffring; Macco, Peter Illing; Compere, Arthur Reynolds; Red Nose, Richard Molinas; Cable Car Conductor, Eric Pohlmann; Sigrist, Hans Moser; Christian, Louis Wiechert; Bartorek, Gerik Schjelderup; Mountain Soldier, Henrik Jacobsen; Lieutenant Prachi, Guido Lorraine; Uncredited: Francks, Alexis Chesnakov; Sophie, Marianne Deeming; Vilnik, Arsene Kirilloff; Joe, Gordon Tanner; Nursing Sister, Pat Neal; State Radio Commentator, Alessandro Tasca

Credits: Director and Screenwriter, Sidney Gilliat; Assistant Director, Guy Hamilton; Assistant to Producer, Cyril Coke; Editor, Thelma Myers; Art Director, Wilfred Shingleton; Assistant Art Directors, John Hawkesworth and Tait McCallum; Cinematographer, Robert Krasker; Camera Operator, Ted Scaife; Additional Photographer, John Wilcox; Costumes, Beatrice Dawson and Ivy Baker; Makeup, Michael Morris; Production Manager, Leslie Gilliat; Sound Recordist, Alan Allen; Sound Editor, Lee Doig; Music, William Alwyn; Musical Conductor, Muir Mathieson; Music played by the Royal Philharmonic Orchestra; Continuity, Paddy Arnold; Language Advisor, Georgina Shield

Song: "Paper Doll" (Black)—sung by Glynis Johns with Olga Lowe and Theresa Van Kye

Location Filming: Fai Della Paganella, Trento, Trentino-Alto Adidge and Dolomites, Italy; Ilesworth, Middlesex, England

Running Time: 99 minutes

Story: Dr. Douglas Fairbanks, Jr. is invited to Vosnia to receive recognition for his development of a new surgical procedure for portal hypertension. Once there, he is asked to perform surgery on a patient who turns out to be Vosnian president Walter Rilla. Colonel Jack Hawkins refuses to allow Fairbanks to leave Vosnia until Rilla fully recovers. If Rilla does not recover, Fairbanks will meet with a fatal "accident." As Fairbanks is allowed to leave, Rilla suffers a setback and dies. Fairbanks makes a break for freedom. In the city, he finds temporary refuge in a theater and persuades entertainer Glynis Johns to shelter him. When Fairbanks has to go on the run, he fears for Johns' life and forces her to accompany him. Fate brings Fairbanks into contact with gangster Herbert Lom, who agrees to help him and Johns get out of the country. Fairbanks and Johns take a cable car to a town high in a mountain range. The cable car conductor recognizes Johns' picture from a newspaper and alerts the authorities. In the mountain town, Lom's associate Hans Moser is to take Fairbanks and Johns on a treacherous mountain climb to safety. Hawkins has arrived in the area to take charge. Soldiers are stationed at various points on the mountaintop. Soldier Henrik Jacobsen spots Moser and shoots him. Jacobsen then confronts Fairbanks; the men struggle but Fairbanks, with help from Johns, is able to overcome Jacobson. They then force him to lead them close to the Vosnian border. Trying to skirt a barracks, Fairbanks encounters a soldier that he's forced to shoot. The shot alerts other soldiers and they begin firing as Fairbanks and Johns attempt to go over a rise to safety. A bullet critically wounds Johns, and Fairbanks refuses to desert her. Both are captured and brought to Hawkins. Hawkins allows Fairbanks to treat Johns even though both will soon be executed. As Fairbanks is about to meet with a shooting "accident," shots are heard over the radio: Rilla's double has been assassinated. The murders of Fairbanks and Johns are no longer necessary so Hawkins allows them to leave Vosnia. On the way to the United States, Fairbanks indicates that Johns would make a wonderful wife.

Notes and Commentary: State Secret was released in England by the British Lion Film Corporation. In most of the United States play dates, Columbia used the alternate title *The Great Manhunt.*

Review: "Mr. Launder and Mr. Gilliat have still made a humdinging film—a film with both color and excitement which Glynis Johns and Douglas Fairbanks, Jr. play in a mood of perpetually rigid terror that is as surely infectious as the plague." *The New York Times*, 10/5/50

"Highly exciting, gripping tale of political intrigue." *Motion Picture Guide*, Nash and Ross

Summation: This espionage noir is basically an excellent chase film. Douglas Fairbanks, Jr. and Glynis Johns react well to the terrors to which they are subjected. Robert Krasker couches the film in noir photography. The darkness adds to the tension and suspense. To go down in the annals of great noir film, the copout ending would have to be replaced. Fairbanks and Johns' escape is thwarted and both are scheduled for fatal "accidents." Only a fortuitous incident allows them freedom. In a memorable noir, both would have been executed.

It's the HIT–AND–FUN AFFAIR of the YEAR!

Strange Affair

(October 1944)

Cast: Bill Harrison, Allyn Joslyn; Jacqueline "Jack" Harrison, Evelyn Keyes; Marie Dumont, Marguerite Chapman; Lt. Washburn, Edgar Buchanan; Frieda Brenner, Nina Foch; Domino, Hugo Haas; Laundry Truck Driver, Shemp Howard; Sgt. Erwin, Frank Jenks; Dr. Brenner, Erwin Kalser; Leslie Carlson, Tonio Selwart; Rudolph Kruger, John Wengraf; Uncredited: Johansen, Erik Rolf; Gloria, Carole Mathews; Motorcycle Officer, Edgar Dearing; Truck Driver, Ray Teal; Dr. Parrish, Edwin Stanley; Superintendent Reynolds, William Forrest; Mike McCafferty, Ralph Dunn; Dr. Igor Baumier, Ivan Triesault; Mac (Police Chemist), Arthur Space; Newsboy, Buddy Swan; B.M. Toman (Nightclub Manager), Eugene Borden; Nightclub M.C., George Sorel; Bank Security Guard, James Flavin; Taxi Drivers, Sam Finn, John Tyrrell, Jack Carr and Tom Coleman; Policemen, Brian O'Hara and Larry Emmons; Mounted Officer, Lane Chandler; Woman with Great Dane, Bess Flowers; Jitterbugs, Dean Collins and Rosemary Wilson; Detective Carey, Hugh Beaumont; Police Psychiatrist, Robert Emmett Keane; Sampson, Jack Lee; Hat Salesman, Harold Minjir; Proprietress, Martha Wentworth; Patrol Car Officer, Kernan Cripps; Irate Woman at Police Lineup, Ruth Warren

Credits: Director, Alfred E. Green; Producer, Burt Kelly; Story, Oscar Saul; Screenwriters, Oscar Saul, Eve Greene and Jerome Odlum; Additional Dialogue, Jack Henley; Editor, Richard Fantl; Art Directors, Lionel Banks and Walter Holscher; Set Decorator, George Montgomery; Cinematographer, Franz F. Planer; Gowns, Jean Louis; Original Music, Marlin Skiles; Musical Director, M.W. Stoloff

Song: "Pistol Packin' Mama" (Dexter)—sung by unknown male vocalist

Production Dates: May 31–June 7, 1944

Running Time: 78 minutes

Story: Dr. Ivan Triesault tells Dr. Erwin Kalser that he fears for his life. Triesault comes to the city to meet Kalser at a dinner honoring refugees. At the dinner, Triesault falls out of his chair, dead. Seated at the table were cartoonist and amateur detective Allyn Joslyn, his wife Evelyn Keyes, Triesault's wife Marguerite Chapman, her companion Tonio Selwart, Kalser, his daughter Nina Foch, astronomer-author John Wengraf and doorman Hugo Haas. Despite the police theory that Triesault died of a heart attack, Joslyn states that he was poisoned by a jab in his temporarily paralyzed left hand. Kalser disappears after taking $200,000 he was keeping for Triesault in his safety deposit box. Haas, who runs errands for Joslyn, tells Joslyn that the poison used was copper thiacide, an ingredient that Joslyn once used to thin paints he used in his comic strip. Stewart owns a warehouse where he stocks paint supplies including copper thiacide. Joslyn gains entrance to the warehouse when he's captured by Eric Rolf. After Joslyn is taken by gunpoint from the warehouse, he is followed by Keyes who, in her sleuthing, showed up looking for Joslyn. In trying to keep up with Joslyn's captors, Keyes runs a red light. She convinces Officer Edgar Dearing that Joslyn is being kidnapped and the trail leads to Martha Wentworth's nightclub. At the club, the police can find no sign of Joslyn. Keyes is arrested and taken to police headquarters. Joslyn is being held in a back room where a bound Kalser is brought. The two face death when ringleader Haas arrives. When obtaining paint supplies for Joslyn, Haas was able to take some of the poisonous material. At the banquet, it was easy for Haas to murder Triesault. The plan is to murder Joslyn, making it look like an accident. Kalser will be killed and his body well hidden to make it look like he murdered Triesault and stole the money. At the last minute, Keyes arrives with the police. Haas and his cohorts are arrested.

Notes and Commentary: The working title for the film was *Stalk the Hunter.*

Reviews: "[The screenwriter] crammed a fair amount of honest laughter in the dishonest goings-on. Alfred E. Green's direction, like everything in sight, was best taken with a sizable pinch of salt." *The Columbia Story*, Hirschhorn

Summation: This noir is for naught. Thanks to Alfred E. Green's brisk directorial skills, he is able to speed through comedic routines, e.g. Shemp Howard's myopic routine, Howard having problems counting articles of clothing and Allyn Joslyn's tussle with a Great Dane, and presenting to audiences a mystery story that has more holes than Swiss cheese. This was a Columbia attempt to rival MGM's Thin Man series. Neither Joslyn nor Evelyn Keyes bring to the screen the necessary sophistication and Oscar Saul's story is lacking in suspense and logic. On the positive side for the adult males in the audience is the eye candy of Keyes, Marguerite Chapman, Nina Foch and Carole Mathews.

He couldn't let her alone...

Strange Fascination

(September 1952)

A Hugo Haas Production

Cast: Margo, Cleo Moore; Paul Marvan, Hugo Haas; Diana Fowler, Mona Barrie; Carlo, Rick Vallin; June Fowler, Karen Sharpe; Shiner, Marc Krah; Yvette, Genevieve Aumont; Walter Fowler, Patrick Holmes; Mary, Maura Murphy; Douglas, Brian O'Hara; Investigator, Anthony Jochim; Dr. Thompson, Dr. Ross Thompson; Nurse, Maria Bibikoff; Mr. Lowell, Gayne Whitman; Uncredited: Jack, Robert Knapp; Mr. Frim, Roy Engel; Printing Foreman, Tom Wilson

Credits: Director, Producer and Screenwriter, Hugo Haas; Assistant Director, Leonard J. Shapiro; Associate Producer, Robert Erlik; Editor, Merrill G. White; Art Director, Rudi Feld; Cinematographer, Paul Ivano; Gowns, Irving-Mitzman; Makeup, Gustaf Nobin; Sound, Victor Appel; Original Music, Vaclav Divina; Musical Director, Adolf Heller; Production Manager, Leon Chooluck; Construction Manager, Don Bruno; Script Supervisor, Jack Herzberg; Dialogue Supervisor, Marc Lowell; Chief Electrician, John Gaudioso

Song: "Nocturne" (Gimpel)—played by Jacob Gimpel

Production Dates: March 19–April 4, 1952

Running Time: 81 minutes

Story: At the piano on the Carnegie Hall stage, Hugo Haas reflects on the last year of his life. Haas was a concert pianist in Europe with a brilliant future. Wealthy widow Mona Barrie offered to be his sponsor in America. Barrie indicated she would be open to romantic overtures from Haas. Barrie had a concert tour set up for Haas. Before departing, Haas borrowed money to pay the premium on an insurance policy to cover a possible injury to his hands that would prevent him from continuing his career. On the successful tour, Haas met Cleo Moore, who performed in a dance routine with Rick Vallin. Moore later contacted Haas in New York and persuaded him to allow her to stay in his apartment. Moore had broken up with Vallin and is afraid he will react violently. Another tour was set up for Haas. Moore found out that she had nothing to fear from Vallin. Haas persuaded Moore to accompany him on the tour and subsequently married her. The tour was highly successful until floods wiped out the last leg. Haas was broke and needed work. Barrie, because of his marriage to Moore, now declined to be Haas' sponsor. Moore tried to obtain jobs to support them. The bosses made sexual advances and Haas forbade Moore to work. Vallin returned to New York to put on a play and wanted Moore as a leading performer. Again Haas forbade it. Haas, in order to obtain money, attempted to see if a piece of music he'd written could be published. He was told that the arrangement had to be changed before it could be published. One of Haas' hands was caught in the publishing company's machinery. Haas insisted that he felt faint and inadvertently placed his hand in jeopardy. As the insurance company was about to pay off, an eyewitness testified that Haas deliberately placed his hand in harm's way. Moore realized the marriage was a mistake and left to be with Vallin, both as lovers and performers. Haas became a derelict. Haas had been playing with one hand as he reviewed his life. As Haas looks up he sees an audience of fellow souls down on their luck. As he looks to the rear of the hall, Haas sees Barrie, who has come to take him to her home.

NOTES AND COMMENTARY: The working title for this film was *Pushover.*

REVIEWS: "Latest Haasean entry has a sordid, sexy theme. It rates as a fine subject for exploitation houses but appears to have a spotty future in general release." *Variety*, 10/1/52

"As with Haas' other films, this is interesting to watch because it is so melodramatic, not because it is a good film." *Motion Picture Guide*, Nash and Ross

SUMMATION: This is a slow, ponderous and boring noir. The climax is telegraphed early on. Haas directs as if his story is of some importance instead of a minor "B." Most of the lines are delivered slowly and without emotion. Only the veteran Mona Barrie comes out unscathed in this turkey.

THE MOST FASCINATING LOUSE YOU EVER MET!

The Strange One

(April 1957)

A Sam Spiegel Production

CAST: Jocko De Paris, Ben Gazzara; Harold Koble, Pat Hingle; Cadet Colonel Corger, Mark Richman; Simmons, Arthur Storch; Perrin McKee, Paul E. Richards; Major Avery, Larry Gates; Col. Ramey, Clifton James; Georgie Avery, Geoffrey Horne; Roger Gatt, James Olson; Rosebud, Julie Wilson; Robert Marquales, George Peppard

CREDITS: Director, Jack Garfein; First Assistant Director, Arthur Steckler; Second Assistant Director, Jack Grossberg; Producer, Sam Spiegel; Assistant to Producer, Sam Rheiner; Screenwriter, Calder Willingham; Editor, Sidney Katz; Art Director, Joseph C. Wright; Production Executive, Harmon Jones; Production Manager, Charles J. Maguire; Cinematographer, Burnett Guffey; Cinematographer Collaborator, Clifford Poland; Wardrobe Master, Arthur Craig; Makeup, Robert E. Jiras; Hair Stylist, Willis A. Hanchett; Sound, Edward Johnstone; Script Supervisor, Sascha Laurence; Dialogue Supervisor, Irving Buchman; Original Music-Musical Conductor, Kenyon Hopkins

FILM LOCATIONS: Gulfport and Winter Park, Florida

PRODUCTION DATES: July 9–August 24, 1956

SOURCE: play and novel *End as a Man* by Calder Willingham

RUNNING TIME: 100 minutes

STORY: After taps at Southern Military College, upperclassmen Ben Gazzara and Pat Hingle invade the room of freshmen George Peppard and Arthur Storch. Gazzara has set up a poker game in which upperclassman James Olson will be cheated out of his money and given whiskey to make him intoxicated so that the noise will attract Cadet Geoffrey Horne, who will report to his father Major Larry Gates. Gates arrives at the barracks to find all in order. Later Horne hears another disturbance and decides to investigate. Gazzara prompts Olson to brutally beat Horne. The next morning, Horne is found unconscious on the grass with empty whiskey bottles around him. When alcohol is found in Horne's bloodstream, it is determined that he broke school rules and he is expelled. Using Storch's enema bag and tubing, Gazzara had inserted alcohol into Horne's stomach. Gazzara had exacted revenge on Horne for reporting him for an infraction of the school's rules. Cadet Paul E. Richards witnessed Gazzara's action and wants him to return his infatuation. Gazzara shrugs Richards off with a half promise to talk with him later. Gates has Gazzara brought to his office and accuses him of pouring whiskey down Horne's throat through a tube. Gazzara tells Gates that Horne had a nervous breakdown. In retaliation, Gates strikes Gazzara. This action costs Gates his position at the school. Peppard tells Storch, Hingle and Olson that Gazzara is against everyone. Peppard plans to leave school. Hingle and Olson, both in their senior years, are afraid of being dishonorably discharged. At the Hair of the Hound Club, Gazzara is brought before a group of cadets led by Olson's roommate Mark Richman. Richman demands Gazzara sign a prepared statement admitting his guilt. Gazzara initially refuses but when faced by witnesses Peppard, Hingle, Olson and Storch, he finally signs. Instead of being allowed to leave the club, Gazzara is blindfolded and placed in a car and driven to a secluded spot near the railroad tracks. Gazzara thinks he is to be thrown in front of the train. Instead as a broken frightened man, Gazzara and his belongings are thrown on the train. As the train pulls away, a screaming Gazzara promises he'll return and exact revenge.

NOTES AND COMMENTARY: The movie differs from Calder Willingham's novel *End as a Man*. The novel follows freshman Robert Marquales' tribulations through his first few months at the military college. Jocko De Paris is responsible for the various violations of the school's rules, which eventually causes him to be expelled and Marquales to be put on probation. Only the poker game in which Cadet Gatt is cheated and Cadet Perrin McKee's infatuation with De Paris made their way into the film.

The working titles for the film were *End as a Man* and *The Young One*.

Because of the Motion Picture Production Code, three minutes of footage pertaining to homosexuality had to be deleted. Sex perversion or its inference could not be shown. However, in the interaction between the characters Perrin McKee and Jocko De Paris, homosexuality is implied.

Members of the Broadway stage production, actors Ben Gazzara, Pat Hingle, Arthur Storch and Paul E. Richards reprised their roles. Jack Garfein was brought in to direct as he had done on Broadway.

REVIEW: "The exploitable film has some excellent performances and is ably directed." *Variety*, 4/3/57

SUMMATION: This noir is an excellent, fascinating study of a psychopath. Ben Gazzara gives a riveting performance as a smart cadet who believes with his slick tongue and brain that no one can stand in his way. Other performances are stellar, especially those of Pat Hingle as Gazzara's roommate and George Peppard as a freshman Gazzara thinks he can use. Willingham's screenplay, Garfein's direction and Burnett Guffey's cinematography are first-rate. The result is a gripping, suspenseful motion picture.

Taut! Torrid! Tremendous! T is for Terror!

The Tall T

(April 1957)

A Scott–Brown Production

CAST: Pat Brennan, Randolph Scott; Frank Usher, Richard Boone; Doretta Mims, Maureen O'Sullivan; Ed Rintoon, Arthur Hunnicutt; Billy Jack, Skip Homeier; Chink, Henry Silva; Willard Mims, John Hubbard; Tenvoorde, Robert Burton; Uncredited: Hank Parker, Fred Sherman; Jeff, Christopher Olsen

CREDITS: Director, Budd Boetticher; Assistant Director, Sam Nelson; Producer, Harry Joe Brown; Associate Producer, Randolph Scott; Assistant to Producer, David Breen; Editor, Al Clark; Art Director, George Brooks; Set Decorator, Frank A. Tuttle; Cinematographer, Charles Lawton, Jr.; Sound, Ferol Redd; Original Music and Musical Conductor, Heinz Roemheld; Technicolor Color Consultant, Henri Jaffa

LOCATION FILMING: Alabama Hills, Lone Pine, California

PRODUCTION DATES: July 20–August 8, 1956

SOURCE: novelette "The Captives" by Elmore Leonard

RUNNING TIME: 78 minutes

Color by Technicolor

STORY: Small ranch owner Randolph Scott, having lost his horse in a bet with Robert Burton, is walking back to his ranch when he gets a ride from stagecoach driver Arthur Hunnicutt. Hunnicutt is driving a special run and his only passengers are John Hubbard and his bride Maureen O'Sullivan, daughter of the richest man in the territory. At the first way station, they're confronted by outlaw Richard Boone and his two confederates, Skip Homeier and Henry Silva. Silva guns down Hunnicutt and wants to shoot Scott but is stopped by Boone. Boone and his men were waiting for the regular stage run. To save his life, Hubbard tells Boone that O'Sullivan's father would pay a nice ransom to get her back. Boone sends Hubbard along with Homeier to make a deal. Boone and Silva take Scott and O'Sullivan to a

***The Tall T* (1957) with Randolph Scott and Arthur Hunnicutt.**

hideout in the hills. Both Scott and Boone want a successful ranch of their own; the difference is that Scott is willing to obtain his by hard, honest work. Hubbard brings back news that the ransom money will be ready the next day. Boone offers Hubbard the choice of staying with O'Sullivan or returning to town. When Hubbard chooses not to stay, Boone has Silva shoot him. Scott realizes that Hubbard and O'Sullivan were not in love. Hubbard wanted the money and influence the marriage would provide. O'Sullivan was afraid of becoming an old maid. Scott and O'Sullivan become romantically attached. Scott knows that after the ransom is paid, Silva and Homeier will insist on killing them. Boone goes to collect the ransom money. Scott plants seeds of distrust and Silva leaves to make sure Boone returns. Homeier is left to guard Scott and O'Sullivan. Scott tells Homeier that both Boone and Silva had their way with O'Sullivan when he was out of the camp. Homeier decides to force himself on O'Sullivan. This gives Scott a chance to jump Homeier and in the struggle, Homeier is killed. Scott and O'Sullivan take refuge in the nearby rocks. Scott wants O'Sullivan to start for his ranch; Scott refuses to leave, stating, "There's some things a man can't ride around." O'Sullivan won't leave without him. Silva returns and finds Homeier's body. With O'Sullivan's help, Scott is able to shoot Silva. When Boone returns, Scott makes him throw down his pistol and the ransom money. Boone keeps his back to Scott and rides out of camp, knowing that Scott remembers that Boone saved his life at the way station. Rifle in hand, Boone later rides back to camp. His shot misses but Scott's shot finds its mark. With arms around each other, Scott and O'Sullivan start for town.

NOTES AND COMMENTARY: Elmore Leonard's short story is followed rather faithfully. Burt Kennedy's screenplay shows how Randolph Scott lost his horse and a dialogue scene was added to show the similarity and differences between Scott and Richard Boone's characters. Leonard's story has Usher killed before Silva. For greater emotional impact, Kennedy's screenplay reverses this.

The working titles for the film were *The*

Captives and *The Tall Rider*. Another film had been registered as *The Captives* so a Columbia executive in New York decided against going to court to obtain rights to use that title. *The Tall T* was finally chosen. The trailer suggests that the T stands for terror. Another source states the T stands for the Tenvoorde ranch, where Scott loses his horse in a bet.

Burt Kennedy's line "There's some things a man can't ride around" would be used again in *Ride Lonesome* (Columbia, 1959).

Reviews: "An unconventional western, *The Tall T* passes up most oater clichés to shape up as a brisk entry.... From a quiet start the yarn acquires a momentum which explodes in a sock climax." *Variety*, 4/3/57

"A marvelous Western." *The Western*, Hardy

"Exceedingly fine Randolph Scott film, well written and taut." *Western Movies*, Pitts

Summation: What a wonderful western noir. Burt Kennedy's fine screenplay follows Elmore Leonard's short story but with a few added scenes and Budd Boetticher's strong direction punches up the storyline, generating exceptional suspense. Charles Lawton, Jr.'s photography captures both the vistas of the Alabama Hills and the claustrophobic atmosphere of the outlaw camp.

BLASTING THE WORLD'S WORST SPY NEST!

Target Hong Kong

(March 1953)

Cast: Mike Lassiter, Richard Denning; Ming Shan, Nancy Gates; Fu Chao, Richard Loo; Lao Shan, Soo Yong; Suma, Ben Astar; Dockery Pete Gresham, Michael Pate; Sin How, Philip Ahn; Dutch Pfeifer, Henry Kulky; Uncredited: Johnny Wing, Victor Sen Yung; Lo Chi, Weaver Levy; Tai Ching, Kam Tong; Wong Lu Cheh, Robert W. Lee; Cashier, Kei Thin Chung; Communist Soldiers, David Chow and George Lee; Pirate, Eddie Lee; Dice Girl, Reiko Sato; Mandarin, Peter Chong

Credits: Director, Fred F. Sears; Assistant Director, James Nicholson; Producer, Wallace MacDonald; Screenwriter, Herbert Purdom; Editor, Richard Fantl; Art Director, Ross Bellah; Set Decorator, James Crowe; Cinematographer, Henry Freulich; Musical Director, Mischa Bakaleinikoff

Production Dates: June 2–7, 1952

Running Time: 66 minutes

Story: Communist China under the rule of Ben Astar plans to gain control of Hong Kong with the help of gambling den owner Soo Tong and her men. Tong believes Astar is working for Nationalist China. Soldier of fortune Richard Denning is persuaded to prevent communist control of Hong Kong. Nationalist China underground leader Philip Ahn knows that money for the communist cause goes through Tong's establishment. At Tong's place Denning becomes romantically interested in Tong's adopted daughter Nancy Gates. Denning gets a lead when he spots known communist agent Richard Loo losing large sums of money at the gambling table. Denning's pals Michael Pate and Henry Kulky follow Loo. Knowing that Astar plans to set off a floating bomb to be followed by warfare in the streets, Loo sends Gates to the mainland to deliver a package to Weaver Levy. Levy is to bring the men to take over Hong Kong. The package contains money and Denning thinks Gates is in league with the communists. To get the men fired up against the communists, Astar has men attack the village. Denning and Levy help Gates get out of the village safely. Levy is killed and Denning is wounded. Ahn and confederate Victor Sen Yung have bugged Loo's hideout and learn of the floating bomb but not its location. The alert Astar has Ahn and Yung captured with plans to take them deep into communist China. Denning leads a rescue attempt and shoots Loo as he is about to kill Ahn and Yung. Even with these setbacks, Astar plans to attack Hong Kong on schedule. Tong goes to arm her men and Astar sends the bomb on its way. Denning and the Nationalist underground agents go to Loo's place. Gates, loyal to Tong, refuses to tell Denning where her mother went. Denning spots the passage to the underground tunnels and everyone races to stop the attack. Denning sees Tong and her men. The battle begins, and other allies of Denning arrive. Pate and Kulky are killed. Only Tong survives as all her men are killed. Gates has followed Denning. When Tong won't reveal the bomb's location, Ahn threatens to kill Gates. Tong relents and Denning and Yung race to find the bomb but find Astar first. Shots are fired, Astar shoots Yung and Denning kills Astar. Denning reaches the bomb and is able to defuse it at the last possible moment. Tong, realizing finally that she had been duped, is now going to the mainland to take up the fight, leaving Denning to watch over Gates.

Reviews: "Action is plentiful and the pace is fast enough to hold interest throughout." *Motion Picture Guide*, Nash and Ross

Summation: This is a fast-moving espionage noir. Although it sustains the interest, it is hardly memorable. Credit director Fred F. Sears' adroit pacing to avoid tedium. Henry Freulich's noir photography adds tension to the story.

EVIL ENTERS THE HOUSE AT 13 WEST STREET...
IT'S SHOCKING AS A SCREAM IN THE NIGHT!!!!

13 West Street

(June 1962)

A Ladd Enterprises Inc. Production

Cast: Walt Sherill, Alan Ladd; Detective Sergeant Koleski, Rod Steiger; Chuck Landry, Michael Callan; Tracey Sherill, Dolores Dorn; Paul Logan, Kenneth MacKenna; Mrs. Landry, Margaret Hayes; Finney, Stanley Adams; Everett, Chris Robinson; Mrs. Quinn, Jeanne Cooper; Bill, Arnold Merritt; Tommy, Mark Slade; Joe Bradford, Henry Beckman; Noddy, Clegg Hoyt; Uncredited: Gang Member, Adam Roarke; Aerospace Engineer, Olan Soule; Jack, Jordan Gerier; Doctor, Robert Cleaves; Negro, Bernie Hamilton; Mexican, Pepe Hern; Mr. Johnson, Frank Gerstle; Baldwin, Ted Knight; Magazine Salesman, Michael Vandever; Old Prisoner, Tom London

Credits: Director, Philip Leacock; Assistant Director, Eddie Saeta; Producer, William Bloom; Screenwriters, Bernard C. Schoenfeld and Robert Presnell, Jr.; Editor, Al Clark; Art Director, Walter Holscher; Set Decorator, Darrell Silvera; Cinematographer, Charles Lawton, Jr.; Makeup, Ben Lane; Sound Supervisor, Charles J. Rice; Sound, Harry Mills; Original Music, George Duning; Orchestrator, Arthur Morton

Source: novel *The Tiger Among Us* by Leigh Brackett

Running Time: 80 minutes

Story: On his way home from work, aerospace engineer Alan Ladd's car runs out of gas. Walking to find help, he is almost hit by a speeding car driven by teenager Michael Callan. When Ladd shouts at them in anger, Callan and his friends Chris Robinson, Mark Slade, Adam Roarke and Arnold Merritt return, surround Ladd and give him a brutal beating. Merritt does not participate because he knows Ladd. Detective Sergeant Rod Steiger is assigned to investigate. When Callan become aware of the investigation, he terrorizes Ladd's wife, Dolores Dorn, in an attempt to get Ladd to drop the case. When these tactics don't work, Callan, Robinson, Slade and Roarke give Ladd another beating, only stopping when a screaming Dorn runs to Ladd's aid. Steiger uncovers Robinson as a suspect but his parents alibi him. Steiger finds that Callan is a close friend of Robinson. Steiger brings pictures of Robinson's friends to the house and Dorn recognizes Merritt, a delivery boy at a local pharmacy. Ladd tries to find Merritt but Merritt sees him first and runs to Callan. Callan tries to calm the frightened Merritt. Ladd goes to Merritt's house, where Merritt is found dead, an apparent suicide. Ladd hires private investigator Stanley Adams to watch Robinson and his friends. Aware that they're under suspicion, Callan and Robinson go into hiding but Adams locates them and calls Ladd at his house with Steiger present. Ladd and Steiger go to meet Adams. When Callan and his friends leave, Adams follows. In a high-speed chase, Callan makes a sudden evasive maneuver. Adams is unable to react in time. His car goes through a guard rail and crashes, killing Adams. Callan has no remorse over Adams' death and admits to his friends that he murdered Merritt so that he wouldn't squeal. As Dorn is talking to Ladd over the telephone, Callan enters the house and begins to terrorize her. He plans to kill Ladd when he returns home. When Dorn begins to taunt Callan, he decides to rape her. To reach Dorn, Ladd has taken a police car.

Ladd approaches his house with sirens blasting. Callan races from the house, leaving his car behind. Ladd get Callan's address from the car's registration. When Callan arrives home, Ladd attacks him and knocks him into a swimming pool. Ladd begins to hold Callan's head underwater before realizing what he's doing. Ladd pulls Callan from the pool as Steiger, Dorn and police officers arrive. Callan is arrested.

Notes and Commentary: The prerelease titles for this film were *The Tiger Among Us* and *13 East Street*.

The basic premise of Leigh Brackett's novel *The Tiger Among Us* is followed. After the beating of Walter Sherris (Walt Sherill in the film), Chuck and his followers become serial attackers. Their latest attack results in a man's murder. One follower, Bill, is appalled and finally calls Sherris. As they are traveling to the police, Chuck and two others corner Walt and Bill in an old barn. Shots are exchanged but no one is hurt. Sherris no longer wants to kill the ones who beat him. Police arrive in time. Chuck and his friends are arrested. Bill, who had no stomach for Chuck's depravity, gets a very light sentence. Sherris becomes a father figure to Bill.

Reviews: "While *13 West Street* may not be Ladd's best picture, the movie's film noir style nonetheless works well with the story." *Motion Picture Guide*, Nash and Ross

"An intriguing little melodrama, in the end, as little more than a thriller whose aim was to exploit the currently popular youth market with yet one more violent excursion into teenage delinquency." *The Columbia Story*, Hirschhorn

Summation: In Alan Ladd's final noir, he gives a good account of himself as a man declaring vengeance on those who beat and terrorized him. Twenty years previously, Ladd played his first noir leading man role in *The Glass Key* (Paramount, 1942), another movie in which he was brutally beaten. It looks like Ladd went full circle. Ladd has good support from Steiger, Dorn and Callan. This is an underrated juvenile noir with no-nonsense, straightforward direction from Philip Leacock. Charles Lawton, Jr.'s photography is first-rate, especially the thrilling car chase sequence.

KILLERS, YOUR HOUR HAS COME!

The Thirteenth Hour

(February 1947)

Alternate Title: The 13th Hour

Cast: Steve Reynolds, Richard Dix; Eileen Blair, Karen Morley; Charlie Cook, John Kellogg; Jerry Mason, Jim Bannon; Don Parker, Regis Toomey; Mabel Sands, Bernadene Hayes; Tommy Blair, Mark Dennis; Uncredited: Voice of the Whistler, Otto Forrest; Truck Driver/Waiter, George Lloyd; Truck Driver, Eddie Parker; Jimmy, Paul Campbell; Donna, Nancy Saunders; Ranford, Anthony Warde; McCabe, Ernie Adams; Judge Collins, Selmer Jackson; Bernie; Charles Jordan; Motorist Who Gets License Number, Robert Kellard; Stack, Jack Carrington; Berger, Robert B. Williams; Secretary, Lillian Wells; Captain Linfield, Cliff Clark; Detectives, Pat O'Malley and Stanley Blystone; Policeman, Kernan Cripps

Credits: Director, William Clemens; Producer, Rudolph C. Flothow; Story, Leslie Edgley; Screenwriters, Edward Bock and Raymond L. Schrock; Editor, Dwight Caldwell; Art Director, Hans Radon; Set Decorator, Albert Rickerd; Cinematographer, Vincent Farrar; Musical Director, Mischa Balaleinikoff; "Whistler" theme music, Wilbur Hatch

Production Dates: October 3–22, 1946

Running Time: 65 minutes

Source: the Columbia Broadcasting System Program "The Whistler"

Story: Freight line owner Richard Dix is framed for the murder of police officer Regis Toomey, his rival for the affections of café owner Karen Morley. Before the murderer knocked out Dix, Dix tore a glove off one of the murderer's hands, and it indicates that the murderer was missing a thumb. Dix has Morley hide the glove. Afraid the police won't believe him, Dix goes on the run. About to give himself up, Dix becomes aware of an unscrupulous freight line run by Jim Bannon and learns that Bannon is the head of a hot car racket. Dix has his mechanic John Kellogg get a job with Bannon. Kellogg tells Dix that hot cars have been brought into Bannon's garage and one of the drivers is missing a thumb. Kellogg tells Dix to get the glove and come to the garage to catch the murderer red-handed. Dix comes to the garage without the glove and finds Bannon's dead body and his safe ransacked. As Dix is investigating, a mysterious figure sneaks up and renders him unconscious. Kellogg encourages Dix to stay on the run. Dix goes to Morley to retrieve the glove and her son, Mark Dennis, shows Dix a cylinder in the glove containing diamonds. Dennis believes Bernadene Hayes, a café waitress, is working with the murderer. Dix follows Hayes to her apartment and overhears her calling the murderer. Dix asks Kellogg to help him capture the murderer, not realizing that Kellogg is the guilty party. Kellogg forces Dix to write a note that will enable Kellogg to retrieve the glove. Dix had removed the diamonds and placed them in his tobacco pouch. When Kellogg goes to see Morley, she insists on accompanying Kellogg back to Dix. Finding that the diamonds aren't in the glove, Kellogg begins to hurt Morley. Dix gives Kellogg the diamonds. Kellogg and Hayes walk out of the apartment into the guns of two policemen. Dennis had alerted the police that Morley and Dix were in danger from Kellogg. Kellogg murdered Toomey because Toomey knew Kellogg was a wanted man and was blackmailing him. Dix will receive a substantial reward for the recovery of the diamonds. He plans to get back in the trucking business and marry Morley.

Notes and Commentary: The working titles for this film were *The Hunter Is a Fugitive* and *Whistler's Destiny*. This was the last film for series star Dix, who died on September 20, 1949.

George Lloyd had two roles in the film, first as a truck driver in the opening scene and then later as a waiter.

Review: "Efficient entry in the Whistler series." *1996 Movie & Video Guide*, Maltin

Summation: Neat noir Whistler story with fate sticking out a leg to trip up Dix at the beginning of the story instead the end. Dix is fine as the fugitive on the run. Again he is given good support, especially by John Kellogg, Karen Morley and Mark Dennis.

It's *The Thirteenth Hour* (1947) for John Kellogg and Richard Dix.

FOR YEARS HE DREAMED OF VENGEANCE ... and a woman!!

Three Hours to Kill

(November 1954)

Cast: Jim Guthrie, Dana Andrews; Laurie Mastin, Donna Reed; Chris Plumber, Dianne Foster; Sheriff Ben East, Stephen Elliott; Niles Hendricks, Richard Coogan; Marty Lasswell, Laurence Hugo; Sam Minor, James Westerfield; Carter Mastin, Richard Webb; Polly, Carolyn Jones; Betty, Charlotte Fletcher; Deke, Whit Bissell; Uncredited: Vince, Francis McDonald; Albert, Paul E. Burns; Cass, Frank Hagney; Esteban, Felipe Turich; Carter Hendricks, Arthur Fox; Ernest, Edward Clark; Dominguez, Julian Rivero; Ranchers, Edward Earle and Boyd Stockman; Townsmen, Stanley Blystone, Franklyn Farnum, Al Hill, Reed Howes, Hank Mann, Frank O'Connor, Pat O'Malley, Syd Saylor; Storekeeper, Robert Paquin; Drunk, Buddy Roosevelt

Credits: Director, Alfred Werker; Assistant Director, Sam Nelson; Producer, Harry Joe Brown; Assistant to Producer, David Breen; Story, Alex Gottlieb; Screenwriters, Richard Alan Simmons and Roy Huggins; Additional Dialogue, Maxwell Shane; Editor, Gene Havlick; Art Director, George Brooks; Set Decorator, Frank Tuttle; Cinematographer, Charles Lawton, Jr.; Second Unit Photographer, Ray Cory; Recording Supervisor, John Livadary; Original Music, Paul Sawtell; Technicolor Color Consultant, Francis Cugat

Location Filming: Hidden Valley, Thousand Oaks; Lake Sherwood; Sherwood Forest and Walker Ranch, California

Production Dates: January 19–February 9, 1954

Running Time: 77 minutes

Color by Technicolor

Story: Dana Andrews returns to his home town to clear his name and reunite with his love, Donna Reed. Andrews was framed for the murder of Reed's brother Richard Webb, who had opposed Andrews' wish to marry Reed. Andrews and Webb had quarreled. Because Andrews had been drinking heavily, he was no match for Webb's fists. When Andrews regained consciousness, he discovered Webb had been killed with two shots from a pistol that was lying on the ground. The townspeople, led by Whit Bissell, Richard Coogan, Laurence Hugo and James Westerfield, stirred up a lynch mob. As he escaped the lynch mob, Andrews' neck was burned by the rope. Andrews convinces Sheriff Stephen Elliott to give him three hours to find the real killer. The only person in town who believes in Andrews' innocence is hotel owner Dianne Foster; she has always loved him and wants him to give up his quest for revenge and leave town with her. Andrews goes to Coogan's ranch only to find that Reed is married to Coogan. Andrews sees Reed's son, Arthur Fox, and realizes he's Fox's father. Reed married Coogan to avoid the stigma of being an unwed mother. In town, Andrews finds the four suspects together. In questioning them, Andrews finds that each left the scene of the crime just before Webb's body was discovered. Andrews confronts Elliott, who admits he killed Webb. Elliott owed Webb money that he was unable to repay. Elliott tries to escape and, in an exchange of shots, Andrews kills him. The townspeople now want Andrews to stay. Andrews knows this would not work out because the rope burn on his neck would be a reminder of the incident. As he rides out of town, Foster rides to catch up with him.

Notes and Commentary: Working titles for the film were *Gunslinger* and *Three Hours to Live.*

Reviews: "Screenplay undertakes too much, resulting in a conflict of themes, none of which is satisfactorily developed. It emerges as a better-than-average western." *Variety,* 9/8/54

"Another superior Western from Werker. Though the script suffers from being the work of many hands, the film and unremittingly bleak vision are unmistakably Werker's." *The Western,* Hardy

"The film benefits from Werker's sure directorial hand and a leathery tone." *Motion Picture Guide,* Nash and Ross

Summation: This is a very good western noir. Director Werker keeps the story taut and suspenseful with some good action sequences. Dana Andrews' performance neatly captures a man tired of running. The story embraces adult themes as his love, Donna Reed, accepts marriage from another suitor (Richard Coogan) to conceal the fact that she was pregnant with Andrews' child. The negatives: a mystery villain who is too easy to guess and a too-pat happy ending as Andrews will find another love.

The Lonesome Whistle of a Train ... bringing the gallows closer to a desperado—the showdown nearer to his captor!

3:10 to Yuma

(August 1957)

CAST: Ben Wade, Glenn Ford; Dan Evans, Van Heflin; Emmy, Felicia Farr; Alice Evans, Leora Dana; Alex Potter, Henry Jones; Charlie Prince, Richard Jaeckel; Mr. Butterfield, Robert Emhardt; Bob Moons, Sheridan Comerate; Bartender, George Mitchell; Ernie Collins, Robert Ellenstein; Bisbee Marshal, Ford Rainey; Uncredited: Bill Moons, Boyd Stockman; Wade Henchmen, Jimmie Booth, John L. Cason, Richard Devon, Joe Haworth, Robert "Buzz" Henry, Tony Mayo, Erwin Neal and Jerry Oddo; Matthew Evans, Barry Curtis; Mark Evans, Jerry Hartleben; Blacksmith, Woody Chambliss; Mrs. Potter, Dorothy Adams; Dave Keene, Bill Hale; Orin Keene, Guy Teague; Hotel Proprietor-Bartender, Guy Wilkerson; Townsman in Contention, Frank Hagney; One-legged Man, Tex Holden; Townsmen, Danny Borzage, William Dyer, Jr., Fred Marlow and William Rhinehart

CREDITS: Director, Delmar Daves; Assistant Director, Sam Nelson; Producer, David Heilweil; Screenwriter, Halsted Welles; Editor, Al Clark; Art Director, Frank Hotaling; Set Decorators, William Kiernan and Robert Priestley; Cinematographer, Charles Lawton, Jr.; Gowns, Jean Louis; Makeup, Clay Campbell; Hair Stylist, Helen Hunt; Recording Supervisor, John Livadary; Sound, Josh Westmoreland; Original Music, George Duning; Orchestrator, Arthur Morton; Musical Conductor, Morris Stoloff

LOCATION FILMING: Dragoon, Elgin, Texas Canyon, Willcox, Sedona and Old Tucson, Arizona

SONGS: "3:10 to Yuma" (Duning and Washington)—sung by Frankie Laine and "3:10 to Yuma" (reprise)—sung by Norma Zimmer

PRODUCTION DATES: November 28, 1956–January 17, 1957

SOURCE: short story "Three Ten to Yuma" by Elmore Leonard

RUNNING TIME: 92 minutes

STORY: Outlaw leader Glenn Ford and his gang hold up a stagecoach carrying a gold shipment. In the holdup the driver is killed. In making their escape, the gang stops at a saloon in Bisbee. The gang leaves but Ford stays to renew acquaintances with bartender Felicia Farr. Farr takes Ford to bed. This delay enables a posse to capture Ford. Sheriff Ford Rainey needs two men to take Ford to Contention to catch the train to Yuma and then on to Yuma Prison. They each would be paid $200. The only volunteers are Van Heflin and Henry Jones. Heflin, an impoverished rancher, needs the money to purchase water rights which would save his herd of cattle. Also, Heflin wants to prove to his wife Leona Dana and his sons that he is not a coward. Heflin refused to come to the stage passengers' assistance during the hold-up. Jones, the town drunk, just wants to prove himself. Heflin and Jones get Ford to a hotel room in Contention. Ford's second-in-command, Richard Jaeckel, learns what's happening and rides to bring gang members. In the hotel room, Ford tries to persuade Heflin to let him walk out. In return, Ford would give Heflin money that would put his ranch on a paying basis. Although tempted, Heflin refuses to give in. Heflin tries to obtain help but the murdered man's brother and friends and other citizens back off, not wanting to face the outlaw gang's guns. Only Jones remains and he is killed by an outlaw's bullet. Stage line owner Robert Emhardt also backs down and releases Heflin from his responsibility. Dana arrives and tries to talk Heflin out of taking Ford to the train depot. Heflin indicates that there are some things a man can't ride around. Heflin gets Ford to the depot and is facing the guns of Jaeckel and the other gang members when Ford suddenly jumps into the moving baggage car. Heflin follows. In an exchange of shots, Heflin downs Jaeckel. Ford, who envies Heflin and his family life, indicates that he'll be able to escape from Yuma Prison. As the train moves toward Yuma, it passes a buckboard with Dana and Emhardt. As Heflin waves to them, rain begins to fall, ending the drought.

Notes and Commentary: In Elmore Leonard's short story, Deputy Marshal Paul Scallen brings outlaw leader Jim Kidd to wait in a hotel room until it's time to board the 3:10 train to Yuma (Kidd has been sentenced to serve a five-year prison term). After shooting Kidd's confederate Charlie Prince at the train station, Scallen prods Kidd into jumping on the train by keeping a gun in his back. Although the thrust of Leonard's story is maintained, many changes are made, especially in the character names.

Glenn Ford turned down the role of Dan Evans, wanting and getting the role of Ben Wade.

3:10 to Yuma (Columbia 2007) was a remake. The plot basically followed the 1957 film rather than Elmore Leonard's story. Rancher Dan Evans had a lot more trouble getting Ben Wade to the Yuma train. The ending deviates from the original: Wade climbs aboard the train. Before Evans can climb aboard, he is mortally wounded by a bullet in the back from Wade's second-in-command, Charlie Prince. After being handed a pistol, Wade guns down Prince and the rest of the gang. Then Wade climbs back on the train, hands over his pistol and sits down. As the train pulls away from the station, Wade whistles and his horse follows the train.

Reviews: "Aside from the fact this is an upper-drawer western, with both quality names and production, *3:10 to Yuma* will strike many for its resemblance to *High Noon*. It still stacks up as a major entry, save for a contrived finale which leaves a bad taste." *Variety*, 8/14/57

"An impressive but somewhat cold film." *The Western*, Hardy

"Sturdy actioner is good entertainment" *Western Movies*, Pitts

Summation: This good noir western consists more of character studies than of action. The strengths lie primarily in the performances of Glenn Ford and Van Heflin as the adversaries. Ford is smooth and confident as a man used to getting his way by either intimidation or bribery. Heflin's role is more complex as an impoverished rancher who finds a way to obtain needed money to save his ranch and to gain respect in the eyes of his family even if might mean his death. Other performances strengthen the film, especially those of Henry Jones as the town drunk and Leona Dana as Heflin's suffering but loving wife. Cinematographer Charles Lawton, Jr. excels both in the claustrophobic confines of the hotel room as well as the outdoor vistas of Arizona. Deficiencies in the screenplay prevent the film from reaching greatness. How can Ford be taken to Yuma Prison before being tried and sentenced? If vengeance is desired, why would the murdered man's brother and friends not want to back Heflin? The ending with Ford doing the "right" thing by voluntarily jumping on the train to save Heflin's life and then having the rain also fall to end the drought makes the movie contrived and unrealistic. It would be interesting to have seen what director Budd Boetticher and screenwriter Burt Kennedy could have done with Leonard's story.

She: "Is that blood?"
He: "I took two bullets through the chest, ma'am. Just routine."

Tight Spot

(May 1955)

Cast: Sherry Conley, Ginger Rogers; Lloyd Hallett, Edward G. Robinson; Vince Striker, Brian Keith; Prison Girl, Lucy Marlow; Benjamin Costain, Lorne Greene; Mrs. Willoughby, Katherine Anderson; Marvin Rickles, Allen Nourse; Fred Packer, Peter Leeds; Mississippi Mac, Doye O'Dell; Clara Moran, Eve McVeagh; Uncredited: Pete Tonelli, Alfred Linder; First Detective, John Larch; Second Detective, Ed Hinton; Warden, Helen Wallace; TV Salesman, Bob Hopkins; Elevator Mechanic, Tom Greenway; Jim Hornsby, Frank Gerstle; Doctor, Tom de Graffenreid; Honeymooners, Kathryn Grant and Robert Nichols; Miss Masters, Gloria Ann Simpson; Judge, Joseph Hamilton; Bailiff, Alan Reynolds; Arny, Norman Keats; Harris, Edward McNally; Carlyle, Robert Shield; Detectives, John Marshall and Will J.

Tight Spot (1955).

White; Policemen, Dean Cromer, Ken Mayer and John Zaremba

Credits: Director, Phil Karlson; Assistant Director, Milton Feldman; Producer, Lewis J. Rachmil; Screenwriter, William Bowers; Editor, Viola Lawrence; Art Director, Carl Anderson; Set Decorator, Louis Diage; Cinematography, Burnett Guffey; Gowns, Jean Louis; Makeup, Clay Campbell; Hair Stylist, Helen Hunt; Recording Supervisor, John Livadary; Sound, Lambert Day; Original Music, George Duning; Musical Conductor, Morris Stoloff; Orchestrator, Arthur Morton

Songs: "The Girl from Cactus Valley"—sung by Doye O'Dell with his band; "Little Brown Jug" (Winner)—performed by Doye O'Dell and his band; "Give My Shoes to Cousin Helen"—sung by Doye O'Dell with his band; "Forbidden Love"—sung by uncredited male singer, and "The Girl from Cactus Valley" (reprise)—sung by Doye O'Dell with his band

Production Dates: September 7–October 28, 1954

Source: play *Dead Pigeon* by Lenard Kantor, produced on the stage by Harald Bromley

Running Time: 97 minutes

Story: Federal attorney Edward G. Robinson's star witness in the trial to deport mob boss Lorne Greene is murdered. Robinson's only chance is to persuade Ginger Rogers, a women's prison inmate, to testify. Police officer Brian Keith and prison matron Katherine Anderson transfer Rogers from prison to a hotel suite in the city. Rogers, a believer in never volunteering, refuses to testify. Little by little in the confines of the hotel suite, Rogers and Keith become attracted to each other. Greene is told where Rogers is being held and sends a gunman to kill her. A shot wounds Rogers and return fire from Keith kills the gunman. After Rogers' wound is cared for, Anderson collapses from a shot that had been fired by the gunman. Keith leaves the hotel to change clothes and is taken by gunmen to Greene. Keith has been in Greene's employ for ten years. Greene reminds Keith that Rogers must not testify. Keith is to open the bathroom window so a gunman can kill Rogers before she is transported to the city jail. Returning to the hotel, Keith lets it slip to Robinson that he knows Rogers is going to the city jail, a fact that Robinson just found out. Rogers gets the news that Anderson's wounds proved fatal and now decides to testify. Keith tries to talk Rogers out of testifying, to no avail. A gunman comes in the window that Keith left open. Keith realizes he can't let Rogers be murdered and rushes into Rogers' bedroom to face the gunman. Shots are exchanged and both men are killed. Rogers testifies and states her occupation as gangbuster.

Notes and Commentary: The working title for this film was *Dead Pigeon*.

Reviews: "Top notch trouping[,] an interesting plot and well-valued direction all contribute to the entertainment." *Variety*, 5/4/55

"*Tight Spot* is a pretty good little melodrama, the kind you keep rooting for, a respectable, if unstriking, entry." *New York Times*, 03/19/55

"An intelligent and gritty crime story." *Motion Picture Guide*, Nash and Ross

Summation: This is exciting, gripping crime noir with fine acting by Rogers, Robinson and Keith. Most of the film takes place in a hotel room and director Phil Karlson uses the claustrophobic atmosphere to build tension and suspense. Cinematographer Burnett Guffey again shows why he is a master of noir, using the darkness to intensify the dramatic sequences of the first-rate screenplay of William Bowers.

HERE'S WHY THEY CALL TIJUANA AMERICA'S BARGAIN BASEMENT OF SIN!

The Tijuana Story

(October 1957)

A Clover Production

Cast: Manuel Acosta Mesa, Rodolfo Acosta; Mitch, James Darren; Eddie March, Robert McQueeney; Liz March, Jean Willes; Linda, Joy Stoner; Peron Diaz, Paul Newlan; Pino, George E. Stone; Reuben Galindo, Michael Fox; Enrique Acosta Mesa, Robert Blake; Alberto Rodriguez, William Fawcett; Paul Coates/Narrator, Paul Coates; Uncredited: Alma Acosta Mesa, Susan Seaforth Hayes; Paul Acosta Mesa, Ralph Valencia; Ricardo (Club Manager), Rick Vallin; Lupe (Bar Girl), Suzanne Ridgeway; Policeman, Abel Fernandez; Miguel Fuentes, William Tannen

Credits: Director, Leslie Kardos; Assistant Director, Leonard Katzman; Producer, Sam Katzman; Screenwriter, Lou Morheim; Editor, Edwin Bryant; Art Director, Paul Palmentola; Set Decorator, Sidney Clifford; Cinematography, Benjamin H. Kline; Production Coordinator, Paul Sperling; Sound, Josh Westmoreland; Music Conductor, Mischa Bakaleinikoff

Location Filming: Tijuana, Baja California Norte, Mexico

Production Dates: May 14–23, 1957

Running Time: 72 minutes

Story: Newspaperman Rodolfo Acosta is waging a vigorous campaign against vice and corruption in Tijuana. Schoolteacher William Fawcett is beaten for giving evidence against gangster William Tannen. Acosta goes to a club secretly run by Paul Newlan, requesting money to pay for Fawcett's hospital bills. When Newlan refuses, Acosta steps up his anti-vice campaign. Newlan pressures newspaper owner Michael Fox to make Acosta tone down his editorials. Acosta does this until young college student James Darren is threatened with arrest for vehicular damage after smoking marijuana cigarettes. Darren dies in an accident while attempting to escape from the police. A decision is now made to murder Acosta. Arrangements have been made to have Tannen leave prison for 24 hours so he can commit the crime. Robert McQueeney, hired by Newlan to give the club respectability, learns of the murder plot. McQueeney, who is aware of the vice element associated with the club, draws the line at murder and is able to warn police of the plot. Police arrive before Tannen can carry out the murder and he is arrested. Newlan figures McQueeney tipped off the police and wants to kill him and Jean Willes, McQueeney's pregnant wife. Newlan and henchman Rick Vallin catch up to McQueeney and Willes. As McQueeney takes a beating from Newlan and Vallin, Willes picks up

Joy Stoner strikes James Darren in *The Tijuana Story* (1957).

a gun that was dropped in the struggle, forcing Newlan and Vallin to leave. McQueeney now decides to return to Tijuana and give information that will damage the criminal organization. Acosta, a marked man, is finally gunned down. Acosta's final editorial is finished and published by his son Robert Blake. Fox admits that he had been a coward and will now help lead the effort to clean up Tijuana. Newlan and Vallin are apprehended by the police.

Notes and Commentary: This was the only starring role for Rodolfo Acosta. Narrator Paul Coates was a real-life newspaperman.

Reviews: "Although based on real-life vice, a mild, routine meller." *Variety*, 10/9/57

Summation: This is a below par crime exposé noir. The acting of the principals is barely passable, the production values almost nonexistent. Leslie Kardos' slack direction produces a story that generates only a modicum of suspense. The prologue promises a hard-hitting story but Lou Morheim's screenplay just doesn't hold up.

A STORY OF SHOCKING IMPACT!

To the Ends of the Earth

(February 1948)

A Sidney Buchman Production

Cast: Mike Barrows, Dick Powell; Ann Grant, Signe Hasso; Shu Pan Wu, Maylia; Nicolas Sokim, Ludwig Donath; Commissioner Lum Chi Chow, Vladimir Sokoloff; Grieg, Edgar Barrier; Shannon, John Hoyt; Commissioner Lariesier, Marcel Journet; Commissioner Alberto Berado, Luis Van Rooten; Binda Sha, Fritz Leiber; Uncredited: Commissioner H.J. Anslinger, Harry J.

Anslinger; Commissioner Hadley, Vernon Steele; Mahmoud, Peter Virgo; Commissioner Hassam, Lou Krugman; Chian Soo, Eddie Lee; Vrandstadter, Ivan Triesault; Joe, Peter Chong; Cassidy, George Volk; Clark, Robert Malcolm; Commissioner Lu, Richard Loo; Professor Salim, Michael Raffetto; Ship's Officers, Douglas Coppin and Horace Brown; Counsel, Harry Kuwahart; Guards, Harry Nogawa and S. Yokota; Counsel's Clerk, S. Nisimura; Judges, M. Okamoto, Y. Kawasaki and Tom Sugiyama; Hernando, Leon Lenoir; Court Clerk, Otto Han; Clerks, Tetsuo Fujita, Hisao Takayama and Chikata Naramura; Chinese Driver, James B. Leong; Sago, James S. Yahiro; Hotel Clerk, Richard Wang; Transportation Captain, Beal Wong; Giant Chinese Man, Henry Kulky; Camel Driver, Frank Lackteen; Egyptian Policeman at Gate, Mahmud Shaikhaly; Chinese Pilot, Victor Sen Yung; Cab Drivers, Nacho Galindo and Julian Rivero; Ship's Doctor, Robert Riordan; Sketch Artist, Nick Volpe; Ship's Captain, Frank Mayo; Ship's Cook who Started Fire, George J. Lewis; Pastry Cook, Fred Godoy; Narcotics Agent, Walter Pietila; Coast Guard Captain, Mack Williams; Midgie, Sally Corner; Ensign, Jack Barnett; Harry Hardt, Harlan Warde; Binda Sha Henchman, Blue Washington; Mary Paine, Florence Wix; Ship Passenger, Bess Flowers; Treasury Agent in Ship's Galley, Tom Coleman

CREDITS: Director, Robert Stevenson; Assistant Director and Second Unit Director (Egypt), Seymour Friedman; Second Unit Director (China), Ray Nazarro; Associate Producer, Jay Richard Kennedy; Assistant to Producer, Gordon Griffith; Story and Screenplay, Jay Richard Kennedy; Editor, William Lyon; Art Directors, Stephen Goosson and Cary Odell; Set Decorators, William Menefee and Frank Tuttle; Cinematographer, Burnett Guffey; Special Effects, Lawrence W. Butler; Gowns, Jean Louis; Makeup, Clay Campbell; Hair Stylist, Helen Hunt; Sound, George Cooper; Original Music, George Duning; Musical Director, M.W. Stoloff

LOCATION FILMING: Santa Catalina Island Channel and Los Angeles Harbor, California; background footage: Shanghai, Cairo, Havana and New York

PRODUCTION DATES: December 6, 1946–February 19, 1947

RUNNING TIME: 109 minutes

STORY: While investigating the possibility that a freighter is transporting narcotics, Treasury agent Dick Powell sees 100 men cast into the Pacific Ocean. The freighter is outside Powell's jurisdiction but he comes close enough to get the name of the freighter and to see the captain. This information takes Powell to Shanghai where, working with Chinese Commissioner Vladimir Sokoloff, he uncovers refining equipment in Ludwig Donath's rickshaw garage. Found out, Donath commits suicide. Powell meets Signe Hasso and her Chinese ward Maylia, and thinks Hasso might have some connection to the narcotics smuggling. Sokoloff believes that the poppies are being grown in Egypt, so Powell works with agents in that country. On one farm, considerable intricate engineering was needed to provide water to grow roses. Powell is suspicious because Hasso's deceased husband was an engineer. At that farm, Powell discovers poppies were grown under the roses. But he is too late: The poppies have been harvested and have left the area. The narcotics have been placed in canisters. Then the canisters were placed in the first stomach of camels being led to slaughter. When Powell learns that Hasso and Maylia have traveled to Cuba, he takes a chance that the package to Havana contains the drugs. The package arrives at Ivan Triesault's place of business. Powell still holds off on grabbing the narcotics, wanting to find the final destination. A shipment is put on a New York–bound ship on which Hasso and Maylia are passengers. An alert agent sees boxes with suspiciously large check marks. Narcotic agents become workers in the ship's galley to keep an eye on any movement of the boxes. As the ship nears the New York harbor, George J. Lewis starts a fire that produces considerable smoke. In the confusion Lewis and his cohorts place the narcotics in garbage cans and these cans are emptied over the bow of the ship. When Powell goes to investigate, he is rendered unconscious. When he awakens, Hasso is there to help. Coast Guard men come aboard the ship. Powell figures the narcotics are in waterproof containers with weights. Powell gives Maylia a note to give to Triesault indicating he knows where the drugs are. In Hasso's stateroom, Powell is expecting a call from Triesault but Maylia calls to see how a romance between Powell and Hasso is progressing. Powell races to Triesault's cabin to find him murdered. After the location of the dumping of the garbage is determined, Coast Guard cutters race to the spot. Powell takes Hasso and Maylia along. Gang members are there to retrieve the narcotics but a short gun battle ensues. The gang members are subdued and the narcotics recovered and placed in Powell's boat. As they begin the return to New York, Maylia grabs Powell's pistol and demands the boat go to a particular point. Maylia also states that she murdered both Triesault and Hasso's husband, the latter because he would not kill Hasso. Then Maylia finds the gun is loaded with blanks. Powell was suspicious because Maylia, who was supposed to be a close friend, was not there when he recovered from being knocked out aboard ship. Maylia, in the employ of Japanese officials, attempts to jump overboard but Powell prevents her from ending her life. The narcotics ring has been broken with cooperation from many nations.

Notes and Commentary: The working titles for the film were *Assigned to Treasury* and *The 27th Day*. Jay Richard Kennedy wrote an original story on the international drug trade, based on exploits of Harry J. Anslinger, the first appointed commissioner of the U.S. Treasury Department's Bureau of Narcotics. Anslinger conducted global investigations between 1917 and 1928. Kennedy sold his story to Columbia for $100,000. Producer Sidney Buchman, uncredited, added material to punch up scenes in the final script. Anslinger provided the filmmakers with classified material and arranged to allow director Robert Stevenson to shoot at Narcotics Control Commission at Lake Success, then the New York headquarters of the United Nations. The subject matter became a concern of the Hollywood Production Code which stated that "illegal drug traffic must never be presented." The Code was amended to allow "the illegal drug traffic to be presented provided it does not stimulate curiosity concerning the use of or traffic in such drugs and provided there shall be no scenes approved which show the use of illegal drugs or their effects in detail."

Reviews: "A fast moving melodrama. Production and direction are neatly keyed to a realistic note, giving maximum credibility to the proceedings." *Variety*, 1/21/48

"An engrossing, globetrotting semi-documentary on the evils of narcotic pushers." *Motion Picture Guide*, Nash and Ross

Summary: Filmed in semi-documentary style, this is a very good crime noir. From an excellent screenplay, directors Robert Stevenson and the uncredited Sidney Buchman fashioned a taut, suspenseful and engrossing motion picture. The acting is good with Dick Powell believable as a tough, smart Treasury agent. Again premier noir cinematographer Burnett Guffey's camerawork is first-rate, capturing the dark, dirty locales that add to the story's suspense.

BOGART'S IN TOKYO ... BATTLING A NEW KIND OF UNDERWORLD...

Tokyo Joe

(November 1949)

A Santana Production

Cast: Joe Barrett, Humphrey Bogart; Mark Landis, Alexander Knox; Trina, Florence Marly; Baron Kimura, Sessue Hayakawa; Danny, Jerome Courtland; Idaho, Gordon Jones; Ito, Teru Shimada; Kanda, Hideo Mori; General Ireton, Charles Meredith; Colonel Dahlgren, Rhys Williams; Anya, Lora Lee Michel; Uncredited: Nani-San, Kyoko Kamo; Kamikaze, Gene Gondo; Major J.F.X. Loomis, Harold Goodwin; Military Police Captain, James Cardwell; Truck Driver, Frank Kumagai; Lt. General Takenobu, Tetsu Komai; Colonel Hara, Otto Han; Najuro Goro, Yosan Tsuruta; Maid, Julia Fukuzaki; Medical Major, Fred F. Sears; Lieutenant at Airport, Harlan Warde; Provost Marshal Major, Hugh Beaumont; Fingerprint Sergeant, Tommy Bond; Photo Sergeant, David Wolfe; Captain Winnow, Whit Bissell; Officer, Scott Edwards; Mrs. Sado, Fumiko Kawabata; Jack (Ireton's Aide), Jack Reynolds; Military Policemen, Ed Randolph, Tony Layng and Ted Jordan; Barkeeper, Yuji Kakuuchi; Nisei Interpreter, Tom Komuro; Policeman, John Yabu; Rickshaw Driver, Lane Nakano; Manservant, Rollin Moriyama; Military Police Sergeant, Michael Towne

Credits: Director, Stuart Heisler; Assistant Director, Wilbur McGaugh; Producer, Robert Lord; Associate Producer, Henry S. Kesler; Story, Steve Fisher; Screenwriters, Cyril Hume and Bertram Millhauser; Adaptor, Walter Doniger;

Editor, Viola Lawrence; Art Director, Robert Peterson; Set Decorator, James Crowe; Cinematographer, Charles Lawton, Jr.; Gowns, Jean Louis; Makeup, Clay Campbell; Hair Stylist, Helen Hunt; Sound, Russell Malmgren; Original Music, George Antheil; Musical Director, Morris Stoloff; Dialogue Director, Jason Lindsey

SONGS: "These Foolish Things" (Strachey, Link and Maschwitz)—sung by Florence Marly; "These Foolish Things" (reprised three times)—by Florence Marly and twice by an unknown Japanese female singer; "London Bridge Is Falling Down" (traditional)—played by Japanese musical instruments; "I Never Knew" (Fio Rio and Kahn)—sung by an unknown Japanese singer

LOCATION FILMING: Tokyo, Japan

PRODUCTION DATES: January 4–February 16, 1949

RUNNING TIME: 88 minutes

STORY: Humphrey Bogart returns to Japan after the conclusion of World War II to visit the bar he co-owned. Bogart was given a permit to stay in Japan for 60 days. At the bar, which is off limits to Allied personnel, Bogart is reunited with his former partner, Teru Shimada. Shimada tells Bogart that Florence Marly is alive. Bogart goes to see Marly, who says that, since he left her the week before Pearl Harbor, after the war she divorced him. Bogart meets Marly's six-year-old daughter, Lora Lee Michel. Marly then married influential lawyer Alexander Knox. Bogart meets Knox and tells him he does not recognize the divorce. Knowing 60 days will not give him time to win back Marly, Bogart enters into an agreement with gangster Sessue Hayakawa to establish a small airline. Trying to cut through red tape, Bogart obtains information that Marly broadcast propaganda over Japanese radio during the War. Marly tells him she did this to be reunited with her daughter. Bogart realizes that Michel is his daughter. Knox wants to defeat Bogart on a level playing field and makes a call to allow Bogart to go through with his airline. Hayakawa initially sends mundane products like frozen frogs but later shows his true colors and wants Bogart to smuggle three war criminals into Japan. These war criminals will restart the Black Dragon Society. Bogart plans to deliver these men to Allied personnel. To make sure Bogart delivers the men to him, Hayakawa kidnaps Michel. Flying from Korea to Japan, the war criminals take over the aircraft and lock Bogart and his pilots in the storage area. On landing the plane at a remote airfield, the criminals set fire to it. Allied forces, which had been monitoring all airfields, arrive and take the war criminals into custody. Bogart and the pilots are rescued. Bogart has only a few hours to find Michel before Hayakawa will kill her. From Shimada, Bogart learns that Hayakawa and Michel are in the basement of the hotel next to their bar. Bogart, with Allied personnel waiting outside the basement, goes in to effect a rescue. Bogart has to fight and defeat guard Hideo Mori to take her into his arms. As he begins to take Michel to safety, Hayakawa begins firing at Bogart. Hearing shots, soldiers rush in and shoot Hayakawa. Knox and Marly, who had been waiting outside, are reunited with Michel. Bogart, mortally wounded, believes Marly will return to him as his life ebbs.

NOTES AND COMMENTARY: Second unit director Arthur Black and cameramen Joseph Biroc and Emil Oster, Jr. shot 40,000 feet of background film in and around Tokyo. They shot an aerial view of Mount Fuji, shots of Haneda airport and a bus ride into the city past burned-out factories and newly built shacks. Black ran into difficulties: The first week it rained each day. To make the shot of a single street backdrop as daylight waned, Black had to shoot one side of one street and one side of another street to make it look like a single street. To make it look like Bogart was in Tokyo, the U.S. Army furnished soldiers to double him. This was the first time an American company was permitted to film in Japan after World War II. Most of the film was shot at Columbia.

Santana Productions wanted Warner Bros. contractee Viveca Lindfors as Bogart's co-star. Negotiations with Warner Bros. fell through.

Tokyo Joe marked the first time Sessue Hayakawa's worked in an American film since 1924. In 1957, he received an Academy Award nomination for Best Supporting Actor as the prison camp commandant in Columbia's *The Bridge on the River Kwai*.

REVIEWS: "What was clearly intended as a typical Bogart thriller emerged as little more than a Bogart parody—and it sank with very little trace." *The Columbia Story*, Hirschhorn

"Although compelling and well-crafted, the film was on par with neither the previous Santana film, *Knock on Any Door*, nor the following one, *In a Lonely Place*." *Motion Picture Guide*, Nash and Ross

SUMMATION: This is good noir that owes a lot to *Casablanca* (Warner Bros., 1942). Bogart is in love with Florence Marly who is married to Alexander Knox. Bogart and Marly's song "These Foolish Things" is heard throughout the proceedings. Bogart's character finally realizes that he has to take action and do the right thing. After saying that, the screenplay generates some good suspense. Bogart is the show with some good support from Alexander Knox as his romantic rival. Again Charles Lawton' photographic talents enhance this film.

"I DON'T DARE SHOW MY FACE!"

The True Story of Lynn Stuart

(March 1958)

CAST: Phyllis Carter aka Lynn Stuart, Betsy Palmer; Willie Down, Jack Lord; Lt. Jim Hagan, Barry Atwater; Uncredited: Edmund G. Brown, Himself; Ralph Carter, Kim Spalding; Hal Bruck, Karl Lukas; Eddie Dine, Casey Walters; Jerry Jackson aka Wilbur Stuart, Harry Jackson; Nora Efron, Claudia Bryar; Doc, John Anderson; Sue Diggins, Rita Duncan; Ben, Lee Farr; Jimmie Carter, Louis Towers; Dr. Freeley, James Maloney; Fred, Carlos Romero; Gus, Art Lewis; Turk, Gavin MacLeod; Linda (Car Hop), Linda Cherney; The Kid, Don Devlin; Priest, Lawrence Green; Father Albert, Edward Le Veque; First Gas Station Attendant, Mack Chandler; Sam (Second Gas Station Attendant), Samuel Colt; Customers, Paul Maxwell and Dorothy Gordon; Buyer, Anita Carrell; Carhops, Shirlee Lewis and Barbara Aler; Lucy, Madeline O'Donnell; Countermen, Lyle Latell, Joey Ray and Jack Kenney; Ginger (Car Hop), Betsy Jones-Moreland; Salesman, Lionel Ames; Officers, Edward McNally and Joe Donte; Mexican, Abel Franco; Truck Driver, Paul Sorensen; Police Sergeant, Larry Thor; Mexican Officer, Manuel Lopez; Doctor, John McNamara; Clerk, Jackson Halliday; Professional Bowler, Ward Brand; Nat, Than Wyenn; Mexican Waitress, Gloria Rhoads; Patron, Gloria Marshall; Policewoman, Audrey Swanson; Plainclothesmen, Paul Lukather and Douglas Wilson; Pin Boy, Jimmy Bates; Girl, Harriette Tarler; Customs Officer, Richard Bull; Bailiff, Tom Coleman; Old Duncan, "Snub" Pollard

CREDITS: Director, Lewis Seiler; Assistant Director, Carter De Haven, Jr.; Producer, Bryan Foy; Screenwriter, John H. Kneubuhl; Editor, Saul A. Goodkind; Art Director, Ross Bellah; Set Decorator, James M. Crowe; Cinematographer, Burnett Guffey; Sound, Lambert Day; Musical Conductor, Mischa Bakaleinikoff

PRODUCTION DATES: August 12–27, 1957

RUNNING TIME: 78 minutes

SOURCE: newspaper articles by Santa Ana reporter Pat Michaels

STORY: Betsy Palmer's nephew is killed in an automobile accident after a high speed chase with the police. Narcotics and syringes are found in the wrecked automobile. In the inquest, Palmer wants to know why the police haven't cracked down on drug traffickers in the area. Lt. Barry Atwater indicates there are not enough law enforcement officers to handle the situation. Palmer volunteers to become an undercover operative but she is turned down. In Tijuana, undercover operative Than Wyenn overhears a drug deal organized by Jack Lord. As Wyenn attempts to alert Atwater, he is murdered by Lord. Desperate to get a handle on the man behind the drug ring, Atwater recruits Palmer. Palmer's husband, Kim Spalding, gives in only if he can call off the arrangement if he feels Palmer is in significant danger. Palmer poses as a parolee from West Virginia and is provided with a new apartment, husband and a job at the drive-in restaurant frequented by Lord and lower level gang members. Palmer and Lord meet and Lord is immediately attracted to her. As Lord begins to trust her, he shows her how the narcotics are distributed to buyers. The drug ring boss is a respected used-car company owner, John Anderson. Anderson checks on Palmer's new identity and Rita Duncan, not knowing Palmer is assuming the former inmate's identity, vouches for her. Palmer's son, Louis Towers, begins to have bad dreams due to being separated from Palmer. Palmer decides that after one more night she'll quit. That night Lord forces Palmer to come with him to Tijuana. Towers has become seriously ill but word does not reach her in time. Atwater begins a search for Palmer. Carlos Romero, a mob informant, tells of a major drug shipment Lord can hijack. Using

***The True Story of Lynn Stuart* (1958) finds Betsy Palmer in the grasp of an Orange County sheriff.**

Palmer with a supposedly disabled car to lure the couriers into a feeling of false security, Lord gets the drop on them. Lord takes them into the bushes and guns down both men. The sudden violence pushes Palmer into hysterics which increase when Lord shoots Romero. Lord divides the narcotics into five smaller lots. Five drivers, including Duncan, will take the spoils to a California motel. At a gas station rest room, Palmer leaves a note for Atwater. At the motel Palmer is terrified knowing that when Duncan arrives, her cover will be exposed. Next she hears a radio request that she immediately contact the hospital about her son. Palmer is unaware that Atwater had received the note and has taken into custody the five couriers, including Duncan, plus Anderson. Lord sees the officers and opens fire. The police fire shots, wounding Lord. To protect Palmer, she is taken to jail also. Palmer delivers damaging testimony at the trial. For their safety, Palmer and her family are then relocated.

NOTES AND COMMENTARY: The working titles for the film were *The Other Life of Lynn Stuart* and *The Grasshopper*. The film's technical advisor was the actual person that Betsy Palmer portrayed as Lynn Stuart. When visiting the set, this woman was masked.

REVIEWS: "Because it's constructed from California fact rather than conjured from Hollywood fiction, *The True Story of Lynn Stuart* manages to assume a semi-documentary flavor that magnifies excitement and instills deep consideration for the plight of the character. On the whole, it is a well-knit piece of work." *Variety*, 2/19/58

"The story is told with gritty honesty and has some fine performances. [Palmer's] performance here lifts the film and is complemented by sensitive direction that works in tandem with the story." *Motion Picture Guide*, Nash and Ross

SUMMATION: This is a taut, tense and sometimes violent crime noir based on fact. The actors' performances are good but it is Betsy Palmer that brings life to the proceedings. Palmer hits no false notes and pulls out all the stops. Palmer's emotions are completely on target for each scenario depicted. Those who want to see a fine performance by an actress who should have gone farther should watch this one. Adroitly directed by veteran Lewis Seiler (his final assignment) and photographed by one of the best cinematographers, Burnett Guffey, this is an example of how a good movie can be made on a limited budget.

They tried to draw the line—Just this side of MURDER!

Two of a Kind

(July 1951)

Cast: Michael "Lefty" Farrell, Edmond O'Brien; Brandy Kirby, Lizabeth Scott; Kathy McIntyre, Terry Moore; Vincent Mailer, Alexander Knox; William McIntyre, Griff Barnett; Todd, Robert Anderson; Maida McIntyre, Virginia Brissac; Uncredited: Father Lanahan, J.M. Kerrigan; Minnie Mitt, Claire Carleton; Chief Petty Officer, Louis Jean Heydt; Woman at Phone Booth, Jessie Arnold; Desk Sergeant, Al Murphy; Man at Police Station, Blackie Whiteford; Ben, James Kirkwood; Deputy, Emory Parnell

Credits: Director, Henry Levin; Assistant Director, Sam Nelson; Producer, William Dozier; Story, James Edward Grant; Screenwriters, Lawrence Kimble and James Gunn; Editor, Charles Nelson; Cinematographer, Burnett Guffey; Art Director, Walter Holscher; Set Decorator, Louis Diage; Gowns, Jean Louis; Makeup, Clay Campbell; Hair Stylist, Helen Hunt; Sound, Frank Goodwin; Musical Score, George Duning; Musical Director, Morris Stoloff

Production Dates: October 10–November 2, 1950

Running Time: 75 minutes

Story: Edmond O'Brien is convinced to join Alexander Knox and Lizabeth Scott in a scam to obtain an inheritance of ten million dollars. O'Brien is to impersonate the son of Griff Barnett and Virginia Brissac.

Their son has been missing since he was three years old. To pull off the scam, O'Brien has to lose the tip of a finger. O'Brien is to be introduced to the family through Terry Moore, a niece. Moore, believing O'Brien to be legitimate, introduces him to Barnett. Moore thinks O'Brien is a crook who can be rehabilitated. Barnett gets Knox to substantiate the claim, not knowing he's part of the scam. Knox verifies the claim, believing Barnett will make O'Brien his heir.

Barnett tells Knox that O'Brien will not be included in his will and in fact will begin liquidating money to charities in his will. Knox decides the answer is to murder Barnett, making it look like an accident, and destroy all copies of his will. O'Brien and Scott, not in favor of murder, want to walk away from the scam. Knox tells them they'll will participate or go to jail. O'Brien calls a meeting and tells Knox that he will confess all to Barnett. Knox then decides to murder O'Brien. Knox's henchman, Robert Anderson, throws O'Brien into the water in an attempt to drown him. O'Brien, formerly an underwater demolition expert, is able to defeat Anderson. Knox quickly goes to Barnett to place all blame of the scam on O'Brien. O'Brien had recorded the last meeting with Knox and plays it for Barnett. Barnett tells Knox to close down his law practice and leave the city.

Barnett had done his own investigation of O'Brien and from the Navy Department received copies of his fingerprints showing no injuries. Barnett knew O'Brien was a false heir but let the deception stand to make Brissac's last days happy. O'Brien is convinced to continue the deception. O'Brien then races to catch up with Scott to kindle a romance.

Notes and Commentary: The working title of this film was *Lefty Farrell.*

Reviews: "Fairly entertaining melodrama of a million dollar shakedown. A generally interesting plot line and good performances help overcome an inclination to wordiness in the script." *Variety*, 6/15/51

"This starts off with an interesting premise, but quickly bogs down to run-of-the-mill suspense action with only a few mild thrills. The dialogue is overly talky and the ending wholly unbelievable. The direction paces itself well, however, and the cast isn't bad, giving performances that are probably better than the script deserved." *The Motion Picture Guide*, Nash and Ross

Summation: This movie was recently released as part of the *Bad Girls of Film Noir* DVD set. Lizabeth Scott's performance is more naughty than bad. Any chance for a worthwhile caper noir is derailed by indifferent performances by Scott and Edmond O'Brien and a script that just isn't believable. Cast-wise, only Alexander Knox, Griff Barnett and Virginia Brissac truly distinguish themselves. It's hard to believe O'Brien is a real lady-killer. Scott doesn't exude the sex appeal needed to put her in the upper rank of film femme fatales. The script makes it impossible for Terry Moore to be convincing. The film's ending is impossible to believe with O'Brien, like a magician, pulling a record out of seemingly nowhere to prove he was going to confess all. In a totally unnecessary bit of scripting, dice are thrown from a car, first appearing to be a six and five but changing to two sixes to symbolize disaster. At the end, dice are again thrown from a car now symbolizing happiness. Pure hogwash!

GIRL VICTIM EXPOSES TOURIST CAMP RACKET...
Charges Mob Used Hundreds of Young Beauties to
Lure Men Into Sinister Resort Chain!

Under Age

(April 1941)

CAST: Jane Baird, Nan Grey; Rocky Stone, Tom Neal; Edie Baird, Mary Anderson; Tap Manson, Alan Baxter; Mrs. Burke, Leona Maricle; Albert Ward, Don Beddoe; Uncredited: Lily Fletcher, Yolande Donlan; Grant, Richard Terry; Rhoda, Wilma Francis; Minnie, Patti McCarty; Boots, Billie Roy; Gladys, Gwen Kenyon; Jackie, Barbara Kent; Nell, Nancy Worth; Hack, John Tyrrell; Downey, Byron Foulger; Mr. Ames, George McKay; Mrs. Ames, Ruth Robinson; Detective, Chuck Hamilton; Judge, Ed Stanley; Driver Who Tries to Pick Up Grey, Earle Hodgins; Johnson, Kenneth MacDonald; Gildersleeve, Frank Mills; Hillard, Ed Bruce; Frane, Al Rhein; Pearson, Lester Dorr; Waiter, Stanley Brown

CREDITS: Director, Edward Dmytryk; Story, Stanley Roberts; Screenwriter, Robert D. Andrews; Editor, Richard Fantl; Art Director, Lionel Banks; Cinematographer, John Stumar

PRODUCTION DATES: February 4–19, 1941

RUNNING TIME: 59 minutes

STORY: Nan Grey and her sister Mary Anderson, who had been serving time in the County Detention Home for Minor Girls, are released. Gangster Alan Baxter offers them jobs as hostesses in a motel chain run by Leona Maricle. Initially they refuse but change their minds and accept when no other job offers are forthcoming. After being interviewed and hired by Maricle, they are transported to a Midwest motel. Their job is to flag down men driving expensive cars and convince them to stay at the motel. Grey gets Tom Neal, the son of a jewelry store owner, to pick her up. Wise to the racket, Neal agrees to go to the motel anyway. At the motel, Baxter learns that Neal is transporting jewelry and steals it. Neal thinks Grey is involved and confronts her. Seeing Grey is innocent, Neal wants her to quit. Grey says she can't. Neal gives Grey a card that tells how he can be reached if she needs him. Baxter sees their meeting and takes her to Maricle for questioning. When Grey's answers are not satisfactory, Maricle has her beaten. Learning of the beating, Anderson plans to get even with Baxter. Baxter is warned by motel manager Wilma Francis. Baxter takes Anderson for a ride, throws her out on the road and then runs the car over her. Grey organizes the girls to avenge Anderson's death and put an end to the tourist camp racket. Grey goes to Neal for help. Neal takes Baxter to an out-of-the-way house where Grey and the girls force Baxter to confess, implicating Maricle. Baxter and Maricle are arrested and convicted. Neal and Grey begin a romance.

NOTES AND COMMENTARY: Richard Terry had a western career as Jack Perrin, starring in oaters for various independent companies from 1930 to 1937. His last starring film was *Wildcat Saunders* (Atlantic, 1936).

Under Age's opening title music would see plenty use as the theme for many Durango Kid westerns.

REVIEWS: "A 'B' film primed for dualers and as such is a fairly neat package." *Variety*, 5/21/41

"*Under Age* again exploited the female form in a serviceable quickie." *The Columbia Story*, Hirschhorn

SUMMATION: This is a pretty strong "B"

crime noir depicting young girls using the physical charms to lure unsuspecting men to motels where girls and gambling are available. Edward Dmytryk's direction is brisk and John Stumar's photography properly sets the somber mood. The film is above average.

SHOCKING BULLET-BY-BULLET STORY OF AMERICA'S SECRET WAR ON THE MOBS!

The Undercover Man

(April 1949)

CAST: Frank Warren, Glenn Ford; Judith Warren, Nina Foch; George Pappas, James Whitmore; Attorney Edward J. O'Rourke, Barry Kelley; Stanley Weinburg, David Wolfe; Inspector Herzog, Frank Tweddell; Joseph S. Horan, Howard St. John; Sergeant Shannon, John F. Hamilton; Sidney Gordon, Leo Penn; Rosa Rocco, Joan Lazer; Maria Rocco, Esther Minciotti; Theresa Rocco, Angela Clarke; Salvatore Rocco, Anthony Caruso; Manny Zanger, Robert Osterloh; Gladys LaVerne, Kay Medford; Muriel Gordon, Patricia White [Patricia Barry]; Uncredited: Narrator, John Ireland; Johnny (Handwriting Expert), Peter Brocco; Judge Allen Parker, Everett Glass; Newsboy, Joe Mantell; Fred Ferguson, Michael Cisney; Alice Ferguson, Marcella Cisney; Harris, Sidney Dubin; Pharmacist, William Vedder; Policemen, Jim Drum and Allen Mathews; Malibu Policeman, Robert Malcolm; Woman in Window, Esther Zeitlin; Gunmen, Tom Coffey and William Rhinehart; Big Fellow (Man in White), Ralph Volkie; Middle-aged Man, Al Murphy; Blonde, Lynn Whitney; Boys, Ronnie Ralph and Billy Gray; Vendor, Silvio Minciotti; Sluggers, Cy Malis and Jack Gordon; Mrs. Weisner, Virginia Farmer; Grocer, John Butler; Tenement Resident, Rose Plummer; Bailiff, Richard Bartell; Court Clerk, Ben Erway; Jury Foreman, Frank Mayo; Judge Parker's Secretary, Wheaton Chambers; District Attorney, George Douglas; Mrs. O'Rourke, Helen Wallace; Customer, Sam LaMarr; Deputies, Brian O'Hara, Pat Lane and Joe Palma; Young Hoodlum, Paul Marion; Cigar Store Owner, Peter Virgo; Horse Parlor Manager, Edwin Max; Horse Parlor Bouncer, Billy Nelson; Gambler, Bill Stubbs; Storekeeper's Wife, Stella LeSaint; Hoodlums, Roy Darmour, Sol Gorss, Ted Jordan, Wally Rose and Harlan Warde; Newsreel Announcer, Tom Hanlon; Big Fellow, Ken Harvey

CREDITS: Director, Joseph H. Lewis; Assistant Director, Wilbur McGaugh; Screenwriters, Jack Rubin and Sydney Boehm; Additional Dialogue, Malvin Wald; Editor, Al Clark; Art Director, Walter Holscher; Set Decorator, William Kiernan; Cinematographer, Burnett Guffey; Gowns, Jean Louis; Sound, Jack Goodrich; Original Music, George Duning; Musical Director, M.W. Stoloff

FILMING LOCATION: Lockheed Airport, Burbank, California; Union Station, Los Angeles, California and North Hollywood, California

PRODUCTION DATES: May 4–June 16, 1948

SOURCE: article "Undercover Man: He Trapped Capone" by Frank J. Wilson (*Colliers*, April 26, 1947) and a story outline by Jack Rubin

RUNNING TIME: 85 minutes

STORY: Treasury investigator Glenn Ford arrives in Chicago to meet with informer Robert Osterloh, who can provide proof of income tax evasion of top mob boss Ralph Volkie. After meeting with Ford, Osterloh is gunned down in the streets. John F. Hamilton, a desk sergeant, gives Ford the name of Anthony Caruso, a mob accountant. Through his mistress Kay Medford, Caruso plans to give Ford a ledger that would help him indict Volkie. Caruso is gunned down before he can turn over the ledger. After a veiled threat to the safety of Nina Foch, Ford's wife, Ford decides to leave the case. Ford is shamed into continuing the investigation by Italian immigrant Esther Minciotti, Caruso's mother-in-law. Minciotti also provides Ford with the missing ledger. After Leo Penn is arrested, he's willing to testify against the mob. All those arrested implicate Volkie. Ford serves the mob's lawyer, Barry Kelley, with a subpoena. Kelley sets up a meeting with Ford to exchange valuable information against Volkie for withdrawal of the subpoena. Ford agrees. Kelly also tells Ford all the prospective jurors have either been bought or frightened off. Leaving the meeting together, mobsters attempt to run down Ford and Kelley. Kelley is killed but Ford avoids the murder attempt and fires bullets into the car.

Nina Foch and Glenn Ford in *The Undercover Man* (1949).

Other jurors are used. Volkie is convicted and sentenced to twenty years in prison.

NOTES AND COMMENTARY: The working title for the film was *Chicago Story*.

Secret Service Agent Frank J. Walton's *Colliers* story was the basis for the film. Walton brought his wife to Chicago on his assignment to nail Al Capone on charges of income tax evasion. Threats were made against him but none were actually carried out. Three ledgers were found by chance and witnesses were located who could tie Capone in to receiving illegal monies. Brought to trial, Capone obtained the list of prospective jurors and either bought off or intimidated each one. The plan was foiled when Judge Wilkerson exchanged this group for the jurors in another court room. These jurors brought in a guilty verdict.

REVIEWS: "Solid documentary-type crimebuster. Standout features are the pic's sustained pace and its realistic quality." *Variety*, 3/23/49

SUMMATION: Although the film holds the viewer's interest, it comes off as an undistinguished crime noir. The basic problem is a screenplay which fails to generate needed suspense. The action quotient is minimal. The major dramatic point occurs when agent Glenn Ford has decided to leave the case due to veiled threats to his wife, Nina Foch. It takes Esther Minciotti, as an immigrant who speaks no English, to shame Ford into doing his duty. Although poignant, the scene is hardly believable. This is one of the talented Joseph H. Lewis' less memorable noir efforts.

THE FACTS ... THE FACES ... THE FILM THAT CRACKS AMERICA'S ORGANIZED CRIME SYNDICATE WIDE OPEN!

Underworld U.S.A.

(May 1961)
A Globe Enterprises Production

CAST: Tolly Devlin, Cliff Robertson; Cuddles, Dolores Dorn: Sandy, Beatrice Kay; Gela,

Paul Dubov; Earl Connors, Robert Emhardt; John Driscoll, Larry Gates; Gus, Richard Rust; Gunther, Gerald Milton; Smith, Allen Gruener; Tolly (age 14), David Kent; Woman, Tina Rome; Connie Fowler, Sally Mills; Officer, Robert P. Lieb; Barney, Neyle Morrow; Dr. Meredith, Henry Norell; Uncredited: Drunks, Bob Hopkins and Tom London; Boy, Alan Aaronson; Vic Farrar, Peter Brocco; Convict, David Fresco; Investigator, Bernie Hamilton; Jenny Menkin, Joni Beth Morris; Mrs. Menkin, Audrey Swanson

Credits: Director, Producer and Screenwriter, Samuel Fuller; Assistant Director, Floyd Joyer; Editor, Jerome Thoms; Art Director, Robert Peterson; Set Decorator, Bill Calvert; Cinematographer, Hal Mohr; Costume Designer, Bernice Pontrelli; Makeup, Ben Lane; Hair Stylist, Helen Hunt; Sound, Josh Westmoreland; Recording Supervisor, Charles J. Rice; Original Music, Harry Sukman; Orchestrators, Leo Shuken and Jack Hayes

Song: "Molly Malone" (Yorkston)

Running Time: 98 minutes

Story: As a 14-year-old, Cliff Robertson witnessed the brutal murder of his father. As the murderers ran away, one of them, mob member Peter Brocco, fell. Brocco was easily recognized by bar owner Beatrice Kay who advised the young boy to remain quiet. The young boy's criminal career escalated until he was sentenced to State Prison, where inmate Brocco was a prison hospital patient. As Brocco is about to die, Robertson compels him to identify the other three murderers. Brocco names Paul Dubov, Gerald Milton and Allan Gruener. Kay tells Robertson that Dubov took over her bar and turned it into a coffee house. Robertson overhears a telephone conversation between Richard Rust and Dolores Dorn, a prostitute who refuses to make a narcotics delivery. Rust is told to murder Dorn. Robertson renders Rust unconscious and takes Dorn to safety. Robertson gets Dorn to take him to the narcotics, which he steals. Dorn is taken to Kay's place. Robertson uses the narcotics to become a member of Dubov's mob. Federal agent Larry Gates is trying to get evidence to arrest Dubov, Milton and Gruener along with crime boss Robert Emhardt. Dorn provides evidence that Gruener murdered one of his prostitutes and he is arrested. Robertson tells Dubov that he can crack the safe in Gates' office and remove any incriminating evidence on Gruener. Robertson, working with Gates, brings a phony report to Dubov and Emhardt stating that Milton is ready to sell out Dubov. Emhardt has Rust murder Milton. Dorn has fallen for Robertson but he doesn't want to marry a prostitute. Robertson makes a phony report that Dubov is meeting with Gates, then arranges for Gates to meet Dubov. The meeting is seen by henchman Neyle Morrow who reports to Emhardt. Emhardt instructs Rust to kill Dubov. Robertson arrives at Dubov's house, stabs him and tells him that he is the last of the four men who murdered his father. When the doorbell rings, Robertson pushes Dubov into the opening and Rust fires two shots into him. His need for revenge sated, Robertson makes a decision to go straight and marry Dorn after all. Before Robertson can clear out, Rust arrives and tells him that Emhardt wants him to murder two people, one of them Dorn. Robertson turns Rust over to the police and names him as Dubov's murderer. To make sure he and Dorn can live a peaceful life, Robertson murders Emhardt. As he leaves, Morrow fires a shot, mortally wounding Robertson. Dorn and Kay find Robertson staggering through the streets. He makes it to the alley where his father was killed and that's where he dies. Dorn still plans to testify against Gruener so that Robertson's death would not be in vain.

Notes and Commentary: Joseph Dinneen's *Saturday Evening Post* articles (eight installments from September 3 to October 22, 1955) on organized crime during the Prohibition years were purchased by Humphrey Bogart for a film to be released by Columbia Pictures. With Bogart's death, the project was put in limbo. Sam Briskin, who succeeded Harry Cohn as Columbia's president, obtained the rights and the project was handed over to Samuel Fuller, who made the decision to update the story. Fuller's reshaping of the story to focus on one man's revenge on those who had murdered his father received the studio's acceptance.

Dinneen's articles were published in book form in 1956. Little was used from the book except the title and the character of mob kingpin Earl Connors. On film Connors, who in the stories abhorred violence and later became more involved in legitimate but profitable operations, became an extremely violent man who dies by violence. Dinneen's story of pickpocket Fingers Tolland who dreamed of the big heist is yet to be filmed.

Reviews: "A gritty tale of vengeance." *Motion Picture Guide*, Nash and Ross

"A conventional crime melodrama with a

strong revenge theme, *Underworld U.S.A.* was raised several notches above the norm thanks to direction by Samuel Fuller that made every shot count. A master at creating intensity and suspense by cunning camera placement, Fuller drew maximum impact." *The Columbia Story*, Hirschhorn

Summation: This is a Samuel Fuller classic. Grim, gripping, violent and exciting, it stays with you long after viewing. Fuller directs to give scenes an added punch. Cinematographer Hal Mohr works in concert with Fuller to give the proper shading to each scene. The acting is fine with exceptional performances.

MURDER STALKS EVERY SHADOW!

The Unknown

(July 1946)

Cast: Rachel Martin, Karen Morley; Jack Packard, Jim Bannon; Nina Arnold, Jeff Donnell; Reed Cawthorne, Robert Scott; Richard Arnold, Robert Wilcox; Doc Long, Barton Yarborough; Edward Martin, James Bell; Ralph Martin, Wilton Graff; Phoebe Martin, Helen Freeman; Uncredited: Joshua, J. Louis Jackson; Captain Selby Martin, Boyd Davis; Colonel Wetherford, Russell Hicks; James Wetherford, Robert Stevens

Credits: Director, Henry Levin; Producer, Wallace MacDonald; Screenwriters, Malcolm Stuart Boylan and Julian Harmon; Adaptation, Charles O'Neal and Dwight Babcock; Editor, Arthur Seid; Art Director, George Brooks; Set Decorator, George Montgomery; Cinematography, Henry Freulich; Musical Director, Mischa Bakaleinikoff

Production Dates: March 25–April 15, 1946

Running Time: 70 minutes

Source: the radio program "I Love a Mystery" written and directed by Carlton E. Morse

Story: Private detectives Jim Bannon and Barton Yarborough escort Jeff Donnell to a Southern mansion in Kentucky where she will attend the reading of her grandmother Helen Freeman's will. Living in the house are Karen Morley, Donnell's mother, who is in a confused and disturbed mental state and still thinks her child is a baby; two uncles, Wilton Graff and James Bell; and a longtime servant, J. Louis Johnson. Lawyer Robert Scott is a guest. Morley's mental state is a result of an incident twenty years previous in which Morley and Wilcox, who were secretly wed, were about to leave the mansion when her father, Boyd Davis, came into the room. Davis ordered Wilcox out of the house at gunpoint. A struggle ensued; a shot was fired as Freeman entered. Freeman ordered Morley to her room. After Morley left, Davis collapsed, mortally wounded. Freeman said she'd accuse Wilcox of murder if he didn't leave without Morley. Davis was laid to rest behind the brick fireplace. Now back to present time: That night, Morley hears a baby's cry and thinks it belongs to her child. Morley comes to Donnell's room where, because of her mental state, Morley doesn't recognize Donnell as her child. Graff says that the will has disappeared from his briefcase. In their investigation, Bannon and Yarborough see a prowler enter the mausoleum on the premises. They follow and find a secret passageway. Meanwhile, an attempt is made on Donnell's life. Believing Wilcox will come to take her away, Morley receives a note to meet Wilcox in the mausoleum. The detectives follow Morley and find Bell stabbed to death and Graff hiding in a crypt. Bannon asks Johnson to go to town and bring the police. Wilcox received a letter promising him money and he returns to the mansion. Wilcox and Morley meet but Morley doesn't recognize him. Bannon goes to the room where Davis was killed and finds Freeman, who had faked her death with Johnson's help. Freeman wants to make amends for the wrongs she's committed. A mysterious intruder silently enters the room through a secret panel, knocks Bannon unconscious and carries Freeman away. Bannon and Yarborough race to the mausoleum where they find the body of Freeman, who has died of shock. They enter the secret passageway and find a room with a doll used to torment Morley. Suddenly, the door is closed and barred. Again Morley is lured to the mausoleum followed by Donnell. They are confronted by Graff, who tells them he killed Bell and now plans to kill them. Johnson frees Bannon and Yarborough. Bannon and Yarborough prevent the murders and, with Johnson's help, capture Graff. In Graff's pocket is the missing will.

Freeman's wish is for Morley to find happiness and love with Wilcox and for Morley, Wilcox and Donnell to live in the mansion.

Notes and Commentary: The working title for the film was *The Coffin*. The screenplay was based on Malcolm Stuart Boylan's radio play "Faith, Hope and Charity Sisters."

Robert Stevens was also billed as Robert Kellard during his fourteen-year career. He was known to avid serial enthusiasts as the young hero in *Drums of Fu Manchu* (Republic, 1940) and also starred in *Perils of the Royal Mounted* (Columbia, 1942) and *Tex Granger* (Columbia, 1948).

Reviews: "The film shapes up as effective spine-tingling fare for the horror hounds." *Variety*, 7/24/46

"A familiar brew of chills and thrills." *The Columbia Story*, Hirshhorn

"The story is filled with all the things that are guaranteed to make audiences jump out of their seats." *Motion Picture Guide*, Nash and Ross

Summation: This time out, the series turns to a gothic noir mystery story, with an old Southern mansion complete with secret passageways, secret rooms and sliding walls. This results in another entertaining story. The cast performs well with Jim Bannon and Barton Yarborough in top form. Karen Morley is a standout. Henry Levin guides the story firmly aided by the fine camerawork by Henry Freulich.

FOR THE FIRST BLAZING TIME ... the spotlight is turned on NAZI PRISONER-OF-WAR CAMPS in AMERICA!

The Unwritten Code

(October 1944)

Cast: Mary Lee Norris, Ann Savage; Sgt. Terry Hunter, Tom Neal; Corp. Karl Richter, Roland Varno; Mr. Norris, Howard Freeman; Mrs. Norris, Mary Currier; Willie Norris, Bobby Larson; Dutchy Schultz, Teddy Infuhr; Uncredited: Narrator, Knox Manning; Roland Cheever, Morton Lowry; McDowell, Holmes Herbert; Henrich Krause, Otto Reichow; Schultz, Fred Essler; Luedtke, Frederick Giermann; Kunze, Tom Holland; Ulrich, Philip Van Zandt; Schroeder, Carl Ekberg; Sheriff, Al Bridge; Nowakowski, Fred Graff; Men in Church, Charles Sherlock and George Magrill; Barricade Corporal, Brian O'Hara; Guard, Peter Michael; Swede, Blake Edwards; Sentries, Joey Ray, Bob Lowell, Melvin Nix and William Hall; Soldiers, Jimmy Clark and Edwin Mills; Brinkin, William Yetter, Jr.; Young Nazi, Frederick Pressel; Nazi, Boyd Bennett; Lieutenant, Larry Thompson; Major Spencer, Theodore von Eltz

Credits: Director, Herman Rotsten; Producer, Sam White; Story, Charles Kenyon and Robert Wilmot; Screenwriters, Leslie T. White and Charles Kenyon; Editor, Gene Havlick; Art Director, Perry Smith; Set Decorator, Joseph Kish; Cinematographer, Burnett Guffey; Musical Director, Mischa Bakaleinikoff

Production Dates: June 26–July 17, 1944

Story: A German U-boat torpedoes an Allied vessel carrying German prisoners of war. On a life raft there are three survivors, German soldiers Roland Varno and Otto Reichow and English soldier Morton Lowry. Varno decides to assume Lowry's identity and pushes him into the ocean to die. Varno is brought to a U.S. hospital; adjacent to it is a German POW camp. Varno becomes enamored with his nurse, Ann Savage. To give Varno more time to recuperate, Savage allows him to stay at her father Howard Freeman's farm. Military policeman Tom Neal, Savage's boyfriend, shows up and becomes jealous. Savage's younger brother, Bobby Larson, takes an immediate dislike to Varno when he shoots a bird with Larson's BB rifle and when Varno makes unwelcome advances on Savage. At the POW camp, Varno spots Reichow, who later makes his escape. Varno and Reichow break into a local hardware store and steal all the guns. Meanwhile Larson and his friend Teddy Infuhr decide to search Varno's room at the farm. When Varno returns, the boys see him with Reichow, whom they recognize as the escaped POW. As Infuhr sounds the alarm, Varno tells Reichow to take care of Larson. Before Reichow can act, Neal arrives. Varno shoots Reichow. Hailed as a hero, he then loads the stolen guns in Savage's car. As he drives off, Neal is waiting and Varno is captured.

Notes and Commentary: The working title was *The Unknown.*

Robert Wilmot directed until July 7 when he was replaced by dialogue director Herman Rotsten. Also, James Nicholson replaced Seymour Ross as assistant director.

Review: "The incredulous tale of Nazi intrigue falls flat due to poorly developed plotting and overall production. Strictly a dualer." *Variety,* 12/13/44

"An unwritten script seems to be the problem with this ill-conceived tale." *Motion Picture Guide,* Nash and Ross

Summation: This wartime noir falls flat, a tepid outing devoid of action and suspense. The opening is promising but the story settles down to less than routine. Third-billed Roland Varno gets most of the screen footage but he's saddled with ludicrous scenes as he begins self-destructing his cover as an English soldier. The code is never explained, perhaps because it was unwritten.

VOLCANIC! VALIANT! VICIOUS!
Violence and Passion the Screen Has Seldom Seen!

The Violent Men

(January 1955)

Cast: John Parrish, Glenn Ford; Martha Wilkison, Barbara Stanwyck; Lee Wilkison, Edward G. Robinson; Judith Wilkison, Dianne Foster; Cole Wilkison, Brian Keith; Caroline Vail, May Wynn; Jim McCloud, Warner Anderson; Tex Hinkleman, Basil Ruysdael; Elena, Lita Milan; Wade Matlock, Richard Jaeckel; Sheriff Magruder, James Westerfield; De Rosa, Jack Kelly; Sheriff Martin Kenner, Willis Bouchey; Purdue, Harry Shannon; Uncredited: Dr. Henry Crowell, Raymond Greenleaf; Mahoney, Frank Ferguson; Mr. Vail, Thomas Browne Henry; Mrs. Vail, Katherine Warren; George Menefee, Peter Hansen; Bud Hinkleman, William Phipps; Jackson, Don C. Harvey; Anchor Man with Gun in Saloon, Ethan Laidlaw; Dryer, Carl Andre; Bill Hinkleman, Walter Beaver; Talkative Anchor Posse Member, Edmund Cobb

Credits: Director, Rudolph Maté; Assistant Director, Sam Nelson; Producer, Lewis J. Rachmil; Screenwriter, Harry Kleiner; Editor, Jerome Thoms; Art Director, Carl Anderson; Set Decorator, Louis Diage; Cinematographers, Burnett Guffey and W. Howard Greene; Gowns, Jean Louis; Makeup, Clay Campbell; Hair Stylist, Helen Hunt; Music, Max Steiner; Musical Conductor, Morris Stoloff; Orchestrator, Murray Cutter; Sound, Lambert Day; Recording Supervisor, John Livadary; Technicolor Color Consultant, Francis Cugat

Location Filming: Alabama Hills, Lone Pine, California, and Old Tucson, Arizona

Production Dates: April 12–May 15, 1954

Source: novel *Smoky Valley* by Donald Hamilton

Running Time: 96 minutes

Color by Technicolor

Filmed in CinemaScope

Story: Glenn Ford, a Civil War vet who came to the West to recuperate from an injury, is pronounced to be healthy again. He now plans to sell his ranch to Edward G. Robinson, marry May Wynn and return East. Ford has a change of heart when Robinson's gun hand Richard Jaeckel murders the sheriff. Wynn uses her sexual charms to change Ford's mind. Ford meets with Robinson, who offers him much less than the ranch is worth. Ford turns Robinson down, knowing that eventually he'll have to accept. The driving force in the quest to obtain all the land in the valley is Robinson's wife, Barbara Stanwyck and Robinson's brother, Brian Keith. Stanwyck and Keith are involved in an adulterous affair. Keith has a mistress, Lita Milan. To convince Ford to sell, Keith has Jaeckel murder Ford's cowhand William Phipps. Ford avenges Phipps' death by killing Jaeckel in a gunfight. Ford decides not to return to the East, causing Wynn to break off their engagement. Ford warns Robinson that he wants to live in peace but will fight if necessary. Stanwyck convinces Robinson that Keith and his men can drive

Ford and his followers out of the valley. Ford leaves his ranch figuring correctly that Keith and his men will burn it down. After Keith and his men set it ablaze, Ford and his men ambush them. Robinson and Stanwyck's daughter, Dianne Foster, goes to Ford's camp to make a plea to end hostilities. Keith knows Robinson will throw him off the ranch when he (Robinson) controls the valley. Ford takes his men to Robinson's ranch, which they set on fire. As Robinson and Stanwyck start to flee the burning ranch house, the crippled Robinson loses his crutches and Stanwyck leaves him to die in the flames.

Stanwyck finds Keith with Milan and tells Keith that Robinson is dead. Keith leaves Milan for Stanwyck.

Milan's pleas to Stanwyck to let her have Keith falls on deaf ears. Foster goes to the smoldering ranch and discovers Robinson crawling in the brush. Believing Robinson dead, Keith convinces Sheriff James Westerfield to brand Ford and his men outlaws. Keith forms a posse to burn out all the ranchers and farmers in the valley. Foster takes Robinson to Basil Ruysdael's farm. Ruysdael gets word to Ford, who decides the only way to end hostilities is for him to face Keith. Ford starts for Robinson's ranch.

Robinson and Foster go with him. Robinson disbands the posse. Ford and Keith face each other. Shots are fired, with Ford's bullets ending Keith's life. Stanwyck runs from the ranch only to be shot by Milan. Ford decides to settle down with Foster and combine his ranch with Robinson's.

Notes and Commentary: The basic premise of Donald Hamilton's novel was kept but important changes were made. Martha Wilkison, Lee Wilkison's wife in the film, is his oldest daughter in the novel. Cole is a gunslinger named Hanson and is not Wilkison's brother. The basic plotline of the novel is followed up to the raid on Wilkison's ranch. Parrish sends his men to raid the ranch so he can sneak into town to help his former fiancée, Caroline Vail. Vail sent Parrish a distress note to draw him into Cole's hands. Cole promised Vail money so she and her new lover George Menefee can go East. News of the raid causes Cole and his men to leave town. Cole finds Caroline only to be attacked by Menefee. Parrish and Menefee have a vicious fight which Parrish wins to great injury to himself. Judith Wilkison comes to Parrish to exchange him for her father and sister, who are in Parrish's men's hands. Cole sends men to kill both Parrish and Judith. The attempt fails. Parrish and Judith begin to fall in love. Parrish challenges Cole to a gunfight. Parrish guns down Cole and decides to settle down with Judith. The Wilkison and Parrish ranches will merge.

The working titles for this film were *Smoky Valley*, *Rough Company* and *The Bandits*.

The novel was serialized in *Collier's* magazine from December 1953 to January 1954.

Broderick Crawford, originally cast as Lee Wilkison, suffered an injury when he fell off his horse, and Edward G. Robinson replaced him.

Stock footage from *The Desperadoes* (Columbia, 1943) was used in the horse stampede sequence.

Reviews: "A conventional feature western of the type that plays best in the outdoor market and to nondiscriminating patrons of action fare." *Variety*, 12/22/54

"Columbia has pulled all the levers in making *The Violent Men*, a broad-beamed and action-crammed western. It has ticked off a well-machined scenario, a three-starred 'big name' cast and a scenic outdoor production that looks mighty grand in CinemaScope. If, at the end, it leaves you feeling you've seen just another horse-opera—it's no wonder, for that's what it is." *The New York Times*, 1/27/55

Summation: This is a satisfactory but unexceptional western with noir overtones thanks to the performances of Barbara Stanwyck and May Wynn. Both actresses use their sexual charms to further their ambitions. Both situations end in failure. Stanwyck displays her prowess as a femme fatale, using her body and greed to pull Brian Keith into her web. Glenn Ford gives a measured performance as he finally becomes a man of action. Edward G. Robinson makes a believable ruthless range baron. As added enjoyment, cinematographers Burnett Guffey and W. Howard Greene capture the grandeur of the Lone Pine landscape.

A HAUNTING BEAUTY DROVE HIM MAD!
A HAUNTING VOICE DROVE HIM TO MURDER!

Voice of the Whistler

(October 1945)

Cast: John Sinclair, Richard Dix; Joan Martin, Lynn Merrick; Ernie Sparrow, Rhys Williams; Fred Graham, James Cardwell; Ferdinand, Tom

Kennedy; Uncredited: Voice of the Whistler, Otto Forrest; Sinclair Executives, Stuart Holmes, Wilbur Mack, Charles Marsh, Harold Miller and Forbes Murray; Paul Kitridge, Douglas Wood; Doctor, John Hamilton; Train Porter, Clinton Rosemond; Tony, Martin Garralaga; Bobbie, Gigi Perreau; Dr. Rose, Frank Reicher; Georgie, Byron Foulger; Georgie's Wife, Minerva Urecal; Waitress, Doris Houck; Pharmacist, Robert Williams

Credits: Director, William Castle; Producer, Rudolph C. Flothow; Story, Allan Radar; Screenwriters, Wilfred H. Pettitt and William Castle; Editor, Dwight Caldwell; Cinematographer, George Meehan; Sound, Jack Goodrich; Musical Director, Mischa Balaleinikoff; "Whistler" theme music, Wilbur Hatch

Production Dates: July 23–August 7, 1945

Running Time: 60 minutes

Source: the Columbia Broadcasting System program "The Whistler"

Story: At the pinnacle of his financial career, Richard Dix decides he wants nothing to interfere with his personal life. Due to stress, he collapses and is told by his physician, John Hamilton, to take a vacation trip. In Chicago, Dix lapses into unconsciousness and cab driver Rhys Williams takes him to a clinic for medical help. Dix is told that he needs good sea air and friends. Dix convinces Williams to accompany him and, believing that he only has months to live, convinces nurse Lynn Merrick to marry him. She agrees, thinking the marriage will be short and then she will inherit Dix's fortune and be free to marry her true love, James Cardwell. Dix converts an abandoned lighthouse into a beach resort. Dix's health miraculously improves and Merrick finds herself in a loveless marriage. Cardwell comes to visit, and he and Merrick rediscover their love for each other. Merrick wants to stay with Dix and see Cardwell on the sly. Dix becomes aware of the situation and tells Cardwell how he could murder him without being caught. Cardwell plans to use Dix's scheme to murder Dix. Dix turns the tables and murders Cardwell. Merrick saw what happened and calls the police. Dix is sentenced and executed. Even though Merrick inherits Dix's money, fate dooms her to a life of solitude in the lighthouse.

Notes and Commentary: The working title for this film was *Checkmate for Murder*.

A pharmacist plays a part in the unfolding of this tale. He supplies a prescription without any label as to ingredients, strength, directions, patient's name and authorization from a physician.

Reviews: "Despite a good idea and the proper atmosphere, the story is not brought to the screen effectively, making for tough going as the plot drags itself out." *Motion Picture Guide*, Nash and Ross

"So-so whodunit of its type." *Variety*, 12/26/45

Summation: While not as suspenseful as the previous Whistler entries, this noir is well-done and well-acted and will hold the viewer's interest.

MURDERING AN FBI MAN IS SIGNING YOUR OWN DEATH WARRANT!

Walk a Crooked Mile

(September 1948)

An Edward Small Production

Cast: Scotty Grayson, Louis Hayward; Daniel O'Hara, Dennis O'Keefe; Dr. Toni Neva, Louise Allbritton; Dr. Ritter Von Stolb, Carl Esmond; Igor Braun, Onslow Stevens; Krebs, Raymond Burr; Dr. Frederick Townsend, Art Baker; Dr. William Forrest, Lowell Gilmore; Anton Radchek, Philip Van Zandt; Dr. Homer Allen, Charles Evans; Carl Bemish, Frank Ferguson; Uncredited: Narrator, Reed Hadley; Woman at Murder Scene, Suzanne Ridgeway; Police Sergeant, Ray Teal; Mr. North, Arthur Space; Agent Alison, Jimmy Lloyd; Agent Gaines, Steve Pendleton; Mrs. Green's Voice on Tape Recorder, Gale Storm; Agent Miller, Keith Richards; Agent Potter, Bert Davidson; G.W. Hunter, John Hamilton; Adolph Mizer, Grandon Rhodes; Agent Thompson, Myron Healey; Fred (FBI Chemist), Fred Coby; FBI Chemists, Marten Lamont and William Tannen; Ivan, Paul Bryar; Feodore, Howard Negley; Curly, Crane Whitley; Mrs. Ecko (Landlady), Tamara Shayne; Policeman, Lee Phelps

Credits: Director, Gordon Douglas; Assistant Director, Ridgeway Callow; Producer, Grant Whytock; Story, Bertram Millhauser; Screenwriter, George Bruce; Editor, James E. Newcom; Art Director, Rudolph Sternad; Set Decorator, Howard Bristol; Cinematographer, George Robinson; Unit Manager, Joseph Small; Wardrobe Manager, Edward Lambert; Sound, John Carter; Original Music, Paul Sawtell

Location Filming: San Francisco, California

Production Dates: May 11–June 12, 1948

Running Time: 91 minutes

Story: An agent is murdered by espionage agent Raymond Burr before he can relay information about Philip Van Zandt and his involvement with the Lakeview Atomic Project to special agent Dennis O'Keefe. Van Zandt is spotted leaving Lakeview for San Francisco and is followed by O'Keefe and agent Jimmy Lloyd. Van Zandt's rooming house is put under surveillance and the only phone is tapped. Van Zandt makes a telephone call to Onslow Stevens. The next morning, Van Zandt is found murdered. Film of persons entering the house show Stevens dressed as a clergyman. Scotland Yard investigator Louis Hayward comes on the scene and tells O'Keefe about paintings being sent to England with mathematical equations hidden in the pictures. The equations relate to a current confidential project at the Lakeview facility. The latest picture shows buildings in a San Francisco neighborhood. The lawmen go to that neighborhood, and then Stevens' apartment is found. Stevens is working on another painting which shows another mathematical formula. Stevens goes to Lakeview to oversee obtaining all the information relative to the project. O'Keefe and Hayward review security protocol at the facility and can find no way that information can be stolen. The possible suspects are narrowed to the persons working on the project, Carl Esmond, Louise Allbritton, Lowell Gilmore and Charles Evans. Their Friday meeting is photographed and recorded. Hayward and O'Keefe see that Allbritton and Esmond are romantically

In *Walk a Crooked Mile* (1948) Tamara Shayne is held by Frank Ferguson while Paul Bryar and an accomplice work over Louis Hayward.

involved. Hayward and O'Keefe see Allbritton take clothes to Frank Ferguson's laundry. Ferguson, a member of Stevens' spy ring, takes a handkerchief from Allbritton's package and places it in another box that is picked up by Burr. On Monday, another painting with a mathematical formula is shipped to England. Believing Ferguson to be involved in the theft, Hayward gets a job working in the laundry. On Friday, Allbritton brings her laundry and Hayward sees the transfer of Allbritton's handkerchief to another package. When the package is picked up by Burr, Hayward signals O'Keefe. O'Keefe jumps Burr and retrieves the package. The handkerchief proves to have the final mathematical equation. Stevens, on learning Ferguson hired a new man, sends Burr and other henchmen to Hayward's rooming house. They quickly capture Hayward and landlady Tamara Shayne. Hayward is beaten but refuses to talk. Burr starts to work on Shayne but she stands up to him. When O'Keefe arrives, he is captured. Burr finds a handkerchief in O'Keefe's briefcase and tells his men to kill all three. Shayne distracts the two men left to carry out Burr's orders. Shayne is fatally shot but O'Keefe and Hayward overpower their captors. Hayward and O'Keefe believe the traitors are Allbritton and Esmond. When questioning Allbritton proves futile, Hayward and O'Keefe go to Esmond's bungalow, only to find him dead. What looked like a suicide proves to be murder. The film of the Friday conference is again reviewed but O'Keefe and Hayward are stumped on how information could be removed from the room. Again the suspects are followed. O'Keefe, while trailing one of the suspects, accidentally figures out how the theft was accomplished. O'Keefe calls Hayward to join him since he's following the traitor. O'Keefe is followed by Stevens and Burr. Burr shoots at O'Keefe, whose car goes off the road into a ravine. With O'Keefe trapped inside, the car catches on fire and the fire creeps closer to the gas tank. Hayward rescues O'Keefe. O'Keefe radios all cars. The sedan in question is spotted and police follow it to a deserted farmhouse. O'Keefe, Hayward and the police surround the house. Stevens refuses to surrender and a gunfight ensues. Stevens and his cohorts are all killed. In an inner room, Hayward and O'Keefe find Evans and charge him with treason. Evans insists he was captured by the gang and he is innocent. At an FBI lab, Keefe places Evans' left hand in a chemical solution and the final formula is revealed. Evans had a chemical solution on his hand and at each meeting would manage to place his hand directly on the formulas. He then would transfer the formula to one of Allbritton's handkerchiefs that he knew would be taken to the laundry.

NOTES AND COMMENTARY: The working title for this film was *FBI Meets Scotland Yard*.

Walk a Crooked Mile was loosely remade as *David Harding, Counterspy* (Columbia, 1950).

Some sources list Carl Esmond's character name as Van Stolb but in writing the names of the suspects, Hayward clearly writes Von Stolb.

REVIEWS: "Film is a solid example of action entertainment with a strong appeal to fans of rugged, exciting spy antics and super sleuthing." *Variety*, 9/8/48

"Brisk little cops-and-spies picture. No use to speak of the action or the acting. It's strictly routine. But the plot is deliberately sensational." *The New York Times*, 10/13/48

"Fast-paced espionage drama presented in a documentary style." *Motion Picture Guide*, Nash and Ross

SUMMATION: This is a good docu-noir with director Gordon Douglas pacing the story nicely with good action and suspense. Louis Hayward and Dennis O'Keefe complement each other perfectly as the agents on the trail of espionage agents. Acting honors go to the unbilled Tamara Shayne and Raymond Burr. Shayne is perfect as a naturalized citizen used to tyranny during World War II and willing to give her life to protect her new country from its enemies. George Robinson's excellent photography adds to the story's suspense.

HOW THE FBI CRACKED SPY RING

Walk East on Beacon!

(June 1952)
A Louis de Rochemont Production

CAST: Inspector Jim Belden, George Murphy; Professor Albert Kafer, Finlay Currie; Mille,

George Murphy (center) briefs fellow FBI agents in *Walk East on Beacon!* (1952).

Virginia Gilmore; Alex Lazchenkov, Karel Stepanek; Elaine Wilben, Louisa Horton; Gino, Peter Capell; Luther Danzig, Bruno Wick; Melvin Foss, Jack Manning; Agent Reynolds, Karl Weber; Dr. Wincott, the Rev. Robert Dunn; Rita Foss, Vilma Kurer; Michael Dorndoff, Michael Garrett; Anna Kafer, Lotte Palfi; Robert Martin, Ernest Graves; Boldany, Robert Carroll; Helmuth, Paul Andor; Nicholas Wilben; George Roy Hill; Harry Mason, Bradford Hatton; Mrs. Martin, Rosemary Pettit; Mrs. Sullivan (Landlady), Eva Condon; Samson, Steve Mitchell; Philadelphia Suspect, Ann Thomas; Uncredited: Narrator, Westbrook Van Voorhis; J. Edgar Hoover, Himself; Old Lady, Mary Young; Taxi Driver, John Farrell

Credits: Director, Alfred Werker; Producer, Louis de Rochemont with the cooperation of the Federal Bureau of Investigation; Associate Producers, Borden Mace and Lothar Wolff; Story and Screenplay, Leo Rosten; Additional Writers, Virginia Shaler, Laurence Heath and Emmett Murphy; Editor, Angelo Ross; Assistant Editor, Peter Ratkevigh; Art Director, Herbert Andrews; Cinematographer, Joseph Brun; Cameramen, George Stoetzel and Edward Horton; Unit Manager, Thomas Whitesell; Sound, Lodge Cunningham; Musical Director, Jack Shaindlin; Casting Director, Shirlee Weingarten; Production Staff, Martin Maloney, Fred Ryle, George Ackerson, James Petrie, William Joyce, Louis de Rochemont III, Marie Kenney, William Graf, Mary Brennan, Fred Ballmeyer, Arthur Burns and Walter Pluff

Location Filming: the New England area including Boston, Massachusetts

Songs: "Sobre las olas" (Over the Waves) (Rosas)—instrumental and "I'm Tickled Pink" (Shaindlin)—Jack Shaindlin with vocal accompaniment

Source: article "The Crime of the Century" by J. Edgar Hoover in *Reader's Digest* (May 1951)

Running Time: 98 minutes

Story: A Communist espionage ring, led by Karel Stepanek, is trying to get information about the Falcon Project. Lead scientist Finlay Currie's son has been kidnapped and taken to East Berlin. Currie is told by Stepanek's agent Virginia Gilmore that upon receipt of the Falcon Project information, his son will be released. Currie arranges a confidential interview with FBI agent George Murphy, who advises Currie to play along in hopes he (Murphy) can arrest the spy ring's members. Currie gives false information to taxi driver Jack Manning who then passes the papers to Gilmore. Within 36 hours the papers are on their way to Moscow. Murphy's agents begin to identify the members of the spy ring. Currie finally has a breakthrough: His theories are proven, which will lead to improvements in many areas of combating espionage, especially with space stations. Afraid of written correspondence, Currie dictates his findings to tape, which is played to the rest of the scientists at the Washington area headquarters. George Roy Hill, a staff member and a member of the spy ring, makes a duplicate copy that he gives to his wife to deliver to Gilmore. After the transfer is made, all three are arrested by FBI agents. The arrests are observed by another agent, Bruno Wick, who relays this information to Stepanek. Stepanek decides to kidnap Currie and take him to Moscow. Following other agents of the spy ring, Murphy learns that Currie is being transported by cabin cruiser to a waiting submarine. Murphy sets plans in motion to rescue Currie and orders the roundup of all of Stepanek's associates in the Boston area. Murphy and his agents board the boat, arrest or kill the spies and rescue Currie. As Currie is being brought back to shore, Murphy tells him that his son has been rescued and is en route to Boston.

Notes and Commentary: Although J. Edgar Hoover's *Reader's Digest* story "The Crime of the Century" is stated as the basis for *Walk East on Beacon!*, the only thing the two have in common is that in both, FBI agents break up Communist espionage rings. In Hoover's story, the FBI arrest spies who have supplied atomic bomb secrets to Russian agents.

Walk East on Beacon! is the only film noir to be given comic book treatment: The story appeared in issue #113 of *Motion Picture Comics* (Fawcett, November 1952). It's extremely faithful to the motion picture. There were only fourteen films adapted for this comic book title.

The film was a Louis de Rochemont production produced in conjunction with RD–DR Corporation (also known as Producers of *Reader's Digest* on the Screen and Dramas of Real Life from *Reader's Digest*). Other *Reader's Digest* stories brought to the screen by de Rochemont were *Boomerang* (20th Century–Fox, 1947), *Lost Boundaries* (Film Classics, 1949) and *The Whistle at Eaton Falls* (Columbia, 1951).

Reviews: "Pic is overly long at 97 minutes, and often gets itself bogged down in tedious details of factual phases. Presentation could have used a sharper pace to help suspense, more excitement and less documentary emphasis." *Variety*, 4/30/52

"The over-all effect of *Walk East on Beacon!* is something less than awesome, but it is a swiftly paced, detail-filled yarn and a tribute to an arm of the law worthy of praise." *The New York Times*, 5/29/52

"This picture eschews phony dramatics and suspense in favor of a realistic depiction of spy operations." *Motion Picture Guide*, Nash and Ross

Summation: This very good docu-noir was filmed on location with the story following FBI procedure. Director Albert Werker brings to the screen a thoughtful, interesting and absorbing account of the FBI breaking up an espionage ring. Finlay Currie's acting stands out. He is able to make the audience feel the torment his character is experiencing. Joseph Brun's cinematography effectively complements Werker's direction.

VIOLENT PASSIONS CLASH IN THE DESERT!

The Walking Hills

(March 1949)

Cast: Jim Carey, Randolph Scott; Chris Jackson, Ella Raines; Shep, William Bishop; Old Willy, Edgar Buchanan; Chalk, Arthur Kennedy; Frazee, John Ireland; Johnny, Jerome Courtland; Bibbs, Russell Collins; Josh, Josh White; Uncredited: King (Father), Houseley Stevens; Cleve, Charles Stevens; Bartender, Frank Yaconelli; King (Son), Reed Howes; Hotel Detective, Ralph Dunn; American Customs Guard, Jack Parker; Bronc Handlers, John McKee and Frank Mario

Credits: Director, John Sturges; Assistant Director, Sam Nelson; Story and Screenwriter, Alan Le May; Additional Dialogue, Virginia Roddick; Editor, William Lyon; Art Director, Robert Peterson; Set Decorator, James Crowe; Cinematographer, Charles Lawton, Jr.; Wardrobe for Miss Raines, Jean Louis; Original Music, Arthur Morton; Musical Director, M.W. Stoloff

Songs: "You Won't Let Me Go" (White)—sung and played by Josh White; "The Riddle Song (I Gave My Love a Cherry)" (traditional)—sung and played by Josh White; "C.C. Rider" (traditional with altered lyrics)—sung and played by Josh White; "Like a Natural Man" (White)—sung by Josh White

Filming Locations: Alabama Hills, Lone Pine, and Death Valley National Park, California

Production Dates: May 10–June 17, 1948

Running Time: 78 minutes

Story: Spotting William Bishop on the streets of a border town, Houseley Stevenson wants private detective John Ireland to arrest him. Bishop slips across the border to the Mexico side and Ireland follows. Bishop enters a bar with a small stakes poker game in the back room. Bishop joins Randolph Scott, Arthur Kennedy, Jerome Courtland and Edgar Buchanan in the game. Ireland sits in also. Courtland mentions that he stumbled upon the ruins of an old wagon train. Buchanan immediately believes this is a lost wagon train transporting $5,000,000 in gold. Gold fever strikes the group. Fearing loose tongues, bar owner Russell Collins and entertainer Josh White are made part of the search party. Scott's ranch hand Charles Stevens goes along. The party sneaks across the border into the United States. Courtland leads them to the spot of the ruins. As they dig for treasure, they are joined by Ella Raines, who has a past with both Scott and Bishop. Bishop tells Raines that he left her because, in an altercation with Reed Howes, Howes was killed. Ireland had been signaling Stevenson and, when he is hiding his signaling device, Courtland jumps him. In the struggle, a shot from Ireland's pistol critically wounds Courtland. Courtland believes that Ireland is looking for him and begs Scott not to send for a doctor. Scott has Stevens hide the horses. Buchanan warns the group that a severe sand storm is imminent. Ireland tells Courtland that the charge against him was bogus. Bishop makes an attempt to leave the camp but is stopped by Ireland. When Ireland begins to strangle Bishop, Scott intercedes. Courtland finally succumbs to his wounds. The sand storm hits and the party attempts to find shelter. Believing Ireland is looking for him, Kennedy stampedes the horses and shoots Ireland. In an exchange of shots, Scott kills Kennedy. Stevens, who believed Ireland was looking for him for smuggling people over the border, is caught in the storm and killed. When the storm abates, the survivors look around and find that the storm has uncovered the wagons. Buchanan announces there is no gold; the wagons were transporting tools. Bishop is tired of running and decides to face the charges. Raines, who has always loved Bishop, follows him. Scott then makes Buchanan admit that he did find some money to be split among the survivors, including Bishop.

Notes and Commentary: The on-screen credit for Josh White stated "Introducing Josh White and his songs." Originally Glenn Ford was announced as the star of the film. This was the first feature film to record sound on tape rather than sound on film.

Review: "An intriguing theme, good cast and tight direction combine to make *The Walking Hills* an out-of-the-way westerner." *Variety*, 12/31/48

"Underrated and highly entertaining melodrama; well worth viewing." *The Western*, Pitts

Summation: This is a fine modern western noir. The streets in the big cities are wet and dark as death changes a rodeo performer's life. Director John Sturges mixes good acting, a taut, suspenseful story, and fine cinematography by Charles Lawton, Jr. Lawton is at home both in the outdoor and the indoor sequences, balancing the darkness with streams of light. The sand storm sequence is outstanding. The fine story balances greed with the paranoia of past sins. This is not in the same class as *The Treasure of the Sierra Madre* (Warner Bros., 1948) but a worthy and compelling attempt all the same. This was the last feature film appearance of famous blues singer and guitarist Josh White, who sings four times. Blues enthusiasts should treasure this film.

WHAT DID SHE HAVE THAT MADE MEN KILL?
What did the walls conceal?

The Walls Came Tumbling Down

(June 1946)

CAST: Gilbert Archer, Lee Bowman; Patricia Foster aka Laura Browning, Marguerite Chapman; George Bradford, Edgar Buchanan; Matthew Stoker, George Macready; Susan, Lee Patrick; Captain Griffin, Jonathan Hale; Catherine Walsh, Elisabeth Risdon; Ernst Helms, J. Edward Bromberg; Dr. Marko, Miles Mander; Bishop Martin, Moroni Olsen; Mrs. Stoker, Katherine Emery; Rausch, Noel Cravat; Uncredited: Anderson (Politician), Arthur Loft; Mario Bianca, Charles La Torre; Girl at Table, Forrest Dickson; Broker, Franklin Dix; Producer, Harold Miller; Roberto (Waiter), Fred Godoy; Carlo (Artist), Julio Abadia; Johnson, Larry Steers; Twin Brother, Ray Hughes; Attendant, Pat O'Malley; Detective Regan, Bob Ryan; Marco's Secretary, Wanda Perry; Tiny, Charles Cane; Hotel Desk Clerk, Charles Marsh; Bradford's Secretary, Mary Field, Newspaper Morgue Clerk, Milton Kibbee; Hotel Clerk, Dick Gordon; Bellboy, Johnny Duncan; Cab Driver, Jack Raymond; Night Clerk, Alfred Allegro; Detectives, Steve Benton, Jack Ellis and Edmund Cobb, Gravediggers, John Tyrrell and William Kahn; Clerk, Dan Stowell, Policeman, Ralph Dunn

CREDITS: Director, Lothar Mendes; Assistant Director, Sam Nelson; Producer, Albert J. Cohen; Screenwriter, Wilfred H. Pettitt; Editor, Gene Havlick; Art Directors, Stephen Goosson and A. Leslie Thomas; Set Decorator, Robert Priestley; Cinematography, Charles Lawton, Jr.; Costumes, Jean Louis; Sound, Jack Goodrich; Original Music, Marlin Skiles; Musical Director, M.W. Stoloff

Lee Bowman menaces J. Edward Bromberg in *The Walls Came Tumbling Down* (1946).

Production Dates: December 10, 1945–February 2, 1946

Source: novel *The Walls Came Tumbling Down* by Jo Eisinger

Running Time: 82 minutes

Story: Columnist Lee Bowman goes to visit a priest, an old friend of his, only to find him dead. It looks like suicide but Bowman believes it was murder. The priest had recently had visitors looking for two Bibles with clues to a valuable Di Vinci painting, "The Walls Came Tumbling Down." Bowman has his name inserted in the newspaper articles as the man who found the body. False missionary George Macready, his wife Katherine Emery and his hired henchman Noel Cravat come to Bowman's apartment looking for the Bibles. For a fee, Bowman tells Macready he will produce the Bibles. Book dealer J. Edward Bromberg is also looking for the Bibles and gives Bowman a retainer to bring them to him. Bowman locates Marguerite Chapman, another suspicious character who may be connected to the mystery, but she won't give any information. Attorney Edgar Buchanan demands that Bowman reveal why his client, Bromberg, gave him money. Bowman tells Buchanan he gave Bromberg a Bible. Returning to his apartment, Bowman finds Police Captain Jonathan Hale and other officers. In his bedroom is the dead body of the priest's sister, Elisabeth Risdon. Risdon's last word before her death was Bible. The Bible that she brought with her is missing. As Bowman leaves his apartment, Cravat forces him, at gunpoint, to go to Macready's residence. Since Bowman cannot produce a Bible, Cravat beats him. The beating stops when Macready realizes Bowman is telling the truth. Bowman is then able to knock Macready to the floor. When Cravat comes back into the room, Bowman strikes him with the gun butt. When Macready tries to reach for a weapon, Bowman kicks him in the head. Bowman then sees Chapman, who finally trusts him. She relates the story of her grandfather who owned the painting and went into hiding. One note was sent telling of the relationship of the Bibles to the painting but death prevented a second letter telling where to find the Bibles. Using good detective work, Bowman realizes the second Bible was buried with Chapman's grandfather. The grave is opened and Bowman retrieves the Bible. Bowman and Chapman hurry to Bromberg's apartment where they find a note stating he has left town in a hurry. Buchanan shows up to give Bromberg money. When he finds Bromberg is not there, he offers to take all of Bromberg's possessions, including a steamer trunk, until Bromberg returns. Bowman takes Chapman to a safe place before returning to his apartment. There he meets Macready, who persuades Bowman to bring the Bible to his residence. Bowman tells Macready that when Bromberg shows up, he will turn over the Bible. At Macready's residence, Buchanan is there to greet him. Cravat arrives and Bowman is told that Bromberg's dead body is in the trunk. Bowman surrenders the Bible but he has removed the page needed to locate the painting. Buchanan and Macready plan to force Bowman to give them the missing page. As they open the door to leave, Hale and other police officers are there to arrest Buchanan, Macready and Cravat. Macready and Cravat murdered the priest to prevent him from giving the Bibles to Chapman. Buchanan had searched for the Bibles in Bowman's apartment. When Risdon came in with the Bible, Buchanan murdered her to get the Bible in her possession. Bromberg was murdered because Bowman told Buchanan he had given him a Bible. With the Bibles now in Chapman's possession, Bowman pieces out the clues needed to find the painting. With the painting safe, Bowman and Chapman now have time for romance.

Notes and Commentary: Changes were made to Jo Eisenger's novel as it came to the screen. Chapter one in which Father Walsh called on newspaper columnist D'Arcy (Gilbert Archer in the film) was omitted. The movie began with chapter two and followed the novel fairly closely until the second Bible was obtained from a grave. Character names were changed for the film. In the novel when D'Arcy was kidnapped, so was the heroine. D'Arcy effected an escape with the result that the heroine now had confidence in him. In the movie, the columnist eluded the police after obtaining the Bible from the grave while in the novel he was nabbed. The police and the columnist then worked together to bring the murderers to justice.

The novel was first adapted for CBS's *Suspense* radio program. It aired June 29, 1944, and featured Keenan Wynn (as D'Arcy), Herb Butterfield, Hans Conried, Wendell Holmes, John McIntire and Jane Morgan. The characters Probiloff (novel)–Matthew Stokes (film) and his henchman Rauch (novel)–Rausch (film) were eliminated. Lawyer Hodakis (novel)–George Bradford (film) was the only murderer. The ending of the radio program had the villainous lawyer firing a pistol, causing a wall to collapse, killing him and uncovering the valuable mural.

In November 1944, Sam Bischoff was announced as the producer of a film adaptation. William Holden was announced as the star in February 1945.

In some extensive cast listings, the role of Father Walsh is credited to Francis Pierlot. His footage ended up on the cutting room floor. My guess is that when chapter one was eliminated, so was Pierlot's part.

Review: "William H. Pettitt's screenplay kept interest simmering." *The Columbia Story*, Hirshhorn

Summation: This is an entertaining but undistinguished mystery noir. Director Lothar Mendes doesn't give the extra punch Wilfred H. Pettitt's screenplay needed to bring the story to an above-average rating. The acting is in the capable hands of Lee Bowman, Marguerite Chapman, Edgar Buchanan, George Macready and Lee Patrick and they do their best to maintain audience interest.

Radio's Master of Mystery ... NOW on the Screen!

The Whistler

(March 1944)

Cast: Earl C. Conrad, Richard Dix; Alice Walker, Gloria Stuart; "Smith," J. Carrol Naish; Gorman, Alan Dinehart; Uncredited: Voice of the Whistler, Otto Forrest; Lefty Vigran, Don Costello; Gus, Cy Kendall; Deaf-mute, Billy Benedict; Police Detective in Alley, Pat O'Malley; Jennings, Charles Coleman; Charlie McNair, Robert Emmett Keane; Telephone Repairman, Clancy Cooper; Bill Tomley, George Lloyd; Antoinette Vigran, Joan Woodbury; Plainclothes Detective, Jack Ingram; Flophouse Desk Clerk, Byron Foulger; Bum, Trevor Bardette; Dock Watchman, Robert Homans; Ship's Purser, Charles Wagenheim; Detective at Dock, Kermit Maynard

Credits: Director, William Castle; Producer, Rudolph C. Flothow; Story, J. Donald Wilson; Screenwriter, Eric Taylor; Editor, Jerome Thoms; Art Director, George Van Marter; Set Decorator, Sidney Clifford; Cinematographer, James S. Brown; Original Theme and Score, Wilbur Hatch

Production Dates: January 21–February 7, 1944

Running Time: 59 minutes

Source: the Columbia Broadcasting System program "The Whistler"

Story: Because of his wife's death, Richard Dix is despondent and hires an unknown killer to murder him. Then Dix receives a telegram telling him that his wife is still alive. He tries to reach the killer and call off the hit on himself. The hired killer, J. Carrol Naish, wants to use a psychological approach and frighten Dix to death. Dix finally meets Naish and asks him to call off the arrangement. Since Naish knows Dix has seen him kill another man, he is afraid that Dix will go to the police. Dix's secretary Gloria Stuart brings him another telegram stating that his wife died on the journey home. Dix still wants to live, having found a new love in Stuart. Naish fires a shot at Dix that misses. Naish is then killed by Kermit Maynard, a detective stationed at the dock.

Notes and Commentary: Richard Dix' health wouldn't allow him to continue in action films. He signed a contract with Columbia to headline the Whistler series.

To get the desired effect of a mood of desperation from Dix, director William Castle first made him go on a diet and give up smoking. Castle also gave him early calls and made him wait until late in the day to film his scenes. This made Dix nervous and jumpy which allowed Castle to get the reactions he wanted. The story was written by J. Donald Wilson, who was responsible for developing the radio series in 1942.

This is the only entry in the series in which the Whistler takes a hand in influencing the storyline. His interference causes Naish's potentially fatal shot to miss, thus, saving Dix' life. The first telegram received by Richard Dix has the date March 8, 1944, the month and year the film was released.

Director William Castle's place in cinema history rests primarily with his gimmicky horror films. Some of his best-known chillers were *House on Haunted Hill* (Allied Artists, 1959), *13 Ghosts* (Columbia, 1960) and *Mr. Sardonicus* (Columbia, 1961).

Gloria Stuart received an Academy Award nomination for Best Supporting Actress in *Titanic* (20th Century–Fox–Paramount 1997). Stuart played Rose, the hundred-year-old survivor.

REVIEWS: "Tense little programmer. Castle never did anything else as effective as this. Dix is excellent... The production values, considering that the film was shot on a budget of less than $75,000, are excellent. A perfect example of the art that could be created in the structures of studio B-unit production." *Motion Picture Guide*, Nash and Ross

SUMMATION: This Whistler entry is a winner. Dix and J. Carrol Naish both give strong performances. The story does not disappoint. The audience knows Naish's efforts to murder Dix would be futile. The fun is seeing how Naish would be tripped up at the last moment.

FOR EVERY MAN WHO BETRAYED HER ...
A HUNDRED MEN HAD TO PAY

Wicked as They Come

(February 1957)

ALTERNATE TITLE: Portrait in Smoke

CAST: Kathy Allen, Arlene Dahl; Tim O'Bannion, Phil Carey; Stephen Collins, Herbert Marshall; Larry Buckham, Michael Goodliffe; John Dowling, Ralph Truman; Frank Allenborg, Sidney James; Sam Lewis, David Kossoff; Virginia Collins, Faith Brook; Mr. Reisner, Frederick Valk; Mike Lewis, Marvin Kane; Pat Clavin; Willie, Patrick Allen; John Salew; Chuck, Gilbert Winfield; Totti Truman Taylor; Larry Cross; Paul Sheridan; Tom Gill; Frank Atkinson; Alastair Hunter; Inspector Caron, Jacques Brunius; Anthony Sharp; Guy De Monceau; Raf De La Torre; Selma Vas Dias

CREDITS: Director and Screenwriter, Ken Hughes; Assistant Director, Philip Shipway; Producer, Maxwell Setton; Screen Story, Robert Westerby and Sigmund Miller; Editor, Max Benedict; Art Director, Don Ashton; Set Dresser, Terrance Morgan II; Cinematographer, Basil Emmott; Camera Operator, Gerry Turpin; Continuity, Beryl Booth; Costumes, Cynthia Tingey; Makeup, Paul Rabiger; Hair Stylist, Betty Sherriff; Wardrobe, Evelyn Gibbs; Production Manager, Fred Gunn; Sound, Fred Ryan and Len Shilton; Music Composer, Malcolm Arnold; Music Director, Muir Mathieson; Orchestra, Sinfonia of London

LOCATION FILMING: Nettleford and Walton on Thames, England

PRODUCTION DATES: December 14, 1955–February 17, 1956

SOURCE: novel *Portrait in Smoke* by Bill S. Ballinger

RUNNING TIME: 94 minutes

STORY: Factory worker Arlene Dahl lives in a tenement house with her stepfather Sidney James. She plans to win a beauty contest that offers a $1,000 cash prize and a paid trip to London. To ensure victory, she plays up to contest promoter David Kossoff, promising sexual favors if she wins.

Kossoff rigs the contest in Dahl's favor. Dahl never planned to submit to Kossoff and just takes her prizes. On the flight to London, television producer Phil Carey tries unsuccessfully to get acquainted with Dahl. In London, finally needing money, Dahl begins a relationship with successful photographer Michael Goodliffe. When Goodliffe is late for a date, Dahl has a drink with Carey and tells him that she wants a job with his firm. Carey tells Dahl she needs to develop secretarial skills before she can be hired.Goodliffe, jealous of Carey, asks Dahl to marry him. Dahl accepts but tells Goodliffe she can't marry until she can afford to purchase her wedding gown. Goodliffe tells Dahl to use his credit at a prestigious department store. Dahl runs up a large bill and pawns some of the items for cash. Department store management does not believe Goodliffe's protests of innocence and has him prosecuted, resulting in a six-month prison sentence. Using some of the money, Dahl obtains secretarial skills and obtains a job with Carey's firm. Her chance to get close to the London head, Herbert Marshall, comes when Marshall needs documents immediately delivered to his hotel room.

Wicked as They Come **(1956): Phil Carey and Arlene Dahl share more than a drink.**

Dahl begins drinking with Marshall, who finally passes out. Dahl then gets undressed and spends the night in the room. The next morning, Marshall believes they must have had sex and makes Dahl his private secretary. Although married to Faith Brook, Marshall falls in love with Dahl. At the same time, Dahl becomes sexually involved with Carey. Dahl tells Carey she plans to marry Marshall; Carey says that will never happen. Dahl forces Marshall to tell her he will leave Brook and marry her. Marshall and Dahl go to a company meeting in Paris. At a company party, Dahl meets the aging president of the company, Ralph Truman. Dahl learns that Brook is Truman's daughter and that if Marshall chooses her, he will lose his position with the company. Brook tries to buy Dahl off. Dahl refuses money but asks to be transferred to the Paris office. Dahl begins seeing Truman, who takes her around Paris and finally proposes marriage. Carey tells Dahl that even though she plans to marry Truman, she really loves him. Carey predicts that Dahl will murder Truman.

After the marriage, Dahl begins receiving threatening phone calls and then a letter which she impulsively burns. When Dahl sees a mysterious figure on the estate grounds, she takes comfort in the pistol she took from Truman's desk. Dahl's bedroom door begins to open and she fires the pistol. Truman falls to the floor, dead. Inspector Brunius believes Dahl is a murderess and arrests her. She is convicted of murder and sentenced to die. At the court, Carey sees a familiar figure, Goodliffe. Carey follows Goodliffe to his room and forces him to confess that he was the threatening figure on the estate the night Truman was killed. Carey convinces Goodliffe to go to the authorities. Dahl's sentence is commuted to manslaughter and she is sentenced to three months in prison.

Carey visits Dahl in prison and walks away not knowing whether on her release they will have a life together.

Notes and Commentary: In Bill S. Ballinger's novel, one plot line is set in the present as Dan April, owner of a small collection agency, finds a newspaper clipping with a picture of a beautiful young girl, Krassy Almauniski (Kathleen

Alanborg in the film), whom he had seen briefly years before. April is transfixed and begins a campaign to locate her. A parallel plot tells of Krassy's travels from the slums to becoming the wife of a wealthy man.

In the final quarter of the book, the two plot threads come together: April finally locates Krassy, now Candice Powers, wife of a multimillionaire. She is able to steal the identity of a prominent businessman. Krassy and April meet and become lovers. Krassy tells April her husband will be out of town for the weekend and they can go to a secluded cabin. When April shows up, he's denied entrance to Krassy's apartment. He forces his way into the living room with Krassy and Powers. Krassy feigns fear and, as April enters the room, brandishes a pistol and fatally shoots Powers. Krassy presses the pistol into April's hand and starts screaming, branding him a murderer. April is able to escape police capture. Krassy moves to France. There is nothing to connect April to the crime, leaving April to live with nightmares. The Dan April character does not appear in the film. The screenplay follows the Krassy plot thread up to the marriage to a wealthy man. After that, it is the work of Ken Hughes, Robert Westerby and Sigmund Miller. In the film, Kathleen is frigid due to an incident in which she was raped by four hoodlums. In the book, Krassy was sexually active to further her ambitions.

In 1957, Dahl sued Columbia Pictures for one million dollars. A composite picture of a man kissing Dahl on the shoulder was used in the promotion of the film. Dahl branded the picture "lewd, lascivious and obscene." It has been reported the judge was not sympathetic to Dahl's case. I do not know the outcome.

Reviews: "Good average entertainment value is provided by this Anglo-American story of a golddigger's rise to fortune. Entertaining yarn." *Variety*, 5/30/56

"This turgid drama is simplistic in its plot and character motivations, but the cast is lively, making this a better drama than it should have been. Dahl is wonderfully icy." *Motion Picture Guide*, Nash and Ross

Summation: This is a gripping, engrossing film noir melodrama. Arlene Dahl and Phil Carey both do a fine job. Ken Hughes' first-rate direction and screenplay doesn't give hope that Dahl will have a happy life. Bravo to Basil Emmott's cinematography, framing scenes as true film noir, heightening the interest and tension. It is to Hughes' credit that there's no happy ending with Dahl and Carey in a romantic embrace.

THAT "STREETCAR" MAN HAS A NEW DESIRE!

The Wild One

(February 1954)

A Stanley Kramer Production

Cast: Johnny Strabler/Narrator, Marlon Brando; Kathie Bleeker, Mary Murphy; Sheriff Harry Bleeker, Robert Keith; Chino, Lee Marvin; Sheriff Stew Singer, Jay C. Flippen; Mildred, Peggy Maley; Charlie Thomas, Hugh Sanders; Frank Bleeker, Ray Teal; Bill Hannegan, John Brown; Art Kleiner, Will Wright; Ben, Robert Osterloh; Jimmy, William Vedder; Britches, Yvonne Doughty; Uncredited: Wilson, Robert Bice; Gringo, Keith Clarke; Mouse, Gil Stratton; Dinky, Darren Dublin; Red, John Tarangelo; Dextro, Jerry Paris; Crazy, Gene Peterson; Pigeon, Alvy Moore; Go Go, Harry Lawrence; Boxer, Jim Connell; Stinger, Don Anderson; Betty, Angela Stevens; Simmonds, Bruno VeSota; Sawyer, Pat O'Malley; Chino Boys, Timothy Carey, Joe Haworth, K.L. Smith, Nicky Blair, Norman Budd and Pepe Hern; Deputies, Sam Gilman, Chris Alcaide, Patrick Miller and Mort Mills; Policeman, Robert Anderson; Racer, Ted Cooper; Race Officials, Frank Hagney and John Doucette; Bee Bop, Danny Welton and Charles Cirillo; Dorothy (Telephone Operator), Eve March; Mrs. Thomas, Mary Newton; Cyclists, George Dockstader, Dude Criswell, Don Fera and Wally Albright

Credits: Director, Laslo Benedek; Assistant Director, Paul Donnelly; Screenwriter, John Paxton; Editor, Al Clark; Art Director, Walter Holscher; Set Decorator, Louis Diage; Cinematographer, Hal Mohr; Sound, George Cooper; Original Music, Leith Stevens; Musical Director, Morris Stoloff; Production Designer, Rudolph Sternad

Location Filming: Conejo Valley, Thousand Oaks and Calabasas and Hollister, California

Production Dates: February 12–March 17, 1953

Source: story "The Cyclists' Raid" by Frank Rooney (*Harper's*, January 1951)

Running Time: 79 minutes

Story: After disrupting a motorcycle race and stealing a trophy, Marlon Brando and his biker gang move on to the next small town. Brando is attracted to Mary Murphy, the niece of café-bar owner Ray Teal. Brando offers Murphy the trophy, which she refuses. He decides to remain in town until Gene Peterson, an injured biker, recovers. Finding that Murphy's father is Sheriff Robert Keith, Brando decides to leave town. Arriving in town is rival biker Lee Marvin, who takes the trophy and starts a fight with Brando. Brando emerges victorious. Town resident Hugh Sanders tries to drive through the bikers and has an altercation with Marvin. Keith decides to arrest only Marvin. Believing Keith's decision to be unfair, bikers storm Sanders' house and throw him in the same cell with Marvin. The bikers start to get out of control. Teal sends Murphy to get Keith. Bikers chase and begin to harass Murphy until Brando shows up and takes Murphy away on his bike. Murphy begins to fall in love with Brando but he spurns her. Murphy runs away and Brando follows. A passerby misunderstands the situation and goes to get help. Brando tells Murphy that he and his gang will leave town. Townsmen break Sanders out of jail and then grab Brando. Murphy sees Brando's capture and finds Keith, who has been drinking. Murphy rouses Keith and they go to help Brando, who is being beaten by the townsmen. Keith's interruption allows Brando to escape, find his bike and try to get out of town. As Brando rides away from the angry townsmen, one man throws a tire iron that hits him. Brando is knocked unconscious and his bike runs out of control, hitting and killing elderly townsman William Vedder. County sheriff Jay C. Flippen and his men arrive and take control. Keith and Murphy stand up for Brando, with Keith telling Flippen how the accident occurred. Flippen releases Brando and his men, telling them to stay out of his jurisdiction. Before leaving the area, Brando returns to give Murphy the trophy as a symbol of his affection for her.

Notes and Commentary: The working titles for the film were *The Cyclists' Raid* and *Hot Blood*. The film was based on Frank Rooney's *Harper's* story. In turn the story was based on an incident that occurred in Hollister, California, on the Independence Day weekend in 1947. Reports of the extent of the cyclists' disturbance vary. In all cases, property was destroyed and townspeople were terrified. The bikers from the two clubs, the Booze Fighters and the Nomads, were invited back to Hollister in 1997 for a 50th anniversary celebration.

Little of Rooney's story made it to the screen. The owner of the hotel-bar was Joel Bleeker. The restaurant-bar owner in the film was Frank Bleeker. Working at both establishments was Cathy (story)-Kathie (film) Bleeker. In the story, Cathy was Joel's daughter. The bikers roar into town. All keep their goggles on except one young member. The bikers finally get out of control and terrorize the town. One biker rides his cycle into the hotel lobby and hits and kills Cathy. The bikers ride out of town. The young biker returns to express his regrets. Joel, out of control, mercilessly beats the biker. Joel knows he not only has to make peace with the dead and also with the living.

Both Marlon Brando and Lee Marvin rode their own motorcycles. Marvin competed in desert races. Marvin based his character Chino on a real-life biker, Willie "Wino Willy" Forkner, a member of the Booze Fighters. Keenan Wynn was the original choice to play Chino. Even though Wynn spent several weeks in pre-production, MGM refused to release him. Marvin was an ideal choice to replace him. It has been stated that Marvin was actually drunk in several scenes in the film.

Stanley Kramer wanted to shoot on location but was voted down by Columbia president Harry Cohn. Cohn insisted the film would be shot in black and white on the Columbia Ranch. The opening scene in which the bikers ride into the first small town was shot in Conejo Valley, Thousand Oaks, California. It is obvious that Brando was not one of the participants on location, with his part shot in front of a process screen. Cohn imposed a strict shooting schedule with little time for revisions or changes.

The famous dialogue exchange ("What are you rebelling against?" "Well, what ya got?") came from an actual conversation between Kramer and one of the cyclists.

The film was released on a double bill in some markets with *The Big Heat* (Columbia, 1953). It was banned in the United Kingdom until

1968 because it was thought that the film would incite British teenagers to acts of violence.

In the Brando–Marvin fight scene, David Sharpe doubled Brando and Tom Steele stood in for Marvin. For other stunt work, Fred Carson doubled Brando. Other notable stuntmen who lent their talents to the film were Richard Farnsworth, Whitey Hughes, Carey Loftin and Larry Duran.

Reviews: "The feature is long on suspense, unmitigated brutality and rampant sadism. What Columbia has is a small epic of human nastiness." *Variety*, 12/23/53

"The first and best biker movie." *Motion Picture Guide*, Nash and Ross

Summation: This is a very good biker noir with Marlon Brando electrifying the screen as the biker leader. The story of bikers who terrorize a small town is tension-packed and told with no wasted moments (a short running time of 79 minutes). Not to be overlooked is a sincere performance by Murphy as a young woman who would like to be a free spirit but knows she never will. The rest of the cast is fine with good acting by Robert Keith who never should have been sheriff but finally stands up and Lee Marvin as Brando's rival, a rough and crude biker. This picture is not to be missed.

FROM EXOTIC CASBAH TO WATERFRONT!
Intrigue explodes into murder!

The Woman from Tangier

(February 1948)

Cast: Nylon, Adele Jergens; Ray Shapley, Stephen Dunne; Ned Rankin, Michael Duane; Captain Graves, Denis Green; Rocheau (Prefect of Police), Ivan Triesault; Parquit, Curt Bois; Paul Moreles, Ian MacDonald; Uncredited: Flo-Flo, Donna Demario; LeDeaux, Anton Kosta; Pedro (Gendarme), Robert Tafur; Martine, Maurice Marsac; LeDeaux, Anton Kosta, Pilot, George J. Lewis

Credits: Director, Harold Daniels; Producer, Martin Mooney; Screenwriter, Irwin Franklyn; Editor, Richard Fantl; Art Director, Walter Holscher; Set Decorator, James Crowe; Cinematographer, Henry Freulich; Musical Director, Mischa Bakaleinikoff

Production Dates: September 22–October 2, 1947

Running Time: 66 minutes

Story: Captain Denis Green steals £50,000 sterling from his ship and buries it on the outskirts of Tangier. To throw authorities off the scent, he murders his purser Michael Dante and blames the crime on him. Prefect of police Ivan Triesault and insurance investigator Stephen Dunne decide to investigate before Green's ship can leave the port. A plane brings known criminal Ian MacDonald to Tangier. Before parachuting from the plane, he shoots the pilot, George J. Lewis. Needing to get in contact with Green so he can move the money out of Tangier, MacDonald enlists the aid of a former lover, Adele Jergens, to bring them together. Jergens is willing to help as long as there is no illegal activity. Green refuses to meet with MacDonald. MacDonald comes to Green's hotel room but Green still refuses to deal with him. Green tells MacDonald that Jergens is working with him. MacDonald goes to Jergens' room and begins to get rough with her. Alerted to the disturbance, Dunne and Triesault rush to help Jergens. MacDonald tries to escape but is shot down by Green. Police bring in a box Triesault tells Green that was found outside the city. Fearing the money was actually found, Green goes to make sure the money is still buried. Triesault and Dunne are present with police to arrest him. Jergens mentioned there was a similar box aboard ship and this was the box used to shake up Green. The incident has brought Jergens and Dunne close and they decide to get married.

Reviews: "An action-filled melodrama [with a story] as basic as a punch on the jaw." *The Columbia Story*, Hirshhorn

Summation: This is a routine action entry that has now been labeled as film noir because of the dark cinematography of Henry Freulich. Stephen Dunne makes for a rather colorless hero. Denis Green and Ian MacDonald add a spark to the story as more-than-competent villains. Adele Jergens' looks help rivet attention to the proceedings. But all in all, it's just filler material.

The suspense—tense surprise of the year!

The Woman in Question

(February 1952)

An Anthony Asquith Production

ALTERNATE TITLE: Five Angles on Murder

CAST: Agnes aka Madame Astra, Jean Kent; Bob Baker, Dirk Bogarde; Michael Murray, John McCallum; Catherine Taylor, Susan Shaw; Mrs. Finch, Hermione Baddeley; Albert Pollard, Charles Victor; Superintendent Lodge, Duncan Macrae; Lana Clark, Lana Morris; Inspector Butler, Joe Linnane; Shirley Jones, Vida Hope; Uncredited: Alfie Finch, Robert Scroggins; Doctor, Ian Fleming; W.T. Gunter, Albert Chevalier; Inspector Wilson, Anthony Dawson; Detective Lucas, John Boxer; Barney, Duncan Lamont; Lipstick Customer, Everley Gregg; Police Sergeant, Richard Dunn; Police Surgeon, Julian D'Albie; Mrs. Hengist, Josephine Middleton; Neighbors, Nora Gordon, Helen Goss and Merle Tottenham; Police Photographer, John Martin

CREDITS: Director, Anthony Asquith; Assistant Director, George Pollock; Executive Producer, Joseph Janni; Producer, Teddy Baird; Story and Screenwriter, John Cresswell; Editor, John D. Guthridge; Art Director, Carmen Dillon; Cinematographer, Desmond Dickinson; Camera Operator, Russell Thomson; Costume Supervisor, Yvonne Caffin; Makeup, W. Partleton; Hair Stylist, Biddy Crystal; Sound Editor, Ken Heeley-Ray; Sound Recordists, John Dennis and Gordon McCallum; Original Music and Music Conductor, John Wooldridge with the Philharmonic Orchestra; Production Manager, Andrew Allen; Continuity, Margaret Sibley

RUNNING TIME: 84 minutes

STORY: When Hermione Baddeley's young son Robert Scroggins discovers the dead body of Jean Kent, Duncan Macrae is assigned to the case. Macrae first talks with Baddeley, Kent's housekeeper, who says that Kent had a stormy relationship with her own sister Susan Shaw. Dirk Bogarde came into Kent's life when he wanted Kent in his mind-reading act. Baddeley believes Kent rejected Bogarde's amorous advances. Later Shaw and Bogarde forced their way into Kent's house and there was a violent argument. When questioned, Shaw admits there was bad blood between her and Kent. Kent wanted nothing to do with her critically injured husband, a patient in a naval hospital. Shaw met Bogarde at Kent's house. There was an immediate romantic attraction. Bogarde and Shaw planned to marry as soon as Bogarde's divorce was final. Shaw told Kent of her plans. Kent's interference threatened Bogarde's divorce plans. Next Macrae interrogates Bogarde, who tells of meeting Kent at an arcade and persuading her to be a part of his mind-reading act. Kent appeared to agree but really only wanted an affair with Bogarde. Bogarde turned Kent down. An argument resulted and an angry Bogarde left Kent's house. Bogarde found out that Kent told private investigator Albert Chevalier that she and Bogarde were romantically involved. Shaw and Bogarde confronted Kent and left her in an angry mood. Charles Victor, the next to be questioned, gave Kent a parrot when her pet bird died. Later Victor performed odd jobs around Kent's house. Victor tells Macrae that Kent had another male visitor, John McCallum. Victor tells Macrae that he comforted Kent after Shaw and Bogarde left. Victor then proposed to Kent and she accepted. After Victor left, two young women, Lana Morris and Vida Hope, arrived at Kent's house to have their fortunes told. In an upper story window, they saw an argument in progress. Then McCallum left the house. Macrae decides the answer is in the murder room at Kent's house. While Macrae is investigating, McCallum enters the room. He is shocked to hear of Kent's death. McCallum, a sailor, met Kent at the arcade. They quickly began an affair. McCallum proposed to Kent. Kent told him that they could't marry until her husband died. After another tour at sea, McCallum returned only to find Kent with another man. After throwing the man out of the house, McCallum knocked Kent to the floor and left. McCallum says the fault was his; Kent had implored him to write but he couldn't find words to put to paper. Macrae has a talk with Scroggins. Scroggins remembers that on the night Kent was murdered, the parrot greeted someone. Macrae then talks with Victor. Macrae deduces that the parrot recognized Victor and cried out. Kent laughed at Victor's marriage proposal. In a rage, Victor murdered Kent.

NOTES AND COMMENTARY: In the United

Kingdom, the film was released by the J. Arthur Rank organization and General Film Distributors. In the United States, the title was changed to *Five Angles on Murder*.

Summation: This is an interesting British mystery noir. Although the acting, direction and photography are first-rate, the story which begins nicely eventually lets the viewer down. Fans of mysteries will spot the murderer early in the game. The break that identifies the killer is a little too convenient. The story is still compelling to watch.

REAL RAW TRUTH ABOUT MAN-SMUGGLING
inside the BIG HOUSE for women!

Women's Prison

(February 1955)

Cast: Amelia van Zandt, Ida Lupino; Brenda Martin, Jan Sterling; Mae, Cleo Moore; Joan Burton, Audrey Totter; Helene Jensen, Phyllis Thaxter; Dr. Crane, Howard Duff; Glen Burton, Warren Stevens; Warden Brock, Barry Kelley; Chief Matron Sturgess, Gertrude Michael; Dottie LaRose, Vivian Marshall; Matron Saunders, Mae Clarke; Don Jensen, Ross Elliott; Grace, Adelle August; Chief Guard Tierney, Don C. Harvey; Polyclinic Jones, Juanita Moore; Sarah Graham, Edna Holland; Uncredited: Deputy Sheriff Green, Lorna Thayer; Frank, Frank Sully; Miss Whittier, Frances Morris; Black Woman, Vera Francis; Mae's Boyfriend, Murray Alper; Carol, Lynn Millan; Head Nurse, Diane DeLaire; Warden's Secretary, Eddie Foy III; Burke, Myra McKinney; Josie, Jana Mason; Matron Enright, Mary Newton; Inmates, Wanda Barbour, Lucille Barkley, June Benbow, Lucia Carroll, Marge Davies, Gay Fairchild, Jean Gale, Julie Gehring, Marcoreta Hellman, Joyce Johnson, Beverly Kidd, Jarma Lewis, Kathy Marlowe, Mara McAfee, Laurie Mitchell, Geraldine Pattison, Lonnie Pierce, Phyllis Planchard, Angela Stevens, Merry Townsend, Dorothy Vernon and Grace Lee Whitney; Hospital Inmates, Sue Carlton, Mary Lou Devore and Ruth Vann; Matrons, Madge Cleveland, Jean Harvey, Beatrice Maude, Riza Royce and Dorothy Ryan; Guards, Jack Kenny, Mike Mahoney, Lee Martin and Tyler McVey

Credits: Director, Lewis Seiler; Assistant Director, Carter De Haven, Jr.; Producer, Bryan Foy; Story, Jack DeWitt; Screenwriters, Crane Wilbur and Jack DeWitt; Editor, Henry Batista; Art Director, Cary Odell; Set Decorator, Louis Diage; Cinematographer, Lester H. White; Recording Supervisor, John Livadary; Sound, George Cooper; Musical Conductor, Mischa Bakaleinikoff

Song: "Home Alone"—sung by Juanita Moore and chorus

Production Dates: August 2–21, 1954

Running Time: 80 minutes

Story: Ida Lupino is the sadistic warden of the women's half of a "coed" prison. Her prison is separated from the men's side only by a wall. A new arrival, the frightened Phyllis Thaxter, is placed in isolation. This is standard procedure but Dr. Howard Duff recommends that she be spared this ordeal. Lupino refuses. Thaxter gets so hysterical that she has to be restrained in a straitjacket. The next morning Thaxter is found unconscious and unresponsive. Lupino allows Thaxter to be sent to the infirmary. When Thaxter breaks rules, Lupino sends her back to her cell while calling her a borderline psychopath. Duff, furious at Lupino's treatment of Thaxter, tells her that the women prisoners have something she can never have, a man's love. Lupino says that her harsh methods will help the women to be rehabilitated. Duff calls her a psychopath. Another woman prisoner, Audrey Totter, learns that her husband Warren Stevens, incarcerated on the men's side, wants to deliver a message in person. Totter works in the laundry. Stevens is able to sneak into the storage room and meet Totter. Knowing Totter is close to parole, Stevens tells her where he hid some money that she can use to hire a lawyer to get his sentence reduced. During an exercise break, Totter remains in the storage room with Stevens. Weeks later, after Totter collapses to the floor, she admits to inmate Jan Sterling that she's pregnant. Sterling takes Totter to the infirmary. Duff tells Lupino and head warden Barry Kelley about Totter's condition. Kelley has

Stevens brought to his office and informs him of his impending fatherhood. Kelley presses Stevens to tell how he enters the women's side. Stevens won't say how until Totter is out on parole. Kelley tells Lupino that if she wants to keep her job, she has one week to find how Stevens did it. Time and again, Totter is brought to Lupino's office during the middle of the night, harassed and beaten in an effort to make her tell how Stevens accessed the women's side. Totter doesn't know. Lupino begins to physically attack Totter. Hearing Totter's screams, Duff intervenes and takes Totter to the infirmary. The word is spread through the cell block that Totter may die. Duff plans to resign after his treatment of Totter is completed. Duff tells Kelley and Lupino that if Totter dies, he'll name them as her murderers. Inmates led by Sterling take over the cell block and take Lupino prisoner. Stevens gains access to the laundry room and then goes to the infirmary. Duff is treating Totter and allows Stevens to have a word with her. Totter tells Stevens to go back to the men's side and she'll be waiting for him when he's finally released. The toll is too much for Totter and she dies. In the hall, Sterling sees Duff and learns the news about Totter. She tells Duff he can't stop them from killing Lupino. Duff tells the women they can win but not if they kill Lupino. Stevens, who has obtained a pistol, starts looking for Lupino. Kelley, aware that Stevens is missing, brings guards to the women's section. Stevens tracks down Lupino and raises his pistol to shoot. Duff prevents Stevens from killing Lupino. Lupino breaks under the strain and has to be restrained in a strait-jacket. Duff tells Kelley that when the meeting is held to review prison conditions, his (Duff's) testimony will cause Kelley to lose his job. Thaxter, who really was not a hardened criminal but convicted of a manslaughter accident, is released from prison.

Notes and Commentary: To increase the cruel aspect of her character, Ida Lupino wore smart clothes, earrings and jewelry in contrast to the women prisoners dressed in unfeminine outfits.

Reviews: "Good entry for the programmer market." *Variety*, 1/26/55

Summation: This may be a "B" prison noir but it is harsh and hard-hitting. Good acting highlights this film: Ida Lupino as a psychotic warden, Audrey Totter a pregnant inmate and Phyllis Thaxter a neophyte inmate. Lewis Seiler's direction is taut and suspenseful. Lester H. White's photography casts shadows among the light to increase the tension. It's obvious from the beginning that Lupino and head warden Barry Kelley's reign will be over by picture's end but the acting, directing and photography make the film a pleasure to watch.

Appendix 1

The Films Listed Alphabetically

Affair in Trinidad September 1952
All the Kings Men January 1950
Anatomy of a Murder July 1959
Angels Over Broadway October 1940
Assignment—Paris October 1952
Autumn Leaves August 1956
Bad for Each Other January 1954
Bait February 1954
Between Midnight and Dawn October 1950
The Big Boss April 1941
The Big Heat October 1953
Blind Spot February 1947
The Brothers Rico September 1957
Buchanan Rides Alone August 1958
The Burglar June 1957
Café Hostess **January 1940**
Cargo to Capetown April 1950
The Case Against Brooklyn June 1958
Cell 2455, Death Row April 1955
Chain Gang November 1950
Chicago Syndicate July 1955
Chinatown at Midnight November 1949
City of Fear February 1959
Comanche Station March 1960
Convicted August 1950
Coroner Creek July 1948
Counter-Espionage September 1942
Counterspy Meets Scotland Yard November 1950
Cowboy March 1958
Criminal Lawyer October 1951
The Crimson Kimono October 1959
The Crooked Web December 1955
Curse of the Demon July 1958
Customs Agent May 1950
Dangerous Blondes September 1943
The Dark Past January 1949
David Harding, Counterspy July 1950
Dead Reckoning January 1947
Death of a Salesman February 1952
Decision at Sundown November 1957
The Devil's Henchman September 1949
The Devil's Mask May 1946
Drive a Crooked Road April 1954
Edge of Eternity December 1959
Escape from San Quentin September 1957
Escape in the Fog April 1945
Experiment in Terror June 1962
Face Behind the Mask January 1941
Face of a Fugitive May 1959
Fire Over Africa November 1954
5 Against the House June 1955
Footsteps in the Fog June 1955
49th Man May 1953
Framed May 1947
The Garment Jungle April 1957
The Gentleman from Nowhere September 1948
Gilda March 1946
The Glass Wall April 1953
The Good Humor Man June 1950
The Guilt of Janet Ames March 1947
Gunman's Walk July 1958
The Harder They Fall April 1956
Hell Is a City November 1960
The Houston Story February 1956
Human Desire September 1954
I Love a Mystery January 1945
I Love Trouble January 1948
In a Lonely Place May 1950
Inside Detroit January 1956
Joe MacBeth February 1956
Johnny Allegro June 1949
Johnny O'Clock January 1947
Jubal April 1956
Key Witness October 1947
Kill Her Gently October 1958
The Killer That Stalked New York December 1950
Knock on Any Door April 1949
Ladies in Retirement September 1941
The Lady from Shanghai June 1948

The Last Posse July 1953
A Lawless Street December 1955
Let No Man Write My Epitaph October 1960
The Lineup June 1958
The Long Haul December 1957
Lust for Gold June 1949
M March 1951
The Man from Colorado December 1948
The Man from Laramie August 1955
Man in the Dark April 1953
Man in the Saddle December 1951
The Man Who Dared May 1946
Mark of the Whistler October 1944
Mary Ryan, Detective January 1950
Miami Expose September 1956
The Miami Story May 1954
The Missing Juror November 1944
Mr. District Attorney February 1947
Mr. Soft Touch August 1949
The Mob October 1951
Murder by Contract December 1958
My Name is Julia Ross November 1945
Mysterious Intruder April 1946
New Orleans Uncensored March 1955
Night Editor March 1946
The Night Holds Terror July 1955
Nightfall February 1957
Nine Girls February 1944
1984 September 1956
On the Waterfront October 1954
One Girl's Confession April 1953
Our Man in Havana March 1960
Over-Exposed April 1956
Pickup July 1951
Pickup Alley August 1957
Power of the Whistler April 1945
Prison Warden December 1949
Pushover August 1954
Queen Bee November 1955
The Reckless Moment November 1949
The Return of the Whistler March 1948
Revenue Agent February 1951
Ride Lonesome February 1959
Rumble on the Docks December 1956
Scandal Sheet January 1952
Screaming Mimi April 1958
The Secret of the Whistler November 1946
711 Ocean Drive July 1950
Shadow on the Window March 1957
Shadowed September 1946
She Played with Fire September 1958
Shockproof January 1949
Sign of the Ram March 1948
Sirocco June 1951
The Sniper May 1952
The Snorkel July 1958
So Dark the Night October 1946
The Soul of a Monster August 1944
Spin a Dark Web October 1956
State Secret October 1950
Strange Affair October 1944
Strange Fascination September 1952
The Strange One April 1957
The Tall T April 1957
Target Hong Kong March 1953
13 West Street June 1962
The Thirteenth Hour February 1947
Three Hours to Kill November 1954
3:10 to Yuma August 1957
Tight Spot May 1955
The Tijuana Story October 1957
To the Ends of the Earth February 1948
Tokyo Joe November 1949
The True Story of Lynn Stuart March 1958
Two of a Kind July 1951
Under Age April 1941
The Undercover Man April 1949
Underworld U.S.A. May 1961
The Unknown July 1946
The Unwritten Code October 1944
The Violent Men January 1955
Voice of the Whistler October 1945
Walk a Crooked Mile September 1948
Walk East on Beacon June 1952
The Walking Hills March 1949
Walls Came Tumbling Down June 1946
The Whistler March 1944
Wicked as They Come February 1957
The Wild One February 1954
Woman from Tangier February 1948
Woman in Question February 1952
Women's Prison February 1955

Appendix 2

The Films Listed Chronologically

Café Hostess **January 1940**
Angels Over Broadway October 1940
The Face Behind the Mask January 1941
The Big Boss April 1941
Under Age April 1941
Ladies in Retirement September 1941
Counter-Espionage September 1942
Dangerous Blondes September 1943
Nine Girls February 1944
The Whistler March 1944
The Soul of a Monster August 1944
Mark of the Whistler October 1944
The Missing Juror November 1944
Strange Affair October 1944
The Unwritten Code October 1944
I Love a Mystery January 1945
Escape in the Fog April 1945
Power of the Whistler April 1945
Voice of the Whistler October 1945
My Name Is Julia Ross November 1945
Gilda March 1946
Night Editor March 1946
Mysterious Intruder April 1946
The Devil's Mask May 1946
The Man Who Dared May 1946
The Walls Came Tumbling Down June 1946
The Unknown July 1946
Shadowed September 1946
So Dark the Night October 1946
Secret of the Whistler November 1946
Dead Reckoning January 1947
Johnny O'Clock January 1947
Blind Spot February 1947
Mr. District Attorney February 1947
The Thirteenth Hour February 1947
The Guilt of Janet Ames March 1947
Framed May 1947
Key Witness October 1947
I Love Trouble January 1948
To the Ends of the Earth February 1948
Woman from Tangier February 1948
The Return of the Whistler March 1948
Sign of the Ram March 1948
The Lady from Shanghai June 1948
Coroner Creek July 1948
The Gentleman from Nowhere September 1948
Walk a Crooked Mile September 1948
The Man from Colorado December 1948
The Dark Past January 1949
Shockproof January 1949
The Walking Hills March 1949
Knock on Any Door April 1949
The Undercover Man April 1949
Johnny Allegro June 1949
Lust for Gold June 1949
Mr. Soft Touch August 1949
The Devil's Henchman September 1949
Chinatown at Midnight November 1949
The Reckless Moment November 1949
Tokyo Joe November 1949
Prison Warden December 1949
All the Kings Men January 1950
Mary Ryan, Detective January 1950
Cargo to Capetown April 1950
Customs Agent May 1950
In a Lonely Place May 1950
The Good Humor Man June 1950
David Harding Counterspy July 1950
711 Ocean Drive July 1950
Convicted August 1950
Between Midnight and Dawn October 1950
State Secret October 1950
Chain Gang November 1950
Counterspy Meets Scotland Yard November 1950
The Killer That Stalked New York December 1950
Revenue Agent February 1951
M March 1951
Sirocco June 1951
Pickup July 1951

Two of a Kind July 1951
Criminal Lawyer October 1951
The Mob October 1951
Man in the Saddle December 1951
Scandal Sheet January 1952
Death of a Salesman February 1952
Woman in Question February 1952
The Sniper May 1952
Walk East on Beacon June 1952
Affair in Trinidad September 1952
Strange Fascination September 1952
Assignment—Paris October 1952
Target Hong Kong March 1953
The Glass Wall April 1953
Man in the Dark April 1953
One Girl's Confession April 1953
The 49th Man May 1953
The Last Posse July 1953
The Big Heat October 1953
Bad for Each Other January 1954
Bait February 1954
The Wild One February 1954
Drive a Crooked Road April 1954
The Miami Story May 1954
Pushover August 1954
Human Desire September 1954
On the Waterfront October 1954
Fire Over Africa November 1954
Three Hours to Kill November 1954
The Violent Men January 1955
Women's Prison February 1955
New Orleans Uncensored March 1955
Cell 2455 Death Row April 1955
Tight Spot May 1955
5 Against the House June 1955
Footsteps in the Fog June 1955
Chicago Syndicate July 1955
The Night Holds Terror July 1955
The Man from Laramie August 1955
Queen Bee November 1955
The Crooked Web December 1955
A Lawless Street December 1955
Inside Detroit January 1956
The Houston Story February 1956
Joe MacBeth February 1956
The Harder They Fall April 1956
Jubal April 1956
Over-Exposed April 1956
Autumn Leaves August 1956
Miami Expose September 1956
1984 September 1956
Spin a Dark Web October 1956
Rumble on the Docks December 1956
Nightfall February 1957
Wicked as They Come February 1957
Shadow on the Window March 1957
The Garment Jungle April 1957
Strange Affair October 1944
The Tall T April 1957
The Burglar June 1957
Pickup Alley August 1957
3:10 to Yuma August 1957
The Brothers Rico September 1957
Escape from San Quentin September 1957
The Tijuana Story October 1957
Decision at Sundown November 1957
The Long Haul December 1957
Cowboy March 1958
The True Story of Lynn Stuart March 1958
Screaming Mimi April 1958
The Case Against Brooklyn June 1958
The Lineup June 1958
Curse of the Demon July 1958
Gunman's Walk July 1958
The Snorkel July 1958
Buchanan Rides Alone August 1958
She Played with Fire September 1958
Kill Her Gently October 1958
Murder by Contract December 1958
City of Fear February 1959
Ride Lonesome February 1959
Face of a Fugitive May 1959
Anatomy of a Murder July 1959
The Crimson Kimono October 1959
Edge of Eternity December 1959
Comanche Station March 1960
Our Man in Havana March 1960
Let No Man Write My Epitaph October 1960
Hell Is a City November 1960
Underworld U.S.A. May 1961
Experiment in Terror June 1962
13 West Street June 1962

Bibliography

Books

Ballinger, Bill S. *Portrait in Smoke*. New York: Harper & Brothers, 1950.

_____. *Rafferty*. New York: Harper & Brothers, 1953.

Blottner, Gene. *Columbia Pictures Movie Series, 1926–1955*. Jefferson, NC: McFarland, 2012.

Brackett, Leigh. *The Tiger Among Us*. Long Preston: Magna, 1991.

Brown, Fredric. *The Screaming Mimi*. New York: E.P. Dutton, 1952.

Carder, Michael. *Decision at Sundown*. Philadelphia, PA: Macrae Smith, 1955.

Chessman, Caryl. *Cell 2455 Death Row*. New York: Prentice-Hall, 1954.

Dinneen, Joseph F. *Underworld U.S.A*. New York: Perma Books, 1957.

Eisinger, Jo. *The Walls Came Tumbling Down*. New York: Crestwood Publishing, 1946.

Ferguson, Margaret. *The Sign of the Ram*. Philadelphia: Blakiston, 1944.

Findley, Ferguson. *Waterfront*. New York: Duell, Sloan and Pearce, 1951.

Finney, Jack. *5 Against the House*. Garden City, NY: Doubleday, 1954.

Flavin, Martin. *The Criminal Code*. New York: Horace Liveright, 1929.

Flynn, T.T. *The Man From Laramie*. New York: Leisure Books, 2009.

Ford, Peter. *Glenn Ford a Life*. Madison, WI: University of Wisconsin Press, 2011.

Fuller, Samuel. *The Dark Page*. Glasgow, Scotland: Kingly-Reprieve, 2007.

Gilbert, Anthony. *The Woman in Red*. New York: Smith and Durrell, 1943.

Gordons, The. *Operation Terror*. Garden City, NY: Doubleday, 1961.

Gorman, Ed, Lee Server and Martin H. Greenberg, editors. *The Big Book of Noir*. New York: Carroll and Graf Publishers, 1998.

Graham, Winston. *Fortune is a Woman*. Garden City, NY: Doubleday, 1953.

Greene, Graham. *Our Man in Havana*. New York: Penguin Books, 2007.

Hamilton, Donald. *Smoky Valley*. West Seneca, NY: Ulverscroft Large Print Books, 1985.

Hardy, Phil. *The Western*. New York: William Morrow, 1983.

Harris, Frank. *My Reminiscences as a Cowboy*. New York: Charles Boni Paper Books, 1930.

Haycox, Ernest. *Man in the Saddle*. Boston, MA: Little, Brown, 1938.

Hirschhorn, Clive. *The Columbia Story*. New York: Crown, 1990.

Huggins, Roy. *The Double Take*. New York: William Morrow, 1946.

Hughes, Dorothy B. *In a Lonely Place*. New York: Feminist Press, 2003.

James, M.R. *Count Magnus and Other Ghost Stories*. New York: Penguin Books, 2005.

Johnson, Malcolm. *On the Waterfront*. New York: Chamberlain Bros., 2005.

Kessel, Joseph. *Sirocco*. New York: Random House, 1947.

King, Sherwood. *If I Die Before I Wake*. New York: Simon & Schuster, 1938.

Lee, Edna. *The Queen Bee*. New York: Appleton-Century-Crofts, 1949.

Leonard, Elmore. *Three-Ten to Yuma and Other Stories*. New York: Harper, 2006.

McCoy, Horace. *Scalpel*. New York: Appleton-Century-Crofts, 1952.

McGivern, William P. *The Big Heat*. Long Preston: Magna, 1980.

Miller, Arthur. *Death of a Salesman*. New York: Penguin Books, 1996.

Mills, Mervyn. *The Long Haul*. New York: Avon Publications, 1957.

Motley, Willard. *Knock on any Door*. New York: D. Appleton-Century, 1947.

_____. *Let No Man Write My Epitaph*. New York: Random House, 1958.

Orwell, George. *Nineteen Eighty-Four*. New York: Harcourt Brace, 2003.

Paley, Frank. *Rumble on the Docks*. New York: Crown, 1953.

Percy, Edward, and Reginald Denham. *Ladies in Retirement*. New York: Dramatists Play Service, 1968.

Petitt, Wilfred H. *Nine Girls*. Chicago, Ill: Dramatic Publishing, 1943.

Pitts, Michael R. *Western Movies*. Jefferson, NC: McFarland, 1986.

Polito, Robert, and David Goodis. *Five Novels of the 1940s & 50s*. New York: Library of America, 2012.

Procter, Maurice. *Hell is a City*. London: Panther Books, 1966.

Roos, Kelley. *If the Shroud Fits: A Jeff & Haila Troy Mystery*. Lyons: Rue Morgue Press, 2005.
Schulberg, Budd. *The Harder They Fall*. New York: Random House, 1947.
Short, Luke. *Coroner Creek*. New York: Bantam Books, 1980.
Silver, Alain, and James Ursini. *Film Noir Reader 4*. New York: Limelight Editions, 1996.
Simenon, Georges. *The Brothers Rico*. New York: Harcourt, 1967.
Storm, Barry. *Thunder Gods Gold*. Tortilla Flat, AZ: Southwest Publishing, 1945.
Traver, Robert. *Anatomy of a Murder*. New York: St. Martins Press, 1958.
Variety Film Reviews (5 volumes), New York: Garland, 1983.
Walsh, Thomas. *The Night Watch*. Boston, MA: Little, Brown, 1951.
Ward, Brad. *Marshal of Medicine Bend*. New York: Dutton, 1953.
Ward, Jonas. *The Name's Buchanan*. Thorndike, MA: G.K. Hall, 1995.
Warren, Robert Penn. *All the King's Men*. Orlando, FL: Harcourt, 2005.
Warwick, James. *Blind Alley*. New York: Samuel French, 1936.
Wellman, Paul I. *Jubal Troop*. Garden City, NY: Doubleday, 1953.
Westerby, Robert. *Wide Boys Never Work*. London, England: John Lehman, 1948.
Willingham, Calder. *End as a Man*. New York: Vanguard Press, 1947.
Wise, Herbert A. and Phyllis Fraser, editors. *Great Tales of Terror and the Supernatural*. New York: Random House, 1944.
Zola, Emile. *La Bête Humaine*. Harmondsworth, England: Penguin Books, 1978.

Magazine Articles

Gallico, Paul. "Trial by Terror." *The Saturday Evening Post*, April 21–June 2, 1951.
Hawkins, John and Ward. "The Missing Witness." *Cosmopolitan*, June 1954.
Holding, Elisabeth Sanxay. "The Blank Wall." *Ladies Home Journal*, October 1947.
Hoover, J. Edgar. "The Crime of the Century: The Case of the A-Bomb Spies." *Readers Digest*, May 1951.
Huggins, Roy. "Appointment with Fear." *The Saturday Evening Post*, September 28, 1946.
Lehman, Milton. "Smallpox the Killer that stalked New York." *Cosmopolitan*, April 1948.
Rooney, Frank. "Cyclists' Raid." *Harper's*, January 1951.
Velie, Lester. "Gangsters in the Dress Business." *Readers Digest*, July 1955.
Wilson, Frank J. "Undercover Man: He Trapped Capone." *Collier's*, April 24, 1947.

Index